The Liability of Arbitral Institutions: Legitimacy Challenges and Functional Responses

Barbara Alicja Warwas

The Liability of Arbitral Institutions: Legitimacy Challenges and Functional Responses

ASSER PRESS

Springer

Dr. Barbara Alicja Warwas
International Bachelor of Law
The Hague University of Applied Sciences
The Hague
The Netherlands

European University Institute

This book has been published with a financial subsidy from the EUI.
This publication is based on an EUI Ph.D. thesis defended at the EUI Law Department on October 7, 2013.

ISBN 978-94-6265-110-4 ISBN 978-94-6265-111-1 (eBook)
DOI 10.1007/978-94-6265-111-1

Library of Congress Control Number: 2016933244

Published by T.M.C. ASSER PRESS, The Hague, The Netherlands www.asserpress.nl
Produced and distributed for T.M.C. ASSER PRESS by Springer-Verlag Berlin Heidelberg

Printed on acid-free paper

This Springer imprint is published by Springer Nature
The registered company is Springer Science+Business Media B.V. Dordrecht

Acknowledgments

The solitude of a writer can be compared to the solitude of a long-distance runner. Although I have not (yet) run a marathon, writing this book helped me understand this phenomenon and appreciate the encouragement offered by the many supporters I met along the way. Upon the completion of this project, I would like to express my gratitude to those who inspired me to get started, those who cheered me on in the course of writing, and those who now await me at the finish line.

I would like to thank my Master thesis supervisor at Wrocław University, Professor Krzysztof Wójtowicz, for his support and inspiration at the early stages of my academic path. I am grateful to my colleagues and the Management from The Hague University. I am also indebted to the current and former members of the European University Institute (EUI) Law Department, particularly to Professors Fabrizio Cafaggi, Hans-Wolfgang Micklitz, Giorgio Monti, Ulrich Petersmann and Wojciech Sadurski. Their academic support during the production of my doctoral dissertation—one of the first seeds of this book—is greatly appreciated. I am also grateful to Professor Sandrine Clavel and Emmanuel Jolivet, whose comments and stimulating discussions on the topic of this book enriched my research.

I am indebted to Tony Cole for the opportunity to participate in the fascinating project for the European Parliament, which shed new insights into the practice of arbitration in Europe and as such contributed to my work in this book. I would also like to thank my Italian family from *Studio Legale Calabresi Guadalupi*, especially Roberto Calabresi and Francesca Boffa. Your professional advice, support, and warmth during the time spent at your legal practice facilitated the drafting of this book and also made it more enjoyable.

My great appreciation goes to Michael McIlwrath and Kai-Uwe Karl, who not only helped me understand the practical importance of the topic at hand but also welcomed me to their legal team introducing me to a number of arbitration puzzles to ponder. Their creativity and openness generated new insights into this project, for which I am eternally grateful. Thanks to my informal mentor, Michael McIlwrath, I was also able to benefit from further consultations with regard to the earlier drafts of this book. Here, I would like to especially thank Professor Catherine A. Rogers and Simon Greenberg for their interest in my work and for their valuable feedback.

I would like to acknowledge the support received from the whole team at T.M.C. Asser Press, especially Philip van Tongeren and Kiki van Gurp, and I am grateful for their tremendous work on the production of this book. I am also thankful to Erin Jackson for language editing this book, which was made possible by the financial support of the EUI Law Department.

My dear friends, it is obvious that I owe you all so much. It is impossible to mention you all but I am particularly indebted to Chiara Altafin, Marija Bartl, Ilze Dubava, Keiva Carr, Joris Larik, Alanna O'Malley, Karolina Podstawa, and Philippe Reyniers for being part of my "shadow committee". I would also like to thank all my friends back in Poland and Joanna and Piotr Liszka. *Chapeau bas!*

I am eternally grateful to Matthew Hoye for his enormous patience and common sense when I felt senseless, and for his moral support and love which I receive every day. Without your help, Matthew, this book would never be finalized. It is my great honour to have you by my side.

Finally, I would like to thank my family: my sister Dagmara Płatek, my grandmother Walentyna Szlufik, my grandfather Władyslaw Szlufik, and my aunt Grażyna Szlufik. This book has been written in the memory of my grandfather's academic career. I am especially grateful to my parents, Jolanta and Krzysztof Warwas. Without you, my beloved parents, I would not be where I am now. This book is dedicated to you.

Contents

Abbreviations

AAA	American Arbitration Association
ADR	Alternative Dispute Resolution
B2B	Business to business
B2C	Business to consumer
BCDR	Bahrain Chamber of Dispute Resolution
CAM	Milan Chamber of Arbitration
CANACO	Chamber of Commerce of the City of Mexico
CBOE	Chicago Board Options Exchange
CEPANI	Belgian Centre for Arbitration and Mediation
CIArb	Chartered Institute of Arbitrators
CICA	Court of International Commercial Arbitration
CIETAC	China International Economic and Trade Arbitration Commission
COMECON	Council for Mutual Economic Assistance
DIA	Danish Institute of Arbitration
DIFC	Dubai International Financial Centre
DIS	German Institution of Arbitration
FAA	Federal Arbitration Act
IACAC	Inter-American Commercial Arbitration Commission
IBA	International Bar Association
ICANN	Internet Corporation for Assigned Names and Numbers
ICC	International Chamber of Commerce
ICDR	International Centre for Dispute Resolution
ICSID	International Centre for Settlement of Investment Disputes
LCIA	London Court of International Arbitration
MAC	Maritime Arbitration Commission
NASD	National Association of Securities Dealers
ODR	Online Dispute Resolution
PCA	Permanent Court of Arbitration
P.R.I.M.E. Finance	Panel of Recognized International Market Experts in Finance

RICO	Racketeer Influenced and Corrupt Organizations Act
SCC	Stockholm Chamber of Commerce
SIAC	Singapore International Arbitration Centre
TTIP	Transatlantic Trade and Investment Partnership
UNCITRAL	United Nations Commission on International Trade Law
VIAC	Vienna International Arbitral Centre

Chapter 1
Introduction

Contents

1.1 Setting the Scene

This book investigates the issue of the civil liability of arbitral institutions (so-called "institutional arbitral liability")[1] by accommodating the changing *legal*, *societal*, and *economic* functions of arbitral institutions in and outside the international arbitration marketplace. The main thesis is that institutional arbitral liability is desirable and, hence, that the current regulations of liability of institutional arbitration actors—for the most part either excluding or strongly limiting any forms of liability for anything done or omitted in connection with arbitrations—are inadequate given the convoluted contractual obligations and the increasing scope of the multifaceted functional objectives underlying the performance of such actors.

[1]The term "institutional arbitral liability" accommodates any potential sources of civil liability of all institutional arbitration actors such as case managers, members of institutional organs and, to a certain degree, institutional arbitrators. In the majority of analyses conducted in this book this term nevertheless excludes the comprehensive regulation of liability of the actors external to institutional arbitration regimes, such as experts appointed by either arbitral tribunals or the parties.

B. Warwas, *The Liability of Arbitral Institutions: Legitimacy Challenges and Functional Responses*, DOI 10.1007/978-94-6265-111-1_1

International arbitration has changed significantly over the past decades. An increasing academic scholarship and many specialized arbitration periodicals have recently focused on the evolution of international arbitration including the explanation of its altering functions. This literature points to the intensification of the international arbitration practice exemplified by its growth in size, changes to the range of disputes and parties involved, procedural complexity, and interchangeability of the roles of the "players" competing for the arbitration market shares.[2] These transformations—suggesting the arrival of a new paradigm in international arbitration—prompt stimulating and well-timed calls for ethical regulation in international arbitration,[3] echoed in escalating requests for increased transparency of international arbitration proceedings.[4]

Another important development concerns the noticeable regionalization of arbitration, especially in the European context, and the implications of this phenomenon for international arbitration practice.[5] Due to the progressive liberalization of the concept of arbitrability at domestic levels of the EU Member States and the latest policies on promoting arbitration at regional, EU level, the interplay between EU law and domestic laws of the EU Member States, on one side, and arbitration, on the other side, has transcended its traditional axis. Regarding EU law developments, not only new, regulatory disputes within the EU regulated markets such as energy and telecommunications have been subject to arbitration and other alternative dispute resolution (ADR) mechanisms.[6] There have also been reforms of consumer arbitration accompanying a number of ADR and online dispute resolution (ODR) means, often based on their traditional commercial models. Furthermore, national practices of arbitration within the EU have revealed the increasing outsourcing of disputes of eminent social and public relevance to arbitration. These kinds of disputes differ significantly from commercial disputes lying at the core of traditional arbitration proceedings. For example, in 2011 Portugal introduced a law on tax arbitration before the Centre for Administrative Arbitration.[7] The 2011 Amendment to Spanish Arbitration Law set forth the framework for institutional arbitration of corporate disputes following similar reforms in Italy tracing

---

[2]Hanotiau and Mourre 2012; Rogers 2014.

[3]Rogers 2014.

[4]Be it as related to international commercial arbitration proceedings or other forms of international arbitration including but not limited to investor-State dispute settlement in the context of the latest EU comprehensive free trade agreements. Cf. McIlwrath and Schroeder 2013; Queen Mary University of London, School of Arbitration, and White & Case. "2015 International Arbitration Survey: Improvements and Innovations in International Arbitration." http://www.arbitration.qmul.ac.uk/docs/164761.pdf. Accessed 25 April 2016; Franck 2005; Stephan Schill, "Transparency as a Global Norm in International Investment Law." Kluwer Arbitration Blog. 15 September 2014. http://kluwerarbitrationblog.com/2014/09/15/transparency-as-a-global-norm-in-international-investment-law/. Accessed 25 April 2016; Ruscalla 2015.

[5]Cole et al. 2014.

[6]Warwas 2014.

[7]Decree-Law No 10/2011.

back to 2003.[8] All these have resulted in the growing allocation of highly sensitive disputes often involving matters of public interest to European arbitration both in regional and national contexts, which is also far-reaching for international arbitration practice.

Together, these developments constitute the incremental privatization of civil justice systems within the EU and suggest an increasing trust by public officials in private arbitration regimes and the eagerness of the EU to engage further in the international arbitration debate in a yet not entirely understood manner. At the same time, however, certain fundamental questions of constitutional nature regarding the fairness of new forms of arbitration—the (un)accountability and democratic-deficits of the emerging arbitration regimes, lack of protecting safeguards for the parties to the new forms of arbitration, and finally the role of private arbitration actors in the determinations of various issues concerning national and EU public policy—remain unaddressed. Although such discussions on the boundaries of arbitration have been subject to lively academic debates in the US, these problems appear novel in continental Europe, requiring new answers specific to the dynamics of both European integration and international arbitration settings.

All the aforementioned changes have one thing in common, namely the involvement of arbitral institutions. Arbitral institutions, be it those traditionally perceived as private, commercial entities, or more regional ones offering expertise in the resolution of specific types of disputes falling beyond commercial nature, have been increasingly active in introducing new instruments aimed at regulating institutional arbitration regimes together with the performance of institutional arbitration actors. This is to respond to new challenges facing contemporary arbitration practice. They do so by means of regular revisions of their arbitration rules or by providing guidance to the parties on the effective management of arbitration cases. For example, a few prominent international arbitral institutions such as the International Court of Arbitration at the International Chamber of Commerce in Paris (ICC Court) and the London Court of International Arbitration (the LCIA) have recently introduced new Arbitration Rules that came into force as of 1 January 2012 and 1 October 2014, respectively. These rules reflect the growing institutional interference with the conduct of the parties and their legal representatives in the course of arbitration proceedings in relation to the appointment of arbitrators, the manner in which legal counsel should and should not act in front of arbitral tribunals, or the ways in which various types of submissions are to be handed to arbitral tribunals, to mention a few. Another example is the recent ICC's Guide for In-House Counsel and Other Party Representatives on Effective Management of Arbitration of 2014. The guide provides an explanation of the basic stages of typical arbitration proceedings together with the institutional recommendation regarding the possible means of improvement to the performance of in-house counsel involved in such proceedings. All of these

[8]Spanish Act 11/2011, of May 20, Reforming Act 60/2003, of December 23, on Arbitration, and Regulating Institutional Arbitration Within the Public Administration.

institutional developments—although refreshing and meritorious—tend to be missing one component: they fail to include any guidelines on the conduct of case managers and other actors involved in the administration of institutional arbitration proceedings.

Consequently, the following logical and timely question arises here: why do regulatory practices of arbitral institutions continuously omit the professional conduct of the actors without whom institutional arbitration would simply lose its standing in the arbitration world, namely case managers and the members of institutional organs? Or, if any regulations of this kind exist, why are they kept behind the closed door of institutional arbitration realms?

There is another aspect of institutional arbitration activity that deserves attention here. Regardless of the natural hostility towards any legal interference with institutional arbitration regimes, arbitral institutions directly or indirectly engage in "public", legal dialogue on arbitration. Some institutions do so by means of adopting specialized sets of arbitration rules relating to the resolution of disputes of non-commercial origins (i.e. the rules of the American Arbitration Association (AAA) on consumer, employment, and the healthcare payroll provider arbitrations). The others amend their existent rules, ordinarily applied to commercial disputes, to attract their usage in either new forms of arbitration—traditionally falling outside the spectrum of commercial institutional services such as investor-State arbitrations or commercial arbitrations yet involving new parties to institutional regimes such as States or state entities (e.g. the recently revised version of the 2012 ICC Rules of Arbitration). This is to say that arbitral institutions respond to the emerging demands placed on them by public actors whose role in the geographical and procedural operation of institutional arbitration becomes less and less marginal.

Arbitral institutions are thus growing in power. Is anything potentially worrisome in that? Whereas at first glance institutional arbitration seems to function perfectly, on closer scrutiny of arbitral institutions deeper problems are revealed. Whether taking into account both traditional commercial arbitration institutions administering commercial disputes between private or public parties, as well as the institutions engaged in the management of more publicly oriented disputes, one thing looms beneath the surface of the exclusive institutional arbitration practices: all these institutions remain unaccountable.

What do arbitral institutions do to invite a discussion on accountability? The mainstream understanding of the primary function of arbitral institutions holds that they merely administer international arbitration cases. Holding to this mantra, we will not be able to escape from the discussion on the contractual obligations and the actual functions of arbitral institutions in and outside arbitration proceedings and how their performance could be improved. Certainly, arbitral institutions do not decide cases. Nevertheless, they draft arbitration rules that empower institutional arbitrators to determine the legal rights of the parties in a clearly defined procedural manner that predetermines the atmosphere and the outcomes of institutional arbitration proceedings. Moreover, the same arbitration rules often fall short of the provisions that would allow arbitrators a required room of manoeuvre to efficiently adjust the phases of arbitration proceedings for the benefit of the parties. Some arbitration counsel have raised concerns regarding the lack of procedures for early depositions in institutional arbitration rules that could largely shorten the conduct of arbitration proceedings while at the same time contributing to their cost-effectiveness.[9] Moreover, there is a wide discrepancy *within* institutional arbitration rules as to the authorization of institutional arbitrators to encourage settlements in the course of the arbitration proceedings, a notion at odds with the original goal of arbitration understood as an amicable and consensual process. Thus, it is not only what arbitral institutions do which directly or indirectly affects the conduct in arbitration proceedings, but also what they do not do that may leave institutional arbitrators with their hands tied when deciding on cases and the parties confused as to their real autonomy in institutional arbitration proceedings. If arbitral institutions keep on acquiring important prerogatives in arbitration processes, why can they not be called into account for their actions or omissions whereas the parties often either bear financial consequences or suffer from procedural irregularities resulting from such actions or omissions?

This book argues that on the margins of the recent corporate, legal, and political debates on the role of arbitration in modern society, arbitral institutions have emerged as powerful players with new procedural and substantive powers in and beyond international arbitration processes. Arbitral institutions no longer only manage international arbitration cases; they design institutional arbitration proceedings in a way that allows them to play with the mandate and discretion of institutional arbitrators and with core principles of international commercial arbitration such as party autonomy. In doing so, they become increasingly exposed to the public authorities involved in legislative and political debates on arbitration (be it legislators, courts, or policy makers) and, hence, they build up their capital also beyond international arbitration marketplace. Institutional arbitration, whether domestic or regional, has serious implications for the functionality of contemporary international arbitration, be it in purely commercial settings or other emerging forms of publicly oriented institutional arbitrations.

The new developments to institutional arbitration could easily give international arbitration a boost through the popularization of the process among new types of disputes. However, it is apparent that any new developments can no longer ignore the current dissatisfaction of arbitration users with the traditional international commercial arbitration. This is not a purely academic concern. This concern would undoubtedly be shared by some commercial parties and practitioners who earn their daily bread as arbitration counsel. It is no longer universally accepted that international arbitration is cost-effective, fast, and procedurally straightforward. To the contrary, international arbitration—in particular as compared to transnational litigation—is increasingly perceived as an expensive,

[9] McIlwrath and Schroeder 2008b.

lengthy, and procedurally intricate process involving burdensome discovery.[10] This is in addition to complaints from the parties and their counsel regarding arbitrators who gradually compromise parties' interest due to their busy agendas. Again, what is the standing of arbitral institutions within this debate?

Whereas this book generally falls within the debate on the possible reforms to international arbitration, it goes much further as it revives an uneasy debate on one of the most intriguing yet unsettled issues in the world of international arbitration, namely the problem of liability in international arbitration. It does so from the perspective of institutional arbitration, hence acknowledging the recent geographical and procedural developments of international arbitration that advanced the position and legal authority of arbitral institutions within the international and regional arbitration communities. At the same time, this book investigates these developments of institutional arbitration also vis-à-vis the actors traditionally perceived as being external to arbitral institutions, that is, various legal authorities engaged in the promotion of arbitration, policy makers, or legislators directly or indirectly influencing the landscape of international arbitration.

This book argues that institutional arbitral liability as a derogative norm is desirable for at least a few reasons. First, from a legal perspective, arbitral institutions operate on a contractual basis and as such there is no good reason to treat arbitral institutions—that are undeniably sophisticated market players—differently than other professional contractors under the general theories of contract law. In this vein, arbitral institutions should not exclude their contractual liability for the performance of their essential contractual obligations.

Furthermore, this book argues that the legal approach to institutional arbitral liability (focusing on the explanation of the contractual bonds and institutional activity through the lens of various contract law theories) *alone* is insufficient to accommodate all aspects of contemporary institutional performance. The contractual obligations of institutional arbitration actors should be analysed in view of the changing societal and economic goals of institutional arbitration regimes. Whereas the *societal goals* correspond to the questions of authority and legitimacy of institutional arbitration in and outside institutional arbitration processes, the *economic aims* relate to the traditional commercial function that arbitral institutions assume in the so-called "market" for international arbitration services. Concurrently, it is claimed that institutional arbitration contracts should be treated as *sui generis* legal instruments that are largely detached from the traditional, contemporary analyses of contract law, hence requiring separate legal and institutional regulations specific to institutional arbitration settings.

The book also identifies the emerging modern public function of institutional arbitration that is in contrast to its traditional commercial function, which long tried to reduce institutional activity to the pure provision of arbitration services.

---

[10] Queen Mary University of London, School of Arbitration, and White & Case. "2015 International Arbitration Survey: Improvements and Innovations in International Arbitration." http://www.arbitration.qmul.ac.uk/docs/164761.pdf. Accessed 25 April 2016.

This public function includes both the increasing *private regulatory powers of arbitral institutions*, exercised in and outside arbitration processes, and the emerging exclusive authority of arbitral institutions in the administration of "regulatory" disputes. Furthermore, the book suggests that while the traditional commercial function of institutional arbitration is in decline, despite the continuous institutional attempts to adapt the arbitration rules to the demands of the new arbitration users, paradoxically, the emerging public function of arbitral institutions becomes the major means of competition between contemporary private arbitration "centres". As such, the proposed model of institutional arbitral liability accommodates the tensions between the traditional, commercial function of institutional arbitration and its emerging public counterpart.

1.2 Why Would Arbitration Users Sue Arbitral Institutions?

Why would they not? Most practitioners engaged in international commercial arbitration would certainly recall the law suit against the AAA with its headquarters in New York City and Mr. Peter Liloia, the arbitrator appointed to determine the construction arbitration under the AAA's rules that had its finale before the Appellate Division of the Superior Court of New Jersey in March 2008.[11] In the case in question, both the arbitral institution and the institutional arbitrator with almost 20 years of experience in hearing AAA's arbitration cases were jointly sued for civil liability for personal injuries allegedly suffered by the defendant as a result of a failure to exercise reasonable control over the conduct of institutional arbitration proceedings by the arbitral institution and the arbitrator. Whereas the dispute underlying the AAA's arbitration was rather straightforward,[12] the events that occurred in the corridors of these arbitration proceedings were rather unconventional. Surprisingly, the events that gave rise to the subsequent liability suit against the AAA and its arbitrator in their majority took place in a parking lot. Let us consider the case more closely.

Mr. Malik, a party to the AAA's arbitration proceedings, objected to the performance of one of the homeowners' legal representatives and requested that the latter be removed from the arbitration hearing. The request was denied by the arbitrator who subsequently ordered a break presumably also aimed at toning down the emotions among the participants to the arbitration hearing. The discussion was nevertheless not over and it moved to the infamous parking space

[11] *Malik v. Ruttenberg et al.* 398 N.J. Super. 489, 495 (App. Div. 2008). ; McIlwrath 2008a.

[12] The AAA's arbitration concerned disagreements between Mr. Malik, hired in order to undertake substantial renovations to the house of the homeowners that acted as the opposing party in the arbitration in question. *Malik v. Ruttenberg et al.* 398 N.J. Super. 489, 495 (App. Div. 2008).

where—as alleged by Mr. Malik—he was assaulted by the same legal representative of the counterparty whom Mr. Malik had previously attempted to challenge.[13]

Although the arbitrator did not witness any such disagreement, as it took place outside the hearing room, Mr. Malik filed a motion in the trial court against both the AAA's arbitrator and the AAA itself. He claimed that the defendants must have known of the temperament and highly unusual oral advocacy skills of the legal representative in question, and hence the failure to exercise their duty to control arbitration proceedings should have resulted in their liability. Needless to say, the AAA and its arbitrator based their defence on the provisions of the New Jersey Arbitration Act[14] that in their view immunized them from liability. The case was decided for the benefit of the plaintiff in the first instance, as the motion court found that the duty of defendants to exercise control in arbitration proceedings fell outside the scope of the doctrine on judicial or quasi-judicial immunity that had been long extended into the performance of arbitrators and arbitration providers in the US. As such, the defendants were denied the motion to dismiss. The Appellate Division of the Superior Court of New Jersey, however, revised this judgement. The Court stated that the act of the arbitrator in question, calling the recess of arbitration proceedings and refusing to remove the legal representative of the party to such proceedings together with any potential corresponding acts of the arbitration provider such as the AAA in their entirety fell within the judicial and quasi-judicial authority of such arbitration actors and therefore should be protected under the doctrine on immunity.

This case, although outrageous and uncommon, attracted lively discussion behind the arbitration scenes on both sides of the Atlantic Ocean.[15] Such debate did not only concern the controversial topic of the desirable scope of immunity covering the performance of arbitration actors in the US, but it also provoked dialogue on the functions of both arbitrators and members of arbitral institutions in and outside the institutional premises where arbitration hearings take place. Such discussions—involving differentiated positions represented by different arbitration practitioners—have not yet led to any firm conclusions. What is certain and relevant for the arguments presented in this book, however, is that they intensified the confusion regarding the scope of contractual obligations of institutional arbitration actors, as well as the modern functions of these actors. Consequently, if no consensus could have been reached by the international arbitration practitioners, why would the parties themselves not be puzzled about the scope of duties of institutional arbitration actors? In addition, if they have the right to be puzzled, they have the legal standing to sue such actors in the courts. Again, why would they not?

Another example of a liability claim against an arbitral institution relates to investment arbitration proceedings that attracted considerable public attention in 2013. The arbitration case concerned the subsequent legal suit against the World

[13] It is also argued that the assault might taken place in the lobby. *Malik v. Ruttenberg et al.* 398 N.J. Super. 489, 495 (App. Div. 2008).

[14] New Jersey Arbitration Act; N.J.S.A. 2A: 23B-14a.

[15] McIlwrath 2008a.

Bank Group, the International Centre for the Settlement of Investment Disputes (ICSID), and the Secretary-General of ICSID, Ms. Meg Kinnear. It was filed in a district court in Washington DC by Mr. Jack J. Grynberg, the President and CEO of RSM Production Corporation, an oil and gas exploration and production company.[16] The lawsuit in question, which entailed the first legal proceedings ever brought against the ICSID, was grounded on the allegation that one of the arbitrators appointed by ICSID to sit in an *ad hoc* Committee charged with the annulment proceedings failed to disclose a conflict of interest.[17] Consequently, on 31 May 2013, Mr. Grynberg published an open letter to Dr. Jim Yong Kim, President of the World Back and Chairman of ICSID, in which he pointed to massive irregularities in the conduct of the arbitration underlying the legal suit discussed here, as well as to the increasing judicial power of ICSID—deprived from any public control—that in his view called into question the transparency and fairness of the entire ICSID arbitration system.[18] The case was eventually dropped by Mr. Grynberg due to a new, favourable deal with the government of Central African Republic, who acted as a defendant in the ICSID arbitration being the subject of the legal suit. However, the case proved the increasing dissatisfaction with the internal work of the ICSID, a major institution dealing with investor-State arbitration cases, by its users. Moreover, regardless of the eventual outcome of the legal proceedings brought against the ICSID in the US district court, yet again the defence line taken by the ICSID, based on the immunity claim, shows that institutional arbitration actors continue to remain unresponsive and nearly indifferent towards increasing legal actions related to any potential irregularities within institutional arbitration regimes. This lack of self-reflection on the institutional end may result in the ever-increasing liability claims against arbitral institutions that, in turn, provoke serious but important questions relating to the functionality of the contemporary institutional arbitration.

1.3 The Two Legitimacy Pressures and Efficiency

Most arbitral institutions, while describing the goals and standards underpinning their operations (be it in the preambles to arbitration rules or in the rules themselves), refer to such values as *ethics*, *fairness*, *transparency,* and *efficiency* of

[16]See an open letter by Mr. Jack Grynberg partially published in a press release: "Jack Grynberg Sues the World Bank Group and ICSID Over Concerns of Conflicts of Interest." 31 May 2013. http://www.prnewswire.com/news-releases/jack-grynberg-sues-the-world-bank-group-and-icsid-over-concerns-of-conflicts-of-interest-209710801.html. Accessed 25 April 2016. This example, which refers to ICSID, also represents the contemporary problems of purely private arbitral institutions.

[17]Ibid.

[18]Ibid.

institutional regimes.[19] Additionally, the drafters of the rules often speak about the institutional *mission* or the *commitment* to the expertise resolution of any arbitrable dispute.[20]

Are contemporary institutional arbitration processes in fact that fair, transparent, and efficient? Do the current practices of arbitral institutions correspond to the initial, core aims of the arbitration users associated with the early arbitral institutions? Are the arbitration rules trustworthy while assuring that they will be applied to all arbitrable disputes regardless of the possible membership of arbitration users in any specific institutional regime?[21] Or, is it rather a facade directed towards the furtherance of the exclusive character of each institutional arbitral regime with an institutional support of "in-house" arbitrators, whether they do a good job or not? The questions at hand touch upon the problems of *legitimacy* and *efficiency* of contemporary institutional arbitration in and of itself.

The questions regarding legitimacy and efficiency of institutional arbitration were identified some time ago in regard to the factors that were to determine the then future role of institutional arbitration in the international arbitration system. In 2009, the then Acting Secretary-General of the ICSID, Mr. Nassib G. Ziade, called for more transparent arbitral procedures, efforts to increase the trustworthiness of institutional arbitration, and identified threats to the legitimacy of arbitral institutions as the biggest challenge facing them.[22] A few years after the speech by Mr. Ziade, it is clear that these problems remained unresolved. In fact, the far-sighted words of Mr. Ziade are increasingly exemplified in the growing dissatisfaction with the institutional involvement in arbitration proceedings, often resulting in legal suits against arbitral institutions themselves.

Why is this so? First, it is a problem of the shifting legitimacy of institutional arbitration. Institutional arbitral liability entails complex issues regarding the institutional responses (or their lack) to the core values and principles of arbitration, all in relation to the arbitration users and institutional arbitrators, on one side (the bottom-up approach) and public authorities, such as courts, legislators, and policy-makers, on the other side (the top-down approach). Broadly speaking, institutional arbitral liability concerns the question of legitimacy of institutional arbitration

---

[19]See: the Preamble to the recently amended 2012 ICC Arbitration Rules, which reads as follows: "These Rules respond to today's business needs. The 2012 Rules of Arbitration remain faithful to the ethos, and retain the essential features, of the ICC arbitration […]. Both sets of Rules define a structured, institutional framework intended to ensure transparency, efficiency and fairness in the dispute resolution process []".

[20]See: AAA President's Letter and Financial Statements 2010, in particular the subsection on "Our Shared Mission". https://www.icdr.org/icdr/ShowProperty;jsessionid=wLyySnLYHphyPpNvT5VvTL2vqG8l26LcQTNZwJS8pYQSWbBQzhvy!-266738542?nodeId=%2FUCM%2FADRSTG_004001&revision=latestreleased. Accessed 25 April 2016.

[21]See: the Preamble to the 2012 ICC Arbitration Rules, where it is stated that: "[…] these Rules are applicable to disputes between parties in any part of the world, whether or not members of the ICC".

[22]Ziadé 2009.

understood as the accommodation by arbitral institutions of the more general and increasingly changing systemic goals of institutional regimes as voiced by the regional and international arbitration communities and public authorities. It also relates to the sources of institutional authority in the arbitration processes and the increasing unaccountable powers of institutional arbitration actors both vis-à-vis the arbitration users and the public(s).[23]

The rise in institutional liability claims is indicative of the decline in legitimacy of institutional arbitration regimes and processes, at least within the internal aspect of such legitimacy (as seen by the traditional institutional arbitration users). This means that the parties to institutional arbitration express not only dissatisfaction with the institutional "services" but also a growing mistrust in institutional values and authority. This situation is getting progressively worse.

Surprisingly, the case of legitimacy of institutional arbitral regimes vis-à-vis State powers (henceforth "external legitimacy") entails the opposite observations. As noted above, legislators have begun to equip arbitral institutions with additional competences concerning regulatory areas of law that fall within public policy domains. Furthermore, the increasing legal and political considerations related to the new forms of arbitration at the regional level (i.e. the EU consumer arbitration and ADR movement or the increasing promotion of arbitration and ADR within the EU regulated markets)[24] require adequate institutional responses to the new public demands placed on institutional arbitration in order to fully expand its potential as a unique private–public dispute resolution mechanisms. At the same time, growing private–public dialogue in the field of institutional arbitration suggests that the external legitimacy of institutional arbitration—aided by the growth of public trust in those institutions—is increasing just as "traditional" arbitration users are increasingly questioning the internal legitimacy of those same institutions. These two problems are therefore mutually aggravating.

The changing interplay between the internal and external legitimacy of institutional arbitral regimes questions the traditional status and functions of institutional arbitration (that is to say, the resolution of commercial disputes arisen among traders), and relates to the emerging public function of arbitral institutions. The public function of institutional arbitration relates to the growing private regulatory

[23]See the question of Mr. Grynberg related to the prospective excessing of the authority by the Secretary-General of ICSID and to the sources of the Secretary-General's authority. "Jack Grynberg Sues the World Bank Group and ICSID Over Concerns of Conflicts of Interest." 31 May 2013. http://www.prnewswire.com/news-releases/jack-grynberg-sues-the-world-bank-group-and-icsid-over-concerns-of-conflicts-of-interest-209710801.html. Accessed 25 April 2016.

[24]Directive 2013/11/EU of the European Parliament and of the Council of 21 May 2013 on Alternative Dispute Resolution for Consumer Disputes and Amending Regulation (EC) No 2006/2004 and Directive 2009/22/EC (Directive on Consumer ADR); Regulation (EU) No 524/2013 of the European Parliament and of the Council of 21 May 2013 on Online Dispute Resolution for Consumer Disputes and Amending Regulation (EC) No 2006/2004 and Directive 2009/22/EC (Regulation on Consumer ODR).

powers of arbitral institutions in institutional regimes and to the limited though significant public powers that have been granted to institutions by means of public acts. This specific public function of institutional arbitration calls for specific regulations of institutional arbitral liability, particularly when taking into account the linkages between the contractual obligations of institutional arbitration actors. The convoluted content of the contractual obligations of institutional arbitration actors—related to the interconnectedness of the functions of arbitral institutions and individual arbitrators—intensifies the confusion about the prospective scope of institutional arbitral liability that is desirable with a view to the discussion on the democratic deficit of institutional arbitration regimes given their increasing public function. As such, the increasing external legitimacy of institutional arbitration contributes to the increasing pressure of public demands relating to institutional arbitration on more traditional, commercial function of institutional arbitration, implying the new alignment of the private–public goals of arbitration regimes.

The *efficiency* of institutional arbitration is also called into question. The main reason for this puzzle is the confusion among institutional arbitration actors themselves as to the role of modern arbitral institutions in and outside arbitration proceedings. Judging from the contents of the liability claims against arbitral institutions, which assume the failure of institutions in the field of efficiency, it seems that arbitration users expect arbitral institutions to ensure "perfect" arbitrations that would result in the rendering by institutional arbitrators of the awards enforceable in law in line with the parties' expectations towards their dispute. Nobody's perfect, one would say, and most arbitration counsel would certainly agree that such statement holds particularly true with regard to international arbitration practice. Stepping aside from the particularities of human nature, international arbitration—unlike most other fields of legal practice—is built upon these perceptions. This is the case when we speak about the self-perceptions of the status of the members of arbitral institutions, case managers, or institutional arbitrators, as well as regarding the perceptions of the ideal outcomes of an arbitration of the arbitration users. It is often the case that the clashes between these perceptions or visions of efficiency result in liability suits against institutional arbitration actors.

Institutional arbitrators understand efficiency in terms of financial and reputational concerns vis-à-vis the parties' expectations but they tend to rely solely on the institutional procedural matrix and authority as the "guarantors" of efficiency of institutional arbitration processes. In many cases, however, institutional arbitrators have a tendency to take these guarantors for granted by allowing schematic resolution of disputes in line with the internal institutional policies.

In turn, the understanding of efficiency by arbitral institutions appears to be linked to the systemic goals of institutional regimes to increase their external legitimacy (meaning the continuous public recognition of institutional arbitration), which often departs from the perception of efficiency and effectiveness by private users. In fact, institutional arbitral regimes cannot do well without an accurate and consistent understanding of the efficiency of institutional arbitration by all institutional arbitration actors.

1.4 How to Respond to the Trend of Increasing Liability Suits? Preliminary Proposals

Although arbitral institutions are sophisticated market players, there is always room for possible misconduct on the side of institutional arbitration actors. Such misconduct can vary from less significant procedural errors that can be corrected during the regular meetings of the members of institutional organs to more serious irregularities that would have real effects for the exercise of the legal rights by the parties to institutional arbitration proceedings. The assessment of the possible institutional misconduct is thus largely dependent on the content of the obligations of arbitral institutions (be it those determined under the contract or more general obligations of due care) and the severity of such misconduct for the parties' rights in the arbitration processes. The latter situations may concern the following: the failure in assisting with the communications between arbitrators and the parties, improper notification of the parties of documents submitted or produced in the arbitration proceedings, ambivalence of institutions with regard to the delays in the work of arbitrators, and non-reaction to the possible conflict of interests concerning arbitrators, among others. In fact, arbitral institutions vary from one to another and so the prospective institutional misconduct will need to be assessed on a case-by-case basis. In addition, there are some arbitral institutions whose standards of conduct may be quite different from the norms established by prominent international arbitration centres, and to this extent, the sophisticated arbitral institutions (acting as trendsetters) should be particularly interested in initiating the necessary reforms.

This book argues that—in view of the existent practical trend among arbitration users to sue arbitral institutions in cases of misconduct—arbitral institutions should take a proactive approach to institutional arbitral liability and initiate the necessary reforms from the bottom, by way of amendments to their arbitration rules. The proposed model of institutional liability is built around *the triad* of institutional functions, and is intended to respond to the main problems faced by modern arbitration systems, that is to say, the problems of legitimacy and efficiency of institutional arbitration in the face of the recent transformations in institutional arbitration regimes. Taking into account the rather vague institutional approach to the liability issue, this book also addresses the question of the optimal scope of institutional liability. It argues that arbitral institutions should become liable not only for their own acts and omission but also for the effects of certain negligent acts or omission of institutional arbitrators. This stems from the particular *sui generis* status and function that arbitral institutions assume in and outside the arbitration processes.

It is also claimed that the commercial and public functions of institutional arbitration should interact in the proposed model of institutional arbitral liability. The added value of this proposal is to bring together, in a single analysis, two different sorts of legitimacy pressures transforming the institutional arbitration regimes that increasingly impact the operability of international arbitration practice. This means that institutional arbitral liability is required not only given the commercial, contractual aspect of institutional activity (bottom-up) but also because of the emerging, public facet of institutional functions that necessitates the public control over institutional arbitrations that concern the matters of the public interest (top-down). Only such proposals are able to accommodate all three pillars of institutional operation, while at the same time responding to the emerging dual role of contemporary institutional arbitration.

The normative goal of this book is not to argue for diminishing the "autonomy" of institutional arbitration in front of the private or public actors involved in arbitration. Rather, the book seeks greater functionality of institutional arbitration regimes, which could eliminate the contemporary shortcomings of institutional arbitration. These shortcomings include: (a) the lack of institutional control over institutional arbitrators; (b) the institutional understanding and further observance of the principle of efficiency that is at odds with the perceptions of the parties; and finally (c) the institutional obliviousness of the societal facet of institutional operation. The last issue should be of particular importance given the spectrum of institutional goals referring to paralegal values, which seem to be emphasized by institutions more in theory than in practice.

1.5 Methodology

This analysis is based on theoretical and, to a certain extent, also empirical research on institutional arbitration and institutional arbitral liability.[25] The theoretical analyses are based largely on the soft-law instruments developed by institutional regimes (such as the arbitration rules, codes of conduct, internal policies and documents) as well as on descriptive, secondary sources (such as the guides to arbitration rules, limited academic studies on institutional arbitration, and in some parts even on the web articles or blogs of prominent arbitrators and legal counsel). This approach is largely a function of the problems with transparency and confidentiality of arbitration.

Given the interdisciplinary character of this book, the analyses of institutional arbitration and civil, contractual liability involve legal theories of contract laws (interpreted in arbitration context), as well as the societal and economic dynamics of institutional regimes. Hence, the legal dimension concentrates on the analyses of the legal instruments of arbitration including the national arbitration laws, case studies, or the international arbitration device such as the New York Convention on the Recognition and Enforcement of Foreign Arbitral Awards of 1958 (New York Convention).[26] Furthermore, the discussion on institutional arbitration contracts uses the terminology and philosophy underpinning the theories of transnational

[25]Conducted in the course of the study for the European Parliament. See Cole et al. 2014.

[26]The New York Convention, 1958.

private regulatory regimes. Moreover, the legal approach concerns the interplay between various contract law theories, different private international laws, and the stances of domestic judges or legislators to arbitration in general and to institutional arbitration in particular, with a view to the particularity of arbitration settings. There is particular focus on the public authorities from jurisdictions where the arbitral institutions under analysis have their assets, namely: France, England, the US, and Sweden. Additionally, the legal dimension concerns the possible transnationality of institutional arbitration and thus the philosophical arguments related to the location of arbitral institutions vis-à-vis sovereign State powers are analysed.

The societal dimension addresses the societal goals and values of institutional regimes and of the local and international arbitration communities. The choice of the leading arbitral institutions under comparative analysis—such as the ICC Court, the Arbitration Institute of the Stockholm Chamber of Commerce (SCC Institute), the LCIA, and AAA with its international branch, the International Centre for Dispute Resolution (ICDR)—is aided by the following objectives. First, it aims at proving the historical evolution of the goals of the arbitration communities associated with the very first (and currently leading) arbitral institutions to show the transformations of the contemporary institutional regimes with a view on the societal, communitarian values of arbitration users. Here, comparison is made with the selected regional arbitral institutions to test the changing commercial, legal, and societal demands of the arbitration users over their preferable arbitral institutions. Second, it intends to show the changing external dynamics of the regimes developed by the institutions under analysis with the *law*. Therefore, although the book focuses on the arbitral institutions commonly perceived as purely *private*, dealing with commercial disputes, the discussion concerns both private law and public law aspects of institutional activities and of civil liability in more general terms. In this vein, references are also made to the new, public functions of the private arbitral institutions, as well as to the arbitral institutions administering disputes arising out of public international law (e.g. investor-State arbitrations). The economic analysis is limited to an explanation of the commercial function of arbitral institutions to demonstrate the significance of the self-regulatory, market-based approach to institutional liability with a view to the competition between arbitral institutions together with its implications for both national economies and international economic order.

1.6 Organization of the Book

Chap. 2 starts with a brief presentation of the shortcomings of the mainstream definitions of the status and function of arbitral institutions, and provides an innovative, functional definition of contemporary institutional arbitration. Chap. 3 provides an analysis of the legal, societal, and economic dimensions of institutional functions (the so-called "triad" of institutional functions) in search of the sources and prospective scope of institutional arbitral liability. Chap. 4 points out the lack of an accurate response by the contemporary regulations of institutional arbitral liability, expressing the trend towards almost blanket exclusion of liability, to the triad of institutional functions. Chap. 5 concentrates on the weaknesses of the public regulation of institutional arbitral liability by looking at the domestic provisions regulating institutional arbitration (if any) as well as at the interpretations of the status, function, and the liability of arbitral institutions by domestic courts (so-called "visions" of liability). To this extent, it involves solely the legal dimension of institutional arbitral liability. Chaps. 6 and 7 put forward a normative model of institutional liability that could respond to the triad of institutional functions. Chap. 6 addresses solely institutional reforms. Chap. 7 proposes changes to national laws on arbitration and domestic contract laws, which could strengthen the efficiency of the proposed institutional reforms. It reflects on both the desirable level of public regulation of institutional liability and the contents of such regulation. The concluding chapter, Chap. 8, reviews the proposals presented in this book in view of the increasing need for arbitral institutions to eventually reform their regulations of liability by means of accepting the risks rooted in the issue in question instead of unremittingly avoiding those risks.

The book aims at contributing to the general academic discourse on institutional arbitration in an innovative manner by identifying its emerging functions and explaining why these functions necessitate institutional arbitral liability. In this view, certain "public life" of institutional arbitration is pointed out that relates to the recent transformations in institutional arbitration regimes. It is argued that the specific public dimension of the work of arbitral institutions can no longer be overlooked in the analysis of the legitimacy of arbitration in general and of institutional arbitration in particular.

References

AAA President's Letter and Financial Statements 2010, in particular the subsection on Our Shared Mission. https://www.icdr.org/icdr/ShowProperty;jsessionid=wLyySnLYHphyPpNvT5VvTL2vqG8126LcQTNZwJS8pYQSWbBQzhvy!-266738542?nodeId=%2FUCM%2FADRSTG_004001&revision=latestreleased. Accessed 25 April 2016.

Cole, Tony, Bantekas Ilias, Feretti Federico, Riefa Christine, Warwas Barbara, Ortolani Pietro. 2014. The Legal Instruments and Practice of Arbitration in the EU, A Study for the Directorate General for Internal Policies Policy Department C: Citizens' Rights and Constitutional Affairs. http://www.europarl.europa.eu/RegData/etudes/STUD/2015/509988/IPOL_STU(2015)509988_EN.pdf. Accessed 25 April 2016.

Decree-Law No 10/2011.

Directive 2013/11/EU of the European Parliament and of the Council of 21 May 2013 on Alternative Dispute Resolution for Consumer Disputes and Amending Regulation (EC) No 2006/2004 and Directive 2009/22/EC (Directive on Consumer ADR). Vol. OJ L 165.

Franck, Suzan D. 2005. The Legitimacy Crisis in Investment Treaty Arbitration: Privatizing Public International Law Through Inconsistent Decisions. Fordham Law Review 73 (4): 1521–1625.

Hanotiau, Bernard, and Mourre Alexis, eds. 2012. Dossier IX - Players' Interaction in International Arbitration. ICC Publication No. 737.

Malik v. Ruttenberg et al. 398 N.J. Super. 489, 495 (App. Div. 2008).
McIlwrath, Michael. 2008a. Arbitrating Dangerously: Eric P. Tuchman on Tribunal Immunity. IDN Podcast 54. http://www.cpradr.org/About/NewsandArticles/tabid/265/ID/437/Arbitrating-Dangerously-The-AAAs-Eric-Tuchman-on-Tribunal-Immunity-IDN-Podcast-54.aspx. Accessed 25 April 2016.
McIlwrath, Michael, and Schroeder Ronald. 2008b. The View from an International Arbitration Customer: In Dire Need of Early Resolution. Arbitration 74 (3): 3–11.
McIlwrath, Michael, and Schroeder Ronald. 2013. Users Need More Transparency in International Arbitration. In: The Rise of Transparency in International Arbitration: The Case for the Anonymous Publication of Arbitral Awards, edited by Alberto Malatesta and Rinaldo Sali JurisNet, LLC, 87–106.
PR Newswire. 2013. Jack Grynberg Sues the World Bank Group and ICSID Over Concerns of Conflicts of Interest. 31 May 2013. http://www.prnewswire.com/news-releases/jack-grynberg-sues-the-worldbank-group-and-icsid-over-concerns-of-conflicts-of-interest-209710801.html. Accessed 25 April 2016.
Queen Mary University of London, School of Arbitration, and White & Case. 2015. 2015 International Arbitration Survey: Improvements and Innovations in International Arbitration. http://www.arbitration.qmul.ac.uk/docs/164761.pdf. Accessed 25 April 2016.
Regulation (EU) No 524/2013 of the European Parliament and of the Council of 21 May 2013 on Online Dispute Resolution for Consumer Disputes and Amending Regulation (EC) No 2006/2004 and Directive 2009/22/EC (Regulation on Consumer ODR). Vol. OJ L 165.
Rogers, Catherine A. 2014. Ethics in International Arbitration. Oxford University Press.
Ruscalla, Gabriele. 2015. Transparency in International Arbitration: Any (Concrete) Need to Codify the Standard? Groningen Journal of International Law. 3 (1): 1–26.
Schill, Stephan. 2014. Transparency as a Global Norm in International Investment Law. Kluwer Arbitration Blog. September 15, 2014. http://kluwerarbitrationblog.com/2014/09/15/transparency-as-a-global-norm-in-international-investment-law/ Accessed 25 April 2016.
Spanish Act 11/2011, of May 20, Reforming Act 60/2003, of December 23, on Arbitration, and Regulating Institutional Arbitration within the Public Administration.
The United Nations Conference on International Commercial Arbitration, Convention on the Recognition and Enforcement of Foreign Arbitral Awards - The New York Convention. 1958.
Warwas, Barbara Alicja. 2014. ADR in B2B Disputes in the EU Telecommunications Sector: Where Does the EU Stand and What Does the EU Stand For? EUI LAW 2014/12.
Ziadé, Nassib G. 2009. Reflections on the Role of Institutional Arbitration Between the Present and the Future. Arbitration International 25 (3): 427–430.

Chapter 2
Status and Functions of Modern Arbitral Institutions

Contents

2.1 Introduction

Chap. 1 set forth the arguments for a discussion on the changing status and functions of arbitral institutions in and outside arbitration proceedings. As early as the turn of the nineteenth and twentieth centuries, arbitral institutions were mostly perceived as facilitators of commercial disputes that were arising between traders within the socio-political context(s) of the time. By contrast, the legitimacy and functions of contemporary arbitral institutions have been subject to new challenges. On the one hand, these reflect the dissatisfaction of business parties with increasingly formalized, lengthy, and costly institutional arbitration services. On the other hand, they include public demands placed on arbitral institutions by new users as a result of the increasing public interest in institutional administration of highly sensitive types of disputes. These new developments of institutional

B. Warwas, *The Liability of Arbitral Institutions: Legitimacy Challenges and Functional Responses*, DOI 10.1007/978-94-6265-111-1_2

arbitration, entailing the shifting and often self-aggravating private–public dichotomy in contemporary institutional arbitral regimes, have not yet been subject to a wide academic debate. In fact, rather scarce definitions of arbitral institutions existent in literature appear to overlook these transformations. Hence, the purpose of this chapter is threefold.

First, the chapter aims at providing a critical analysis of the current mainstream definitions of institutional arbitration by pointing to the inadequacy of these definitions, interpreted in isolation from one another, due to the emerging functions of contemporary arbitral institutions. Given the fact that, to date, no single comprehensive definition of institutional arbitration has been developed, this chapter puts together the existent discussion on arbitral institutions. It distinguishes between the following categories in which the concept of institutional arbitration can be captured: (1) the legal definition of arbitral institutions as provided in the legal textbooks of prominent arbitration scholars and practitioners; (2) the internal, institutional definition stemming from arbitration rules, guides to these rules and public appearances of the members of institutional regimes; and (3) the scholarly definition of institutional arbitration provided by academics not necessarily predominantly specialized solely in arbitration such as sociologists, political scientists, and economists. Second, the chapter presents an innovative functional definition of the contemporary dual function of institutional arbitration, incorporating the traditional, commercial function of arbitral institutions together with its changing variables and the emerging public function of institutional arbitration. Lastly, the chapter analyses the interplay between the efficiency and legitimacy of the traditional commercial function of arbitral institutions and the emerging public function of institutional arbitration, especially with regard to the goals of traditional institutional arbitration users. This analysis serves as an explanation of the emerging trends among contemporary commercial arbitration users to increasingly challenge the legitimacy of institutional arbitration and eventually sue arbitral institutions in the courts of law.

2.2 Arbitral Institutions as Service Providers? The Mainstream Definitions of Institutional Arbitration Condemned

2.2.1 International Legal Textbooks

The leading treatises on international commercial arbitration mention private arbitral institutions next to *ad hoc* arbitration in the context of the organization of the arbitration process. Most of these textbooks are written by prominent legal academics that are also renowned practitioners in the field of international arbitration. To this extent, the explanation of institutional arbitration appearing in these textbooks should be regarded as the major source of information on the practicalities of institutional arbitration that reflects the prevailing contemporary legal approach to the objectives and functions of arbitral institutions.

These interpretations of institutional arbitration usually focus on the following features: (a) the private nature of commercial arbitral institutions; (b) their administrative functions in the organization of arbitrations expressed in institutional arbitration rules; and (c) the advantages and disadvantages of institutional arbitration in juxtaposition to *ad hoc* arbitration.[1] Moreover, most of the treatises in question provide brief explanations of the leading arbitral institutions such as the ICC Court, the LCIA, or the SCC Institute. They point out the divergences among institutional infrastructures and procedural rules that usually concern different methods of costs allocations developed by arbitral institutions, and the level of institutional involvement in the conduct of arbitrations (be it reflecting the "hands-off" or "hands-on" administrative models).[2] These variables are said to be the major determinants of the parties' consent regarding the recourse to a particular institutional arbitration regime.

Only a few legal commentaries on arbitration, including the famous *Fouchard, Gaillard, Goldman on International Commercial Arbitration* published in 1999, go beyond such conventional understanding of institutional arbitration and explain more complex and often problematic issues that institutional arbitration may entail. These include the potential impact of institutional procedural competences on both the limits to party autonomy and the outcomes of institutional arbitrations or the possible contractual matrix in institutional arbitration.[3] By way of comparison, most contemporary commentaries on arbitration point to rather superficial characteristics suggest that arbitral institutions, as purely private law organizations, provide nothing beyond flexible and neutral arbitration services to disputing parties, entailing solely procedural and logistical frameworks for the resolution of disputes by institutional arbitrators. In sum, according to the mainstream legal definition, private arbitral institutions solely administer international arbitration cases, with varying degree of institutional involvement in the conduct of arbitration proceedings.

Additionally, the authors of arbitration commentaries often describe private arbitral institutions vis-à-vis public international law institutions such as the Permanent Court of Arbitration (PCA) or the ICSID, and the specialized arbitral institutions that have been established and operate within the auspices of national or international professional organizations such as the Grain and Feed Trade Association in the UK.[4] The former institutions deal mostly with the resolution of

---

[1]Born 2009, 150–151; Lew et al. 2003, 36–37; Moses 2012, 9–10.

[2]Moses 2012, 10. The two models reflect the level of institutional involvement in arbitration proceedings, with the hands-on model (i.e. the ICC Court, the CAM) providing for an in-depth institutional supervision of the process and the "hands-off" model (i.e. Belgian Centre for Arbitration and Mediation (CEPANI), Danish Institute of Arbitration (DIA), SCC Institute) entailing more procedural freedom for the parties to tailor the various stages of arbitration proceedings according to their expectations associated with dispute resolution and business goals.

[3]Gaillard and Savage 1999, 450.

[4]Lew et al. 2003, 41–42.

investor-State or inter-State disputes to which a State or State-like entity is a party, and as such the consent to arbitrations administered by the public law institutions is usually based on the international treaty underlying the arbitration in question. The latter institutions enjoy jurisdiction over the disputes covered by the model arbitration clauses included in the codes of practice or general conditions referring to the sale of goods binding upon the members of the relevant professional organization. The consent to such institutional arbitrations is hence rooted in those codes or conditions. Additionally, special purpose arbitral institutions are distinguished from private arbitral institutions that concern various tribunals operating under international law conventions or other international law instruments such as the Iran-US Claims Tribunal.[5]

As opposed to the explanation of private arbitral institutions, the analysis of public law arbitral institutions provided in the textbooks on arbitration brings about more compound arguments stemming from the private–public dichotomy inherent in institutional arbitrations involving public actors. These rather sensitive issues mostly concern the role of public international law institutions in the formulation of the standards of independence and impartiality of arbitrators, the appointment of arbitrators or additional institutional obligations of ensuring the confidentiality of arbitration proceedings given the sensitive subject matter that such arbitrations usually entail. It is questionable, however, whether the distinction between private arbitral institutions and public law or specialized institutions, as contained in the conventional definition of arbitration provided in the textbooks, is still accurate in view of the contemporary status and functions of private arbitral institutions. In fact, the mainstream legal definition of private institutional arbitration appears ambiguous and incomplete for various reasons. This is mainly because it continues to view institutional arbitration as a purely private animal, according little or no public functions to private arbitral institutions.

Regarding the legal nature of institutional arbitration, the mainstream definition of private arbitral institutions does not fully explain the legal status of these institutions in the arbitration process. Moreover, it does not analyse all potential sources of institutional powers acquired by institutions, or accorded to them, both within and outside arbitration proceedings (whether rooted in traditional, private interest in arbitration of arbitration users or in the increasing public interest in arbitration as expressed by State/public authorities). Take, for example, a recent lively debate on the possible involvement of the private arbitration sector (including private arbitral institutions) in the resolution and/or administration of a variety of disputes under the Transatlantic Trade and Investment Partnership (TTIP).[6]

The legal textbooks ordinarily do not refer to the statutes or constitutions of arbitral institutions, which constitute a useful indicator of their organizational form as legal entities (whether operating as private or public legal entities) as well as of their purpose, objectives, and financial organization (whether for-profit or

[5]Lew et al. 2003, 41–42.

[6]Cole et al. 2014, 269–270.

not-for-profit oriented). The detailed analysis of the internal documents of arbitral institutions may therefore shed light on the original purpose of early arbitral institutions, while at the same time helping to confront such purpose with the contemporary institutional activity.

The fact that most private arbitral institutions aim at promoting arbitration and ADR by responding to the commercial goals of the parties involved in arbitrations does not necessarily exclude the existence of limited yet important public aims underlying the activity of such institutions. In fact, not only have arbitral institutions started to popularize and represent more general aims of either regional or international arbitration communities towards the public but there has also been a growing public interest in the operation of arbitral institutions from some legislators. The first situation can be illustrated by institutions promoting institutional regimes among different sectors traditionally falling beyond the scope of arbitration,[7] by institutions entering the market for mediation services as a result of legislative reforms at the EU and domestic levels,[8] or when acting as *amicus curiae* in judicial proceedings that involve legal questions on arbitration.[9] The second argument can be seen in the increasing powers to administer particular types of arbitrations granted to some arbitral institutions through legislative acts or on the basis of the self-regulatory practices of multinational corporations. Some national laws on arbitration (e.g. Italian or Spanish) established exclusive institutional authority in the organization and/or administration of arbitration concerning corporate law.[10] In Malta, the only arbitral institution, namely the Malta Arbitration Centre, was granted exclusive power to administer mandatory arbitration that constitutes a distinctive feature of Maltese arbitration law. Additionally, the Registrar of the Malta Arbitration Centre enjoys distinctive authority in collecting evidence in the course of arbitration proceedings that usually lie within the prerogatives of the parties or arbitral tribunals such as to produce documents or to issue subpoenas to compel witnesses to provide evidence in domestic arbitration.[11] Notably, under Romanian arbitration law parties must comply with institutional arbitral rules at all stages of arbitration proceedings and any derogations from such rules are allowed solely

[7]For example, the ICC encouraging arbitration in international tax disputes in: ICC Commission on Taxation. 2000. "Policy Statement: Arbitration in International Tax Matters." ICC Publication No. 180/438.

[8]Cf. the Italian Legislative Decree No. 69 of 21 June 2013 (which entered into force on 24 June 2013) that introduced mediation in certain civil and commercial matters following the enactment of Directive 2008/52/EC of the European Parliament and of the Council of 21 May 2008 on Certain Aspects of Mediation in Civil and Commercial Matters.

[9]David 1985, 37.

[10]Cf. the amendments to Spanish and Italian arbitration laws: Spanish Act 11/2011, of May 20, Reforming Act 60/2003, of December 23, on Arbitration, and Regulating Institutional Arbitration within the Public Administration; and the Italian Legislative Decree No. 5 of 17 January 2003 (which entered into force on 1 January 2004) introducing the regulation of certain facets of arbitration in unlisted corporations.

[11]Cole et al. 2014, 39.

upon the consent from particular arbitral institutions.[12] The fact that more and more national arbitration laws have outlined such a broad scope of exclusive institutional authority not only favours institutional arbitration over *ad hoc* proceedings in those jurisdictions,[13] but also encourages institutions to further expand the scope of their arbitration services. In this vein, few European arbitral institutions entered in coalitions with regulatory organizations to support their distinct dispute resolution practices. For example, the Czech Arbitration Court through its Arbitration Centre for Internet Disputes acts as the Internet Corporation for Assigned Names and Numbers (ICANN) approved service provider by managing ICANN's mandatory administrative proceedings that are said to resemble traditional arbitration.[14]

These facts imply that contemporary arbitral institutions have expanded their "arbitration services" beyond their traditional scope. Furthermore, there are clearly additional goals underlying statutory mission of arbitral institutions, different from the objectives of typical institutional arbitration users in particular and of international arbitration community in general.[15] This not only makes a discussion on the non-profit character of institutional services more puzzling but also questions the legitimacy of contemporary institutional arbitration in and of itself.

As for the sources of institutional powers, the mainstream definition—regardless of its focus on the consensual aspect of institutional arbitration—tends to disregard the nature of contractual provisions that *de facto* bind arbitral institutions and the parties at the moment of the emergence of institutional contracts and in the course of arbitration proceedings. Although arbitral institutions operate on the basis of the parties' arbitration agreements or submissions to institutional arbitration that are deemed to expressly reflect the parties' consent, no consensus exists on the matter of whether, and if so, *when* and *how*, institutional contract (or contracts) come into existence in institutional arbitration. It is also unexplored how the institutional contract relates to the parties' initial arrangements regarding the organization of arbitration. Does the institutional contract constitute a separate legal instrument (or instruments) which somehow links to the arbitration agreement, or is the institutional contract contained in the arbitration agreement and only complements or "perfects" the latter once the actual arbitration proceedings

[12]Cole et al. 2014, 39.

[13]In fact, some national laws tend to limit the use of *ad hoc* arbitration within national borders by imposing restrictive provisions regarding the effectiveness of *ad hoc* arbitration. For example, Latvian arbitration law states that the awards rendered in the course of domestic *ad hoc* arbitration will be refused enforcement in Latvian courts. Moreover, Czech law requires that all arbitration agreements referring to arbitral rules of arbitral institutions other than Czech permanent institutions be accompanied by a relevant copy of the arbitration rules of the institution in question. See: Cole et al. 2014, 41–42.

[14]See List of Approved Dispute Resolution Service Providers. https://www.icann.org/resources/pages/providers-6d-2012-02-25-en. Accessed 25 April 2016.

[15]On the discussion of arbitration actors on the new challenges to the European arbitration see: Alison Ross, "What Lies Ahead for Europe?" Global Arbitration Review 6, no. 5. http://globalarbitrationreview.com/news/article/29866/europe-ahead. Accessed 25 April 2016.

commence? The prevailing statement that arbitration rules, once referred to by the parties in their arbitration agreement or the submission to arbitration, are incorporated into the contracts containing arbitration clauses does not address the above concerns related to the contractual matrix in institutional arbitration. Little has also been said on the interplay between institutional arbitration rules and the parties' consent to arbitration. Some authors provide studies on the contractual relations involving arbitral institutions.[16] However, none of them examine the actual sources of authority of arbitral institutions in and outside the arbitration process in isolation from the arbitrator's contract, and in relation to a *single* party to arbitration. These issues appear theoretical only superficially. In fact, contractual analysis of institutional arbitration has significant practical implications inasmuch as it serves as an explanation of the precise moment the institutional contractual duties come into existence and of the content of these duties vis-à-vis the parties and arbitrators, which is determinative of the nature and scope of institutional arbitral liability.

These issues become even more problematic once confronted with the analysis of the "judicialization" of institutional arbitration and its impact on the possible decrease in the role of party autonomy in designing the outlook of private institutional arbitration proceedings. The process of judicialization of arbitration, which has been widely discussed in literature for at least two decades,[17] can be defined as the formalization of arbitration procedures in a litigation-like manner, though "in a private setting".[18] Already in the mid-1990s, in their ground-breaking piece on the sociology of arbitration, Professors Dezalay and Garth spoke about the practical implications of the "ICC bureaucracy" for the "Americanization" of the European arbitration.[19] Dezalay and Garth noticed the then increasing efforts of the ICC to proceduralize arbitration process by introducing Terms of Reference and reviving the scrutiny of arbitral awards by the ICC Court, which was seen as a tool to maintain the universality of the ICC arbitration by inviting new arbitrators of new nationalities into the ICC institutional regime.[20] Discussing institutionalization of arbitration, also Professor Gaillard pointed to the risks emerging from the arbitration clauses contained in general conditions of trade binding upon a party which do not fall within the membership scheme of professional association that ordinarily relies on institutional arbitration.[21] Today, however, such "judicialization", "proceduralization", or "formalization" of arbitration,[22] especially in its institutional variant, is often explained by arbitral institutions as being the result of

[16]Clay 2001; Schöldström 1998; Onyema 2010.

[17]Stipanowich 2010; Stipanowich et al. 2010; Drahozal 2009; Horvath 2011; McIlwrath and Schroeder 2008 where arbitration is analysed vis-à-vis court litigation.

[18]Gaillard and Savage 1999, 32.

[19]Dezalay and Garth 1998, 46–47.

[20]Ibid.

[21]Gaillard and Savage 1999, 34.

[22]All these expressions mean precisely the same thing.

responding to the demands placed on institutions by parties relating to the proper administration of arbitration cases by institutions.[23] In turn, the parties themselves have increasingly begun to criticize the formalization of institutional arbitration because of the higher costs and the increasing length of time that this type of arbitration involves.[24] Although both sides seem to make valid points in this discussion, formalization of arbitration has undeniably put arbitral institutions in a position to influence the way parties would usually tailor various steps of arbitration proceedings according to their business needs and procedural expectations, hence in line with the core principle of party autonomy in arbitration. The questions remain whether such institutional interference in the conduct of arbitration went too far and whether arbitral institutions misunderstood the judicialization of arbitration by focusing on the pedantic drafting of the details of almost every aspect of their arbitration rules (in a "rules for rules' sake" spirit),[25] instead of on enforcement of such rules, in particular vis-à-vis institutional arbitrators.[26]

In view of these arguments, the mainstream definition of arbitral institutions also does not address the question: what kind of service do arbitral institutions in fact provide to the parties? Institutional arbitration "service" is said to concern the procedural support for institutional arbitration actors, and the remuneration of institutional arbitrators directly by institutions in order to ensure the "material detachment" of arbitrators from the parties.[27] Indeed, institutional arbitration, especially as presented in front of *ad hoc* arbitration, is usually seen as being suitable for both repeat users of institutional services and parties with little or no knowledge of arbitration. The former prefer in-depth logistical and procedural support in the course of the proceedings because of their relative satisfaction with institutional involvement in arbitration, while the latter require institutional assistance due to their lack of awareness of technicalities of arbitration in more general terms. It is questionable, however, whether institutional arbitration is still such a good alternative to *ad hoc* arbitration and whether it would not be more accurate today to list its advantages (if any) next to litigation, given the increasing similarity of these two processes. Additionally, the advantages of institutional arbitration, defined in this manner, only increase confusion about the scope of the administrative support of arbitral institutions and the nature of the interplay between the members of institutional organs, parties, and arbitrators, as well as other actors

---

[23]Justice Stream B2; Premise: Arbitral Institutions Can Do More To Further Legitimacy. True or False? Legitimacy: Myths, Challenges, Realities. ICCA Miami 2014. http://www.arbitration-icca.org/conferences-and-congresses/ICCA_MIAMI_2014-video-coverage/ICCA_MIAMI_2014_B2.html. Accessed 25 April 2016.

[24]Queen Mary University of London, School of Arbitration, and White & Case. 2015 International Arbitration Survey: Improvements and Innovations in International Arbitration. http://www.arbitration.qmul.ac.uk/docs/164761.pdf. Accessed 25 April 2016.

[25]Sabharwal and Zaman 2014, 709.

[26]Bernini 2007 as cited in Horvath 2011, 263.

[27]Lew et al. 2003, 37.

participating in arbitration proceedings, particularity in view of the interconnectedness of the work of such actors in arbitration.

What does *administrative institutional support* mean in the context of a day-to-day arbitration practice? Where does institutional arbitration service end and where does the work of arbitrators begin, and *vice versa*? Is the institutional arbitration service provided only to the parties or, additionally, to other actors such as arbitrators (and potentially their secretaries), experts, counsel of the parties,[28] and witnesses, just to mention a few? If so, how are the interests of all institutional arbitration actors balanced by arbitral institutions? Finally, are arbitral institutions the only actors providing a specific type of service in the course of the arbitral proceedings today? Is it plausible that the parties themselves as well as institutional arbitrators provide certain service to arbitral institutions as a result of the response to the demands put on them by contemporary arbitral institutions? None of these issues has been addressed comprehensively in legal literature, whereas more and more arbitration practitioners openly call for more transparency on the side of arbitral institutions regarding the methods adopted by them to both appoint and monitor the work of arbitrators.[29] This information is crucial for the parties to understand the changing functions of institutional arbitration that to date still leave arbitration users confused about the work behind institutional arbitration doors.

These observations allow the assumption that arbitral institutions, notwithstanding their ordinary definition as service providers, may assume additional powers in the arbitration process that surpass even the parties' prerogatives in arbitration. Clearly, arbitral institutions have transformed into independent private actors endowed with limited but important public powers. Meanwhile, these same institutions have begun to assume additional private powers in the arbitration processes through the modifications of arbitration rules that increasingly call into question the preferences of institutional arbitration users, as well as the freedom of contract and party autonomy in arbitration. These developments are often missing from contemporary mainstream definitions of institutional arbitration.

2.2.2 Arbitration Rules and Guides to the Rules

Another way to learn about the status and functions of institutional arbitration is through the information provided by arbitral institutions themselves. Here, it is essential to begin with the analysis of the legal status and objectives of arbitral institutions as determined in the founding documents of such institutions, before

[28]At least in situations in which the reputation of such counsel expressed by tight bonds with one of the institutional local communities (such as the ICC National Committees) increases the probability of the future nomination of the counsel in question as arbitrator within a particular institutional infrastructure.

[29]McIlwrath and Schroeder 2013, in particular 97–105.

proceeding with the explanation of the functions of institutional arbitration as provided by arbitral institutions in their arbitration rules, guides to these rules or in the course of public appearances of the members of institutional bodies.

Most internationally recognized arbitral institutions, such as the ICC Court or the SCC Institute, are independent bodies of their home institutions (the ICC and the SCC, respectively), which were established as not-for-profit organizations under relevant national laws.[30] The others, such as the AAA and the LCIA themselves function as complex not-for-profit legal entities. While the AAA, founded in 1926 under the Membership Corporation Act, is a not-for-profit public service organization committed to the service and education in the field of ADR, the LCIA, whose roots date back to 1891, operates as a not-for-profit company limited by guarantee, providing administrative service for the conduct of arbitrations and other types of ADR procedures.[31] In both cases, arbitral institutions claim to be independent from any judicial or governmental bodies, and to operate largely on the basis of the voluntary membership of the representatives of local or international business communities.

The non-profit status of institutional activity of most prominent arbitral institutions is problematic given the progressing professionalization and specialization of these arbitral institutions, in particular in the eyes of arbitration users who have faced increasing costs of institutional services in the past decades. The arbitral institutions mentioned above, while offering their support in the conduct of arbitrations, are said to fulfil more general aims underlying their own policies or the policies of their home institutions such as the preservation of the "communitarian" or societal values of business communities through a fair and expertise resolution of commercial disputes. In this vein, the ICC Court is supposed to execute the ICC's goals, enshrined in the ICC Constitution, to further develop an open world economy through the facilitation of international economic exchanges.[32] Similarly, the SCC Institute, as a third neutral party, assists businesses in the maintenance of business relations to continue the SCC's goals to "realize the vision of Stockholm as the centre of economic growth in Northern Europe".[33]

It is questionable, however, whether such broad and idealistic objectives contained in the founding documents of these arbitral institutions—drafted decades ago in different economic and political circumstances—can still easily explain the financial organization of contemporary arbitral institutions. It is no secret that

[30]The ICC was established as an association under the French law of 1901. Derains and Schwartz 2005, 1; for the SCC see: About the SCC. http://www.sccinstitute.com/about-the-scc/. Accessed 25 April 2016.

[31]"Events in the History of the AAA and Alternative Dispute Resolution"; http://www.lectlaw.com/files/adr07.htm. Accessed 25 April 2016 "LCIA—The London Court of International Arbitration—History of the LCIA. Based on the Report from the Law Quarterly Review; 1898." http://www.lcia.org/LCIA/history.aspx. Accessed 25 April 2016.

[32]See the Preamble and Article 1 of the ICC Constitution. http://www.iccwbo.org/constitution/. Accessed 25 April 2016.

[33]See About the SCC. http://www.sccinstitute.com/about-the-scc/. Accessed 25 April 2016.

arbitration is not a charity, a fact that is supported by the institutionalization of arbitration. Perhaps the not-for-profit character of institutional arbitration services had its *raison d'être* in the post-war reality, when institutional arbitration was to contribute to the rebuilding of the market economy, and when arbitral institutions, assuming almost gratuitous tasks, were not the sophisticated market players that they are today. Even though the financial organization of most arbitral institutions is confidential, it is conventional knowledge that arbitral institutions administer cases with millions of US dollars at stake, and that they charge the parties for their services according to certain percentage or hourly rates. In this view, the non-profit nature of arbitral institutions as defined in their statutes or constitutions appears to have little correlation with the demands of business people wishing to resort to institutional arbitration today, who still want to perceive arbitral institutions as nothing more than the providers of cost-effective arbitration services. Paradoxically, however, what arbitration users can witness is the growing formalization of institutional arbitration entailing additional arbitration costs; all these under the shield of elaborate institutional goals to serve as guarantors of the prosperity of global or regional economic growth. In fact, one could ask the question why arbitral institutions, as non-profit organizations, have been so actively involved in competition for institutional fees within the market for arbitration services. The most likely explanation emerges with regard to the potential need for institutions to secure the best quality arbitrators to act within institutional structures and to increase the yearly caseload that can be subsequently published on the institution's website to attract new users.[34]

This is not to suggest that remuneration of institutional members and employees constitutes the high percentage of financial contributions to the budget of arbitral institutions. Rather, the discussion of the not-for-profit nature of arbitral institutions may be indicative of the changing reasons why arbitration users tend to choose one arbitral institution over another (and why future users may, potentially, begin to favour new arbitral institutions with more transparent financial accounts over those institutions with convoluted financial organization). Some academic studies have shown that the financial organization of dispute resolution service providers may influence the selection of particular service providers by commercial parties in that non-profit service providers (as well as public service providers) appear to be more dependable, thus acting more in line with parties' expectations than for-profit service providers.[35] Although such theory requires further verification based on reliable empirical data, it is likely that due to the confusion about the nature of prominent arbitral institutions by their users (whether

[34]Joshua Karton in his recent book on *The Culture of International Arbitration and the Evolution of Contract Law* claims that the major reason why arbitral institutions—as, after all not-for-profit entities—compete for their clients by means of institutional fees relates to the institutional desire to gain a greater share in the arbitration market, which is indicative of the efficiency of particular institutional regime. Karton 2013, 64–65.

[35]Davis 2012, 222–229 with further references.

for-profit or not-for-profit oriented) some arbitration users will recourse to new arbitral institutions whose financial structure appears relatively clear as compared to prominent arbitral institutions. Furthermore, the parties may start to rely more often on truly commercial, for-profit dispute resolution service providers (only because they will see no difference in provision of such services by for-profit providers as compared to the services offered by traditional arbitral institutions). Additionally, business parties may begin to increasingly request more transparency regarding the allocation of institutional fees. This observation has standing on its own in view of the complex organizational structure of most prominent contemporary arbitral institutions, highlighted by the increasing costs of their institutional services. The not-for-profit organization of arbitral institutions therefore calls for more accountability of institutional regimes, both in front of international arbitration community and the public.

To add to this debate, prominent arbitral institutions, traditionally perceived as administrators of purely commercial, private disputes fail to define their contemporary goals in a fashion that would reflect the engagement of these institutions in new types of arbitration beyond purely commercial institutional objectives. The self-proclaimed mission of the institutional arbitration "sector", with solely commercial values of business communities underpinning such mission, seems inaccurate for two reasons. First, this is due to the already-mentioned public international law objectives of some pioneer arbitral institutions. Second, it is because of the increasing expansion of institutional arbitration services as discussed in Sect. 2.3.1.1.

Although prominent arbitral institutions boast of their independence from public powers, many cooperate with governmental authorities in numerous programmes involving dispute resolution, even in regulated industries. Reading from the AAA's leaflet, every year the AAA administers "thousands of cases under governmental authority".[36] The AAA's tight bonds with the US government and Congress were established at the outset of the AAA's operation, which was dictated by the specificity of the American arbitration. Undoubtedly, such cooperation popularized other forms of arbitration involving also statutory or civil rights (i.e. consumer or employment arbitrations), and confirmed the AAA's authority in the administration of the emerging forms of arbitrations in the US, often without an express consent from the parties interested in the case. Even if these observations are relevant mostly in the American, domestic setting, they show that the profile of the AAA goes beyond purely commercial aims, which in practice may have an impact on the (in)correct application of specific sets of institutional arbitration rules to commercial or other types of disputes administered by the AAA or other institutions. In fact, the alleged misapplication by the AAA of its rules resulted in the legal proceedings against the AAA in the past that largely showed the

---

[36]The American Arbitration Association: A Long History of Working with Government. http://www.adr.org/aaa/ShowPDF?doc=ADRSTG_017603. Accessed 25 April 2016.

arbitrariness of the AAA in determining the set of applicable arbitration rules to the case in question, contrary to the expectations of the parties.[37]

Another troubling issue regarding the scope of institutional services against the background of the early objectives of the most prominent arbitral institutions concerns the lack of the proper explanation of the casework of these institutions relating to other, non-commercial types of disputes or commercial disputes involving States or State-like entities. Although the statistics of most prominent institutions have been increasingly detailed, they still remain rather vague when it comes to the explanation by arbitral institutions of the application of traditional, commercial arbitration rules to new types of disputes and the possible alteration of these rules given the particular nature of arbitrations that new disputes entail. The latter observation has significant practical implications for business parties that may have legitimate expectations to be better informed by institutions whether, and if so, how the amendments to the rules compromise the business goals of the parties for whom the commercial rules were, nota bene, originally designed. The major limitation for arbitral institutions to provide detailed information in this regard is undoubtedly rooted in the confidentiality of the highly sensitive types of institutional arbitration, possibly involving matters of public policy. Bearing in mind, however, that most prominent arbitral institutions such as the ICC Court and the LCIA, offer to all parties solely one set of arbitration rules (including schedules of costs valid for all types of arbitrations), it appears well grounded to require from these institutions that the growing adaptability of their rules is clarified with regard to both business parties and new arbitration users.

Consistent with the preceding discussion is the growing popularity of new, regional arbitral institutions with somewhat more transparent statutes and objectives, as defined by the internal documents of these institutions. For example, Section 1(3) of the Statutes of the German Institution on Arbitration (DIS) states:

> The Association solely and directly pursues only non-profit ("gemeinnützige") objectives within the meaning of the Chapter "Tax Exempt Objectives" of the Tax Code. The Association is non-profit oriented; it does not primarily pursue its own commercial aims. The means of the Association may be used only for purposes in conformity with the statutory objectives. Members do not receive any grants out of the funds of the Association. No

[37] *Strategic Resources Co. v. BCS Life Insurance Co. No. 26022, 2005 WL 1943536* (S.C. Aug. 15, 2005) discussed in detail in Chap. 5. To be more precise, the alleged misapplication of the rules concerned the choice of the AAA's Supplementary Rules for the Resolution of Intra-Industry United States Reinsurance and Insurance Disputes instead of the AAA's Commercial Rules. It should also be noted that the international branch of the AAA, the ICDR adopted new rules in addition to its standard rules and procedures to be used in the resolution of commercial disputes. These include: ICDR Procedures for Final Review of Perceived Inconsistent or Unreasonable String Confusion Objection Expert Determinations of 2015, or the Final Offer Supplementary Arbitration Procedures of 2015, to mention a few.

person may benefit from expenditures which are not compatible with the objectives of the Association or receive disproportionately high remunerations.[38]

Furthermore, as set forth in Section 5(1) of the Statutes in question entitled "Contribution and Financial Year":

The Association is financed by:

(a) membership contributions,
(b) grants,
(c) fees derived from the conduct of arbitral proceedings,
(d) revenues from the conduct of events and the distribution of publications.

DIS, which operates as a registered non-profit association ("eingetragener Verein") with its seat in Berlin,[39] also clearly defines its main objectives in Section 1 of the DIS Statutes. Accordingly, DIS aims at promoting arbitration by means of the following activities: (1) through "the preparation, support and administration of arbitral proceedings" by the DIS Court of Arbitration; (2) the organization of various academic and training events in the field of arbitration, including the support of research projects; and (3) knowledge dissemination in relation to arbitration through publications and information events.[40] Moreover, the involvement of DIS in different forms of arbitration has been specified by means of different sets of arbitration rules offered by DIS for particular types of disputes, including but not limited to, corporate disputes or disputes relating to sport.[41] Although the language of some provisions contained in DIS Statues may require further precision (i.e. the expression on the necessary avoidance of "disproportionately high remunerations" for DIS officials calls for further explanation), both the financial organization and the objectives of DIS appear relatively straightforward and more transparent, in particular as compared to the financial structures and aims of more international arbitral institutions such as the ICC Court, LCIA, and the SCC Institute.

In the same vein, the Preamble to the Arbitration Rules of another regional arbitral institution, the Chamber of Arbitration of Milan (CAM), in its Section on the "Tasks and bodies of the Chamber of Arbitration", specifies the nature and

---

[38]DIS Statutes are available at the DIS website: *Deutsche Institution Für Schiedsgerichtsbarkeit (DIS) e.V.—German Institution of Arbitration—Statutes.* http://www.dis-arb.de/en/13/content/satzung-id9. Accessed 25 April 2016.

[39]According to the information provided on DIS' website, DIS started its operation in 1992 following the merger of the German Arbitration Committee (*Deutscher Ausschuss für Schiedsgerichtswesen e.V.*, DAS) (founded as early as in 1920) and the German Arbitration Institute (*Deutsches Institut für Schiedsgerichtswesen*, DIS) (established in 1974). As such, DIS should be regarded as the most prominent arbitral institution operating in Germany after its reunification in 1990. "About the DIS". http://www.dis-arb.de/en/57/content/about-the-dis-id46. Accessed 25 April 2016.

[40]Section 1 "Aims and objectives of the Association" in: *Deutsche Institution Für Schiedsgerichtsbarkeit (DIS) e.V.—German Institution of Arbitration—Statutes.* http://www.dis-arb.de/en/13/content/satzung-id9. Accessed 25 April 2016.

[41]DIS Rules. http://www.dis-arb.de/en/16/rules/overview-id0. Accessed 25 April 2016.

objectives of the CAM. Hence, the CAM, as an entity of the Chamber of Commerce of Milan, performs arbitration services that fall within the following categories: (1) the administration of arbitration proceedings under the CAM Rules; (2) acting as appointing authority under arbitration rules different than CAM Rules; and (3) acting as appointing authority under the UNCITRAL Arbitration Rules. The Commentary to the CAM Rules adds to the understanding of the nature and functions of the CAM. Hence, the CAM, established in 1986 as a "special operating unit" ("azienda speciale") of the Milan Chamber of Commerce, has been entrusted to perform a wide scope of ADR services including arbitration and mediation, as well as, more broadly, the promotion of the dispute resolution "culture".[42] In line with these objectives, and in addition to the standard arbitration services administered under the CAM Rules, the CAM offers its services for the resolution of domain name disputes pursuant to the rules developed by international authorities in this field such as the Internet Assigned Numbers Authority and ICANN.[43]

Although the broad scope of CAM's activities may at first glance correspond with the objectives of the prominent arbitral institutions, the CAM certainly appears as a significant competitor vis-à-vis the renowned international arbitral institutions mostly because of its strong regional profile that entails less complex questions regarding both the scope of its institutional goals and the "universalization" of its arbitration rules as opposed to the rules of most prominent arbitral institutions. This observation appears relevant for the discussion on the changing legitimacy of prominent arbitral institutions, as it suggests that the universalization or internationalization of arbitration rules is no longer the major determinant of the parties' choices to rely on particular institutional infrastructure. Beyond any doubt, the proliferation of arbitral institutions as well as the progressive specialization of their services contributed to the increased diversity among arbitral institutions, both with regard to their organizational (here also, financial) structure and the scope of their arbitration services. Hence, arbitral institutions are not and will never become universal enough to share the same characteristics in front of their users. Be that as it may, arbitral institutions should, to the utmost degree, ensure clarity regarding their services to avoid confusing their users as to the scope of their modern activities. This is valid especially with regard to the most prominent arbitral institutions whose objectives have become ambiguous in front of their early, commercial goals, as well as vis-à-vis relatively straightforward activity of the emerging, regional arbitral institutions attracting more and more business people from local arbitration communities.

The question also arises regarding the scope and character of institutional arbitration *services* in the eyes of the arbitral institutions. It was already noted that the scope of institutional involvement in the conduct of arbitrations differs from

---

[42]Fumagalli 2012, 9–13.

[43]See CAM: Domain Names Disputes, http://www.camera-arbitrale.it/en/Domain+Names+Disputes/index.php?id=13. Accessed 25 April 2016.

one institution to another, with some institutions providing an in-depth administration of disputes and other institutions allowing for more freedom of the parties to tailor the procedural aspects of their proceedings. While trying to find a common denominator for both models, one could enlist the following stages of institutional work: (a) assistance to the parties in the composition of the arbitral tribunal; (b) setting time limits; (c) allocation of institutional arbitration costs; and (d) further monitoring of various stages of arbitration proceedings. In any event, the institutional administration of arbitration is supposed to be efficient, that is cost-effective and fast, and it is advertised as such by most arbitral institutions.

Regrettably, such promotion of institutional services does not correspond to the actual character of these services, nor does it truly reflect on the character of institutional involvement in arbitration proceedings. Are all institutional decisions purely administrative in their nature? Do all such decisions, even in arbitration proceedings entailing an in-depth institutional involvement in the conduct of arbitration, concern only procedural support of the work of arbitrators? Some, by now rather isolated, opinions of current or former officials of arbitral institutions suggest contrary answers.

At the ASA Seminar on "Arbitral Institutions under Scrutiny", held on 9 September 2011 in Zurich concerning the functions of the ICC Court, the former Deputy Secretary General of the ICC, Simon Greenberg pointed to some possible pitfalls in the ICC's process of the scrutiny of arbitral awards, which concerned, inter alia, the ICC Court's interference with the liberty of decision of the arbitral tribunal.[44] There are some substantive aspects of the ICC's scrutiny procedure that can be visible from the moment of the evaluation by the ICC counsel of the conformity of an award with the ICC rules and practices until the deliberations of the ICC Court on the draft awards. The ICC Court's recommendations that result from such evaluations, as noted by Greenberg, "can cause a change in the outcome of the award".[45] However, according to Greenberg, this falls under the arbitrators' control while rendering the awards.[46] Additionally, an interesting explanation of the rationale of Article 40 of the 2012 ICC Arbitration Rules on Limitation of Liability of the ICC arbitration actors sheds light on the functions of ICC officials in the course of arbitration proceedings as seen by those same officials. A commentary note to Article 40 states that: "where such bodies and individuals [including the ICC and its employees] were exposed to liability, this could hinder their work, making it difficult for them to provide the required level of service".[47] Although it is challenging to capture the understanding of the nature of the ICC arbitration services from this, rather vague statement of the drafters of the ICC Guide, justification of limitation of liability, as noted above, suggests that the ICC service together with the work of ICC arbitrators taken as a whole falls beyond

[44]The speech has been written up into an article. See Greenberg 2013.

[45]Greenberg 2013, 105.

[46]Ibid.

[47]A commentary note in: Fry, Greenberg, and Mazza 2012, 421.

pure provision of services in the meaning of any known contractual law theory. If this were not the case, why would ICC employees as professional lawyers be excluded from liability for the performance of their duties, whereas other professional contractors cannot enjoy such a privilege?

Such declarations, coming from the members of institutional organs, intensify doubts about the scope and nature of all institutional acts. The complex institutional involvement in arbitration creates room for more substantive context of arbitral institutions' decisions. This may be especially important in situations in which an institution steps in between the parties and arbitrators or decides jurisdictional challenges. This observation also makes procedural institutional authority in formation of contracts in institutional arbitration more problematic. As stated by the Commentary to the CAM Rules, "the performance by the CAM, through its bodies […] leads to, and/or is based on, the creation of legal relations between all the subjects involved in arbitration".[48] How does the contract formation in institutional arbitration look like in practice? Regrettably, neither the CAM nor any other arbitral institution, at least as known to the author, provides the answer to this issue.

2.2.3 Other Disciplines

A few sociologists and political scientists have devoted attention to arbitral institutions in a more general context of the interplay between arbitration and *lex mercatoria*, which—according to them—are "intriguing cases" of private ordering.[49] Dirk Lehmkuhl recalls the aforementioned sociological study on arbitral institutions conducted by Professors Dezalay and Garth, and points out the institutional "shares" in a globalized arbitration industry.[50] Lehmkuhl notes the linkages between the competing dynamics between arbitration service providers and the creation and subsequent evolution of self-regulatory transnational commercial arbitration. This adds to the multifaceted objectives of institutional arbitration, and shifts the mainstream discussion on arbitral institutions to the transnational level, in which particular institutional objectives meet. Hence, the socio-political aspects of institutional arbitration involve intriguing questions regarding the traditional understanding of legitimacy of institutional arbitration regimes, and suggest additional functions that contemporary arbitral institutions assume in transnational arbitration systems, on behalf of international arbitration community as a whole.

Institutional arbitration has also become an interesting case study for economists. In the 1990s, Alessandra Casella provided an analysis of the interplay between international commercial arbitration (involving also arbitral institutions)

[48]Fumagalli 2012, 10.

[49]Dezalay and Garth 1998; Lehmkuhl 2006, 101–125.

[50]Lehmkuhl 2006, 101–125, in particular 112–113.

and the emergence of supranational arbitration jurisdiction through the production of "self-made economic law" by international traders.[51] In her equilibrium model, Casella shows that arbitration "centres", as specific forms of "private coalitions of individuals", do have an impact on the expansion of international trade, as they facilitate the accumulation of public goods that are necessary for efficient trade.[52] Casella also argues that the attempts of arbitral institutions to publish the extracts of arbitral awards of precedential value contribute to the development of the legal doctrine on arbitration, which is created from the bottom, by the very members of the "arbitration club".[53] Yet again, the economic analysis of institutional arbitration substantiates the emerging functions of arbitral institutions in a more global context of market integration. Even if these functions overlap with the goals of such complex institutions as the ICC Court, they might appear as new, and not yet well-mapped dynamics to the smaller centres whose primary aims were directed towards the demands of local business communities. Furthermore, Casella notices a particular dialogue between the work of institutions and the law, which requires an analysis of the "legalization" of arbitration procedures, especially in view of the recent demands for the increased legality and certainty of the arbitration processes.[54]

Moreover, more and more legal practitioners and scholars have begun to depict institutional arbitration within the broader context of sociological interactions within international and local arbitration communities. In addition to the already-mentioned sociological studies of Professors Dezalay and Garth[55] and Joshua Karton,[56] Professor Gaillard most recently presented the sociological "representation" of arbitration in which arbitral institutions appear as "merchants of recognition" with whom the local and international communities of arbitration actors (including parties and arbitrators) are associated.[57] These studies point to the changing landscape of institutional arbitration, the new allocation of power among institutional arbitration players, and suggest novel functions of these players within new academic disciplines such as behavioural economics.

The above presentation showed both the shortcomings of the mainstream definition of institutional arbitration and the inaccuracy of the institutional explanation of their own mission and of the scope and character of the contemporary institutional arbitration services. The major arguments involve the following:

(1) The simplification of the definition of private arbitral institutions in the comparative legal discourse based mainly on the reduction of institutional status and goals to purely private arbitration services.

[51] Casella 1996, 155–186.

[52] Ibid.

[53] Casella 1996, 161.

[54] Ibid.

[55] Dezalay and Garth 1998.

[56] Karton 2013.

[57] Gaillard 2015.

(2) Confusion regarding the character of institutional arbitration services, particularly in the context of the recent increased specialization of institutional arbitration, which calls into question the original mission of arbitral institutions and suggests the emergence of the new functions of arbitral institutions, often in response to the public interest in arbitration.
(3) The possible interdisciplinary approach to institutional activity, which explains additional functions of arbitral institutions and questions the orthodox understanding of the legitimacy of institutional arbitration as a purely commercial dispute resolution process.

Against this background, in the following part of Chap. 2, an innovative functional definition of institutional arbitration is proposed. This should both address the above-mentioned doctrinal and practical shortcomings and accommodate the novel trends in the field of contemporary institutional arbitration.

2.3 Dual Function of Arbitral Institutions in the Contemporary Arbitration System

In view of the preceding discussion on the shortcomings of the contemporary mainstream definitions of institutional arbitration, the following part of this chapter presents the emerging, public function of institutional arbitration against the background of the traditional, commercial function of arbitral institutions, stemming from the provision of institutional arbitration services. This book proposes that institutional arbitration be treated as a hybrid that simultaneously assumes dual commercial and public functions. The commercial function encompasses the dynamics of competition between arbitration institutions, and to this extent it ensures the maintenance by institutions of traditional demands placed on institutional arbitration by business parties, corresponding to the *efficiency* of institutional regimes. In contrast, public function embodies the emerging public role of arbitral institutions in governing the private arbitration system as a whole, which, in turn, is stipulated by the need for *legality* in arbitration called for by both institutional arbitration actors and public authorities.

The dual function analysis intends to demonstrate the evolving profile of the typical users of particular institutional regimes, together with its implications for the changing understanding of efficiency of institutional arbitration, both internally (that is, in the eyes of the arbitration users, institutional arbitrators, and arbitral institutions themselves) and externally (as seen by representatives of public powers). It will be shown that the emergence of the public function influences the development of additional dynamics of competition between arbitration centres, which brings into question the efficiency of the traditional, commercial function of institutional arbitration. These variables, entailing the ongoing interaction between commercial and public functions, will be of particular importance for the discussion on the necessary improvements in the modern institutional liability regimes.

2.3.1 *Traditional Commercial Function*

As already noticed, the commercial function involves an analysis of the dynamics of competition between arbitration centres. Arbitral institutions (referred to as "arbitration centres" in this section) are therefore presented here as repeat market players that compete for their users within the market for institutional arbitration services. The dominant paradigm of the commercial function concerns the efficiency of arbitration services from the perspective of business parties to institutional arbitration proceedings. The notion of *efficiency* in the context of institutional arbitration does not fully conform to the explanation of efficiency by the law and economics nomenclature. Rather, it reflects the efficiency of institutional services through the institutional response to the traditional demands of arbitration users such as cost-effectiveness of institutional services and expeditiousness of institutional arbitration proceedings.[58] These demands are regarded as traditional because they correspond with the original goals of arbitral institutions as defined in early institutional statutes or constitutions. In this sense, the commercial function of institutional arbitration is also considered as traditional to the extent that it addresses the gradual evolution of commercial services by institutional arbitration centres.

2.3.1.1 Evolving Profile of Institutional Arbitration Users: New Challenges for the Leading Arbitral Institutions

In order to assess the implications of the competing dynamics in the institutional arbitration market for the efficiency of institutional regimes, as understood by business parties, it is necessary to first examine the changing nationality of the users of different institutional arbitration regimes. Given the context of the analysis involving the commercial function of institutional arbitration, the focus will be placed on the geographical origins of the business parties to the institutional arbitration. Moreover, the question will be posed whether particular centres are better suited to administer disputes between the parties representing certain legal traditions and geographical areas, and, if so, how this affects the competition between the studied institutions. The major assumption concerns the possible effects of the universalization of institutional arbitration rules, stimulated by the forces of globalization and professionalization of institutional arbitration services, on the decline in the efficiency of institutional regimes, at least as perceived by traditional institutional arbitration users.

The ICC and its Court of Arbitration aimed high from the very outset of its operation, which has been reflected in the current, truly international aspect of the ICC Court's activities. The founding goal of the ICC spoke to the institutional aspiration to manage disputes between international businessmen on a more

[58] The notion of efficiency will be further elaborated in the course of the following analysis.

horizontal level, as opposed to domestic disputes. Both the early ICC structure (concerning the activity of numerous ICC National Committees) and the policy underlying the early ICC Rules of Procedure expressed institutional interest in transcending any particular geographical area by serving the business community as a whole and at the international level.[59] According to the statistics provided for by the ICC,[60] the ICC arbitration is used by a variety of parties from Asian, Latin American, and African countries.[61] The ICC arbitration has continuously tried to respond to the demands of European users, with the rising number of disputants coming from Central and Eastern Europe in 2007.[62] As such, the ICC Court has undoubtedly secured its position as the most international and the most prominent arbitral institution in the world.

In this vein, the organizational structure of the Secretariat of the ICC Court reflects the geographical diversity of the ICC parties, as it comprises nine different case management teams (with the latest one established in New York), each headed by the counsel and supported by two or three deputy counsel and secretaries.[63] The teams represent the following language groups or geographical areas: (a) French, (b) American, (c) Latin American, (d) German, (e) UK, (f) Italian, Swiss, and Austrian, and (g) Eastern-European.[64] Moreover, the Secretariat of the ICC Court launched its Hong Kong branch in November 2008, which constituted the eighth team to oversee the arbitral proceedings involving Asian parties.[65] The members of the Hong Kong team supervise the cases and provide ordinary reports on the progress of the caseload during the weekly ICC staff meetings organized in the form of teleconferences. The launch of the Hong Kong branch of the ICC Court's Secretariat, which was a response to the growing demand for arbitration services in the Asia-Pacific region, proves the indefatigable attempts of the ICC to increase the worldwide applicability of the ICC Arbitration Rules to the disputes between arbitration users from various cultural and legal backgrounds. The ICC's ambition to "cover all major time zones" has recently been emphasized by the

[59] Kelly 2001.

[60] "ICC Arbitration: A Ten Year Statistical Overview." 2008. ICC International Court of Arbitration Bulletin 19, no. 1; Tercier 2008.

[61] Ibid.

[62] As far as Eastern Europe is concerned, Polish parties were strongly represented in 2007, while Turkish parties maintained their lead in Central Europe. There was also an increase in the number of Czech and Ukrainian parties. "2007 Statistical Report." 2008. ICC International Court of Arbitration Bulletin Vol. 19 No. 1.

[63] See Secretariat of the Court. http://www.iccwbo.org/About-ICC/Organization/Dispute-Resolution-Services/ICC-International-Court-of-Arbitration/Secretariat-of-the-Court/. Accessed 25 April 2016.

[64] Ibid.

[65] "ICC Court Focuses on Hong Kong and Eastern Europe" 2008. 3 Global Arbitration Review 6. http://globalarbitrationreview.com/journal/article/15641/icc-court-focuses-hong-kong-eastern-europe. Accessed 25 April 2016.

ICC's opening of an office of the ICC Court's Secretariat in New York.[66] This established an additional case management team to work on North American cases.

In case of the LCIA, which for a long time remained reluctant to publish its Statistical Reports, the English parties prevail as the LCIA typical users.[67] Two following observations should be pointed out: (1) the long-established perception of the LCIA as a London-based institution, and (2) the recent shift in the international expansion of the LCIA involving the foundation of two prominent partnerships such as the LCIA India and the Dubai International Financial Centre LCIA (the DIFC-LCIA)[68]. Although the LCIA promotes itself as a "thoroughly international" institution, providing flexible administration of the cases for "all parties, regardless of their location, and under any system of law",[69] it has long been perceived as a London-centric institution with limited "international" tools for the administration of cross-border disputes. This was mainly due to the provisions of Articles 16.1 and 17.1 of the 1998 LCIA Rules, which determined London as the default seat of arbitration and English as the default language of the proceedings for non-participating parties as well as for the purpose of the communications with the Registrar.[70] Regardless of the rationale underpinning these provisions, such as to decrease the staying of the proceedings when the parties fail to stipulate the place of their arbitration, the LCIA's attachment to the institutional seat was for a long time seen as a sign that the LCIA's procedure did not fully express the international spirit of arbitration.[71] However, the time for more variability has also come for London. The recently amended LCIA Rules that entered into force as of 1 October 2014, authorize an arbitral tribunal as soon as it is constituted to change the default seat of arbitration (which remained London in cases in which the

[66]"ICC to Open Office of the Court in New York. http://www.iccwbo.org/News/Articles/2012/ICC-to-Open-Office-of-the-Court-in-New-York/. Accessed 25 April 2016.

[67]Pursuant to the statistical data presented in LCIA's Report of 2013, English parties were the leading national group of the common parties to the LCIA arbitration in both 2013 and 2012, representing 18.6 % of all LCIA arbitration users in 2013 and 16 % in 2012. Registrar's Report 2013. http://www.lcia.org/LCIA/reports.aspx. Accessed 25 April 2016.

[68]As of 1 June 2016 the LCIA will administer disputes between users in India from its London offices. See: "LCIA Adopts a Changed Approach to Indian Arbitration Market", http://www.lcia-india.org. Accessed 25 April 2016.

[69]About the LCIA: Introduction. http://www.lcia.org/LCIA/introduction.aspx. Accessed 25 April 2016.

[70]Turner and Mohtashami 2009, Sect. 1.14.

[71]The already-mentioned section on Arbitration of the LCIA website confirms that in the cases in which one of the parties will still insist on an alternative default seat of arbitration other than London, the LCIA Court will decide on the issue. See: LCIA—The London Court of International Arbitration—LCIA Arbitration. http://www.lcia.org/Dispute_Resolution_Services/LCIA_Arbitration.aspx. Accessed 25 April 2016. See also: Koepp et al. 2013, 261–262.

parties fail to agree on a seat of their choice) upon written submissions from the parties.[72] Moreover, the new Article 17.1 of the 2014 LCIA Rules no longer specifies English as the default language for non-participating parties and for the purposes of the communications with the Registrar. The recent cooperation between the LCIA and the Financial Centre of Dubai,[73] as well as the foundation of the LCIA India,[74] is also evidence of the growing international aspirations of the LCIA. However, it remains to be seen if the LCIA manages to truly universalize its activity in line with its contemporary efforts.

As far as the ICDR is concerned, the two following variables appear particularly significant with regard to internationalization and universalization of its activities: (a) the development of the ICDR as an international branch of the AAA in 1996, and (b) the maintenance by the ICDR of its Global Strategic Alliances. To start with the launch of the ICDR in the late 1990s, the ICDR was established as an international branch of the AAA that was originally perceived as an American arbitral institution aided by the promotion of the arbitration among *peoples* and within different industrial sectors in the US.[75] This does not mean, however, that prior to this date the AAA did not administer international cases via its network of local offices in the US. It was not until the launching of the ICDR in the mid-1990s, when the international activity of the AAA's hub was popularized due to the hiring of the international staff as part of the ICDR's Case Management Teams.[76] Today, the members of the ICDR's teams come from a number of countries, including Brazil, Colombia, Mexico, Italy, Ireland, Germany, Romania, Russia, Iran, Ghana, and Sri Lanka.[77] Moreover, in addition to its standard International Dispute Resolution Procedures (ICDR Procedures), with the recent

---

[72]Article 16.1 of the 2014 LCIA Rules.

[73]The DIFC-LCIA was founded in February 2008 as a joint venture of DIFC and the LCIA for the administration of international arbitration and mediation. The arbitration centre of DIFC-LCIA adopted its own Arbitration Rules that are modelled on the LCIA Rules. For more information, visit the LCIA website at: "LCIA: International Offices & Overseas." http://www.lcia.org/LCIA/international.aspx. Accessed 25 April 2016. "DIFC/LCIA Arbitration Centre". http://www.difc-lcia.org/Default.aspx. Accessed 7 July 2016.

[74]The LCIA India was launched on 18 April 2009 as the first independent overseas office of the LCIA. Also the Arbitration Rules of the LCIA India were adopted as a "legal transplant" of the LCIA Rules. As of 1 June 2016 the LCIA will administer disputes between users in India from its London offices on the basis of the LCIA Rules (for new referrals under these Rules) and the LCIA India Rules (for existing cases and new referrals under these Rules based on existing contracts and arbitration and/or meditation clasues). See: LCIA Adopts a Changed Approach to Indian Arbitration Market. http://www.lcia-india.org. Accessed 25 April 2016. "LCIA: International Offices & Overseas." http://www.lcia.org/LCIA/international.aspx. Accessed 25 April 2016.

[75]See: the analysis of the historical emergence of the AAA provided in Sect. 3.3.1.1 of Chap. 3.

[76]Luis Manuel Martinez 2012, 7.

[77]See: the information provided in The ICDR International Arbitration Reporter. 1, 2011, no. 2: 1–8.

version effective as of 1 June 2014, the ICDR most recently adopted the Canadian Dispute Resolution Rules and Procedures as a result of the establishing of the ICDR Canada for the resolution of Canadian domestic disputes.[78]

Furthermore, the emergence of the ICDR was not the last of the AAA's attempts to respond to the demands of a worldwide group of its arbitration users. Within the above-mentioned policy of the Global Strategic Alliances, the ICDR maintains partnerships with different organizations including: the Bahrain Chamber of Dispute Resolution (BCDR-AAA),[79] the SIAC (ICDR Singapore),[80] the CANACO[81], and the IACAC.[82] Moreover, the ICDR also operates via its established offices in Dublin (the only Europe–based ICDR office), Mexico, Bahrain, and Singapore. All these support the growing interest in the ICDR arbitrations of the arbitration users from the Americas, Asia, and also European countries such as Spain or Portugal.

In contrast, the SCC Institute is still viewed as a more local institution that only recently started to compete for arbitration business and that has served the most homogenous group of arbitration users since its foundation in 1917. However, the slow evolution of the SCC arbitration users is also visible in the case of the SCC Institute. The popularity of the SCC arbitration is a complex issue insofar as it concerns the involvement of the external political factors in the SCC position within the arbitration market. These factors include the development of the so-called "Optional Arbitration Clause for Use in Contracts in US–USSR Trade 1977" as a result of cooperation between the then USSR Chamber of Commerce and Industry, the AAA, and the SCC itself,[83] and the establishment of the new Swedish Arbitration Act of 1999, which inspired the SCC Institute to amend its

[78]Canadian Dispute Resolution Rules and Procedures (Including Arbitration and Mediation) effective 1 January 2015.

[79]The Bahrain Chamber for Dispute Resolution (BCDR-AAA) was established in January 2010 in partnership with the Kingdom of Bahrain. The institution, which administers arbitration cases pursuant to different sets of arbitration rules (including the ICDR International Rules of Procedures and the BCDR-AAA's own Rules), was meant to provide state-of-the-art arbitration facilities which would address the unique, legal and cultural tradition in Bahrain and neighbouring countries. See: "ICDR International Arbitration Reporter" 2010, 1, no. 1, 3.

[80]The ICDR Singapore is the ICDR's Asian Centre, established as a joint venture with the Singapore International Arbitration Centre (SIAC) in order to maintain the ICDR arbitration services in collaboration with the practitioners from Asia. See: Ibid

[81]Within the cooperation with the Mediation and Arbitration Commission of the Mexico City National Chamber of Commerce (CONACO), which was inspired by the creation of the NAFTA, the ICDR opened its office in Mexico City to facilitate and promote the ICDR international arbitrations throughout Mexico. See: Ibid.

[82]The ICDR is the member of the Inter-American Commercial Arbitration Commission (IACAC) that maintains a network of institutions from the Americas, Spain, and Portugal in order to provide a consistent dispute resolution through arbitration for the parties coming from the above territories. See: Ibid.

[83]Hope 2008, 23.

Rules of Arbitration to address the objectives of a wider group of arbitration users.[84] The Optional Arbitration Clause was an impulse for the SCC arbitration in a sense that it brought considerable attention to Stockholm as a major arbitration venue within a specific, East-West niche.[85] Despite this impulse, the number of cases handled by the SCC Institute remained relatively small until the adoption of the new Swedish Arbitration Act of 1999, which constituted the grounds for the modern Swedish arbitration law.[86] Even though the SCC statistics prove the historical reliance on the SCC arbitration predominantly by Swedish, Russian, German, North American or Nordic parties, there is a growing interest in the SCC arbitration services coming from disputants from the UK, France, China and the Middle East, Caribbean, as well as Eastern Europe.[87] Today, the SCC Institute promotes itself as an international dispute resolution centre with the parties of around 40 different nationalities using its dispute resolution services every year.[88] Out of the most prominent commercial arbitral institutions under analysis here, the SCC Institute is also one of the most popular administrators of investment arbitration cases worldwide.[89]

This brief presentation of the changing nationality of typical institutional arbitration users demonstrates that within each of the prominent arbitral institutions under analysis—even in the most modest SCC system—there has been an increasing tendency for the expansion and universalization of institutional arbitration rules to attract the parties from any jurisdiction, representing any legal tradition. This also means that the competition between the most prominent arbitration centres has gone far beyond their original local communities and shifted towards more unified international level. Even though the institutional services still bear some degree of divergence, the universalization of arbitration rules in the course of the twentieth century has resulted in the increased unification of the practices of most prominent arbitral institutions. This has also certainly increased their reputation beyond traditional arbitration communities and even among parties with little or no knowledge of arbitration. In line with this observation is the changing profile

[84]Dezalay and Garth 1998.

[85]Dezalay and Garth 1998, 188.

[86]Dezalay and Garth 1998, 182–196.

[87]Indeed, in 2014 Swedish and Russian parties continued to be the most frequent SCC arbitration users, with English, Chinese, German, and French users constituting the other common nationalities relying on the SCC arbitration services. http://www.sccinstitute.com/statistics/. Accessed 25 April 2016.

[88]"Dispute Resolution Services. http://www.sccinstitute.com/dispute-Resolution/. Accessed 25 April 2016.

[89]The SCC Institute claims to be the second largest arbitral institution, next to the ICSID, to administer investment arbitration cases worldwide. See The Administration of Investment Disputes. http://www.sccinstitute.com/dispute-Resolution/investment-Disputes/. Accessed 25 April 2016; and also A Record Year for Investment Treaty Disputes. http://www.sccinstitute.com/statistics/investment-disputes-2015/. Accessed 25 April 2016.

of arbitration users of the predominant institutions under analysis, involving States or State-like entities or disputants from more specialized business industries. The 2012 version of the ICC Arbitration and ADR Rules (2012 ICC Arbitration Rules) serves as a pivotal example for the escalated adaptability of the arbitration rules. The recent changes in the ICC Rules respond to the complexity and demands of emerging institutional arbitration users such as States or State-like entities, even in situations in which States act in arbitration proceedings solely in their commercial capacity. Although, as already noted, such universalization tendencies appear as a generally positive development for arbitral institutions (meaning the increased caseload), it seems that the prominent arbitral institutions, now more than ever, need to reassure the traditional business parties to institutional arbitration that the adaptability of their rules did not proceed at the expense of these parties.

It appears as though the compromises proposed by the institutions, even if guided by the need for greater efficiency of institutional arbitration regimes as a whole, have either directly or indirectly contributed to the way in which the typical institutional arbitration users perceive the most prominent arbitration centres today. This implies the decline in the efficiency of the traditional commercial function of institutional arbitration, at least as seen by those typical users. This is the potential reason why more regional arbitral institutions have gained prominence among parties from more local business communities that prefer to rely on less sophisticated and perhaps less reputed arbitral institutions with potentially higher flexibility as to business expectations and desires of traditional arbitration users and less costly arbitration services. This is the case with the Vienna International Arbitration Centre (VIAC) with its increasing popularity in Eastern Europe, the Swiss Chambers' Arbitration Institution with regard to international arbitration in Switzerland, the CAM in relation to Italian and North African parties,[90] and the Singapore International Arbitration Centre (SIAC) in Asia, to mention a few.[91]

2.3.1.2 Features of the Institutional Arbitration Market: Introduction to the Competition Dynamics

The market for institutional arbitration services can be characterized by means of two major variables. First, by relatively low barriers for the entry to the market. Second, by the dynamics of competition based, in particular, on the following instruments: (1) differences within the sets of various institutional arbitration rules; (2) soft-law mechanisms; and (3) the marketing techniques aiming at the promotion of particular institutions and/or arbitration in general.

[90]Cole et al. 2014, 57, 122, 185.

[91]There are also other regional arbitral institutions that have witnessed an increased caseload, also concerning international arbitration cases, such as the Madrid Court of Arbitration, the Brussels-based CEPANI, the Hong Kong International Arbitration Centre (HKIAC), DIS, DIA, or the Netherlands Arbitration Institute (NAI).

There have been many studies of the proliferation of arbitral institutions worldwide.[92] It is also usually implied that arbitration centres, unless based in jurisdictions providing for heavy legal regulations for the establishment of arbitral institutions,[93] do not face serious obstacles when entering the arbitration market. There are even some jurisdictions with an unreasonably high amount of arbitration institutions in place. For example, over 200 arbitral institutions have been reported to exist in Latvia,[94] with 130 arbitral institutions operating in Slovakia due to the relatively liberal regime for the establishment and operation of arbitral institutions under Slovak law.[95] In addition to more regional arbitral institutions established in different geographical locations in the 1980s and 1990s, such as the CAM in Italy or DIS in Germany, more and more specialized arbitral institutions have recently come into existence. This is the case with the Panel of Recognized International Market Experts in Finance in The Hague (P.R.I.M.E. Finance). The example of P.R.I.M.E. Finance is particularly intriguing as it shows that arbitral institutions can even spring from the individual initiative of academics representing strong moral and financial capital for starting up the institutional arbitration business.[96]

P.R.I.M.E. Finance was founded upon the idea of Jeffrey Golden, a prominent academic and practitioner, to advance the resolution of disputes related to financial products.[97] Note that in the case of P.R.I.M.E. Finance, as in the case of any other arbitral institution that wishes to gain international or local recognition upon its establishment, the prerequisites for entering into the arbitration market involve the prior affiliations of the founders of the institutions with the existing players in the arbitration field (be it distinguished international arbitrators, academics specializing in arbitration and/or arbitration practitioners). What cannot be forgotten is the importance of institutional networks and cooperation with most prominent arbitral institutions that increases the legitimacy of small institutions that begin to operate more locally. As such, the market for institutional arbitration services comprises the dynamics of both competition and complementarity of all arbitration actors operating on a local or international arbitration platform.

As for the means of competition, arbitration centres are said to compete based mostly on the differences in the sets of their arbitration rules, which, as already noted, are regularly amended to accommodate the possible demands of

---

[92]Law Guides at Harnish Law Library: International Arbitration. Pepperdine University School of Law; Arbitral Institutions & Rules: Index of Arbitral Institutions Rules. http://lawguides.pepperdine.edu/c.php?g=399520&p=2715723. Accessed 25 April 2016. Davidson et al. 1992.

[93]This is the case with the laws of the Czech Republic, Greece, and Hungary. Cole et al. 2014, 39.

[94]According to the recent Study on the Legal Instruments and Practice of Arbitration in the EU Member States and Switzerland 214 permanent arbitral institutions were registered with the Register of Companies of the Ministry of Justice in Latvia in March 2014. See: Cole et al. 2014, 126–128 with further references.

[95]Cole et al. 2014, 163–164.

[96]"P.R.I.M.E. Finance (Panel of Recognized International Market Experts in Finance)" http://primefinancedisputes.org/about-us/. Accessed 25 April 2016.

[97]Brabandere 2011.

institutional arbitration users. Here, although progressively applied by other arbitral institutions (i.e. CEPANI and the Arbitration Centre of the Chamber of Commerce of the Grand-Duchy of Luxembourg), the ICC's distinctive provisions regarding the process of scrutiny of arbitral awards by the ICC Court should be recalled. Also, tracing back to 2010, one should not forget the then pioneering role of the SCC Institute in introducing the framework for modern emergency arbitrator proceedings by means of its 2010 Rules.[98] Similarly, the provisions of both the 1998 and 2014 LCIA Rules making London a default arbitration seat in respective cases reflect the distinctive aspect of the LCIA procedural regime.

In fact, between 2010 and 2015 the majority of arbitration rules of the most prominent arbitral institutions have been amended. Beginning with the changes to the SCC Rules in 2010, the ICC amended its rules in 2012, and finally the LCIA as well as the ICDR in 2014. Furthermore, the most prominent arbitral institutions internalized some soft-law international arbitration guidelines into their respective regimes as means of competition. Hence, in the spirit of the 2014 International Bar Association (IBA) Guidelines on Party Representation in International Arbitration, the LCIA annexed to its 2014 Rules the "General Guidelines for the Parties' Legal Representatives" that need to be complied with by each party's representative upon the instructions from the parties. Moreover, in 2014 the ICC published a document entitled: "Effective Management of Arbitration—A Guide for In-House Counsel and Other Party Representatives". Similarly, the wordings of the model arbitration clauses proposed by institutions should also be perceived within the meaning of dynamics of competition. The competition among the most prominent arbitral institutions regarding their rules and other soft-law mechanisms, however, has proven increasingly problematic.

An increasing amount of scholars and arbitration practitioners have criticized the introduction of soft-law guidelines by arbitral institutions, with a few authors even trivializing the increasing convergence of procedural rules of the most prominent arbitral institutions. As argued argued by Sabharwal and Zaman, although in 2010 the SCC Institute was an isolated arbitral institution offering emergency arbitrator procedures to its users, today most other prominent arbitral institutions provide similar services[99]. In a similar vein, although it was the SCC who first addressed the issue of third-party treatment and consolidation of arbitration proceedings in its 2010 Rules, today the ICC, the LCIA, as well as the ICDR provide their own rules that regulate these issues. One question that has been recently addressed by arbitration scholars and practitioners is whether such convergence of procedural rules and policies (i.e. the ones on party representatives in arbitration) is still the function of thoughtful competition between arbitral institutions or rather the expression of the growing imitation of the rules with a view of simply not staying behind the competitors or multiplying procedural errors "in a good company".[100] Sabharwal and Zaman rightly observe that it is

[98]Sabharwal and Zaman 2014, 704. See also: Warwas, 2012, 44-54.

[99]Sabharwal and Zaman 2014, 704–705.

[100]Sabharwal and Zaman 2014, 711 with further references.

also questionable whether the unification of arbitration rules of the prominent arbitral institutions, in fact, reflects and continues to prioritize the preferences of arbitration users relating to their desirable outlook of institutional arbitration procedures.

Leaving these questions open for now, the means of competition (and collaboration) adopted by other, more local arbitral institutions appear as a positive alternative to the competition mechanisms developed by more sophisticated institutions such as the ICC and LCIA. One particular example emerges in this regard. Four arbitral institutions, the CAM, DIS, VIAC, and the SCC Institute, conventionally known under the name "Gang of Four", an informal coalition of small or medium-size arbitral institutions, have been organizing a number of events during which the institutions exchange their practices in relation to the management of institutional arbitration cases.[101] Interestingly, they do so by pointing to the divergences in their handling of arbitration cases rather than by focusing on similarities in their rules.[102] This is a remarkable initiative in that it brings together the Secretaries General of these institutions and practitioners who can discuss different ways in which arbitration services are provided to the parties (although often still relating to similar procedural rules) rather than by simply pointing to the universalization of arbitration rules as in the case of the most prominent institutions such as the ICC and the LCIA.

Translations of arbitration rules, which address the heterogeneity of institutional users, also constitute an instrument of competition between arbitral institutions. Even though most institutions name the native versions of their arbitration rules as the official versions in case of any discrepancy or inconsistency, a number of institutions translate their rules into several languages, which corresponds to the cultural diversity among institutional arbitration users. While the ICC Court provides its rules in 13 languages, the previous version of the LCIA rules was available in 10 language versions, in both cases with the rules referring to the origins of the parties representing large economies such as China, Germany, Russia, or the Arab countries, as well as the emerging arbitration users coming from Eastern Europe. The recent set of the LCIA Rules of 2014 is, by now, available in two language versions (English and Russian), but it seems to be just a matter of time before the LCIA will provide further translations. The ICDR Procedures, originally available in English, were translated into Spanish, Arabic, and Portuguese, whereas the SCC Rules are offered in English, Swedish, Russian, and Chinese. Although these means of competition might not seem significant at first glance, in fact the quality of the translation of different rules (in particular of model institutional arbitration clauses) has an enormous impact on both the decisions on jurisdiction and the duration of institutional arbitration proceedings. The recent research on "100 Translation Errors in Institutional Arbitration Rules" conducted

---

[101]Cole et al. 2014, 58, 123.

[102]Cole et al. 2014, 58; Michael, McIlwrath, "The Gang of Four Rides Again: Pathological Clauses." 30 July 2015. Kluwer Arbitration Blog. http://kluwerarbitrationblog.com/2013/07/30/the-gang-of-four-rides-again-pathological-clauses/. Accessed 25 April 2016. For the comparison of certain rules of arbitral institutions falling within the "Gang of Four" see Coppo 2010.

by Isabelle Liger unveils that the translations of arbitration rules into different languages within the same arbitral institution often contain contradictions, which may affect the diligence and expeditiousness of institutional arbitration proceedings with regard to the parties coming from different geographical locations.[103]

Additionally, arbitral institutions compete by virtue of different marketing strategies, including publications on institutional arbitration and the organization of conferences or educational events concerning recent developments in the institutional arbitration practice. Most institutions also publish specialized brochures in different language versions explaining particularities of institutional regimes along with the distinctiveness of national laws on arbitration in jurisdictions where institutions have their assets. These attempts appear especially helpful for the accidental and new users, which, unlike repeat market players, are not familiar with the general features and objectives of a specific arbitral institution. In this light, the organization of seminars and other educational events is aided by the promotion of arbitration services as a product for both repeat market players and new, potential users of arbitration from the emerging economies.

Moreover, some international events of arbitral institutions take the form of international trainings for young lawyers.[104] As such, institutional marketing strategies expand the competition beyond arbitration users, and prove institutional interest in educating future institutional arbitration actors such as parties' legal representatives, arbitrators, or even the future institutional employees. In addition to such purely competitive strategies, arbitral institutions participate in numerous political and academic events regarding international arbitration, which address both policy-making in the field of arbitration (such as the vivid discussion on the future of the EU investor-State arbitration[105]) and the emerging juridical problems in the context of arbitration.[106] These initiatives also demonstrate the growing private, institutional awareness of the public challenges facing modern institutional arbitration practice. In this way, they will be relevant for the analysis of the public function of institutional arbitration in Sect. 2.3.2.

2.3.1.3 "Cost-Effective Arbitration Without Delay?" Understanding Competition Dynamics

When traditional arbitral institutions were emerging at the turn of the nineteenth and twentieth centuries, arbitration was relatively cheap and rapid, particularly in

---

[103] Liger 2011.

[104] The ICC actively participates in various academic events and legal trainings. "Opportunities and Materials for Arbitrators and Legal Practitioners". http://www.iccwbo.org/Products-and-Services/Arbitration-and-ADR/Arbitration/Introduction-to-ICC-Arbitration/Opportunities-and-materials-for-arbitrators-and-legal-practitioners/. Accessed 25 April 2016.

[105] Ross 2011.

[106] "The ICC 2012 Programme Action." http://www.iccwbo.org/news/brochures/. Accessed 25 April 2016.

comparison to litigation. Regrettably, this is not the case today. Progressively, the critics of arbitral institutions have flagged the increasingly high price of institutional arbitration services, as well as the inefficiency of these institutions in terms of controlling the duration of the proceedings in general and the timely rendering of the awards by arbitrators in particular.[107] The criticism has come mainly from arbitration users themselves, including in-house counsel who has less financial incentives to support lengthy arbitration proceedings than external counsel working based on high hourly rates. In fact, the increasing complaints regarding the bureaucratization of institutional arbitration and its implications for time and costs of the proceedings should be depicted from a more holistic perspective, in that they point to the (il)legitimacy of the contemporary international arbitration system as a whole.[108] All these require new institutional responses that have been reflected in new dynamics of competition visible among the arbitral institutions.

2.3.1.3.1 Competition Regarding Institutional Arbitration Costs

To understand the dynamics of competition among arbitral institutions in terms of arbitration costs, it is necessary to examine the following issues: (1) what kind of fees constitute institutional arbitration costs; (2) how they are calculated; and (3) what the institutional tools to decrease these costs are (if any).

Generally, the costs of institutional arbitration are comprised of: (a) arbitrators' fees; (b) expenses of the arbitral tribunal; and (c) administrative fees of an arbitral institution.[109] In principle, it is the arbitration centre itself that stipulates arbitrators' fees, within its own discretion and in accordance with the arbitration rules and schedules of costs developed within each institutional regime. The scope of institutional authority to fix arbitrators' fees is remarkable to the extent that it diminishes any form of direct stipulations of arbitration costs by parties and arbitrators and therefore places arbitral institutions at the epicentre of all contractual relations coming into existence in institutional arbitration. In this way, from the contractual perspective, the institutional authority regarding the determination of arbitration costs has another practical implication for the parties. It affects the assessment of the parties of who in fact bears any potential responsibility for the conduct of arbitration proceedings (be it arbitrators who decide on the outcomes of a dispute or arbitral institutions that administer the proceedings and enjoy almost ultimate authority in fixing the costs for their services, including the fees and expenses of arbitral tribunals). This has further significance when identifying a plausible claimant in relation to liability claims against arbitral institutions (and/or arbitrators). The correlations between institutional contractual authority and the liability of institutional arbitration actors will be discussed further in Sect. 2.3.2.

---

[107] See Draetta 2011.

[108] See generally QC Menon 2012.

[109] There are also the costs that might be directly incurred by the parties in connection with arbitration.

The way in which arbitrators' fees are fixed by arbitral institutions varies among the four main institutions under analysis. Both the ICC Court and the SCC Board determine these charges on the basis of the amount of the dispute in question according to the Scales of Arbitrators' Fees.[110] The ICC also provides for a special regulation that forbids any separate fee arrangements between the parties and arbitrators.[111] The ICC arbitral tribunals may only decide on the costs *other* than those to be fixed by the ICC Court, including the fees and expenses of the experts appointed by the arbitral tribunal in accordance with Article 25(4) of the ICC Arbitration Rules, the parties' reasonable legal and other costs, total costs of arbitration to be included in the final award, and parts of the costs of arbitration to be fixed or allocated between the parties.[112] By contrast, the LCIA and the ICDR set the fees of the arbitral tribunal according to the time to be spent on the dispute by arbitrators (i.e. hourly rates in the case of the LCIA[113] and daily or hourly rates in the case of the ICDR).

Interestingly, in the case of the LCIA arbitration, the LCIA Court determines the fees and expenses of LCIA arbitral tribunals at the outset of each arbitration proceeding, and it normally also secures such costs of its own deposits.[114] Prior to their appointment, the members of the LCIA arbitral tribunal agree in writing to be bound with the rates contained in the LCIA Schedule of Fees and, at the time of the appointment, these rates are communicated to the parties by the Registrar, including a reservation that they are subject to change should the duration of the proceedings or change in the circumstances so required.[115]

The ICDR (through its Case Administrators) consults with the parties and arbitrators regarding the rate of compensation due to arbitral tribunal at the beginning of arbitration with regard to the arbitrators' stated rate of compensation in view of

[110]See Scale of Arbitrators' Fees in the Appendix III to the 1998 ICC Rules (Article 4); Scale of Arbitrator's Fees in the Appendix III to the 2012 ICC Arbitration Rules (Article 4); Appendix II to the SCC Rules(Article II), respectively.

[111]Any separate fee arrangements are contrary to the ICC Rules. See Article 2 Section 4 of the Appendix III to the 1998 ICC Arbitration Rules. The 2012 ICC Arbitration Rules provide for the same solution. Additionally, the fact that separate fee arrangements between the parties and arbitrators are not permitted is clarified in the Statement of Acceptance, Availability, Impartiality and Independence that shall be signed by all arbitrators before being considered for the confirmation or appointment.

[112]See Article 31(2) of the 1998 ICC Arbitration Rules and Article 37(3) of the 2012 ICC Arbitration Rules. See a commentary note to Articles 37(1) and 37(3)-(5) in: Fry, Greenberg, Mazza, 2012, 404–411.

[113]See: "Hourly rates for arbitrators shall not exceed £450 save in exceptional circumstances when they can be higher". In: "Schedule of LCIA Arbitration Costs." http://www.lcia.org//Dispute_Resolution_Services/schedule-of-Costs-Lcia-Arbitration.aspx. Accessed 25 April 2016.

[114]A commentary note to Article 28 of the 2014 LCIA Rules in: Wade et al. 2015, 305–314.

[115]"Schedule of LCIA Arbitration Costs." http://www.lcia.org//Dispute_Resolution_Services/schedule-of-Costs-Lcia-Arbitration.aspx. Accessed 25 April 2016.

the size and complexity of the arbitration in question.[116] In addition, the ICDR case administrator has an exclusive authority to decide on any dispute regarding the fees and expenses of the arbitrators between arbitrators and the parties.[117] In ICC and SCC arbitrations, it is the ICC Court and the Board, respectively, that fix the arbitrators' remuneration at the end of every arbitration proceeding. These assessments should keep in line with: (a) the advance stipulation of the arbitration costs; (b) the decision on costs in the arbitration award; and (c) the exceptional circumstances which appeared in the course of the proceedings. The SCC Rules expressly oblige the arbitrators to recourse to the Board before rendering the award to finally determine the costs of arbitration.[118]

Since the arbitrators' fees are said to constitute the major part of all costs in institutional arbitration, it is also significant to understand the factors that arbitral institutions take into account while fixing arbitrators' fees, and whether any mechanisms have been implemented by these institutions to contribute to a considerable decrease of such fees. Usually, relevant members of institutional bodies will determine the amount of arbitrator's fees on a case-by-case basis, taking into account the duration of the proceedings, the workload (hence the number of submissions made by the parties and the complexity of a dispute), diligence of arbitrators in fulfilling their tasks and any other circumstances that may affect the work of arbitral tribunal (i.e. resignation of co-arbitrators, the highly contentious character of arbitration proceedings requiring additional workload from arbitrators).

The ICC reported that it departed from its average arbitrator's fee and set a lower fee on many occasions. For example, in cases of extensive delays in submitting the final award by arbitral tribunal (with at least partial responsibility on the part of arbitrators), where the arbitral tribunal waited too long to prepare a brief addendum to a partial award, or in cases in which the amount in a dispute was simply too high, therefore providing for equally high arbitrator's fees that turned out to be disproportionate to the amount of arbitrators' work in arbitration in question.[119]

At the same time, most leading arbitral institutions, including the ICC Court itself, appear eager to increase the amount of arbitrator's fees against the average fee contained in a schedule of costs should the complexity of the case, high efficiency on the part of arbitrators, or other circumstances require. This makes it particularly challenging for the parties to truly understand the institutional mechanisms that are applicable when fixing arbitrator's fees on a case-by-case basis. Here, a remarkable document prepared by the SCC should be noted. The SCC issued a special guide for its arbitrators that deals with the framework for arbitrators' fees, and which mentions the possibility of reducing fees for arbitrations in special cases, including situations in which the award was rendered

[116]Article 35.2 of the ICDR Procedures.

[117]Article 35.3 of the ICDR Procedures.

[118]See: Article 43(2) of the 2010 SCC Arbitration Rules.

[119]A commentary note: Articles 37(1) and 37(2) in: Fry, Greenberg, Mazza, 2012, 392–404.

without ruling on the merits of the case and/or when the arbitrators had been previously released.[120] Although this document is clearly directed to SCC arbitrators, it also serves as a practical tool for the parties to SCC arbitration proceedings in that it allows them to understand the complexity of the costs' allocation within the SCC framework, including the potential impact of arbitrator's inefficiency on the final institutional arbitration costs. The LCIA, in turn, suggests to its prospective parties to carefully consult the fees of their advocates and counsel in order to further decline the cost of the LCIA arbitrations.[121]

Regarding institutional administrative costs, the ICC, the SCC Institute, and the ICDR take into account the amount of the dispute as the major determinant of these costs. Unlike these institutions, the LCIA Court calculates the LCIA's fees, as in the case of the LCIA arbitrators, according to the time spent by the Registrar and the Secretariat on the dispute on the basis of the hourly rate.[122] As for the registration fee, the SCC Institute collects the lowest amount of €2,000, whilst the ICC and LCIA require the fee of US$3,000[123] and £1,750, respectively, to be paid by the claimant at the outset of each arbitration.[124] The ICDR offers two administrative fee options including the Standard and the Flexible Fee Schedule. The basic difference between the two schedules relates to the number of instalments that should be paid to the ICDR (i.e. a two payment schedule in the standard option and a three payment schedule in the flexible option), depending on whether the parties prefer to pay a higher amount upfront or if they chose to have the administrative costs spread out into slightly smaller payments in the course of the proceedings.[125]

It is remarkable that, unlike in the case of arbitrators' fees that are subject to readjustment (e.g. they are usually decreased or increased based, to a certain degree, upon the performance of arbitrators), in practice, arbitral institutions rarely use their discretion to lower the amount of arbitration costs corresponding to their own services.[126] For example, it appears that the ICC Court derogated from its scales contained in the schedule of costs only on a few occasions; when it was

[120]The SCC Arbitrator's Guidelines 2014. http://sccinstitute.com/about-the-scc/legal-resources/arbitrators-guidelines/. Accessed 25 April 2016

[121]Information on the LCIA website in the Section "About the LCIA" as provided in 2009.

[122]This includes: £250 per hour for the Registrar/Deputy Registrar, £225 per hour for a Counsel, and between £175 and £150 per hour for Case Managers and other personnel providing casework accounting functions, respectively. "Schedule of LCIA Arbitration Costs." http://www.lcia.org//Dispute_Resolution_Services/schedule-of-Costs-Lcia-Arbitration.aspx. Accessed 25 April 2016.

[123]This filling fee was set in the new 2012 ICC Arbitration Rules.

[124]"Schedule of LCIA Arbitration Costs." http://www.lcia.org//Dispute_Resolution_Services/schedule-of-Costs-Lcia-Arbitration.aspx. Accessed 25 April 2016.

[125]Administrative Fees, which are attached to the ICDR Procedures.

[126]See, for example, Article 2(5) of Appendix III to the 2012 ICC Arbitration Rules, that authorizes the ICC Court to deviate from the scales included in the schedule of costs and set the amount of costs at either lower or higher rates.

necessitated by the number of frivolous challenges against arbitrators and in the case where arbitral tribunal proved to be highly unprofessional so as to affect the level and quality of communications in the course of the proceedings, at the same time calling for a more in-depth assistance from the ICC Secretariat.[127] Based on these examples, the readjustment of the administrative costs in institutional arbitration can be seen as the function of the interconnectedness of the work of arbitral institutions and institutional arbitrators, all in view of the performance of the parties that requires institutional arbitration services to be tailored to the level of cooperativeness of both the arbitrators and the parties to the proceedings. Although such justification seems more than legitimate, it is surprising that arbitral institutions do not provide for a possible decline in the amount of their administrative costs due to the error or misconduct on the part of institutional staff or officials (should such behaviour occur), in particular if similar situations gave rise to the decrease in the amounts due to institutional arbitrators as visible from institutional practices in the field of arbitration costs.

Against this background, there is no clear-cut formula for identifying the most attractive institutional regime regarding the costs of institutional arbitration from the perspective of its users. Consequently, it is difficult to assess whether hourly rates are better suited for the parties than calculations based on the amount of disputes to be collected by an institution. Some commentators have noted that the SCC Institute provides relatively cheap arbitration service.[128] To the contrary, the ICC arbitration costs are relatively high in the arbitration market, which can be seen as the result of the in-depth involvement of the ICC Court in the administration of the arbitration cases.[129] It is reasonable to think that the LCIA system of the hourly rates could, in principle, affect dilatory tactics on the part of arbitrators, institutions, or even the parties to arbitration proceedings, which could increase the hazard of overrating, especially given the limited procedural tools for the parties to control arbitrators, the institutions, and recalcitrant parties in cases of the possible delays. At the same time, it is also hard to determine which system of cost allocation offers more transparency, and therefore also more predictability to the parties from the start until the closure of the proceedings. Given that, it appears particularly important for the parties to remain proactive and cautious when determining the degree of their involvement in arbitration proceedings both prior to and in the course of such proceedings. This can be achieved by carefully drafting arbitration agreements to avoid them being pathological, when appointing arbitrators and making submissions in the course of arbitration, when appointing witnesses or experts, or managing other logistical costs.[130] The effectiveness of the parties' arrangements in these regards will depend, inter alia, upon the flexibility of the institutional arbitration rules and the level of cooperation from their

[127] A commentary note 3–1475 in: Fry, Greenberg, and Mazza 2012.

[128] Hope 2008, 25–27.

[129] For a general discussion on the costs of arbitration see: Bühler 2005.

[130] Cf. Chao and Schurz 2007.

counterparties. Here, the parties should first and foremost examine the institutional techniques and tools aiming at controlling both the costs and the length of arbitration proceedings.

2.3.1.3.2 Competition Regarding the "Effective" Case Management Techniques

In light of the progressing pressure placed on arbitral institutions under overwhelming criticism regarding institutional arbitration costs and speed, the majority of institutional rules and policies increasingly reflect the greater need for improving the efficiency of institutional arbitration proceedings and the diligent performance of arbitrators and the parties. Accordingly, the 2012 version of the ICC Rules contains a number of provisions dealing exclusively with effective case management techniques, which should be taken into account by parties and arbitrators for controlling time and costs of the proceedings. Such techniques are mentioned in Appendix IV to the 2012 ICC Arbitration Rules and have been reflected in the main body of these rules. Hence, Articles 22(1) and 22(2) expressly set forth general duties with regard to the parties and arbitrators concerning the effective management of arbitration proceedings. Furthermore, Article 24(1) in accordance with Article 24(4) requires that arbitral tribunals organize and conduct the obligatory case management conference at the outset of the proceedings. The latter rule is tailored at the early consensus between the parties and arbitrators regarding all procedural matters and case management techniques relevant for the quick and cost-effective resolution of a dispute. Additionally, the ICC published the aforementioned "Guide for In-House Counsel and Other Party Representatives" to address the need for effective management of ICC arbitration proceedings that is also applicable to any other institutional arbitration proceedings should the parties to such proceedings wish to rely on the guidance contained in the Guide.[131] Indeed, the ICC's Guide for In-House Counsel serves as a detailed toolkit for the parties, their legal representatives, and arbitrators in securing the effective conduct of almost all stages of their arbitration proceedings. It should be emphasized here that already in 2012 the ICC adopted a similarly noteworthy document entitled "Techniques for Controlling Time and Costs in Arbitration" that also provides a guidance for the parties and an arbitral tribunal concerning the procedural support for the conduct of arbitration.[132]

Similarly, other leading arbitral institutions have also recently adopted certain case management techniques aimed at reducing the time and costs of arbitration.

---

[131]ICC Commission on Arbitration and ADR. 2014. Effective Management of Arbitration: A Guide for In-House Counsel and Other Party Representatives. International Chamber of Commerce.

[132]ICC Arbitration Commission Report on Controlling Time and Costs of Arbitration of 2012. http://www.iccwbo.org/Advocacy-Codes-and-Rules/Document-centre/2012/ICC-Arbitration-Commission-Report-on-Techniques-for-Controlling-Time-and-Costs-in-Arbitration/. Accessed 25 April 2016.

The SCC Institute, in Article 23 of its Rules, authorizes the arbitral tribunal to establish a provisional timetable for the conduct of the arbitration.[133] Once the timetable is sent to both the parties and the Secretariat, the SCC should observe whether the proceedings are delayed per the agreed upon schedule. The SCC Rules also require that arbitral tribunals conduct arbitration proceedings in "practical" and "expeditious" fashion in any case with respect of due process requirements in arbitration.[134] Furthermore, the SCC itself is obliged, under Article 9 of the SCC Rules, to ensure the expeditious conduct of the SCC arbitration.

The ICDR Procedures also offer to the parties the possibility of participating in the conference organized at the start of the proceedings.[135] Article 4 provides for the possibility of the organization of an administrative conference by the ICDR Administrator, even before the constitution of the arbitral tribunal, "to facilitate party discussion and agreement on issues such as arbitrator selection, mediating the dispute, process efficiencies, and any other administrative matters". In the same spirit, the ICDR Procedures encourage the parties and arbitrators (once appointed) to conduct the proceedings in an expedited manner to eliminate any possible delays and additional costs to be incurred in the course of arbitration proceedings.[136] Although the ICDR to date did not issue any guidelines for the parties' legal representative, it leaves such possibility open through the new provision of Article 16 of the ICDR Procedures that sets forth a broad authority for the ICDR to regulate the conduct of legal counsel in the future.

In addition, the recent amendments to the LCIA Rules as well as new LCIA policies regarding the conduct in arbitration by the parties and arbitrators put more emphasis on the need for the increased cost-effectiveness and expeditiousness of LCIA arbitration proceedings. One notable feature can be seen in the wording of Article 14.1 of the 2014 LCIA Rules, under which the parties and the arbitral tribunal must get in contact with one another within 21 days as of the composition of the arbitral tribunal. This provision, although potentially problematic,[137] makes it mandatory for LCIA arbitrators and the parties to liaise at the outset of the arbitration proceedings to decide on any potential procedural issues in an expedited manner. In addition, Article 28.4 of the 2014 LCIA Rules introduces, for the first time, the specific authority of LCIA arbitrators in allocation of both the legal costs to be borne by the parties and the arbitration costs. Under this new provision, LCIA arbitrators are entitled to decide on the costs' allocation also based on the performance and cooperativeness of the parties to a dispute. Should the parties' conduct

---

[133]See Article 18(1) which provides for the conclusion of the Terms of Reference by the parties and the arbitrators, and Article 23 of the SCC Rules.

[134]See Article 19(2) of the SCC Rules.

[135]See Article 20(2) of the ICDR Procedures.

[136]See in particular: Articles 20(2) and 20(7) of the ICDR Procedures.

[137]As explained by Remy Gerbay, it is unclear how a 21-day deadline set forth in Article 14.1 of the 2014 LCIA Rules will apply in view of the requirement provided for in Article 24.3 of the LCIA Rules preventing the arbitral tribunal to proceed with arbitration if the initial deposits have not been covered by the parties. See Gerbay, forthcoming 2016.

appear to be in bad faith, LCIA arbitrators will be allowed to reflect on this behaviour in their decisions regarding the apportionment of arbitration costs. In fact, two other new provisions introduced under the 2014 LCIA Rules make express reference to the obligation of "good faith" with regard to the parties' conduct and, to some degree, in relation to the conduct of LCIA arbitrators and the LCIA itself.

Under Article 14.5 of the 2014 LCIA Rules: "[A]t all times the parties shall do everything necessary in good faith for the fair, efficient and expeditious conduct of the arbitration, including the Arbitral Tribunal's discharge of its general duties". Furthermore, Article 32.2 states that: "For all matters not expressly provided in the Arbitration Agreement, the LCIA Court, the LCIA, the Registrar, the Arbitral Tribunal and each of the parties shall act at all times in good faith, respecting the spirit of the Arbitration Agreement [...]". These amendments aim at encouraging the cooperation between the LCIA arbitration actors in order to potentially increase the efficiency of LCIA arbitrations. On top of the changes to the LCIA Rules, the LCIA has also introduced some soft-law instruments (called "LCIA Notes for Parties" and "LCIA Notes for Arbitrators") that explain the procedural matrix of the LCIA arbitration to the parties, their legal representatives and LCIA arbitrators in order to improve the efficiency in the performance of these actors in the course of the arbitration proceedings. In addition, as already noted, the LCIA has also included in its 2014 Rules (Articles 18.5 and 18.6) as well as in the Annex to its Rules, the "General Guidelines for the Parties' Legal Representatives" that should be understood as the code of conduct for legal counsel of the LCIA parties to arbitration. Without a doubt, such a soft-law instrument aimed at increasing the quality of performance of litigation counsel in the course of the LCIA arbitration should be read as a remarkable step vis-à-vis other arbitral institutions in that the LCIA is undoubtedly the first most prominent arbitral institutions that codified loose ethical norms and standards for legal representatives in arbitration proceedings. Given the increased calls for ethical regulation in international arbitration,[138] the LCIA efforts in this field certainly strengthens the LCIA's position within the institutional arbitration market, while at the same time further contributing, at least indirectly, to the increase in the effectiveness of the counsel's conduct in arbitration.

2.3.1.3.3 Competition in the Field of the Length of Arbitration Proceedings: Time Limits and Expedited Proceedings

One of the institutional techniques to control the length of arbitration (that, at the same time, is strongly interlinked with the institutional efforts to decrease the costs of the proceedings) concerns the supervision of the time of both the arbitration proceedings and of issuing of the awards by arbitrators. Increasingly, the majority of institutional arbitration rules also contain procedures for the expedited

[138] Rogers 2014.

formation of arbitral tribunal in extraordinary circumstances, which, at least at first glance, serve as an efficient tool for the parties wishing to secure the prompt resolution of a dispute, especially in view of the unstable financial situation or the insolvency of one or more parties to arbitration proceedings. The efficiency of these solutions will now be analysed in greater detail.

Most leading arbitral institutions set forth time limits for the completion of different stages of arbitration proceedings. By way of illustration, different sets of arbitration rules promulgated by the leading arbitral institutions often provide for default time frames for the receiving of the response to the request of arbitration, and for the constitution of the arbitral tribunal or the appointment of a sole arbitrator, to mention a few.

Regarding the time frame for the submission of the answer to the request of arbitration to be transmitted to arbitral institutions, the 2012 ICC Arbitration Rules set the time limit of 30 days from the moment of the receiving of the request by the ICC Secretariat;[139] the 2014 LCIA Rules provide for the answer to the request to be submitted within 28 days from the commencement of arbitration (compared to 30 days from the delivery of the request to arbitration to respondent as provided for in the 1998 version of the LCIA Rules);[140] the ICDR Procedures set forth the time frame of 30 days after the commencement of the arbitration;[141] and the SCC Rules leave the time limit for the submitting of the answer to the request within the discretion of the SCC Secretariat.[142]

As far as the time limits for the constitution of a three-member arbitral tribunal in cases in which the parties have agreed that a dispute shall be decided by three arbitrators is concerned, the ICC first invites the parties to nominate the co-arbitrators in their request for arbitration and the answer to the request. Here, the deadlines for submitting these documents apply. If the parties fail to do so, the ICC Court would invite each party to nominate the co-arbitrator as soon as practicable and normally within the extendable deadline of 15 days.[143] If respondents fail to nominate the co-arbitrators within the specified time, in most cases the ICC Court will refuse to extend the time limit and will itself proceed with the nomination of co-arbitrators.[144] The parties to the ICC arbitration should also fix a time limit for the nomination of the president of the ICC arbitral tribunal. If they fail to do so, the default time limit of 30 days from the date of the confirmation or appointment of the second co-arbitrator will apply under the new provision included in Article 12(5) of the 2012 ICC Arbitration Rules. This time frame, however, may still be

[139]Article 5(1) of the 2012 ICC Arbitration Rules.

[140]Cf. Article 2.1 of the 2014 LCIA Rules and Article 2.1 of the 1998 LCIA Rules.

[141]Article 3 of the ICDR Procedures.

[142]Article 5 of the SCC Rules.

[143]A commentary note to Article 12(4) of the 2012 ICC Arbitration Rules in: Fry, Greenberg, Mazza, 2012, 142–144.

[144]There is a slightly different procedure to be followed by the ICC Court in cases in which the parties have fixed their own deadlines for the nomination of co-arbitrators in their arbitration agreements. See: Ibid.

altered by the ICC upon the request of the parties and/or one of the parties or on its own imitative; similarly, the parties themselves are free to agree on the extension of such deadline even in cases in which the time limit was fixed by the ICC Court. The ICC Rules concerning the deadlines regarding the appointment of a sole arbitrator are equality flexible as in the case of time limits for the nomination of co-arbitrators in a three-member arbitral tribunal. Under Article 12(3) of the ICC Arbitration Rules, the parties are encouraged to nominate a sole arbitrator within 30 days of the date in which the respondents received the request for arbitration. If they fail to meet this deadline, they may be granted extension, and if they fail to meet the extended time limit, a sole arbitrator will be appointed by the ICC Court.

In turn, in the case of the LCIA arbitration the arbitral tribunal and a sole arbitrator will be appointed "promptly" by the LCIA after the receipt of the Response to Arbitration by the Registrar. Additionally, if no response has been transmitted to the Registrar, the LCIA Court will appoint members of the arbitral tribunal and a sole arbitrator within 35 days from the start of arbitration. The SCC Rules do not provide for any time limit for the appointment of a three-member tribunal by the parties or the SCC itself (which is authorized to appoint the chair of the arbitral tribunal). In case of the appointment of a sole arbitrator, the SCC provides for the joint appointment by the parties within 10 days or, failing such procedure, for the appointment by the SCC itself. The ICDR Procedures provide for a time limit of 45 days from the commencement of the ICDR arbitration for the appointment of arbitrators (or a sole arbitrator) by the parties. If the parties fail to do so within this time frame, or within the alternative time limit as agreed by them, the ICDR Case Administrator will appoint all arbitrators unless the parties have agreed otherwise within 45 days from the commencement of arbitration.[145]

Most importantly, arbitral institutions also set time limits for arbitrators to render arbitral awards or require from arbitrators to inform relevant institutional organs or staff members about the provisional time frame within which the arbitral tribunal or a sole arbitrator expects to render an award. Both the ICC and the SCC Rules require the arbitral tribunal to render an award within 6 months from the moment of: (a) the drafting of the Terms of Reference (or upon the notification to the arbitral tribunal of the approval of the Terms of Reference by the ICC Court), as in case of the ICC Rules;[146] and (b) referring the arbitration to the arbitral tribunal, as for the SCC arbitration.[147] The LCIA Rules are again silent in this respect, however, Article 15.10 of the LCIA Rules obliges the arbitral tribunal to "seek to make its final award as soon as reasonably possible following the last submission from the parties (whether made orally or in writing), in accordance with a timetable notified to the parties and the Registrar as soon as practicable". In turn, the

[145]Article 12.3 and 12.5 of the ICDR Procedures.

[146]Article 30(1) of the 2012 ICC Arbitration Rules.

[147]Even if these time limits can be successively extended, they "ethically oblige" an arbitrator to deal with arbitrations in a relatively short time.

ICDR Procedures mention that the award should be rendered "as quickly as possible after the hearing" in no case later than 60 days from the date of the closing of a hearing.[148] Additionally, the ICC Rules state that, on the closing of the proceedings, the arbitral tribunal must indicate to the ICC Secretariat when it expects to submit a draft award.[149] This may increase the pressure on arbitrators to complete their work expeditiously. From the practical perspective, however, the provisions setting time limits for the issuance of arbitral awards have little effect, in that such time limits can be easily extended, in some cases even on institution's own initiative. Furthermore, the lack of specific time limits for the LCIA arbitrations may bring serious economic consequences for the parties, especially while considering the hourly rate as a general basis for fixing the arbitrators' remuneration and the LCIA's administrative fees.

Another particular feature of the competition between the leading arbitral institutions is that the majority of the arbitration rules of these institutions provide for accelerated arbitration procedures. This is ensured either by means of the specific sets of arbitration rules for the so-called "fast track" institutional arbitrations (as in the case of the SCC Expedited Arbitration Rules of 2010) or through the limited provisions included in the main sets of institutional arbitration rules that support the parties' decisions regarding expedited stages of different phases of arbitration proceedings (as in the case of the ICC, LCIA, and ICDR Rules).

The SCC advertises its expedited procedures mainly in relation to small-value disputes.[150] In contrast, the ICDR Expedited Procedures will be applied by default to disputes where "no disclosed claim and counterclaim exceeds US$250,000 exclusive of interest and the costs of arbitration" and to any other disputes in which the parties expressly agree on the application of these Procedures. In turn, the specific provisions on expedited arbitration contained in the ICC and LCIA Rules (such as the provision of Article 38 of the ICC Arbitration Rules authorizing the parties to request for shortening the time limits set forth in the ICC Rules,[151] and the provisions of Article 9A and 9C of the LCIA Rules regarding the expedited formation of arbitral tribunal and of the replacement of arbitrator, respectively) can be invoked in any case if any party to the proceedings wishes to conduct their arbitration in a fast-track manner.

Two questions arise with regard to the efficiency of these solutions. First, are expedited procedures realistic in complex arbitrations? Second, how would the

[148]Article 30.1 of the ICC Rules and Procedures.

[149]See Article 27(b) of the 2012 ICC Arbitration Rules (Cf. former Article 24(1) of the 1998 ICC Arbitration Rules).

[150]Expedited Arbitration. http://www.sccinstitute.com/dispute-Resolution/expedited-Arbitration/. Accessed 25 April 2016.

[151]In any case, even when parties to ICC arbitration decide on the expedited conduct of their proceedings and the arbitral tribunal further approves the parties' decision in this regard, the ICC Court, on its own initiative, may subsequently extend such time limits "if it decides that it is necessary to do so in order that the arbitral tribunal and the Court may fulfil their responsibilities in accordance with the Rules." See Article 38(2) of the ICC Arbitration Rules.

parties' choices on accelerated conduct of certain stages of arbitration impact arbitration costs? By way of example, as reported by a prominent chief litigation counsel of a multinational company, in one dispute where the arbitration agreement provided for an arbitral tribunal to issue the award within 9 months from the appointment of a chairman (which was in fact slightly longer than the time limit contained in the applicable institutional arbitration rules), the institution qualified the clause in the meaning of the fast-track arbitration proceedings and doubled the advance of costs calculated in the dispute in question[152]. This forced the parties to redraft their arbitration clause and refer their dispute to *ad hoc* arbitration instead where the award was rendered within 10 months from the appointment of a chairman and the costs of arbitration appeared to be 50 % lower than the provisional costs determined by the institution. This example shows that some arbitral institutions in fact have little understanding of the provisions on expedited treatment and that, in any case, the reference to such provisions by the parties may mean additional costs to be borne by the parties. Consequently, it is questionable whether the provisions on accelerated arbitration as included in institutional arbitration rules correspond with the institutions' commitment to efficient arbitration proceedings that seems to be emphasized more in theory rather than in actual arbitration practice.

2.3.1.3.4 Competition Regarding the Procedural Framework Encouraging Settlement, in Particular by Means of the Mediation Attempts

Although encouraging settlement in the course of arbitration proceedings lies usually within the arbitrators' responsibility, the institutional arbitration rules certainly do build procedural framework within which such settlement can be facilitated and eventually reached by the parties. Most arbitration rules of the leading arbitral institutions regulate the context in which the award by consent can be rendered following the settlement between the parties.[153] More interestingly, however, some arbitration rules facilitate settlement by means of encouraging parties to mediate their dispute (either prior the commencement of arbitration proceedings or in parallel to the proceedings that have already started). As already noted, most arbitral institutions include provisions regulating mediation in their sets of arbitration rules.[154] Certainly, the recent increased popularity of mediation and other ADR

[152]McIlwrath and Schroeder, 2008, 4–5.

[153]Article 32 of the ICC Arbitration Rules, Article 26.9 of the LCIA Rules, Article 32.1 of the ICDR Procedures, and Article 39(1) of the SCC Rules.

[154]The ICC Mediation Rules are in force as of 1 January 2014; the LCIA adopted its Mediation Rules in 2012, the SCC Mediation Rules came into force on 1 January 2014, and the recent version of the ICC Rules and Procedures contains the ICDR Mediation Procedures that entered into force in 2014.

services, supported by legal regulations at national and regional levels, allowed most prominent arbitral institutions to feel the momentum for new means of competition in this field. Leaving aside the significance of institutional mediation rules in and of themselves, the question arises regarding the efficiency of the provisions encouraging mediation in the context of the future and pending arbitration proceedings (to be) initiated by the parties, in particular in so far as the costs are concerned. In other words, it is crucial for the parties to arbitration proceedings to understand if the mediation services in the forms offered by arbitral institutions can in fact facilitate settlement in the context of their arbitration and, if so, how much it will cost.

The relationship between the provisions encouraging the use of mediation and the potential mediation and arbitration costs is not entirely straightforward. In the cases of most arbitral institutions, the parties can initiate mediation proceedings, even concurrently to arbitration proceedings, that will simply mean parallel costs to be borne by the parties for two different types of services provided by arbitrator(s) and mediator under the institutional shield. The recent set of the ICDR Procedures provide for a particularly interesting solution in that the rules not only encourage the parties to express their potential interests in mediation in the notice of arbitration, the answer to the notice, or during the preparatory conference (Articles 2, 3, and 4, respectively) but also authorize the ICDR Case Administrator to expressly invite the parties to mediate following the submission of the answer (Article 5). Article 5 also allows the parties to seek for mediation at any stage of arbitration proceedings. Notwithstanding the remarkable innovation that such rules entail, it is questionable whether they are in fact cost-effective. It is therefore unclear whether the parties can expect any refund from an arbitral institution in cases in which they settle by means of mediation while the arbitration proceedings are still pending. Out of four leading arbitral institutions under analysis only the ICC provides for a straightforward provision that states that when a mediation is preceded by the request of arbitration under the ICC Arbitration Rules submitted with regard to the same parties and the same or parts of the same dispute, the "filing fee paid for such arbitration proceedings shall be credited to the administrative expenses of the mediation", provided that the total administrative expenses covered by the parties to the underlying arbitration exceed US$ 7,500.[155] Given the limited regulation of the relationship between the costs of arbitration and the parallel mediation in arbitration and/or mediation rules of the institutions under analysis, it appears that arbitral institutions have not yet developed efficient competition means in this regard.

[155]Article 4 of the Appendix to the 2014 ICC Mediation Rules. Although the ICDR provides for a tiered schedule of costs that allows refunds in certain circumstances, the relationship between the costs of arbitration and the parallel mediation under the ICDR schedule remains unclear.

2.3.1.3.5 On Why the Institutional Efforts in Terms of Controlling Time and Costs Remain Inefficient

In view of the preceding discussion, it should be apparent that arbitral institutions have implemented increasing numbers of rules and/or techniques aimed at decreasing the time and costs of arbitration. The following question, however, remains open. Why are institutional arbitration rules and other soft-law instruments, despite continuous alteration to respond to the challenges to the efficiency of institutional arbitration proceedings, still largely inadequate and therefore inefficient from the perspective of institutional arbitration users?

One possible explanation is that the institutional provisions concerning the allocation of cost and time are more arbitrator-oriented than party-oriented. Each arbitration centre has their own policy referring to the institutional costs, which comprises, in most cases, the exclusive institutional power to fix the arbitrators' fees and to increase the diligence of arbitrator's performance in view of the costs of arbitration. Arbitrators' authority is largely minimized to simply allocate the costs fixed by arbitral institution between the parties in the final award. Some institutional arbitration rules allow respective institutional organs to adjust those costs with regard to the efficiency of arbitrators in rendering arbitral awards. For example, the ICC Court may take into consideration the "diligence and efficiency of the arbitrator, the time spent, the rapidity of the proceedings" while setting the arbitrators' fees.[156] Although not expressly provided in the arbitration rules of other leading arbitral institutions, it is reasonable to assume that efficient conduct of an arbitrator may be a determinative factor in fixing arbitrator's fees also in the case of other arbitral institutions.

The main problem remains, however, regarding the vagueness of such potential institutional actions, especially in view of the relative flexibility of institutional time limits for rendering arbitral awards by arbitrators. In this vein, it seems necessary for the arbitration centres to take responsibility for their own policies and procedural rules regulating arbitrators' fees. Yet, arbitral institutions seem to lack the authority over arbitrators to execute and enforce such rules and policies. This is particularly striking when taking into account the fact that some arbitration centres rely on the lists of arbitrators, which create different pools of institutional arbitrators, that would require certain accountability of the "affiliated" arbitrators vis-à-vis their "home" arbitral institution. Why do arbitral institutions not place more emphasis on the reputational dynamics when dealing with diligence and efficiency of arbitrator's performance at the stage when the arbitrator's fees are determined? Could they do better when encouraging new, less reputed arbitrators with more flexible agendas to offer their services to the parties? Or, would it not be helpful for the parties to understand in which cases they can expect that the arbitrators' fees be decreased due to the poor performance of arbitrators and to increase the transparency of institutional practices in this regard? Professor Ugo Draetta, an

[156] Article 2(2) of the Appendix III to the 2012 ICC Arbitration Rules.

experienced international arbitrator and a former in-house counsel, openly admits that arbitration centres simply assume no power to monitor the work of individual arbitrators, which resembles the case of "responsibility with no authority".[157] Surprisingly, this is so in view of the broad contractual authority that arbitral institutions enjoy in regards to the legal relationships that come into existence in institutional arbitration.

In contrast, arbitral institutions have designed various means for securing the payment of the arbitration costs from the parties. Both the LCIA and the SCC adopted provisions expressly stating that the parties are jointly and severally liable to the institution and to arbitral tribunal for the costs of arbitration.[158] The ICDR established an alternative rule for securing the payment of the arbitration costs, which provide for the suspension or termination of the proceedings in the situation that parties did not cover the deposits required by the ICDR Case Administrator.[159] The SCC Institute and the ICC established similar provisions, which involve the consequences of the non-payment of the advance of costs by the parties.[160] In the same spirit, Article 2(7) of Appendix III to the ICC Arbitration Rules introduces the so-called "Abeyance Fee" in that it authorizes the ICC Court to request the additional payment of the ICC administrative fees corresponding to putting arbitration in abeyance.[161] These provisions, despite being necessary for the proper functioning of institutional arbitration, can be seen by the arbitration users as too "disciplinarian", in particular in view of the less rigid provisions aiming at increasing the diligence and efficiency of institutional arbitrators. Arbitral institutions, on a number of occasions, suggest to the parties how to plausibly decrease the arbitration costs. One example can be seen in the increasing guidelines for the parties and their legal representatives on effective case management techniques. Another example concerns the recommendations by arbitral institutions to the parties regarding more accurate negotiations of the fees of their attorneys, with the implication that this is the most burdensome part of institutional arbitration costs. All these certainly appear in line with the "best practices" in institutional arbitration. Arbitration is expensive and it is the parties that should first and foremost bear the responsibility of any delays or counterproductive practices that contribute to the increase in arbitration costs. Be that as it may, there are complex arbitration cases, where the relationships between the parties are far beyond friendly, that require the arbitral institutions to act in their professional spirit more than in other, more straightforward cases. This concerns institutional responsibility in both ensuring the speed and cost-effectiveness of arbitration within institutional powers and the adequate institutional control of arbitrators.

---

[157]Draetta 2011, 104.

[158]Articles 28.1 and 28.6 of the LCIA Rules and 43(6) of the SCC Rules.

[159]Articles 32.2 and 32.3 of the ICDR Procedures.

[160]Article 30(4) of the 1998 ICC Arbitration Rules (Cf. Article 36(6) of the 2012 ICC Arbitration Rules) and Article 45(4) of the SCC Rules.

[161]A commentary note to Articles 37(1) and 37(2) in: Fry, Greenberg, Mazza, 2012, 403.

From the perspective of individual arbitration users, it is desirable that institutional rules address the efficiency of all arbitration actors in a similar manner so that the parties are treated as serious and sophisticated entities in the course of arbitration proceedings. Doing so could bring the institutional authority in line with the original commercial function of institutional arbitration that placed at its core the parties' satisfaction with the arbitration process.[162] This could be achieved by increasing the transparency of institutional arbitration regimes. Indeed, as seen in recent requests for greater time and cost efficiency in institutional arbitration, the transparency of institutional practices, as well as the "clarification" of the rules and best practices of arbitral institutions applied in different stages of arbitration proceedings, is increasingly "on demand".[163] The lacklustre institutional response in this regard is surprising because the opening up of the institutional practices, currently conducted behind closed doors of arbitral institutions, would enhance the parties' understanding of the institutional control. By now, what the parties are left with is the frustration relating to the fact that they often do not understand the intricacies of institutional internal operation and how their disputes are handled. More transparency could decrease this frustration. This could also increase the parties' compliance with institutional decisions made to reduce the time and address the cost-effectiveness of the arbitration, even where the final outcome of such decisions is unfavourable to individual parties. This could happen only when the parties are duly informed by arbitral institutions of the crucial aspects of their arbitration proceedings, together with the rationale behind the institutional decisions.[164]

Three preliminary observations arise with regard to the efficiency of institutional arbitration proceedings. First, different institutional arbitration actors define efficiency in different ways. Second, the dynamics of competition between arbitration centres are aided more by the understanding of the efficiency by institutional arbitrators rather than by the institutional arbitration users. Finally, due to the emerging bureaucratization of institutional arbitration entailing the intensification of procedural tactics (in a convergent manner), arbitral institutions are no longer able to ensure the efficiency in terms of costs and speed, as expected by the traditional parties to institutional arbitrations. Rather, the increased formalization of institutional procedures implies more expensive and lengthier arbitration

[162]The parties' satisfaction is difficult to be measured. Some commentators state that a satisfactory decision in the arbitration context does not need to imply only the winning of the case, but "rather having a fast procedure, well managed, with a complete exchange of memoranda." See Philippe-Gazon 1997, 463.

[163]Cf. Gillion 2012.

[164]One of the recent examples of the institutional practices in increasing the transparency of the proceedings concerns the announcement of 8 October 2015 by the ICC that it will begin to communicate the reasons for many administrative decisions issued under the ICC Arbitration Rules. See ICC Court to Communicate Reasons as a New Service to Users. http://www.iccwbo.org/News/Articles/2015/ICC-Court-to-communicate-reasons-as-a-new-service-to-users/. Accessed 25 April 2016.

processes, contrary to the core principle of efficiency of the commercial function of institutional arbitration.

Institutional arbitration actors understand the efficiency of the commercial function of arbitral institutions in different and often discordant ways. Whereas business parties demand cost-effectiveness and expeditiousness of the proceedings that would be guaranteed by both arbitral institutions and institutional arbitrators, institutional arbitrators, seem to largely rely on the institutional support as the "guarantors" of efficiency of institutional arbitration processes.[165] Yet, the understanding of efficiency by arbitration centres remains largely affected by the need to facilitate the resolution of disputes by prominent arbitrators with extremely busy agendas. The analysis of the implications of the competition between arbitration centres suggests that arbitral institutions are usually directed into individual arbitrators and the arbitrators' community as such when ensuring the efficiency of arbitrations.[166] For example, in terms of costs and time, institutional competition shows that different institutional policies aim mostly at attracting the participation of prominent arbitrators in institutional arbitrations (to increase the reputation of arbitral institutions themselves). Arbitral institutions are more aided by offering a friendly environment to arbitrators rather than by responding to the individual demands of traditional arbitration users expressed in the calls for relatively cheap and fast arbitration services. Again, this is because, as continuously explained by arbitral institutions, in most cases it is the parties and their counsel that could do better.

There exists considerable differentiation regarding the calculation of institutional arbitrators fees within the studied regimes. However, the reason for these differences is not necessarily due to arbitral institutions trying to decrease the costs of institutional arbitrations for the sake of the disputing parties. Instead, it is largely to attract new arbitrators to institutional regimes by corresponding to the methods of calculating legal fees established in the jurisdictions in which these arbitrators practice. Moreover, arbitral institutions remain reluctant to decrease the costs of their administrative fees in cases of poor performance of institutional case managers or members of institutional bodies. In light of this, some commentators have proposed that institutions should adopt more flexible and realistic measures for reducing both the arbitrators' and administrative fees, should the amounts of disputes decrease in the

[165]This argument appears valid with regard to both prevailing perceptions of the role of arbitrators (whether acting as service providers or private judges whose mandate should be understood in terms of "status" that arbitrators enjoy in the course of the proceedings) in the eyes of the arbitrators themselves. Both perceptions seem to correspond with the need for the "furtherance" of institutional goals as expressed in institutional rules by institutional arbitrators, with different incentives for arbitrators associated with these perceptions. In cases in which institutional arbitrators perceive themselves as service providers they would need to obey institutional rules and policies to receive their remuneration. In the case in which institutional arbitrators perceive themselves as private judges, they would need to follow the arbitration rules at hand to ensure the due process requirements in the course of arbitration.

[166]See Draetta 2011, 102.

course of the proceedings, that could actually respond better to the expectations of the arbitration users.[167] This does not only concern the refunds to the parties that are already provided for in the arbitration rules. The important step would also be to respect the institutional provisions on fast-track arbitration by arbitral institutions themselves that, as noted in the preceding analysis, are often enforced in the manner detrimental to arbitration users, contributing to the increase in the costs of arbitration, instead of ensuring the cost-effectiveness of arbitration proceedings. Such institutional interpretations of their own rules simply appear to be counterproductive.

Moreover, it appears necessary that the provisions on costs of arbitration correspond in a better way with the principle of party autonomy and the freedom of contract. The parties themselves have little to say on the costs of their arbitration when the arbitration centre amends its schedule of costs or the amount of the hourly rate for the institutional charges after drafting institutional arbitration agreement by the parties. All of the amendments regarding the issue at hand are effective upon the publication of the new institutional instruments, and the parties to arbitrations commenced after that date need to comply with the new institutional schedules regardless of the date in which their arbitration clause or agreement came into force. This not only limits the role of the parties' consent in relying on carefully chosen schedules of costs but also proves the institutional arbitrariness in the field of the costs of institutional arbitrations. Such arbitrariness also decreases the predictability of the costs of institutional arbitration, which is said to be one of the advantages of institutional regimes over *ad hoc* arbitrations. In this view, the institutional regulations in the field of costs of arbitration do not seem to fully respect the parties' legitimate expectations and commercial goals regarding the institutional arbitration proceedings at the moment of the drafting of institutional arbitration clauses.

This critique also applies to the topic of institutional control over the length of arbitrations. Although arbitral institutions do not settle disputes themselves, and therefore they do not render arbitral awards, it seems they could exercise more control over the observance of time limits in institutional arbitration proceedings (be it with relation to the parties, arbitrators, or institutional own actions) in order to increase efficiency. This brings us to the last preliminary observation concerning the question of whether sophisticated and bureaucratized arbitral institutions are, in fact, still capable of ensuring the efficiency of institutional regimes from the perspective of their traditional commercial arbitration users. It appears that the intensified procedural supervision of the relationships between the parties and arbitrators *de facto* contributes to the decline in the flexibility and expeditiousness of the institutional arbitration procedures. Perhaps it is relevant for the arbitral institutions to reflect further on this tendency, in particular in view of the possibility of more frequently encouraging the parties to mediation, for example by offering the parties the provisions to set off some proportions of their arbitration costs when settlement is reached by means of meditation. The following analysis of the public function of arbitral institutions will further address the concerns related to the increased formalization of institutional procedures.

---

[167]Draetta 2011, 108.

2.3.2 *Emerging Public Function*

Undoubtedly, it may appear controversial to identify the emerging public function of such a private process as institutional commercial arbitration. Although some of the literature introduces certain accidental public functions underlying the rationale of contemporary international arbitration[168] (in particular with regard to the investor-State arbitration[169]), none of the authors consider the transformation of the activity of private arbitral institutions in the context of the legal, political, and ideological denotations of arbitration. This part of the chapter aims at addressing this gap.

This chapter looks at arbitral institutions from a broader perspective of the democratic legitimacy of arbitration as dispute resolution, which concerns the responses of arbitral institutions to the increasing legal and political considerations regarding the regulation of arbitration at national, regional (e.g. European), and international levels. The term "public function" denotes the tendency that arbitral institutions as private actors have been increasingly taking on roles traditionally understood as public, often with no express consent in this regard from disputing parties. This is in contrast with the principle of party autonomy and therefore may invite public criticism regarding the increasing functions of arbitration (and arbitral institutions). By way of illustration, not only have arbitral institutions developed new procedural functions that often limit party autonomy in traditional, commercial arbitration proceedings, but also, mostly due to the universalization and formalization of institutional arbitration rules, arbitral institutions have begun to adapt their rules to new types of disputes involving public entities or non-commercial parties by compromising the traditional commercial model of arbitration procedure. This, in turn, questions the traditional understanding of private institutional arbitration as a process of solely private dimension, hence limiting to the resolution of individual disputes with no impact on third parties.[170] Notably, these changes have occurred with either express or tacit support from the broader

[168]Werlauff 2009.

[169]Schill 2010.

[170]The use of the expression an "impact on third parties" is not intended to claim that the procedural decisions of arbitral institutions are outcome-determinative in and beyond a single institutional arbitration proceeding. Rather, it is stated that the procedural changes in institutional arbitration rules have sanctioned the increasing applicability of the private model of commercial dispute resolution to non-commercial disputes or disputes of any sorts (be it public or private disputes) involving public entities that sheds light on the truly private function of these new types of arbitration proceedings. As such, the distinction between private and public function presented in this chapter largely corresponds to the definition of private and public functions of dispute settlement mechanisms as presented by Stephan Schill in his article on "Crafting the International Economic Order: The Public Function of Investment Treaty Arbitration and Its Significance for the Role of the Arbitrator." As stated by Schill: "[t]he distinction, as used here, relates to the purpose, function, and effect a dispute settlement proceedings has in relation to the parties to the proceedings. The private function is one that is limited to the solution of the dispute; any function beyond that is understood as a public function." See Schill 2010, 407.

arbitration community and/or public authorities such as policy-makers in the field of arbitration and legislators.

The public function is analysed here from two angles: bottom-up and top-down.[171] The *bottom-up* dimension of the public function refers to the institutional procedural safeguards developed to ensure the *legality* of institutional arbitration processes. To this extent, it involves institutional powers assumed on behalf of the parties to ensure the enforceability of institutional arbitral awards, as well as the exclusive powers developed by arbitral institutions against the background of the changing democratic legitimacy of institutional regimes that corresponds to the increasing pressure of new public demands on more traditional, commercial function of arbitration. In contrast, the *top-down* dimension of the public function entails more problematic variables, namely the increasing exclusive authority of arbitral institutions in the administration of new types of public disputes, based on statutory or private rights of the parties. The term public disputes as well as the expression "public function" should be understood here broadly, including but not limited to: (1) disputes between private actors (e.g. investors) and public actors (e.g. States or State-like entities) emerging from public international law relationships; (2) disputes between private actors and public actors acting in their commercial capacity; (3) disputes of public policy relevance arising in various contexts such as consumer disputes, tax disputes, financial disputes, etc., broadly called "regulatory disputes". Moreover, the public function tackled from the top-down perspective has additional implications in the US, which concern the institutional authority in stipulating parties' consent regarding the participation in class arbitrations. The following analysis will grasp both understandings of the public function and their consequences. This analysis will conclude with legal and political questions regarding the condition of the contemporary institutional arbitration regimes. It will be conducted, in particular, in view of the potential *democratic deficits* of the emerging forms of institutional arbitration that call for increasing public accountability of institutional arbitration regimes and hence distort the traditional private–public axis in commercial arbitration.

2.3.2.1 Bottom-up Analysis of the Public Function

Professors W. Michael Reisman and Brian Richardson, in their article on the architecture of international commercial arbitration, consider the changes to the private regime of international commercial arbitration.[172] After looking back to mediaeval times, when arbitration represented a truly private and self-sufficient dispute resolution system, they argue that:

---

[171]This distinction is made from the perspective of institutional arbitration regimes (bottom-up approach) vis-à-vis the law and public demands placed on arbitration processes externally to traditional, private dynamics developed within institutional arbitration regimes (top-down approach).

[172]Reisman and Richardson 2012.

> international commercial arbitration, no less than arbitration within nation-states, while conducted in the sphere of private law, is a public legal creation whose operation and effectiveness is inextricably linked to prescribed actions by national courts.[173]

Reisman and Richardson then claim that arbitration actors have to decide on the level of the necessary relationship between arbitral tribunal and national courts in the field of enforceability of arbitration agreements and arbitral awards in order to make the process more functional.

In this part of the chapter, it will be argued that arbitral tribunals and public courts are not the only architects designing the public facet of private international arbitration. Furthermore, it will be claimed that arbitral institutions possess increasing *private regulatory powers* that are exercised in the conduct of arbitration proceedings in front of the parties in all types of arbitration (whether involving traditional private arbitration users or public actors or both) and institutional arbitrators. Moreover, it will be argued that these powers make arbitral institutions independent actors and therefore as significant as arbitrators and national courts in the discussion on the public enforceability of private institutional settings. Although there have not been any studies conducted heretofore showing that national judges are more eager to enforce institutional awards than *ad hoc* awards, it can be speculated that the name of an arbitral institution with a good reputation standing behind the institutional arbitral award increases the confidence of the judges at the enforcement stage.[174]

In this context, the following analysis will address the question of how arbitral institutions in fact ensure the legality of institutional arbitration processes. This discussion goes beyond the debate regarding the qualifications of institutional involvement in arbitrations in either purely "administrative" or "jurisdictional" terms.[175] Rather, it distinguishes the institutional tasks in relation to the principle of party autonomy to grasp the development of private regulatory functions of arbitral institutions vis-à-vis the traditional understanding of institutional functions by private arbitration users. Hence, the following part contains the discussion on the institutional tasks assumed on behalf of the parties as a continuation of case management techniques, as well as on the exclusive prerogatives developed by arbitral institutions from the perspective of the more generalist and holistic administration of arbitration cases. In the second case, institutional performance is organized around the exclusive, unquestioned, and inherent authority of arbitral institutions to decide on the conduct of arbitration proceedings pursuant to the set(s) of rules adopted by a particular arbitral institution and also the institutional policies based on different soft-law mechanisms. The majority of the institutional powers (falling within both groups) respond to the legal requirements for arbitration, as enshrined in the only legal instrument governing arbitration at the

[173] Reisman and Richardson 2012, 17.

[174] Lew et al. 2003, 38–39.

[175] For an excellent discussion on the theoretical "representations" of the functions of arbitral institutions see: Gerbay, forthcoming 2016.

international level, that is the New York Convention.[176] To this extent, the institutional activity within the public function is guided by broader legal prerequisites concerning the *legality* of the arbitration process itself, which may have divergent meaning for different institutional arbitration actors. This is primarily because of the vagueness of certain provisions enshrined in the New York Convention itself that invite varying legal interpretations.[177]

The disputing parties understand legality primarily in the meaning of institutional arbitration service to ensure the enforceability of institutional awards issued in institutional arbitration proceedings concerning these parties directly, thus satisfying their commercial goals associated with the transaction underlying arbitration in question. Arbitral institutions, in turn, seem to be responding rather to the broader, systemic requirements existent in the public realm of arbitration to have a vital voice in the architecture of international commercial arbitration by ensuring legality of any and all arbitration processes understood as the most formalized form of contemporary ADR mechanisms. This means that the understanding of legal certainty by institutions corresponds more with the legal standards for institutional arbitration processes, *even though* the context of institutional activity also involves the private goals of institutional arbitration users. In other words, arbitral institutions have begun to perceive the arbitration process from additional perspectives external to the understanding of arbitration by individual parties to a dispute. This perspective corresponds, on the one hand, to the understanding of institutional arbitration as a holistic private arbitration process that requires a certain level of uniformity, even at the cost of party autonomy, due to the minimal legal requirements placed on it. On the other hand, this more generalist understanding of the private function of institutional arbitration in the legal context invites the further "legalization" of institutional arbitration rules to allow their applicability to disputes that traditionally fell outside the scope of arbitration. At the same time, arbitration users still treat institutional safeguards as a contractual service, which makes them overlook the systemic role which institutions exercise in the arbitration proceedings. This dissonance regarding the legality of arbitration proceedings underlying the rationale of the institutional public function has a significant impact on the parties' objectives while filing liability claims against arbitral institutions in cases in which the institutional processes simply fail to accommodate the parties' expectations. This argument will be returned to in Sect. 2.3.2.

To recognize the development of the public function of institutional arbitration from bottom-up it is crucial to first understand the legal requirements for the validity and enforceability of arbitration settings as enshrined in the New York Convention. The grounds for refusing enforcement, or for setting aside arbitral awards under Article V of the New York Convention, are thus the following: (1) incapacity of the parties under applicable law, and the procedural and substantive invalidity of the arbitration agreement; (2) lack of due process, (3) lack of jurisdiction and extension of the scope of arbitration agreement; (4) improper composition

[176]The New York Convention, 1958.

[177]Gerbay, forthcoming 2016 with further references.

of the arbitral tribunal and the irregularities in the procedure in comparison with the arbitration agreement; (5) award not binding, set aside or suspended; and lastly (6) violation of public policy. As will be shown in the following analysis, most institutional safeguards address these legal concerns to assure that institutional awards are enforceable in law.[178] While some of those safeguards can be seen as the continuation of the parties' expectations regarding the institutional arbitration process based on the principle of party autonomy, arbitral institutions have also developed exclusive prerogatives that concern the supervisory powers in the institutional arbitration processes that often appear to be at odds with the autonomy of the parties to design their arbitration processes as they see fit. In this vein, the analysis below distinguishes between two groups of institutional prerogatives that correspond to: (a) the institutional safeguards provided on behalf of the parties, and (b) the exclusive procedural autonomy of arbitral institutions understood within the meaning of the private regulatory functions of arbitral institutions.

2.3.2.1.1 Safeguards on Behalf of the Parties

Although the level of institutional involvement varies considerably from one institution to another, there are certain shared features of most institutional arbitration processes that correspond to the original demands of arbitration users concerning the formal organization of institutional arbitration proceedings. The institutional activity in this regard is exercised in the continuation of the parties' will to have their dispute resolved with the institutional support (as opposed to *ad hoc* arbitration). This activity concerns: (a) the institutional assistance in the communications between the parties and to some extent also between the parties and the members of the arbitral tribunal or sole arbitrators; (b) the assistance with regard to the composition of the arbitral tribunal or the appointment of a sole arbitrator and also involving the oversight of the standards of independence and impartiality of arbitrators; and (c) the general responsibility of arbitral institutions to ensure the proper application of the rules by institutional arbitrators and that the institutional award will be enforceable at law. Thus, each of these will be considered in turn.

2.3.2.1.1.1 Assistance Regarding Communications

The assurance of proper communications between and by the parties increases the legality of arbitration award in the sense that it addresses due process standards as well as the right of the parties to a fair hearing set forth in Article V(1)(b) of the New York Convention. Based on the wording of the aforementioned article, recognition and enforcement of arbitral award may be refused if "the party against whom the award is invoked was not given a proper notice of […] the arbitration proceedings or was otherwise unable to present its case".

---

[178] Article V of the New York Convention.

Beside the formal requirements regarding time limits for the completion of different procedural stages of institutional arbitration proceedings, discussed in detail in one of the preceding sections,[179] as well as regarding the necessary content of parties' submissions, most arbitration rules regulate the delivery of submissions and service of documents in the course of arbitration and the post-arbitration proceedings. In practice, proper communication with and between the parties as well as between the parties and the arbitral tribunal (and the arbitral institution) is crucial for the proper understanding by *all* parties of the developments of their arbitration case. This is especially the case because the notification of such developments usually triggers the time limits for the parties to react to the pleadings and submissions of the counterparty and/or the procedural orders issued by arbitrators and/or arbitral institutions. Although the parties are generally free to determine how the communications will be handled in their arbitration agreement, the institutional arbitration rules set up default standards that aim at addressing the legal regulations of the delivery of documents under mandatory provisions of national laws. Since no universal legal framework exists in this regard, it is usually the case that any provisions of national laws on the delivery of documents and communications between the parties will apply in the absence of the agreement of the parties themselves. Hence, arbitration rules on the service of documents and communications can be seen as a specific proxy between the parties' arrangements and the mandatory provisions of national laws governing arbitration in question. This proxy increases the likelihood that the parties will be able to be notified of any and all procedural steps in the course of arbitration as well as that they will be given the chance to fully present their case. The institutional safeguards regarding the service of documents and the communications between the parties, as well as the communications by arbitrators and institutions themselves to the parties have significant practical implications. They are particularly relevant when the delivery of the request of arbitration and the answer to the request is concerned, so that the parties can enjoy the sufficient amount of time prescribed for the submission of those documents in the arbitration rules. If, for example, the delivery of the request of arbitration is delayed due to the institutional error in notifying the erroneous respondent or the respondent proper yet at the wrong postal address, the party may find it problematic to prepare the answer to the request within the prescribed period of time. This is especially problematic if the claims presented in the request reflect a complex legal and commercial relationship between the claimant and the respondent. Although there is still the room for the parties' agreement regarding the application for a possible extension of time limits for the submission of counterclaims or pleadings to arbitral institution, if the relationship between the parties to arbitration is hostile, the institutional errors in the field of parties' notifications can prove to be particularly weighty to the parties in that they can determine the atmosphere of arbitration and even the outcome of a particular arbitration case.

[179]See Sect. 2.3.1.3.3.

For this reason, arbitral institutions have developed a number of procedural rules that aim at minimizing the consequences of improper notifications, lack of communications between the parties and by the arbitrators and arbitral institutions themselves, and finally the potential issues concerning the delivery of documents in the course of arbitration proceedings as well as following the issuance of the arbitral award by arbitrators.[180] As reads from *The Secretariat's Guide to ICC Arbitration*, the ICC provisions of Article 3 of the 2012 ICC Arbitration Rules set forth the requirements regarding "how to send communications, to whom, in how many copies, and to which address". Such framework will usually be set forth also by other arbitral institutions.[181] Hence, most arbitration rules contain provisions specifying the exact number of copies of documents (e.g. the request for arbitration, the answer to the request, or other communications in the course of the arbitration) which the respective party (or parties) are to submit to the specific organ of the arbitral institutions—mainly the Secretariat—at each stage of the proceedings.[182] Arbitral institutions require copies of all written communications and pleadings, which both secures the validity of the "legal" actions in the course of the proceedings for the sake of due process requirements and increases the institutional oversight of the whole institutional arbitration proceedings.[183] Although some arbitration rules of the leading arbitral institutions under analysis provide for the institution to transmit the copies of certain documents, such as the request for arbitration to the respondent (e.g. the ICC Rules,[184] the SCC Rules[185]), other arbi-

[180]Since the detailed analysis of the institutional arbitration rules regarding communications, notifications, and the delivery (or service) of the documents submitted or produced in the course of arbitration proceedings falls outside the scope of this section, the discussion here concerns mostly the common institutional patterns that aim at securing the requirements set forth in Article V(1)(b) of the New York Convention regarding due process standards and the proper notification of the arbitration proceedings.

[181]It is necessary to stress here that in any case the parties and the arbitrators are free to decide on how the documents will be submitted in the course of the proceedings as well as on the ways the arbitral tribunal will notify the parties to the proceedings. Arbitrators can also issue directions to the parties in this regard.

[182]Article 3(1) of the 2012 ICC Arbitration Rules, Article 1.2 of the LCIA Rules, Article 2 of the ICDR Procedures, which do not expressly refer to the number of copies to be provided by the party but require the party to give due notice to the other party of the commencement of arbitration.

[183]See: Article 3(1) of the 2012 ICC Arbitration Rules and Article 13.1 of the LCIA Rules that requires simultaneous copies of all correspondence between arbitral tribunal and the parties to be sent to the Registrar. The 2012 ICC Arbitration Rules also require from the arbitral tribunal that all written documents submitted in the course of the proceedings are sent to the Secretariat which supervises the particular arbitration file. This has also a consequence for the effectiveness of the ICC's process of scrutiny of the awards, which will be discussed in Sect. 2.3.2.1.2.4 of this chapter.

[184]Article 4(1) of the 2012 ICC Arbitration Rules.

[185]Article 5 of the SCC Rules.

tration rules (e.g. the LCIA Rules[186] and the ICDR Procedures[187]) will require the claimant itself to serve a notice of arbitration to the respondent. In both cases, arbitral institutions secure the proper notification to the respondent due to the provision requiring the parties to obtain the receipt of each notice, which increases the probability that all parties will be duly informed of all the exchanges and submissions. This is particularly important given the wide range of communications allowed by the institutions due to modern technological developments.[188]

In addition, institutional provisions require the parties to provide institutions with their most recent address as well as the address of their representatives (together with the power of attorney) to potentially eliminate the probability that the documents will be served and notifications will be made at erroneous address.[189] Furthermore, most arbitration rules set out the circumstances under which documents are deemed to have been served by default. This rule also relates to the determination of the effective date of the written communications that under most arbitration rules should be a date of their receipt.[190] Thus, the date of the receipt of the request for arbitration (notice of arbitration)—which is said to be a date of the commencement of the proceedings under most arbitration rules[191]—is of particular importance, as it guarantees that all parties are duly informed that their arbitration was actually set in motion, which is necessary for the award to be enforceable at law.

In addition, there are a number of instances in post-arbitration proceedings in which arbitral institutions have become increasingly active with regard to the enforcement of institutional arbitral awards. These include: the institutional rules providing for the transmission of the award to the parties by arbitral institutions themselves,[192] the institutional assistance with the correction and/or interpretation of arbitral awards,[193] or even the institutional involvement in certification and authentication of arbitral awards for enforcement purposes.[194] These competences

[186]The notification of the Request for Arbitration under the LCIA Rules is the responsibility of the claimant and as such it falls within Article 4 of the LCIA Rules. See Wade et al. 2015, 57.

[187]Article 2 of the ICDR Procedures.

[188]Cf. Article 3(2) of the 2012 ICC Arbitration Rules and Article 18.1 of the ICDR Procedures.

[189]Cf. Article 4(3) of the 2012 ICC Arbitration Rules, Article 2 of the SCC Rules, Article 1.1(a) of the LCIA Rules.

[190]Article 3(3) of the 2012 ICC Arbitration Rules, Article 4.4 of the LCIA Rules, Article 8(3) of the SCC Rules.

[191]Article 4(2) of the 2012 ICC Arbitration Rules, Article 4 of the SCC Rules, Article 1.2 of the LCIA Rules, and Article 2.2 of the ICDR Procedures.

[192]Article 34(1) of the 2012 ICC Arbitration Rules, 26.7 of the 2014 LCIA Rules, Article 30.4 of the ICDR Procedures. In contrast, the provisions of Article 36(6) of the SCC Rules require the arbitral tribunal to deliver the copies of the award to all parties and the SCC.

[193]See, for example, Article 35(4) of the 2012 ICC Arbitration Rules.

[194]This is the case with SIAC that has been authorized by means of Section 19C of the Singapore International Arbitration Act of 1994 (with further amendments) to certify and authenticate arbitral awards. See Gerbay, forthcoming 2016.

certainly increase institutional involvement in the final oversight of the legal products of each institutional arbitration proceeding and also in assisting the parties (at least the winning party) in obtaining the court's decision regarding the recognition and enforcement of the arbitral award in the jurisdiction where such legal actions are being sought.

2.3.2.1.1.2 Proper Composition of Arbitral Tribunals Versus Independence and Impartiality of Arbitrators

Institutional activities concerning the composition of an arbitral tribunal fall within the group of the most significant, and hence the most developed, tasks assumed by institutions. They are crucial because they assure that arbitral tribunals will be constituted in accordance with the parties' will expressed in their arbitration agreement,[195] and that each party will be given a full right to present its case.[196] Moreover, as due process requirements and the impartiality of arbitrators are also enshrined in the concept of public policy, institutional activities concerning the issue at hand secure the enforceability of an arbitral award under Article V(2)(b) of the New York Convention. The institutional role is even more significant while appointing arbitrators in cases in which the parties fail to do so in the arbitration agreement or in the submission to arbitration.

Numerous arbitral institutions, while appointing arbitrators, try to ensure the neutrality, ability, and the expertise of the arbitrators.[197] This concern arises not only from the original goals of the arbitration process such as neutrality of arbitration but also from the professionalization of the arbitration practice, which results in the fact that different arbitration actors play interchangeable roles in different arbitration proceedings. Today it is already a given for arbitration practitioners who act as arbitrators in one case to act as counsel of the same parties in another proceeding, and *vice versa*, often within the same institutional arbitration regime. To this extent, institutions tend to ensure high standards for the neutrality, independence, and impartiality of arbitrators in each particular case. This gives institutions, at least in theory, certain powers to exercise quality control over the arbitration proceedings.

Most of the rules require that the presiding arbitrator and the sole arbitrator are not of the same nationality as any of the parties to a dispute.[198] Although all stud-

[195]See Article V(1)(d) of the New York Convention.

[196]See Article V(1)(b) of the New York Convention.

[197]As regards the prospective arbitrator's ability, the ICC Court should take into consideration whether an arbitrator-to-be will be able to conduct the ICC arbitration for the following reasons: (1) the language abilities of arbitrator are good enough to assume that he/she manages to decide a case, (2) the legal qualifications of an arbitrator fall within the subject matter of a dispute, and (3) an arbitrator is experienced enough not only in arbitration in general but also in ICC arbitration in particular. Derains and Schwartz 2005, 158.

[198]Article 13(5) of the 2012 ICC Arbitration Rules, Article 13(5) of the SCC Rules, and Article 6.1 of the LCIA Rules.

ied arbitral institutions have developed divergent models for the appointment of arbitrators, the ICC's system requires particular attention here, as it involves the assistance of the ICC National Committees in the composition of the arbitral tribunal. Moreover, the ICC Court exercises a distinctive function that authorizes the Court to confirm each arbitrator, even in situations in which an arbitrator had been previously nominated by a party (or the parties).[199]

The ICC National Committees—comprising organizations, legal entities, or individuals, which assist the ICC Court on a case-by-case basis—represent the chief economic interest of the country in which they were established.[200] In this way, the ICC National Committees are perceived as lobby groups (local networks) among business communities of the respective State. The 2012 version of the ICC Rules sets forth the requirement for the ICC Court to rely on the National Committees in each case in which institution appoints arbitrators.[201] However, the ICC Court gained the power to directly appoint an arbitrator under the following circumstances: (a) one or more of the parties is a State or claims to be a State-like entity; (b) the Court decides that it is reasonable to appoint an arbitrator from a country or territory where there is no ICC National Committee; (c) a direct appointment is appropriate in the eyes of the President of the ICC Court.[202] The new Rules still allow the Court to choose a sole arbitrator or a chairman of an arbitral tribunal from the country where there is no National Committee, provided that suitable circumstances arise and the parties do not object.[203] The interplay between the ICC Court and its National Committees involves the following two issues: (a) the question of which National Committee is appropriate to deal with the proposal of an arbitrator to the ICC Court; and (b) whether the ICC Court should accept the proposal made by that Committee.

There are a number of circumstances to be considered by the ICC Court while deciding upon which National Committee will be suitable to make a proposal of an individual arbitrator to the Court. The first concerns the nationality of the parties, which, as already stated, is the most relevant issue to be taken into account while composing the arbitral tribunal. Thus, the ICC Court will ordinarily begin the nomination of the National Committee by excluding the Committee operating in the country of origin of the parties to arbitration.[204] Then, the ICC Court will

[199]See the discussion on the contractual relations in institutional arbitration in Sect. 3.2.1.1.2.2 of Chap. 3.

[200]Craig 1985, 53; ICC Constitution. http://www.iccwbo.org/constitution/. Accessed 25 April 2016.

[201]Article 13(3) of the 2012 ICC Arbitration Rules.

[202]Article 13(4) of the 2012 ICC Arbitration Rules.

[203]Article 9(4) of the 1998 ICC Arbitration Rules and Article 13(5) of the 2012 ICC Arbitration Rules.

[204]The explanation of the ICC Court cooperation with its National Committees provided in this part of the chapter is based on the information included in: Derains and Schwartz 2005, 168–176. See also: Article 13 of the 2012 ICC Arbitration Rules.

usually send its request to the Committee which, in the opinion of the Court, could be of help for selecting an arbitrator concerning such circumstances as: (a) the language of arbitration; (b) the nature of a dispute; (c) the place of arbitration; and (d) the law governing a dispute (provided that these issues were specified by the parties in their agreement). In some cases, the ICC Court will send more than one request in order to ensure that at least one satisfying proposal is sent back to the Court. Whenever the ICC National Committee fails to nominate an arbitrator or the ICC Court is not satisfied with the work of the selected ICC National Committee and the ICC Court refuses to accept the candidate proposed by the Committee, the Court will either repeat its request or address the new request to another committee that it considers appropriate. This demonstrates that the 2012 ICC Arbitration Rules establish an appointment mechanism that gives the ICC Court great room to manoeuvre with regard to the reliance on the assistance of National Committees. In any case, it is the ICC Court that has the last word regarding the appointment of an arbitrator. The understanding of the interactions between the Court and the National Committees shows how the ICC Court makes all efforts to eliminate the composition of a tribunal that may appear to favour one of the parties. Some authors, however, have criticized the ICC's cooperation with its National Committees, in particular when the National Committee does not represent the prominent "epistemic community" of a particular region.[205] To this extent, some doubts arise about the functionality of the ICC dialogue with its regional "branches".

Leaving aside the peculiarities of the ICC arbitration, it seems sufficient to address here all safeguards developed by the leading arbitral institutions under analysis to secure the impartiality and independence of arbitrators. Every LCIA arbitrator is required, under Article 5.3 of the LCIA rules, "to be and remain impartial and independent of the parties; and none shall act in the arbitration as advocate for or representative of any party. No arbitrator shall advise any party in the parties' dispute or the outcome of the arbitration". Moreover, pursuant to Article 5.4 "before appointment by the LCIA Court, each arbitral candidate shall furnish to the Registrar (upon the latter's request) a brief written summary of his or her qualifications and professional positions (past and present) […]; the candidate shall give a written declaration stating: (i) whether there are any circumstances currently known to the candidate which are likely to give rise in the mind of any party to any justifiable doubts as to his or her impartiality or independence and, if so, specifying in full such circumstances in the declaration […]". These provisions, that impose obligation of impartiality and independence of arbitrators both vis-à-vis arbitrators themselves and the parties, result in the situation in which every LCIA arbitrator is required to sign the Statement of Impartiality and Independence, as well as the Consent to Appointment in which all potential

[205] Draetta 2011, 97–117.

circumstances pertaining to conflict of interest must be disclosed.[206] There are two different versions of the Statement of Impartiality and Independence under the LCIA arbitration regime; Statement A in which the arbitrator affirms his independence and impartiality and Statement B, also known as a "qualified" statement, in which the arbitrator expresses his or her willingness to serve in the case in question yet leaving any potential justifiable grounds creating conflict of interest for further consideration of the LCIA Court.[207] This allows the latter to make a relevant decision regarding the appointment of arbitrators and invites the parties to oppose to the appointment in the form of a challenge.

As for the ICDR, Article 13 of the ICDR Procedures sets forth the standards for independence and impartiality of ICDR arbitrators. Under Sections 1 and 2 of Article 13, arbitrators accepting their appointments should sign a Notice of Appointment in which they should disclose any and all potential circumstances that may give rise to justifiable doubts as to their independence and impartiality. Moreover, Article 13.6 states that neither the party nor its representative shall *ex parte* communicate with an arbitrator in the course of an arbitration nor should the party or its representative initiate such communications, except while needing information for the proper assessment that the arbitrator is suitable to resolve the case. Under no circumstances should the parties or their representatives contact *ex parte* a candidate for a presiding arbitrator. Any forbidden communication may result in further challenge to, or the replacement of, the allegedly biased arbitrator.

The SCC has also developed mechanisms to secure the impartiality and independence of its arbitrators. The confirmation by an SCC arbitrator that there are no circumstances that could question her independence or impartiality shall be provided by an arbitrator-to-be before and after his/her appointment. Before the appointment, the arbitrator shall disclose any facts that show her connections with any party to a dispute, whereby upon the appointment an arbitrator has to provide the Secretariat of the SCC with a signed statement of impartiality and independence.[208] Subsequently, the Secretariat will send a copy of the statement to the parties and other members of the arbitral tribunal (if any) so that the further steps regarding the prospective challenges to, and replacements of, a biased arbitrator may be taken.

The ICC also provides for elaborate provisions regarding the independence and impartiality of ICC arbitrators. Each ICC arbitrator needs to sign a Statement of Acceptance, Availability, Impartiality and Independence, in which an arbitrator-to-be shall disclose any facts or circumstances that may shed light on his or her independence *in the eyes of the parties*.[209] An arbitrator has two options while signing

[206]Wade et al. 2015, 63–81.

[207]Ibid.

[208]Article 14(2) of the SCC Rules.

[209]See: Article 7(2) of the 1998 ICC Arbitration Rules and Article 11(2) of the 2012 ICC Arbitration Rules. Cf. also: ICC's Arbitrator's Statement of Acceptance, Availability and Independence 2010 (1998 ICC Arbitration Rules).

this statement. The first option is to confirm that there are no facts or circumstances that may question his or her independence ("nothing to disclose" option).[210] The second option is for "acceptance with disclosure" in cases where there:

> exists any past or present relationship, direct or indirect, between an arbitrator and any of the parties, their related entities or their lawyers or other representatives, whether financial, professional or any of any other kind. Any doubt must be resolved in favour of disclosure. Any disclosure should be complete and specific, identifying inter alia relevant dates […], financial arrangements, details of companies and individuals, and all other relevant information.[211]

The catalogue of circumstances to be disclosed by an arbitrator-to-be is provided for in a Statement that supplements Article 11(2) of the 2012 ICC Arbitration Rules. Here, the rather vague expression "[in] the eyes of the parties" is used regarding the prospective facts that may call into question the arbitrator's independence.[212]

Regardless of the development of the procedural safeguards for the appointment of arbitrators on behalf of the parties, some procedural aspects of the selection and appointment of arbitrators often transcend the principle of party autonomy and allow arbitral institutions to issue procedural decisions on their own initiative. This also means that the institutional prerogatives to select arbitrators could be regarded as decisions of certain jurisdictional relevance that fall outside pure case management tasks. Some national authorities recognize the relevance of institutional appointments of arbitrators. For example, the provisions of the UK Arbitration Act of 1996 grant arbitral institutions immunity concerning the appointment of institutional arbitrators.[213] Similarly, the institutional decisions regarding the challenges to arbitrators, which will be analysed in detail in Chap. 4, may take the form of more authoritative procedural orders issued in the continuation of the parties' initial authorization of arbitral institutions to supervise the proceedings, yet in the absence of the express agreement of the parties in this regard.

---

[210]The most recent version of the document, Arbitrator's Statement of Acceptance, Availability, Impartiality and Independence of 2012, is available via the ICC Dispute Resolution Library. http://www.iccdrl.com/itemContent.aspx?XSL=arbSingle.xsl&XML=\PRACTICE_NOTES\SNFC_0001.xml&CONTENTTYPE=PRACTICE_NOTES&TOC=ltocPracticeNotesAll.xml&TITLE=Arbitrator's%20Statement%20of%20Acceptance,%20Availability,%20Impartiality%20and%20Independence%20(2012%20ICC%20Rules%20of%20Arbitration). Accessed 11 July 2016. For the discussion on the most recent changes to the Statement cf. Hauser 2010.

[211]ICC's Arbitrator's Statement of Acceptance, Availability and Independence 2010 (1998 ICC Arbitration Rules). The wording of this paragraph remained practically unchanged in the recently amended Statement 2012.

[212]Article 11(2) of the 2012 ICC Arbitration Rules.

[213]Sect. 5.2.1.2.3 of Chap. 5.

2.3.2.1.1.3 Provisions Ensuring the Application of Institutional Rules

The majority of arbitral institutions contain in their rules provisions obliging arbitrators and all other institutional actors to act in the spirit of the relevant set of arbitration rules in order to ensure that the award is legally enforced.[214] To this extent, institutions secure the legal requirement set forth in Article V (1) (d) of the New York Convention relating to compliance of the arbitral procedure with the parties' arbitration agreement. This is mostly achieved by means of the encouragement in the arbitration rules of the parties to participate in a preparatory conference during which the parties may submit proposals regarding the conduct of the proceedings and agree on procedural issues even before the arbitral tribunal is constituted.[215] Some arbitration rules, including the ICC Rules, make the participation in a case management conference at the outset of the proceedings mandatory.[216] The ICC additionally secures these provisions by means of Article 23 of the 2012 ICC Arbitration Rules, which sets forth the components of the unique document called "Terms of Reference".

The Terms of Reference is a document prepared by arbitrators and signed both by the members of an arbitral tribunal and the parties to a dispute. The Terms of Reference deal with the procedural aspects of arbitration, and, if the ICC arbitral tribunal decides so, they may also contain the list of the main substantive concerns of a dispute. To this extent, the Terms of Reference may be regarded as the provisional plan of the matters to be resolved by means of arbitration. Under Article 23(3) of the 2012 ICC Arbitration Rules, the ICC Court approves the Terms of Reference only in cases in which either of the parties refuses to sign them. However, in practice, the ICC Court examines these documents on a case-by-case basis to support the work of arbitrators and, whenever it seems sufficient to the Court, to oversee the arbitrators' performance in this regard.[217] In this way, both the establishment of Terms of Reference by the ICC Arbitration Rules and the equipment of the ICC Court with the respective supervisory powers over such a document ensure, at the beginning of every arbitral process, that the subject matters of the particular arbitration will be determined in accordance with the agreement of the parties.

2.3.2.1.2 Private Regulatory Powers of Arbitral Institutions

There are several stages of institutional arbitration proceedings in which institutional activity limits party autonomy and determines the conduct of arbitrations at

[214] See: Articles 7(5) and 35 of the 2012 ICC Arbitration Rules, Article 32.2 of the LCIA Rules, Article 48 of the SCC Rules, Article 36 of the ICC Rules and Procedures.

[215] Article 4 of the ICDR Procedures, Article 14 of the LCIA Rules, and Article 24 of the 2012 ICC Arbitration Rules.

[216] Article 24 of the ICC 2012 Rules.

[217] Craig et al. 2001, 23.

the discretion of the arbitral institution even before the relevant decision of an arbitral tribunal is made. These "exclusive" institutional prerogatives can be understood as private regulatory powers developed by arbitral institutions in the course of their supervisory activities in the arbitration proceedings and as such they should be analysed in the context of self-regulatory functions of institutional arbitration regimes. In this particular understanding of arbitral institutions, the concept of transnational private regulation appears particularly relevant inasmuch as it set up a framework in which various private self-regulatory regimes operate today in a transnational context. Such a framework involves rule-making, monitoring, and enforcement[218]. Although it is not the purpose of this analysis to present the functions of arbitral institutions in view of all components of the above-mentioned framework, the concept of transnational private regulation is particularly relevant when distinguishing the private regulatory functions of arbitral institutions that fall beyond a single arbitration proceeding. In a sense, these functions can be perceived as setting forth the standards and requirements for all institutional arbitration actors (including the future parties and arbitrators). This also means that private regulatory functions of arbitral institutions are not limited to individual disputes (where they still may appear to be contrary to the principle of party autonomy). Instead, these functions have effects for the whole group of arbitration users of a particular institutional regime, as well as the arbitrators working within such a regime, and even on other institutional regimes in that the prerogatives of particular institution inform the self-regulatory framework of other arbitral institutions.[219] This latter observation can be illustrated by means of the aforementioned universalization of the institutional arbitration policies and rules at more horizontal, transnational level that results in the situation in which most leading arbitral institutions offer to the parties similar procedural frameworks for the resolution of disputes that are often at odds with the parties' demands placed on institutional arbitration regimes. These demands mostly arise because such frameworks appear burdensome and too formal to traditional arbitration users.

In this vein, private regulatory functions are seen here as having broader implications for the public function of institutional arbitration taken as a whole and at the transnational level simply because they fall beyond the private function of any single arbitral institution understood in the context of the resolution of individual disputes. These functions explain, to a certain degree, why some arbitral institutions amend their rules to incorporate the recent procedural developments of other institutional regimes even if such amendments do not necessarily correspond to the legal framework for arbitration in the jurisdiction where a particular institution

---

[218]Cafaggi, 2014, 71.

[219]In this vein, institutional settings of procedural norms in arbitration bear resemblance to "experimentalist governance architecture" as defined by Professors Jonathan Zeitlin and Charles Sabel, meaning that arbitral institutions learn through and from comparison of various approaches to the governance of arbitration processes. See Sabel and Zeitlin 2008.

has its assets.[220] It is necessary to emphasize here that most exclusive prerogatives of arbitral institutions differ from one institution to another due to the different models of institutional involvement in the arbitration proceedings as adopted by arbitral institutions. However, there are some shared private regulatory functions that can be distinguished among the leading arbitral institutions within the following categories: (1) institutional decisions on jurisdictional challenges; (2) decisions regarding non-signatories and consolidation of the proceedings; and (3) the institutional choices regarding the applicability of the altered arbitration rules with regard to the parties' arbitration agreement.

2.3.2.1.2.1 Institutional Decisions on Jurisdictional Challenges

The nature of the institutional decisions regarding the admissibility of an arbitration case has raised a number of controversies, mostly concerning the administrative versus jurisdictional character of such decisions. As already mentioned, the members of the ICC organs openly discuss the possibility for such decisions to be jurisdictional in nature.[221] Even though the mechanisms for the scrutiny of the arbitration agreement differ from one institution to another, these mechanisms determine whether the arbitration may preliminarily proceed in regard to the parties, be it those disclosed or undisclosed in the arbitration agreement. In any event, this institutional prerogative ensures the requirements of the New York Convention concerning the procedural validity of the arbitration agreement.

There are only a few arbitral institutions whose arbitration rules authorize them to make decisions on jurisdiction instead of allowing the arbitrators to exclusively rule on the jurisdiction pursuant to the doctrine of competence–competence.[222] Most institutions, however, have developed mechanisms that either create an implicit procedural framework for arbitral institutions to *prima facie* allow or disallow the case or that directly authorize the relevant institutional bodies to issue *prima facie* decisions on jurisdiction. Hence, the significance of the institutional determinations of jurisdiction can be classified into two groups. The first group involves institutions such as the LCIA and the ICDR, which do not expressly provide for the exclusive competence of the institution to allow or disallow the case in the arbitration rules but that invite the analyses of jurisdictional challenges by the members of institutional organs by means of the established institutional practices. The second group comprises arbitral institutions such as the ICC and the SCC, which explicitly authorize the relevant organ of the institution to preliminarily determine jurisdiction.[223]

---

[220] This concerns the argument that emergency orders may not be treated as final decisions in some jurisdictions. See Sabharwal and Zaman 2014, 710–711 with further references.

[221] Sect. 2.2.2 of this chapter.

[222] These include: the CIETAC, CMAC, and the Beijing Arbitration Commission (BAC). See Gerbay, forthcoming 2016.

[223] Article 6(4) of the 2012 ICC Arbitration Rules and Articles 6, 9(i) and 10(i) of the SCC Rules.

Within the first group, the LCIA Secretariat exercises implicit combined authority with the LCIA arbitral tribunal regarding possible jurisdictional challenges.[224] Once a request for arbitration has been submitted to the LCIA, the LCIA Secretariat writes a letter to the parties in which it refers to the relevant arbitration agreement and alerts the parties of any possible queries the Secretariat may have regarding jurisdiction.[225] Consequently, where there are justified reasons for believing that the provisions of the contract (including the arbitration clause itself) signed by the parties are vague and/or when the respondent questions the LCIA's jurisdiction, it is standard procedure for the LCIA Secretariat's to address jurisdictional challenges. These decisions will mostly be issued to confirm that the arbitration agreement does not refer to the arbitration rules of other arbitral institutions and to draw the parties' attention to arbitration agreements that do not contain the reference to any arbitral institution and/or institutional arbitration rules.[226] Subsequently, the LCIA arbitral tribunal needs to issue a final decision concerning jurisdiction.

As for the ICDR, the *prima facie* jurisdictional issues fall within the responsibility of the ICDR's case management team. This means that the case management staff of the ICDR, in instances where one party objects to arbitral jurisdiction, will contact the party in question, requesting the party to support its standing with further comments and supplementary documentation.[227] Therefore, the provisional institutional determinations on this matter are based on the written materials provided for by the parties. Usually, preliminary jurisdictional controversies are resolved within 30 days of receiving a notification of arbitration.[228] Again, as in the case of the LCIA, the ICDR arbitral tribunal will make subsequent determinations either in the preliminary decision or in the final award.[229]

Regarding the second group of institutions, both the ICC Arbitration Rules and the SCC procedures provide for more elaborated institutional involvement in determinations of jurisdictional challenges. The new 2012 ICC Arbitration Rules empower the ICC Court to preliminarily determine whether: (1) arbitration should be set in motion based on the valid arbitration agreement; (2) the arbitration file should be dismissed due to the invalidity of the arbitration agreement; (3) arbitration should proceed in relation to all or some parties referred to in the arbitration

---

[224]Pursuant to Article 23 of the LCIA Arbitration Rules "the Arbitral Tribunal shall have the power to rule upon its own jurisdiction and authority, including any objection to the initial or continuing existence, validity, effectiveness or scope of the Arbitration Agreement".

[225]Chan 2009, 410.

[226]Wade et al. 2015, 262.

[227]Chan 2009, 411.

[228]Ibid.

[229]Moreover, the preliminary jurisdictional controversies "raised prior to the constitution of the tribunal shall not preclude the [ICDR] from proceeding with administration and shall be referred to the tribunal for determination once constituted." See Article 19.4 of the ICDR Procedures.

agreement; and (4) arbitration should proceed with regard to all or certain claims submitted in the request for arbitration.[230] Moreover, pursuant to the modifications incorporated into the new Article 6(3) of the 2012 ICC Arbitration Rules, it is the Secretary General who may refer the case to the ICC Court for preliminary determination of jurisdiction once he or she decides that the circumstances require such determination.[231] In the case of the SCC, Article 9 of the SCC Arbitration Rules authorizes the Board to rule on jurisdiction *ex officio*, not only when the Board is not *prima facie* satisfied that the alleged arbitration clause constitutes a proper basis for an arbitration to be set in motion in whole or in part, but also when there are justified reasons for assuming that a respondent against whom a request for arbitration was filed is not bound by an alleged arbitration agreement.[232] In such cases, the Board will likely raise a jurisdictional issue on its own motion.[233] Subsequently, if it finds that arbitration cannot proceed, the Board will dismiss the arbitration case when the SCC Institute manifestly lacks jurisdiction over a dispute concerning the existence of the SCC arbitration clause in general or its existence with regard to the particular party to arbitration.

In all cases concerning the institutional mechanisms analysed here, every arbitral institution preliminarily screens arbitration agreements in order to assess: (1) whether such arbitration agreements in fact exist (control over the procedural validity); and (2) if the institution which received the request for arbitration has *de facto* authority to supervise the case (the screening of the accurate wording of the institutional arbitration agreement). Although the determinations made by the LCIA or the ICDR are not final, they set forth all the prerequisites for the arbitral tribunal, which largely determine the ultimate ruling of the latter. Although it is up to the arbitral tribunal to finally determine the jurisdiction, the institutional assistance is of great importance for such determination as it points to the potential gaps in arbitration agreements, which may eventually result in the refusal by the arbitral tribunal to hear the case.

Finally, the dynamics established in the ICC Arbitration Rules expressly entail the finality of the ICC Court's preliminary decisions on jurisdiction, rendered pursuant to Article 6(3) in accordance with Article 6(4) of the 2012 ICC Arbitration Rules. Hence, the Court's decisions concerning the dismissal of the case in regard to some parties or some claims will not be referred to the ICC arbitral tribunal for

---

[230] A commentary note to Article 6(3) of the 2012 ICC Arbitration Rules in Fry, Greenberg, Mazza, 2012, 71–74.

[231] Article 6(3) in accordance with Article 6(4) of the 2012 ICC Arbitration Rules.

[232] It happened so in the following cases: SCC case 121/1998 and SCC case 90/1999, reported in Stockholm Arb. Rep. 2000:2, 178, and SCC case 87/2002, reported in Stockholm Arb. Rep. 2004:2, 57.

[233] Magnusson and Shaughnessy 2006, 46.

further deliberation. Although such decisions may still be challenged in any court having jurisdiction in the case giving rise to arbitration, they prove the private regulatory functions of arbitral institutions—exercised by the ICC Court in front of the ICC arbitrators and the parties. These functions are fulfilled in the arbitration, self-regulatory sense, not in a purely legal meaning. If the parties against whom the "negative" decision on jurisdiction has been issued still wish to have their dispute resolved by means of institutional arbitration, they must submit a new request to the ICC Secretariat accompanied by the new registration fee.

2.3.2.1.2.2 Decisions Regarding Non-Signatories, Joinders, and Consolidation of the Proceedings

The institutional decisions on jurisdiction also take the form of determinations regarding the effects of the arbitration agreement with respect to the parties who did not originally sign the arbitration agreement (so-called "non-signatories"), the joinder of third parties, and the consolidation of the proceedings under more than one arbitration agreement into a single arbitration. These issues become even more problematic in disputes arising out of complex, multiparty contracts. Different institutional arbitration rules grant arbitral institutions different levels of autonomy in these regards vis-à-vis institutional arbitrators. However, there is a visible trend among most leading arbitral institutions to shift certain powers to preliminary determine the validity of arbitration agreements with regard to non-signatories or in the context of the consolidations of the proceedings from arbitrators to arbitral institutions. This shift can be viewed yet again in the context of the increased formalization of arbitration rules in similar direction at the transnational level. In many cases, institutional private regulatory functions in the above-mentioned procedural aspects of the proceedings may have significant practical implication for the parties to the proceedings, as they often run contrary to the principle of party autonomy. Thus this allows arbitral institutions increasing discretion when deciding on who shall be bound by the arbitration agreement and whether the arbitral institution in question (together with institutional arbitrators) is in fact authorized to proceed with the arbitration case.

It is generally acknowledged under different theories of national contract laws that arbitration agreements do not necessarily need to bind only the parties that actually signed them.[234] Arbitral institutions such as the ICC follow this reasoning by "extending" the effects of the arbitration agreements to parties that did not sign the original agreement, though actively participated in the negotiations, performance, and termination of the contract containing the ICC arbitration clause. These theories, known as "group of companies", "alter ego", or "piercing the

[234] See generally Brinsmead 2007.

corporate veil" have long been applied by the ICC arbitrators and for some time now have also been referred to by the ICC Court.[235] As reads from *The Secretariat's Guide to ICC Arbitration*, the ICC Court will allow the continuing of the proceedings with regard to non-signatories in the following situations:

> (i) [...] the non-signatory has participated in the negotiation, performance, and/or termination of the contract (e.g. in its capacity as a parent or other company related to the signatory); (ii) [...] the non-signatory is an assignee of the original signatory's obligations under the contract; (iii) [...] the non-signatory is the guarantor of a signatory (although some additional evidence of its acceptance of the arbitration agreement will usually be required).[236]

The ICC decisions on the effects of arbitration agreements on non-signatories are particularly sensitive as they deal with the interpretation of the implied consent of the parties to be bound by the arbitration agreement or the interpretation of the agreement binding upon the non-signatory sometimes even "in disregard of corporate personality" of the original signatory to the arbitration agreement.[237] These issues also enjoy different treatment by various national laws and hence the enforceability of the decisions on non-signatories largely depends on the case law developed in this regard by national courts. This is why the analyses of the treatment of the effects of arbitration agreements for non-signatories shall also be done in the context of the laws governing different arbitration proceedings.

The institutional decisions regarding non-signatories appear even more ambiguous in regards to arbitration proceedings involving States or State entities, where the consent to arbitration is usually expressed tacitly by means of the compliance with various provisions of international law such as international treaties. In these cases, the authority to determine the implied consent of public actors to arbitration may be particularly controversial in situations where the preliminary decisions are made by arbitral institutions (or even private arbitrators authorized to decide on their jurisdiction at the later stage).

In addition, the arbitration rules of the leading arbitral institutions have increasingly granted more elaborate powers to arbitral institutions in the field of joinder of third parties to arbitration. The new 2012 ICC Arbitration Rules empower the ICC Secretariat to collect requests for the joinder of additional parties, provided that the arbitral tribunal has not yet been constituted and that the arbitrators have not yet been confirmed by the ICC Court.[238] By means of such requests, the additional parties will almost automatically be added to the pending arbitration proceedings.[239] Yet the ICC Court (and, at the further stage, the ICC arbitral tribunal)

---

[235] Vidal 2005; Besson 2010; Youssef 2010.

[236] A commentary note to Article 6(4) of the 2012 ICC Arbitration Rules in: Fry, Greenberg, Mazza, 2012, 78.

[237] Section 1.14–1.16 Park 2009.

[238] Article 7(1) of the 2012 ICC Arbitration Rules.

[239] A commentary note to Article 7 of the 2012 ICC Arbitration Rules in: Fry, Greenberg, Mazza, 2012, 94–104.

has the power to remove the additional party from the proceedings if it is not *prima facie* satisfied with the continuation of the proceedings with regard to this party based on the provisions of Articles 6(3) and 6(4) of the 2012 ICC Arbitration Rules.[240] Similarly, the ICDR Procedures also authorize the parties to submit the notice of arbitration against an additional party until the constitution of the arbitral tribunal unless otherwise agreed by the parties.[241] The new LCIA Rules, although leaving the decision on joinders within the scope of arbitrators' prerogatives, have also created the possibility for the arbitral tribunal to join the parties to arbitration proceedings even with no express consent of the remaining parties that only need to "be given a reasonable opportunity to state their views" in this regard.[242]

Moreover, arbitral institutions tend to exercise greater control over the consolidation of arbitration proceedings. For example, under the 2012 ICC Arbitration Rules, the ICC Court gained the power to preliminary determine the consolidation of the proceedings arising from different arbitration agreements,[243] which requires the Court to both decide on the compatibility of arbitration agreements and to interpret the parties' initial consent regarding the prospective consolidation of the arbitrations.[244] While deciding on the compatibility of the arbitration agreements, the Court will ordinarily assess whether disputes arise out of the same legal relationship, and for that reason the Court will look at the *place* where arbitration agreements were signed, and the respective *intentions* of the parties. Correspondingly, the SCC Board may decide on the consolidation of the proceedings following the request for the party and after conducting relevant consultations in this regard with all parties to the proceedings as well as with arbitrators.[245] Notably, under the new provision of Article 22.1 of the LCIA Rules the LCIA arbitral tribunal was empowered with the possibility to order, <u>with the approval of the LCIA Court</u>:

> (ix) […] the consolidation of the arbitration with one or more other arbitrations into a single arbitration subject to the LCIA Rules where all the parties to the arbitrations to be consolidated so agree in writing;
>
> (x) […] the consolidation of the arbitration with one or more other arbitrations subject to the LCIA Rules commenced under the same arbitration agreement or any compatible arbitration agreement(s) between the same disputing parties, provided that no arbitral tribunal has yet been formed by the LCIA Court for such other arbitration(s) or, if already formed, that such tribunal(s) is(are) composed of the same arbitrators […].

What is more, the LCIA Court, by means of Article 22.6 of the LCIA Rules, was directly authorized to decide on the consolidations of the proceedings where

[240] Ibid.

[241] Article 7.1 of the ICDR Procedures.

[242] Article 22.1(viii) of the 2014 LCIA Rules. Wade et al. 2015, 246.

[243] Article 6(3) of the 2012 ICC Arbitration Rules.

[244] Article 4(ii) in accordance with Article 10 of the 2012 ICC Arbitration Rules.

[245] Article 11 of the SCC Rules.

arbitrations were commenced under the same arbitration agreement, in relation to the same parties, and the arbitral tribunal has not yet been constituted in the arbitrations in question. This new function of the LCIA Court can be exercised even without express consent from the parties.[246]

Institutional decisions regarding joinder or consolidation of the proceedings whether of preliminary or final nature[247] have in fact significant relevance for both the parties to the pending arbitration proceedings and the additional parties. This is mostly visible with regard to the additional parties' rights to affect the composition of the arbitral tribunal in consolidated proceedings.[248] By way of illustration, the Arbitration Rules of the Swiss Chambers' of Commerce Association for Arbitration and Mediation (Swiss Chambers) of 2012 provide for the institutional authority to revoke the appointment or confirmation of arbitrators, and apply the new procedure, once the Court decides on the consolidation of the new arbitration with the pending proceedings.[249] In other words, the Swiss Chambers' Rules waive the right of the parties to appoint an arbitrator, should the consolidation occur. Moreover, the rules further allow the arbitral tribunal to decide on the joinder of the new parties even *without* consent from the joining party or the parties to the pending proceedings. Naturally, the last argument does not fully support the private regulatory functions of all arbitral institutions. However, it gives a general picture of the system of the Swiss Chambers regarding the further implications of the consolidation of the proceedings and joinders for the conduct of the proceedings. The institutional determinations in this regard—whether they are supported by arbitrators' rulings or not—deal with the matters which touch upon party autonomy and the consent of the signatories or non-signatories to arbitration. Regardless of the possibility of the parties to move institutional decisions on jurisdiction in the courts of law, the institutional determinations may, in practice, be final. It may also be extremely difficult to challenge such decisions, especially in jurisdictions that protect institutional activity under the doctrine on immunity.

We see this, for example, in the judgement of the US Southern District Court for New York in *Global Gold Mining, LLC v. Peter M. Robinson et al*, where the US Court was faced with a claim filed by the unsatisfied non-signatory to the ICC arbitration agreement (Mr. Vardan Ayvazin, the Armenian Minister for the

[246]Wade et al. 2015, 254.

[247]Usually, the institutional decisions regarding the joinder of the parties will be subject to the further review by the arbitral tribunal. In contrast, the institutional decisions concerning consolidations of the proceedings will have more autonomous character and thus will be rarely reviewed by arbitral tribunals.

[248]Some authors present other plausible scenarios where institutional decisions regarding joinder of the parties or the consolidation of the proceedings will impact the conduct of arbitrations. See Gerbay, forthcoming 2016 where the relationship between the decisions on consolidation of the arbitration proceedings is discussed in view of its potential influence on the seat of arbitration.

[249]Article 4(1) of the Arbitration Rules of the Swiss Chambers' Arbitration Institution.

Environment) to review the ICC Court's decision refusing the participation of Mr. Ayvazin in the ICC arbitration.[250] The US Southern District Court of New York questioned the admissibility of the legal action against the ICC. It also stated that in any case judicial actions against institutional arbitration actors should not violate the rule on immunity protecting arbitration organizations, and therefore should not be brought in ill-considered manner.[251] This ruling demonstrates the interplay between the preliminary decisions of arbitral institutions on the early conduct of arbitration and the public review of such decisions, which may be governed by general national approach to institutional arbitration, developed to support the integrity of the arbitration processes.

2.3.2.1.2.3 Which Rules Shall Apply?

The clarification of the institutional rules stemming from the parties' respective choices of the arbitral procedure guarantees that arbitration proceeds in accordance with the rules under which the parties in fact meant to resolve their dispute. It is a general rule that once the parties agreed to submit to arbitration, they shall be deemed to have submitted to the rules in effect on the date of the commencement of arbitration unless the parties agreed otherwise.[252]

However, institutions often do not expressly clarify the issue of which rules shall apply once an institution adopts new set of arbitration rules after the parties sign the arbitration agreement. This is not an unusual case in recent institutional arbitration practice. Shall all new rules apply immediately? If not, and if the parties remain tacit as to the applicability of the new rules, will the arbitration proceed in accordance with: (a) the rules in effect on the date of the signature of the arbitration agreement; (b) the rules in force on the date of submitting the request for arbitration by the claimant; or (c) the rules in effect when the actual arbitration proceedings begin? The 2012 ICC Arbitration Rules should apply to all arbitrations commenced after the date when the new rules came into force, that is, after 1 January 2012. Although the new ICC Arbitration Rules seem to provide for transitional measures regarding their applicability (i.e. the parties that signed the arbitration agreement prior to the coming into force of the new Rules should not be bound by the new provisions on the Emergency Arbitrator),[253] there is a risk that if the parties are not equipped with the possibility to opt in or opt out of the new

[250]Cf. Chan 2009; *Global Gold Mining, LLC v. Peter M. Robinson et al.*, No. 636 United States District Court, Southern District of New York, 6 February 2008, 07 Civ. 10492 (GEL), with a commentary in Yearbook Commercial Arbitration Vol XXXIII, 1117–1125, in particular 1117.

[251]*Global Gold Mining, LLC v. Peter M. Robinson et al.*, No. 636 United States District Court, Southern District of New York, 6 February 2008, 07 Civ. 10492 (GEL), with a commentary in Yearbook Commercial Arbitration Vol XXXIII, 1117–1125.

[252]See Article 6(1) of the 2012 ICC Arbitration Rules.

[253]See Article 29(6) of the 2012 ICC Arbitration Rules. See also: Steindl 2012.

rules, the latter will affect the parties' procedural safeguards. This may eventually impact the predictability of the institutional arbitration proceedings, the feature of institutional arbitration that is said to constitute one of the advantages of institutional arbitration over *ad hoc* arbitration. Similar concerns arise with regard to the recent LCIA Rules. According to the LCIA Notes for Parties:

> 8. The LCIA Arbitration Rules presently in force are the LCIA Arbitration Rules 2014, which came into effect on 1 October 2014 (the 2014 Rules). With the exception of the Emergency Arbitrator provisions (discussed below), the 2014 Rules apply to all arbitrations subject to the LCIA Rules commenced on or after 1 October 2014, regardless of when the underlying agreement to arbitrate was concluded.[254]

And further:

> 9. The LCIA Rules effective 1 January 1998 (the 1998 Rules) continue to apply to arbitrations that were commenced before 1 October 2014, as well as to arbitrations where the parties' agreement expressly refers to the LCIA Rules 1998 or, for example, to "the LCIA Rules in force as at the date of the agreement" (where that date was before 1 October 2014).[255]

Although this commentary certainly provides useful guidance regarding the applicability of the new LCIA Rules, some issues remain open mostly because the parties to the new Rules (that is the parties to arbitration agreements referring to the LCIA Rules concluded on or after 1 October 2014) were not granted the right to opt out of all new provisions contained in the LCIA Rules. This is the case with the provisions on the joinder and consolidation of the proceedings under Article 22 of the LCIA Rules, as discussed above.[256] The fact that the parties to newly effective rules are faced with entirely new provisions that they cannot derogate from puts the LCIA Court in the position of the private rule-maker vis-à-vis both the repeat and accidental LCIA arbitration users as well as the arbitrators working under the LCIA aegis. Thus the LCIA Court is a specific private regulator with the powers exceeding the party autonomy in any and all arbitration proceedings.

Similarly, the provisions of Article 1 of the new ICDR Procedures grant certain discretionary powers to the ICDR itself when determining the applicability of its international arbitration rules to disputes submitted to the ICDR/AAA arbitration. Under Article 1.1 of the Rules:

> Where parties have agreed to arbitrate disputes under these International Arbitration Rules ("Rules"), or have provided for arbitration of an international dispute by the International Centre for Dispute Resolution (ICDR) or the American Arbitration Association (AAA) without designating particular rules, the arbitration shall take place in accordance with these Rules as in effect at the date of commencement of the arbitration, subject to modifications that the parties may adopt in writing.

---

[254] LCIA Notes for Parties. http://www.lcia.org/adr-services/guidance-notes.aspx. Accessed 25 April 2016.

[255] Ibid.

[256] Wade et al. 2015, 239.

Further, in accordance with Article 1.3 of the same Rules:

> When parties agree to arbitrate under these Rules, or when they provide for arbitration of an international dispute by the ICDR or the AAA without designating particular rules, they thereby authorize the ICDR to administer the arbitration.

These provisions in fact authorize the ICDR to make respective decisions regarding the applicability of its set of international arbitration rules. This is because the ICDR may exercise its discretion when determining the international character of arbitration even when the parties themselves predetermine such dispute as being of domestic nature.[257]

Moreover, the new provision contained in Article 6(2) of the 2012 ICC Arbitration Rules expressly limits the principle of party autonomy, as it excludes the possibility for the parties to participate in the "combined" arbitration proceedings with the ICC Court administering the arbitration case in accordance with the rules of another arbitral institution and *vice versa*; which was possible, at least in theory, under the previous ICC arbitration regime. Under the 2012 ICC Arbitration Rules, the ICC Court became the only ICC organ capable of both administering the ICC arbitration and assuring the compliance with ICC procedure.[258] This provision cannot be altered even by means of dispositive arrangements of the parties.[259] Keeping in mind that the ICC has exclusive authority to both fix the costs of arbitration and arbitrators' fees at its own discretion and to apply the new schedule of costs to the new arbitration proceedings without the consent of the parties, this proves the increasing private regulatory functions of the ICC Court, exercised within the meaning of the public function. Although the extension of the authority of the ICC Court aims at securing the legality and enforceability of the arbitration proceedings and awards, it interferes with the autonomy of the parties to fully control the conduct of their arbitrations.

2.3.2.1.2.4 The ICC Court of Appeal versus Supervisory Functions of Other Institutions

The bottom-up analysis of the public function of arbitral institutions would remain incomplete without reference to the ICC's peculiar mechanism concerning the scrutiny of draft ICC arbitral awards. Under Article 33 of the 2012 ICC Arbitration Rules,[260] the ICC Court is authorized to lay down mandatory modifications as to the form of arbitral awards, and also to draw the attention of the ICC arbitrators to the points of substance of the ICC awards. By exercising its function under Article 33 of the Rules, the ICC Court contributes to the better compliance of the ICC arbitral awards with the scope of the parties' agreements to arbitrate and the Terms of Reference, while, at the same time, the ICC Court secures that the ICC arbitral tribunal will not exceed its jurisdiction.

---

[257] Gerbay, forthcoming 2016.

[258] Article 6(2) of the ICC Arbitration Rules.

[259] Steindl 2012, 236

[260] See Article 27 of the 1998 ICC Arbitration Rules.

In practice, the authority of the ICC Court to review the draft awards resembles the procedural review of the lower court's decision by a court of appeal. Whenever the ICC Court determines that arbitrators decided on the issue which was not determined at the outset of arbitration or is contrary to the parties' agreement, it will ordinarily invite the ICC arbitral tribunal to reconsider its ruling. It will do so by listing all the matters which need to be re-examined in accordance with the parties arrangements, or by pointing out all of the issues which go beyond the parties' submission. To this extent, the ICC Court—even prior to respective review of the public court having jurisdiction to decide on the enforcement of the ICC award—secures the fulfilment of the legal requirement set forth in Article V(1)(c) of the New York Convention, that the award would deal with a difference contemplated by or falling within the terms of the submission to arbitration and that it would contain decisions on matters determined in parties' submission. This does not mean that the ICC Court decides on the merits of the dispute, however, and as confirmed by the members of the ICC, in some cases the ICC Court may affect the procedural liberty of the ICC arbitrators to ensure procedural integrity of the ICC arbitral awards. This prerogative, increasingly adopted by other arbitral institutions,[261] could have significant implications for the operation of the whole institutional arbitration system. It could further increase the private regulatory powers of arbitral institutions in arbitration proceedings and also strengthen the institutional "position" in the architecture of international commercial arbitration, as analysed by Reisman.[262]

The analyses of both institutional safeguards on behalf of the parties and the institutional private regulatory functions ensuring enforceability of institutional arbitral awards prove the shared public function of all arbitral institutions under analysis in the international arbitration system and also vis-à-vis public actors such as domestic courts. Some of the institutional prerogatives are exercised in verbatim continuation of the parties' arbitration agreement and as such they fall within the meaning of the management of arbitration cases and are often called by commentators and arbitral institutions themselves "administrative" tasks. This concerns, for example: assistance regarding communications, assistance in the composition of the arbitral tribunal, and the ensuring of the applicability of institutional rules by all institutional arbitration actors. Other prerogatives are consonant with the private regulatory powers of arbitral institutions that, although building off of the principle of party autonomy, often run contrary to this core principle in arbitration resembling the decisions of a jurisdictional nature. This involves, for example: decisions on jurisdictional challenges, decisions regarding non-signatories, amendments to the institutional rules and schedules of costs, and the additional ICC Court's prerogatives such as the scrutiny of the ICC awards. In other

[261]Some arbitral institutions such as SIAC, and CIETAC, and the Arbitration Centre of the Chamber of Commerce of the Grand-Duchy of Luxembourg adopted similar mechanisms of the scrutiny of the awards. Cf. Greenberg 2013, 94–96.

[262]Sect. 2.3.2.1.

words, arbitral institutions exercise their private regulatory powers vis-à-vis both repeat and accidental arbitration users by limiting party autonomy in the arbitration process. They also exercise these powers vis-à-vis institutional arbitrators by controlling, at least by means of monitoring their compliance with arbitration rules, the consistency of the decision-making of individual arbitrators that work under the aegis of particular institutions on a case-by-case basis.

The institutional competences falling within both groups are interconnected and so they are assumed in a general context of self-regulatory dynamics of institutional regimes rather than as accidental institutional supervisory powers in single arbitration proceedings. Additionally, in some cases arbitral institutions use their private regulatory powers also vis-à-vis public courts, either tacitly, when the courts assume higher procedural compliance of institutional awards while assessing the enforceability of these awards, or more explicitly, when the courts refuse to move institutional decisions on jurisdiction under the doctrine on judicial immunity. As such, institutional attempts to secure the legality of arbitration proceedings and arbitral awards can be viewed within the meaning of the concept of the *managerial rule of law* that forces the arbitral institutions to ensure the enforceability of their own rules vis-à-vis all institutional arbitration actors (including the parties, arbitrators, experts, etc.). At the same time this concept encourages the members of arbitral institutions to seek the convergence with public regulatory framework for institutional arbitration proceedings, as enshrined in the New York Convention and further enforced by courts at domestic levels.

2.3.2.2 Top-Down Analysis of the Public Function

As noted in the introduction to this part of the chapter, the top-down understanding of the public function concerns the authority of arbitral institutions to administer new types of disputes that traditionally fell outside the scope of interest of early institutional arbitration communities. Broadly speaking, these new types of disputes should be understood as any types of disputes that bear "public" relevance and therefore fall beyond the determination of rights and obligations of disputants in any individual disputes.

The expression "public relevance" also has a broad meaning, as it pertains to any potential legal, societal, and political influence by institutional arbitration of new types of disputes on the repeat or future members of institutional arbitration communities but also the publics, hence the subjects external to institutional arbitral regimes. More specifically, the top-down analysis of the public function presents the arguments on the interrelation between the legal and political (public) goals associated with arbitration by public actors (i.e. legislators, policy-makers, public users of private commercial arbitration regimes) and the scope of disputes that are today increasingly subject to institutional arbitration. In other words, the public function from the top-down aims at explaining the increasing institutional involvement in the administration of disputes involving public actors (States and State entities) whether arising out of or in connection with commercial law relationships (e.g. commercial arbitrations) or public law settings (e.g. investment disputes). It also concerns disputes involving commercial and non-commercial parties that have been increasingly encouraged to rely on private commercial arbitration rules in so-called regulatory disputes that have long been subject to the resolution by administrative authorities or public courts at national levels. Moreover, the additional dimension of the public function as analysed from the top-down perspective concerns the responses of arbitral institutions in the US to the legal questions regarding the consent of the parties to rely on class arbitration.

The following top-down analysis of the public function turns to normative arguments. Since the recent developments involving exclusive institutional competence in administering new types of arbitration cases stem, indirectly, from national regulations of arbitrability, the discussion will concern the existent and emerging implications of the recent changes in domestic arbitration laws for the architecture of arbitration at the international and transnational levels. Against this background, the following part starts with the increasing liberalization of the concept of arbitrability both in the selected EU Member States and in the US. Here, the focus is first made on the developments of the notion of arbitrability in jurisdictions in which the leading arbitral institutions under analysis have their assets in order to present how such developments inform the liberalization of the concept of arbitrability at the international level, which, in turn affects the regional peculiarities of the notion of arbitrability. It continues with the debate on the emergence of new dynamics of competition within the public function, in light of the proliferation of institutional arbitration due to the liberalized arbitrability as defined by domestic legislatures. Furthermore, the analysis focuses on the consequences of this liberalization for the public function of arbitral institutions, as well as for the efficiency of their traditional commercial function assumed within the market for arbitration services. Questions of the legitimacy of these transformed institutional regimes are also raised. This leads to the concluding discussion regarding the interplay between a dual function of institutional arbitration and the corresponding responsibility of arbitral institutions in the arbitration process, particularly in view of the increasing liability lawsuits against arbitral institutions.

2.3.2.2.1 Liberalization of Arbitrability Versus New Institutional Authority in Public Disputes

Regardless of the parties' freedom concerning their contractual arrangements in the context of arbitration, public determination of arbitrable disputes (so-called substantive or objective inarbitrability[263]) also affects the contractual inarbitrability of disputes that the parties may wish to settle by means of arbitration. The

[263]While the first term refers to the distinction under American law, the other term deals with the relevant "definition" of arbitrability provided by the French jurisprudence. See Carbonneau and Janson 1994, 210.

extension of the category of arbitrable disputes is a matter of national laws, and to this extent no international body may, in a binding fashion, impose the stipulations of arbitrability into national legislation. However, since the emergence of early institutional arbitration regimes at the beginning of nineteenth century, there has been an ongoing liberalization of arbitrability in many jurisdictions. On the one hand, this opens national arbitration to new disputes, and, on the other hand, it adds to the understanding of "international" or "transnational public policy" in arbitration, hence informing the increasing liberalization or autonomy of international arbitration. These changes, which imply the shifting recognition of the arbitration process by national and regional legislators as well as by international regulatory bodies in the field of arbitration, appear particularly significant for arbitral institutions. This is due to the increasingly formalized and universalized arbitration rules adopted by arbitral institutions that contribute to the growing trust of public authorities to further extend the concept of arbitrability to new types of disputes often falling beyond traditional commercial arbitration. It is thus hypothesized below that arbitral institutions have become important actors in shaping the regulation of arbitrability, at least indirectly, by signalling their readiness to take on new types of disputes mostly by means of their private regulatory powers as exercised in and outside arbitration regimes thus vis-à-vis institutional arbitration communities and public actors.

The discussion on the liberalization of arbitrability should begin with the comparison of the regulations of arbitrability in the US, the UK, France, and Sweden, thus in jurisdictions in which the leading arbitral institutions have their assets.[264] On the one hand, the statutory law and case law developed in the US, France and Sweden seem to have expressed the most adaptable approach to the notion of arbitrability. On the other hand, the UK—ordinarily perceived as an inflexible arbitration forum—also seems to be responding to the trend of liberalization of arbitrability.

As the provisions on arbitrability codified in the Federal Arbitration Act of 1925 (FAA) are not exhaustive,[265] the US judges have been consequently extending the category of arbitrable disputes, which stays in line with the US policy

[264] The discussion on the potential role of other arbitral institutions in the development of the scope of arbitrability at national levels follows at the end of this section. It is necessary to stress here that the focus on the leading arbitral institutions is made here with regard to the evolution of the relationship between arbitration and the law (involving the regulations of arbitrability) in the course of the development of arbitration practice in traditional arbitration jurisdictions.

[265] Cf. Section 2 of the Federal Arbitration Act; Pub.L. 68–401, 43 Stat. 883, Enacted February 12, 1925, Codified at 9 U.S.C. § 1 et Seq., which reads as follows:

"Section 2.

A written provision in any maritime transaction or a contract evidencing a transaction involving commerce to settle by arbitration a controversy thereafter arising out of such contract or transaction, or the refusal to perform the whole or any part thereof, or an agreement in writing to submit to arbitration an existing controversy arising out of such a contract, transaction, or refusal, shall be valid, irrevocable, and enforceable, save upon such grounds as exist at law or in equity for the revocation of any contract."

favouring arbitration.[266] Already at the moment of promulgation of the FAA, labour disputes were admissible for arbitration. Doubts stemming from domestic public policy concerns still existed, however, as to arbitrability of statutory disputes involving securities or consumer cases. The situation changed with the judgement in *Southland Corp. v. Keating* in 1984,[267] where arbitration was encouraged in domestic cases arising out of the relationships in the securities market (be it statutory claims based on securities acts, antitrust laws or the Racketeer Influenced and Corrupt Organizations Act (RICO)),[268] or in business-to-consumer (B2C) transactions involving a broad context of health care, selling of goods, or finance.[269] In addition, the use of international arbitration in regulatory disputes was confirmed.[270] Since the judgement in *Allied-Bruce Terminix Companies, Inc. v. Dobson* in 1995, the US judges further promoted arbitration of consumer disputes. This extreme liberalization of arbitrability in the US was recently subject to open criticism, especially because of the increased enforcement by the US judges of pre-dispute arbitration agreements binding consumers in standard business-to-business (B2B) transactions.[271] This observation will be relevant for the further discussion in the course of this chapter.

Similarly, French authorities encourage the emancipation of arbitration, and thus also the liberalization of arbitrability. French law distinguishes between the

---

[266] Such policy, according to Carbonneau, was preliminarily determined in *Moses H. Cone Memorial Hosp. v. Mercury Constr. Corp.* in 1983 (460 U.S. 1 1983), where Section 2 of the FAA was defined as a congressional intention of implementing the policy favouring arbitration agreements. See: Carbonneau and Janson 1994, 203.

[267] See: Ibid. quoting *Southland Corp. v. Keating* (465 US, 1, 1984).

[268] For example, in *Shearson/American Express v. McMahon*, No. 86-44 argued 3 March 1987 decided 8 June 1987 482 U.S. 220, the US Supreme Court stated that: "The Arbitration Act establishes a federal policy favouring arbitration, requiring that the courts rigorously enforce arbitration agreements. This duty is not diminished when a party bound by an agreement raises a claim founded on statutory rights. The Act's mandate may be overridden by a contrary congressional command, but the burden is on the party opposing arbitration to show that Congress intended to preclude a waiver of judicial remedies for the statutory rights at issue. Such intent may be discernible from the statute's text, history, or purposes. [...]". Moreover, in the case at hand the Court encouraged the use of arbitration also in Respondents' claims under both the Securities Exchange Act of 1934 and the RICO.

[269] Cf. Brunet et al. 2006.

[270] It is said that the promotion of arbitration and of the concept of arbitrability in international disputes was determined by the American economic interest in arbitration. One of the most prominent cases introducing the reformed stance to arbitrability in international transactions concern the so-called "Mitsubishi case", in which the US Supreme Court held that antitrust claims could be submitted to international arbitration. Cf. *Mitsubishi v. Soler Chrysler-Plymouth*, 473 U.S. 614 (1985) US Supreme Court.

[271] Cf. the text of H.R. 2087: the Arbitration Fairness Act of 2015 and the text of H.R. 1844 (113th): the Arbitration Fairness Act of 2013.

notion of arbitrability in domestic and international arbitration. The regulation of arbitrability was provided in Articles 2059, 2060 and 2061 (Book III, Title XVI) of the French Civil Code.[272] Under Article 2059 of the Civil Code, the parties may refer to arbitration all disputes involving the contractually accessible rights ("*droits disponibles*"). Furthermore, Article 2060 sets forth the limits to the contractual inarbitrability by indicating the following categories of disputes, which are not arbitrable: (a) matters of status and personal capacity concerning divorce or judicial separation; (b) controversies concerning public bodies and institutions (exclusive of the bodies or institutions of an industrial or commercial character that were authorized to enter into arbitration agreements under a relevant decree); and (c) public policy-related matters. Moreover, in accordance with the provision of Article 2061 of the French Civil Code, an arbitration clause regarding certain statutory provisions may be valid for contracts coming into existence as an effect of professional activity of the parties. The codification of these provisions has been an outcome of a long debate in the French courts over the appropriate approach to public policy issues.

Already in the judgment in *Tissot v. Neff* of 1950, it was confirmed that the very fact that contractual dispute touches upon public policy matters did not make the case inarbitrable *per se*.[273] This decision contributed to the French doctrine on the "selective inarbitrability of statutory rights", which constituted permissible submission to arbitration of statutory rights, provided that the right was admissible in individual cases under specific circumstances.[274] As a result of this decision, the French approach to arbitrability has been progressively liberalized, and currently the employment rights claims,[275] consumer disputes, securities disputes, antitrust or intellectual property (IP) rights are arbitrable, *only if* the courts control the application of public policy by arbitrators after the arbitral awards in these matters are issued.[276]

As for arbitrability in international arbitration, two prominent French decisions need to be presented here, namely the judgement of the Paris Court of Appeal in *Société Ganz v. Société Nationale des Chemin de Fers Tunisiens* of 1991,[277] and

[272]The major changes regarding arbitrability were introduced by means of the reform of 2001. See: Jean de la Hosseraye, Stéphanie de Giovanni and Juliette Huard-Bourgois "Arbitration in France", CMS Guide to Arbitration Vol I (2012), 333–334

[273]See the judgment of 28 November 1950, Cass. Com [1950] Bull. Civ., No. 316, together with the commentary in: Carbonneau and Janson 1994, 213; Gaillard and Savage 1999, 334.

[274]See Carbonneau and Janson 1994 referring to the work of Patrice Level, *L'Arbitrabilite*, Revue de L'Arbitrage 213, 219 (1992).

[275]In particular after the expiration of the employment contract. See Carbonneau and Janson 1994, 215–216.

[276]Cf. Honlet et al. 2010.

[277]*Société Ganz v. Société Nationale Des Chemin de Fers Tunisiens*. 1991. *Revue de L'Arbitrage 478 (1991) Cour d'appel de Paris*; Carbonneau and Janson 1994, 218.

the *Mors/Labinal* case decided by the Paris Court of Appeal in 1993.[278] In *Ganz*, the Paris Court of Appeal authorized arbitrators to apply the rules of international public policy to international arbitrations. This included giving the green light to arbitrators to impose contractual sanctions on the parties in cases of their incompliance with the international public policy. This specific "rule of law for international arbitration"[279] was subsequently acknowledged in the decision in *Mors/ Labinal*, in which any interdependency of the national understanding of the arbitrability of statutory rights on international arbitration was eventually rejected.

As far as Sweden is concerned, the Swedish Arbitration Act of 1999 follows the solutions developed by its predecessor (the Act of 1927), and provides for the broad autonomy of the parties to contractually regulate the resolution of their disputes by means of arbitration.[280] Thus, the category of arbitrable disputes under Swedish law involves similar disputes to those from the already-presented jurisdictions, namely: controversies involving consumers (provided that the consumer contract was issued after a dispute had arisen), certain disputes concerning the application of mandatory statutory provisions, or matters involving environmental law and financial markets.[281] Yet again, the very fact that certain disputes involve public policy concerns does not automatically rule out the possibility of arbitration of those cases in Sweden. Apart from the general trends presented above, the arbitrability of each dispute will be assessed on a case-by-case basis by the Swedish courts once the controversy in this regard is raised by one of the parties. This was also the case in the recent judgment of the Supreme Court of Sweden dated 23 November 2012, which declared that disputes should be non-arbitrable if they concern matters not designed for out-of-court dispute settlement, and in particular dealing with the application of the peremptory laws that involve the interest of the society or a third-party interest.[282]

The presentation of the regulation of arbitrability in the UK needs to begin with the emphasis on the traditional hostility of the UK public authorities to arbitration. It seems, however, that the traditional UK approach to the issue at hand has also witnessed some changes. The UK Arbitration Act of 1996 distinguished between

[278]Jarrosson 1993; Redfern et al. 2004, 140.

[279]See Carbonneau and Janson 1994, 218.

[280]See Section 1 of the Swedish Arbitration Act of 1999, which reads as follows: "Disputes concerning matters in respect of which the parties may reach a settlement may, by agreement, be referred to one or several arbitrators for resolution. Such an agreement may relate to future disputes pertaining to a legal relationship specified in the agreement. The dispute may concern the existence of a particular fact. In addition to interpreting agreements, the filling of gaps in contracts can also be referred to arbitrators. Arbitrators may rule on the civil law effects of competition law as between the parties."

[281]Sundin and Wernberg 2007, 64.

[282]Swedish Arbitration Portal: The Supreme Court. http://www.arbitration.sccinstitute.com/Swedish-Arbitration-Portal/Supreme-Court/The-Supreme-Court2/The-Supreme-Court/. Accessed 25 April 2016. The website contains relevant links to the decision at hand, both in English and in Swedish language versions.

contractual and non-contractual disputes that may be submitted to arbitration. The non-contractual disputes involve tort claims, IP rights, and other statutory claims concerning civil proceedings.[283] To this extent, criminal matters shall not be arbitrable in the UK. As for the contractual disputes, the recent judgment of the UK Court of Appeal in *Fiona Trust & Holding Corporation and others v. Yuri Privalov and others* may suggest the liberalization of the UK approach to arbitration in general and to arbitrability in particular under English law. [284] In *Fiona Trust,* the Court of Appeal underlined the necessity of a more *liberal construction* of arbitration agreements due to the demands of international commerce. This allows one to look prospectively also into the future developments of the concept of arbitrability in the UK. When discussing the concept of arbitrability in the UK it is also necessary to notice the particular UK approach to consumer arbitration. Under English law, the consumer arbitration clauses should be unfair if the claim involves less than £5,000.[285] This distinct stance to consumer arbitration in England, unlike the US approach, is determined by the particular regime for the consumer protection in Europe. In the same way, pre-dispute arbitration clauses, which are rather easily enforced in the US, would be considered unfair in most European jurisdictions, including the UK.[286]

It can therefore be speculated that the national regulations of arbitrability have had an impact on the admissibility of new categories of disputes also at international level in that the determinations of arbitrability in the context of international arbitration have often been conducted by judges or legislators directly in contrast to more rigid provisions in this regard relating to domestic arbitrations. Albeit each jurisdiction distinguished between national and international concept of arbitrability in view of the necessary interpretations of national and international public policy, and even if the latter seems to escape from any public regulation, it appears that the prior liberalization of arbitrability at domestic levels has largely informed and determined the expansion of international arbitration. Such expansion proceeded with an active involvement of arbitral institutions. This has at least two implications for the public function of arbitral institutions analysed from the top-down perspective. First, arbitral institutions have gained more credibility in front of domestic authorities deciding on arbitrability (mostly due to the increased formalization of institutional regimes), and therefore some national or regional arbitral institutions have been awarded exclusive competence to administer new category of disputes that fall within so-called "grey zones" of arbitrability. These "grey zones" encompass categories of disputes falling between the universally

[283]Miles and Davies 2013.

[284]*Fiona Trust & Holding Corporation & Ors v Yuri Privalov & Ors [2007] EWCA Civ 20 (24 January 2007).*

[285]Cf. the UK Arbitration Act 1996, Chapter 23, Section 91(1); The Unfair Arbitration Agreements (Specified Amount) Order 1999.

[286]See generally Drahozal and Friel 2003.

arbitrable disputes and the obviously non-arbitrable disputes.[287] Second, arbitral institutions have received an increased recognition by regional and international authorities that can be recently seen in the debate on the inclusion of the investor-State arbitration into the TTIP and other international agreements entered into by the EU following the adoption of the Lisbon Treaty. On the one hand there has been continuous criticisms by the European public(s) of the potential determination of regulatory and public policy issues by private arbitrators due to the lack of the democratic legitimacy of the latter, making the final regulation of investor-State arbitration within the EU unsure. On the other hand the current debate concerns the arguments of some public functions of private arbitral institutions in the arbitration process, especially as far as the procedural safeguards and transparency of new forms of arbitrations are concerned. Overall, the expansion and liberalization of arbitrability at the domestic levels, that also informed the public understanding of international arbitration, have contributed to the new dynamics of competition between arbitral institutions within the public sphere thus transcending the traditional commercial function of institutional arbitration activity.

2.3.2.2.2 Proliferation of Arbitral Institutions and the Development of Additional Dynamics of Competition

The growing external recognition of institutional arbitration not only contributed to the proliferation of institutional arbitration but also implied the changing dynamics of competition between arbitration centres. This can be illustrated by the following examples. First, as already noted, the category of disputes that may be arbitrated under the supervision of arbitral institutions has been expanded at national and international levels that prompted arbitral institutions to reflect these developments in institutional arbitration rules. Second, the dynamics under discussion directly or indirectly contributed to the creation of new arbitral institutions that deal solely with new forms of arbitrations allowed by means of recent changes to the regulation of arbitrability. Lastly, the emergence of new forms of arbitration was promoted that hardly correspond to the original goals of commercial arbitration, which questions the traditional commercial function of arbitral institutions in the arbitration system.

Only the first two issues, which concern the interplay between the increasing proliferation of institutional arbitration in view of the national liberalization of the scope of arbitrability and the emergence of new dynamics of competition between arbitral institutions (be it traditional ones or emerging institutions), will be analysed here. The latter issue entails the interaction between the new forms of arbitration in a more general context of the transformation of the ADR and the role of

[287] Cole et al. 2014, 10.

institutional service providers in facilitating these forms of ADR mostly as a consequence of the public encouragement of out-of-court dispute settlement in new types of disputes—and, to this extent, it falls outside the scope of this book.[288]

Moving back to the discussion at hand, the emerging public function of arbitral institutions encourages the existent arbitral institutions to expand their traditional goals beyond the administration of purely *commercial* disputes at national level. This trend is mostly visible within the institutional regime of the AAA that expresses a particular dialogue with the US authorities. The AAA actively participates in numerous governmental programmes involving the Automobile Industry Special Binding Program, the former cooperation with the US Department of Justice in a 2010 antitrust case settlement, the cooperation with federal Centres for Medicare & Medicaid Services (CMS), or the AAA's involvement in the resolution of disputes under the United States Anti-Doping Agency (USADA) Protocol for Olympic Movement Testing and the AAA Olympic Sport Doping Disputes Supplementary Procedures—to name a few.[289] The last AAA's activity in sports arbitration is particularly absorbing, as it concerns the AAA's cooperation—through its international division, the ICDR with the Court of Arbitration for Sports in Lausanne in anti-doping arbitrations. These two institutions offer a common pool of arbitrators specialized in anti-doping disputes. Moreover, the AAA

[288]This is indicated by, among other developments, the encouragement of arbitration and ADR in the resolution of various EU sectorial disputes (Warwas 2014) and the introduction of consumer ADR across the Union (Cole et al. 2014, 52–52; 204–212). There are intriguing questions that relate to the developments of the new forms of ADR, especially at the EU level that imply the growing privatization of civil justice systems within the EU. Moreover, the encouragement of new forms of ADR in increasingly sensitive disputes such as consumer disputes, often administered by for-profit service providers, as well as the interplay between the activity of arbitral institutions in some specific "regulatory" sectors such as sports arbitration call for further questions. What are the linkages between the new forms of arbitration, so-called new "laws" (e.g. *lex sportiva, lex informatica* or even *lex energetica*) whose normativity the new variants of institutional arbitration are to support (such as the Court of Arbitration for Sport) and the traditional arbitral institutions? To what extent do traditional arbitral institutions respond to the external dynamics concerning the development of new laws? Do the new forms of arbitration entail the necessity for the emergence of new arbitration service providers such as e-associations or simplified arbitral institution to provide quasi-arbitration services? And finally, what would be the implications of these developments for the functionality and legitimacy of traditional institutional arbitration? One of the effects can be identified already now against the background of the additional dynamics of competition between traditional arbitration centres and newly established arbitral institutions.

[289]See the AAA Government Programmes via: Government & Consumer: Federal, State, Local Governments. http://www.adr.org/aaa/faces/aoe/gc/government?_afrLoop=735865533092255&_afrWindowMode=0&_afrWindowId=null#%40%3F_afrWindowId%3Dnull%26_afrLoop%3D735865533092255%26_afrWindowMode%3D0%26_adf.ctrl-state%3Dagxlw73i2_4. Accessed 25 April 2016.

provides for specialized rules in the field of employment, consumer, and labour arbitration.[290] The AAA even adopted the Consumer Due Process Protocol that constitutes a form of private regulation of consumer arbitrations in the US. Moreover, many European arbitral institutions went beyond the purely commercial patterns of dispute resolution and expanded their services into new areas. As already noted, DIS implemented rules for corporate law disputes.[291] Similarly, the CAM and the Czech Arbitration Court Arbitration Centre for Internet Disputes offers Rules for Domain Name Disputes that correspond with the ICANN's regulation of the Internet.[292]

In view of the progressive liberalization of national laws on arbitration, the wider use of institutional arbitration has also been permitted in various company-related disputes. For example, the Italian law through the Legislative Decree No. 5 of 17 January 2003 (which took effect on 1 January 2004) allowed arbitration of disputes regarding the operation of close corporations, though without a reference to publicly held or listed corporations.[293] Furthermore, the recent reform of Spanish arbitration law expressly confirmed the possibility of arbitration of company law disputes.[294] These changes authorize arbitral institutions to exclusively administer company-related disputes (Spain), or to appoint an arbitral tribunal once the use of arbitration in companies' by-laws or statutes has been approved by the majority of two-thirds of the votes reflecting the corporate capital (Italy). All this accords Spanish—and to some extent also Italian—arbitral institutions extraordinary prerogatives in the management of company-related disputes, which even *ad hoc* arbitrators cannot enjoy.

Similarly, some national laws such as Hungarian law and Maltese law, empowered arbitral institutions with competences that cannot even be exercised by *ad hoc* arbitrators in these jurisdictions. Yet, in some aspects, they mirror the powers of national courts. Hungarian arbitration is governed by Act LXXI of 1994 on Arbitration (HAA) that has recently imposed restrictive rules regarding arbitrability that increased the authority of domestic arbitral institutions in Hungary. Under Section 2(3) of the HAA parties to the disputes over a right in rem relating to the real estate located in Hungary (as well as its lease and tenancy) may submit these types of disputes only to institutional arbitration seated and administered in

---

290See: the AAA Consumer, Employment and Labour Rules in the section on: Rules & Procedures https://www.adr.org/aaa/faces/rules/searchrules?_afrLoop=1533029715880923&_afrWindowMode=0&_afrWindowId=eulkhplnj_32#%40%3F_afrWindowId%3Deulkhplnj_32%26_afrLoop%3D1533029715880923%26_afrWindowMode%3D0%26_adf.ctrl-state%3Deulkhplnj_114. Accessed 25 April 2016.

291See: DIS Rules. http://www.dis-arb.de/en/16/rules/overview-id0. Accessed 25 April 2016

292Domain Names Disputes. http://www.camera-arbitrale.it/en/Domain+Names+Disputes/index.php?id=13. Accessed 25 April 2016.

293The Italian Legislative Decree No. 5 of 17 January 2003.

294Spanish Act 11/2011, of May 20, Reforming Act 60/2003, of December 23, on Arbitration, and Regulating Institutional Arbitration within the Public Administration.

Hungary. The requirement is that all the parties to the contract underlying the right in rem or to the lease or tenancy agreement have their seats or permanent establishments in Hungary.[295] Moreover, Hungarian law sanctions the exclusive jurisdiction of some arbitral institutions conferred to them by the act of the Hungarian Parliament. For example, the most prominent Hungarian arbitral institution, the Arbitration Court attached to the Hungarian Chamber of Commerce and Industry (HCCI) enjoys exclusive jurisdiction to administer international arbitration proceedings, unless otherwise stipulated by an act of the Hungarian legislators. This means that whenever the parties agree on international arbitration administered by an arbitral institution to be seated in Hungary in their arbitration agreement or the submission to arbitration, they have no other choice than to select the HCCI Arbitration Court as an administrator of their dispute, unless a specific legislative act authorizes them to chose another arbitral institution.

Likewise, the Malta Arbitration Centre, the only arbitral institution that was established in Malta (nota bene by means of Malta's arbitration law[296]) enjoys extensive powers in the arbitration proceedings that some authors even compare to the functions of domestic courts.[297] The members of the main organ of the Centre, namely the Board, are elected by the Prime Minister of Malta. The Centre is authorized to administer both domestic and international arbitration proceedings, and, most importantly, also the mandatory arbitration that constitute a particular feature of Malta's arbitration law. In addition to these prerogatives, the Registrar of the Centre was equipped with extensive functions relating to document production and collection of evidence in the course of arbitration that usually fall within the scope of arbitrators' duties or the competences of national courts.

As noted, some existent arbitral institutions also engage in the resolution of new types of disputes at the international level. For example, some private commercial arbitral institutions such as the SCC and the ICC, have been occasionally participating in both commercial arbitrations and investment law arbitrations involving States and State-like entities. The way in which the ICC Court responded to the new dynamics of competition in this regard can be illustrated by the recent changes to the ICC Arbitration Rules (2012). The recent developments in the ICC Rules are meant to further attract States and State-like entities to the ICC arbitration.

States or State-like entities may use ICC arbitration either in commercial or investment disputes.[298] In order to make the rules adaptable to investment arbitra-

[295]See: 2012 Amendments to the HAA, Cole et al. 2014, 114–115.

[296]Arbitration Act, Ch. 387 of the Laws of Malta of 1996, as Subsequently Amended with the Major Changes Implemented in 2004 by Means of the Legal Notice 421.

[297]Cole et al. 2014, 136.

[298]For a study on the involvement of commercial arbitral institutions in all types of arbitrations concerning States and State-like entities see: Cole et al. 2014, 229–246.

tion involving States, in the 2012 ICC Arbitration Rules the requirement provided for in the previous version of the Rules that the ICC arbitration refers to business disputes was deleted. Moreover, and as already analysed in the previous section on the procedural dimension of the public function, the 2012 ICC Arbitration Rules authorize the ICC Court to directly appoint a sole arbitrator or presiding arbitrator. This amendment was underpinned by the rationale that investment arbitrations would need more neutrality for the appointment of arbitrators, which apparently, some ICC National Committees were not able to offer. The new ICC provisions also strengthened the principle of impartiality of the arbitral tribunal by adding an express requirement of impartiality in new Articles 11 (dealing with the appointment) and 14 (concerning the challenges to arbitrators) of the 2012 ICC Arbitration Rules.

Another significant change involves the limitation of the ICC's arbitral tribunal autonomy to apply provisions of contract or trade usages. Since the application of trade usages to investment arbitrations was one of the major concerns of States and State-like entities concerning the ICC arbitration,[299] the new Article 21(2) of the 2012 ICC Arbitration Rules states that arbitral tribunals shall take into account the provisions of contract, *if any* (since majority of investment arbitrations would arise out of Bilateral Investment Treaties), and any relevant trade usage. This is a serious departure from the previous Article 17(2) of the 1998 ICC Arbitration Rules, which required arbitral tribunal to take account of provisions of contract and trade usages *in all cases*. To this extent, the 2012 ICC Arbitration Rules seem to also undermine the original goals of the business community to have any dispute resolved under *lex mercatoria*.

Furthermore, the recent ICC practice allows the modification of the general arbitration features such as confidentiality and transparency of arbitration proceedings, by encouraging the new ICC arbitration users (State and State-like entities) to make their submissions, proceedings, or awards public.[300] Although such practices respond to the continuous critique of the lack of transparency in arbitration, it is dubious whether it will correspond with the demands of traditional arbitration users who tend to keep all the aspects of arbitration (even the very fact of the emergence of a dispute) secret. All these amendments create room for the ICC to manoeuvre to further broaden its horizons by administering investment disputes possibly arising out of the EU investment treaties. The members of leading European arbitral institutions confirmed their eagerness to deal with investment disputes at the EU level during the European Forum for New Ideas, which was held in Poland on 26–28 September 2011.[301] Currently, although the debate on the resolution of investment disputes within the EU has taken various directions, the

[299]ICC Arbitration Commission Report 2015. Arbitration Involving States and State Entities under the ICC Rules of Arbitration.

[300]Ibid.

[301]Ross 2011.

fact that arbitral institutions remain significant actors within such debate demonstrates the institutional involvement in the public dialogue on arbitration (pertaining to policy-making in this field) at the international level.

Under the Lisbon Treaty, the EU was accorded an exclusive competence in the field of foreign direct investment within the EU Common Commercial Policy. This allows the EU to enter into international investment or trade agreements with the investors from outside the EU (either within the EU's exclusive capacity or jointly with other EU Member States). These developments require novel dispute settlement procedures to be contained in future free trade agreements and investment agreements, as well as transitional mechanisms for the BITs—already binding upon EU member states and third countries. Since the EU does not have a capacity to become a signatory of the ICSID Convention—the most prominent regime for the resolution of investment disputes—new solutions need to be found to address the existent gap. The current proposals at the EU level relying on the ICSID mechanisms are thus insufficient.[302] It seems that the recent transformations of arbitral institutions in general, and the recent amendments to the 2012 ICC Arbitration Rules in particular, point to the adaptability of institutional arbitration regimes in view of the public challenges and demands placed on them (even if only indirectly). Although this argument is of the utmost normative character, this may have additional consequences for the traditional arbitration users. The necessary revisions of the traditional commercial arbitration rules, required in view of the need for the increased transparency and confidentiality of the new institutional arbitration processes, may be viewed as adopted in order to undermine the traditional features of institutional commercial arbitration.

The final implication of the liberalization of arbitrability and the emergence of new dynamics of competition in the institutional arbitration regime concerns the development of new arbitral institutions that focus exclusively on "regulatory" arbitrations. This is the case of the P.R.I.M.E. Finance that was established in order to "assist judicial systems in the settlement of disputes on complex financial transactions".[303] This means that P.R.I.M.E. Finance, while fulfilling its private goals ensured by the independence of the institution from any industry associations and participants to financial market,[304] also assumes certain public function in mixed, private–public regulation of financial markets. In line with this, P.R.I.M.E. Finance not only competes with other private arbitral institutions that developed similar tools regarding regulation of financial disputes, but also enters into the competition with public courts by offering complementary resolution of financial disputes for the members of the industry. This new dimension of competition affects not only the market for institutional arbitration services, but also the

---

[302]Cf. Regulation (EU) No 1219/2012 of the European Parliament and the Council of 12 December 2012 Establishing Transitional Arrangements for Bilateral Investment Agreements between Member States and Third Countries; Happ and Tietje 2013.

[303]"P.R.I.M.E. Finance (Panel of Recognized International Market Experts in Finance)" http://primefinancedisputes.org/about-us/. Accessed 25 April 2016.

[304]Ibid.

system of *ad hoc* arbitration, which seems to be loosing its significance vis-à-vis newly established arbitral institutions that cooperate with public actors. In addition, arbitral institutions have begun to split their shares in the institutional arbitration market with public courts.

2.3.2.2.3 Additional Components of the Public Function in the US

The particular relationship between public regulations of arbitration and institutional activity to potentially extend the scope of its "services" concerns the AAA's interference with the parties' consent regarding their participation in class arbitrations previously sanctioned by means of the decision of the public court. Although the issue at hand, as it relates to the specificity of the arbitration in the US, does not yet seem to have broader implications outside the US, it is significant to the extent that it proves the AAA's *public* authority vis-à-vis AAA's arbitrators, the parties, and the US courts in setting up the framework for class arbitrations.

Without a doubt, the admissibility of class arbitration in the US has long been a subject of stormy debate between Republicans and Democrats, and to this extent such debate entails mostly political questions.[305] The judgement of the US Supreme Court in *Green Tree Financial Corp. v. Bazzle*,[306] together with the subsequent promulgation by the AAA of the Supplementary Rules for Class Arbitrations (AAA's Class Arbitrations Rules)[307] on 8 October 2003, unquestionably added to this debate. It is striking that the AAA, while adopting its Class Arbitration Rules, responded immediately to the possibility for class arbitrations created by a public court. The US Supreme Court in *Green Tree* decided that, when the arbitration clause is silent as to the recourse to class arbitration, it is a matter for the arbitral tribunal to determine the admissibility of class action. The AAA did not wait long to make the most of this ruling. The AAA's Class Arbitration Rules—which mirror the Federal Rule of Civil Procedure 23,[308] and to this extent they show the "public" authority of the AAA over its arbitrators and arbitration users—allow class arbitration once a party resorted to the AAA's arbitration in the agreement, and when the party submits the dispute against or on behalf of a class.[309] If there is doubt regarding the admissibility of the class relief in view of the parties' original intentions, the dispute will be resolved by the AAA's arbitrators instead of the US courts. Moreover, the AAA's Class Arbitration Rules applied even to pending arbitrations, which questioned the very consent of the parties to the already pending proceedings to rely on the new AAA's Class

[305]Park 2012.

[306]*Green Tree Financial Corp. v. Bazzle Et. Al.* 2003. *539 U.S. 444 US Supreme Court.*

[307]"AAA's Supplementary Rules for Class Arbitrations" 2003.

[308]Braken II and Dixon 2004, 215–217; see also Rau 2011.

[309]Braken II and Dixon 2004, 215–217.

Arbitration Rules in case of the submission of the class action by other disputants. It is particularly important to notice that the Class Arbitration Rules do not provide for confidentiality of the proceedings, and all submissions and documents produced in the course of class arbitration should be made available on the AAA's website. The awards rendered as a result of class actions can also be accessed upon the filing of the relevant fee.[310]

The above presentation indicated the increasing public function of the AAA, which on the one hand stems from the specific nature of arbitration in the US, and on the other hand, permits the AAA to regulate various legal issues concerning the arbitration proceedings. The question comes to mind here what is the permissible level of such regulation, and how does it correspond with the *consensuality* and *fairness* of the arbitration proceedings in the US? Although the increased transparency of the AAA's class arbitration should be regarded as a positive development, it remains unclear who exercises control over these socially oriented processes, in particular while taking into consideration the exclusion of liability of both the AAA and its arbitrators for any acts provided in the course of class arbitrations.[311] Given the limited right of appeal in institutional arbitration, the transparency and legitimacy of the AAA's class arbitration may be easily undermined vis-à-vis democratic principles and constitutional rights, which the AAA's users should be able to enjoy in the course of the arbitrations, as well as at the post-arbitration level. This appears to overlap with more general concerns regarding "the outsourcing" of public disputes to private institutional arbitration regimes corresponding to the discussion on the "unaccountable private power" in decision-making.[312]

These points are definitely generalizable: uncontrolled private authority in regulating the design of dispute settlement aggravates the problems of democratic legitimacy of private, institutional arbitration vis-à-vis private arbitration users, as well as the *public*—be it the US government or social and political order taken as a whole. This is mostly because of the lack of sufficient accountability mechanisms (be it of private or public nature) of those institutional arbitration regimes that have been increasingly empowered with new public functions. These observations

[310]Ibid. Rule 16(b).

[311]Ibid. Rule 12.

[312]"Chomsky.info: The Noam Chomsky Website. Radical Democracy, Noam Chomsky Interviewed by John Nichols." Chomsky notes that: "There are plenty of good arguments, in my opinion, against centralized government authority. On the other hand, there's a much worse danger right outside. The centralized government authority is at least to some extent under popular influence, and in principle at least under popular control. The unaccountable private power outside is under no public control. What they call minimizing the state—transferring the decision-making to unaccountable private interests—is not helpful to human beings or to democracy or, for that matter, to the markets. In this time when we are told there is "a triumph of the market", the markets are threatened themselves, aren't they? What's developing is a kind of corporate mercantilism with huge centralized, more or less command economies, integrated with one another, closely tied to state power—relying very heavily on state power, in fact—and enforcing social policies and a conception of social and political order that happen to be highly beneficial to the interests of the top sectors of the population, the richest sectors."

lead us to the conclusion of this chapter, which stresses the interdependence of the emerging public function of institutional arbitration, and the changing dynamics of efficiency and legitimacy of institutional processes, by calling for more responsibility of institutional arbitral regimes in and outside arbitration processes.

2.4 Conclusion in the Context of Institutional Liability: On the Relationship Between the Emerging Public Function, Efficiency, and Legitimacy of Institutional Regimes

This chapter argued that arbitral institutions have increasingly started to assume public function in international commercial arbitration system. The distinction between traditional commercial function and the emerging public function of arbitral institutions pointed out the following issues: (1) the evolving profile of arbitration users of particular arbitration regimes from traditional commercial arbitration parties to public actors including States and/or State-like entities; (2) the expanding category of institutional arbitration "services"; that (3) contributes to the development of the new types of disputes administered by arbitral institutions and vis-à-vis new public actors which surpasses classical understanding of arbitral institutions as private service providers; and finally (4) the declining efficiency of the traditional commercial function of institutional arbitration in view of the changing legitimacy of traditional institutional regimes.

The arbitral institutions that ordinarily competed in the field of cost and speed of arbitration proceedings universalized their arbitration procedures which started to resemble formalized judicial proceedings, entailing additional private regulatory powers of arbitral institutions, exercised on top of the institutional safeguards on behalf of the parties thus in continuation of the principle of party autonomy. Such additional prerogatives, analysed from the internal, *bottom-up* perspective of the public function, as well as the increasing liberalization of arbitrability presented from the *top-down* perspective of the public function, also encourage arbitral institutions to expand their arbitration "services" towards a new, more publicly oriented disputes. This is achieved by attracting the new, usually non-arbitrable categories of disputes to be administered by arbitral institutions, or different arbitration users such as public actors (e.g. States and State-like entities) or non-commercial parties to rely on institutional arbitration.

The analysis of the commercial function showed that arbitral institutions are no longer able to respond effectively to the demands of traditional arbitration users, which still require their arbitrations to be fast and cost-effective, and at the same time providing the parties with the perfect outcomes of arbitration cases. Instead, the amendments of the institutional arbitration rules are aided by the increasing public interests in institutional arbitration. It appears therefore that the traditional commercial function is declining, notwithstanding the institutional attempts to offer arbitration rules of worldwide applicability, and that—paradoxically—the emerging public function of arbitral institutions becomes a major means of competition between private arbitration centres.

The declining efficiency of the commercial function is exemplified in the recent liability claims against arbitral institutions, which are indicative of the failure of arbitral institutions in providing efficient administration of commercial disputes from the perspective of traditional arbitration users. This dissatisfaction of traditional parties to arbitration is often rooted in the confusion about the role of arbitral institutions in the arbitration proceedings in the context of the emerging public function of arbitral institutions.

In contrast, the top-down analysis of the public function showed the increasing public trust in private institutional arbitration process. Public regulation of arbitrability (which deals with the content of the legal norms on arbitration) has been developed in conjunction with private actors as represented by arbitral institutions. Thus, just as private arbitration users are increasingly questioning the efficacy, efficiency, and ethical neutrality of institutional arbitral regimes, the public actors regulating arbitrability are increasingly opting to use private arbitration exactly because these private systems are perceived to be effective, efficient, and ethically neutral. This trend shows no sign of abating.

This results in the transformations of private institutional arbitration regimes based on two different legitimacy pressures: bottom-up (legitimacy stemming from institutional private regulatory functions) and top-down (democratic legitimacy of institutional arbitration as dispute resolution). This also means that the effectiveness of new, public forms of institutional arbitration is not indicative of the national, regional, or international hard or soft laws but runs in parallel with the changes being adopted by private institutional arbitration regimes. In other words, although different public officials have begun to encourage institutional arbitration in disputes of public interest, the effectiveness of such laws or policies—including the potential introduction of democratic safeguards into arbitration processes—are still largely dependent on the recognition of such policies by private institutional arbitration actors. These conflicting legitimacy pressures also imply a new private–public axis in institutional arbitration regimes that requires arbitral institutions to address the legitimacy concerns of traditional commercial arbitration users, thus from the perspective of the traditional commercial public function of institutional arbitration. At the same time, it calls for the adoption of certain democratic safeguards into institutional regimes in order to respond to public values and the necessary democratic legitimacy of the new forms of institutional arbitration.

Against this background, the following chapter will argue that the public accountability of institutional arbitration process, as well as the legal responsibility of institutional arbitration actors (which are desirable under the recent changes in institutional arbitration regimes), could be addressed by means of the institutional arbitral liability. Modern institutional liability regimes are required in order to respond to the emerging public function of institutional arbitration. Additionally, such liability regimes are needed in view of the traditional commercial function of arbitral institutions that confirms that arbitral institutions operate on a contractual basis and triggers civil liability of private arbitral institutions for the potential misconduct in the course of arbitrations. In view of this, Chap. 3 will analyse the sources, and the optimal scope, of institutional arbitral liability.

References

2007 Statistical Report. 2008. ICC International Court of Arbitration Bulletin Vol. 19 No. 1.

About the DIS. http://www.dis-arb.de/en/57/content/about-the-dis-id46. Accessed 25 April 2016.

About the LCIA: Introduction. http://www.lcia.org/LCIA/introduction.aspx. Accessed 25 April 2016.

About the SCC. http://www.sccinstitute.com/about-the-scc/. Accessed 25 April 2016.

Appendix II to the SCC Rules of 2010.

Arbitration Act, Ch. 387 of the Laws of Malta of 1996, as Subsequently Amended with the Major Changes Implemented in 2004 by Means of the Legal Notice 421. Accessed 10 July 2016.

A Record Year for Investment Treaty Disputes. http://www.sccinstitute.com/statistics/investment-disputes-2015/. Accessed 10 July 2016.

Bernini, Giorgio. 2007. The Future of Arbitration: Flexibility or Rigidity? In: Julian D.M. Lew and Loukas A. Mistelis, eds. Arbitration Insights: Twenty Years of the Annual Lecture of the School of International Arbitration Alphen aan den Rijn: Kluwer Law International, 47–62.

Besson, Sébastien. 2010. Piercing the Corporate Veil: Back on the Right Track. In: Bernard Honotiau and Eric A. Schwartz, eds. Dossier VII of the ICC Institute of World Business Law: Multiparty Arbitration. ICC Publication No. 701E, 147–161.

Born, Gary. 2009. International Commercial Arbitration. Kluwer Law International, Alphen aan den Rijn.

Brabandere, Eric De. 2011. P.R.I.M.E. Finance: The Role and Function of the New Arbitral Institution for the Settlement of Financial Disputes in The Hague (Online Version). American Society of International Law Insights 16, no. 3.

Braken II, Lawrence J., and Dixon, Caroline H. 2004. AAA Releases Rules on the Administration of Class Actions. Franchise Law Journal Volume 23, no. 4 Franchise Law Journal: 215–217.

Brinsmead, Simon. 2007. Extending the Application of an Arbitration Clause to Non-Signatories: Which Law Should Apply? Unpublished. http://papers.ssrn.com/sol3/papers.cfm?abstract_id=980483. Accessed 25 April 2016.

Brunet, Edward, Speidel, Richard E., Sternlight, Jean E, and Ware, Stephen H. 2006. Arbitration Law in America: A Critical Assessment. Cambridge University Press.

Bühler, Michael W. 2005. Costs of Arbitration: Some Further Considerations. In: Gerald Aksen, Karl-Heinz Böckstiegel, Paolo Michele Patocchi, and Anne Marie Whitesell, eds. Global Reflections on International Law, Commerce and Dispute Resolution Liber Amicorum in Honour of Robert Briner Publication No. 693 ICC Publishing, 179–190.

Cafaggi, Fabrizio, 2014. A Comparative Analysis of Transnational Private Regulation: legitimacy, quality, effectiveness and enforcement. http://www.eesc.europa.eu/resources/docs/a-comparative-analysis-of-transnational-private-regulation-fcafaggi_12062014.pdf. Accessed 25 April 2016.

Carbonneau, Thomas E., and Janson François. 1994. Cartesian Logic and Frontier Politics: French and American Concepts of Arbitrability. Tulane Journal of International and Comparative Law 2: 193–222.

Casella, Alessandra. 1996. On Market Integration and the Development of Institutions: The Case of International Commercial Arbitration. European Economic Review 40, no. 1: 155–86.

Chan, Calvin. 2009. Of Arbitral Institutions and Provisional Determinations on Jurisdiction. The Global Gold Case. Arbitration International 25, no. 3: 403–426.

Chao, Cedric C., and Schurz James. 2007. International Arbitration: Selecting The Proper Forum. MEALEY's International Arbitration Report: 57–68.

Chomsky.info: The Noam Chomsky Website. Radical Democracy, Noam Chomsky Interviewed by John Nichols. http://www.chomsky.info/interviews/19970303.htm. Accessed 25 April 2016.

Clay, Thomas. 2001. L'arbitre. Dalloz.
Cole, Tony, Bantekas Ilias, Feretti Federico, Riefa Christine, Warwas Barbara, Ortolani Pietro. 2014. The Legal Instruments and Practice of Arbitration in the EU, A Study for the Directorate General for Internal Policies Policy Department C: Citizens' Rights and Constitutional Affairs. http://www.europarl.europa.eu/RegData/etudes/STUD/2015/509988/IPOL_STU(2015)509988_EN.pdf. Accessed 25 April 2016
Coppo, Benedetta. 2010. Comparing Institutional Arbitration Rules: Differences and Similarities in Developing International Practice. International Arbitration Law Review: 100–110.
Craig, W. Laurance, Park William W., and Paulsson Jan. 2001. International Chamber of Commerce Arbitration. Third Edition. Oxford University Press, USA.
Craig, W. Laurence. 1985. International Ambition and National Restraint in ICC Arbitration. Arbitration International 1, no. 1: 49–81.
David, René. 1985. Arbitration in International Trade. Kluwer Law and Taxation Publishers.
Davidson, Paul J., Kos-Rabcewicz-Zubkowski L., International Federation of Commercial Arbitration Institutions, Canadian Arbitration Conciliation, and Amicable Composition Centre, and Inter-American Commercial Arbitration Commission. 1992. Commercial Arbitration Institutions: An International Directory and Guide. Second Edition Oceana Pubns.
Davis, Kevin A. 2012. Privatizing the Adjudication of International Commercial Disputes: The Relevance of Organizational Form. In: Fabrizio Cafaggi, ed. Enforcement of Transnational Regulation: Ensuring Compliance in a Global World. Edward Elgar, 211–237.
de la Hosseraye, Jean, de Giovanni, Stéphanie, and Huard-Bourgois, Juliette. 2012. In: Arbitration in France, CMS Guide to Arbitration Vol I 333–362.
Derains, Yves, and Schwartz Eric A. 2005. A Guide to the ICC Rules of Arbitration, 2nd Edition Revised. Kluwer Law International.
Deutsche Institution Für Schiedsgerichtsbarkeit (DIS) e.V.—German Institution of Arbitration—Statutes. http://www.dis-arb.de/en/13/content/satzung-id9. Accessed 25 April 2016.
Dezalay, Yves, and Garth Bryant G. 1998. Dealing in Virtue: International Commercial Arbitration and the Construction of a Transnational Legal Order. University Of Chicago Press.
DIFC/LCIA Arbitration Centre. http://www.difcarbitration.com/index.html. Accessed 25 April 2016.
Directive 2008/52/EC of the European Parliament and of the Council of 21 May 2008 on Certain Aspects of Mediation in Civil and Commercial Matters.
Dispute Resolution Services. http://www.sccinstitute.com/dispute-resolution/. Accessed 25 April 2016.
DIS Rules. http://www.dis-arb.de/en/16/rules/overview-id0. Accessed 25 April 2016.
Domain Names Disputes. http://www.camera-arbitrale.it/en/Domain+Names+Disputes/index.php?id=13. Accessed 25 April 2016.
Domain Names Disputes. Camera Arbitrale Milano. http://www.camera-arbitrale.it/en/Domain+Names/index.php?id=13. Accessed 25 April 2016.
Draetta, Ugo. 2011. Behind the Scenes in International Arbitration. JurisNet, LLC.
Drahozal, Christopher R. 2009. Business Courts and the Future of Arbitration. Cardozo Journal of Conflict Resolution: 491–507.
Drahozal, Christopher R., and Friel Raymond. 2003. Consumer Arbitration in the European Union and the United States. North Carolina Journal of International Law and Commercial Regulation 28: 357–394.
Events in the History of the AAA and Alternative Dispute Resolution. The Lectic Library Law. http://www.lectlaw.com/files/adr07.htm. Accessed 25 April 2016.
Expedited Arbitration. http://www.sccinstitute.com/dispute-resolution/expedited-arbitration/. Accessed 25 April 2016.
Fiona Trust & Holding Corporation & Ors v Yuri Privalov & Ors [2007] EWCA Civ 20 (24 January 2007).
Fry, Jason, Greenberg Simon, Mazza Francesca, The Secretariat's Guide to ICC Arbitration. 2012 Edition ICC Publication No. 729.
Fumagalli, Luigi. 2012. Tasks and Bodies of the Chamber of Arbitration. In Ugo Draetta and Riccardo Luzzatto, eds. The Chamber of Arbitration of Milan Rules: A Commentary JurisNet, LLC: 9–33.

Gaillard, Emmanuel. 2015. Sociology of International Arbitration. Arbitration International: 1–17.
Gaillard, Emmanuel, and Savage, John.1999. Fouchard, Gaillard, Goldman On International Commercial Arbitration. Kluwer Law International.
Gerbay, Remy. 2014. Neither Savile Row nor Quite Vivienne Westwood: The Verdict on the 2014 LCIA Arbitration Rules. Les Cahiers de l'Arbitrage: 675–685.
Gerbay, Remy. The Functions of Arbitral Institutions. Kluwer Law International. Forthcoming 2016.
Gillion, Frederic. 2012. Impact of the New ICC Rules (2012) on the Management of Construction Arbitration Cases. Fenwick Elliot: The Construction & Energy Law Specialists: International Quarterly: 1–5.
Global Gold Mining, LLC v. Peter M. Robinson et al., No. 636 United States District Court, Southern District of New York, 6 February 2008, 07 Civ. 10492 (GEL) Yearbook Commercial Arbitration Vol XXXIII. 29: 1117–1125.
Government & Consumer: Federal, State, Local Governments. http://www.adr.org/aaa/faces/aoe/gc/government?_afrLoop=735865533092255&_afrWindowMode=0&_afrWindowId=null#%40%3F_afrWindowId%3Dnull%26_afrLoop%3D735865533092255%26_afrWindowMode%3D0%26_adf.ctrl-state%3Dagxlw73i2_4. Accessed 25 April 2016.
Greenberg, Simon. 2013. Arbitral Award Scrutiny under Scrutiny: An Assessment. In: Philipp Habegger, Daniel Hochstrasser, Gabrielle Nater-Bass, and Urs Weber-Stecher, eds. Arbitral Institutions Under Scrutiny. ASA Special Series 40 JurisNet, LLC, 89–108.
Green Tree Financial Corp. v. Bazzle et al. 539 U.S. 444 US Supreme Court.
Happ, Richard, and Tietje Christian, eds. 2013. EU, Investment Treaties, and Investment Treaty Arbitration—Current Developments and Challenges—Editorial Note. Transnational Dispute Management Journal 2.
Hauser, Maria. 2010. The New International Chamber of Commerce Statement of Acceptance, Availability and Independence for Arbitrators. Arbitration E-Review no. 2: 24 et seq.
Honlet, Jean-Christophe, Legum Bart, and Dufêtre Anne-Sophie. 2010. Know-How Commercial Arbitration—France—Global Arbitration Review. http://globalarbitrationreview.com/reference/topics/61/jurisdictions/28/france/. Accessed 25 April 2016.
Hope, James. 2008. Why Choose Stockholm: Reflections of an English Lawyer After Two Years Practising International Arbitration in Sweden. Stockholm International Arbitration Review no. 2: 21–38.
Horvath, Günther J. 2011. The Judicialization of International Arbitration: Does the Increasing Introduction of Litigation-Style Practices, Regulations, Norms and Structures into International Arbitration Risk the Denial of Justice in International Business Disputes? International Arbitration and International Commercial Law: Synergy, Convergence and Evolution. Kluwer Law International, 251–271.
H.R. 1844 (113th): Arbitration Fairness Act of 2013. http://www.govtrack.us/congress/bills/113/hr1844/text. Accessed 25 April 2016.
H.R. 2087: Arbitration Fairness Act of 2015. https://www.govtrack.us/congress/bills/114/hr2087. Accessed 25 April 2016.
ICC Arbitration: A Ten Year Statistical Overview. 2008. ICC International Court of Arbitration Bulletin 19, no. 1.
ICC Arbitration Commission Report. 2015. Arbitration Involving States and State Entities under the ICC Rules of Arbitration.
ICC Arbitration Rules (1998).
ICC Arbitration Rules (2012). http://www.iccwbo.org/products-and-services/arbitration-and-adr/arbitration/icc-rules-of-arbitration/. Accessed 25 April 2016.
ICC Constitution. http://www.iccwbo.org/constitution/. Accessed 25 April 2016.
ICC Commission on Arbitration and ADR. 2014. Effective Management of Arbitration: A Guide for In-House Counsel and Other Party Representatives. International Chamber of Commerce.
ICC Arbitration Commission Report on Controlling Time and Costs of Arbitration of 2012. http://www.iccwbo.org/Advocacy-Codes-and-Rules/Document-centre/2012/ICC-Arbitration-Commission-Report-on-Techniques-for-Controlling-Time-and-Costs-in-Arbitration/. Accessed 25 April 2016.

ICC Commission on Taxation. 2000. Policy Statement: Arbitration in International Tax Matters. ICC Publication No. 180/438.

ICC Court Focuses on Hong Kong and Eastern Europe. 2008. Global Arbitration Review 3:6. http://globalarbitrationreview.com/journal/article/15641/icc-court-focuses-hong-kong-eastern-europe. Accessed 25 April 2016.

ICC Court of Arbitration. 2010. Arbitrator's Statement of Acceptance, Availability and Independence (1998 ICC Arbitration Rules). http://www.rwi.uzh.ch/lehreforschung/alphabetisch/domej/archiv/HS11-1/izvr/ICC-Arbitrator-Acceptance-Form-2010.pdf. Accessed 25 April 2016.

ICC Court of Arbitration. 2012. Arbitrator's Statement of Acceptance, Availability, Impartiality and Independence (2012 ICC Rules of Arbitration). http://www.iccdrl.com/itemContent.aspx?XSL=arbSingle.xsl&XML=\PRACTICE_NOTES\SNFC_0001.xml&CONTENTTYPE=PRACTICE_NOTES&TOC=ltocPracticeNotesAll.xml&TITLE=Arbitrator's%20Statement%20of%20Acceptance,%20Availability,%20Impartiality%20and%20Independence%20(2012%20ICC%20Rules%20of%20Arbitration). Accessed 11 July 2016.

ICC Court to Communicate Reasons as a New Service to Users. 2015. http://www.iccwbo.org/News/Articles/2015/ICC-Court-to-communicate-reasons-as-a-new-service-to-users/. Accessed 25 April 2016.

ICC to Open Office of the Court in New York. http://www.iccwbo.org/News/Articles/2012/ICC-to-open-office-of-the-Court-in-New-York/. Accessed August 25, 2015.

ICDR Procedures (2014). https://www.icdr.org/icdr/ShowProperty;jsessionid=wL65TGcH2Kl6QdzHPG1Zh9vL2tB2V1J5Mm8HvxPqf96wpGgd2dPh!102604678?nodeId=/UCM/ADRSTAGE2020868&revision=latestreleased. Accessed 25 April 2016.

ICDR International Arbitration Reporter. 2011. 1, no. 2: 1–8.

ICDR International Arbitration Reporter. 2010. 1, no. 1: 1–4.

Italian Legislative Decree No. 69. 2013.

Jarrosson, note. 1993. Mors/Labinal Case: Decision of May 19, 1993, [1993]. Revue de L'Arbitrage 546.

Justice Stream B2; Premise: Arbitral Institutions Can Do More To Further Legitimacy. True or False? Legitimacy: Myths, Challenges, Realities. ICCA Miami 2014. http://www.arbitration-icca.org/conferences-and-congresses/ICCA_MIAMI_2014-video-coverage/ICCA_MIAMI_2014_B2.html. Accessed 25 April 2016.

Karton, Joshua D. H. 2013. The Culture of International Arbitration and The Evolution of Contract Law. Oxford University Press, USA.

Kelly, Dominic. 2001. The Business of Diplomacy: The International Chamber of Commerce Meets the United Nations. CSGR Working Paper No. 74/01.

Koepp, Johannes, Farah Dorine, and Webster Peter. 2013. Arbitration in London: Features of the London Court of International Arbitration. In: Giuditta Cordero-Moss, ed. International Commercial Arbitration: Different Forms and Their Features. Cambridge University Press, 217–270.

Law Guides at Harnish Law Library: International Arbitration. Pepperdine University School of Law. Arbitral Institutions & Rules: Index of Arbitral Institutions Rules. http://lawguides.pepperdine.edu/c.php?g=399520&p=2715723. Accessed 25 April 2016.

LCIA Arbitration Rules (1998). http://www.lcia.org/Dispute_Resolution_Services/LCIA_Arbitration_Rules.aspx. Accessed 25 April 2016.

LCIA Arbitration Rules (2014). http://www.lcia.org/Dispute_Resolution_Services/lcia-arbitration-rules-2014.aspx. Accessed 25 April 2016.

LCIA India. http://www.lcia-india.org. Accessed 25 April 2016.

LCIA: International Offices & Overseas. http://www.lcia.org/LCIA/international.aspx. Accessed 25 April 2016.

LCIA Notes for Parties. http://www.lcia.org/adr-services/guidance-notes.aspx. Accessed 25 April 2016.

LCIA—The London Court of International Arbitration—History of the LCIA. Based on the Report from the Law Quarterly Review; 1893. http://www.lcia.org/LCIA/history.aspx. Accessed 25 April 2016.

LCIA—The London Court of International Arbitration—LCIA Arbitration. http://www.lcia.org/Dispute_Resolution_Services/LCIA_Arbitration.aspx. Accessed 25 April 2016.

Lehmkuhl, Dirk. 2006. Resolving Transnational Disputes: Commercial Arbitration and Linkages Between Multiple Providers of Governance Services. In: Mathias König-Archibugi and Michael Zürn, eds. New Modes of Governance in the Global System. Exploring Publicness, Delegation and Inclusiveness. Palgrave Macmillan, 101–125.

Lew, Julian D. M., Mistelis Loukas A., and Kröll Stefan. 2003. Comparative International Commercial Arbitration. Kluwer Law International.

Liger, Isabelle. 2011. 100 Translation Errors in Institutional Arbitration Rules. Unpublished. http://papers.ssrn.com/sol3/papers.cfm?abstract_id=1781078. Accessed 25 April 2016.

Luis Manuel Martinez. 2012. A Guide to ICDR Case Management. ICDR Awards and Commentaries. Juris Net, LLC.

Magnusson, Annette, and Shaughnessy, Patricia. 2006. The 2007 Arbitration Rules of the Arbitration Institute of the Stockholm Chamber of Commerce. Stockholm International Arbitration Review no. 3: 33–66.

McIlwrath, Michael. 30 July 2015. The Gang of Four Rides Again: Pathological Clauses. Kluwer Arbitration Blog. http://kluwerarbitrationblog.com/2013/07/30/the-gang-of-four-rides-again-pathological-clauses/. Accessed 25 April 2016.

McIlwrath, Michael, and Schroeder Ronald. 2008. The View from an International Arbitrat- Tion Customer: In Dire Need of Early Resolution. Arbitration: Vol. 74, No. 3, 3–12.

McIlwrath, Michael, and Schroeder Ronald. 2013. Users Need More Transparency in International Arbitration. In: Alberto Malatesta and Rinaldo Sali, eds. The Rise of Transparency in International Arbitration: The Case for the Anonymous Publication of Arbitral Awards. JurisNet, LLC, 87–106.

Miles, Wendy, and Davies Kate. 2013. England & Wales Chapter—International Arbitration 2013 (Online Edition). ICLG—Publication Chapters.

Mitsubishi v. Soler Chrysler-Plymouth. 473 U.S. 614 (1985) US Supreme Court.

Moses, Margaret L. 2012. The Principles and Practice of International Commercial Arbitration. Cambridge University Press.

Onyema, Emilia. 2010. International Commercial Arbitration and the Arbitrator's Contract. Routledge.

Opportunities and Materials for Arbitrators and Legal Practitioners. http://www.iccwbo.org/Products-and-Services/Arbitration-and-ADR/Arbitration/Introduction-to-ICC-Arbitration/Opportunities-and-materials-for-arbitrators-and-legal-practitioners/. Accessed 25 April 2016.

Park, William W. 2009. Non-Signatories and International Contracts: An Arbitrator's Dilemma. Multiple Party Actions in International Arbitration. Oxford University Press.

Park, William W. 2012. The Politics of Class Action: Jurisdiction, Fairness and Vindication of Rights: A Comment on Stolt-Nielsen SA v AnimalFeeds Intl Corp and AT&T Mobility LLC v Concepcion. In: Patrick Wautelet, Thalia Kruger, and Govert Coppens, eds. The Practice of Arbitration: Essays in Honour of Hans van Houtte. Oxford and Portland, Oregon, Hart Publishing, 169–187.

Philippe-Gazon, Mirèze. 1997. Rôle de La Cour Internationale d'Arbitrage de La CCI (Role of the ICC International Court of Arbitration). Revue de Droit Des Affaires Internationales: 443–70.

P.R.I.M.E. Finance (Panel of Recognised International Market Experts in Finance) http://primefinancedisputes.org/about-us/. Accessed 25 April 2016.

QC Menon, Sundaresh. 2012. Joint Plenary Opening Session A1 International Arbitration: The Coming of a New Age for Asia (and Elsewhere). Keynote Address, ICCA Singapore 2012. http://www.arbitration-icca.org/AV_Library/ICCA_Singapore2012_Sundaresh_Menon.html. Accessed 25 April 2016.

Queen Mary University of London, School of Arbitration, and White & Case. 2015. 2015 International Arbitration Survey: Improvements and Innovations in International Arbitration. http://www.arbitration.qmul.ac.uk/docs/164761.pdf. Accessed 25 April 2016.

Rau, Alan Scott. 2011. Arbitral Power and The Limits of Contract: The New Trilogy. American Review of International Arbitration 22: 435–550.

Redfern, Alan, Hunter Martin, Blackaby Nigel, and Partasides Constantine. 2004. Law and Practice of International Commercial Arbitration. Fourth Edition, Sweet & Maxwell.
Registrar's Report 2013. http://www.lcia.org/LCIA/reports.aspx. Accessed 25 April 2016.
Regulation (EU) No 1219/2012 of the European Parliament and the Council of 12 December 2012 Establishing Transitional Arrangements for Bilateral Investment Agreements between Member States and Third Countries. OJ L 351/40 of 20.12.2012.
Reisman, W. Michael, and Richardson, Brian. 2012. The Present—Commercial Arbitration as a Transnational System of Justice: Tribunals and Courts: An Interpretation of the Architecture of International Commercial Arbitration. In: Albert Jan Van Den Berg, ed. Arbitration: The Next Fifty Years. ICCA Congress Series No. 16. Wolters Kluwer, 17–65
Rogers, Catherine A. 2014. Ethics in International Arbitration. Oxford University Press.
Ross, Alison. 2011. What Lies Ahead for Europe? Global Arbitration Review 6, no. 5. http://globalarbitrationreview.com/news/article/29866/europe-ahead/. Accessed 25 April 2016.
Rules & Procedures. 2013. American Arbitration Association. https://www.adr.org/aaa/faces/rules/searchrules?_afrLoop=1533029715880923&_afrWindowMode=0&_afrWindowId=eulkhplnj_32#%40%3F_afrWindowId%3Deulkhplnj_32%26_afrLoop%3D1533029715880923%26_afrWindowMode%3D0%26_adf.ctrl-state%3Deulkhplnj_114. Accessed 25 April 2016.
Sabel, Charles F., and Zeitlin Jonathan. 2008. Learning from Difference: The New Architecture of Experimentalist Governance in the EU. European Law Journal: 271–327.
Sabharwal, Dipen, and Zaman, Rebecca. 2014. Vive La Difference? Convergence and Conformity in the Rules Reforms of Arbitral Institutions: The Case of the LCIA Rules 2014. Journal of International Arbitration 31:6,701–717.
Scale of Arbitrators' Fees in the Appendix III to the 1998 ICC Rules.
Scale of Arbitrator's Fees in the Appendix III to the 2012 ICC Arbitration Rules.
SCC Arbitration Rules. 2010. http://sccinstitute.com/dispute-resolution/rules/. Accessed 25 April 2016.
SCC Statistics 2014. http://www.sccinstitute.com/statistics/. Accessed 25 April 2016.
Schedule of LCIA Arbitration Costs. 2014. http://www.lcia.org/Dispute_Resolution_Services/schedule-of-costs.aspx. Accessed 25 April 2016.
Schill, Stephan W. 2010. Crafting the International Economic Order: The Public Function of Investment Treaty Arbitration and Its Significance for the Role of the Arbitrator. Leiden Journal of International Law: 401–430.
Schöldström, Patrik. 1998. The Arbitrator's Mandate: A Comparative Study of Relationships in Commercial Arbitration under the Laws of England, Germany, Sweden and Switzerland. Elanders Gotab.
Secretariat of the Court. http://www.iccwbo.org/About-ICC/Organization/Dispute-Resolution-Services/ICC-International-Court-of-Arbitration/Secretariat-of-the-Court/. Accessed 25 April 2016.
Shearson/American Express v. McMahon. No. 86-44 Argued 3 March, 1987 Decided 8 June, 1987 482 U.S. 220 US Supreme Court.
Société Ganz v. Société Nationale Des Chemin de Fers Tunisiens. Revue de L'Arbitrage 478 (1991) Cour d'appel de Paris.
Spanish Act 11/2011, of May 20, Reforming Act 60/2003, of December 23, on Arbitration, and Regulating Institutional Arbitration within the Public Administration.
Steindl, Barbara Helene. 2012. Party Autonomy under the 2012 ICC Arbitration Rules. Czech and Central European Yearbook of Arbitration—2012: Party Autonomy versus Autonomy of Arbitrators II: 231–51.
Stipanowich, Thomas J. 2010. Arbitration: The New Litigation. University of Illinois Law Review, 1–60.
Stipanowich, Thomas J., von Kann Curtis E., and Rothman Deborah. 2010. Protocols for Expeditious, Cost-Effective Commercial Arbitration: Key Action Steps for Business Users, Counsel, Arbitrators & Arbitration Provider Institutions. College of Commercial Arbitrators.
Strategic Resources Co. v. BCS Life Insurance Co. No. 26022, 2005 WL 1943536 (S.C. Aug. 15, 2005).

Sundin, Per, and Wernberg Erik. 2007. The Scope of Arbitrability Under Swedish Law. An Extract from the 2007 European Arbitration Review, a Global Arbitration Review Special Report: 63–65.
Supplementary Rules for Class Arbitrations. 2003. American Arbitration Association. https://www.adr.org/aaa/ShowPDF?url=/cs/groups/commercial/documents/document/dgdf/mda0/~edisp/adrstg_004129.pdf. Accessed 25 April 2016.
Swedish Arbitration Portal: The Supreme Court. http://www.arbitration.sccinstitute.com/Swedish-Arbitration-Portal/Supreme-Court/The-Supreme-Court2/The-Supreme-Court/. Accessed 25 April 2016.
Swiss Chambers' Arbitration Institution. Swiss Rules 2012. https://www.swissarbitration.org/Arbitration/Arbitration-Rules-and-Laws. Accessed 25 April 2016.
Techniques for Controlling Time and Costs in Arbitration. 2012. ICC Dispute Resolution Library. http://www.iccdrl.com/CODE/LevelThree.asp?tocxml=ltoc_CommReportsAll.xml&page=Commission%20Reports&L1=Commission%20Reports&L2=&tocxsl=Double.
Tercier, Pierre. 2008. ICC Rules of Arbitration: A Decade of Use. ICC International Court of Arbitration Bulletin 19, no. 1: 33–50.
The Administration of Investment Disputes. http://www.sccinstitute.com/dispute-resolution/investment-disputes/. Accessed 25 April 2016.
The American Arbitration Association: A Long History of Working with Government. http://www.adr.org/aaa/ShowPDF?doc=ADRSTG_017603. Accessed 25 April 2016.
The Federal Arbitration Act; Pub.L. 68–401, 43 Stat. 883, Enacted February 12, 1925, Codified at 9 U.S.C. § 1 et Seq.
The ICC 2012 Programme Action. http://www.iccwbo.org/news/brochures/. Accessed 25 April 2016.
The Italian Legislative Decree No. 5 of 17 January 2003.
The SCC Arbitrator's Guidelines. 2014. http://sccinstitute.com/about-the-scc/legal-resources/arbitrators-guidelines/. Accessed 25 April 2016.
The Swedish Arbitration Act of 1999 (SFS 1999:116). http://www.sccinstitute.com/about-the-scc/legal-resources/legislation/. Accessed 25 April 2016.
The Unfair Arbitration Agreements (Specified Amount) Order 1999. Vol. No. 2167. http://www.legislation.gov.uk/uksi/1999/2167/contents/made. Accessed 25 April 2016.
The UK Arbitration Act 1996, Chapter 23. http://www.legislation.gov.uk/ukpga/1996/23/contents. Accessed 25 April 2016.
The United Nations Conference on International Commercial Arbitration Convention on the Recognition and Enforcement of Foreign Arbitral Awards—The New York Convention. 1958.
Turner, Peter, and Mohtashami Reza. 2009. A Guide to the LCIA Arbitration Rules. OUP Oxford.
Vidal, Dominique. 2005. The Extension of Arbitration Agreements within Groups of Companies: The Alter Ego Doctrine in Arbitral and Court Decisions. ICC International Court of Arbitration Bulletin 16, no. 2: 63–76.
Wade, Shai, Clifford Philip , and Clanchy James. 2015. A Commentary on the LCIA Arbitration Rules 2014. London: Sweet & Maxwell.
Warwas, Barbara Alicja. 2014. ADR in B2B Disputes in the EU Telecommunications Sector: Where Does the EU Stand and What Does the EU Stand For? EUI LAW 2014/12.
Warwas, Barbara, 2012. The Function of Emergency Arbitrator in Emergency Arbitrator Proceedings—The New Solutions Adopted by the Court of Arbitration at the Polish Confederation of Private Employers Lewiatan in Light of the International Regulations: a Comparative Perspective, Court of Arbitration Lewiatan, Arbitration e-Review, 3–4 (10–11)/2012). http://www.sadarbitrazowy.org.pl/repository/e-przeglad-do_pobrania/ENG/10-11.EPA10-11ENGfinal.pdf. Accessed 25 April 2016.
Werlauff, Erik. 2009. Private Arbitration of Incidental Public Law Issues. European Business Law Review 20, no. 4: 565–577.
Youssef, Karim. 2010. The Limits of Consent: The Right or Obligation to Arbitrate of Non-Signatories in Groups of Companies. In: Bernard Honotiau and Eric A. Schwartz, eds. Dossier VII of the ICC Institute of World Business Law: Multiparty Arbitration. ICC Publication No. 701E, 71–110.

Chapter 3
The Triad of Modern Functions of Arbitral Institutions—in Search of the Sources and Scope of Institutional Arbitral Liability

Contents

3.1 Introduction

This chapter aims at identifying both the sources and optimal scope of the modern institutional liability regimes, by analysing three major pillars of institutional activity (so-called "triad" of modern institutional functions): the *legal*, *societal*, and *economic* dimensions of institutional arbitration. The major assumption of Chap. 3 is that the legal approach to institutional arbitral liability, which analyses contractual bonds and institutional activity by means of different contract law theories, *alone* is insufficient insofar as it cannot account for the particular status and the actual scope of the contemporary functions of arbitral institutions.

B. Warwas, *The Liability of Arbitral Institutions: Legitimacy Challenges and Functional Responses*, DOI 10.1007/978-94-6265-111-1_3

Institutional activity—even if based on contract—also encompasses the *societal* and *economic* goals of arbitral institutions. These goals are embedded in the particular status of arbitral institutions within, and outside of, institutional arbitration regimes. This means vis-à-vis the local arbitration communities associated with particular arbitral institution and the international arbitration community taken as a whole, on the one side, and public, State authorities, on the other side. They also include broader, systemic functions of institutional arbitration performed in and outside such regimes, therefore in the continuation of the commercial and public functions of institutional arbitration. *Societal goals* concern questions of the authority and legitimacy of institutional arbitration vis-à-vis both local and international arbitration communities and sovereign State powers. *Economic aims* refer to the traditional commercial function of institutional arbitration in the market for arbitration services (commercial goals), as well as to the institutional role in fostering development of international commerce (economic goals). Given the emerging public function of institutional arbitration, and the changing dynamics of competition within the institutional arbitration market stemming from this new public function as identified in Chap. 2, the societal and economic aims are governed by the continuous private–public interplay in the field of arbitration, which should be reflected in the modern institutional liability regimes.

This chapter is organized in three main parts that correspond with the analyses of the triad of institutional functions. The first part presents the legal, contractual aspect of institutional arbitration to allocate the possible sources of institutional arbitral liability. Subsequently, the second part of the chapter continues with the presentation of the societal facet of institutional activity to depict the changing legitimacy of the institutional arbitration process in view of the progressing formalization and legalization of institutional arbitration. Finally, the analysis of the economic dimension of institutional functions presented in the third part of this chapter sketches the interplay between institutional activity and the international economic order. The chapter concludes with an explanation of the plausible scope of institutional arbitral liability within this above-mentioned triad of institutional functions.

3.2 The Legal Dimension

As already observed in the previous discussion in Chap. 2, no consensus currently exists among practitioners and academics regarding the legal status of arbitral institutions in the arbitration process and the legal basis under which the institutional legal relationships come into existence with regard to all institutional arbitration actors.[1] Notably, this confusion has been particularly visible among the members of arbitral institutions and institutional arbitrators, as well as the business

[1] Sect. 2.1.1 of Chap. 2.

parties to arbitration proceedings that often take for granted the legal facet of arbitration in general and the impact of specific arbitration rules on their legal situation in arbitration in particular.

The possible explanation of such legal "obliviousness" is that most business parties would rather focus on how arbitral institutions can address their commercial goals relating to arbitration, whereas the legal questions regarding the organization of arbitration play a secondary role, at least at the outset of arbitration proceedings. In fact, the realization of the existence of legal relationships in institutional arbitration by business parties often takes place in cases of irregularities, when the parties were denied undertaking certain procedural action in the conduct of the arbitration (e.g. refusal by an institution to allow parties' challenge of an arbitrator) and when it is often too late for the parties to move such institutional decisions. All these issues are significant insofar as they may trigger the civil liability of arbitral institutions as a result of the parties' dissatisfaction with the conduct of their arbitration rather than as a consequence of the breaches by arbitral institutions of their specific contractual obligations. Therefore, the lack of clear determination of institutional obligations at the outset of proceedings and in relation to all actors involved, gives rise to legal uncertainty and deepens the parties' confusion regarding the sources and scope of institutional obligations and liability. All of this only invites liability claims against arbitral institutions. In this vein, the analysis of the legal dimension of institutional arbitration below addresses these questions from two different angles.

The first part of the analysis interprets institutional arbitration within the parameters of the jurisdictional and contractual theories of arbitration in order to depict the sources of institutional liability and of institutional obligations. The second part, dealing with the territoriality of institutional arbitration, concerns the *location* of institutional arbitration vis-à-vis public powers (be it at a national or a-national, transnational level), and the autonomy (if any) of institutional arbitration within the international arbitration community on the one side, and in front of the State authorities, on the other side. As such, the second part examines the prospective authority of national courts to assess the scope of institutional arbitral liability and to award damages to unsatisfied parties given the misconduct or negligent performance of arbitral institutions.

3.2.1 The Legal Basis for Institutional Liability: Contract or Status or Both?

The following section refers to the major assumptions of the legal theories of arbitration—jurisdictional and contractual theories—that address the relationship between arbitration vis-à-vis the sovereign, State power and the will of the parties to be bound by an arbitration agreement. Although such theories are often invoked in the debate on the nature of the arbitration process, none of them have been analysed with respect to institutional arbitration, whose interaction with State powers has recently been particularly intriguing. The framework for such interaction was provided in Chap. 2 which, especially in the context of the increasing public recognition of institutional arbitration regimes, showed the relinquishing of certain public authority to arbitral institutions with regard to new forms of arbitrations that extend beyond the traditional concept of arbitrability concerning purely commercial disputes. The major objective of the following discussion is to identify the legal basis of institutional obligations and therefore also of institutional arbitral liability.

3.2.1.1 Jurisdictional and Contractual Theories of Arbitration

In brief, the jurisdictional theory assumes significant public involvement in the arbitration process. Following Samuel, there are three branches of jurisdictional theory, namely: (1) the judgment theory, (2) the delegation theory, and (3) the municipal law theory.[2] The first variant of jurisdictional theory, represented mainly by Pillet, invoked the adjudicatory function of arbitrator whose authority as a judge does not stem *solely* from the parties' arbitration agreement.[3] In this regard, arbitrators presumably substitute judges while rendering arbitral awards that, in turn, should be regarded as acts of arbitrators' jurisdiction.[4]

The second branch of jurisdictional theory focused exclusively on the source of arbitrators' authority to act as temporary judges. The propagators of the delegation theory (Motulsky) claimed that arbitrators perform their function (understood as a public function) not under the parties' agreement but instead as delegates of the legal systems of different States.[5] In this regard, arbitrators "take on lease" certain areas from the state administration of justice, and therefore the arbitration process and the arbitrators' work are dependent upon the level of flexibility offered to them by relevant municipal (local) State authorities.[6] In light of this, an arbitral award is subject to certain restrains determined by municipal laws.

The most recent variant of the jurisdictional theory—municipal law theory—was developed mainly by Mann.[7] Mann emphasized the significance of the law of the place of arbitration for the arbitrator's activity by stating that such law not only

[2]Samuel 1989, 51–60.

[3]According to Pillet: "the arbitration agreement is necessary to give the arbitrators their authority, but once that authority has been conferred on them, provided they keep within the limits of the task given to them, their freedom is absolute and the arbitration agreement has no influence on their award which is based on quite different matters." See Pillet 1923. Translation in Samuel 1989, 52.

[4]See generally Yu and Sauzier 2000.

[5]See: Motulsky et al. 1974, 14; translation in: Samuel 1989, 55.

[6]Some commentators argued that the *sine qua non* condition for the performance of arbitrator's mandate was a *concession* granted to him/her by relevant public authorities. See: Samuel 1989, 55.

[7]See Mann 1967a; in Samuel 1989: 56–60.

constitutes a basis for the arbitrators' authority but also affects the scope of the arbitrator's competences.[8] Moreover, Mann claimed that the necessity to respect parties' will (which lies at the heart of the arbitrator's function) does not emerge from an arbitration agreement but from the legal norms developed in the place of arbitration.[9] This is also why any non-compliance with such norms by the arbitrator shall be treated as the infringement of the State's sovereignty.[10]

In contrast, contractual theory refers exclusively to the consensual character of arbitration and presumes that each arbitration device stems *exclusively* from the will of the parties that was originally expressed in the arbitration agreement.[11] Given that, both the status of an arbitrator vis-à-vis the parties and State powers (hence, also the character of the acts falling within the arbitrator's mandate) and the character of arbitral awards originate in, and are determined by, contractual arrangements previously made by disputants.

The contractualists can be divided into two groups. The first group comprises the founders of the classical contractual theory such as Merlin, Foelix, and Lainé, while the second group consists of the propagators of the modern version of the contractual theory, including inter alia Bernard and Klein.[12] Classical contractual theory underlines the linkages between the arbitration agreement and the contractual character of arbitral awards, as well as the authority of arbitrators. Merlin argued that: "an arbitral decision is the natural consequence of the agreement to arbitrate with which it forms a single entity".[13] Moreover, according to Merlin, an arbitration agreement is the only instrument that gives power to arbitrators whose subsequent acts are nothing more than the continuation of such an agreement. In this regard, arbitrators are the agents of the parties, not judges exercising state powers or performing any form of a public function.[14] Thus, the jurisdiction of arbitrators is territorially unbounded, which means that arbitral awards may be enforced everywhere.[15]

Foelix basically agreed with Merlin and only restated that the authority of arbitrators does not require any kind of public support, as the arbitrators' power lies in the realm of the parties' contract.[16] However, Lainé criticized some arguments of other classical contractual theorists such as the application to arbitrators of the assumptions of the agency theory.[17] Lainé's critique was based upon the following

---

[8]See Samuel 1989, 57.

[9]Mann 1967b, 167; in Samuel 1989, 52.

[10]Mann 1967b, 164–166; Mann 1967b; see Samuel 1989, 57.

[11]Cf. *Reily v Russel, 34 Mo 524 (1864) 528*; Carlston 1952, 631.

[12]Samuel 1989 33–50.

[13]Merlin 1829; in Samuel 1989, 34.

[14]Samuel 1989, 35–39.

[15]Ibid.

[16]Samuel 1989 34–35.

[17]Ibid.

controversies. First, no agent can be empowered to act in the capacity of the parties in situations in which his/her principal is incapable of acting himself/herself.[18] Second, an arbitrator, whose task is to render an award on behalf of both parties, cannot act as an agent of a particular disputant,[19] as it disturbs the principle of impartiality of arbitrators. Finally, assuming that arbitrator's authority is, in principle, irrevocable, the whole idea of agency theory can be undermined, as each agency can be easily revoked.[20] By adopting the agency theory to arbitration, arbitrators need to comply with all instructions of their principals, even in cases in which a party instructs an arbitrator not to render an award, which a disputant is not authorized to do under the general arbitration rules.[21] Furthermore, Lainé called the pure contractual character of arbitral awards into question by stating that if an arbitrator is not a parties' agent, it will be difficult to imagine that his/her act involving the rendering of an arbitral award (that additionally was subject to a judicial review) could express the continuation of the parties' initial agreement.[22]

Lainé's scepticism became the foundation of the modern contractual theory. Even though its major propagators—Bernard and Klein—still believed in a private and contractual nature of arbitration,[23] they entirely rejected the agency theory with respect to arbitrators. Both Bernard and Klein claimed that the process of making the arbitral award could be qualified as the arbitrators' performance of the parties' contract under which the arbitrators were appointed,[24] that, in turn, could be classified as a contract *sui generis*.[25] Moreover, as Klein observed, arbitration encompasses a number of contractual instruments that stem from an arbitration agreement, and to this extent, it is rather a network of contractual acts and not an exclusive authority of a single, initial contract that determines the outcome of the arbitration process.[26]

Due to the underdevelopment of most arbitral institutions at the time when the legal theories of arbitration were formed, those theories say very little about institutional arbitration. This is unsurprising given that the modern functions of arbitral institutions (such as the public function identified in Chap. 2) are a relatively new phenomenon that has not yet triggered an adequate debate. In view of this, it

[18]Samuel 1989 36–39.

[19]Ibid.

[20]Ibid.

[21]Ibid.

[22]Ibid.

[23]Bernard regards arbitration agreement and arbitral award as instruments delivered in two phases of *the same* operation. Klein speaks about the awards which form a *single* entity within an arbitration agreement. Cf. Bernard 1937, 289; Merlin 1829; see Samuel 1989, 43.

[24]Ibid.

[25]Ibid.

[26]As defined by Klein: "The arbitral agreement is the work of the parties alone. The award is the work of the arbitrators. The appointment of the arbitrators is the work of the parties and arbitrators together". In Samuel 1989, 44

is obvious that neither jurisdictionalists nor contractualists were in the position to address the specific institutional status and role in the arbitration process. In fact, it is the emerging public function of institutional arbitration that entails a fascinating discussion on the interplay between *sovereignty* and *private power* in the same manner in which the classical analysis of the authority of arbitrators engaged the then theorists in the debate on the sources of arbitrators' functions. As such, the analysis below will focus on the explanation of institutional arbitration through the lenses of both jurisdictional and contractual theories of arbitration, pertaining to the inability of those theories to accommodate both the status and functions of contemporary arbitral institutions.

3.2.1.1.1 On Why Institutional Arbitration Is not Purely Jurisdictional

There are some evident features of institutional arbitration that dismiss the assumption of the purely jurisdictional nature of institutional arbitration. Pure jurisdictional theory is therefore inadequate to explain the emergence of traditional institutional arbitration, as well as the dual function of contemporary arbitral institutions.

Arbitral institutions do not themselves settle disputes, but rather safeguard the application of the rules by arbitrators.[27] Albeit the public function of institutional arbitration, as defined in Chap. 2, could correspond with certain arguments of the delegation theory of arbitration, the interconnectedness of the public aspect of institutional activity and its inseparable commercial facet does not allow further defence of the assumption that public function automatically implies the applicability of jurisdictional theory to institutional arbitration.

Notwithstanding the declining efficiency of their traditional commercial function, arbitral institutions are continuously aiming at responding to the demands of business parties. Hence, the traditional, private goals of institutional arbitration counterbalance its public component, which should not be overstated in view of the status of traditional arbitral institutions. Institutional arbitration—regardless of its judicialization—is still a private process, and it is hard to argue that the authority of contemporary arbitral institutions stems *exclusively* from the increasing public recognition of institutional arbitration. At the same time, there remain some doubts about the possible interplay between the institutional activity and the law of the seat of arbitration in the meaning of the municipal law theory.[28] Although this analysis falls within the territoriality of institutional arbitration, which will be addressed in Sect. 3.2.2 of this chapter, it seems necessary to consider already now how institutional arbitration rules address the authority of the law of the arbitral *situs*.

---

[27]For example: Article 1(2) of the 2012 ICC Arbitration Rules that states that: "the Court itself does not resolve disputes. It administers the resolution of disputes by arbitral tribunals, in accordance with the Rules of Arbitration of the ICC".

[28]Cf. Yu 2008.

In general, institutional interference in the matters concerning the seat of arbitration[29] amounts to two interrelated institutional capacities. Many arbitration rules empower the respective decisive bodies of arbitral institutions to fix the place of arbitration when the parties fail to do so.[30] Depending on the wording of the arbitration clause, such provisions can give the institution the authority to decide on the major determinants of the arbitration, concerning (1) the conduct of the proceedings and (2) post-arbitration challenges. The former observation implies institutional powers to stipulate the mandatory provisions of the procedural law of the *situs* to be applicable to arbitration, or simply the institutional context of arbitration meaning the local stances to arbitration determining, to a certain extent, the supportiveness of arbitration by local courts and judges.[31] The latter argument concerns mostly the institutional influence on the "nationality" of arbitral awards understood also in the meaning of the procedural laws applicable to the recognition, enforcement, and setting aside of arbitral awards.[32]

In fact, most arbitration rules connect the institutional awards with the law of the *situs* for the sake of finality and enforceability of the arbitration process. For example, Article 6 of the Internal Rules of the ICC Court requires that the ICC Court, while scrutinizing draft arbitral awards, consider the requirements of mandatory law of the place of arbitration.[33] Such prerogatives indeed bring the institutional activity closer to the legal system within which the arbitration proceeds; nonetheless, they should not be regarded as being conferred on arbitration centres solely by the laws of the *situs* (as jurisdictionalists would claim).[34] Some of the institutional prerogatives, as already presented in Chap. 2 (Sect. 2.3.2.1.1), stem from the will of the parties to have their dispute resolved within the general legal framework designed for arbitration such as the New York Convention, to ensure the legality of the proceedings and awards. Some of these prerogatives, however, remain strongly interlinked with the law of the arbitral *situs*, especially as far as the concept of arbitrability is concerned, which authorizes arbitral institutions to exclusively administer certain category of disputes under national arbitration laws. This controversy will be further addressed in the presentation on the mixed nature of institutional arbitration in Sect. 3.2.1.2.

---

[29]The seat of arbitration should not be confused with the place of institutional arbitration proceedings.

[30]Article 20 of the SCC Rules, Article 18 of the 2012 ICC Arbitration Rules, and Article 17 of the ICDR Procedures. See also the new wording of Article 16.2 of the 2014 LCIA Rules under which the default seat of arbitration shall be London failing the agreement of the parties in this regard, "unless and until the Arbitral Tribunal orders, in view of the circumstances and after having given the parties a reasonable opportunity to make written comments to the Arbitral Tribunal, that another arbitral seat is more appropriate".

[31]For an in depth discussion regarding the importance of the seat of arbitration for the conduct of arbitration proceedings, as well as in the context of the post-arbitration proceedings see: McIlwrath and Savage 2010, 20–35.

[32]Ibid.

[33]See: Appendix II to the 2012 ICC Arbitration Rules: Internal Rules of the International Court of Arbitration.

[34]Sect. 3.2.1.1.

3.2.1.1.2 On Why Institutional Arbitration Is not Purely Contractual

As shown above, pure contractualists reject any aspect of State interference in the arbitration process and place exclusive emphasis on the authority of the arbitration agreement when defining the foundation of arbitration. This assumption cannot be accepted against the background of the recent developments in arbitration in general, and in institutional arbitration in particular, which altogether shed a new light on the spectrum of the potential new public challenges facing institutional arbitration. The following discussion will be divided into two subsections that analyse (1) the inaccuracy of the pure contractual theory for the explanation of institutional arbitration due to the particular status of arbitral institutions in and outside the arbitration processes (the status approach), and (2) the multifaceted functions of arbitral institutions in designing and tailoring the matrix of contractual relationships in institutional arbitration (the contractual approach).

3.2.1.1.2.1 The Status Approach: Sources of Institutional Powers Outside Contract

As already noted, one of the main weaknesses of the contractual theory was the complete rejection of any public aspect of arbitraion. This argument does not seem to hold up as it cannot explain the rationale and transformations of institutional arbitration in post-communist countries, the extensive authority of arbitral institutions in the administration of arbitrations in non-democratic States such as China, as well as the recent emergence of the exclusive institutional authority to administer certain category of disputes under the express authorization from national laws. Although most arbitral institutions were inspired by purely private goals, in some geographical areas the proliferation of institutional arbitration took the form of a more publicly oriented process. This has certain implications for the development of the modern arbitral institutions in Central and Eastern Europe, as well as the ways in which those institutions operate today in States from these geographical regions.

Considering the Soviet Union and Eastern bloc countries, the only legal variant of arbitration concerned institutional arbitration.[35] Arbitral institutions "functioned [there] as a mere transmission of state directives and control," but at the same time they pretended to address all the characteristics of a truly private process.[36] According to Professor Uzelac, arbitral institutions in the Soviet Union could be regarded as "para-governmental organs" which fell within the "structure of political power." This also meant that arbitral institutions rather than institutional arbitrators decided on cases, which was a result of tight bonds linking the institutional hierarchy and State powers.[37] Moreover, as regards the basis of arbitration proceedings involving some of the then members of the Soviet Union, it was an act provided by law (such as the Moscow Convention binding upon the Council for Mutual Economic Assistance (COMECON) countries) rather than a voluntarily negotiated arbitration agreement.[38]

[35]Uzelac 1996, 75; Kirchner and Marriott 1993, 5 with further references.

[36]Uzelac 1996, 76.

[37]Ibid., 87.

[38]Ibid., 75.

This peculiar "status approach" to institutional arbitration does not, however, aim at proving the general interdependence of institutional arbitration and the sovereign. In fact, the use of private arbitration by controlled economies neither reflected the very nature of arbitration process *per se*, nor did it claim global applicability. What is striking here, however, is the continuing tradition of the contemporary arbitral institutions operating in the post-communist countries, which, to a certain extent, reflects the early treatment of institutional arbitration as a State domain.

The introductory remarks to the "controlled institutional arbitration" entail further questions concerning the outlook of institutional arbitral activity *after* the fall of communism. Although the claim that the dissolution or succession of socialist States contributed to the creation of the modern arbitration centres solely by means of public acts is highly controversial, there are several less contentious cases worth analysing, which call into question the purely private goals and functions of institutional arbitration originated in the former socialist countries. These cases concern the following issues: (1) the relationship between the continuity of an arbitral institution and the *private authority* of an arbitration agreement; (2) the interaction between the continuity of an arbitral institution and the *validity* of an arbitration agreement; and (3) the impact of a succession of a State on the "succession" of the arbitration tradition established in a given territory.[39]

The first case is the so-called "transitional institutional arbitration" in the Czech Republic after the dissolution of Czechoslovakia in 1992. The former Arbitration Court of the Czechoslovak Chamber of Trade and Industry was transformed into the Arbitration Court at the Czech Chamber of Commerce and Czech Chamber of Agriculture under the Czech Statute No. 223/94 of 1 January 1995.[40] The major legal problem underlying this transformation concerned the provision of Section 3/3 of the Statute, which stated that the existing arbitration clauses referring to the Czechoslovak Chamber should constitute a valid reference to the Arbitration Court of the Czech Chamber of Commerce and Agriculture.[41] This means that the continuity of an arbitral institution (declared nota bene by a legal act) was interrelated with the *public* regulation of arbitration in the meaning of the modification of the previously expressed parties' will concerning the choice of the particular administrator of their disputes.[42] Such modification, even if dictated by the necessary political and economic changes, emphasized a strong interrelation of *law* (legislative bodies) and the authority of private, newly formed arbitral institution. In this way, it is arguable that in the case at hand the status of the arbitration centre under analysis originated strictly in the private, contractual arrangements of the parties.

The second example refers to the possible impact of the continuity of an arbitral institution on the validity of arbitration agreements signed by the parties prior to the unification of West and East Germany in 1990. The story of "transitional"

---

[39] These case studies largely follow the examples provided for by Professor Uzelac in Uzelac, 1996.

[40] Uzelac 1996, 77.

[41] See: the fragment of § 3/3 of the Czech statute, quoted in Uzelac 1996, 77.

[42] The shock was dual as it concerned not only a 'new' institution but also the foreign arbitration (on the side of the Slovak parties) as compared with the previous domestic arrangements. See: Ibid.

institutional arbitration in Germany was different as compared to the situation in former Czechoslovakia, as it concerned the merger, not dissolution of the German States. Therefore, it implied the necessity of the consolidation of arbitration practice on both sides of the former Iron Curtain. In a nutshell, the former Arbitration Court at the Foreign Trade Chamber in Berlin was transferred into the Arbitration Court Berlin (*Schiedsgericht Berlin*) that claimed the authority over each dispute referring to "Berlin arbitration".[43] Even if the organizational staff of the "new" institution argued that: "the change of sponsorship of the *Schiedsgericht Berlin* [had no impact] on the validity of any arbitration agreement entered into previously",[44] the issue soon became highly controversial and had its finale in the German Federal Court of Justice in Karlsruhe.[45] The Federal Court affirmed the previous decisions of the appellate courts and held, inter alia, that: (1) the liquidation of an arbitral institution selected by the parties resulted in the arbitration agreement becoming null and void, and (2) the authorisation of a particular arbitral institution was not transferable to a different organization without a prior agreement of the parties.[46] Although this decision seems, at first glance, to support the principle of party autonomy and the private nature of institutional arbitration, on closer scrutiny this decision again expressed specific public stipulation of the parties' consent to arbitration. It was commonly claimed by the propagators of the validity of the "initial" arbitration agreements that the additional submission of the parties to a "new" arbitral institution should be a sufficient instrument to express the parties' will to rely on this "new" institution without a necessary recourse to the public determination of the parties' consent. The strictness of the Court in Karlsruhe in interpreting the parties' will in relation to institutional arbitration in the case at hand not only showed the uneasy relationship concerning public interference with private arbitration processes but also underscored the supremacy of the German judiciary over private arrangements of the parties to German institutional arbitration.

The last example relates to the unchanged tradition of institutional arbitration in the Russian Federation after the dissolution of the Soviet Union. One fact is especially relevant for the this discussion. The arbitral institutions such as the Court of International Commercial Arbitration (CICA) and the Maritime Arbitration Commission (MAC) in Moscow, after the fall of communism, simply continued their operation without even amending their rules on arbitration.[47] The continuity of these arbitral institutions was rooted in the Decree of the Presidium of the Supreme Soviet of the Russian Federation of January 1993 and further confirmed by Annexes 1 and 2 of the Russian Federation Law No. 5338-1 of 7 July 1993 on

---

[43]Uzelac 1996, 81; Melis 2013, 182–185.

[44]Strohbach 1992, 186–187.

[45]Before reaching the highest German federal court, the issue had been examined by the courts in Berlin and Itzehoe (which confirmed the validity of the arguable arbitration clause) and, subsequently, by the appellate courts in Hamburg and Frankfurt on the Main (which refuted the effectiveness of such clauses).

[46]Uzelac 1996, 82.

[47]Ibid.

International Commercial Arbitration.[48] It is therefore not an overstatement that the soviet tradition of "controlled arbitration" also affected the activity of modern arbitration centres in the Russian Federation, at least by both preserving the tight relationships between those arbitral institutions and State authorities and placing those relationships in the epicentre of all legal bonds coming into existence within the CICA's and MAC's arbitration regimes.

Notably, similar patterns were also found in the arbitral institutions that started to proliferate in other post Soviet States in that they appeared to have followed the organizational and procedural solutions of the Moscow institutions.[49] Although it is hard to argue that the controlled model of institutional arbitration in the Soviet Union was transplanted into all arbitral institutions in all post-communist countries, it may be claimed that the general rationale of controlled institutional arbitration inspired a particular private-public status of some of those institutions and the manner they function vis-à-vis the parties also today.

This is the case with the already-mentioned Arbitration Court attached to the HCCI that operates under the explicit public authorization contained in the Hungarian Arbitration Act granting to it exclusive functions in the administration of certain types of arbitration including international arbitration proceedings.[50] Some authors even argue that such authorization implies the public law nature of the relationships between the Arbitration Court attached to the HCCI and the parties to the proceedings administered by this institution.[51] Leaving aside for now the discussion on the nature of the institutional contracts that will be addressed in the following section of this chapter, the Hungarian example shows that the domestic regulations of arbitration may impose clear restrictions regarding the party autonomy in deciding on the desirable forum of their dispute resolution (whether institutional or *ad hoc* arbitration) mirroring the infamous tradition of institutional arbitration in the Soviet Union.

Similarly, the provisions of the Fourth Book of the Romanian Code of Civil Procedure of 1993 [52] empowered Romanian arbitral institutions to ultimately decide whether the institutional rules referred to by the parties are in fact effective and applicable to a dispute in question.[53] In cases of the institutional doubts in this regard, arbitral institutions can stipulate the parties' will by referring a dispute to *ad hoc* arbitration even if such a referral seems contrary to the principle of party autonomy.[54] The newly amended Romanian Code of Civil Procedure that entered into force on 15 February 2013 restated these provisions by reaffirming the broad

[48]Gerbay, forthcoming 2016; Uzelac 1996, 77–78 with further references.

[49]Uzelac 1996, 75–77.

[50]Sect. 2.3.2.2.2 of Chap. 2.

[51]Timár 2013, 109 with further references to the work of László Ujlaki (footnote 23).

[52]Law no. 59 of 1993

[53]Florescu and Cristina 2011, 107–108.

[54]Ibid.

autonomy of arbitral institutions with regard to the decisions regarding the parties' choices on applicable arbitration rules.[55]

Furthermore, the Czech Act No. 216/1994 Coll. on Arbitration Proceedings and Enforcement of Arbitration Awards (Czech arbitration law), as well as the Czech courts including the Czech Supreme Court, long favored the arbitration agreements referring to institutional arbitration (to be more precise, the permanent arbitral institutions established by law) over *ad hoc* arbitration agreements entered into in the Czech Republic.[56] The preferential treatment of institutional arbitration agreements was mostly a consequence of the ruling of the Czech Supreme Court of 11 May 2011[57] that declared arbitration agreements that did not refer to the rules of a permanent arbitral institution established by law and did not include the names of the arbitrators null and void.[58] The situation has been slightly improved together with the recent amendments to the Czech arbitration law of 20 December 2011 (effective from 1 April 2012) that validated the parties' references to the rules of non-permanent arbitral institutions provided that the copy of those rules has been attached to their arbitration agreement or a contract containing the reference to such an agreement.[59] What is more, the public recognition of institutional arbitration in the Czech Republic even resulted in the decision of the Czech Constitutional Court in which it was held that the arbitral awards produced in the course of the institutional arbitration proceedings should be regarded as being issued by arbitral institutions themselves rather than individual arbitrators. This eventually proved the broad institutional autonomy in arbitration in the Czech Republic.[60]

The above examples demonstrate particular powers of contemporary arbitral institutions in post-communist countries that reflect the specific treatment of institutional arbitration in the then Soviet block that largely limited the use of *ad hoc* arbitration and treated arbitral institutions as the continuation of State powers in the field of dispute resolution. This particular "legacy" of institutional arbitration in post-Soviet countries serves as an argument against the adequacy of the pure contractual theory of institutional arbitration. It demonstrates that the limitations to the parties' consent to institutional arbitration occur in both domestic and international proceedings. This is so because even if the public authorization of institutional arbitration takes place domestically in the post-Soviet countries under analysis, it has been largely insipred by the general tradition of controlled arbitration in the former Soviet Union. This also places the discussion on the public interference with the arbitration process beyond purely national regulations of arbitration. In fact, this public legacy of institutional arbitration can be seen today with regard to arbitral institutions operating in other countries of controlled market

[55]Cretu 2013.

[56]Cole et al. 2014, 76–78.

[57]No. 31 Cdo 1945/2010.

[58]Cole et al., 76–78.

[59]Ibid.

[60]Ibid.

economies such as China where the tight bonds between arbitral institutions and State "apparatus" also reflect the extensive institutional competences in the administration and supervision of arbitration proceedings.[61]

Finally, the status approach to the inadequacy of the pure contractual theory of institutional arbitration is incomplete without pointing out the linkages between sovereign public power and institutional private authority in administering new types of arbitration based on the relevant authorization contained in legal provisions. This is the case with the already-mentioned company-related disputes under the recent amendments to national laws in Spain and Italy, and the extensive powers of Maltese Arbitration Centre under Malta's Arbitration Act.[62] In light of the discussion on the proliferation of institutional arbitration in the context of domestic liberalization of arbitrability,[63] it should be clear that certain public powers have been delegated to arbitral institutions, which even *ad hoc* arbitrators do not enjoy. This means that institutional authority has been—to a certain extent—rooted also in public acts, and that the prior public recognition of the role of arbitral institutions in some jurisdictions complements private "power" to recourse to these arbitral institutions by means of private agreements between the parties. Pure contractualists would have trouble explaining these dynamics.

3.2.1.1.2.2 The Contractual Approach and the Schöldström's Model: Private Regulatory Powers of Arbitral Institutions in Contract Formation

Given the inadequacy of the pure contractual theory because of the particular status of arbitral institutions as analysed in the preceding section, it is now necessary to study the applicability of this theory to multifaceted functions of arbitral institutions from the contractual perspective. Although some assumptions of the modern contractual theory could justify the operation of arbitral institution,[64] it is uncertain how the modern contractualists would treat the institutional involvement in the creation of the contractual bonds emerging in institutional arbitration, especially in view of certain limitation of the parties' autonomy under institutional arbitration rules. There are at least three controversies that call into question the applicability of the arguments of the classical contractualists to the contractual situation in the institutional variant of arbitration.

The first controversy addresses the question of which legal instrument: whether an arbitration agreement or a request for arbitration, or, accordingly, the answer to the request for arbitration, or even some other act produced in the course of institutional proceedings, constitutes the contractual ties between institutional arbitration

[61] See the discussion on the connections of such institutions as the CIETAC, BAC and CMAC in China with the State authorities in Gerbay, forthcoming 2016 (with further references). See also: Ortolani 2013.

[62] Sect. 2.3.2.2.2.

[63] Ibid.

[64] For example, the interdependency of arbitration agreement and the nexus of contracts coming into existence between institutional arbitration actors.

actors. This issue sheds light on the authority of institutional arbitration agreements in institutional contracts' formation, by questioning the exclusive role of such agreements to confer the arbitration powers to *all* institutional arbitration actors. The second problem refers to the academic debate over the individual versus triangular character of institutional contractual relations.[65] It is plausible that institutional arbitration contracts come into existence at different times with regard to individual institutional arbitrators, each party to arbitration, and the arbitral institution itself. Finally, the third controversy deals with the possible legal qualification of institutional arbitration contracts under the assumptions of the classical contractual theory that could imply treating institutional contracts as agency contracts in a similar manner as some contractualists treat arbitrators as agents of the parties.

In order to address these controversies the following analysis will present the Schöldström's model of institutional contractual relationships, which also aims at further explaining a particular dual function of institutional arbitration as presented in Chap. 2, in this part *exclusively* in the contractual context. This mainly concerns the accommodation of both commercial and legal goals of arbitral institutions understood within the meaning of the commercial and public functions of arbitral institutions, with the former dealing with traditional goals of early institutional arbitration users and the latter corresponding to the institutional authority in ensuring the public enforceability of the private institutional arbitration settings. To start with, it is necessary to first provide a context for the second controversy regarding the individual versus triangular character of institutional contractual relations as the debate in this regard naturally determines the foundation and structure of the model of contractual institutional relations.[66]

The proponents of the triangular theory claimed that institutional arbitration features linkages between arbitrators (regarded as one body), the parties (acting also in their joint capacity) and the relevant arbitral institution serving as *pater familias*, with its rules of arbitration lying at the heart of each of the contractual institutional settings.[67] Despite being popular, such theory is debatable as it overlooks the practical side of both the arbitrators' and institutional "mandate". In response to the practical problems associated with triangular theory, an alternative model of contractual relations emerged in literature, which was underpinned by the major hypothesis that each of the institutional arbitration actors is entangled—at least at the stage of pre-arbitration proceedings—in a direct legal relationship.[68] The author of this theory, Patrik Schöldström, further claimed that such an individualized theory of institutional relations addresses in the most comprehensive way a dual character of the arbitrator's mandate, including the twofold role of the arbitrator as a service provider and decision-maker (private adjudicator). Following Schöldström, it will be argued below that this theory also reflects the specific

[65]This debate will be addressed in the following part of this section.

[66]The two other controversies will be addressed in the course of the following examination of Schöldström's model of the institutional contractual design.

[67]Rubino-Sammartano 2001, 368; Fouchard 1995; Lew et al. 2003, 267.

[68]Schöldström 1998, 405.

status of arbitral institutions in contract formation in institutional arbitration vis-à-vis parties and individual arbitrators. Schöldström's model will therefore be used to expose the role of arbitral institutions in conferring the judicial status on arbitrators, and in the subsequent supervision of the judicial function of arbitrators *in relation to*, yet not necessarily *under* the authority of the earlier arbitration agreement. To this extent, the following analysis will address the inadequacy of the pure contractual theory with regard to the organization of institutional arbitration. It will also point out that certain institutional obligations—interrelated with the work of institutional arbitrators—may be embedded in such particular institutional status in the formation of institutional contractual settings.

A hypothetical case, proposed by Schöldström,[69] arises under the arbitration agreement referring to the 1998 ICC Arbitration Rules,[70] in which the parties agreed on three arbitrators in accordance with the provision expressed in Article 8(1) of the 1998 ICC Arbitration Rules.[71] It is sufficient to state from the outset that institutional arbitration involves the incorporation of the relevant institutional arbitration provisions to each contractual bond that arises among institutional arbitration actors. This means that, once the parties express their consent with regard to a particular arbitration centre to act as an administrator of their future or already arisen dispute, the procedural rules of such institution become determinative upon all the provisions (also substantive terms) of all contracts concluded by the parties and arbitrators or arbitral institution. To this extent, the rules also stipulate the initial will of the parties with regard to the conduct of the proceedings.[72] This issue will be explained in detail below, while referring to the mandatory provisions included in institutional arbitral rules.

The case discussed by Schöldström reflects the chronological order of the stages of the ICC arbitration and analyses the following five relations involving[73]:

(1) the Claimant (P1) — the Arbitrator (A1);
(2) the Claimant (P1) — the ICC Court (the Court);
(3) the Respondent (P2) — the Arbitrator (A2);

[69]See generally: Schöldström 1998 (with references to ICC arbitration) and 2010 (with references to SCC arbitration).

[70]Schöldström's model is based on the 1998 version of the ICC Arbitration Rules, and therefore the analysis follows the Schöldström's assumptions based on the 1998 ICC Arbitration Rules. Given the particular character of the ICC arbitration, which was not undermined in the new 2012 ICC Arbitration Rules, the basic assumptions of this model as well as the following conclusions should have applicability also to the arbitrations conducted under the 2012 ICC Arbitration Rules.

[71]Pursuant to Article 8(1) of the 1998 ICC Arbitration Rules, dispute shall be decided either by a sole arbitrator or by three arbitrators.

[72]Some institutional arbitration provisions are of mandatory character meaning that the parties cannot derogate from such provisions or change the wording of a particular arbitration rule unless they want to risk that an institution dismisses their claim.

[73]As noted by Schöldström, the case does not claim general applicability. It therefore focuses on the basic relationships between the parties, arbitrators and the ICC Court without the recourse to the involvement of experts, witnesses or multiparty claimants/respondents in ICC arbitration proceedings.

(4) the ICC Court — the Respondent (P2);
(5) the ICC Court — the Chairman (A3) and the other Arbitrators (A1) (A2).

In order to address in a comprehensive manner the problems of the present discussion, Schöldström's observations regarding each stage of the proceedings will be explained. This discussion will be accompanied with a general analysis of the ICC arbitration practice.[74]

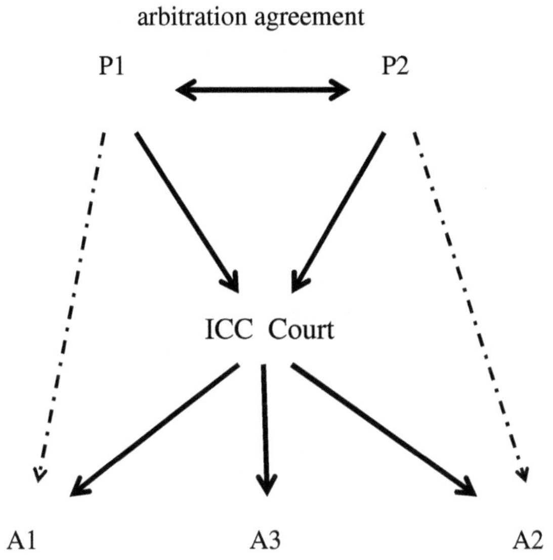

(1): (P1-A1) Contract for a provision of service with the arbitrator A1

(2): (P1-ICC Court) Request for ICC Arbitration

(3): (P2-A2) Contract for the provision of service with the arbitrator A2

(4): (P2-ICC Court) Answer to the Request for Arbitration

(5): (ICC Court-A3) Appointment of the Chairman

(ICC Court-A1) Confirmation of the arbitrator A1

(ICC Court-A2) Confirmation of the arbitrator A2

[74]The author was an intern at the ICC Court of Arbitration within the period from 3 January 2011 until 25 February 2011. Therefore, the observations on the general ICC practice concern the practical experience obtained by the author during this internship.

(1) In the model proposed by Schöldström, the prospective Claimant (P1) decides to commence the ICC arbitration against the prospective Respondent (P2) thus he/she contacts a suitable person asking him/her to act as arbitrator in accordance with the ICC Rules. Once the Claimant receives a *confirmation* from this person expressing his/her *consent* to act in the arbitrator's capacity, the result should be a contract between them in which the nominee undertakes to settle a dispute according to the ICC Rules in return for remuneration being paid to him/her pursuant to the same provisions.[75] In principle, each party to a dispute (here, the Claimant in the ICC arbitration) is authorized to propose his/her own arbitrator before the actual proceedings commence.[76] Leaving aside the problem of neutrality of party-appointed arbitrators, which is of particular relevance especially in the context of American arbitration,[77] it is important to consider what sort of information an individual to be appointed as arbitrator can access at this stage of the pre-arbitration proceedings. According to the results of the questionnaire undertaken and published by the ICC, an arbitrator-to-be should be informed of the nature of a dispute, the identity of the parties, the law applicable to the dispute, as well as the language and the place of arbitration[78]. Even though such pre-disclosure serves mainly for the arbitrator's assessment of his/her own competence with regard to the future arbitration, it should be secured by the initial pre-contractual arrangements—as proposed by Schöldström—under which the prospective arbitrator should bear, inter alia, the duty of confidentiality concerning the information he/she received from the Claimant. This is significant for the prospective civil liability of the nominee for the disclosure of secret business information even before arbitration commences.[79]

(2) The second step of Schöldström's contractual framework concerns the Claimant's submission of the Request for Arbitration to the Secretariat of the ICC Court. The Request contains, inter alia, the nomination of the previously chosen arbitrator (A1). Once the Claimant pays the filing fee and the ICC Court begins to organize the proceedings,[80] the contract between the Claimant and the ICC Court comes into existence with the Claimant undertaking to pay the ICC arbitration costs and the ICC Court obligating itself to oversee arbitral proceedings in accordance with its Rules.[81]

---

[75]Schöldström 1998, 406.

[76]Anecdotal evidence reveals, however, that in the majority of arbitration cases it is the legal staff of the ICC Court's Secretariat who appoints the most experienced and suitable arbitrators on behalf of the parties.

[77]For example, Hans Smit notes that in the US party-appointed arbitrators are basically the advocates of the parties on the arbitration panel. Smit 2011.

[78]The ICC Commission on Arbitration. "Final Report on the Status of Arbitrator." ICC International Court of Arbitration Bulletin 1996. Vol. 7 No. 1.

[79]Cf. Schöldström 1998.

[80]See Article 4(1) and 4(4) of the 1998 ICC Arbitration Rules.

[81]Schöldström 1998, 406.

This aspect of Schöldström's model may seem controversial, in particular while taking into account both the claims of pure contractualists regarding the exclusive authority of an arbitration agreement in arbitration proceedings and the wording of Article 4(2) of the 1998 ICC Arbitration Rules which states that: "the date on which the Request is received by the Secretariat shall, *for all purposes*, be deemed to be the date of the commencement of the arbitral proceedings".[82] Schöldström explains the emergence of a direct contract between the Claimant and the ICC Court under the Request for Arbitration by stressing the assumption of his model that each party and each arbitrator should be regarded as an individual whose contractual ties with arbitral institutions do not necessarily have to be created at the same time. This hypothesis requires further explanation regarding the character of the arbitration rules and the consequences of the incorporation of such rules into the arbitration agreement.

In mainstream theoretical discourse arbitration rules are said to constitute a *permanent offer to contract*.[83] Generally, there are two prevailing theories regarding the actual moment of the acceptance of such an offer by disputing parties. The first theory assumes that the offer is accepted—with regard to both parties—once the parties enter into arbitration agreement in their contracts and—regarding the institution—upon the filing of the request for arbitration by the claimant.[84] The second theory implies that the offer is accepted—with regard to the parties—once the claimant commences the arbitration and—with regard to the institution—when the institution accepts to act under the claimant's submission.[85] The second theory seems to correspond with certain assumptions of Schöldström's model. The second theory is more convincing regarding the moment of the acceptance of the offer by the claimant (and of the further confirmation to proceed with the arbitration by the ICC), however, both theories do not respond well to the theory of individualized relationships provided by Schöldström. Moreover, the first theory unnecessarily emphasizes the role of arbitration agreement in the acceptance of the institutional offer.

Assuming that an arbitration agreement expresses the exclusive power that stipulates *all* the subsequent arbitral acts (of arbitrators, arbitral institutions, and the parties themselves) would result in the situation in which the parties' signature on the contract containing arbitration agreement would be determinative upon their contractual relationships with an arbitration institution without an awareness of the latter of the existence of such relationships. Even while presupposing that arbitration rules are some sort of a public offer to contract, the general principles of contract law ordinarily require that the offerees (here the parties to arbitration agreement) indicate an assent to the offer by sending their acceptance to the institution (offeror) within the reasonable time (as in the case

[82]Cf. Article 4(2) of the 2012 ICC Arbitration Rules.

[83]Rubino-Sammartano 2001, 367–368.

[84]Cf. Fouchard 1995; Greenberg 2013.

[85]Greenberg 2013.

in which no time limit was fixed by the offeror for the acceptance of an offer).[86] This necessary conclusion should be recognized not only by theorists but also by practitioners. As was also rightly observed by Schöldström, arbitration proceedings can be launched even several years after the arbitration agreement has been negotiated by the parties, or may not occur at all with regard to the contracting parties. In line with this, it is arguable that arbitral institutions entangle themselves in contractual relationships with all the parties that inserted an institutional arbitration clause in their original contract.

Moreover, it is also controversial whether an arbitration agreement could be classified as an initial contract that has been "perfected" *for both parties* once the claimant submits the request for arbitration to the administrator of his/her dispute and the institution decides to commence the proceedings.[87] Schöldström is right in saying that at this stage of the pre-arbitration proceedings, a direct relationship emerges only between the institution (the ICC) and the Claimant who pays the initial fee (so-called "provisional advance"[88]) and provides the name of the arbitrator, whereas the ICC Court undertakes to organize the arbitration, meaning that the ICC Court proceeds with the *prima facie* determination of the validity of the arbitration agreement. The wording of the aforementioned Article 4(2) of the 1998 ICC Arbitration Rules is not in fact straightforward. The interpretation of the ICC provision—which relates to the moment of the commencement of the proceedings upon the date of receiving the Request for Arbitration by the Secretariat—should be limited to the coming into existence of the obligations of the ICC Court (and, accordingly, those of the Claimant) to investigate whether an agreement exists between the parties-to-be, and furthermore to proceed with the Request for Arbitration.[89] It could be implied from Schöldström's assumption regarding the contract between the ICC Court and the Claimant that once the ICC Court decides that there is no binding ICC arbitration agreement between the parties, the institutional contract between the Claimant and the ICC Court will be treated as fully executed and hence the obligations of the ICC Court will be discharged. This means that institutional contracts could be classified as autonomous contracts vis-à-vis the initial arbitration agreement concluded by the parties. Finally, at this stage of institutional contract formation, Schöldström claims that the ICC Court undertakes, inter alia, to conclude the contract with prospective arbitrators and with the prospective Respondent provided that the latter is validly bound under the arbitration clause.[90]

---

[86]For example: von Bar et al. 2009.

[87]Cf. Gaillard and Savage 1999, 602; Schöldström 1998, 402.

[88]Cf. Article 1 of the Appendix III: Arbitration Costs and Fees to the 2012 ICC Arbitration Rules.

[89]Article 4(2) of the 1998 ICC Arbitration Rules.

[90]Cf. *Ceskilovenska Obchodni Banka A.S. (Cekobanka) C/Chambre de Commerce Internationale. 1986. Rev. arb. (1987) Tribunal de grande instance de Paris 1986.*

(3) The third stage of the Schöldström's model includes the contractual bond between the Respondent and an individual to be approached by him/her to become an arbitrator. After having received a copy of the Request for Arbitration from the Secretariat, the Respondent obtains the arbitrator's (A2) consent to decide the dispute. This, according to Schöldström, results in the contract between the Respondent and his/her nominee (A2) in which the arbitrator undertakes to settle the dispute pursuant to the ICC Rules in return for remuneration fixed under the ICC Schedule of Costs and Fees.

These arguments bring us back to the initial stage of the contractual arrangements between the Claimant and his/her nominee. It is indeed reasonable to treat each party and each arbitrator individually (at least at the level of pre-arbitral proceedings as proposed by Schöldström). It seems that the ICC Court would also support such distinction, which can be shown by the fact that the ICC Arbitration Rules provide for the joint appointment of arbitrator(s) *only* in the case of multiparty proceedings.[91]

(4) Once the respondent files the Answer to the Request for Arbitration (including, inter alia, the counterclaims) at the ICC Court's Secretariat, the latter fixes the amount of the advance of costs, which, in principle, is to be paid by the Claimant and the Respondent in equal shares.[92] This, according to Schöldström, should result in the contract between the Respondent and the ICC Court, which may be concluded at the moment in which the ICC Court receives the Answer to the Request together with the nomination of the arbitrator (A2).[93] Schöldström further argues that the contract's notable terms would be the respondent's undertaking to pay the costs of the ICC arbitration in return for the ICC Court's undertaking to supervise the dispute in accordance with the ICC Rules.

Schöldström's hypothesis appears even more credible if we take into account the provision of Article 30(2) of the 1998 ICC Arbitration Rules, which states that if—in addition to the claims—counterclaims are also submitted, the ICC Court may fix *separate* advance on costs for the claims and counterclaims which should be paid by the Claimant and the Respondent accordingly. This means that at this stage the Respondent will be bound under a direct contract with the ICC Court, which will stipulate the amount due to the ICC Court's Secretariat from the Respondent only, necessary for the further examination of his/her counterclaims. This is particularly important given that the ICC Arbitration Rules (be it in their 1998 or 2012 version) do not provide for the filing fee to be paid by the respondent.

(5) The last stage of Schöldström's model concerns the confirmation by the ICC Court of the parties' nominees. As such, it addresses the two aforementioned

[91]See: Article 10 of the 1998 ICC Arbitration Rules.

[92]See: Article 30(3) of the 1998 ICC Arbitration Rules.

[93]Schöldström has doubts as to the exact moment of the conclusion of this contract. However, in my opinion, it should be the date on which the Secretariat receives the Answer to the Request (cf. the discussion on the institutional public offer to contract).

controversies reflecting the inadequacies of the arguments of pure contractualists to the relationships arising in institutional arbitration, namely: (1) a dual character of the arbitrator's mandate (and also, to a certain extent, a dual nature of institutional activity), and (2) the adaptation of agency theory to institutional arbitration settings. Schöldström suggests looking at the ties between each arbitrator and each party at both contractual and adjudicatory level, which can help in respecting the dual character of the arbitrators' work. Furthermore, he claims that the conferment of the adjudicatory powers on arbitrators occurs at the moment of the confirmation by the ICC Court of the individuals previously nominated by each party, who, until the moment of confirmation, are individually and contractually bound only to each of their "nominators".

In order to provide a better understanding of the Schöldström's arguments, as well as of the weaknesses of the classical variant of the contractual theory in the case of institutional arbitration, it is necessary to follow here the process of the arbitrator's confirmation by the ICC Court. As stated in Article 8(4) of the ICC Rules, each party shall nominate in the Request and the Answer, respectively, one arbitrator for confirmation. The Secretariat of the ICC Court requires each nominated arbitrator to fill out two forms,[94] a Curriculum Vitae and a Statement of Acceptance, Availability and Independence,[95] in which the nominees should disclose any facts or circumstances which might be of such a nature as to call into question the arbitrator's independence "in the eyes of the parties".[96] If no comments from the parties follow, the ICC Court confirms the nominees what, according to Schöldström, should result in the coming into existence of two contracts: one between the ICC Court and the arbitrator nominated by the Claimant (P1), and the other between the ICC Court and the nominee of the Respondent (P2). These contracts, according to Schöldström, supplement or even supersede each original contract between the arbitrators and their nominators to the extent that the post-confirmation by the ICC Court transfers the adjudicatory powers to arbitrators to bind *both parties* with their decision.[97] The Final Report of the ICC Commission on Arbitration on the status of an arbitrator also states that:

> the contractual relationship between the parties and each arbitrator, and the arbitration centre itself, is ultimately concluded at the moment that the last of the said contracting parties expresses its acceptance.[98]

---

[94]Unless the CV of an arbitrator to be confirmed has already been submitted to the ICC Court's arbitrators' database.

[95]ICC Court of Arbitration 2010 Arbitrator's Statement of Acceptance, Availability and Independence (1998 ICC Arbitration Rules). http://www.rwi.uzh.ch/lehreforschung/alphabetisch/domej/archiv/HS11-1/izvr/ICC-Arbitrator-Acceptance-Form-2010.pdf. Accessed 25 April 2016.

[96]See: Article 7(2) of the 1998 ICC Arbitration Rules. Cf. Ibid.

[97]Schöldström 1998, 408–409.

[98]The ICC Commission on Arbitration. "Final Report on the Status of Arbitrator." ICC International Court of Arbitration Bulletin 1996 Vol. 7 No. 1.

This means that it is the ICC Court whose ultimate decision as to the suitability of the relevant arbitrator imposes all the duties on arbitrators which, from the moment of confirmation, become private judges with a duty to render an award for *both* disputants, instead of the hitherto provision of services by the arbitrators-to-be whose initial task was to prepare an arbitration case. Moreover, as Schöldström argues, from the moment of the confirmation, arbitrators are contractually bound only with the ICC Court, which undertakes to remunerate their work from the fees provided by the parties.[99]

The next step of the ICC Court in Schöldström's model would be to appoint the Chairman provided that the parties had failed to agree upon the alternative procedure for such appointment.[100] A separate appointment of a chairman, which is carried out by the ICC Court with a particular duty of care (given the presiding role of the chairman in the arbitration tribunal), only supports Schöldström's argument that each arbitrator shall be bound with the ICC Court under a separate contract. Under Article 9(3) in accordance with Article 9(5) of the 1998 ICC Rules, both the ICC Court and a relevant National Committee of the Court shall be particularly cautious about the nationality of the Chairman-to-be to ensure maximum level of independence and impartiality of the umpire of an arbitral tribunal. Unless the chairman-to-be fails to submit the Statement of Acceptance, Availability and Independence to the Court's Secretariat and the parties oppose to his/her appointment, the ICC will produce a contract with the Chairman whose terms will be similar to the contractual provisions binding upon the other two arbitrators and the ICC Court. In addition, this contract will include the particular obligations of the chairman such as making of the award alone in case the award cannot be given by a majority decision.[101]

3.2.1.1.2.3 On How Schöldström's Model Informs the Legal Basis and the Scope of Institutional Arbitral Liability

Schöldström's conclusions relating to the relationships in institutional arbitration in the scenario above concern the existence of five contracts: two between each of the parties and the ICC Court and three between each of the three arbitrators and the ICC Court.[102] As already stated, Schöldström also proves that before the confirmation of the arbitrators (and the appointment of the Chairman) by the ICC Court no adjudicatory relation emerges between the arbitrators and the parties. Ergo, one may conclude that furnishing arbitrators with adjudicatory powers with regard to each party to arbitration proceedings is a special function of the ICC Court.

It seems plausible that the advocates of the triangular theory would question the emergence of five contracts under Schöldström's model. Triangular theorists

[99] Cf. with SCC model in Schöldström 2010 453–457.

[100] Article 8(4) of the 1998 ICC Arbitration Rules.

[101] Article 25(1) of the 1998 ICC Arbitration Rules.

[102] Schöldström 1998, 408.

could argue that once the ICC Court confirms the arbitrators, triangular relationships could emerge between all institutional arbitration actors (the arbitral institution, the parties and the arbitral tribunal). This would require the parties as well as the arbitrators to be treated as one body vis-à-vis each other and the ICC Court. Such assumption seems arguable, especially under the ICC Arbitration Rules that underpinned the above-presented model.

Even though the adjudicatory bond that appears at the moment of the arbitrators' confirmation supersedes the individualized relations between each party and each arbitrator, both the Claimant and the Respondent act in the arbitration process on their own behalf and for their own benefit.[103] In this regard, there are no grounds for treating the parties as one body vis-à-vis an arbitration tribunal *even after* the conferment on such a panel of the adjudicatory powers with regard to both parties.[104] Additionally, the individualized contractual relationship between each member of the arbitration panel and the ICC Court is more telling than the understanding of the arbitral tribunal as one body bearing the collective responsibility vis-à-vis the ICC Court. This is reflected in both the ICC Arbitration Rules and the ICC internal arbitration practice. Thus, the arbitrators' fees under the ICC Schedule of Costs and Fees differ, respectively, depending on the arbitrator's function assumed within the arbitration tribunal.[105] The ICC Court also has exclusive authority to terminate the contract with a particular arbitrator in cases in which the Court decides that he or she is prevented *de jure* or *de facto* from fulfilling his/her functions.[106] Given that, the triangular theory should be rejected under the proposed model.

The triangular theory—as already stated—is strongly interrelated with the arguments of traditional contractualists concerning the exclusive power of an arbitration agreement to confer the arbitration authority to *all* arbitration actors. Although the contractual situation in institutional arbitration indeed reflects a complex network of contractual arrangements, the special function of the ICC Court involving the conferment of the adjudicatory powers on arbitrators distorts the authority of arbitration agreement in stipulating *all* contractual situations arising in institutional arbitration settings.[107] This special function of the ICC Court—while confronted with the public function of institutional arbitration presented in Chap. 2—implies particular observations for the sources of both contractual authority and obligations of institutional arbitration actors.

[103]This observation is also reflected in the ICC Arbitration Rules. The ICC Rules, apart from the cases of multiparty or multi-contract arbitrations, do not provide for joint acts of the parties in the course of the proceedings.

[104]Rather, the arbitral tribunal itself shall be regarded as one body in front of both parties, which seems crucial for the assurance of the neutrality, independence and impartiality of the members of the arbitral tribunal.

[105]30/40/30 scheme: 30 % for the party-appointed arbitrators and 40 % for the chairman.

[106]Article 12(2) of the 1998 ICC Arbitration Rules on the replacement of arbitrators on the Court's own initiative.

[107]Even though the confirmation of arbitrators has long been perceived as a distinctive feature of the ICC arbitration, more and more arbitral institutions started to follow the ICC's provisions on confirmations (see: CEPANI Arbitration Rules of 2013).

It is argued that it is not only the ICC Court that has a voice in eventual conferring of all the duties on institutional arbitrators, but that all the contracts with institutional arbitrators under *different* arbitration rules are ultimately concluded under the authority of arbitral institutions. This means that arbitral institutions—notwithstanding the methods of appointment of arbitrators agreed on by the parties, as well as the fact whether institutional design provides for confirmation of arbitrators or not—have the major authority to stipulate the arbitrators' contractual situation (implying also the arbitrators' adjudicatory functions). This stems from the institutional rules and other soft-law instruments developed within institutional regimes, which require all arbitrators to comply with the institutional rules and policies at the outset of arbitration, and to carefully apply the rules of a particular regime in the further course of the proceedings.[108] No institution will allow the arbitrator to proceed without such confirmation from an arbitrator-to-be that he/she will act in the spirit of the institutional rules.

Having said that, arbitral institutions enjoy particular *private regulatory powers* in the formation of institutional contracts that supersede the authority of the arbitration agreements previously concluded between the parties. Such powers concern also *institutional authority to re-determine the authority of institutional arbitrators* by furnishing them with the adjudicatory powers after the prior nomination by the parties of individual arbitrators. This also means that after the conferment of adjudicatory powers on institutional arbitrators there are no direct contractual relationships between the parties and the institutional arbitrators who are contractually linked only with arbitral institutions. Hence, the institutional arbitrators, from the moment of their confirmation, should report on the progress of the cases to arbitral institutions rather than directly to the parties.

The institutional private regulatory powers in contract formation imply two further questions. In which capacity—its own or on behalf of the parties—does the arbitral institution enter into institutional contracts with institutional arbitrators? And, what kind of contract emerges between arbitral institutions and each party, and each arbitrator? These issues will also be addressed in view of the assumptions of the contractual theory of arbitration that could imply the existence of agency contracts between arbitral institutions, the parties and institutional arbitrators.

Some authors suggest that arbitral institutions, while appointing or nominating the arbitrators, act either as principals or agents of the parties.[109] It is claimed here, however, that arbitral institutions enter into contractual relationships with each party and each arbitrator as independent actors. In view of this, arbitral institutions should not be perceived as agents of the parties either in the meaning of the contractual theory of arbitration or under any traditional theory of agency.

---

[108] In any case, before proceeding with the case, arbitrators need to provide the relevant body of the institutional organ with the information regarding their independence and impartially, or with the CV which constitutes contractual bonds between such arbitrators and an institution.

[109] Cf. the case studies (from 8 to 12) provided by Onyema in: Onyema 2010, 93–102.

Schöldström suggested that the first contract, which comes into existence between the ICC Court and the Claimant, might involve certain provisions of agency contract, namely, that the ICC Court will undertake to conclude—on behalf of the Claimant—further contracts with each arbitrators and the Respondent. The analysis of the public function provided in Chap. 2 (Sect. 2.3.2) also distinguished between institutional prerogatives "on behalf of the parties" and the exclusive institutional authority in ensuring the enforcement of institutional arbitration processes and awards to be understood within the meaning of the institutional "private regulatory functions." However, this terminology should not be confusing as it does not imply the activity of arbitral institutions as agents or even principals of the parties.

If there was a contract of agency with regard to each party and arbitral institutions, it would also entail the existence of the contract between these parties and arbitrators after the conferment of adjudicatory function on arbitrators,[110] the possibility of which was already excluded under Schöldström's model. Even assuming that certain institutional functions are fulfilled *in the continuation of* the parties' initial will as expressed in the arbitration agreement (competences on behalf of the parties), these functions are strongly interlinked with the exclusive institutional prerogatives exercised in the further stages of arbitration proceedings. These competences concern, inter alia, the confirmations or appointments of institutional arbitrators on behalf of the parties. Once they are invoked by the parties in their submission to institutional arbitration (in the request for arbitration or the answer to the request), they mostly fall within the authority of the institutional rules and the private regulatory powers of arbitral institutions that have been developed by means of the continuous adjustments of these rules.

In other words, even if in some stages of arbitration proceedings such competences may resemble the authority of agents, the more comprehensive functional understanding of all institutional prerogatives does not justify the classification of institutional contracts as agency contracts. This is also because—as explained in Sect. 2.3.2.1.2.4 of Chap. 2—the institutional competences on behalf of the parties and the exclusive institutional prerogatives overlap and cannot be easily separated under institutional contracts. This specific "agency" of arbitral institutions is thus enshrined in the *sui generis* character of institutional operation. To this extent, the institutional contracts should be themselves regarded as *sui generis* contracts of a dual nature: commercial and legal. From the commercial law perspective, institutional contracts are to secure the commercial goals of the business parties (e.g. the appointment and/or confirmation of arbitrators suitable for the resolution of particular types of disputes because of their expertise and availability). From the purely legal perspective, however, institutional arbitration contracts empower arbitral institutions to determine the legal rights and duties of all institutional arbitration actors for two reasons. First, because arbitral institutions have been authorized by means of institutional arbitration rules to do so mostly to ensure the enforceability of arbitration processes and of institutional arbitral awards. Second, because

[110] Onyema 2010, 96.

institutional arbitration rules, once incorporated into all contracts concluded in the course of institutional arbitration predetermine the contractual obligations of all institutional arbitration actors. In this vein, those rules can be treated as specific "terms and conditions" of institutional arbitration contracts that list the contractual duties of all actors involved in institutional arbitration proceedings. The latter observation may explain why arbitral institutions remain reluctant to increase the transparency of the internal institutional practices regarding the appointment of arbitrators or issuance of procedural orders in the course of proceedings. It is plausible that the increased transparency would run contrary to the principle of confidentiality underlying these specific terms and conditions of institutional arbitration contracts. The further analysis of institutional contracts under different contract law theories will be provided in Sect. 7.3.2.

3.2.1.2 Institutional Arbitration as a Hybrid Versus the Contractual and Extra Contractual Sources of Institutional Duties

The inadequacy of both pure jurisdictional and contractual theories for the illustration of the status and function of arbitral institutions, as explained in the preceding discussion, implies the hybrid nature of institutional arbitration. The mixed (hybrid) theory of arbitration was formed by Professor Sauser Hall.

Hall argued that both the contractual and jurisdictional elements are visible in the arbitrator's function, as well as in the modern national laws of arbitration.[111] Hall claimed that the contractual arbitration facet concerns the private authorization of arbitrators by the parties in the form of the arbitration agreement. According to Hall, arbitrators perform specific quasi-judicial functions that are not conferred on them directly by a State, as a State may vest such power only to its own public officials. Therefore, arbitrators enjoy only quasi-judicial status to the extent that they are bound by the law of the arbitral *situs*. Conversely, a purely jurisdictional aspect of arbitration appears at the enforcement level, when a judge from a relevant jurisdiction recognizes the legality of the award, thus, he or she confers the powers of a State on the arbitral act by applying to it a procedure of the place of the enforcement. To this extent, arbitration is not free from national legal systems as long as the two interrelated issues such as the arbitrability of a particular dispute and the enforceability of the award come into question. This seems to be supported also by other commentators. As Redfern and Hunter observe:

> International commercial arbitration is a hybrid. It begins as a private agreement between the parties. It continues by way of private proceedings, in which the wishes of the parties are of great importance. Yet it ends with an award which has binding legal force and effect and which, on appropriate conditions being met, the courts of most countries of the world will be prepared to recognise and enforce. The private process has a public effect, implemented by the support of the public authorities of each state expressed through its national law.[112]

[111] Yu 2008, 274–277.

[112] Redfern et al. 2004, 11; Yu 2008, 275.

Some commentators claim that mixed arbitration theory constitutes an unsatisfactory compromise, which is not capable of expressing the nature of the arbitral process, as it artificially reduces the arbitration instruments, either to the contractual aspect of the process or to its jurisdictional facet.[113] Regardless of these concerns, it is argued here that the mixed theory of arbitration is best suited for the explanation of both the dual function and the particular status of institutional arbitration in the formation of contracts in institutional arbitration and hence on the stipulation of legal relationships in institutional arbitration.

On the one hand, institutional arbitration by no means operates on the contractual basis, and yet—in most cases—this is the parties' authorization that *presupposes* the institutional and arbitrator's activity. Arbitral institutions still owe contractual duties toward the parties, especially to ensure the efficiency and flexibility of arbitration proceedings in the field of the costs and speed of arbitration. Moreover, it seems that the "guarantee" concerning enforceability of arbitration processes and awards also falls within the group of contractual obligations of arbitral institutions. On the other hand, however, the emerging public function of institutional arbitration gives additional context to contractual obligations of arbitral institutions. This means that—similar to arbitrators' duties which originate in both the arbitrators' contract and the arbitrator's status[114]—institutional obligations are also embedded in both private contractual arrangements and particular *status* of institutional arbitration in and outside arbitration proceedings. These observations also have implications for the scope of the liability of the institutional arbitration actors.

Before analysing the scope of institutional arbitral liability, however, it is necessary to explain the terminology that will be applied to the authority of institutional obligations. The discussion will distinguish between the institutional status as the *ability to act*,[115] the institutional status as the *authority to re-determine the authority of institutional arbitrators* and the authority of contractual duties. Hence, institutional obligations originating from the status as the *ability to act* involve the institutional "authorization" by either private parties or public authorities (in recent regulatory arbitrations), or both. The private "authorization" occurs once the parties refer to particular arbitration regime in their arbitration clause or arbitration agreement. The public authorization emerges under the legislative actions of national legislatures concerning the scope of arbitrability, and under the international recognition of institutional arbitration by States acting within their sovereign capacities, external to institutional regimes. Furthermore, the institutional duties that originate in contract arise once either of the parties submits their request for arbitration or the answer to the request to the chosen arbitral institution that, in turn, proceeds with arbitration with regard to each party. Contractual duties

[113] Samuel 1989, 60–63.

[114] See generally Gal 2009.

[115] Cf. Gal 2009, 424. In Part Four Gal summarizes his observations regarding the dual nature of arbitrators' mandate, originating in his/her "ability" understood as a power to act, and in the contract in the meaning of a "duty" to act.

of arbitral institutions arise then under "shared" authority of the parties, institutions, and institutional arbitrators, as they are based on the institutional arbitration rules (with limited possibility for any alterations by the parties). This means that, once the parties presuppose the institutional *ability to act*—within their own private authority—they also stipulate the authority of institutional contractual duties. Consequently, the authority of arbitral institutions to *re-determine the authority of institutional arbitrators* is embedded in the contractual duties that imply the public function of arbitral institutions under the institutional rules. Now, what are the implications of such a distinction for the institutional liability regimes?

In light of the analysis above, it should be clear that arbitral institutions work on a contractual basis and therefore could be contractually liable to other institutional arbitration actors for their essential contractual obligations. Moreover, it is also argued that regardless of the fact that all institutional obligations are based on contract (within the legal dimension of institutional functions) there is additional context for the performance of such obligations that stem from the particular status of arbitral institutions in and outside arbitration proceedings. This concerns the institutional exclusive competence in the administration of regulatory disputes *under* some national arbitration laws, but also the more systemic goals of institutional regimes vis-à-vis traditional arbitration users. These goals will be explained in detail in Sect. 3.3 of this chapter. Institutional arbitral liability should then accommodate both contractual obligations of institutional arbitration actors and the systemic values and goals underlying the institutional regimes.

Moreover, institutional liability should also respond to the particular institutional status *within* institutional regimes, which means institutional *authority to re-determine the authority of arbitrators*. The fact that arbitral institutions enjoy broad regulatory powers in institutional contracts under which the institutions confer the adjudicatory powers on institutional arbitrators implies that arbitral institutions could be also liable in front of the disputing parties for certain acts of institutional arbitrators. This should not imply liability stemming from agency contracts as understood in its classical, contractual sense. Rather, the liability of arbitral institutions for certain arbitrators' acts should fall within the obligations distinct to arbitral institutions. For example, the obligation to ensure efficient conduct in arbitration proceedings in the spirit of the institutional arbitration rules.

Lastly, the hybridity of institutional arbitration also necessitates the increased accountability of institutional regimes, understood in both private and public contexts. This is required given the particular institutional status within, and outside of, arbitration regimes. "Private accountability" addresses the institutional commitment to the values of arbitration processes and the legitimacy of institutional regimes in front of the local and international arbitration communities. As such, it concerns the mechanisms of compliance and responsibility developed within arbitral institutions, hence enforced internally vis-à-vis all actors involved in institutional arbitration proceedings. These mechanisms are to be seen as aiming at increasing both the standards of private participation in arbitrations and the private control over any forms of irregularities in the course of arbitrations. "Public accountability" means the transparency and fairness of institutional processes concerning publicly oriented aspects of those processes developed in the course of the formalization and legalization of arbitration practice in general and in view of the emerging public function of institutional arbitration, in particular. The latter, public form of accountability should be seen within Kelsen's conceptualization of private law that appears as "no less the arena of political power than the public law created in legislation and administration."[116] Therefore, public accountability in the field of arbitration relates to the ways in which institutional arbitration regimes respond (or not) to the public challenges rooted in the increasing institutional mission of "the democratic self-rule by a collective" of private individuals engaged in arbitration proceedings vis-à-vis law.[117]

3.2.2 Theorizing Territoriality of Institutional Arbitration: Courts' Jurisdiction and the Law Applicable in Liability Lawsuits

After identifying the sources and the prospective scope of institutional arbitral liability together with their consequences, it is necessary to analyse the possible authority of public courts to assess institutional arbitral liability. The following section will therefore examine the territoriality of institutional arbitration, including its prospective autonomy vis-à-vis public authorities that shape the legal framework of arbitration at national and international levels. This section begins with the presentation of the autonomous theory of arbitration in the context of the emerging debate on the transnational arbitral legal order(s).[118] References are then made to Professor Gaillard's representations of international arbitration that concern the philosophical visions of the validity and territoriality of international arbitration in the eyes of the sovereign States.[119] The discussion concludes with the presentation of the allocation of the authority among domestic courts regarding the territorial jurisdiction in institutional liability suits.

3.2.2.1 On the Autonomy of Arbitration

The author of the autonomous theory of arbitration, Rubellin-Divichi, claimed that arbitration should be perceived not necessarily through its contractual or jurisdictional nature but rather from a broader perspective involving the goals of the

---

[116]Curtin and Senden 2011, 4–5.

[117]Ibid., 5.

[118]The term "*transnational arbitral legal order*" was adopted after Thomas Schultz, who speaks about the interaction of law with transnational arbitral legal orders. Cf. Schultz 2012. See also Gaillard 2012.

[119]See generally Gaillard 2010b.

system, as viewed by its users.[120] Arbitration, according to Rubellin-Divichi, aims at filling the gap regarding dispute resolution existent at international level, and operates as an instrument for the resolution of international disputes of an international community.[121] Rubellin-Divichi looked at the practical aspect of the arbitration process by scrutinizing the social and economic demands placed upon it by the parties. Based on this analysis, Rubellin-Divichi argued that the autonomous character of arbitration needs to be recognized, preferably at supra-national level.[122]

The formation of autonomous theory of arbitration by Rubellin-Divichi, accompanied by the subsequent socio-political changes driven by the forces of globalization and the resulting proliferation of new forms of arbitration, inspired commentators to postulate a full detachment of arbitration from both the municipal law and traditional positive law thinking. Such claims began to include the popular arguments concerning the operation of arbitration as an autonomous transnational legal order.[123] These arguments deal with the territoriality of arbitration to be understood either as territoriality of arbitration process *per se* or as territoriality of arbitration concerning the law applicable *in* arbitration cases.[124]

Firstly, according to "transnationalists", arbitral order derives its authority from the plurality of legal systems, which, in turn, enables arbitration to reach its "transnational representation" of the community of States.[125] To this extent, arbitration constitutes a delocalized instrument that should not be reduced to any particular legal system.

Secondly, the arbitral order makes use of transnational norms created by the spontaneous community of merchants, that is, the *lex mercatoria.* Given that, the autonomous theory of arbitration takes a more systemic approach to arbitration than contractual, jurisdictional and hybrid theories. It will be argued below that the autonomous theory, notwithstanding its applicability to some aspects of institutional arbitration, does not adequately represent the authority and the functions of the contemporary arbitral institutions.

3.2.2.2 On Why Institutional Arbitration Is Not Purely Autonomous

There are at least three arguments that could at first glance support the autonomous nature of institutional arbitration in front of national laws. Firstly, the private

---

[120]See: Samuel 1989; Yu and Sauzier 2000.

[121]Yu and Sauzier 2000, 114–121

[122]Ibid.

[123]The early doctrine of transnational arbitration was developed mainly by French Professors associated with the University of Dijon such as: Berthold Goldman, Philippe Kahn, Philippe Fouchard, and Eric Loquin (the so-called "School of Dijon"). For the more recent publications, see Paulsson 2011; Gaillard 2011; Gaillard 2010a; Schultz 2012.

[124]Cf. the analysis of the law which governs the arbitration in Paulsson 2011.

[125]Paulsson 2011, 12.

goals of arbitral institutions, such as the support of efficient and effective dispute resolution by institutional arbitrators, advances the major assumption of the autonomous theory. This assumption suggests that arbitration shall be perceived from the perspective of its purpose, that is to say, the institutional correspondence with the societal and economic demands of the parties. Secondly, the institutional authorization given to arbitrators to apply rules of law (next to or instead of national laws) and trade usages supports the arguments that arbitral institutions are willing to contribute to the development of the transnational system of private norms.[126] Thirdly, arbitration procedures which claim global applicability to all categories of disputes regardless of the legal tradition of their users, also appear to support the argument of institutional autonomy.

Despite the fact that all the above observations seem convincing at first glance, the following observations eventually undermine their validity under the pure autonomous theory of arbitration. First, the perception of institutional arbitration only through its private goals overlooks the significance of the public function of institutional arbitration. The increasing public function, especially in its variant in which it interplays with the public regulation of arbitrability and the exclusive competences of arbitral institutions in regulatory arbitrations, proves that arbitral institutions are to a certain extent interlinked with national legal orders that indirectly support the validity and normativity of institutional arbitration regimes. Ergo, institutional operations are not territorially unlimited. Moreover, the assumption that institutional arbitration responds exclusively to the private goals of arbitration users seems inadequate if one takes into account the growing reliance of the States on institutional arbitration, or the extraordinary competences of the AAA in stipulating the consent of the parties with weaker bargaining power regarding class actions.

Additionally, the problem of the application by arbitrators of *lex mercatoria* under institutional arbitration regimes is a complex issue. The statistics of the pioneering "European" arbitral institution—the ICC—concerning the law applicable to ICC arbitrations within the last years show that national law of different jurisdictions is still more popular among the parties than the general principles of international law or trade usages.[127] Hence, parties would rather rely on national laws than on the vague and uncodified "rules of law" with which most lawyers drafting the arbitration clauses are unfamiliar. Moreover, the analysis of the recent

[126]Article 21 of the 2012 ICC Arbitration Rules, Article 14.2 of the LCIA Rules, Article 28 of the ICDR Procedures, Article 22 of the SCC Rules.

[127]Based on the ICC statistics it can be seen that the use of the so-called *lex mercatoria* and trade usages by the parties to the ICC arbitration is declining. The 2004 ICC Statistical Report demonstrates the use by the parties of the laws and principles other than national laws while the Statistics for the year 2012 report that 98 % of the choice of law clauses in the cases referred to the ICC in 2012 specified a state law. See 2004 Statistical Report. 2005 ICC International Court of Arbitration Bulletin 16, No. 1. 2012 Statistical Report. 2013 ICC International Court of Arbitration Bulletin 24, No. 1.

amendments to the ICC rule on the application by arbitrators of the provisions of contracts and trade usages provided in Chap. 2[128] also shows that the ICC changes its policy regarding the worldwide applicability of *lex mercatoria* to all ICC arbitration cases. This means that, whereas arbitration processes (also institutional ones) may be regarded as an instrument proving the transnational character of *lex mercatoria,*[129] such reasoning does not work the other way around. Therefore, the use of *lex mercatoria* by institutional arbitrators (in any event, in the limited number of cases) cannot itself prove the transnationality of (institutional) arbitral order.

Furthermore, the issue of delocalization of both the arbitral procedure and arbitral awards is also a subject of controversy. As seen in the discussion on the bottom-up public function of arbitral institutions in the course of Chap. 2,[130] arbitral institutions address the international legal framework designed for arbitration by the New York Convention, and therefore the institutional arbitration proceedings do not exist in a vacuum. Additionally, the ICC Court's internal procedures provide for the compliance of the arbitral awards with the law of the seat of arbitration. Combined, these arguments undermine the notion of the autonomous character of institutional arbitration.

3.2.2.3 Gaillard's Third Representation of International Arbitration, the Public Function, and the Jurisdiction of Domestic Courts

Professor Gaillard looks at the concept of international arbitration through a philosophical lens and distinguishes between three different mental constructs called "*representations*".[131] Gaillard considers international arbitration in a way in which people view it, and therefore the representations are not theories of arbitration. Rather, they reflect the internalization of different concepts of international arbitration by different "observers".[132]

Gaillard identifies three representations of international arbitration. The first one (so-called "monolocal vision"[133]) addresses the work of arbitrators as an equivalent of the function of the local judge of the seat of arbitration.[134] In view of this, the law of the seat determines the validity and legality of the whole international arbitration process. The second representation points out the significance of the place or places of the enforcement of the award on the whole arbitration

[128]Sect. 2.3.2.2.2.

[129]See Gaillard 2011.

[130]Sect. 2.3.2.1.

[131]See generally Gaillard 2010b. Cf. Gaillard 2010a.

[132]The expression "observers" concerns all actors—whether private or public—involved in arbitration.

[133]Berg 2012, 68.

[134]Gaillard 2010b, 277–278.

process.[135] This is a Westphalian vision that explains the legitimacy of international arbitration through the recognition of the process by the plurality of legal orders.[136] Finally, the third representation (the transnational vision)[137] emphasizes the role of States taken collectively on the validity and legitimacy of both arbitration agreements and arbitral awards.[138] The third representation justifies the international role of arbitrators to administer justice on behalf of the international community. In this way, Gaillard distinguishes between the two further meanings of the third representation: *jusnaturalist* and positivist. The *jusnaturalist* aspect refers to the work of Opetit and David, who claimed that the validity of the arbitration process stems from the "higher values" resulting in the "nature of things or society".[139] The positivist aspect emphasized the "normative activity of States taken collectively" as the main source of validity of international arbitration.[140] What do these representations mean for the institutional arbitration then?

In the current analysis, Gaillard's third representation (in its positivist aspect) will be applied to institutional arbitration settings. This should help explain—and visualize—both the particular status and the emerging public function of institutional arbitration as assessed in the prospective liability claims and in other forms of judicial proceedings involving arbitral institutions. Again, it should be stressed here that this is not a theory of institutional arbitration. The interpretation of the institutional arbitration within the parameters of Gaillard's third representation aims at elucidating practical problems relating to the authority of public courts to determine liability claims (choice of forum), and the problems concerning the law applicable to such claims.[141]

The standpoint of the practical effects of the Gaillard's third representation on institutional arbitration concerns the validity and the legitimacy of institutional arbitration which arise out of the normative activity of the States taken collectively. Although the public authorization of some arbitral institutions to exclusively administer certain categories of disputes under national arbitration laws could fall within the Westphalian vision of international arbitration, it is argued here that the third representation is better suited to explain the public function of arbitral institutions that is also assumed on behalf of "international sovereign." Even if some competences are transferred to arbitral institutions within a particular legal order, arbitral institutions—due to their status in international arbitration—also assume their new functions on behalf of all sovereign States that

[135]Gaillard 2010b, 277–278.

[136]See generally Berg 2012.

[137]Berg 2012, 68.

[138]Ibid.

[139]Ibid.

[140]Ibid.

[141]This stays in line with Gaillard's aims concerning his concepts of representations which were to address practical controversies relating to arbitration process in the eyes of all actors involved in arbitration. Gaillard 2012.

are subject to the legal regime on international arbitration under the New York Convention. By submitting to the public regime for international arbitration, States undertook to support the institutional arbitration system (i.e. through their domestic regulations), which derives from international obligations of States imposed on them by the international public regime on arbitration. These obligations should not be interpreted strictly as obligations in the meaning of public international law, nor should they contain only the duties to recognize arbitration agreements and enforce foreign arbitral awards based on domestic frameworks for arbitration. Such obligations should reflect the general commitment of the States to facilitate the standards for international arbitration and the emerging functions of institutional arbitration also at the international level thus respecting the local developments of (institutional) arbitration from a holistic perspective.

The consequences of Gaillard's representations for the public judges should now be conceptualized. For the sake of clarity, this part of the book does not address in a comprehensive manner the choice of forum and choice of law issues referring to the institutional liability claims. Instead, it presents a theoretical framework for the discussion on the necessary legal reforms aimed at facilitating the assessment of institutional arbitral liability by domestic courts that will be proposed in Chap. 7.

Normally, the performance of arbitral institutions in accordance with their obligations is assessed by national courts of the seats of relevant institutions. It is also plausible that the court of the forum will be determined pursuant to the habitual residence of the parties to arbitration,[142] or that the choice of forum will be connected with the place where the enforcement of the institutional award was originally refused (should the judicial proceedings against institutional arbitration actors be related to the prior vacatur proceedings against the arbitral award).[143] Finally, depending on the intention of the parties to find the most suitable forum for the judicial interpretations of their claims against institutional arbitration actors, judicial proceedings against institutional arbitration actors can be initiated in the most surprising forum with little or no connection with arbitration giving rise to such proceedings.

For example, the parties may wish to manipulate the local provisions regarding jurisdiction of courts given the parochial understanding of such provisions by judges whose understanding of arbitration is minimal or whose approaches to arbitration are hostile. Judges, as a result, may sanction the parties' forum shopping. This was the case with one of the recent liability claims against the ICC that involved the proceedings against the ICC in the Slovak Republic initiated by HND Software.[144] Given such divergence, it is necessary that judges in all jurisdictions adopt a unified approach to the status and functions of institutional arbitration. Gaillard's third representation of arbitration could be a useful hint in this regard. The understanding of institutional arbitration within this representation may be significant for the determination of the law applicable to liability claims insofar as

---

[142]Cf. the majority of the US cases dealing with the institutional liability (or immunity).

[143]Cf. Rutledge 2004, 158.

[144]A brief discussion on this case was conducted by the author and General Counsel of the ICC, Mr. Emmanuel Jolivet, during a meeting at the ICC headquarters in Paris on 20 October 2015.

the assessment of contractual liability requires determination of the court's jurisdiction under the mandatory provisions of the forum. Let us analyse different consequences of all three representations for the determinations of law applicable to the liability claims through a hypothetical scenario.[145]

The hypothetical case concerns the party seeking damages against arbitral institution in the court of the seat of arbitral institution. First, under the monolocal vision, the court of the institutional seat—after accepting its territorial jurisdiction—will apply the law of the forum to the liability claim (notwithstanding the nationality of the party which filed the claim), and either grant damages to the party or reject the claim should the mandatory provisions of the law of the forum provide for the immunity of arbitral institutions.

Furthermore, the same party will seek damages in the court of its habitual residence once the court of the institutional forum refused the claim due to the institutional performance falling within the local doctrine on institutional immunity. Under both the Westphalian and transnational visions, the courts of the habitual residence of the party will make their own determinations regardless of the previous determination of the court of the institutional seat.[146] The Westphalian approach will allow the court of the forum to deliver its own decision (meaning also the re-determination of the judgement of the court of the institutional seat) pursuant to its own mandatory provisions on arbitral liability (if any).[147] The transnational vision, in turn, will allow the court of the habitual residence of the party to determine the claim pursuant to the international approach to institutional arbitral liability (once it has been developed) as a consequence of the commitment of the State where the liability claim was raised to promote the international standards for such liability.[148] These hypothetical scenarios have practical implications for both the authority of domestic courts to rule on institutional liability (potential jurisdictional objections and forum shopping) and the laws or approaches that the domestic courts will apply to the institutional liability claims.

It is suggested that the courts should perceive institutional function and institutional arbitral liability through the lens of Gaillard's third representation of international arbitration (in its positivist variant). This could diminish the inconsistency within the judicial decisions regarding jurisdiction in liability and other types of claims against arbitral institutions, as well as within the assessment of the role of arbitral institutions and the scope of prospective institutional liability. Currently, because there is no consensus regarding institutional arbitral liability amongst private or public actors, domestic judges are invited to apply the local provisions on jurisdiction as well as their parochial visions of arbitration to liability claims

[145]The analysis follows the observations of Professor Gaillard provided in his examination of the practical consequences of the representations for the practice of the public courts relating to the enforcement of foreign awards. See Berg 2012, 69–70.

[146]See Gaillard's observations in: Berg 2012, 70.

[147]Ibid.

[148]Ibid.

initiated by the parties. This further increases the forum shopping of the parties to sue arbitral institutions basically anywhere where it is possible based on any possible domestic legal provisions that can offer the parties satisfactory outcomes of such claims.

Once the common approach to institutional liability is found, domestic courts will be able to make relevant determinations on liability within the general commitment of the States to contribute to the functionality of transnational arbitral order, regardless of the parochial regulations of arbitral liability under national arbitration laws that could apply to domestic arbitral institutions but not necessarily to international institutions. This proposal should not decrease the significance of national arbitration laws. Rather, it may encourage national legislative authorities to re-examine the necessary domestic provisions on liability in accordance with the international practice of arbitral institutions, which will stay in line with the international obligations of the States regarding their recognition of the arbitration process.

3.2.3 Additional Sources of Institutional Arbitral Liability—Introduction to the Societal and Economic Dimensions of Institutional Functions

The analysis of the sources of institutional arbitral liability within the legal dimension of institutional functions showed that there are additional contexts that underlie the contractual institutional obligations let alone the legal dimension of institutional arbitration. This resulted in the assumption that institutional arbitral liability should also respond to these additional layers of institutional function. As such, they should help conceptualize and interpret the legal, contractual obligations stemming from institutional arbitration contracts by accommodating the overall standards of performance inherent in institutional arbitration practice from a holistic perspective.

This is done in particular in view of the original goals and values (or in the words of Professor Gaillard "rituals"[149]) relating to the nascent institutional arbitration regimes. As already discussed on a number of occasions in this book, the general organization of arbitration (in particular in its institutional variant) has changed drastically over the past decades, having transformed into a more formalized and law-centric process. This process has begun to respond to the progressive challenges of international and national laws related to arbitration. These challenges concern, inter alia, the privatization of domestic justice systems that entails the emerging public function of institutional arbitration. At the same time, however, the core business goals of institutional arbitration must not be consigned to

[149] Gaillard 2015, 3.

oblivion. It appears that arbitral institutions are particularly well positioned to take up the challenge of maintaining those original aims and values of business communities. Without these communities, institutional arbitration would have never gained its popularity since, at the moment of its emergence, it would have simply ceased to exist before it was popularized if not for the business parties.

It is said that early arbitral institutions were created to protect the business community by offering a satisfactory level of "social harmony" and communitarian justice to their early users.[150] The access to the initial systems of business justice was thus ensured by the responsibility of institutional members and institutional arbitrators, which in turn entailed the trust of arbitration users in the communitarian, societal values expressed by the early institutional regimes. The responsibility of early institutional arbitration actors originated in both the socio-economic dynamics within that arbitration community and the internal mechanisms of compliance and accountability developed by early arbitral institutions.

Against this background, the following presentation will refer to both the societal and economic dimensions of institutional function. The part on the societal dimension will analyse how the institutional "transition into legality"[151] affected the traditional societal, communitarian values of institutional regimes. The discussion of the economic dimension will deal with the continuation of the private, commercial tradition of institutional arbitration by the modern arbitration centres and also sketch the changing interplay between institutional arbitration regimes and the international economic order.

It should be emphasized that neither the societal nor the economic dimensions of the functions of arbitral institutions constitute a direct source of institutional arbitral liability understood in a legal sense. As such it is proposed not to regard these dimensions as any potential sources of in tort, extracontractual liability. Rather, they should be seen as the interpretative context for the legal, contractual obligations and the contractual civil liability of arbitral institutions. In this vein, the following analysis will also investigate the interplay between the proposed civil liability of arbitral institutions to be based on contract (therefore understood as a legal tool) on the societal and economic contexts of the contractual bonds governing institutional arbitration actors. Although the legal norms and obligations cannot directly *express* the societal and economic values of the institutional regimes, it will be argued that the legal instruments—such as institutional arbitral liability—are able to *secure* such values, especially given the increased legalization of modern institutional arbitration regimes. In other words, it will be assumed below that civil liability of arbitral institutions can accommodate the recently contested legitimacy of institutional arbitration by traditional commercial arbitration

[150] See generally Auerbach 1984.

[151] Auerbach 1984, 17.

users, while at the same time responding to the necessary calls for the increased democratic legitimacy of institutional arbitration given its emerging public function.

3.3 The Societal Dimension

The discussion on the societal dimension of institutional arbitration is organized in two parts that follow the distinction between internal and external legitimacy of institutional arbitration regimes. The term "internal legitimacy" involves the relationship between the arbitration users, arbitral institutions (together with institutional arbitrators), and the arbitration community connected with the particular arbitral institution as well as the international arbitration community taken as a whole, in view of the changing perception within such communities as to the societal role of arbitration as a dispute resolution mechanism. In turn, the expression "external legitimacy" concerns the ongoing interaction between institutional arbitration regimes and the *law*, be it at national, international and a-national (transnational) levels. Such distinction aims at pointing out the consequences of the two legitimacy pressures (internal versus external) for the evolution of the accountability mechanisms developed within the early institutional regimes. In line with this, it also links the discussion on the accountability of institutional regimes with institutional liability.

3.3.1 The Internal Legitimacy

Arbitral institutions that continue to operate today appeared on the commercial arbitration scene at the end of the 19th century. The initial goal underpinning the emergence of institutional arbitration was to systemize the spontaneous trade practices related to the settlement of differences between merchants outside courts of law and pursuant to trade usages governing the then economic exchange. Together with the growth of cross-border commerce and the changes in the organization of the modern state, the complexity of dispute resolution naturally increased. Merchants started to cast about for a more formalized and permanent forum that could determine their commercial disputes still pursuant to the original goals concerning private justice, fairness and equity. In this view, the activity of arbitration centres originated in the medieval tradition of merchant law and in the spontaneous arbitration practice, and was a natural continuation of the private merchants' courts such as the Courts of Pie Powder in England.[152]

[152]The Courts of Pie Powder in England were medieval spontaneous courts which operated during fairs or as bodies attached to the market in order to provide the traders with the expeditious and *ad hoc* resolution of their disputes.

In light of this, arbitral institutions engaged in trade practices within different commercial markets, which in most cases involved strong institutional cooperation with the local business communities. Given that, the discussion on the internal institutional legitimacy will concern the informal dynamics of cooperation and compliance developed within the hierarchy of early arbitral institutions vis-à-vis arbitrators and the then arbitration users.

3.3.1.1 Components of the Early Internal Legitimacy

In order to analyse the informal relationship between the early trade and business markets and the initial status and functions of arbitral institutions exercised within these markets, the following presentation will focus on the historical emergence of the studied arbitral institutions, that is the LCIA, the AAA, the ICC with its Court of Arbitration, and the SCC Institute. This presentation will be preceded with the brief analysis of the discussion on the dynamics of the business communities of the time when the said arbitral institutions began their arbitration activities.

To begin with, Anglo-American commercial activity in the 19th century quickly came to require institutional structures to secure the self-governance practices of merchants. In 1883, the Court of Common Council of the City of London delegated to a specialized committee drawing up the suggestions for the development of a tribunal to deal with "domestic and trans-national commercial disputes arising within the ambit of the City".[153] The committee's plan of 1884 was subsequently adopted in 1891 upon the creation of the City of London Chamber of Arbitration.[154] The formal inauguration of the Chamber, dated 23 November 1892, turned into a prominent event attended by, among others, the then President of the Board of Trade.[155] The original principles underlying the operation of the tribunal, which was supervised by the committee comprising the members of the London Chamber and the City Corporation, reflected the concerns of the commercial community such as "celerity", costs of private disputes, and the facilitation of self-regulation and self-governance.[156] According to Sir Manson, the newly established institution was to respond to these objectives, which had been already stressed in "the old Court of Pied Poudre, in the alderman arbitrators of the fifteenth century, in the committees of the Stock Exchange, Corn Exchange, Coal Exchange".[157] The internal legitimacy of the Chamber was therefore predetermined by the cooperative behaviour of medieval merchants, based on the internal standards of

[153] LCIA—The London Court of International Arbitration—History of the LCIA. Based on the Report from the Law Quarterly Review, 1893. http://www.lcia.org/LCIA/history.aspx. Accessed 25 April 2016.

[154] Ibid.

[155] Ibid.

[156] Manson 1893, 86.

[157] Ibid.

performance of the commercial actors in the trade market. To this extent, such legitimacy was purely "animated by a natural sense of justice" of the society of commercial men.[158]

As regards the origins of American arbitral institutions (in particular the AAA), it was again a remarkable social consensus existent among various interest groups that contributed to the creation of institutional arbitration in the US. The model of American arbitration appears unique to the extent that it encompassed the active role of lawyers (next to the representatives of business community and academics), which shaped the general American arbitration picture for the following decades and also determined the way in which American arbitral institutions such as the AAA operate today.[159] The prominent role of the American lawyer and social activist, Frances Kellor deserves particular attention here.

Kellor promoted arbitration as an "ideal" dispute resolution tool that could ensure international peace and security.[160] To this extent, discussion on the roots of American institutional arbitration, notwithstanding its inspiration by the spontaneous medieval law merchant, has always involved broader goals that American arbitration was to address including the necessary formal, legal structures of arbitration at both national and international levels. Moreover, such discussion should not omit the active engagement of both legal actors and representatives of academia in the developments of arbitration in the US. This cooperative engagement, however, does not diminish the spirit and ideals of the early American arbitral institutions created within the realm of the spontaneous commercial arbitration practice.

Three factors must be taken into account while analysing the pre-establishment of the AAA. The first regards the creation of the first permanent arbitration tribunal known as "The New York Chamber of Commerce's Arbitration Committee" (the Chamber) in the late nineteenth century. In fact, the Chamber, was not very popular among the potential arbitration users, even though it sought the State's support for the arbitral decisions that originally lacked legal sanctions.[161] The reason for the

---

[158]Ibid.

[159]See generally Kellor 1999.

[160]For more information, see Partridge 2012.

[161]See Benson 1995, 488; Jones 1956, 216. Jones observes that: "[...] Around the period of the Civil War, it [the Chamber] began to seek support from the state in its efforts to provide adjudicatory facilities for its members outside the court system. Thus, its charter was amended in 1861 to provide specifically for an arbitration committee (the act was on an amendment to the act removing doubts concerning the powers of the Chamber of Commerce of the State of New York), and to provide that awards of the committee might be entered as judgments of courts of records if the parties so agreed. In general its effect was to bring these proceedings under the New York arbitration statutes. In 1874 this act was amended to provide for the appointment by the governor of an arbitrator of the chamber of commerce of the State of New York to be paid by the Chamber. Members could be summoned to arbitrate mercantile disputes arising within the port of New York, although they could escape jurisdiction of the arbitrator by filling an objection with him. In 1875 the act was again amended so that the members of the Chamber could be required by, requisition' to bring their cases before this court whose judge was to be paid by the state. The judge was actually appointed by the governor and appropriation made for his salary for two years. He continued to sit without pay for many years thereafter."

limited popularity of the Chamber's arbitration activity is therefore explained by means of the extensively formalized organization of the Chamber (that contributed to the merchants' incapacity of choosing their own private arbitrator) vis-à-vis the natural aim of the commercial groups to rely on the internal, moral sanctions linked to the operation of spontaneous commercial arbitration rather than on the sanctions imposed on them by law.[162] This was particularly emphasized by Benson who argued that the Chamber—at a certain moment of its operation—started to lose its prestige "to other arbitration arrangements" which lacked any legal support thus providing the parties with more flexible procedural framework for arbitration.[163] Given that, it can be seen that the early development of institutional arbitration in America was also inspired by the internal dynamics of legitimacy, which involved mainly the informal compliance by private arbitration users with the core values of private disputing notwithstanding the existence of other arbitration regimes that were equipped, already by that time, with legal sanctions.

The second remarkable fact within the pre-history of the AAA involves the emergence of the Arbitration Society of America (the Society) in 1922. Reading from the archival New York Times' issue of 24 May 1922, the Society, which gathered together the representatives of business and legal fields,[164] was perceived as a "people's tribunal" with an aim to determine all disputes, except from criminal and divorce matters.[165] Even though the initial core goals of the Society were directed toward commercial issues, the Society's activity quickly transformed to encourage more specialized industrial companies to implement arbitration provisions into their internal regulations. For instance, in 1923 an arbitration system was established in the Film Boards of Trade for the motion picture industry.[166] The function of the Society assumed within the period of its operation (between 1922 and 1926) was twofold. Firstly, the Society institutionalized and acknowledged the tradition of commercial arbitration between businessmen.[167] Secondly, the activity of the Society, including successful marketing strategies such as the publication of the first "Arbitration News", infiltrated a wider group of Americans by popularizing among them the very idea of arbitration as an alternative method of dispute

[162]Benson 1995, 480–481.

[163]Ibid.

[164]The first officers elected by the board after the enactment of the by-laws and the constitution of the organization were the following: Emerson Mcmillin (the President) banker and the President of the American Light and Traction Company, Samuel Maccune Lindsay (vice-President), President of the American Academy of Political and Social Science, and Moses H. Grosmann, head of the law firm of Grosmann & Vorhaus; Executive Secretary J.W. Slaght, Secretary, J. Noble Braden. *New York Times* (Archival Issue) of 24 May 1922. "People's Tribunal Will Open Today—Arbitration Society to Hear First Controversy Outside of the Courts. Hall of Justice Offered. Arnold Rothstein Proposes to Donate Quarters–Emerson McMillin Is President."

[165]Ibid.

[166]Kellor 1999, 13.

[167]Such particular dynamics involved, inter alia, the interdependency of the American commercial society on the operation of the legal actors in the US.

resolution.[168] This resulted in better public awareness of arbitration, and encouraged citizens to set up new organizations dealing with arbitration.

The last important fact about the history of the AAA concerns the emergence of the Arbitration Foundation in 1925. The Foundation came into being by dint of the financial contribution of the Chamber of Commerce of the State of New York.[169] The Foundation, which was headed by the then Chairman of the Arbitration Committee of the New York's Chamber of Commerce, Charles L. Bernheimer, had different goals and financing methods as compared to the aims and financial model of the Society of America.[170] While the Society was driven by more mainstream objectives to contribute to the increasing recognition of arbitration among its potential users, the Arbitration Foundation mainly aimed at conducting research on arbitration and providing facilities for the development of arbitration law and practice. Hence, the operation of the American Foundation was more egalitarian, yet it "lacked the democratic approach to people"[171] which, in the case of the Society, was the major factor underpinning its success. Moreover, the American Foundation's financial sources were based on both unstable substantial contributions and the insurance funds payable to the Foundation upon the death of Bernheimer, its first Chairman. In turn, the Society sought more democratic and transparent financial methods based on the contributions of its members (be it individuals or organizations).[172] These basic differences between the Arbitration Foundation and the Society led to a conflict of interest between the two institutions, which was eventually prevented by setting up two committees (one within each organization) to establish the common strategy for times of crisis. The members of the committees, who were mainly the representatives of business,[173] organized themselves in one body that recommended to the institutions the merger of their efforts and the creation of a joint association. Once more, the consensus between business leaders (a recurrent feature of the arbitration world) prevailed, and gave rise to the establishment of the AAA in 1926.

The AAA was the first national arbitral institution in the US and was founded under federal law—the Membership Corporation Law.[174] Moreover, the organization of the AAA was subject to the AAA's Charter and Bylaws (stemming from the modes of organization of both the Society of Arbitration and the Arbitration Foundation[175]), which authorized the institution to supervise and facilitate the

[168] Kellor 1999, 12.

[169] Kellor 1999, 15.

[170] Ibid.

[171] Ibid.

[172] Ibid.

[173] Ibid.

[174] Ibid.

[175] As can be read from the historical reports on the emergence of the AAA, the AAA inherited from the Society the Panel of Arbitrators, memberships and a Commercial Arbitration Tribunal, while from the Foundation it gained *conservative business leadership* which has stimulated the future direction and growth of the AAA in the US and abroad. Kellor 1999, 17.

work of the AAA's Tribunals under the AAA's Rules of Procedure.[176] The main objective of the AAA's Tribunals and the AAA itself was to meet the conventional demands of business people such as the desire for the exclusive, self-governed, inexpensive and neutral dispute resolution system. The AAA's contribution involved the adaptation of the original assumptions of commercial arbitration to the wider category of social agreements, and the promotion of the spirit of arbitration through new ideas and organizational competences.

Two observations come to mind regarding the origins of American institutional arbitration. On the one hand, all early arbitral institutions in the US described above were built around the commercial needs and values, and therefore they aimed at creating an exclusive system of private disputing which could preserve the goals of their existent and potential users. On the other hand, however, the origins of institutional arbitration in the US reflect the particular tensions between arbitration and law and between private and public goals of the arbitration process in North America. In other words, although arbitration as a process, as well as arbitral institutions as organizations sponsoring arbitration in the US, were perceived as *private* creatures, institutional arbitration, already from the moment of its emergence, exercised public functions that mostly related to the types of disputes it could then accommodate.

This brings us back to the already discussed active participation of the AAA in governmental programmes and to the authority of the AAA regarding the stipulations of "regulatory" arbitrations often falling beyond individual disputes such as consumer, employment or labour arbitrations. This should not be seen as diminishing the role of the early commercial goals of the AAA. Rather, this particular dual function of arbitral institutions in the US, although controversial, brought together two conflicting legitimacy pressures on the American arbitral institutions from the beginning of their operation by confronting the private, purely commercial goals of business people with public aims associated with the arbitration process. This could be classified as private enforcement of legal rights by means of arbitration. This is the reason why the debate on the fairness of American arbitration has for decades been connected with the activity of arbitral institutions in the US.

There are a number of questions that emerge in the context of this observation. To what extent are private arbitral institutions such as the AAA able to provide unbiased arbitration service to all contemporary arbitration users (including non-commercial parties or commercial parties participating in arbitrations outside their commercial relationships) within the American arbitration market? Is the AAA legitimate to set up the standards for class arbitrations, in which the consumers arbitrate their disputes (in most cases without a prior, *express* consent to arbitrate) with sophisticated corporations? One could claim that the AAA's arbitration regime is not suitable for such actions as it is inherently tied with the powerful business communities or industry-based organizations, which questions the

[176] First Code of Arbitration Practice and Procedure of the AAA was published in 1931. Events in the History of the AAA and Alternative Dispute Resolution, http://www.lectlaw.com/files/adr07.htm. Accessed 25 April 2016.

fairness of "regulatory" arbitration *per se*. Again, when addressing these questions one should take into consideration the specific private-public interplay developed at the creation of the institutional arbitration in the US that cannot be easily translated into the European arbitration settings.

Regarding the origins of the ICC arbitration in Paris, the sophisticated character of the ICC as an institution with international ambitious needs to be addressed from the outset. As rightly noticed by Dominic Kelly, the ICC, which was created in 1919:

> [...] emerged from a network of nationally and locally based chambers of commerce in the XIX century and it assumed the form, after the World War I, of a federation of national chambers with a Paris-based secretariat and an extensive web of specialist committees covering most of the key areas of concern to business community.[177]

The ICC, from the moment of its foundation, has expressed the voice of international business community, while at the same time it has been engaged, at least indirectly, in the public law activity at the international level, which involved the reparations in the interwar period.[178] Moreover, as stated in the Constitution of the ICC, its initial goals comprised: (a) the promotion of international trade, services and investment; (b) the rise of the market economy system; and (c) the fostering of the economic growth of developed and developing countries.[179] This demonstrates that the emergence of the ICC—and therefore also the boundaries of its internal legitimacy—concerned the international community of traders, not only the local business markets that co-operated with the London-based and American arbitral institutions. In this sense, the ICC Court of Arbitration should also be treated as one of the several tools that the ICC developed to achieve its more general functions to be exercised with a view of the goals of the international business community of the time. We will now analyse the various steps taken by the ICC to establish its Court of Arbitration, together with the early mechanisms of cooperation and compliance that ensured the early efficiency of the ICC arbitration regime.

The first step involved the establishment by the ICC Council of the International Committee on Arbitration (the International Committee) headed by M. Lyon-Caen, the Permanent Secretary of the *Acadèmie des Sciences morales et politiques* and the former Dean of the *Facultè de Droit de Paris*. The Committee drafted the Plan of Conciliation and Arbitration between traders of different countries (the Plan).[180] The Plan, after its approval by the London Congress of the Chamber on 1 July 1921[181] was subsequently readopted as the Regulations on Conciliation and Arbitration, which came into force after their confirmation by the

---

[177]Kelly 2001, 3.

[178]Ibid.

[179]Preamble to the ICC Constitution: ICC Constitution. http://www.iccwbo.org/constitution/. Accessed 25 April 2016.

[180]The Introductory Note to the first set of the ICC Court of Arbitration Rules of Procedure of 1922.

[181]Ibid., 15.

ICC's Council on 10 July 1922.[182] As stated in the Introductory Note to the Regulations:

> They [these Regulations] are the result of a great deal of very difficult work, owing to the wide differences regarding commercial arbitration which exist between the various legislations of the countries affiliated to the Chamber. The members of the Committee were obliged to make strenuous efforts in order to conciliate as far as possible the various national points of view.[183]

The Regulations renamed the International Committee on Arbitration "the Court of Arbitration of the International Chamber of Commerce". The main activity of the new institution was to address the administration of controversies between commercial actors worldwide:

> […] the International Chamber of Commerce believes that it should encourage the use of conciliation and arbitration. It therefore puts itself freely at the disposal of financiers, manufacturers and business men of all countries, for the purpose of facilitating, in so far as may be possible, through the exercise of its good offices, the settlement of disputes in this manner.[184]

The International Committee of the ICC (the predecessor of the ICC Court) was a joint initiative of the representatives of different professions and nations (involving France, the UK, Belgium, Italy, Netherlands and the US[185]) which, as founding fathers of the ICC arbitration system, worked on a common arbitration strategy that could address the joint business concerns at the international level. The early structure of the International Committee of the ICC also informed the further work of the ICC National Committees. Each National Committee had to appoint an Administrative Commissioner who was to reside in Paris in order to maintain the international cooperation from the ICC headquarters.[186] Moreover, in the countries in which the ICC did not operate through its National Committees, the ICC's network was attained through the affiliation with various "Organization Members" such as "chambers of commerce and similar organizations, the associations of bankers, manufacturers or traders".[187] In this sense, the ICC Court of Arbitration, from the very outset, was an "umbrella institution" which covered the interrelated interests and ambitions of the evolving, modern international community of merchants.

The contents of the very first set of rules of the ICC Court of Arbitration of 1922 show how the early mechanisms of the ICC arbitration addressed the traditional commercial concerns of the early ICC arbitration users. The latter can be

[182]Ibid.

[183]Ibid.

[184]Ibid.

[185]Ibid.

[186]Excerpt from the Constitution of the ICC (Article VII, para 2): "There shall be an Administrative Commission of which the Secretary General of the International Headquarters shall be Chairman […]. "ICC Rules of Arbitration and Conciliation of 1927". Document obtained during an internship at the ICC.

[187]Constitution of the ICC. see: Article I para 3.

classified into the following categories: (1) the expeditiousness of the arbitration proceedings; (2) cost-effectiveness of early ICC arbitrations; and (3) the exclusiveness of the early ICC arbitration regime understood as both the expertise determinations of disputes ensured by the ICC Court and the ICC internal enforcement mechanisms. The dynamics of compliance were secured by moral sanctions, the ICC Court's disciplinary measures, and by the honourable character of the ICC arbitrators.

Regarding the expeditious character of the early ICC arbitration proceedings, the ICC Court of Arbitration was authorized to control members of the ICC's organs to deal promptly with the case management and to monitor the ICC arbitrators to render the arbitral awards without unnecessary delay.[188] As regards the exclusive responsibilities of the ICC Court of Arbitration, it was not only the procedural orders concerning time limits that stood for the expedited character of the ICC Court's activity.[189] What requires particular attention is the fact that, for the sake of the speed, the Court provided a special method of communications between the parties and the Court itself which involved the delegation by the Court of the organization or individual from the country to which one party to arbitration proceedings belonged to serve as a recipient of the documents which were to be delivered to a party.[190]

As far as the cost-effective character of the early ICC arbitrations is concerned, the ICC arbitrators performed their work on a pro-bono basis. Pursuant to Article XIX(XL) (e) of the Rules of 1922:

> The arbitrators shall be entitled to re-imbursement of all expenses but, shall render their service gratuitously; except that in so far as it is recognized that in such countries and industries fees are customarily provided for arbitrators, the Court of Arbitration may in its discretion, allow arbitrators fees to be included in the costs of arbitration at rates customary to such countries or industries.[191]

In a sense, such philosophy underlying the early remuneration of the ICC arbitrators reflected the organization of the medieval fair courts that provided for the judgements of notable men serving the commercial community as a whole rather than their own interests. Therefore, under the above-mentioned Article XIX(XL) (e) of the ICC Rules of 1922 arbitrators, in principle, worked with no remuneration and the stipulation of the arbitrators' fees was only possible to the extent that

---

[188] As regards the work of arbitrators, pursuant to Article XV of the ICC Court of Arbitration Rules of Procedure of 1922:

"(a) The Court of Arbitration shall fix the period within which the Arbitrators shall render their award and wherever possible, the date from which that period commences. Normally the period should not exceed 60 days.

(b) The Court of Arbitration reserve the right to extend this period of delay as circumstances may warrant."

[189] Here, see i.e. Article XI and Article XXXI(a) and (b) of the ICC Court of Arbitration Rules of Procedure of 1922.

[190] Article XI(XXXI) of the ICC Court of Arbitration Rules of Procedure of 1922.

[191] ICC Court of Arbitration Rules of Procedure of 1922, 37.

the commercial custom developed within a geographical location where an arbitrator was based required so. In these cases, the fixing of the arbitrator's fees also lied within the discretion of the ICC Court that was authorized to make relevant stipulations on a case-by-case basis. The gratuitous nature of the arbitrator's mandate also meant that the reputation of the early ICC arbitrators stemmed from their status in the relevant business community, and that the arbitrator's tasks were more a matter of honour than a legal profession, which is in opposition to what arbitration users are witnessing today. Already, the subsequent version of the ICC Rules of Arbitration and Conciliation of 1927 amended this provision upon the recommendation made by several National Committees which referred to the need of the then arbitration practice "to secure the services of expert arbitrators" by granting them payment "when allowed".[192] It is, however, significant that the ICC Court was continuously trying to allocate very little payments to its arbitrators and it was not until after the Second World War that the scale of the ICC costs was introduced and made public as an annex to the ICC Rules.[193]

As for the exclusiveness of the early ICC arbitration system, both the exclusive function of the ICC Court vis-à-vis arbitrators and the internal mechanisms for the parties' compliance with the ICC arbitration awards should now be addressed. The early ICC arbitration model did not provide for the nomination of the ICC arbitrators by the parties, who had to rely on the ICC Court in this regard.[194] The Court—by its National Committees—maintained a list of "technically qualified arbitrators",[195] which served as a pool of recognized practitioners suitable for the resolution of the disputes within the ICC arbitration regime. In the case of early ICC arbitration, it was therefore the ICC Court who represented the parties vis-à-vis arbitrators, which maintained the commercial tradition of the medieval courts.[196] This early goal of the ICC Court to respect the particularities of the transactions between merchants in a highly professional and expert manner was further reflected in the work of the National Committees that assisted the ICC Court in the appointment of arbitrators from the local pools of prominent experts in a number of different business fields. The second version of the ICC Rules of Conciliation and Arbitration of 1927 enabled the parties to chose their own arbitrators in cases in which a dispute was to be resolved by three arbitrators, provided

[192]See: Arbitration. Revision of the Rules of Conciliation and Arbitration. Report of the Secretary General Comparing the Old and New Rules and Describing the Principal Amendments, The ICC's Brochure No. 50, Fourth Congress Stockholm, June 27-July 2, 1927, Appendix 5 to the Rules of Procedure of 1927. The new Article 22 (para 2) of the Rules of 1927 stated: "The costs of the arbitration shall include fees of arbitrators, when such are allowed, fees of experts if any, and all expenses of the arbitration."

[193]ICC Publication No. 412, 1984, 394.

[194]Article XII(XXXII) of the ICC Court of Arbitration Rules of Procedure of 1922.

[195]Article VI(XXVI) of the ICC Court of Arbitration Rules of Procedure of 1922.

[196]Yet again, the early ICC mechanism of the appointment of arbitrators by the ICC Court might have been inspired by the operation of the medieval fair courts, where the parties referred their already arisen disputes to the jurors which were not individually chosen by disputants but served during the medieval fairs on a permanent basis.

that the umpire was still to be appointed by the ICC Court after the relevant nomination made by the ICC National Committee.[197]

While focusing on the second aspect of the exclusiveness of early ICC arbitration, that is the parties' compliance with the ICC arbitral awards, it is sufficient to start with the particular distinction made in the first set of the ICC Rules of Procedure of 1922 between conciliation and arbitration *with* and *without* legal sanctions. Undoubtedly, such distinction responded to the level of recognition by various national laws of the arbitration process *per se*. For the parties from the jurisdictions that did not, at the time, secure arbitration instruments with legal sanctions, the ICC designed informal mechanisms of compliance. Broadly speaking, the early ICC arbitration system encompassed significant internal dynamics of cooperation that are not visible within the current ICC institutional framework. These dynamics involved the following overlapping features: (a) honourable character of the early ICC arbitration; (b) the disciplinary measures of the ICC Court; and (c) the so-called moral sanctions for the parties' non-compliance with the ICC awards.

Medieval commercial arbitration and early institutional arbitration were generally founded upon an informal honour code that stipulated the performance of the duties of both arbitrators and the parties. Similar observation can be made of the early ICC arbitration, which not only gathered noble and specialized arbitrators, but also relied upon the honourable behaviour of the parties to the ICC arbitration when the compliance with the ICC awards came into question. Article XX (XLI) of the Rules of Procedure of 1922 stated that: "the parties were in honour bound to carry out the award of arbitrators". This provision, which was to guarantee the outcome of ICC arbitration, imposed moral obligations on the ICC parties that they will perform their duties in an honourable manner, which also stemmed from the societal values shared by the business communities within which the recalcitrant parties operated. These societal values were embedded in the relationship between single parties to arbitration and the local or international community of traders and concerned mostly the trust underlying the pending and future business transactions, the perception of natural justice among traders, and honourable or even to say egalitarian character of the early ICC arbitration. Notably, the ICC Court was authorized to invoke moral sanctions against the parties who did not comply with the ICC awards, by informing a relevant organization or chamber of commerce to which such parties were members to apply suitable disciplinary measures against them.[198] Moreover, the ICC Court had a supplementary right to request that the

---

[197] Article II(2) of the Rules of Conciliation and Arbitration of 1927.

[198] Article XX(XLI) of the ICC Court of Arbitration Rules of Procedure of 1922 provided that: "(b) In the event that the party against whom the award has been rendered fails to comply with the terms thereof within a period of 30 days, counting from the date fixed for pronouncement of the award, the party in whose favour the award has been rendered may notify the National Committee or the Organization Member of the International Chamber of Commerce, as the case may be, that the award has not been carried out by the opposite party; thereupon the Court shall notify the Chamber of Commerce or other business organization to which such defaulting member may belong and shall request such Chamber of Commerce or business organization to apply such disciplinary measures as it may think fit and proper under the circumstances, in respect of the defaulting member".

name of the defaulting party be published in the official publications of both the ICC and its National Committees together with the text of the arbitration award that had not been executed.[199] In a nutshell, the early mechanism of enforcement of the ICC arbitral awards was underpinned by disciplinary measures and moral sanctions which could be imposed on defaulting parties in cases of their misconduct or breaches of their commitments to be bound with the ICC internal sanctions made at the moment of the submitting of a dispute to the ICC arbitration. The role of the ICC Court of Arbitration vis-à-vis other ICC arbitration actors in imposing such measures was remarkable to the extent that the Court was regarded as an ultimate moral authority thanks to which the ICC arbitration process had a chance to function without any State-sanctioned support.

Although the early exclusiveness of the ICC arbitration regime was solely rooted in the moral standards of cooperative behaviour, with time such standards were ousted by the changing dynamics of compliance visible among arbitration actors, which began to be progressively ensured by the coercive legal sanctions guaranteeing the enforcement of the ICC arbitral awards. Already the ICC Rules of Conciliation and Arbitration of 1927 modified the wording of the previous ICC provision on the enforcement of arbitral awards. The new version of the former Article XX of the 1922 ICC Rules (Article 25 of the 1927 ICC Rules) no longer referred to honour while determining the parties' compliance with arbitration awards.[200]

Moreover, the moral authority of the disciplinary measures against recalcitrant parties weakened, as the ICC Court withdrew from the idea of the publication of the names of such parties in the internal ICC periodicals. Yet, the ICC Court preserved the right to contact a relevant National Committee or business organization of the recalcitrant party to implement suitable measures in cases of the parties' non-compliance with the arbitral awards.

The logic behind such changes to the Rules revised by the ICC's Arbitration Committee was the following. The Committee admitted that the publication of "black lists" was without practical value, as the award not complied with could be annulled by public courts, in which case the party whose name had been published could subsequently sue the ICC Court of Arbitration for libel, which could result in damages against the ICC for injury sustained.[201] This is a very intriguing fact, as it shows the interplay between the informal mechanisms of compliance of the early ICC regime, the legalization of arbitration, and the ICC's fear of liability for the inaccurate assessment of the parties' non-compliance with the awards.

Hence, informal moral sanctions started to lose significance and legitimacy in front of the legal sanctions developed for the legal enforcement of the arbitral awards. In addition, the emergence of the dual (moral and legal) standards for the

[199] Section c) of Article XX(XLI) of the ICC Court of Arbitration Rules of Procedure of 1922.

[200] As follows from the said provision: "the parties shall be bound to comply with the award".

[201] See: the Comments on the Measures against recalcitrant parties: Arbitration. Revision of the Rules of Conciliation and Arbitration. Report of the Secretary General Comparing the Old and New Rules and Describing the Principal Amendments, The ICC's Brochure No. 50, Fourth Congress Stockholm, June 27-July 2, 1927, Appendix 5 to the Rules of Procedure of 1927, 6.

determination of the parties' compliance with the awards continuously discouraged the ICC Court from relying on its early informal compliance methods. This was not necessarily because they were inefficient but because they could result in monetary damages against the ICC. These observations will be of particular importance for the discussion on the external legitimacy of institutional arbitral regimes.

It is time now to change spot on the arbitration map and move to Stockholm, where the Arbitration Institute of the SCC was established in 1917. Although the information on the history of the SCC arbitration is rather scarce, some important characteristics need to be addressed here with regard to the internal legitimacy of the Stockholm-based institution itself. It seems that the SCC arbitration, from the outset, served mostly domestic businessmen that sponsored their own system of dispute resolution. To this extent, the local businessmen created "from the bottom" an arbitration institution that was to address their original goals. The SCC was sponsored by the prominent Swedish Wallenberg family.[202] The Wallenbergs not only provided ample financial support but also the moral authority, which together bolstered the early reputation of the SCC.[203] It is said that the SCC inherited the traditional Swedish neutrality that was reflected in high standards of performance of the early SCC arbitration actors.[204]

The fact that the SCC arbitration maintained its remarkable domestic position vis-à-vis locally organized commercial actors for the following years proves, on the one hand, the very strong internal legitimacy of the institution itself and, on the other hand, the exclusive nature of Swedish economic cooperation. To this extent, the SCC Institute was for long operating as a local institution that was responding to traditional values and demands of the Swedish business community. All this may serve as evidence of the existence of strong internal mechanisms of compliance within the SCC business community that reflected moral authority of the SCC, underpinned by the good arbitration practice and neutrality of the early SCC arbitration regime.

The historical analysis above provided a general understanding of the components of the early internal legitimacy of institutional regimes. Notwithstanding the particularity of every institutional arbitration regime, it should be clear that internal legitimacy of the early institutional regimes supported the validity and normativity of arbitral institutions vis-à-vis the business communities affiliated with the early institutions (be it at local or international levels or both).

Each of the arbitral institutions analysed above originated from the traditional concept of private justice, as practiced in medieval times, which involved the desire of businessmen to have their own system of dispute resolution that would be cheap, expeditious, fair and neutral. The institutional arbitration in its early outlook addressed all these demands and—due to the informal tools stipulating the internal cooperation of institutional arbitration regimes—it created a self-sufficient system based on moral sanctions and reputational dynamics as the major means of private enforcement.

---

[202]Dezalay and Garth 1998, 188.

[203]Ibid.

[204]Ibid.

Against this background, the following components of the early internal legitimacy of arbitral institutions should be distinguished: (1) *participation*, (2) *performance*, and (3) *moral sanctions*. *Participation* is understood as the informal affiliation of an individual party to both a society of traders and to the relevant institutional arbitration regime. *Performance* is regarded as the preservation by the institutional arbitration actors of internal standards of behaviour and traditions of traders based on informal norms prescribed to the members of the relevant society of traders. As such, it can be related to the voluntariness of the early institutional arbitration actors. Finally, *moral sanctions* can be seen as the internal regimentation of the informal norms through the moral authority of a particular institutional arbitral regime stemming from the common values shared by the participants in both the relevant society of traders and the institutional arbitration regime.

3.3.1.2 The Early Sources of Private Accountability

Given the significance of the informal mechanism of compliance within the early institutional arbitration regimes, it will be argued in this section that the mechanisms of compliance presented above can also be perceived as the early accountability mechanisms of these institutional regimes. The concept of accountability is presented here in a private sense, meaning the private standards of institutional arbitration actors adopted to increase the efficiency of private arbitration settings and also their enforcement within institutional arbitration regimes.

Private accountability refers to the early standards of performance of institutional arbitration actors in the conduct of arbitrations (i.e. vis-à-vis one another within a particular institutional regime), enforced or executed in the shadow of the private powers corresponding to the authority of the early arbitral institutions as well as of the institutional arbitrators. The following classification of the early sources of private accountability is built around the early ICC informal mechanisms of cooperation presented above together with the soft-law instruments—such as the Code of Ethics for Arbitrators of 1946 (the Code)—employed by the AAA.[205] The aim of the section below is to conceptualize private accountability in

[205]The Code was adopted by the American Law Institute and issued as a guide for members of the Panel of the AAA in 1946. As reads from the Introduction to the Code (Some Basic Principles of Right Conduct): […] The following description of the powers, duties and responsibilities of the Arbitrator and the standards pertaining to his office are observed in all Tribunals organized; maintained and administered by the American Arbitration Association; and in all of the instances where the Association acts in an advisory or consulting capacity; and in the Inter-American, Canadian-American and International Tribunals in which this Association participates; and in the manner specified in the Rules of these respective organizations". This suggests that the Code was designed as an exclusive instrument of the AAA arbitration and to this extent it should correspond with the internal dynamics of legitimacy of this institution. AAA Code of Ethics for Arbitrators 1946 in: Kellor 1999, 235–244.

the context of early self-governance and the responsibility of private institutional arbitration systems taken as a whole that can produce common outcomes for all early arbitral institutions under analysis here. In sum, the private accountability of the ICC arbitration regime stemmed from the following devices:

- Honourable character of the ICC's arbitrators' mandate strengthened by the gratuitous work of the ICC arbitrators;
- Nomination of the ICC arbitrators by the ICC Court of Arbitration;
- Lists of technically qualified arbitrators;
- Self-enforcement of the ICC arbitral awards under the reputational and moral sanctions such as:
  - Disciplinary measures against the parties failing to comply with the awards exercised by the ICC National Committees and business organizations at the request of the ICC Court;
  - Publications of the black lists of the recalcitrant parties in the official booklets of the ICC and its National Committees together with the texts of the arbitral awards which were not executed.[206]

These devices developed within the ICC arbitration regime regulated the accountability of the early ICC arbitration actors, which originated in the honourable character of the early ICC arbitration. What is particularly striking is that the early ICC accountability system referred to all actors participating in the proceedings from the parties themselves through the ICC Court and the ICC arbitrators. Accordingly, it constituted the closed, self-sufficient scheme of internal standards of behaviour, the breach of which had immediate consequences for all these actors.

Hence, the accountability of the parties towards the ICC Court, National Committees, and the institutional arbitrators was rooted in the consequences of their non-compliance with the ICC awards that could involve moral sanctions imposed on the parties by the local business communities including through the ICC Court. The ICC arbitrators were accountable towards the ICC Court and the parties themselves under reputational concerns. In the case of misconduct of an arbitrator, he/she could be deleted from the ICC Court's list of arbitrators, therefore being excluded from the participation in the ICC arbitration system for many following years.

What is important is that these potential exclusions were more severe to arbitrators themselves than is the case today since they affected the reputation of individual arbitrators understood through the lens of their nobility rather than financial incentives. Therefore, the accountability of early ICC arbitrators—secured by means of the internal mechanisms of the ICC Court—was also a guarantor of the noble nature of the whole ICC arbitration, and the individual perception of arbitrators by the parties and institutional bodies was different than it is today. Arbitrators

[206] Cf. Sect. 3.3.1 and the practice of commercial arbitration in England, which also involved the publications of disobeying parties in the commercial black-lists.

were perceived through the institutional function they were to fulfil rather than through their individual roles in the ICC arbitration system. Finally, the accountability of the ICC Court itself originated in the position of the ICC Court vis-à-vis the then local and international business communities. This position translates into the understanding of the ICC Court more like a guardian of the system of private justice, and the ultimate moral authority that established the rules of private ordering together with the enforcement mechanisms and sanctions. This guaranteed both the strong moral capital underpinning the whole system of ICC arbitration and its effectiveness and efficiency vis-à-vis its users.

The early status of the ICC Court was therefore far from qualifying as the pure provision of services to individual parties and the ICC arbitration community, a discussion that is particularly valid today with regard to the contemporary nature of the arbitration activity of both the ICC Court and other arbitral institutions. The noble nature of the early ICC accountability mechanisms—so self-contained and interdependent on the performance of all institutional arbitration actors—also minimized the possible frivolous challenges to the authority of both the ICC Court and arbitrators. This is because the parties themselves felt a strong responsibility to perform to the best of their ability in the course of arbitrations simply because of their perception of being part of the noble system of private justice understood as a privilege rather than in the meaning of the service.

In support of these arguments, we will look at the selected provisions of one of the first regulations of the professional conduct of arbitrators and the ethics in arbitration, namely at the AAA's Code of Ethics for Arbitrators of 1946. The specific provisions of this Code clearly demonstrate the honorary nature of the arbitrator's mandate in the early AAA's arbitrations:

> HONORARY POSITION OF THE ARBITRATOR
> Carrying on an ancient tradition, the office of the Arbitrator is honorary […] Men have not hitherto been attracted to it either as a profession or as a source of regular income. The office as a rule seeks the man.
> […]
> When the office is honorary, the Arbitrator is freed from all financial interest in the matter before him. He has none of the obligations or handicaps that attach to an advocate or employee paid by a party naming him; he is free to proceed expeditiously, for he is not interested in prolonging hearings; and he is holly independent, being beholden to no man for an office that he did not seek.
>
> PERSONAL RESPONSIBILITY
> Arbitration is, in itself, nothing but a word, save as the Arbitrator clothes it with dignity, integrity, and authority. The office is precisely what the Arbitrator makes it. If he is conscientious, deliberate, fair, painstaking in arriving at the truth, and bases his decision upon the facts, arbitration becomes an instrument for advancing the justice. If he follows the principles laid down in the Rules and those indispensable attributes of law of evidence which makes the parties feel that they have had a fair trial, arbitration becomes a safeguard of society, for it eliminates disputes and promotes amity and contributes to the well-being of those it serves and those it influences. The responsibility of the Arbitrator is, therefore, to act to the best of his ability and with a conscientious regard for his office.[207]

[207] AAA Code of Ethics for Arbitrators 1946 in Kellor 1999, 235–244.

It is evident that the AAA's Code expressly stressed the *sui generis* nature of the arbitrators' accountability and responsibility, which was not interlinked with the arbitrators' remuneration by an institution but solely with the unique features of institutional arbitrator's mandate involving *dignity, integrity* and *authority.* Moreover, the proper conduct of the AAA's arbitrator (meaning the compliance with the authority of the institutional rules) stemmed from the responsibility of an arbitrator to act *to the best of his ability* under his good reputation.

The enforcement of the AAA's Code was also guaranteed by means of moral sanctions. Under the Code, the AAA appointed arbitrators to its own Panel of Arbitrators, which served as an incentive for arbitrators to conduct the proceedings in a responsible manner, and pursuant to the AAA's internal policy, having in mind the noble nature of the arbitrator's appointments by an institution.[208] This mechanism of accountability also aimed at fostering both the integrity of the AAA arbitration and private confidence in the AAA arbitration regime.[209]

As shown, the private accountability of institutional regimes was interrelated with the status of arbitral institutions in the arbitration processes understood through the lens of both categories identified in the preceding discussion, namely: *the institutional ability to act* and *the institutional authority to re-determine the authority* of institutional arbitrators. This is in line with the legal analysis of the sources of institutional arbitral liability provided in the first part of this chapter. This preliminary observation also implies that there is an interplay between early institutional accountability originating in the institutional status and the necessity for the adoption of institutional arbitral liability that emerges from the increased "legalization" of the modern institutional relationships, which took the form of, inter alia, intensification of contracts within institutional regimes. This brings about the question of the increasing external legitimacy of institutional arbitral regimes, especially in the context of the progressive public recognition of institutional arbitration. It will be argued that the increasing external legitimacy diminished the significance of the early private accountability of institutional regimes discussed above, which altogether has consequences for the discussion on contemporary institutional liability.

---

[208]See the wording of the last provision of the AAA Code of Ethics for Arbitrators 1946: "UPHOLDING THE HONOR OF THE PANEL:

Members of Panels are the judicial branch of the organization that appoints them. Their appointment implies recognition of their high degree of qualification, by non-partisan, non-profit-making, wholly non-partisan, scientific and educational organizations that are devoted to the maintenance of high standards of arbitration.

The behaviour of a Panel member when he acts as an Arbitrator either adds prestige or dignity to, and confidence in, the Panel as a whole, or reflects adversely upon it. Therefore, in justice to the parties who choose him by preference from the Panel and his colleagues on the Panel and to the organization that appointed him to the Panel, his faithful observance of this Code is of high importance.

This concern for integrity of the Panel should extend to the making of statements that would seem to identify them with the Panel as a whole, but which do not necessarily reflect its views. It is, therefore, advisable in making public statement for the Arbitrator to avoid implying that such statement are associated with his Panel membership". In Kellor 1999, 243–244.

[209]Ibid.

3.3.2 The External Legitimacy

The external legitimacy of institutional arbitration is a broader concept than internal legitimacy in that it deals with the external, public life of institutional arbitration. In this vein, the analysis of the external legitimacy provided below deals with the interaction of institutional arbitration regimes with law and the public, State powers.

That is with the legal instruments that have been developed in the course of the twentieth century to increase the public recognition of (institutional) arbitration, as well as its formal, legal framework. As such, the following discussion aims to address the question of how the legal framework for arbitration informed the activity of institutional arbitration (and vice versa). The goal of this analysis is therefore twofold. First, it is to understand how arbitral institutions (and the business community or communities affiliated with them) influenced their relationship with the public authorities at the national and international levels. Second, it is to determine the implications of the changing dialogue between institutional arbitration and law on the internal standards of performance of institutional arbitration actors presented above as private mechanisms of accountability.

3.3.2.1 Institutional Approach to the Law: The "Young System"

Many historical studies of arbitration present arbitration as a regime that emerged in opposition to the national judiciary, and that expressed the natural "aversion of business men to courts of law".[210] The historical note on the establishment of the LCIA (the then City of London Chamber of Arbitration) emphasized that:

> This Chamber is to have all virtues which the law lacks. It is to be expeditious where the law is slow, cheap where the law is costly, simple where the law is technical, a peacemaker instead of a stirrer-up of strife.[211]

The debate on the "legalization" of institutional arbitration, and also on the status of arbitral institutions vis-à-vis the law began with the speech of Owen Young, the then Chairman of the Board of the Radio Corporation of America and the Chairman of the Commercial Arbitration Committee of the US Chamber of Commerce, which was delivered in 1921, shortly after the foundation of the ICC.[212] There, Young presented his ideas related to the operation of the ICC within the broader regime of arbitration "outside the law" (Young's postulates are called hereinafter the "Young system"):

---

[210]See Macassey 1938, 179.

[211]Manson 1893; LCIA—The London Court of International Arbitration—History of the LCIA. Based on the Report from the Law Quarterly Review; 1893. http://www.lcia.org/LCIA/history.aspx. Accessed 25 April 2016.

[212]Excerpts of the speech in: Paulsson 2011, 21–22.

> The field of international commercial arbitration is one in which the International Chamber of Commerce may well play an important and influential part. Its success, however, will depend on the recognition by the Chamber and by its individual members of the inherent difficulties and complexities of the situation. The most important of these difficulties lies in the fact that, generally speaking, the business men of continental Europe rely upon a legal sanction for the carrying out of arbitral decisions, whereas in the United States, as well as in England and the South American countries, a moral sanction has been shown to be, certainly for the present, more effective than a legal sanction. To ensure the cooperation of these countries, therefore, some system of arbitration outside the law must be provided.[213]
>
> [...]
>
> International Chamber of Commerce itself, and by member National Committees, with all the force that business men of a country can bring to bear upon a recalcitrant neighbour. Before agreeing to conduct an arbitration outside the law, even when both parties should join in a request, the International Chamber should be convinced that the business men of both countries concerned are sufficiently well organized and that the business organizations are willing to exert moral pressure, if need be, in favor of carrying out the arbitration decision outside the law, and are sufficiently influential to make such pressure effective.[214]

These excerpts from Young's speech raise fundamental and still pertinent questions of the (inter)relation between the status of commercial arbitration and arbitral institutions vis-à-vis *the law*. Did the Young system mean the illegality of institutional arbitration? Is arbitration an equivalent of, or an alternative to, state justice? Or, is it a *sui generis* concept that escapes traditional legal thinking and definition? Before addressing these questions, it is crucial to first present the academic debate concerning the Young system, featuring the enduring yet intriguing disagreement among academics and practitioners as to the role that the law should play in arbitration, and *vice versa*.

The academic debate on the Young system mostly involved the arguments presented by Heinrich Kronstein in his article on "Business Arbitration—Instrument of Private Government" of 1944[215] and Jan Paulsson's criticism of Kronstein's postulates set out in 2008 in an article entitled "International Arbitration is not Arbitration" and further developed in Paulsson's recent publication "The Idea of Arbitration".[216] The basis of a disagreement between these authors lurked in the opposing interpretation of Young's concept of arbitration "outside the law". Kronstein claimed that such a concept meant nothing more than "lawlessness" because arbitration as a process was "divorced from an ideal of social justice and have been designed to avoid the law".[217]

Paulsson, over sixty years later, disagreed with Kronstein for the following reasons. First, according to Paulsson, Kronstein misinterpreted Young's desire to

---

[213] Ibid.

[214] Paulsson 2011, 21–22.

[215] Kronstein 1944.

[216] Paulsson 2008; Paulsson 2013, 125–129.

[217] Kronstein 1944, 67.

create an arbitration system operating within the law. Confusion stemmed from the misinterpretation of Young's expression: "outside the law" by Kronstein. Paulsson claimed that Young just used an unclear expression, which in fact was supposed to reflect the reliance of the ICC arbitration on moral sanctions rather than outlawing the arbitration process.[218] Moreover, Paulsson argued that Kronstein's argumentation referring to the arbitration of competition law, that was seen by the latter as a threat to public policy alongside other forms of arbitration of publicly oriented disputes, should not be applicable to all types of arbitration, just as "the sea elephant does not have to mean an elephant".[219] Finally, Paulsson criticized Kronstein's idea of restoring arbitration within the law by ensuring national and international control over the private process (preferably through both the restitution of the revocability of arbitration agreements and the adoption of the mechanism of appeal against arbitral awards in the courts of law) in order to ensure that "organized arbitration does not violate the principles of law, social justice and national interest".[220]

It needs to be further explained that Kronstein presented a vision of organized arbitration (hence, of the Young system) in the context of Kelsen's theory of law under which the people who exercise certain power (be it legislative or political) seem to be justified to create their own "kind of law" which is, nevertheless, "colorless, without aim [...] and constitutes just a ready tool of those who would make use of it".[221] Broadly speaking, Kronstein's arguments amounted to a severe criticism of the Young system simply because he perceived an arbitration process *per se* as a private ordering tool securing abusive practices of trade associations and other industry-based organizations that had invented it.

Taking into account the preceding discussion on the components of the early internal legitimacy of institutional regimes, Kronstein's arguments can be seen as slightly exaggerated. Kronstein's fear of arbitration as a form of private government operating against *law,* and as distorting the basic social and moral principles of justice for the sake of the shady commercial private goals, seems ungrounded.

As already stated, the early ICC arbitration not only provided for the procedure to be applied to arbitration "with legal sanctions" but it also used the instrument of moral sanctions exclusively as a safeguard of the core values of business communities with which the ICC was affiliated. As rightly noted by Young, the effectiveness of the moral sanctions was still dependent upon the geographical location of businessmen and, to this extent, it was also determined by the legal ramification for arbitration process, which had been established in the territory where specific arbitration users operated. As such, the original idea of institutional arbitration had a strong communitarian capital and the potential abuses of the process within the Kronstein's criticism had little to do with the potential "unlawful" aspect of arbitration. Rather, and as will be seen from the following discussion, the damages to

[218] Paulsson 2011, 22.

[219] Paulsson 2008.

[220] Kronstein 1944, 68.

[221] Ibid.

the original idea of institutional arbitration occurring in parallel to the process of legalization of arbitration were mainly the function of the impact of formalization of arbitration on the early moral capital of institutional arbitration. The disagreement concerning the "ideal" role of the law in the arbitration process is nothing striking. Academics and practitioners have long been trying to work out a satisfactory compromise concerning this issue.[222]

Against the background of this discussion, the following part of this chapter will address the interplay between the law and institutional arbitral regimes. This will involve the analysis of the legislative efforts resulting in the legalization of arbitration at both national and international levels in parallel to the transformations of the institutional regimes. The question, which the following analysis will address, is twofold. Firstly, it concerns the problem whether the progressive proliferation of institutional arbitration was in fact dependent upon the public, legal recognition of the commercial arbitration process as such. Secondly, the question involves the effects of such private-public interplay on the early private accountability mechanisms developed by the early institutional arbitration regimes.

3.3.2.2 The Support of National Public Authorities for Arbitral Institutions

In England, the first official act of the Parliament referring to arbitration between traders was passed in 1698 under the name "An Act for determining differences by arbitration".[223] The Act of 1698 acknowledged the finality and enforceability of the awards secured by the possible sanction of imprisonment. However, each party could revoke the submission to arbitration at any time up to the making of the award.[224] Such revocation was said by the traders to be immoral and forced the legal authorities in England to pass another act (Act 3 & 4 Will, c.42) in 1833, which, in order to make the authority of arbitrators irrevocable, required the incorporation to the contracts of the express provision that the submission to arbitration should be made a rule of the Court.[225] Even though such an amendment was perceived as a move forward, it did not establish a general rule of irrevocability of arbitration agreements until the enactment of the Common Law Procedure Act of 1854.[226] The Common Law Procedure Act provided that any submission to arbitration could constitute a rule of the Court unless the parties had expressly excluded such possibility in their contract.[227] Notwithstanding the above efforts, it

[222]Jan Paulsson noted that "other Kronsteins appear in every generation" with the most recent criticism of arbitration process presented by Drahozal 2007. See: Paulsson 2013, 127.

[223](9 & 10 Will. 3, c. 15) referred to in: Macassey 1938. For a discussion on the history of arbitration and dispute resolution in England see Roebuck 2006; Martin and Hunter 1985.

[224]Macassey 1938, 188.

[225]Ibid.

[226]Ibid.

[227]Ibid.

was only the Arbitration Act of 1889 that guaranteed both the absolute irrevocability of arbitration agreements and the true enforceability of arbitral awards.

As noted, the City of London Chamber of Commerce was established in 1891, shortly after the adoption of the modern legal instrument dealing with commercial arbitration in England. It is, however, arguable whether the emergence of the first English arbitral institution was absolutely determined by the legal framework for arbitration developed by the public authorities. The Committee of the Court of Common Council of the City of London started its work on the modern arbitration procedure in 1883 when commercial arbitration was already operative.[228] Undoubtedly, the external support to arbitration coming from national authorities was an additional factor that enabled the early operation of the London arbitral institution. However, it needs to be underlined that this factor was not an exclusive impulse for the organization of institutional arbitration in England. The London institution based its legitimacy mainly on the commercial goals and values of the spontaneous arbitration practice that had been prospering in an efficient fashion already for some time.

Notably, however, it was not until the early 1980s when commercial arbitration in London began to gain its international impetus by means of the adoption of the Arbitration Act of 1979 (Chapter 42). Prior to this date, arbitration practice in the UK (and especially in London) remained predominantly local, witnessing the increasing caseload of the ICC in the field of international disputes with a tacit jealousy.[229] The increased recognition of London as a seat of international arbitration was strongly interlinked with the changes adopted under the already-mentioned Arbitration Act of 1979 that decreased the judicial intervention in arbitration process, mostly by means of abolishing the so-called "special-case procedure" as well as the authority of the High Court to set aside arbitral awards potentially issued in error of facts and/or law.[230]

The private-public dialogue in the field of arbitration in the US took a slightly different direction. Unquestionably, the enactment of the first Arbitration Act in the State of New York in 1920 was an influential event for the popularization of the arbitration process in the US. This is because it offered to the parties legal support in affirming the irrevocability of arbitration agreements and the enforceability of the awards. This external encouragement for the evolution of the American arbitration also mobilized the first arbitration organization in the US—the American Society—to promote the concept of private disputing among citizens and, subsequently, it gave rise to the establishment of the AAA. The creation of the AAA followed the adoption of the US Federal Arbitration Act in 1925.

The emergence of institutional arbitration in the US reflects the particular nature of the interaction between the arbitration society and the US authorities. The AAA, from the outset, needed an external support, hence, the legal background for

---

[228] Macassey 1938, 199.

[229] Dezalay and Garth 1998, 129–150.

[230] Sanders 1999, 29–30.

the arbitration process, that could confirm the idea of arbitration in a legal sense in the variety of disputes. The AAA also needed public support for another reason. As already mentioned, the AAA became quickly involved in industry-based dispute resolution. The early AAA's arbitration of industry-based disputes can be perceived, at least in an academic sense, as falling beyond truly private, individual disputes. This is so because of its reliance on arbitration clauses often contained in adhesion contracts imposed within different industries, and, hence, having broader, societal implications for the members of those industries. This is why the early industry-based arbitration offered by the AAA, although bearing the characteristics of the private process, simultaneously required increasing public recognition to accommodate the public relevance of the disputes it entailed. In this sense, already the provisions of the AAA's Code of Ethics for Arbitrators of 1946 also spoke about the "public responsibility" of the AAA arbitrators:

> PUBLIC RESPONSIBILITY
> Such are the social implications of modern business society and so integrated are modern human relations that the old concept that a dispute is personal matter between the parties and of no public concern no longer holds. A labor dispute is of public concern. When a trade association sets up an arbitration system for its members, it admits that disputes are the concern of the whole industrial group. When a chamber of commerce establishes facilities, it is with a view to serving not only the members but the community. When national and international organizations set up systems they have in mind something more than settling disputes between individuals, namely contributing to international peace and security. Private though the proceedings may be, friends, relatives, associates, organizations and communities may come to know of it. The office is, therefore, not only one of personal responsibility but of public importance.[231]

In conclusion, the private-public dialogue between institutional arbitration and the law in the US called for the external legitimacy of institutional regimes, in addition to pure internal legitimacy. This may also explain the subsequent development in American case law of the doctrine of legal immunity for all arbitration actors irrespective of the contractual dimension of institutional arbitral liability invoked by the parties to institutional contracts in the liability claims.

Turning to France, it was already noted that the emergence of the ICC in 1917 reflected the very ambitious goals of the French business association, which were never limited to purely private initiatives. Moreover, the ICC arbitration system responded to the demands of the *internationally organized* business community. In line with this, any discussion of the external legitimacy of the ICC arbitration regime involves the ICC's prospective search for the public recognition of the process at the international level. Also, the domestic approach favouring arbitration in France largely supported the international activity of the ICC.

The French approach to arbitration reflects the traditional French hospitality toward this process. Already the French Revolution declared arbitration as *droit naturel* and the French Constitution of 1793 proclaimed the constitutional right of

[231]AAA Code of Ethics for Arbitrators 1946 in Kellor 1999, 238. See the discussion on the private responsibility of the early AAA's arbitrators in Sect. 3.3.1.2.

citizens to rely on arbitration.[232] The French Code of Civil Procedure of 1804 (the French Code) also contained relevant provisions relating to arbitration.[233] This means that the concept of arbitration was not unfamiliar to French law and that arbitration rights fell within the group of the fundamental constitutional principles. This tradition continues to date and defends the original choice of the ICC to maintain the headquarters of its Court of Arbitration in Paris.

The SCC arbitration regime is a perfect example of the influence of public support on the growth of the arbitration caseload of the SCC, and thus on strengthening the internal legitimacy of the SCC regime. The SCC was established upon the financial contribution of local businessmen. It operated for long merely as a domestic institution supported by the moral authority of the Swedish arbitration community. In addition to this moral support, the Swedish courts, similar to the French legislature, were ensuring the functionality of the SCC arbitration by providing it with the relevant legal support.[234] The international function of the SCC arbitration was eventually acknowledged in the 1970s together with the conclusion of the cooperative agreement called "The Optional Clause for Use in Contracts in the U.S.A.—U.S.S.R. Trade 1977," which provided for the East/West arbitration exclusively in the Stockholm venue. This political confirmation of the SCC contributed to the proliferation of SCC cases and the international recognition of the Stockholm arbitration. It should be therefore evident that the SCC needed external public support more than any other institution studied here.

3.3.2.3 The International Support of Institutional Arbitration

This section concerns the private-public interactions in the field of arbitration at the international level. The following part will present only selectively the development of the international legal framework for arbitration. However, the relevant role of the arbitral institutions (mainly the ICC) in influencing the international legal instruments of arbitration will be emphasized.

Three events define private-public dialogue at the international level: (1) the adoption by the League of Nations of the Geneva Protocol on Arbitration Clauses in 1923 (the Geneva Protocol);[235] (2) the enactment of the Geneva Convention on the Execution of Foreign Arbitral Awards in 1927 (the Geneva Convention);[236] and (3) the adoption by the United Nations (UN) of the New York Convention on 10 June 1958.[237]

---

[232]The French Constitution in Article 83 stated that: "the right of the citizens finally to resolve their disputes through arbitrators of their choice cannot in any respect be decreased by law." The quotation in: Rutledge 2013, 2.

[233]von Mehren 1986, 1046.

[234]Dezalay and Garth 1998, 116–118.

[235]The Geneva Protocol on Arbitration Clauses, 1923.

[236]The Geneva Convention on the Execution of Foreign Arbitral Awards, 1927.

[237]The United Nations Conference on International Commercial Arbitration Convention on the Recognition and Enforcement of Foreign Arbitral Awards—The New York Convention, 1958.

The essential assumptions of these instruments were the following. Firstly, the Geneva Protocol obliged each of the Contracting States to recognize the validity of arbitration agreements in which the parties had decided to refer to arbitration for their existing or *future* disputes. Secondly, the Geneva Convention provided that the Contracting States would enforce arbitral awards rendered in conformity with the provisions of the Geneva Protocol. Finally, the New York Convention ensured the almost unfettered enforcement of foreign arbitral awards by eliminating the previous requirement of double exequatur of the awards.[238]

Regarding the institutional involvement in the shaping of the international legal framework for arbitration, two events need to be addressed with regard to arbitral institutions. The first one refers to the fact that the enactment of both the Geneva Protocol and the Geneva Convention was stimulated by a domestic growth of arbitration that occurred mainly due to the emergence of arbitration centres within the respective jurisdictions. The second fact involves the activity of the ICC in developing the international legal framework for arbitration.

The ICC participated in the adoption of the New York Convention of 1958. It included the preparation and the subsequent submission to the UN of a draft version of the New York Convention by the ICC. The New York Convention, which was a milestone in the development of the modern commercial arbitration practice, not only inspired the further development of arbitration laws on the national level, but also gave rise to the proliferation of arbitral institutions internationally (including, notably, in those countries where economic exchange fell within the realm of state powers).

Reflecting these changes, the names of the two prominent arbitral institutions (the London Court of Arbitration and the ICC Court of Arbitration) were modified into the London Court of *International* Arbitration[239] and the ICC *International* Court of Arbitration, respectively, marking a new age of international arbitration. Moreover, in 1996 the AAA launched its international division, called the International Centre for Dispute Resolution. To this extent, the ICC's diplomatic efforts contributed to the functionality of the modern arbitration processes and to the proliferation of institutional arbitration within the international legal framework for arbitration, in parallel to domestic legislative attempts to increase the functionality of international arbitration as described in the section above.

---

[238]See Course on Dispute Settlement: International Commercial Arbitration. Module 5.1: International Commercial Arbitration, UNCTAD 2005.

[239]LCIA—The London Court of International Arbitration—History of the LCIA. Based on the Report from the Law Quarterly Review; 1893. http://www.lcia.org/LCIA/history.aspx. Accessed 25 April 2016.

3.3.3 On How the Need for Public Accountability Diminished Private Accountability: Consequences of the Weakening of the Societal Dimension

As shown in the analysis of the internal and external legitimacy of institutional arbitration in Sects. 3.3.1 and 3.3.2 above, institutional arbitration emerged "from the bottom", namely from the spontaneous commercial practices in various geographical locations. It was originally built off of the internal mechanisms of compliance developed within the early institutional regimes. Such mechanisms of compliance, related to the goals of the early members of different business communities such as the celerity and cost-effectiveness of institutional arbitration, also underpinned the private accountability of the early institutional regimes. The discussion on internal legitimacy in Sect. 3.3.1 demonstrated that the early goals of the parties to institutional arbitration proceedings were largely cohesive. This was the function of relative exclusiveness of the early arbitral institutions. Those cohesive, unified goals and values of early businessmen relying on institutional arbitration also correspond to the "solidaristic" model of arbitration as defined by Professor Gaillard, who depicted early arbitrations as accommodating "a strong common set of shared values" of its early players.[240]

Indeed, as shown in the case of the early rules of the ICC Court of 1922, arbitral institutions benefited from the notable features of early institutional regimes that were contingent upon a high level of respect from both early arbitration users and arbitrators participating in institutional arbitration proceedings of the times. These proceedings were rooted in the shared values and goals of early institutional arbitration regimes. The ICC Court, for example, played a significant role in ensuring the continuation of such values that were seen in the private accountability of early ICC arbitrations. The ICC Court was authorized, by means of its first set of rules, to discipline recalcitrant parties to comply with arbitral awards based on moral sanctions and reputational dynamics. It also exercised its authority vis-à-vis arbitrators who could be expelled from the ICC arbitration regime in cases of their misapplication of the ICC procedure. These powers of the ICC Court were much more significant than the contemporary authority of arbitral institutions in front of arbitrators. This was mostly so because of the severity of the potential exclusions of the then arbitrators from arbitration proceedings. This amounted to the possible loss of the "symbolic capital" of arbitrators not only in front of the parties to the individual disputes and the ICC Court but also vis-à-vis the whole community of traders in the sectors in which the then arbitrators operated.

As such, the misconduct of arbitrators in the early institutional arbitrations could amount to the end of their professional career even beyond a single arbitration. This was plausible because arbitrators served in this capacity only occasionally, whereas on a daily basis they were ordinary traders with a high level of expertise in the commercial fields relevant for the resolution of particular disputes.

[240] Gaillard 2015, 13–17.

By way of illustration, it is assumed that the first case submitted to the ICC arbitration in 1923 was decided by the Dutch arbitrator who was a gum merchant appointed to determine the differences in the quality between two deliveries of gum by a British and French company.[241] All this was possible due to the strong communitarian values shared by all actors participating in early institutional arbitration regimes.

With time, the inevitable interaction of arbitration with *the law* increased the legal recognition of arbitration processes, which contributed to the development of the so-called external legitimacy of arbitral institutions meaning the public, legal recognition underpinning their activity. The increasing external legitimacy, developed with the active participation of arbitral institutions, contributed to the growing public confidence in institutional arbitration processes. The growth of the external legitimacy of arbitral institutions took place at both the national and international levels in response to the room created for arbitral institutions by the changing political, legal, and economic contexts underlying the evolution of commercial arbitration.

Here, arbitral institutions, whether directly or indirectly, contributed to the creation of the formal frameworks facilitating the development of arbitration and hence also to their increasing caseloads concerning both the number of domestic and international disputes capable of being resolved by means of arbitration. This was due to the growing formal, public recognition of arbitration and the liberalization of the concept of arbitrability being the function of this increasing public recognition of the arbitration process. As presented in the sections above, the AAA, by means of its close collaboration with the US government, popularized arbitration in a number of industry-based disputes. The ICC contributed to the development of the New York Convention, as well as to the popularization of the idea of international arbitration vis-à-vis the French legislators and also their counterparts in the UK serving as an example of a pivotal success in the field of administration of international arbitrations. This indirectly affected the liberalization of arbitration in the UK that, in turn, contributed to the flourishing of the international arbitration administered by the LCIA. Finally, the SCC made use of the political support of arbitration in Scandinavia by responding to the increasing need for a neutral administrator of arbitrations arising out of or in connection with the Optional Clause. All these institutional efforts undertaken in the shadow of the external legitimacy of institutional arbitration had positive and negative implications for the internal functioning of the arbitral institutions, and hence for the societal values securing the private accountability of the early institutional arbitration actors.

Regarding the positive developments related to the gradual "transition into legality" of arbitral institutions, without a doubt arbitral institutions witnessed an

[241] Arbitration Report no. 3, July 1924, 8 as presented in the Historic Changes in ICC arbitration; a document prepared by the ICC Documentation and Research Centre, ICC International Court of Arbitration, June 2008.

increasing number of disputes being submitted to arbitration.[242] This was the result of the changing nationality of the parties to arbitration due to the internationalization of institutional arbitration practices[243] and the liberalization of the concept of arbitrability that can be recently seen in the emergence of the public function of arbitral institutions.[244] In fact, it can be argued that the legalization of the arbitration processes had more consequences for institutional arbitration than for *ad hoc* proceedings. The public function of institutional arbitration has recently proven that the proceedings under the auspices of arbitral institutions started to resemble court proceedings, which was indirectly supported by the public recognition of the institutional regimes. This was not the case in *ad hoc* arbitrations that, although benefiting from the public, legal framework of arbitration, were and still are conducted in accordance with the core principle of party autonomy that has not been significantly altered as in the case of increasingly formalized institutional arbitration proceedings. Moreover, the emergence of the public function of institutional arbitration, sanctioning the exclusive resolution of certain categories of publicly oriented disputes by means of institutional arbitration, contributed to the novel institutional powers that even *ad hoc* arbitrators do not assume.

Also the parties to the proceedings and institutional arbitrators, at least in the early period of the legalization of institutional arbitration, have gained more powers. As relates to the parties to arbitration, the legal changes affecting the evolution of the arbitration rules invited the growing involvement of the parties in tailoring the arbitration process according to their altering demands, which was called by the ICC the "increasing personalisation of cases" in the period between 1983 and 1992.[245] In the same vein, more and more sophisticated parties began to enter into more complex arbitration clauses by means of which they started to substitute the original exclusive functions of arbitral institutions (such as the ICC Court) to predetermine the basic aspects of their arbitrations such as the place of arbitration or the selection and the number of arbitrators.[246] As far as the changing functions of arbitrators are concerned, all adjudicatory functions have been shifted from the

[242]For example, as reads from the statistical data provided by the ICC, "After more than 30 years' existence, the Court of Arbitration had dealt with fewer than 1,000 cases (most resolved by conciliation); since then there has been a great of flood of cases that the number comes close to 300 cases per year, so much than in the near future the total of number of cases will have reached 5,000." See ICC Publication No. 412 1984, 397. And further: "between 1983 and 1992 the ICC caseload for the past ten years represents approximately forty per cent of all requests filed with the ICC International Court of Arbitration since its founding in 1923." See Ten Years of ICC Arbitration (1983-1992): A Statistical Survey. 1993 ICC International Court of Arbitration Bulletin 4, no. 1: 3–7.

[243]See Sect. 2.3.1.1 of Chap. 2.

[244]See Section 2.3.2.2.1.

[245]Ten Years of ICC Arbitration (1983-1992): A Statistical Survey. 1993 ICC International Court of Arbitration Bulletin 4, no. 1: 3–7.

[246]Ibid.

respective institutional organs on arbitrators, who also began to receive more substantial remuneration for their particular services.[247]

All these developments appear positive at first glance to the extent that they seem to have responded well to the altering goals of institutional arbitration actors. This, however, should not be misleading because the positive aspects of the evolution of internal institutional rules need to be analysed also in the context of the most recent changes in institutional arbitration. The trend toward „personalisation" of arbitration cases contributed to the recent enormous professionalization of institutional arbitration practices, which in fact diminishes the significance of all internal reforms undertaken by institutions in the course of the past decades. Why is this so? In answering this question two issues will be confronted: the effects of the recent professionalization of institutional arbitration, on one side, and the decline in the societal dimension of institutional arbitration, on the other side.

The professionalization of arbitral institutions led to the progressive adversarial, if not to say, litigious nature of the behaviour of the parties not only during arbitration proceedings but also outside them. This is exemplified by the increasing dissatisfaction of the parties with the functions and the attitudes of arbitral institutions toward the parties and with the growing costs of institutional arbitration proceedings (also due to the increasing fees of institutional arbitrators for their highly professional services). Moreover, the values of the changing parties to institutional arbitration regimes were "polarized"[248] vis-à-vis the early uniform goals associated with institutional rules due to the legalization of institutional arbitration that allowed for the developments of the new yet shared functions of arbitral institutions such as the public function.

Although the traditional, commercial parties to institutional arbitrations still opt for the cost-effectiveness and expeditiousness of their arbitrations, the new parties to new types of disputes administered by institutions within their public function (such as State actors) started to express purely legal concerns relating to their arbitration proceedings. Such concerns include increased independence and impartiality of arbitrators that led toward the resolution of such new disputes by a three-member arbitral tribunals or the longer periods for nominating the arbitrators by State parties, just to mention the few.[249] These, often conflicting, goals of the contemporary parties to institutional arbitration result in the decline in authority of arbitral institutions vis-à-vis the parties (and also institutional arbitrators) in the meaning of the societal dimension of arbitral institutions.

Notably, the early institutional authority corresponding to the strong societal, symbolic capital of early arbitral institutions have now been minimized, particularly in view of the already noted relinquishing of certain original powers in early

[247]As stated in ICC Publication No. 412 1984, 397: "Since 1955 the division of tasks between the arbitrators and the Court is more in keeping with the nature of their respective functions—essentially administrative for the Court and judicial for the arbitrators."

[248]Gaillard 2015, 13–17.

[249]ICC Arbitration Commission Report 2015. Arbitration Involving States and State Entities under the ICC Rules of Arbitration.

arbitration process by arbitral institutions to the parties and arbitrators themselves. It seems that arbitral institutions, in order to regain their original symbolic capital, derive their contemporary statuses mostly from the legal, contractual authority of their rules that have expressed private regulatory powers of arbitral institutions in the increasingly complex legal relationships between contemporary institutional actors. This is partly the function of the progressing formalization and judicialization of arbitration proceedings that, paradoxically, occurred indirectly because of the increasing sophistication of the commercial parties. This also attracted the new types of legally complex disputes of increasing public relevance to institutional arbitration, which only further supported the growing legal authority of arbitral institutions.

Concurrently with this growing formalization of institutional arbitration in the shadow of the legal changes to arbitration, there have been increasing calls for more public accountability of institutional regimes. They concern the responsibility of arbitral institutions in front of both the public authorities that have supported institutional arbitration and the new parties from outside the original business communities surrounding early arbitral institutions. For example, the AAA began to publish all documents produced in class arbitrations in order to make their processes more transparent. Regrettably, the need for public accountability of the transformed institutional regimes has not been addressed in a uniform manner by arbitral institutions. This means that the efforts to increase the transparency of institutional arbitration practices remain largely fragmented and undertaken on selective bases, responding more to accidental public concerns regarding the functionality of institutional arbitration in disputes involving new users than to the calls for transparency voiced by the traditional, commercial parties.

Consequently, public accountability diminished the early private accountability of institutional regimes by indirectly leading to the atrophy of all informal mechanisms of compliance and moral sanctions developed by the early institutions. Because arbitral institutions have failed to keep up with the demands of their traditional users, they also lost the societal capital in front of those users. This, in turn, resulted in the weakening of the standards of performance of parties and institutional arbitrators.[250] This can be seen in reference to the evolutional changes to the ICC arbitration rules.

Without a doubt, external legitimacy also contributed to the proliferation of institutional arbitration. However, it was in a way contrary to the original goals of business communities that—although opted for the increasing legal enforcement of institutional arbitration settings—still wanted their arbitration processes to be conducted in the spirit of their original commercial goals such as speed and efficiency. This resulted in a paradoxical situation in which external legitimacy ensured the emancipation of institutional arbitration from the original goals of the early institutional arbitration users. Some authors currently claim that the legitimacy of the legalized arbitration process is no longer derived from the informal features of arbitration but that it stems from the public nature of the formalized arbitration proceedings (which have begun to resemble litigation).[251]

---

[250]Compare the discussion in Section 3.3.1.2 with the arguments on the "personalisation" of ICC arbitration cases earlier on in this section.
[251]Dezalay and Garth 1996, 299.

The discussion on the interplay between the private and public mechanisms of accountability also connects with institutional arbitral liability. This is so through the assumption that the implementation of institutional liability clauses could be justified given the recent legalization of institutional functions that increasingly link the institutional authority with the legal prerogatives of arbitral institutions based on contract. This is vis-à-vis traditional and new commercial parties, and the new non-commercial parties to institutional arbitration. Moreover, the introduction of institutional liability based on negligence (rather than the strict, in tort liability) could potentially correspond to the original societal capital of arbitral institutions in front of their traditional, commercial users. Hence, the concept of liability for negligence could bear restorative functions understood within the early internal legitimacy dynamics of institutional regimes. Finally, civil liability clauses might encourage arbitral institutions to reintroduce the early informal mechanisms of compliance within the institutional regimes, once the institutions begin to fear of damages awarded against them in the courts of law, that would require the institutional restatement of its early authority deriving from its societal, symbolic capital.

3.4 The Economic Dimension

It is now necessary to refer to the economic aspect of institutional arbitration, which will be presented below from a twofold perspective. The following analysis distinguishes between the economic dimension understood from bottom-up and top-down.

On the one hand, the bottom-up analysis concerns the competing dynamics between arbitral institutions and their competitors, that is other providers of similar dispute resolution services. Consequently, it aims at analysing the institutional arbitration services within the parameters of the economic theories on the perfect and imperfect competition relating to the market's structures. This, in turn, aims at sketching the linkages between those competing dynamics and the institutional arbitral liability together with their implications on the increased competition within the market for institutional arbitration services. Hence, the bottom-up analysis deals with the traditional commercial function of institutional arbitration stimulated by the efficiency of institutional regimes in the eyes of the arbitral institutions themselves and of the traditional institutional arbitration users. To this extent, the discussion should be read in the context of the analysis of the traditional commercial function of institutional arbitration provided in Chap. 2 (Sect. 2.3.1).

On the other hand, the top-down analysis of the institutional economic functions portrays institutional activity in the context of the competing dynamics *outside* the market for institutional arbitration services to depict the role of arbitral institutions in fostering international trade as well as the possible institutional contribution to the production of public goods. The latter, top-down dimension of institutional economic functions largely amounts to the conceptualization of the economic incentives for domestic authorities such as legislators and national judges to support the regime for institutional arbitration liability pre-developed from the bottom, that is by the institutional arbitration actors.

3.4.1 Bottom-up

The competition concerning the institutional arbitration market involves the following dynamics: (a) the competition between arbitration centres (internal dynamics); (b) the dynamics of competition between institutional arbitration and *ad hoc* arbitrations (internal dynamics); (c) the competition between institutional arbitration centres (and *ad hoc* arbitrations) on the one side, and the other forms of arbitration including both "regulatory" arbitrations and various ADRs on the other side (internal dynamics); and (d) the competition between arbitration centres and public courts (internal/external dynamics). The last category is the result of the emerging public function of institutional arbitration, which, as already presented, diminished the traditional means of competition between arbitral institutions and encouraged competition between private centres with the public courts and with proliferating arbitral institutions dealing with public regulatory disputes. Now, how do these changing dynamics inform the discussion on institutional arbitral liability?

To start with, the emergence of the new dynamics of competition concerning regulatory arbitrations further divides the original aims of the business communities understood within the meaning of the internal legitimacy of the institutional regimes. This has economic implications for such commercial parties that may now consider submitting their disputes to other, competing *fora* for dispute resolution (e.g. courts, *ad hoc* arbitrations, or any other dispute resolution service providers dealing with ADR).

Moreover, the formalization of the institutional processes in the parameters of the external legitimacy of institutional regimes hinders the market-based regulation of arbitration services. Such regulation is largely stimulated by the dynamics of competition that are external to institutional arbitration services including the legal requirements for arbitration. Similar observations are valid with regard to institutional arbitral liability. The contemporary contractual liability clauses excluding the liability of arbitral institutions without negotiating the scope of institutional liability with the disputing parties (so called "contractual immunity"[252]) prevents the systems competition between the arbitration centres in the meaning of the traditional commercial function of institutional arbitration. The modern institutional regulations of liability interact mostly with the national laws on liability (if any), and to this extent, they do not respond to the traditional components of the

[252]Cf. the "contractual immunity" with the terminology used by Peter Rutledge in: Rutledge 2004.

internal legitimacy of institutional regimes. All these distort the competition within the market for institutional arbitration services, making such competition imperfect to the detriment of the users of those services, thus the parties to institutional arbitration proceedings, as well as of the arbitral institutions themselves.

One of the reasons for such imperfect competition is the incomplete information regarding the functioning of the internal bodies of arbitral institutions provided to arbitration users that also affects the quality signalling by arbitral institutions vis-à-vis the institutional arbitration users. For example, neither the repeat users nor accidental parties to institutional regimes are aware of the exact steps undertaken by arbitral institutions while selecting institutional arbitrators, in particular in the context of the suitability of those professionals to determine individual commercial disputes between the parties.[253] This has implications for the ways in which arbitral institutions could possibly signal the quality of arbitrators to the parties. Similarly, signalling behaviour is also missing regarding the existence and enforceability of the internal, institutional accountability mechanisms (if any) whose explanation to the parties could, potentially, serve as an indicator of the quality of the services provided for by the institutions. Neither the parties nor their counsel in fact realize the alternative instruments within arbitral institutions that could have similar preventive functions in relation to the misconduct of institutional arbitration actors as the civil liability might have. For example, arbitration users are not fully aware of the internal enforcement mechanisms of the codes of conduct for institutional members or arbitrators (if any) because the institutional regimes are not transparent when it comes to the explanation of such mechanisms to the parties or identifying the particular organs or institutional employees whose responsibility lies in the enforcement of internal mechanisms of compliance. Yet again, this affects quality signalling by arbitral institutions and indirectly encourages the parties to immediately sue an institution or the institutional arbitrator in cases of any kind of irregularity of institutional arbitration actors. Moreover, due to the general tendency of most arbitral institutions to maintain the information regarding their internal operation behind closed doors, the competition between these institutions again appears imperfect. This is so because the parties cannot make informed, rational choices concerning their desirable arbitral institutions based on the information on the institutional policies in the field of internal mechanisms of compliance.

It is therefore proposed that the more flexible approach of arbitral institutions to the contents of the institutional liability clauses together with the possibility for the waivers from such liability may restore the traditional commercial function of arbitral institutions and increase the competition among arbitral institutions within the market for institutional arbitration services. These issues will be analysed in detail in the following parts of this book (specifically in Sect. 6.4.3.1 of Chap. 6). Chapter 6 will address the issue of whether quality signalling (through voluntary institutional arbitral liability) or exogenous quality requirements (e.g. through

[253] Drahozal 2005, 175–176.

insurance schemes) may in fact increase the dynamics of competition between arbitration centres. This analysis will also concern the private incentives for institutional arbitration actors concerning the implementation of institutional liability clauses.

3.4.2 Top-Down

States seem to have economic interests in fostering the use of arbitration insofar as they perceive arbitration to be an enabler of international commerce. Additionally, arbitral institutions can be seen by public authorities as serving certain public goods. All these may contribute to the realization of the State authorities that the support of institutional arbitral liability can further enable international trade.

Unsurprisingly, the operation of institutional arbitration in any jurisdiction may bring profits for States, as the conduct of the hearings at the given territory attracts foreign capital. Generally, States try not to interfere in private institutional proceedings to the extent that they connect the neutrality of such proceedings with the perspective of the future profits that may stem from the organization of specific arbitration proceedings within a given teritory. The same is valid for the discussion on the domestic treatment of institutional liability clauses.

Although it may not appear straightforward how private arbitral institutions engage in the international economic order[254] (unlike arbitral institutions dealing with the administration of investment disputes),[255] some commentators have linked the operation of institutional arbitration with the general prosperity of international trade. This means that the private arbitration processes may facilitate international business transactions in a more effective manner than State systems of justice.[256]

This was the case with in the Casella's equilibrium model, which was based on the following variables: (a) the economic role of individual market players, (b) the failure of national courts to meet the transaction costs, and (c) the emergence of arbitral institutions vis-à-vis the economic interests of the individuals.[257] Casella

[254]To date, there have only been accidental contributions relating to the prospective impact by private arbitral institutions on the expansion of international trade. Moreover, no empirical studies have been conducted that could provide quantitative or qualitative data explaining the interplay between the operation of institutional arbitration and the growth of international trade. See: Alain Plantey, "The International Court of Arbitration of the International Chamber of Commerce in the New Economic Trends." Eastern Bloc Joint Ventures: A Collection of the Papers delivered at the International Bar Association Regional Conference, Warsaw, Poland 22–24 April 1990, where the role of the ICC in the "drafting of a universal commercial language and acceptable international standards" was presented. Additionally, Plantey speaks there about the influence of the ICC on the qualitative changes in international trade.

[255]See Schill 2010.

[256]Cf. Casella 1996; Casella and Feinstein 2002.

[257]Cf. Casella 1996.

concludes that international commercial arbitration and the associated therewith private arbitral institutions are frequent and influential enough to affect the creation of a new jurisdiction, which is directed towards the further market integration and the growth of international trade. What is particularly important in Casella's model is the following argument:

> market and public goods coalitions are determined together: trade influences the formation of jurisdictions, and the partition into jurisdictions shapes the public goods necessary to support private trade, and thus the formation of markets.[258]

Is it then plausible that institutional arbitration shapes the public goods or even represents such goods by means of its own operation? Some authors, such as Professor Rogers, support such thinking, though in the context of a non-administered arbitration.[259] Rogers argues that international arbitration as such generates public goods concerning: (a) the procedural rule making, and (b) the production of substantive commercial standards by arbitrators.[260]

It can also be argued that international institutional arbitration, once equipped with additional private accountability mechanisms and with more transparent procedures, could itself be regarded as a global public good. This will, however, imply the following, additional assumptions.[261] First, that notwithstanding the competitive character of institutional arbitration within its commercial function, institutional arbitration is a non-rivalrous good (in the sense that it provides the parties with a non-exclusive pool of institutional arbitrators). Second, that institutional arbitration constitutes a non-excludable public good (probably due to the private authority of the parties to recourse to any kind of institutional arbitral regime). Finally, institutional arbitration is available worldwide (which should not be at all problematic).

These observations demonstrate that in order to implement necessary reforms of private liability regimes public authorities will need to analyse different public incentives which should overlap with the general public perception of the role of institutional arbitration in building up the national and international economy. Institutional arbitral liability itself may increase the public recognition of institutional arbitration, which may imply additional dynamics of competition from the bottom-up. This means that States—once institutional liability is assumed by private arbitral institutions—may start to increasingly recourse to institutional regimes or grant more public powers to such regimes. This is mostly because the potential liability of arbitral institutions will correspond to the problems with democratic deficits of current institutional regimes, which may have further implications on the developments of the international economic order. These observations will be further addressed in Chaps. 5 and 6.

Finally, the political and economic decisions undertaken by public authorities may also impact the operation of institutional arbitration in a negative manner in

---

[258]Ibid.

[259]Rogers 2011.

[260]Rogers 2011, 173–179.

[261]Cf. Rogers, 2011

that various public decisions or acts may restrict the autonomy of institutional arbitration actors resulting in the prospective liability claims against these actors. This may be the case with the recent economic sanctions imposed on certain Russian (and Crimean) parties to potential institutional arbitration proceedings administered by EU-based institutions.

Since March 2014, various sanctions including trade bans and export/import embargos in different economic sectors have been introduced by the EU against the Russian Federation in the response to the illegal annexation of Crimea.[262] The implementation of these economic sanctions by EU authorities raised certain concerns from Russian parties regarding the independence and impartiality of arbitration processes administered by arbitral institutions based in the EU. This is so given the possible introduction by those institutions of additional administrative measures in arbitrations involving Russian parties relating to asset-freezing restrictions implying the necessity of additional information to be provided by these parties regarding their ownership or control structure.[263] The major concern related to the effects the EU sanctions may directly or indirectly have on the length and procedural flexibility in the conduct of institutional arbitrations involving the parties being subject to the sanctions. This situation proves the plausible implications of trade barriers on the functionality of institutional arbitration, which, in turn, can demonstrate the strong relationship between the activity of arbitral institutions and the developments of international trade. Although the implementation of EU sanctions in the case at hand could be mitigated by arbitral institutions on a case-by-case basis, yet again the correlation between the activity of States and public authorities of various kinds and institutional arbitration demonstrates that the role of private dispute resolution in international economic order should not be underestimated.

Therefore, various political and economic decisions undertaken by public, State authorities in the field of international trade should take into account the private interests of the actors engaged in international commerce (such as private arbitral institutions). Also, any public incentives to interfere with arbitration should be set up in a way allowing it to flourish rather than to undermine its significance for the developments of international trade. These issues particularly concern the above discussion on the public incentives of State actors to support institutional liability clauses in a manner designed by private institutional arbitration actors.

---

[262]European Union: Newsroom: EU Sanctions against Russia over Ukraine Crisis. http://europa.eu/newsroom/highlights/special-Coverage/eu_sanctions/index_en.htm. Accessed 25 April 2016. ICC, LCIA, and SCC. The Potential Impact of the EU Sanctions against Russia on International Arbitration Administered by EU-Based Institutions. http://www.sccinstitute.com/media/80988/legal-Insight-Icc_lcia_scc-on-sanctions_17-June-2015.pdf. Accessed 25 April 2016.

[263]The Potential Impact of the EU Sanctions against Russia on International Arbitration Administered by EU-Based Institutions http://www.sccinstitute.com/media/80988/legal-Insight-Icc_lcia_scc-on-sanctions_17-June-2015.pdf.

3.5 Conclusion: The Sources and Optimal Scope of Institutional Arbitral Liability

This chapter argued that although civil liability *per se* is a matter of contract law, the contractual approach to institutional arbitral liability *alone* is not able to accommodate all aspects of institutional status and functions. Although institutional activity is based on contract (that reflects the legal dimension of institutional functions), there are additional pillars of institutional functions that concern the societal and economic goals of institutional arbitral regimes in and outside arbitration proceedings. In this view, it was proposed that the institutional arbitral liability should accommodate the triad of institutional activity, namely: the legal, societal and economic dimensions of institutional functions.

Regarding the **legal dimension**, the discussion showed that arbitral institutions could be held liable for the poor performance of their contractual obligations given that the institutional activity is based on contract. At the same time, arbitral institutions could also be liable for the acts of institutional arbitrators. This stems from the particular status of arbitral institutions vis-à-vis the arbitrators, which was defined as the institutional authority to re-determine the authority of institutional arbitrators after the conferment on the arbitrators of the adjudicatory powers by institutions. This particular institutional authority is largely the function of the legal changes within the institutional arbitration regimes that shifted the early institutional societal capital into the contractual powers of contemporary arbitral institutions understood within the meaning of private regulatory powers in contract formation. This means that contemporary arbitral institutions exercise increasing legal powers vis-à-vis the parties and institutional arbitrators and that they no longer derive their autonomy from the symbolic capital that underpinned the early operation of arbitral institutions. The civil liability that is embedded in this particular institutional status should not be, however, explained within the parameters of the agency theory. The institutional obligations concerning the supervision of the work of institutional arbitrators after the conferment on the arbitrators of the adjudicatory powers by arbitral institutions fall within the *sui generis* authority of institutional rules that encapsulates private regulatory powers of arbitral institutions in institutional regimes. In practical terms this indicates that even the misconduct of individual arbitrators could fall within the institutional obligation to ensure the efficient and effective conduct of the proceedings in the spirit of institutional arbitration rules.

Additionally, the analysis of the territoriality of institutional arbitration proved the authority of national judges to hear institutional liability cases, which was explained within the parameters of Gaillard's third representation of international arbitration. It was proposed that the harmonized approach to institutional arbitral liability be worked out by domestic judges given the international function that arbitration and arbitral institutions play on behalf of the so-called international sovereign. This could minimize the forum shopping of the parties to potential liability claims often resulting in the "abuse of process"-like behaviour of the parties that wish to bring a legal claim against arbitral institutions often without a proper legal basis and cause of action.

Regarding the **societal dimension** of institutional arbitration, it was noted that the restoration of private accountability in the sense of both the early internal legitimacy of institutional regimes and the early sources of private accountability based on shared, societal capital enshrined in institutional arbitration is required. The progressive legalization of institutional arbitration processes being the function of the increasing external legitimacy of institutional arbitration diminished the societal aspect of institutional activity. Moreover, the increasing external legitimacy of institutional regimes boosted the public confidence in the efficacy and effectiveness of institutional regimes. This, however, did not imply any legal control over the institutional arbitration process, which has been increasingly accorded certain public functions. This explained the linkages between institutional arbitral liability and private and public accountability mechanisms that are desirable in order to both restore the private trust in institutional authority and make the processes more transparent in front of the public. In this sense, institutional arbitral liability was presented as a legal tool that could secure the performance of institutional arbitration actors under institutional contracts in front of the arbitration users.

In addition, it was explained that institutional liability—once supported by additional private accountability mechanisms—could ensure the private internal control of the compliance of institutional arbitration actors with the traditional goals and values of early arbitral institutions. It was also noted that in tort, strict liability does not correspond to the societal dimension of institutional functions. In turn, civil liability for negligence has a strong potential to restore both the possible wrongdoings for the parties and the confidence in arbitration undermined by such wrongdoings. Consequently, civil liability for negligence could be treated as the ultimate guarantor of societal harmony and the original communitarian goals of institutional arbitration actors. Moreover, institutional liability responded to the calls for the fairness and transparency of institutional processes, hence, for the public accountability of institutional regimes in view of the emerging public function of arbitral institutions.

The analysis of the **economic dimension** of institutional functions linked institutional arbitral liability with the dynamics of competition within the arbitration markets. It was shown that institutional liability clauses might in fact restore the competition within the arbitration centres so as different provisions on civil liability—once implemented by different arbitral institutions—may correspond to the signalling behaviour regarding the quality of institutional arbitration processes. The possible divergence between institutional arbitration provisions on liability could increase the rational choices of arbitration users to rely on a particular arbitration regime mostly because such a regime would send a clear signal to the parties regarding how the regulations of liability address its internal policies and practices.

In addition, the discussion on the economic functions of arbitral institutions demonstrated the possible linkages between the operation of private arbitral institutions and the growth of international trade. Once public, State authorities recognize such correlation, they may also realize that the support of the internal provisions of arbitral institutions including those on institutional arbitral liability can be beneficial for public actors. This is largely so because of the role that such provisions may have on the developments of international economic order. Based on these observations, Chap. 4 will present the weaknesses of the current institutional liability clauses in the context of the proposed triad of institutional functions, namely the legal, societal, and economic functions of arbitral institutions.

References

2004 Statistical Report. 2005. ICC International Court of Arbitration Bulletin 16, No. 1.

2012 Statistical Report. 2013. ICC International Court of Arbitration Bulletin 24, No. 1.

AAA. 1946. Code of Ethics For Arbitrators.

Arbitration. Revision of the Rules of Conciliation and Arbitration. Report of the Secretary General Comparing the Old and New Rules and Describing the Principal Amendments, The ICC's Brochure No. 50, Fourth Congress Stockholm, June 27-July 2, 1927, Appendix 5 to the Rules of Procedure of 1927.

Auerbach, Jerold S. 1984. Justice Without Law? Oxford University Press, USA.

Benson, Bruce L. 1995. An Exploration of the Impact of Modern Arbitration Statutes on the Development of Arbitration in the United States. The Journal of Law, Economics & Organization 11, no. 2: 479–501.

Bernard, A. 1937. L'Arbitrage Volontaire En Droit Privé. 937th ed Brussels: Bruylant.

Bourque, Jean-François. 1993. Ten Years of ICC Arbitration (1983-1992): A Statistical Survey. ICC International Court of Arbitration Bulletin 4, no. 1: 3–7

Carlston, Kenneth S. 1952. Theory of the Arbitration Process. Law and Contemporary Problems 17, no. 4: 631–651.

Casella, Alessandra. 1996. On Market Integration and the Development of Institutions: The Case of International Commercial Arbitration. European Economic Review 40, no. 1: 155–86.

Casella, Alessandra, and Feinstein Jonathan. 2002. Public Goods in Trade: On The Formation of Markets and Jurisdictions. International Economic Review 43, no. 2: 437–462.

Ceskilovenska Obchodni Banka A.S. (Cekobanka) C/Chambre de Commerce Internationale. 1986. Rev. arb. (1987) Tribunal de grande instance de Paris.

Christian von Bar, Clive Eric, and Schulte-Nölke Hans et al., eds. 2009. Principles, Definitions and Model Rules of European Private Law: Draft Common Frame of Reference (DCFR). Sellier: European Law Publishers.

Cole, Tony, Bantekas Ilias, Feretti Federico, Riefa Christine, Warwas Barbara, and Ortolani Pietro. 2014. The Legal Instruments and Practice of Arbitration in the EU, A Study for the Directorate General for Internal Policies Policy Department C: Citizens' Rights and Constitutional Affairs. http://www.europarl.europa.eu/RegData/etudes/STUD/2015/509988/IPOL_STU(2015)509988_EN.pdf. Accessed 25 April 2016.

Constitution | ICC—International Chamber of Commerce. ICC Constitution. http://www.iccwbo.org/constitution/. Accessed 25 April 2016.

Course on Dispute Settlement: International Commercial Arbitration. Module 5.1: International Commercial Arbitration. 2005. UNCTAD. http://unctad.org/en/docs/edmmisc232add38_en.pdf. Accessed 25 April 2016.

Cretu, Sorina Olaru. 2013. New Civil Procedure Code Improves Arbitration Procedure. International Law Office, Newsletters. http://www.internationallawoffice.com/Newsletters/Arbitration-ADR/Romania/Nestor-Nestor-Diculescu-Kingston-Petersen/New-Civil-Procedure-Code-improves-arbitration-procedure. Accessed 25 April 2016.

Curtin, Deirdre, and Senden Linda. 2011. Public Accountability of Transnational Private Regulation: Chimera or Reality? Amsterdam Centre for European Law and Governance; Working Paper Series 2011—06: 1–32.

Dezalay, Yves, and Garth Bryant. 1996. Fussing About the Forum: Categories and Definitions as Stakes in a Professional Competition. Law & Social Inquiry 21, no. 2: 285–312.

Dezalay, Yves, and Garth Bryant G. 1998. Dealing in Virtue: International Commercial Arbitration and the Construction of a Transnational Legal Order. University Of Chicago Press.
Drahozal, Christopher R. 2005. Arbitrator Selection and Regulatory Competition in International Arbitration Law. In: Christopher R. Drahozal and Richard W. Naimar, eds. Towards a Science of International Arbitration: Collected Empirical Research. Kluwer Law International: 167–187.
Drahozal, Christopher R. 2006. Is Arbitration Lawless. 40 Loyola of Los Angeles Law Review: 187–216.
European Union: Newsroom: EU Sanctions against Russia over Ukraine Crisis. http://europa.eu/newsroom/highlights/special-Coverage/eu_sanctions/index_en.htm. Accessed 25 April 2016.
Events in the History of the AAA and Alternative Dispute Resolution. The Lectic Library Law. http://www.lectlaw.com/files/adr07.htm. Accessed 25 April 2016.
Fouchard, Philippe. 1995. Relationships between the Arbitrator and the Parties and the Arbitral Institution. The ICC International Court of Arbitration Bulletin, Special Supplement.
Gaillard, Emmanuel, and Savage John. 1999. Fouchard, Gaillard, Goldman On International Commercial Arbitration. Kluwer Law International.
Gaillard, Emmanuel. 2010a. Legal Theory of International Arbitration. Martinus Nijhoff.
Gaillard, Emmanuel. 2010b. The Representations of International Arbitration. Journal of International Dispute Settlement 1, no. 2: 271–281.
Gaillard, Emmanuel. 2011. Transnational Law: A Legal System or a Method of Decision Making? Arbitration International 17, no. 1: 59–71.
Gaillard, Emmanuel. 2012. International Arbitration as a Transnational System of Justice. In: Albert Jan Van Den Berg, ed. Arbitration—The Next Fifty Years (ICCA Congress Series 16). Kluwer Law International: 66–73.
Gaillard, Emmanuel. 2015. Sociology of International Arbitration. Arbitration International: 1–17.
Gal, Jens. 2009. Die Haftung des Schiedsrichters in der internationalen Handelsschiedsgerichtsbarkeit. Mohr Siebeck.
Geneva Convention on the Execution of Foreign Arbitral Awards. 1927.
Gerbay, Remy. The Functions of Arbitral Institutions: Kluwer Law International. Forthcoming 2016.
Greenberg, Simon. 2013. Liability of Players in Arbitration. Presented at the VIAC/UNCITRAL/YAAP Joint Conference, March 22, Vienna Economic Chamber, Stubenring 8-10, 1010 Vienna.
Grigore Florescu, and Florescu Cristina. 2011. Part I: International Commercial Arbitration, Chapter 5: The Latest Developments in Commercial Arbitration in Romania. International Arbitration and International Commercial Law: Synergy, Convergence and Evolution. Kluwer Law International, 97–121.
ICC Arbitration Commission Report. 2015. Arbitration Involving States and State Entities under the ICC Rules of Arbitration.
ICC Arbitration Rules 1998.
ICC Arbitration Rules 2012. http://www.iccwbo.org/products-and-services/arbitration-and-adr/arbitration/icc-rules-of-arbitration/. Accessed 25 April 2016.
ICC Court of Arbitration. 2010. Arbitrator's Statement of Acceptance, Availability and Independence (1998 ICC Arbitration Rules). http://www.rwi.uzh.ch/lehreforschung/alphabetisch/domej/archiv/HS11-1/izvr/ICC-Arbitrator-Acceptance-Form-2010.pdf. Accessed 25 April 2016.
ICC Court of Arbitration Rules of Procedure of 1922.
ICC, LCIA, and SCC. 2015. The Potential Impact of the EU Sanctions against Russia on International Arbitration Administered by EU-Based Institutions. http://www.sccinstitute.com/media/80988/legal-Insight-Icc_lcia_scc-on-sanctions_17-June-2015.pdf. Accessed 25 April 2016.
ICC Publication No. 412. 1984. 60 Years on. A Look at the Future: ICC Court of Arbitration 60th Anniversary.
ICC Rules of Arbitration and Conciliation of 1927.
ICDR Procedures 2014. https://www.icdr.org/icdr/ShowProperty; jsessionid=wL65TGcH2Kl6QdzHPG1Zh9vL2tB2V1J5Mm8HvxPqf96wpGgd2dPh!102604678?nodeId=/UCM/ADRSTAGE2020868&revision=latestreleased. Accessed 25 April 2016.

Jones, William C. 1956. Three Centuries of Commercial Arbitration in New York: A Brief Survey. Washington University Law Review 1956, no. 2: 193–221.

Kellor, Frances A. 1999. American Arbitration: Its History, Functions and Achievements. Reprinted by Beard Books.

Kelly, Dominic. 2001. The Business of Diplomacy: The International Chamber of Commerce Meets the United Nations. CSGR Working Paper No. 74/01.

Kirchner, Jörgand, and Marriott Arthur L. 1993. International Arbitration in the Aftermath of Socialism—The Example of the Berlin Court of Arbitration. Journal of International Arbitration: 5–16.

Kronstein, H. 1944. Business Arbitration—Instrument of Private Government. Yale Law Journal 54, no. 1: 36–69.

LCIA Arbitration Rules. 1998. http://www.lcia.org/Dispute_Resolution_Services/LCIA_Arbitration_Rules.aspx. Accessed 25 April 2016.

LCIA Arbitration Rules 2014. http://www.lcia.org/Dispute_Resolution_Services/lcia-arbitration-rules-2014.aspx. Accessed 25 April 2016.

LCIA—The London Court of International Arbitration—History of the LCIA. Based on the Report from the Law Quarterly Review. 1893. http://www.lcia.org/LCIA/Our_History.aspx. Accessed 25 April 2016.

Lew, Julian D. M., Mistelis Loukas A., and Kröll Stefan. 2003. Comparative International Commercial Arbitration. Kluwer Law International.

Macassey, Lynden. 1938. International Commercial Arbitration: Its Origin, Development and Importance. Transactions of the Grotius Society 24: 179–202.

Mann, F. 1967a. State Contracts and International Arbitration. B.Y.I.L. 42, no. 1.

Mann, F. 1967b. Lex Facit Arbitrum. In: Peter Sanders, ed. International Arbitration: Liber Amicorum for Martin Domke. Martinus Nijhoff.

Manson, Edward. 1893. The City of London Chamber of Arbitration. Law Quarterly Review.

Martin, J., and Hunter, H. 1985. Arbitration Procedure in England: Past, Present and Future. Arbitration International 1, no. 1: 82–102.

McIlwrath, Michael, and Savage, John. 2010. International Arbitration and Mediation: A Practical Guide. Kluwer Law International.

Melis, Werner. 2013. The Effects of Changes in Eastern Europe on International Arbitration. In: Pieter Sanders, Werner Melis, Contemporary International Law Issues: Opportunities at a Time of Momentous Change: Proceedings of the Second Joint Conference Held in the Hague, the Netherlands, July 22-24, 1993 Martinus Nijhoff, 182–193.

Merlin, P. 1829. Recueil Alphabétique de Questions de Droit. 4th Edition. Vol. 9 Tarlier.

New York Times (Archival Issue) of 24 May 1922. People's Tribunal Will Open Today—Arbitration Society to Hear First Controversy Outside of the Courts. Hall of Justice Offered. Arnold Rothstein Proposes to Donate Quarters–Emerson McMillin Is President.

Onyema, Emilia. 2010. International Commercial Arbitration and the Arbitrator's Contract. Routledge.

Ortolani, Pietro. 2013. The Role of Arbitration Institutions in China. Transnational Dispute Management Journal. 10(4):1–22

Partridge, Sandra K. 2012. Frances Kellor and the American Arbitration Association. Dispute Resolution Journal 67, no. 1.

Paulsson, Jan. 2008. International Arbitration Is Not Arbitration. Stockholm International Arbitration Review no. 2: 1–20.

Paulsson, Jan. 2011. Arbitration in Three Dimensions. LSE Legal Studies Working Paper no. 2.

Paulsson, Jan. 2013. The Idea of Arbitration. Oxford University Press.

Pillet, Antoine. 1923. Traité pratique de droit international privé. Imprimerie J. Allier.

Plantey, Alain. 1990. The International Court of Arbitration of the International Chamber of Commerce in the New Economic Trends. Eastern Bloc Joint Ventures: A Collection of the Papers delivered at the International Bar Association Regional Conference, Warsaw, Poland 22-24 April 1990.

Redfern, Alan, Hunter Martin, Blackaby Nigel, and Partasides Constantine. 2004. Law and Practice of International Commercial Arbitration. Fourth Edition, Sweet & Maxwell.
Reily v Russel, 34 Mo 524 (1864) 528.
Roebuck, Derek. 2006. The Prehistory of Dispute Resolution in England. Arbitration 72, no. 2: 93–103.
Rogers, Catherine A. 2011. International Arbitration's Public Realm. In: Arthur W. Rovine, ed. Contemporary Issues in International Arbitration and Mediation: The Fordham Papers (2010) Martinus Nijhoff Publishers, 165–185.
Rubino-Sammartano, Mauro. 2001. International Arbitration Law. 1st edn., Kluwer Law International.
Rutledge, Peter B. 2004. Toward a Contractual Approach to Arbitral Immunity. Georgia Law Review 39: 151–214.
Rutledge, Peter B. 2013. Arbitration and the Constitution. Cambridge University Press.
Samuel, Adam. 1989. Jurisdictional Problems in International Commercial Arbitration: A Study of Belgian, Dutch, English, French, Swedish, Swiss, U.S., and West German Law. Schulthess Polygraphischer Verlag.
Sanders, Pieter. 1999. Quo Vadis Arbitration? Sixty Years of Arbitration Practice. Kluwer Law International.
SCC Arbitration Rules. 2010. http://sccinstitute.com/dispute-resolution/rules/. Accessed 25 April 2016.
Schill, Stephan W. 2010. Crafting the International Economic Order: The Public Function of Investment Treaty Arbitration and Its Significance for the Role of the Arbitrator. Leiden Journal of International Law: 401–430.
Schöldström, Patrik. 1998. The Arbitrator's Mandate: A Comparative Study of Relationships in Commercial Arbitration under the Laws of England, Germany, Sweden and Switzerland. Elanders Gotab.
Schöldström, Patrik. 2010. Contractual Relations in Institutional Arbitration. In: Kaj Hobér, Annette Magnusson, and Marie Öhrström, eds. Between East and West: Essays in Honour of Ulf Franke. Juris Publishing, 451–459.
Schultz, Thomas. 2012. The Concept of Law in Transnational Arbitral Legal Orders and Some of Its Consequences. Journal of International Dispute Settlement 2, no. 1: 59–85.
Smit, Hans. 2011. The Pernicious Institution of the Party-Appointed Arbitrator. In: Karl P. Sauvant, Lisa Sachs, Ken Davies, and Ruben Zandvliet, eds. FDI PERSPECTIVES Issues in International Investment. Vale Columbia Center on Sustainable International Investment. http://academiccommons.columbia.edu/item/ac:134503. Accessed 25 April 2016.
Strohbach, Heinz. 1992. Arbitration in Berlin. Arbitration International: 185–188.
The Geneva Protocol on Arbitration Clauses. 1923.
The ICC Commission on Arbitration. 1996. Final Report on the Status of Arbitrator. ICC International Court of Arbitration Bulletin Vol. 7 No. 1. Online version available at the website of the ICC Dispute Resolution Library.
The United Nations Conference on International Commercial Arbitration Convention on the Recognition and Enforcement of Foreign Arbitral Awards—The New York Convention. 1958.
Timár, Kinga. 2013. The Legal Relationship between the Parties and the Arbitral Institution. ELTE Law Journal: 103–122.
Uzelac, Alan. 1996. Succession of Arbitral Institutions. Croatian Arbitration Yearbook 3: 71–89.
Van den Berg, Albert Jan. 2012. Arbitration—The Next Fifty Years (ICCA Congress Series 16). Edited by Albert Jan Van Den Berg Kluwer Law International.
von Mehren, Arthur Taylor. 1986. International Commercial Arbitration: The Contribution of the French Jurisprudence. Louisiana Law Review 46, no. 5: 1046–1059.
Yu, Hong-Lin, and Sauzier E.. 2000. From Arbitrator's Immunity to the Fifth Theory of International Commercial Arbitration. International Arbitration Law Review 3: 114–121.
Yu, Hong-Lin. 2008. A Theoretical Overview of the Foundations of International Commercial Arbitration. Contemporary Asia Arbitration Journal 1, no. 2: 255–286.

Chapter 4
On How the Current Institutional Regulations of Liability Do Not Respond to the Triad of Institutional Functions

Contents

4.1 Introduction

Against the background of the optimal scope of institutional arbitral liability proposed in Chap. 3, this chapter aims at demonstrating the lack of an accurate response by the current institutional regulations of civil liability to the triad of institutional functions reflecting the desirable pillars and scope of institutional arbitral liability. In view of this, this chapter provides a critical analysis of the current institutional liability clauses contained in the arbitration rules of the leading arbitral institutions under analysis.

B. Warwas, *The Liability of Arbitral Institutions: Legitimacy Challenges and Functional Responses*, DOI 10.1007/978-94-6265-111-1_4

The core problem is that the majority of institutional liability clauses support the so-called "contractual immunity"[1] of institutional arbitration actors, which precludes the parties from successfully seeking damages against arbitral institutions in the courts of law unless the acts or omission in the course of arbitration constitute an action (or the lack thereof) implying severe consequences to the parties that amounts to gross negligence or wilful misconduct. As such, any form of civil liability for negligence is excluded by institutional arbitration rules. This creates confusion among the parties to institutional arbitrations regarding the scope of potential responsibility of those actors in the arbitration process. This confusion, that is further intensified by the lack of understanding by the arbitration users themselves of the category of acts or omission that could, in fact, be interpreted by domestic judges within the concept of gross negligence and wilful misconduct, eventually invites any party dissatisfied with arbitration to initiate ungrounded and even frivolous legal actions against arbitral institutions.

All these concerns are even more substantial when considering the diversified cultural backgrounds of all institutional arbitration actors that usually picture the performance in the course of arbitration in the context of their cultural expectations and legal standards inherent in their local traditions. Imagine the situation in which one actor in arbitration proceedings seeing that the staff person in charge of handling the case within the institutions signs letters as a member of the secretariat assumes that this person is a woman. This belief is based on the misconception and stereotype that a secretariat is composed of secretaries and that secretary is a profession predominantly occupied by females. The discovery of the opposite circumstances (that the secretary was, in fact, a male) would usually not constitute a ground for any action by most actors in arbitration. In one case this was however raised among other reasons, by a dissatisfied arbitrator who initiated a legal suit against an arbitral institution for the misrepresentation and misapplication of its arbitration rules. This was one of the recent liability claims against the ICC.[2]

Although this rather trivial story should not raise major controversies, it serves as an excellent example of the frequent clashes between the societal (understood here as cultural) and legal (contractual) expectations placed upon the institutional arbitration process by its different arbitration actors including its users. Those clashes may have even more severe consequences for both the parties and institutional arbitration actors when the arbitration process is disrupted by an actual breach of arbitration rules by arbitrators or institutional officials in cases in which the arbitral institution disregards a conflict of interest between arbitrator(s) and the party or parties, or when the accumulation of acts or omission contributes to the slowing down of the arbitration proceedings. Could such acts or omissions potentially amount to gross negligence and wilful misconduct under laws applicable in liability claims and, as such, result in damages to be paid by an arbitral institution to the party initiating the liability claim?

[1]The term "contractual immunity" is inspired by the terminology used in: Rutledge 2004.

[2]This information was generously provided to the author by General Counsel of the ICC, Mr. Emmanuel Jolivet, during a meeting at the ICC headquarters in Paris on 20 October 2015.

This chapter is organized in three main parts that correspond to the presentation of the triad of institutional arbitration functions provided in Chap. 3. The first part of the chapter deals with the legal controversies concerning institutional liability clauses in view of the legal dimension of institutional status and functions. This part scrutinizes the problems stemming from contractual immunity granted to *all* institutional arbitration actors under most arbitration rules. Moreover, it points out the issues emerging from the contractual immunity from process protecting institutional arbitration actors from participating in any and all legal proceedings in connection with arbitration, especially in view of the lack of the clear procedural rights of the parties to lodge a compliant concerning the misconduct of institutional arbitration actors within the institutional regimes.

The second part analyses the weak response of the current institutional regulations of liability to the societal dimension of institutional functions as defined in Sect. 3.3 of Chap. 3. This part intends to show that neither the contemporary institutional liability clauses, nor the current internal mechanisms of private accountability, reflect the societal values and arbitration ethos that was the substance of the early internal legitimacy of institutional arbitration. The major critique concerns here the legal context underlying the adoption of the limitation of liability clauses by arbitral institutions, which disregards the *private* contractual rights of the parties to negotiate the content of these clauses. This prevents the business parties to institutional arbitration contracts from taking active part in minimizing the commercial risks relating to their involvement in institutional arbitration proceedings. In addition, the second part analyses the inability of arbitral institutions to oversee the performance of the members of institutional organs and institutional arbitrators within the meaning of the early components of the internal legitimacy of institutional regimes presented in Sect. 3.3.1.1 of Chap. 3.

The last part investigates the interplay between the current institutional regulations of liability and the economic dimension of institutional arbitration regimes. In line with this, it analyses the impact of the current contractual immunity of institutional arbitration actors on both the parties' choices while selecting a particular institutional regime and the decrease in the traditional commercial function of institutional arbitration. The third part of the chapter also focuses on the interplay between the imperfect competition within the institutional arbitration market—that stems from the mandatory character of institutional liability clauses—and the understanding and awareness of the quality of institutional arbitration services by the traditional institutional arbitration users.

4.2 Legal Problems with Institutional Contractual Immunity

The meaning of institutional contractual immunity in the course of the following analysis is twofold. First, it involves the contractual immunity granted to *all* institutional arbitration actors by means of institutional arbitration rules for acts and omissions in the course of the arbitration proceedings, which is a mandatory provision under institutional arbitration rules. This means that the rule providing for contractual immunity is automatically incorporated into institutional arbitration contracts once such contracts are concluded. Hence, this rule excludes the prospective liability of institutional arbitration actors from the start of every arbitration proceedings. Second, institutional contractual immunity concerns the immunity protecting all institutional arbitration actors from participating in legal proceedings in the courts of law that arose out of, or in connection with, arbitration proceedings (henceforth referred to as "the contractual immunity from process"). The contractual immunity from process has been adopted mostly by arbitral institutions that have their seats in common law countries. Both meanings of the contractual immunity, together with the implications they have in the arbitration process, will be addressed below.

4.2.1 "We Are Contractors but We Do Not Assume Liability:" On Why Absolute Contractual Immunity Appears Paradoxical

Already the French Civil Code of 1804 (also called the Napoleonic Code) contained a statement that "everyone is liable for the damage he causes not only by his acts, but also by negligence or imprudence".[3] The concept of contractual liability also prevails in contemporary business transactions and most companies would rarely enter into contractual relationships without carefully defining the scope of their potential contractual liability by negotiating the exclusion or limitation of liability clauses. Indeed, when a commercial lawyer has one hour to review a 60-page contract, he or she would be advised to predominantly focus on the provisions on limitation on liability before looking at any other aspects of the transaction in question.[4] In addition, the parties to contracts—although generally free to stipulate the commercial relationships as they see fit within the concept of the freedom of contracts—may rely on legal instruments designed to control unfair contractual terms that aim at excluding or limiting the liability assumed under a contract to the detriment of the opposing party.[5]

That being said, regulations of liability of institutional arbitration actors generally do not constitute the major concern of the parties to arbitration proceedings, at least at the moment when arbitrations are being commenced. This results in the situation in which exclusion of liability clauses drafted by the authors of relevant arbitration rules become the major source of contractual liability of institutional arbitration actors. Needless to say, such exclusion of liability clauses, in principle,

[3]§1382, §1383 and §1384 of the French Civil Code of 1804.

[4]This anecdotal scenario is based on GE training materials on Limitation of Liability, 2013.

[5]See, for example, Unfair Contract Terms Act 1977—Chapter 50.

largely limit the contractual liability of all institutional arbitration actors for the acts or omission in arbitration, at least to the extent that laws applicable to any potential liability claims against institutional arbitration actors allow such limitations. For example, the 2012 ICC Arbitration Rules provide for "blanket" exclusion of liability for all participants in ICC arbitrations unless such exclusion is prohibited under applicable laws.[6] Similar provisions can be found in Article 38 of 2014 ICDR Procedures. Correspondingly, the 2010 SCC Arbitration Rules contain provisions limiting the liability of the SCC and its arbitrators to the acts or omission that constitute wilful misconduct or gross negligence.[7] The new version of Article 31 of 2014 LCIA Rules also provides for the "qualified" exclusion of liability of LCIA arbitration actors, meaning that the liability of such actors is limited to conscious and deliberate wrongdoing and/or to situations in which the law applicable will not allow the limitations of liability established by the LCIA.[8]

From a legal perspective, there are two problems stemming from the current exclusion of liability or limitation of liability clauses: the problem concerning purely contractual controversies relating to such clauses, and the second problem regarding the commercial aspect of institutional arbitration contracts. First, given the contractual basis of institutional activity, most exclusion and limitation of liability clauses of professional contractors (whether contained in institutional contracts or any other contracts under general contract law theories) can usually be stricken down by courts in cases in which these clauses cover breach of material obligation under the contract or gross negligence.[9] This means that blanket exclusion of liability clauses, at least from the perspective of general contract law, often appear unenforceable, meaning that the protection of contractors imposing or agreeing on such clauses is frequently illusionary and left for the further determination by courts. Taking into account this general rule that professional contractors (at least in commercial transactions) being sophisticated parties should not, in principle, exclude or largely limit their own responsibility for prospective breach of their substantial contractual obligations, there seems to be little if no arguments supporting the opposite statement with regard to arbitral institutions. Bearing in mind that arbitral institutions operate as sophisticated market players in the field of arbitration services, it is surprising if not paradoxical that the contractual liability of institutional arbitration actors is so limited simply because no legal argument seems to exist that could justify such exclusion, in particular with a view on the statutory protection of the parties to unfair contractual terms. This argument seems to hold true even if treating institutional arbitration contracts as *sui generis* contracts that fall outside any contract law theories known thus far. For example, if we recall the explanation of the rationale underpinning contractual immunity

[6] Article 40 of the 2012 ICC Arbitration Rules. For both the wording of the current institutional exclusion of liability clauses and their analysis see: Table 4.1 in Sect. 4.3.1.

[7] See: Table 4.1 in Sect. 4.3.1.

[8] Wade et al. 2015, 323–326.

[9] France is the case; see Rambaud 2007.

contained in the 2012 ICC Arbitration Rules that the policy for such immunity can be seen in the necessary protection of the effectiveness of arbitration, one could question the relationships between the policy favouring immunity and the contractual basis (or bases) of institutional arbitration.[10] Looking further at the explanation for immunity provided for in *The Secretariat's Guide to ICC Arbitration,* that the limitation of liability of the ICC arbitration actors provided for under Article 40 of the 2012 ICC Arbitration Rules corresponds with the immunity of courts in most jurisdictions, the link between immunity and contractual aspect of the ICC arbitration becomes even more puzzling.[11]

Secondly, analysing the exclusion of liability clauses contained in institutional contracts from the perspective of commercial law and commercial goals of contractors, the fact that blanket exclusion of liability clauses may be stricken down by judges in jurisdictions in which such clauses will not be enforced due to local legal restrictions leaves the transaction risk associated with arbitration proceedings by arbitral institutions unquantified and unlimited. In other words, arbitral institutions cannot manage or levy such risk because the determination of their contractual liability has in fact been left in the hands of national judges that assess the scope of negligence and/or breach of contractual obligations under law applicable to liability claim. Yet again, it appears largely surprising that arbitral institutions—acting as sophisticated market players—do not take a proactive approach to regulating the scope of their contractual liability from the bottom, in accordance with general provisions of contract law and with a view to the commercial goals of arbitral institutions associated with the arbitrations in question. This results in a situation in which the conclusion of institutional arbitration contracts implies a high degree of legal and commercial uncertainty for both arbitral institutions and the parties, with the former counting on a favourable decision regarding liability from the judge of the law of the forum and the latter being unable to properly assess all arbitration risks related to the transaction in question.

4.2.2 "Do Not Attack Our Experts:" On Why Contractual Immunity Should Not Apply to All Institutional Arbitration Actors

It was concluded, while analysing the model of institutional contractual relations, that arbitral institutions enjoy particular authority to re-determine the authority of institutional arbitrators.[12] This resulted in the observation that arbitral institutions could be—to some extent—liable for the acts of institutional arbitrators. This, in turn, could justify the contractual immunity granted by institutions to arbitrators

[10] A commentary note to Article 40 of the 2012 ICC Arbitration Rules, in Fry, Greenberg, Mazza, 2012, 421–423.

[11] Ibid.

[12] Sect. 3.2.1.1.2.3.

that work under their aegis on a case-by-case basis. It is, however, questionable whether the institutional authority as explained in Sect. 3.2.1.1.2.3 involves the institutional powers to accord immunity to *all* members of institutional organs, as well as to institutional employees, or even to any other persons participating in arbitration proceedings such as experts appointed by an arbitral tribunal.

Although contractual relations with experts were not addressed in the model on contractual relationships presented in Chap. 3, it is doubtful that arbitral institutions are in a position to conclude contracts with the experts appointed by arbitral tribunals. Rather, the arbitral tribunal itself will enter into contractual relationships with experts whose essential obligations under the contracts will concern the issuance of the expert's opinion or report in line with the internal policies and rules of particular institutional regime in return for remuneration. The experts will need to be impartial and independent from the parties and comply with the provisions on confidentiality of arbitration proceedings (if any).

Even assuming that the performance of the experts acting within the particular institutional regime is regulated under soft-law mechanisms developed within such a regime, the institution does not seem to be in a position to exclude the contractual liability of occasional experts, as it does not have the authority to grant any powers to the experts which are only service providers in the meaning of traditional contract law theories. This means that the role of experts in arbitration is rather straightforward and it does not involve the conferment on them of any adjudicatory powers by the institution as in the case of institutional arbitrators. Moreover, some arbitration rules of the institutions under analysis expressly state that the arbitrators should be responsible for ensuring the payment by the parties of the fees and expenses of the experts.[13] This suggests that it is the arbitral tribunal not the arbitral institution that has a direct legal relationship with experts. In addition to this argument, arbitral institutions have little (if any) control over the conduct of experts, and so it is surprising that they grant contractual immunity to those actors under broad institutional exclusion of liability clauses. Therefore, what safeguards exist for the parties that the expert appointed by the arbitral tribunal is neutral, and that his/her service is of the highest standards and corresponds with the technical background of the dispute?[14] Currently, parties seem to be deprived of such safeguards, and—what is more—any liability of experts is excluded under the prominent arbitration rules, such as the 2012 ICC Arbitration Rules, even in cases of the misconduct of plausible experts.

In addition, a particularly interesting observation stems from the provision of Article 31.1 of the 2014 LCIA Arbitration Rules where the contractual immunity was extended to experts appointed by arbitral tribunals but not by the parties.[15]

[13]See Article 1(12) of Appendix III to the 2012 ICC Arbitration Rules.

[14]Some institutional arbitration regimes provide the parties with the possibility to question the opinion of an expert at a hearing (see Article 25.4 of the ICDR Procedures). Other than that, however, no mechanisms exist that would formally assure the neutrality of an expert or his or her accountability toward the parties.

[15]Wade et al. 2015, 324.

This provision is controversial to the extent that it not only supports the artificial distinction between party-appointed and tribunal-appointed experts, assuming different levels of neutrality of experts from either of these categories, but also due to the potential preferential treatment by arbitral institutions of tribunal-appointed experts in the LCIA arbitrations. Be that as it may, the reformed regime of contractual liability of experts could respond to these problems. The liability of professional contractors is the conventional method of ensuring the performance of the contract with due care, as the reputation of the contractors cannot be the only guarantee of their proper conduct.

The contractual immunity of the members of institutional organs and of the institutional employees is also controversial. The issue is problematic because many members of institutional organs are also the employees of the arbitral institution. This legal relationship could amount to, at least in certain jurisdictions, some forms of vicarious liability of arbitral institutions for the acts or omission of their employees in the course of their employment. It should be clear the arbitral institutions, while excluding the liability of all arbitration actors, aim at protecting the integrity of institutional arbitration processes. The institution, however, has no guarantee—other than the CV and good reputation of its employee—that he or she fulfils his or her duties in a diligent way. Moreover, most arbitral institutions do not provide for any codes of conduct for the members of institutional organs, leaving the performance of these members beyond the control of the arbitral institution or at least making it secret in front of the parties to arbitration proceedings.[16]

Regarding the contractual immunity of institutional arbitrators, the situation becomes even more complex once confronted with the institutional authority in re-determining the authority of arbitrators in the wake of the procedures providing for the confirmation or the appointment by the institutions of arbitrators previously nominated by the parties. In the discussion of the model on contractual relations in institutional arbitration it was proposed that—given the institutional status concerning the confirmation of the adjudicatory powers of arbitrators—arbitral institutions could be held liable for certain acts of arbitrators.[17] In view of this, the contractual immunity granted by arbitral institutions to arbitrators can be somehow justified, as arbitral institutions should have the right to grant the private adjudicators that deliver arbitral awards within a particular institutional regime the freedom of discretion while deciding arbitration cases. However, even in such cases arbitral institutions should take responsibility for the work of their arbitrators, either by means of institutional liability for the acts of arbitrators or through the effective mechanisms of private accountability that could increase the standards of performance of the arbitrators vis-à-vis both the parties and the institution itself. The current contractual immunity of institutional arbitrators does not meet these objectives.

[16]This also concerns lack of institutional regulations of the independence and impartiality of the members of institutional bodies. For the statistical data on the topic in question see Hofbauer et al. 2013, 20.

[17]Sect. 3.2.1.1.2.2.

Lastly, the enforceability of institutional liability clauses under various mandatory provisions of national laws concerning arbitral liability should be addressed. Given the hybrid nature of institutional arbitration, as well as the status of arbitral institutions understood as the ability to act,[18] it should be apparent that the contractual liability clauses do not function in a vacuum and that in each liability suit the scope of liability will be assessed in accordance with the applicable law determined by the court of the forum.[19] Already in the course of the analysis of Gaillard's representations of international arbitration, several scenarios of the determination by the public courts of the institutional liability were presented.[20] It is necessary, therefore, to stress here that even the mandatory provisions on immunity of institutional arbitration actors may be overridden by domestic judges should the national laws contain different solutions for the regulation of responsibility of institutional arbitration actors (e.g. when the applicable law provides for some forms of liability of these actors).[21] This observation is important to the extent that it shows that some institutional contractual immunity clauses may *de facto* constitute a legal loophole, which calls into question the rationale underpinning the adoption of such clauses by arbitral institutions. This problem will be further explained in Sect. 4.3.1 of this chapter. Moreover, given the interdependence between the limitation of liability clauses concerning institutional arbitration actors and the law of the forum, arbitral institutions, by making institutional liability clause a blanket provision, expose themselves to unknown legal risks. These risks relate to the possible interpretations of the prospective liability of arbitral institutions based on the laws with little or no connection with arbitration underlying the liability claim by judges from *fora* not necessarily favouring or understanding arbitration as a result of the parties' forum shopping. Again, this was the case with the recent liability claim initiated against the ICC in the Slovak Republic where the parties relied on specific local provisions and doctrines that in fact sanctioned the jurisdiction of the Slovak court in the liability claim against the ICC, although the underlying arbitration had no direct connection with Slovak law.

4.2.3 What Happens in Arbitration Stays Behind Closed Doors of Arbitral Institutions: Immunity from Process and Its Consequences

As already noted on many occasions in this book, the calls for increased transparency have been recently particularly popular in regards to both traditional

---

[18]Sect. 3.2.1.2.

[19]Especially in cases in which the parties themselves have not agreed on the law governing the institutional contract and the liability clause contained therein.

[20]Sect. 3.2.2.3.

[21]For the analysis of selected national laws on prospective liability of institutional arbitration actors, see Chap. 5.

commercial arbitrations administered by arbitral institutions and arbitrations involving publicly oriented disputes falling within the emerging public function of institutional arbitration. Whereas the arguments concerning opening up towards the public (meaning also the future institutional arbitration users) by arbitral institutions can be easily counterbalanced by the arguments of implied confidentiality of commercial arbitration proceedings, it seems that the increased transparency of publicly oriented institutional arbitrations is something that arbitral institutions can no longer underestimate. The major problem in this regard concerns the already noted contractual immunity from process protecting institutional arbitration actors. Some institutional regimes—such as those of the AAA, ICDR, and the LCIA—have developed rules that diminish the possibility for institutional actors to participate in any proceedings arising out of or in connection to the arbitration.[22] In parallel, all arbitration rules of the leading arbitral institutions analysed in this book provide for a default "waiver of the right to object" with regard to the party that fails to notice the irregularities in the organization of the arbitration proceedings within due time.[23] These regulations require particular attention in the context of the democratic deficits of the institutional arbitration regimes, which concern the lack of transparency and sufficient procedural safeguards to be exercised by the parties within the arbitration processes. What is striking, however, is that institutional rules providing for immunity from process are drafted in response to the domestic protection granted to some of these institutions by means of national arbitration laws.

For example, the US policy underlying the rationale of the absolute legal immunity accorded to all arbitration actors (including the arbitral institutions) is based on the public goal to protect the integrity of arbitration processes by means of eliminating the possibility of any legal actions against arbitration actors.[24] This, in turn, is

[22]Section b of the Rule R-48 of the AAA 2009 Commercial Arbitration Rules provides that: "Neither the AAA nor any arbitrator in a proceeding under these rules is a necessary or proper party in judicial proceedings relating to the arbitration." Section (e) of the Rule R-52 of the AAA 2013 Commercial Arbitration Rules states that: "Parties to an arbitration under these rules may not call the arbitrator, the AAA, or AAA employees as a witness in litigation or any other proceeding relating to the arbitration. The arbitrator, the AAA and AAA employees are not competent to testify as witnesses in any such proceeding". Article 31.2 of the 1998 LCIA Rules stated that no party shall "seek to make any of the LCIA arbitration actors a witness in any legal or other proceedings arising out of the arbitration. The current version of Article 31.2 of the 2014 LCIA Rules provides that: "After the award has been made and all possibilities of any memorandum or additional award under Article 27 have lapsed or been exhausted, neither the LCIA (including its officers, members and employees), the LCIA Court (including its President, Vice-Presidents, Honourary Vice-Presidents and members), the Registrar (including any deputy Registrar), any arbitrator, any Emergency Arbitrator or any expert to the Arbitral Tribunal shall be under any legal obligation to make any statement to any person about any matter concerning the arbitration; nor shall any party seek to make any of these bodies or persons a witness in any legal or other proceedings arising out of the arbitration". See: Table 4.1 in Sect. 4.3.1.

[23]Article 39 of the 2012 ICC Arbitration Rules, Article 32 of the 2014 LCIA Rules, Article 28 of the 2014 ICDR Procedures, and Article 31 of the SCC Rules.

[24]Sect. 5.2.1.2.2.3 of Chap. 5.

bolstered by federal policies supporting arbitration to ensure the liberty of arbitrator's decision-making, as well as to facilitate the participation of arbitration actors in the arbitration system in the US.[25] In view of this, the 2009 AAA Commercial Arbitration Rules expressly state that neither the AAA nor any AAA arbitrator is a "necessary" or "proper" party to any judicial proceedings relating to the arbitration.[26] What is more, the 2013 AAA Commercial Arbitration Rules extend the immunity from process as defined in their previous version by expanding the category of AAA arbitration actors covered by such immunity (in the current version of the rules the provisions on immunity from process relate to the AAA, the AAA employees and the AAA arbitrators).[27] The same 2013 AAA Commercial Rules clearly state that none of these actors should participate in litigation or any other proceedings relating to the arbitration whether as a party or a witness in judicial or any other proceedings relating to the arbitration.[28] A similar provision was contained in the AAA's Supplementary Rules for Class Arbitrations.[29]

The institutional provisions establishing the AAA's immunity from process are particularly striking insofar as they are supported by the express sanctions that may be imposed on the parties that filed an "unnecessary" claim against the organization sponsoring arbitration by the US courts under the Revised Uniform Arbitration Act (RUAA).[30] Such a combination of private regulations of contractual immunity and the legal framework for arbitration in the US *de facto* prevents any control over proper conduct in arbitration proceedings. In brief, institutional provisions on immunity—supported by US policy (including certain public regulations of non-interference with arbitration process)—sanction the well-known statement among participants to any arbitration proceedings that what happens behind arbitration doors should remain there for the sake of the integrity of the arbitration process.

The LCIA Arbitration Rules follow the trend established by the US authorities and further continued by the AAA by according to both the LCIA arbitrators and the members of the LCIA almost absolute immunity from process when it comes to making a statement concerning the arbitration or acting as a witness in any form of proceedings in relation to the arbitration.[31] In contrast, neither the ICC nor the SCC adopted similar provisions in their sets of arbitration rules. The LCIA's immunity from process is naturally dictated by the necessity of the observance of the principle of confidentiality, which is regarded as the major advantage of the

---

[25]Ibid.

[26]Cf. Rule R-48 (b) entitled "Applications to the Court and Exclusion of Liability" of the AAA Commercial Arbitration Rules 2009.

[27]Cf. Rule R-52(e) of the AAA Commercial Arbitration Rules 2013.

[28]Ibid.

[29]Rule 12 of the AAA 2003 Supplementary Rules for Class Arbitrations.

[30]Comment 6 to Section 14(e) of the Uniform Arbitration Act (Last Revisions Completed Year 2000).

[31]Article 31.2 of the 2014 LCIA Rules. Cf. Wade et al. 2015, 325–326.

arbitration process itself. Moreover, it is interlinked with the finality of arbitration proceedings (and of the award), which should mean the reduction of any possibility of the recourse against the award that was rendered as a result of the parties' submission to arbitration. However, confronting such regulations with the general protection of institutional arbitration actors from civil liability, the arbitral immunity from process creates a situation in which the parties have been left with no safeguards to protect their rights in and outside arbitration proceedings. This is especially the case when some irregularities take place that would require witness testimony in the subsequent judicial proceedings relating to the arbitration. Imagine a situation in which a party to the LCIA proceedings, after filing a liability claim against the LCIA, wishes to call an LCIA employee as a witness to testify against the LCIA. This possibility is largely restricted by the LCIA provisions on immunity from process. An even more controversial scenario would arise if such requests were filed in the context of the investor-State arbitration administered by the LCIA.

In addition, the finality of arbitration (reflecting the concept of *res judicata* in the judicial proceedings) applies only to the disputants involved in the particular arbitration case. Therefore, the internal institutional regulations should not eliminate the possibility for other interested parties to request an arbitrator or the members of institutional organs to testify in the legal proceedings arising out of the arbitration cases. Again, this issue may be particularly relevant in investor-State arbitrations administered by the LCIA (and other arbitral institutions), as it limits the possibility of institutional arbitration actors in making statements concerning such arbitrations, testifying in judicial proceedings involving such prior arbitrations, or appearing in any other legal proceedings concerning such arbitrations. The possible violations of the rights of investors under the international investment treaties come to mind here, where transparency and the observance of due process in the course of arbitration proceedings is particularly sought today. These questions appear relevant in view of the United Nations Convention on Transparency in Treaty-based Investor-State Arbitration adopted on 10 December 2014,[32] as well as the UNCITRAL Rules on Transparency in Treaty-based Investor-State Arbitration that came into effect on 1 April 2014 with a view on the need to increase the accessibility to the public of investor-State arbitration proceedings.[33] Should the parties to institutional arbitration proceedings or even third parties not have a right to seek for greater transparency concerning the arbitration if the arbitration engages publicly oriented matters?

If the answer to these issues is positive, another question emerges regarding how the institutional arbitration rules securing the immunity from process correspond with the recent trends visible at the international level to open up closed doors of arbitral institutions to the public by making arbitration proceedings more

[32]United Nations Convention on Transparency in Treaty-Based Investor-State Arbitration 2014 was open for signature on 17 March 2015.

[33]UNCITRAL Rules on Transparency in Treaty-Based Investor-State Arbitration, 2014.

transparent. The UNCITRAL Rules on Transparency in Treaty-based Investor-State Arbitration of 2014 can also be applied to arbitrations conducted under any other arbitration rules than the UNCITRAL Arbitration Rules or even in *ad hoc* proceedings.[34] Moreover, in cases in which a conflict arises between such other applicable rules and the UNCITRAL Arbitration Rules on Transparency in Treaty-based Investor-State Arbitration of 2014, the latter rules should prevail. This provision makes it clear that the possible clashes between the institutional rules providing for the immunity from process and the UNCITRAL Arbitration Rules on Transparency in Treaty-based Investor-State Arbitration of 2014 may result in situations in which the former rules remain ineffective. This may be the case when the arbitrators deciding on the case exercise their discretion in the application of the UNCITRAL Rules on Transparency in Treaty-based Investor-State Arbitration of 2014 even if the Rules provide for the concurrent regulations of transparency as compared with the regime provided for by the institutional arbitration rules having application to the arbitration in question.[35]

Furthermore, all leading arbitral institutions analysed here incorporated into their arbitration rules a provision which constitutes a *waiver* on the side of the parties of the right to raise a timely objection to the organization of the arbitration and to the application by institutional arbitrators of any rules applicable to the proceedings.[36] Such a waiver, even if aiming at ensuring the expeditiousness of arbitration proceedings by eliminating possible dilatory tactics of the parties, seems detrimental to the parties should we consider the immunity from process of institutional arbitration actors mentioned above.

This begs the following questions. How do arbitral tribunals or arbitral institutions assess the weight of these provisions with regard to different procedural issues in the course of arbitration? For example, should the waiver of the parties' rights to object have similar implications in the following situations? First, for one's party non-reaction to procedural order of an arbitral tribunal inviting the possibility to comment on the document submitted by the opposing party within the time period prescribed by the arbitral tribunal? Second, in cases in which the party suspected the partiality of an arbitrator but did not have sufficient evidence to challenge this arbitrator before the award has been rendered? How is the "knowledge" or the "awareness" of the parties of the circumstances giving rise to a possible objection in a timely manner interpreted? How is the "reasonableness" of time assessed by an arbitral tribunal in deciding the timely objection by a party? Why are the time limits set out for the arbitrators to either render the award within reasonable time, or to comply with any procedural stage in institutional arbitration, often prolonged and adjusted to the arbitrators' tight schedules? Why do the

[34]Article 9 of the UNCITRAL Rules on Transparency in Treaty-Based Investor-State Arbitration 2014.

[35]Article 3(b) of the UNCITRAL Rules on Transparency in Treaty-Based Investor-State Arbitration 2014.

[36]See Article 39 of the 2012 ICC Arbitration Rules, Article 32.1 of the LCIA Rules, Article 28 of the ICDR Procedures, and Article 31 of the SCC Rules.

parties not enjoy the possibility of pointing out the irregularities on the side of arbitrators or institutional organs within a similarly flexible approach? All these question the equality of the procedural rights in institutional arbitration, especially in view of the institutional immunity from process, which eliminates any control of the institutional enforcement of such rights *prior to* the assessment of the enforceability of the arbitral award by judges.

4.3 On the Problems with the Societal Dimension

Considering the discussion on the internal legitimacy of institutional arbitration and on the influence of the growing public recognition of institutional arbitration (called external legitimacy) on the early mechanisms of private accountability, the following analysis will aim at proving the following hypothesis. That is, that the particular character of the public–private interplay in the field of arbitration resulted in the weakening of the early mechanisms of compliance developed by arbitral institutions.[37] The following part will first explicate the effects of the public regulations of arbitral liability on the wording of institutional liability clauses as adopted by private arbitral institutions under analysis. Secondly, the analysis will point out the insufficiency of the contemporary mechanisms of private accountability in regards to the significant internal legitimacy enjoyed by the early institutional regimes.

4.3.1 Public Rationale Behind Institutional Contractual Immunity

This analysis addresses both the rationale underlying the adoption of the exclusion of liability clauses by arbitral institutions (defined above as contractual immunity) and the changing effects of the private–public interplay on the wording of such clauses. The discussion incorporates the following terminology: the "blanket" (absolute) exclusion of liability provided under the 2012 ICC Rules and the recent version of the 2014 ICDR Procedures, and the "qualified" exclusion of liability under the LCIA and SCC arbitration rules.[38] The internal legitimacy of the early institutional arbitration regimes will be understood here as a private confidence in the early institutional arbitration processes—hence as an arbitration ethos which ensured the high quality of the early institutional services (Table 4.1).

[37] Sect. 3.3.3.

[38] For both the wording of the current institutional exclusion of liability clauses and their analysis see: Table 4.1 in Sect. 4.3.1.

Table 4.1

WORDING OF THE RULES	
ICC	**1998 Rules**: Article 34 Exclusion of Liability: Neither the arbitrators, nor the Court and its members, nor the ICC and its employees, nor the ICC National Committees shall be liable to any person for any act or omission in connection with the arbitration.
	2012 Rules: Article 40 Limitation of Liability: The arbitrators, any person appointed by the arbitral tribunal, the emergency arbitrator, the Court and its members, the ICC and its employees, and the ICC National Committees and Groups and their employees and representatives shall not be liable to any person for any act or omission in connection with the arbitration, except to the extent such limitation of liability is prohibited by applicable law.
SCC	**2010 Rules**: Article 48 Exclusion of Liability: Neither the SCC nor the arbitrator(s) are liable to any party for any act or omission in connection with the arbitration unless such act or omission constitutes wilful misconduct or gross negligence.
AAA	**2009 Commercial Arbitration Rules**: R-48 Applications to Court and Exclusion of Liability: (a) No judicial proceeding by a party relating to the subject matter of the arbitration shall be deemed a waiver of the party's right to arbitrate. (b) Neither the AAA nor any arbitrator in a proceeding under these rules is a necessary or proper party in judicial proceedings relating to the arbitration. (c) Parties to an arbitration under these rules shall be deemed to have consented that judgment upon the arbitration award may be entered in any federal or state court having jurisdiction thereof. (d) Parties to an arbitration under these rules shall be deemed to have consented that neither the AAA nor any arbitrator shall be liable to any party in any action for damages or injunctive relief for any act or omission in connection with any arbitration under these rules.
	2013 Commercial Arbitration Rules: R-52 Applications to Court and Exclusion of Liability: (a) *[Wording of the provisions remains the same];* (b) *[Wording of the provisions remains the same];* (c) *[Wording of the provisions remains the same];* (d) *[Wording of the provisions remains the same];* (e) *[Added]* Parties to an arbitration under these rules may not call the arbitrator, the AAA, or AAA employees as a witness in litigation or any other proceeding relating to the arbitration. The arbitrator, the AAA and AAA employees are not competent to testify as witnesses in any such proceeding.
ICDR	**2009 International Dispute Resolution Procedures**: Article 35 Exclusion of Liability: The members of the tribunal and the administrator shall not be liable to any party for any act or omission in connection with any arbitration conducted under these Rules, except that they may be liable for the consequences of conscious and deliberate wrongdoing.

(continued)

Table 4.1 (continued)

WORDING OF THE RULES	
	2014 International Dispute Resolution Procedures: Article 38 Exclusion of Liability: The members of the arbitral tribunal, any emergency arbitrator appointed under Article 6, any consolidation arbitrator appointed under Article 8, and the Administrator shall not be liable to any party for any act or omission in connection with any arbitration under these Rules, except to the extent that such a limitation of liability is prohibited by applicable law. The parties agree that no arbitrator, emergency arbitrator, or consolidation arbitrator, nor the Administrator shall be under any obligation to make any statement about the arbitration, and no party shall seek to make any of these persons a party or witness in any judicial or other proceedings relating to the arbitration.
LCIA	**1998 Rules**: Article 31 Exclusion of Liability: 31.1 None of the LCIA, the LCIA Court (including its President, Vice Presidents and individual members), the Registrar, any deputy Registrar, any arbitrator and any expert to the Arbitral Tribunal shall be liable to any party howsoever for any act or omission in connection with any arbitration conducted by reference to these Rules, save where the act or omission is shown by that party to constitute conscious and deliberate wrongdoing committed by the body or person alleged to be liable to that party.
	31.2 After the award has been made and the possibilities of correction and additional awards referred to in Article 27 have lapsed or been exhausted, neither the LCIA, the LCIA Court (including its President, Vice Presidents and individual members), the Registrar, any deputy Registrar, any arbitrator or expert to the Arbitral Tribunal shall be under any legal obligation to make any statement to any person about any matter concerning the arbitration, nor shall any party seek to make any of these persons a witness in any legal or other proceedings arising out of the arbitration.
	2014 Rules: Article 31 Limitation of Liability: 31.1 None of the LCIA (including its officers, members and employees), the LCIA Court (including its President, Vice-Presidents, Honourary Vice-Presidents and members), the Registrar (including any deputy Registrar), any arbitrator, any Emergency Arbitrator and any expert to the Arbitral Tribunal shall be liable to any party howsoever for any act or omission in connection with any arbitration, save: (i) where the act or omission is shown by that party to constitute conscious and deliberate wrongdoing committed by the body or person alleged to be liable to that party; or (ii) to the extent that any part of this provision is shown to be prohibited by any applicable law.
	31.2 After the award has been made and all possibilities of any memorandum or additional award under Article 27 have lapsed or been exhausted, neither the LCIA (including its officers, members and employees), the LCIA Court (including its President, Vice-Presidents, Honourary Vice-Presidents and members), the Registrar (including any deputy Registrar), any arbitrator, any Emergency Arbitrator or any expert to the Arbitral Tribunal shall be under any legal obligation to make any statement to any person about any matter concerning the arbitration; nor shall any party seek to make any of these bodies or persons a witness in any legal or other proceedings arising out of the arbitration.
ANALYSIS	
ICC	**1998 Rules**: "Blanket" exclusion of liability.
	2012 Rules: "Blanket" exclusion of liability unless such exclusion is prohibited by applicable law.

(continued)

Table 4.1 (continued)

ANALYSIS	
SCC	**2010 Rules**: "Qualified" exclusion of liability" in cases of wilful misconduct and gross negligence.
AAA	**2009 Rules**: "Blanket" exclusion of liability" for AAA and AAA arbitrators. Immunity from process for AAA and AAA arbitrators.
	2013 Rules: "Blanket" exclusion of liability" for AAA and AAA arbitrators. Immunity from process extended; now concerning the non-participation by AAA, AAA employees, and AAA arbitrators in litigation or any other proceedings relating to the arbitration as witnesses.
ICDR	**2009 Rules**: "Qualified" exclusion of liability; liability allowed in cases of the consequences of conscious and deliberate wrongdoing.
	2014 Rules: "Blanket" exclusion of liability unless such exclusion is prohibited by applicable law. Immunity from process; concerning the non-participation by the ICDR arbitrator, emergency arbitrator, consolidation arbitrator, and the Administrator (ICDR) as party or witness in judicial or any other proceedings relating to the arbitration. These actors are also protected from making any statements relating to the arbitration.
LCIA	**1998 Rules**: "Qualified" exclusion of liability; liability allowed in cases of conscious and deliberate wrongdoing (needs to be shown by the interested party). Immunity from process; the LCIA, the LCIA Court (including its President, Vice Presidents and individual members), the Registrar, any deputy Registrar, any arbitrator or expert to the Arbitral Tribunal have no obligation to make any statement to any person about anything concerning the arbitration. No party may seek to make any of these persons a witness in any legal or other proceedings arising out of the arbitration.
	2014 Rules: "Qualified" exclusion of liability; liability allowed in cases of conscious and deliberate wrongdoing or unless exclusion of liability is prohibited under applicable law. Immunity from process; neither the LCIA nor its Court, Registrar, any arbitrator or any expert to the Arbitration Tribunal should be under no legal obligation to make any statements in relation to arbitration nor should any party seek to make any of these bodies or persons a witness in any legal or other proceedings arising out of the arbitration.

4.3.1.1 Blanket Contractual Immunity Under the 1998 and 2012 Versions of the ICC Arbitration Rules and the Public Regulations of Liability

The 1998 version of the ICC Arbitration Rules provided for an absolute exclusion of liability that granted the contractual immunity to all ICC arbitration actors including the ICC and its Court of Arbitration, its employees and agents, as well as the ICC institutional arbitrators.[39] Such blanket immunity was uncertain and questionable from the moment of the promulgation of the 1998 ICC Arbitration Rules

[39] Article 34 of the 1998 ICC Arbitration Rules. See Table 4.1 in Sect. 4.3.1.

not only because of the legal concerns—involving the question regarding the enforceability of such clauses in different jurisdictions—but also from the institutional point of view. The 1998 Rules prompted a stormy debate within the ICC Working Group on Arbitration concerning the admissibility of such contractual immunity within the ICC arbitration regime.[40]

According to some commentators, Article 34 of the 1998 ICC Arbitration Rules aimed purely at protecting both the ICC—together with the members of its institutional bodies, employees, and the National Committees—and the ICC arbitrators from *any* potential claims raised by the parties, which could result in institutional liability.[41] As further explained, however, the ICC believed that the provision of Article 34 was not in contrast with other possibilities of the parties for the recourse against ICC arbitration actors in the actions for the annulment of the ICC arbitral awards.[42] Moreover, the ICC perceived the mechanism of challenging its arbitrators as a sufficient equivalent of the liability claims.[43] The fact that the ICC concerned mostly the cases in which the work of arbitrators might be questioned while deliberating on the possible ICC's liability means that the ICC did not assume any possibility of its own legal responsibility in the arbitration processes. This was the private rationale behind the first and almost absolute institutional contractual immunity of ICC arbitration actors as established by the 1998 ICC Arbitration Rules.

We should now consider the possible public rationale underpinning the ICC clause on the contractual immunity. Even though it is difficult to present a particular *legal doctrine* that stood behind the 1998 ICC provision on the exclusion of liability,[44] it seems that the ICC followed a take-it-or-leave-it approach to the interpretation of the liability of ICC arbitration actors by judges. As argued in the prominent guide to the ICC Arbitration Rules, the ICC, while adopting this controversial provision, was aware of the fact that its exclusion of the liability clause may be ineffective in various jurisdictions and under different national laws.[45] This means that the ICC—knowing that the clause may be enforced in *some* jurisdictions (e.g. possibly in the US and to a certain extent also in the UK)[46]—preferred to promote the blanket contractual immunity notwithstanding the fact that it was more plausible that the exclusion of liability will be held ineffective in *most* European jurisdictions including France, where the ICC is headquartered.

---

[40]Derains and Schwartz Eric 2005, 381–383.

[41]Ibid.

[42]Bond et al. 2010, 389–390.

[43]Ibid.

[44]Especially given that most contract laws (including French contract law) will not be favourable toward absolute exclusion of liability of contractors for their essential contractual obligations.

[45]Derains and Schwartz Eric 2005, 382.

[46]Given the doctrine of arbitral immunity applied to arbitral institutions in these jurisdictions.

The problems with the 1998 ICC absolute exclusion of liability clause concern the fact that the ICC ignored the societal dimension of its own operation. By granting contractual immunity to ICC institutional arbitration actors, the ICC not only neglected the very commercial aspect of institutional functions but also diminished the private confidence in ICC arbitration from the perspective of its traditional arbitration users. This means that the ICC adjusted its provision on contractual immunity to the uncertain public regulations. Yet, it again exercised its public function vis-à-vis the parties by limiting the parties' freedom to stipulate the provisions of liability. Albeit the early arbitral institutions (especially the ICC Court) also exercised unlimited autonomy with regard to the regulation of performance of institutional actors, these institutions developed additional mechanisms of accountability that—as already shown in Sect. 3.3.1.2 of Chap. 3—aimed at monitoring the work of institutional actors internally, from the bottom. The ICC Court cannot recourse to such mechanisms under the modern ICC arbitration rules simply because they do not exist. This situation supports the argument that the 1998 ICC exclusion of liability provisions were determined by the public rationale of institutional liability/immunity. The public rationale involves here both the institutional response to certain legal provisions or precedents regarding the arbitral immunity and the institutional regulation of the performance of institutional arbitration actors within its public function thus diminishing the involvement of the parties to arbitration proceedings in negotiating their desirable scope of liability to be included in the contracts with the ICC.

The 1998 ICC exclusion of liability provided for immunity for ICC arbitration actors concerning any act or omission in connection with arbitration vis-à-vis "any person".[47] This meant that the 1998 ICC system of contractual immunity eliminated the possibility of filing any liability claims against the ICC also by the third parties to the proceedings (such as the experts or the parties which were refused to participate in arbitration as a result of jurisdictional challenges). That observation raises controversies regarding the possible application of Article 34 of the 1998 ICC Arbitration Rules to the actors that did not enter into contractual relationships with the ICC Court. Both the time and the public approach to the 1998 ICC exclusion of liability clause encouraged the ICC to reconsider the wording of its provision on liability. Paradoxically, it was the French court that first found the ICC exclusion of liability clause unenforceable under French law.[48]

The fact that the parties began to challenge the ICC's clauses on the exclusion of liability in domestic courts that, in turn, increasingly acknowledged the unenforceability of such clauses, put pressure on the ICC to reformulate its provisions on liability. Hence, the new version of the Article 34 of the former 1998 ICC Rules calls the ICC's contractual immunity "limitations of liability" and expressly states

[47] Article 34 of the 1998 ICC Arbitration Rules. See: Table 4.1 in Sect. 4.3.1.

[48] *Société SNF v. International Chamber of Commerce. Cour d'appel de Paris (1. Ch.)* 2009. See also Sect. 5.2.1.2.1.

that the ICC's exclusion of liability is dependent on the relevant law applicable.[49] This means that the ICC strengthened the public rationale underpinning the scope of responsibility of the ICC arbitration actors (by making the assessment of its liability dependent on domestic courts and the law of the forum). However, it did not depart from the private rationale of the exclusion of liability (by sanctioning the non-participation of the arbitration users in shaping the scope of contractual liability of institutional arbitration actors). In other words, the material scope of the exclusion (*ratione materiae*) remained unchanged, and the major amendment involved the express connection of the exclusion of liability with the law applicable to liability claims. It is surprising that the ICC again left the regulation of liability to the public courts without seeing the necessity and opportunity for the possible negotiations of such clauses with the parties, which could ensure the authority of such clauses vis-à-vis the parties, and, in a longer term perspective, perhaps eliminate the risk of liability claims against arbitral institutions.[50]

Moreover, the new Article 40 of the 2012 ICC Arbitration Rules expanded the personal scope of the exclusion of liability clauses (*ratione personae*). As a result, from the 1 January 2012 (that is, when the new rules came into force), contractual immunity also concerns any person appointed by the tribunal, the ICC Groups and their employees, together with their representatives, *in addition to* the institutional arbitrators, members of institutional organs and institutional employees, and the ICC National Committees.[51] This demonstrates that, in fact, nothing has changed with regard to the rationale of the previous ICC exclusion of liability clauses, apart from the fact that the personal scope of the exclusion has been expanded and that the ICC confirmed the authority of the national laws to override its own provisions on liability. As already noted, *The Secretariat's Guide to ICC Arbitration* explains that if the bodies or individuals that are currently protected from civil liability under Article 40 of the 2012 Rules were exposed to liability, "this could hinder their work, making it difficult for them to provide the required level of service".[52] Does this observation imply that civil liability is a general obstacle for the contractors to perform their duties in accordance with the provisions of contracts? If so, this is a highly controversial claim.

---

[49]See: Article 40 of the 2012 ICC Arbitration Rules and Table 4.1 in Sect. 4.3.1.

[50]It is understood here that the parties—once involved in the stipulation of the institutional arbitral liability—could regain their private trust in the institutional arbitration processes as well as in the exclusiveness of such processes. If that was the case, the parties would not be particularly eager to ask judges to assess the scope of institutional liability, especially if the institutional regimes were equipped with the additional mechanisms of accountability in a manner proposed in Chap. 6. This argument should correspond with the early internal legitimacy of institutional regimes.

[51]Article 40 of the 2012 ICC Arbitration Rules. See Table 4.1 in Sect. 4.3.1.

[52]A commentary note to Article 40 of the 2012 ICC Arbitration Rules in: Fry, Greenberg, Mazza, 2012, 421–422.

4.3.1.2 Blanket Exclusion of Liability Under the ICDR Procedures

Notably, the 2014 ICDR Procedures also mimic the ICC trend classified as a "blanket" exclusion of liability, even though the 2009 ICDR Procedures followed the patterns regarding liability established by its home institution, the AAA. This concerned the long-standing provisions of the AAA, responding to the legal doctrine on the arbitral immunity, developed in the US.[53] The 2009 ICDR Procedures provided for a qualified exclusion of liability of the ICDR itself to the extent that any act or omission of the ICDR did not constitute conscious and deliberate wrongdoing. In this vein, the ICDR—even if regarded as an international branch of the AAA—has long been linking its regulations on liability with the federal, US policy concerning the institutional arbitral immunity.

The recent provisions on liability of the ICDR largely correspond with the ICC's limitation of liability clause provided for in Article 40 of the 2012 ICC Arbitration Rules. Indeed, the members of the ICDR arbitral tribunal, any emergency and consolidation arbitrator appointed under the ICDR Procedures, and the ICDR itself should not be liable to any party for any act or omission in connection with any arbitration under the ICDR Procedures unless such limitation of liability is prohibited by applicable law. This means that not only did the ICDR Procedures reduce the connection of the scope of its liability with the general protection of arbitration actors under the immunity doctrine developed in common law jurisdictions but also the same rules expanded the interdependence of the ICDR's liability and the laws applicable to liability claims internationally, given the international nature of the ICDR operation. In essence, the evolution of the ICDR Procedures on liability took place more in the context of any current and prospective public regulations on liability instead of responding to private, internal reasoning behind institutional liability.

4.3.1.3 Qualified Contractual Immunity Under the LCIA and the SCC Rules

In comparison, the LCIA and the SCC Institute both provide for a general exclusion of liability of their own organizational bodies, members, and arbitrators, however, they also allow the institutional arbitration actors to be held liable in exceptional circumstances.[54] These exceptions involve: conscious and deliberate wrongdoing of institutional actors in the case of the LCIA, and the wilful misconduct or gross negligence of institutional actors in the case of the SCC Institute.[55] Moreover, in the case of the LCIA it is the party who starts the liability claim that bears the burden of proof that the act or omission done in connection with the

[53]Sect. 5.2.1.2.2.

[54]Article 31.1 of the 2014 LCIA Arbitration Rules and Article 48 of the SCC Arbitration Rules. See Table 4.1 in Sect. 4.3.1.

[55]Ibid.

arbitration constituted a conscious and deliberate wrongdoing of the body or person alleged to be liable to that party.[56] These rules do not define what kind of acts or omission might result in liability of institutional arbitration actors. Yet again, it will be a matter to be assessed by the national courts in accordance with the law applicable to the liability disputes. This public rationale underpinning the LCIA and the SCC provisions on qualified immunity stays in line with the goals associated with the contractual immunity of the ICC presented above.

Two observations can be drawn from the analysis above. The first concerns the already-known impact of the national laws on the exclusion of liability. The second concerns the interpretation of the prospective misconduct of institutional arbitration actors under the provisions presented above. Let us consider both in turn.

It seems that the LCIA followed the domestic regulations on institutional liability reflecting a qualified approach of the UK authorities to the issue at hand.[57] Some commentators claim that the provisions of the UK Arbitration Act of 1996, which exclude the liability of arbitral institutions for acts or omission performed in the arbitrators' capacity, resemble the so-called "Himalaya clause" under English law.[58] This reasoning stays in line with the rationale of the preliminary proposals of this book concerning the prospective connection between the acts of arbitrators and the status and function of arbitral institutions. However, it does not comply with the content of such proposals; it was proposed that the particular status and function of arbitral institutions should justify the contractual liability of arbitral institutions for certain acts of arbitrators.[59] Therefore, the rationale behind the LCIA exclusion of liability does not conform to the actual authority that the LCIA should be able to exercise within the LCIA institutional regime.

Moreover, even though Swedish arbitration law does not provide for the express regulation of the arbitration conduct, it can be argued that in view of the lack of the relevant regulation, the SCC Institute came to the conclusion that a moderate stance regarding the institutional liability corresponded better to the contemporary inconsistencies of national approaches to the institutional arbitral liability. Again, the SCC's provisions on liability—which follow the private–public rationale standing behind exclusion of liability as regulated by the most leading arbitral institutions—does not seem to respect the societal dimension of the institutional operation.

The second observation concerns the uncertainty involving the prospective determination by judges of a group of acts or omission that could actually constitute the degree of misconduct of institutional arbitration actors as defined by the selected arbitration rules under analysis. Although this matter falls within the exclusive competence of domestic courts, it seems plausible that the institutional prior determination of proper conduct or of good practice concerning arbitration

[56]Article 31.1 of the 2014 LCIA Arbitration Rules.

[57]Section 74 para 2 of the UK Arbitration Act 1996, Chapter 23.

[58]Schöldström 1998, 78–79.

[59]Section 6.3 of Chap. 6.

proceedings (e.g. in the internal codes) could clarify which acts should be qualified as gross negligence or wilful misconduct. Domestic judges may have problems with such interpretations given the lack of public regulations of due care and diligence in arbitration, which is required given the unique character of arbitration processes. Institutional clarifications in this regard would then appear as important guidelines for both the parties, considering suing arbitral institutions in the courts of law, and also—indirectly—for domestic judges whose interpretations of institutional acts or omission in the course of arbitrations could fall within the internal language of arbitration proceedings, specific to each institutional arbitration regime.

As already noted, the parties are now left with confusion regarding the prospective classification of institutional acts or omission within the meaning of severe irregularities that could in fact result in liability of institutional arbitration actors under applicable laws. Would the appointment of an incapable arbitrator by an arbitral institution amount to wilful misconduct? What if an arbitral institution replaces an arbitrator, whom it sees unfit to perform his or her functions, and the newly appointed arbitrator fails to fulfil his or her duties due to the conflict of interests? Will this "carelessness" on the side of the arbitral institution be interpreted within the meaning of gross negligence? All these questions remain open thus far and the parties tend to seek answers to them in the courts of law.

Arbitral institutions could be more proactive in addressing these issues, if not by formal clarifications or institutional soft-law instruments, then specifically by means of conferences and workshops during which the prospective interpretation of institutional errors could be openly discussed in the context of the laws on civil liability in jurisdictions in which arbitral institutions have their seats. This appears particularly relevant given the strong interplay between the prospective institutional liability for negligence and the societal dimension of institutional arbitration. This societal dimension, at least in its early outlook, created a strong interdependence between honorary performance in the course of arbitration and the arbitration ethos underpinning the early dynamics of institutional arbitration regimes. It appears that the interrelation between institutional arbitral liability for negligence and the performance of institutional arbitration actors could entail similar consequences today. The current suppression of the topic resembles swiping it under the carpet, which does not appear to be a fortunate solution for either the parties or the arbitral institutions themselves.

The above analysis therefore shows that institutional contractual immunity does not correspond well with the components of the early internal legitimacy of arbitral institutions. The general critique involved the non-compliance of the institutional exclusion of liability clauses with the parties' autonomy in the arbitration processes (private rationale), in particular in view of the non-existence or insufficiency of the internal mechanisms of compliance developed within the institutional regimes. In this context, contractual immunity granted to institutional arbitration actors by means of arbitration rules gives a clear signal to the parties that both the institutional arbitrators and arbitral institutions themselves are no longer accountable for their performance, which used to be the case at the moment of the emergence of arbitral institutions. Honour, which served as a threshold for early accountability of institutional arbitration actors, is no longer a guarantor of responsibility in institutional arbitration. It has been replaced by the legal provisions of selective applicable laws under which arbitral institutions "hide" before their users. This situation only invites arbitration users to a particular "hide-and-seek" game (with different versions of the game being played around the world), in which arbitral institutions are not necessarily turning out to be the winners.

4.3.2 *Insufficiency of the Modern Mechanisms of Accountability*

The stipulation of the contractual immunity of institutional arbitration actors by arbitral institutions would have certain *raison d'être* if arbitrators or the members of institutional organs were in some way accountable to such institutions by means of internal mechanisms of accountability. First, such a solution could reaffirm private confidence in the legitimacy and authority of institutional arbitral regimes vis-à-vis the parties, which, in turn, could limit the parties' recourse against arbitral institutions in the courts of law by filing liability claims against them. Second, it could ensure the double private–public control of the performance of both institutional arbitrators and the members of institutions; by the supervisory body developed within the arbitral institution, and by the public judges in cases in which the parties eventually decide to sue arbitral institutions. There are few provisions within the modern institutional arbitration rules and policies that deal with the issues at hand. Three institutional devices require particular attention here: (1) the replacement of an arbitrator on the initiative of the institution; (2) the adoption by some institutions of the codes of ethics or codes of conduct for arbitrators; and (3) the lists of institutional arbitrators. Each will be analysed below.

4.3.2.1 Replacement of the Arbitrator at the Discretion of the Institution

The institutional authority to replace an arbitrator is the only explicit provision within the studied arbitration rules that expresses a truly supervisory power of the institutional bodies over institutional arbitrators. Replacement of an arbitrator is a natural consequence of a challenge,[60] usually made by the parties, which in most cases needs to be confirmed by the administering institution. However, in some cases the arbitral institution itself, at its own discretion, may replace the arbitrator.

[60] Replacement of an arbitrator needs to be considered in case of the death of an arbitrator or as a result of an unexpected disability to further fulfil his or her function. See Article 15(1) of the 2012 ICC Arbitration and Rules.

The wording of the institutional rules on the replacement of arbitrators, however, differs from one centre to another, oscillating between the *absolute* and *limited* institutional authority to determine the arbitrator's incapability to further perform his or her duties.

Undoubtedly, the ICC Court, as compared to other institutions, enjoys the broadest liberty in the issue at hand, as Article 15 (2) of the 2012 ICC Arbitration Rules explicitly states that an arbitrator should be replaced in the case in which the ICC Court itself decides that such arbitrator is *de jure* or *de facto* unable to fulfil his or her function.[61] It is arguable in which situations the ICC Court would actually exercise its power to expel the unsuitable arbitrator. The authors of the *Guide to the ICC Rules of Arbitration* point out that the Court's practice in this regard within the period between July 1988 and the end of the year 1994 involved only a narrow group of cases that were "either unusual or extreme".[62] *The Secretariat's Guide to ICC Arbitration* provides a comprehensive table of the number of arbitrators removed on the Court's initiative between 2007 and 2011, with a total of 8 arbitrators removed within the aforementioned period.[63] The 2012 ICC Arbitration Rules provide an indicator in this regard stating that the arbitrator should be replaced on the ICC's own motion if the arbitrator fails to fulfil his or her functions in accordance with the ICC Rules or within the prescribed time limits.[64]

By way of comparison, the new provisions of Article 10 of the 2014 LCIA Arbitration Rules also grant the powers to the LCIA Court to revoke "any arbitrator's appointment upon its own initiative, at the written request of all other members of the Arbitral Tribunal or upon a written challenge by any party" in a number of circumstances provided for in the LCIA Rules.[65] These cases amount to an arbitrator's resignation, serious illness, refusal to act, inability to act, unfitness to act and circumstances that give rise to justifiable doubts as to the arbitrator's impartiality and independence.[66] The provision of Article 10.1 of the 2014 LCIA Arbitration Rules can be considered revolutionary in that it expanded the LCIA Court's authority to make independent decisions regarding the removal of arbitrators whose standards of performance or capacities prevent these arbitrators from fulfilling their functions in accordance with the parties' arbitration agreement and the LCIA Rules, regardless of the fact whether the emergence of the obstacles is

---

[61]See the former Article 12 of the 1998 ICC Arbitration Rules.

[62]See: Derains and Schwartz Eric 2005, 197. The authors mention there a "venomous" conflict between two arbitrators, and the further impossibility to act as arbitrators in one case in which the partial award rendered by the arbitral tribunal was annulled and another award was to be made in the same subject matter. The ICC Court determined there that the arbitral tribunal was prevented *de facto* from continuing the arbitration.

[63]A commentary note to Article 15(2) in: Fry, Greenberg, Mazza, 2012, 184–186.

[64]Article 15(2) of the 2012 ICC Arbitration Rules.

[65]Article 10.1 of the 2014 LCIA Rules.

[66]Wade et al. 2015, 130–131.

the function of the arbitrator's culpability or not.[67] Usually, it would be the President or a Vice President of the LCIA Court or a Division composed of three members of the LCIA Court that decides on the revocation of an LCIA arbitrator.[68] Since the detailed analysis of all situations in which the LCIA Court can revoke an arbitrator falls beyond the scope of this book, it is important to stress here the other prerogative of the LCIA Court in the case at hand, concerning the possible determination that an arbitrator is unfit to act. This function was established under Article 10.1 of the LCIA Arbitration Rules to address the situations where that arbitrator: (i) acts in deliberate violation of the Arbitration Agreement; (ii) does not act fairly or impartially as between the parties; or (iii) does not conduct or participate in the arbitration with reasonable efficiency, diligence and industry".

This provision, together with the rule stated in Article 10.1 of the LCIA Rules begs certain questions concerning the interpretations by the LCIA Court of the situations in which the behaviour or quality of arbitrator's performance may in fact result in his or her revocation by the LCIA Court. For example, as reads from *A Commentary on the LCIA Arbitration Rules 2014*, in LCIA Arbitration Reference No. 0256 an arbitrator was challenged by the party as the result of the lack of the proper notice of an arbitration hearing to this party's counsel that led to the LCIA Court's decision stating that the arbitrator in fact deliberately violated the LCIA Rules.[69] Consequently, the LCIA Court revoked the appointment of the arbitrator. In another case (LCIA Arbitration Reference No. 5665), however, a presiding LCIA arbitrator was subject to the procedure under Article 10.2 of the LCIA Rules where the LCIA Court was requested by the parties to consider an arbitrator unfit to act. The issue that gave rise to this procedure concerned the alleged violation by the arbitrator in question of the parties' arbitration agreement by means of including the names of the parties together with the fact that the arbitrator had been appointed by them to hear their dispute in the arbitrator's CV that was further made available on the Internet.[70] The LCIA Court did not find the violation of the LCIA Rules in the case at hand to be deliberate mostly because, in the eyes of the LCIA Court, the information concerning the parties and their dispute published on the Internet was not significant to the extent that it could not result in "substantial injustice being suffered by any party".[71] As such, the arbitrator's appointment was not revoked by the LCIA Court.

---

[67]The previous version of the LCIA Rules of 1998 provided for different solutions. Article 10.2 of the Rules only enabled the LCIA Court to "consider an arbitrator unfit" in situations in which that arbitrator deliberately violated arbitration agreement together with the LCIA Rules contained therein, or whenever he or she did not conduct or participate in the arbitration proceedings with reasonable diligence. Moreover, pursuant to Article 11 of the 1998 LCIA Rules, in the event in which the LCIA Court found the arbitrator to be unsuitable or in violation of principles of independence or impartiality, the Court had "complete discretion" to determine whether the original nominating procedure should actually be applied.

[68]Wade et al. 2015, 129.

[69]Wade et al. 2015, 143–144 with further references.

[70]Ibid., 144.

[71]Ibid.

These two examples illustrate that, in practice, the LCIA Court, and also—presumably—other arbitral institutions that exercise powers to remove arbitrators at their own discretion, often issue unpredictable decisions in this regard that need to be analysed on a case-by-case basis. It is very likely, therefore, that these decisions will meet the dissatisfaction of the parties who, rather justifiably, will find it challenging to understand the reasoning of the LCIA Court in one case regarding the revocation of an arbitrator but not in another. This is largely the function of the fact that the institutional decisions on arbitrators' removals are often authoritative, which leaves the parties with little power to appeal such decisions within institutional regimes and hence they need to accept institutional orders regardless if they agree with them or not.[72] This often leaves their dispute in the hands of the arbitrator who they no longer trust and whose authority lacks the honourable dimension that was part of the accountability mechanisms of early institutional regimes.

Regarding the ICDR, the previous version of the 2009 ICDR Procedures did not contain any provision that would expressly authorize the ICDR to decide on the replacement of arbitrators. However, there used to exist certain procedural safeguards that granted the members of the arbitration panel the power to continue the proceedings without the arbitrator who had failed to participate in the arbitration without providing a justification of his or her disability to act.[73] Although this provision did not constitute the explicit authority of an institution to intervene between arbitrators, it marks the development of some kind of institutional means to ensure that the proceedings would not be obstructed due to the misconduct of one undisciplined arbitrator. Similar solutions were also adopted by other arbitration institutions analysed here.[74] The current 2014 ICDR Procedures expressly authorize the ICDR to decide, on its own initiative, on the removal of an arbitrator who fails to perform his or her duties.[75] Moreover, under Article 14.3 of the 2014 ICDR Procedures, the ICDR is empowered to eventually decide on the challenge

[72]Usually, the parties will have the possibility to refer to the relevant court in cases in which their challenge is rejected. This is the case under the UK Arbitration Act 1996 Chapter 23. Section 24. Wade et al. 2015, 129.

[73]Article 11.1 of the 2009 ICDR Procedure, which reads as follows: "If an arbitrator on a three-person tribunal fails to participate in the arbitration for reasons other than those identified in Article 10, the two other arbitrators shall have the power in their sole discretion to continue the arbitration and to make any decision, ruling or award, notwithstanding the failure of the third arbitrator to participate. In determining whether to continue the arbitration or to render any decision, ruling or award without the participation of an arbitrator, the two other arbitrators shall take into account the stage of the arbitration, the reason, if any, expressed by the third arbitrator for such nonparticipation and such other matters as they consider appropriate in the circumstances of the case. In the event that the two other arbitrators determine not to continue the arbitration without the participation of the third arbitrator, the administrator on proof satisfactory to it shall declare the office vacant, and a substitute arbitrator shall be appointed pursuant to the provisions of Article 6, unless the parties otherwise agree".

[74]See Article 15(5) of the 2012 ICC Arbitration Rules, Article 17(2) of the SCC Arbitration Rules, Article 12 of the 2014 LCIA Rules.

[75]Article 14.4 of the 2014 ICDR Procedures.

to an arbitrator if there is a disagreement between the parties in this regard or when the challenged arbitrator does not withdraw. All these new ICDR prerogatives demonstrate the increasing importance of the controlling mechanisms of arbitrators by arbitral institutions to be included within the institutional arbitration structures. As in the case of the LCIA and the ICC, however, time will tell whether the powers of the ICDR do not prove to be arbitrary thus making the rationale underpinning the institutional competence to remove individual arbitrators unclear in front of the parties. This, in fact, may only aggravate the parties' frustration regarding the bonds between arbitral institutions and arbitrators.

Regarding the SCC, the SCC Board has limited means to sanction arbitrators who fail to perform their duties. However, the SCC Arbitration Rules stress the finality of the Board's decisions concerning the preliminary challenge made by the party in cases in which the other party to arbitration remains silent as to the arisen circumstances. This supports the efficiency of the challenge even if the opposing party delays the proceedings.[76] What is more, Article 16(1)(iii) of the SCC Arbitration Rules authorizes the SCC Board to "release an arbitrator from appointment" whenever, among other things, an arbitrator "fails to perform his/her function in an adequate manner".[77] This means that the SCC Board may examine the arbitrator's misconduct in accordance with the standards established in this regard within the SCC arbitration practice, and in this sense the SCC Board enjoys certain control over its own arbitrators.

The comparison of the arbitration rules above shows how arbitral institutions have developed certain mechanisms for assessing the possible dismissal of fractious arbitrators on their own initiative. The institutional replacement of arbitrators is a good development insofar as it reflects some kind of supervisory power of arbitral institutions over the arbitrators' conduct. However, as demonstrated by the analysis, it seems doubtful whether the institutional authority to replace an arbitrator is a real authority that could be regarded as the informal institutional sanctions within the meaning of the early internal legitimacy of institutional regimes.

The major issue relates to the way in which the parties understand the institutional authority to revoke arbitrator's appointments. In fact, it is the opinion of the author that the institutional authority to replace an arbitrator has more significance for the parties rather than for the arbitrators who are subject to such procedures. This is so because the institutional decisions on the replacement of arbitrators are to signal to the parties that, in cases of violation by arbitrators of the parties' arbitration agreements or institutional rules, the parties have someone

[76]Article 15(4) of the SCC Arbitration Rules, which states that: "If the other party agrees to the challenge, the arbitrator shall resign. In all other cases, the Board shall make the final decision on the challenge".

[77]Article 16(1)(iii) of the SCC Arbitration Rules, which obliges the SCC Board to release an arbitrator from appointment in the case in which he or she is otherwise prevented from fulfilling his or her duties.

to refer to, counting on the transparent decision that could "compensate" the lost trust toward the fractious arbitrator. Yet again, the replacement of arbitrators by arbitral institutions could have societal implications for the relationships and dynamics within institutional arbitration proceedings that were disrupted not necessarily only because of legal irregularities (such as violation of due process standards by an arbitrator). The replacement of arbitrators could have relevance also when the arbitrator's behaviour simply made parties feel that the parties' case only insignificantly appeared in his or her agenda to increase the reputation of an arbitrator rather than being subject of a serious analysis to be conducted in an impartial and independent manner. Perhaps, in order to increase the societal significance of the institutional replacement of arbitrators, the arbitral institutions could allow the parties' access to the quasi-hearings. This would create an opportunity for the parties to express their concerns regarding arbitrators' challenges leading to removals of arbitrators. At the same time, the appropriate members of institutional organs could face such concerns and provide the justification of such decisions in front of the parties instead of contemplating on them alone behind closed institutional doors. The parties would certainly appreciate if they were taken seriously.

In addition, the replacement of arbitrators, even if called here a *sanction*, does not seem to have any preventive function vis-à-vis the fractious arbitrators. The reason for this is that the arbitrators are not members of arbitral institutions under the aegis of which they operate. This means that even if the arbitrator had been removed by the arbitral institution in the past, there is no formal obstacle for this arbitrator to be appointed in future arbitrations within the same institutional regime. The anecdotal evidence suggests that even in cases of serious and deliberate irregularities on the side of arbitrators, arbitral institutions often return to these arbitrators after a short period of time following their misconduct. The reason for that is simple: there are not enough arbitrators specialized in the fields occupied by previously fractious arbitrators whom arbitral institutions could approach. Given that, it is hard to claim that the institutional replacement of arbitrators constitutes a sufficient mechanism to increase the compliance by institutional arbitrators with the institutional arbitration policies. Even though the replacement of arbitrators usually results in the revocation of their outstanding fees, it is difficult to assume that such a financial sanction may in fact be detrimental to a professional arbitrator (who would most likely have a few parallel arbitrations on his or her agenda at the same time). Also, the arbitral institution that removed the arbitrator may easily "compensate" such revocation in future arbitration cases.

4.3.2.2 Codes of Ethics and Codes of Conduct for Institutional Arbitrators

From the leading arbitral institutions analysed here, only the AAA and its international branch, the ICDR, developed its own internal code of ethics for arbitrators.[78] This may be connected with the fact that both the AAA and the ICDR established the most formal relationship with its own arbitrators. For example, the ICDR maintains the Panel of Arbitrators and Mediators and the standards for the ICDR arbitrators-to-be are relatively strict.[79] The vacancy openings for joining the Panel are limited (usually appearing every year) and the candidates must meet a range of requirements in order to be accepted as the ICDR Arbitrators, including demonstrating the dedication to "upholding the AAA Code of Ethics for Arbitrators".[80]

The modern AAA Code of Ethics for Arbitrators in Commercial Disputes (the Code) was originally prepared in 1977 as a joint initiative of the AAA and the American Bar Association (the ABA).[81] Subsequently, the Code was amended in 2003 and approved by the ABA House of Delegates on 9 February 2004 as well as by the Executive Committee of the Board of Directors of the AAA.[82] The Preamble to the Code reads as follows:

> The use of arbitration to resolve a wide variety of disputes has grown extensively and forms a significant part of the system of justice on which our society relies for a fair determination of legal rights. Persons who act as arbitrators therefore undertake serious responsibilities to the public, as well as to the parties. Those responsibilities include important ethical obligations.[83]

---

[78]See AAA's Code of Ethics for Arbitrators in Commercial Disputes 2004. https://www.adr.org/aaa/ShowProperty?nodeId=/UCM/ADRSTG_003867. Accessed 25 April 2016. However, it should be stressed here that some other arbitral institutions, such as the CAM considered as regional arbitral institution implemented the codes of ethics for their own arbitrators that seem to be equipped with efficient enforcement mechanisms. See: the later part of the discussion included in this section.

[79]See the information available at the AAA's website under the section on International Center for Dispute Resolution: ICDR Arbitrators & Mediators. https://www.icdr.org/icdr/faces/icdr-resources/icdrarbitratorsmediators?_afrLoop=316706666705919&_afrWindowMode=0&_afrWindowId=18iyqqkovq_171#%40%3F_afrWindowId%3D18iyqqkovq_171%26_afrLoop%3D316706666705919%26_afrWindowMode%3D0%26_adf.ctrl-state%3D18iyqqkovq_247. Accessed 25 April 2016.

[80]See Application Information for Becoming an ICDR Arbitrator and Mediator. https://www.icdr.org/icdr/faces/icdrresources/icdrarbitratorsmediators?_afrLoop=316706666705919&_afrWindowMode=0&_afrWindowId=18iyqqkovq_171#%40%3F_afrWindowId%3D18iyqqkovq_171%26_afrLoop%3D316706666705919%26_afrWindowMode%3D0%26_adf.ctrl-state%3D18iyqqkovq_247. Accessed 25 April 2016. There the ICDR sets forth the necessary qualifications of the prospective ICDR arbitrators (including, inter alia, minimum of 15 years of senior-level business or professional experience, and a membership in a professional organization.

[81]The information provided in: AAA's Code of Ethics for Arbitrators in Commercial Disputes 2004. https://www.adr.org/aaa/ShowProperty?nodeId=/UCM/ADRSTG_003867. Accessed 25 April 2016.

[82]Ibid.

[83]Ibid., Preamble.

> [...] this Code sets forth generally accepted standards of ethical conduct for the guidance of arbitrators and parties in commercial disputes, in the hope of contributing to the maintenance of high standards and continued confidence in the process of arbitration.[84]

Pursuant to its Preamble, the Code applies to every arbitration apart from labour cases (that are governed by a separate code of ethics). However, it does not form part of the organization structure of the institutions which decide to adopt it nor does it constitute part of the arbitration rules of such institutions unless they expressly provide so.[85] This signifies that the AAA Code can also be applied by other arbitration organizations in the US (and perhaps also outside the US), not only by the AAA or the ICDR.[86] However, regardless of the idealistic goals of the Code, the AAA's experience concerning the significance of the Code showed the practical problems with the enforcement of the canons expressed in the Code against fractious arbitrators.[87] The absence of any efficient enforcement mechanism, which would help the institution discipline or sanction AAA arbitrators, also showed a lack of accountability of the AAA arbitrators to the AAA itself. Some commentators stress that arbitral institutions do not have economic incentive to increase the "unwanted publicity and lawsuits", which the enforcement of such codes would imply.[88] Therefore, most institutions are not interested in maintaining public lists of unsuitable arbitrators that did not comply with the codes, and so the major sanction against such arbitrators involves the already discussed replacement of the arbitrators. The replacement procedure, however, only applies to an ongoing arbitration case. To this extent, it does not constitute a harmful sanction for an *international* arbitrator because such an arbitrator will still be able to decide future arbitration cases within the AAA's regime as well as the pending cases within other institutional arbitration regimes. Both the unwillingness and hesitance of arbitral institutions to enforce their codes of conduct can be further evidenced by

---

[84] Ibid., Preamble.

[85] Ibid.

[86] The ICDR Arbitrators should comply with the provisions of the Code, which was made clear already in the Application Information for future ICDR arbitrators or mediators. See: Requirement 4—Reputation: "(b) Dedicated to upholding the AAA Code of Ethics for Arbitrators." In "Application Information for Becoming an ICDR Arbitrator and Mediator." https://www.icdr.org/icdr/faces/icdrresources/icdrarbitratorsmediators?_afrLoop=316706666705919&_afrWindowMode=0&_afrWindowId=18iyqqkovq_171#%40%3F_afrWindowId%3D18iyqqkovq_171%26_afrLoop%3D316706666705919%26_afrWindowMode%3D0%26_adf.ctrl-state%3D18iyqqkovq_247. Accessed 25 April 2016.

[87] See: the forthcoming discussion on the speech of the former President of the AAA, Robert Coulson: The Arbitrator's Duty to the Process in: Arbitration 1988 Emerging Issues for the 1990s Proceedings of the 41st Annual Meeting National Academy of Arbitrators (Gladys W. Gruenberg ed., 1988), cited—by reference to Steven J. Goering Note, The Standard of Impartiality as Applied to Arbitrators by the Federal Courts and Codes of Ethics, 3 GEO. J. LEGAL ETHICS 821, 831 (1990)—in Sabin 2001, 1356.

[88] Sabin 2001, 1356.

the approach of the former President of the AAA, Mr. Robert Coulson, presented during the meeting of the National Academy of Arbitrators in 1988, in which he said:

> Arbitrators who engage in improper or unethical behaviour are listed less frequently or not at all. Usually, the arbitrator's failures are discussed when such action is taken, but not always. The AAA is not eager to be sued.[89]

This justification, coming from a president of an organization which—as one of the few arbitral institutions analysed here—adopted the code of ethics for its own arbitrators, shows that the protection of the parties under the codes of ethics is illusionary, and that the prospective enforcement of these codes is non-existent. This observation demonstrates that the inefficiency of the codes of ethics is connected with the legal concerns and economic goals of institutional arbitration, which lose with the societal dimension of institutional activity. In other words, legal and economic issues prevail when arbitral institutions consider the application of the codes of ethics to institutional arbitration proceedings. This undermines their significance from the perspective of the parties' aims to have their dispute decided by the independent and impartial arbitrators in accordance with the highest professional and ethical standards. Moreover, it is questionable why—even within the economic dimension—the AAA or other institutions are hesitant to implement effective enforcement means within their institutional regimes, as it could only foster the competition between arbitral institutions.

Regarding the three other arbitration institutions analysed here, it seems very plausible that some of the ICC's, SCC's, and the LCIA's arbitrators would at the same time also be members of the Chartered Institute of Arbitrators (CIArb) or its regional branches,[90] which is a self-regulated organization in the field of arbitration.[91] The CIArb adopted its own Code of Conduct for Arbitrators.[92] The CIArb's Code expressly defines the prospective misconduct of its members by also providing certain enforcement mechanisms against fractious arbitrators.[93] The neutrals who participate in the arbitration proceedings as CIArb's members must comply with the provisions of the Code, otherwise the CIArb will be authorized to screen

[89]Ibid.

[90]The CIArb boasts a global membership of around 12,500 individuals. See: About: Welcome to the Chartered Institute of Arbitrators (CIArb). http://www.ciarb.org/about. Accessed 25 April 2016.

[91]The CIArb is a London-based, not-for-profit charity that maintains worldwide educational and promotional activities in the field of arbitration and dispute resolution through its international branches. For more information see: The Chartered Institute of Arbitrators: Royal Charter Bye-Laws and Schedule to the Bye-Laws 2013; About: Welcome to the Chartered Institute of Arbitrators (CIArb). http://www.ciarb.org/about. Accessed 25 April 2016.

[92]The Chartered Institute of Arbitrators Code of Professional and Ethical Conduct for Members 2009.

[93]Ibid.

the complaints on the misconduct of arbitrators. The CIArb cannot, however, review the arbitrators' awards that resulted from the poor performance of arbitrators. The compliant procedure follows the exchange of documents, which should provide evidence for the arbitrator's misconduct, as defined in para 15.2 of the CIArb's By-laws.[94]

Pursuant to para 15.2, the misconduct of an arbitrator may involve, inter alia, "a significant breach of professional or ethical conduct which shall include the Code of Professional and Ethical Conduct or other similar document published from time to time by the Institute".[95] Even though it is not certain what sanctions the CIArb enforces against its members in practice, the solutions adopted by the Institute seem more convincing than those developed by the AAA. The questions remains, however, how effective the CIArb's compliant procedure remains in practice, as it seems to have mostly reputational value for the conduct of arbitrators. Moreover, the question is how such horizontal regulations of arbitrators' conduct (that can be compared to the those stemming from the IBA Guidelines on Conflict of Interests in International Arbitration) correspond with their domestic counterparts (if any). Given the interchangeability of the roles in institutional arbitration and the jurisdictional cocktail coming into existence in international arbitration proceedings, some of these codes of ethics or conduct may in fact become unenforceable due to the confusion regarding the applicability of these codes to the institutional arbitration actors in question.[96] In this view, it is arguable whether any of the studied arbitral institutions had an express or tacit control over the institutional arbitrators, which, from a broader perspective, undermines the private accountability of any particular arbitration regime. [97]

That being said, there are certain arbitral institutions that not only draft codes of ethics for arbitrators that contain the provisions that allow certain sanctions to be applied in front of the arbitrators but also make the provisions of these codes an integral part of the arbitration rules of these arbitral institutions. This is the case

[94]The Chartered Institute of Arbitrators: Royal Charter Bye-Laws and Schedule to the Bye-Laws 2013.

[95]Paragraph 15.2.2 of the The Chartered Institute of Arbitrators: Royal Charter Bye-Laws and Schedule to the Bye-Laws 2013. See also: CIArb: Complaints Booklet. Pursuant to para 15.2 of the aforementioned Bye-laws the other grounds for a prospective misconduct of arbitrators should be the following:

(1) conduct which is injurious to the good name of the Institute, renders a person unfit to be a member of the Institute or is likely to bring the Institute into disrepute;
(2) [...]
(3) falling significantly below the standards expected of a competent Practitioner or a competent professional person acting in the field of private dispute resolution;
(4) a failure without reasonable excuse to comply with a direction and/or a recommendation of a Peer Review Panel constituted under Bye-law 15.1;
(5) a significant breach of any of the Articles of the Charter or of these Bye-laws (or any Regulation or rule published thereunder from time to time).

[96]See Rogers 2014.

[97]Through a tacit control I understand the institutional reliance on the external codes of conduct or ethics for institutional arbitrators.

with the CAM, which in Article 13 of its Code of Ethics of Arbitrators clearly states that the arbitrators who fail to comply with the Code of Ethics "shall be replaced by the Chamber of Arbitration, which may also refuse to confirm him on subsequent proceedings because of this violation".[98] Usually, compliance with this provision is achieved by means of: trainings, the express provisions on arbitrators' duties and the institutional system of sanctions.[99] In fact, the CAM appear to have designed a comprehensive system of enforcement of the duties of the CAM's arbitrators mainly by means of Articles 18.4 and 20.1 of the CAM Rules, as well as through the already mentioned provisions of the Code of Ethics of Arbitrators. Pursuant to Article 18.4 of the Rules, each arbitrator needs to be confirmed by the CAM's internal organ, the Arbitral Council, after signing the declaration of independence.[100] Correspondingly, under Article 20.1(e) of the CAM Rules, an arbitrator may be removed *ex officio* if he or she violates the duties of the Arbitral Tribunal under the CAM Rules or on other serious grounds. Although these two controlling mechanisms at first glance do not seem to differ from the powers of the previously studied arbitral institutions to replace arbitrators on their own initiative, a closer analysis reveals that in CAM arbitration it is not the authority of the arbitration rules alone that allows the CAM to exercise its control over recalcitrant arbitrators. Instead, it is a combination of sanctions included in the CAM Rules and other soft-law mechanisms such as the Code of Ethics that together contribute to the increased effectiveness of the enforcement of CAM's controlling mechanisms in front of individual arbitrators.

The fact that the CAM enjoys broad autonomy in refusing the confirmation of arbitrators in future arbitrations and that it is willing to use this autonomy in practice speaks for a relative success of the CAM's disciplining methods vis-à-vis arbitrators. Yet again, the major strength of the CAM's sanctioning regime lies in the CAM's willingness to limit the participation of certain arbitrators in their arbitration system for a longer period of time following their poor performance in an individual case, which, as already stated, is not the case with most leading arbitral institutions. The reason for that is that usually the institutional bonds between the prominent international arbitrators seem to be stronger in the case of leading arbitral institutions rather than in the event of the regional centres. For example, the fact that the CAM is increasingly open to the idea of developing young arbitrators gives this institution more freedom in choosing new players (and banning the old ones) than in the case of the prominent institutions that remain reluctant to appoint new arbitrators. In the case of the latter institutions, the tight bonds with the experienced international arbitrators also prevent these institutions from further

[98]CAM, Code of Ethics of Arbitrators. http://www.camera-arbitrale.it/en/Arbitration/Arbitration+Rules/Code+of+ethics.php?id=104. Accessed 25 April 2016.

[99]Orlandi 2012, 649.

[100]Ibid., 656.

restricting the appointments of the prominent, repeat players simply because there are not enough arbitrators falling beyond the exclusive club connected with the relevant institution.

Lastly, it is unclear why arbitral institutions do not develop codes of ethics or codes of conduct for employees of arbitral institutions and the members of institutional organs that, in fact, render decisions concerning the performance of the parties and arbitrators. As already noted in Chap. 2, there has been an increasing trend among arbitral institutions to adopt codes of conduct or guidelines for the parties or their representatives.[101] Leaving aside the content of such guidelines that falls beyond the present discussion, the non-inclusion by arbitral institutions of the provisions on the standards of their own conduct appears highly unequal. This is for two reasons. First, because arbitral institutions should signal to all participants in arbitration proceedings that high standards of performance and arbitration ethos are applicable to any and all institutional arbitration actors (not only institutional arbitrators and the parties). Second, the lack of codes of conduct or ethics for the members and employees of arbitral institutions, as well as experts participating in institutional arbitration proceedings, indirectly weakens the enforcement of the existent codes of conduct and ethics for arbitrators. Why would individual arbitrators wish to comply with the internal codes of conduct if those who are enforcing such codes do not appear accountable based on such codes at all? Once again, this undermines the efficiency of the internal mechanisms of accountability within institutional arbitration regimes that appears at odds with the early operation of institutional arbitration that was largely based on arbitration ethos.

4.3.2.3 Lists of Arbitrators

Some arbitral institutions maintain lists of qualified arbitrators, which serve as a suggestion to the parties deciding to recourse to a particular arbitral institution or are taken into account by relative organs of arbitral institutions when appointing arbitrators on behalf of the parties.[102] Although the LCIA, the ICC, or the SCC Institute did not provide for such a straightforward co-operation with arbitrators as the ICDR or the AAA, all these institutions maintain databases including the CVs of the arbitrators that already participated in their arbitration proceedings. This allows the arbitral institution to develop a network of informally affiliated arbitrators—regarded as the members of institutional "clubs" (often in the manner that is

[101] ICC Commission on Arbitration and ADR 2014. Effective Management of Arbitration: A Guide for In-House Counsel and Other Party Representatives. International Chamber of Commerce and the Annex to the 2014 LCIA Rules entitled General Guidelines for the Parties' Legal Representatives.

[102] In fact, some arbitral institutions operating in industries other than commercial arbitration maintain mandatory lists of arbitrators and the parties cannot select an individual falling beyond these lists. This is the case with the CAS, which maintains a so-called closed list system.

not entirely transparent to the public). These lists or databases seem to be a relict of the early institutional lists of the expertise arbitrators developed by early arbitral institutions. However, they do not appear to have the similar significance as their predecessors, in the meaning of the very societal dimension of the early institutional regimes. Following the argumentation of the former President of the AAA, Mr. Coulson,[103] they are stipulated by the economic aims of the institutions to participate in the market for arbitration services rather than to discipline the misconduct of the arbitrators. These observations should be kept in mind for the proposals of the reforms to the modern institutional liability regimes provided in Chap. 6.

4.4 Imperfect Competition and the Harmonized Contractual Institutional Immunity: On the Problems with the Economic Dimension

Given the discussion on the lack of institutional response to the commercial aspect of limitation of liability clauses, it is assumed that the public rationale underpinning institutional contractual immunity clauses distorts the competition between arbitral institutions. As a result, arbitral institutions comply with the public regulations on liability (if any), which shifts the dynamics of competition from the private to the public level. This leads to the situation in which the wording of institutional liability clauses of different institutions is often similar or the same as a consequence of the desire of institutions to exclude their liability to the largest extent possible under any, potentially applicable, national law. This can be illustrated by the recent changes introduced in both the 2014 ICDR Procedures and the 2014 LCIA Rules that largely mimic the provisions of Article 40 of the 2012 ICC Arbitration Rules. That is, these rules seek for almost absolute exclusion of liability unless such exclusion is shown to be prohibited by the law applicable.

In this vein, arbitral institutions diminish the exclusive nature of their services and instead they follow the linear trend towards the universalization of their rules and practices by minimizing the inputs from individual arbitration users in this regard. This is why arbitral institutions eliminate any possible negotiations of the liability clauses by the private arbitration parties. This is surprising to the extent that by doing so arbitral institutions expose themselves to unknown financial risks relating to liability claims. This is because arbitral institutions allow the liability claim to be initiated in the court of any forum, which invites a judge to subsequently determine the law applicable to this claim in a manner that may turn out to be extremely unfavourable to arbitral institutions. Would not the possibility for the parties to affect the scope of liability of arbitral institutions (e.g. by means of

[103]Sect. 4.3.2.2.

negotiation) be more favourable to arbitral institutions than the almost blank exclusion of liability? Would not the financial cap on liability or the clear-cut catalogue of acts or omission for which arbitral institutions would not be liable as a result of negotiation, decrease the current uncertainty faced by arbitral institutions as a consequence of leaving the interpretations of their liability to unknown judges under unknown law and in the unknown forum? Such parties' participation in determining the scope of institutional liability could restore the competition among arbitration centres, as understood in the meaning of the traditional commercial function of arbitral institutions. Naturally, the implementation of liability clauses into institutional regimes would also imply the reliance by such institutions on insurance schemes in order to protect the institutional misconduct. All these variables could in practice be used by institutions as additional means of competition.[104]

The competition between arbitral institutions is currently incomplete also because the parties have incomplete information regarding the ways in which the internal organization of arbitral institutions is structured to increase the effectiveness of the performance of all institutional arbitration actors. In other words, arbitration users (whether repeat or accidental) do not know whether hierarchical institutional structures provide for any mechanisms of accountability that could justify the exclusion of liability of most arbitral institutions. This situation was already presented in Chap. 3 in the context of the problems with the quality signalling by arbitral institutions. That is why the parties, when choosing the arbitration centre to administer their dispute, have limited information to rationally decide on which institutional liability regime, accompanied by informal mechanisms of accountability, would best fit their preferences and expectations associated with the dispute in question.

For example, if arbitral institutions provided more information regarding the internal technicalities in using the lists of arbitrators or enforcing the codes of ethics or codes of conduct to the parties, this could in fact increase the recourse to these institutions by the parties who currently seek for more transparency in regards to these issues. To the contrary, some parties who remain uninterested in exposing themselves to any risks relating to the increased transparency of institutional arbitration proceedings would refer their dispute to an arbitral institution who do not provide for more transparency in this regard. All in all, the quality signalling through the institutional explanations and clarifications of the internal mechanisms of accountability could in fact increase the rationality of the parties when making choices on their preferable arbitral institution. Currently, the parties cannot make fully informed choices simply because the provisions on liability of the leading arbitral institutions—being largely similar and opaque—prevent them from doing so.

As illustrated in the analysis of the enforcement means relating to in the CAM's Code of Ethics of Arbitrators, it appears that the development of new

---

[104]See: Sect. 6.4.3 of Chap. 6 and the response of the proposed liability clauses to the economic dimension of institutional operation.

models of internal sanctions may also further contribute to the new competition dynamics. Arbitral institutions, by drawing a connection between their internal sanctions and arbitrators' performance, could open up toward new arbitrators. This could lead toward the development of a new generation of arbitrators and hence encourage the competition between new arbitrators and internationally renowned arbitrators that are now regarded as monopolists within the international arbitration market.

4.5 Conclusion

The analysis above showed that the contemporary institutional regulations of liability—which involve the institutional contractual immunity of *all* arbitration actors, and in some cases also the contractual immunity from process—are insufficient, as they do not address the optimal scope of institutional arbitral liability proposed in Chap. 3. It was proposed in the previous chapter that institutional arbitral liability should accommodate the triad of institutional functions: the legal, societal, and economic dimensions of institutional arbitration (see Sects. 3.2–3.4). As demonstrated in this chapter, this is not the case with the modern institutional regulations of liability contained in the arbitration rules of the leading arbitral institutions.

From **the legal perspective** the major controversies involved:

- The contractual immunity in its current form, hence granting arbitral institutions exclusive authority to exclude their own liability (and the liability of other institutional arbitration actors) in an almost absolute manner, which does not correspond to the contractual and commercial goals of arbitral institutions as professional contractors. From the contractual point of view, sophisticated contractors are rarely allowed to largely limit or exclude the liability for the performance of their crucial contractual obligations. Even if this happens, such clauses can be regarded as unfair contractual terms and therefore be refused enforcement by public courts. From the perspective of the commercial goals of contractors, it was demonstrated that the solutions adopted by arbitral institutions to disallow negotiations of limitation of liability clauses with the parties are highly controversial. The reason for such controversy was that arbitral institutions increasingly opt for the public interpretations of the scope of their liability by public judges in unknown courts and under the unknown applicable laws.
- The contractual immunity of experts and other persons appointed by arbitral tribunal, institutional arbitrators, members of institutional organs, and institutional employees (when applicable) granted by means of the authority of the arbitral institutions. On the one hand, it was demonstrated that arbitral institutions do not posses legal authority to grant contractual immunity to all institutional arbitration actors (such as tribunal-appointed experts). On the other hand, it was shown that although such authority seem to exist in relation to some actors

(arbitrators, members of institutional organs, or employees), it does not necessarily justify the exclusion of liability of arbitral institutions for acts or omission of these actors.
- The contractual immunity from process of both arbitral institutions and institutional arbitrators in the jurisdictions providing for both the absolute arbitral immunity and the monetary sanctions against the parties who decided to sue arbitration actors without the proper grounds. This was particularly striking given the lack of procedural safeguards for the parties to formally complain about the misconduct of institutional arbitration actors within the institutional regimes operating in these jurisdictions.

From **the societal perspective** the major problems concerned:

- The public rationale standing behind the institutional arbitration clauses, which undermines the private authority in institutional regimes, as defined by the internal legitimacy of the early institutional regimes. In other words, the regulations of liability in their current forms, which exclude any form of participation of the parties in negotiation of their wordings, diminish the societal, communitarian values associated with the early institutional arbitration process. Consequently, arbitral institutions put more emphasis on the public, external regulations of liability that ultimately serve as a protection of the integrity of institutional arbitration.
- Non-existence or inefficiency of the internal mechanisms of accountability, which undermines the very private confidence of the parties in institutional arbitration. This proved particularly worrisome when considering the lack of any forms of institutional influence on the conduct of institutional employees and the members of institutional organs as confronted with the sporadic institutional attempts to subject arbitrators, the parties, and the parties' representatives to internal codes of ethics and codes of conduct. Such lack of balance regarding the internal mechanisms of accountability largely distorts the equality in institutional proceedings and further undermines the institutional authority to enforce informal sanctions in front of institutional arbitrators or the parties. This is mostly because of the unaccountability of arbitral institutions themselves to any other actors participating in arbitration proceedings.

From **the economic perspective** the major insufficiency involved:

- The impact of the unified contractual immunity clauses—expressing the international trend of arbitral institutions toward almost blanket exclusion of liability, if permissible under relevant national law—on the incomplete competition within the market for institutional services. This meant the orientation of the institutional goals to public authorities instead of toward private parties in the field of competition.
- The impact of incomplete information regarding the institutional liability and accountability regimes on: (a) the selection of arbitral institutions by the parties in the sense of forum shopping, and (b) the perception of quality of institutional arbitration services by the parties to arbitration.

In view of these insufficiencies of the institutional regulations of liability, the next chapter will focus exclusively on legal regulations of liability in the selected jurisdictions (if any). The analysis will concern the interplay between the national regulations of, and the views on, the arbitral liability (if any) with the triad of institutional functions proposed in Chap. 3. This will serve the assessment of the issue on how the current national regulations and visions regarding institutional arbitral liability in fact relate to the optimal scope of institutional arbitral liability defined in Chap. 3.

References

AAA. 2003. Supplementary Rules for Class Arbitration https://www.adr.org/aaa/ShowPDF?url=/cs/groups/commercial/documents/document/dgdf/mda0/~edisp/adrstg_004129.pdf. Accessed 25 April 2016.

AAA. 2009. Commercial Arbitration Rules and Mediation Procedures (including Procedures for Large, Complex Commercial Disputes).

AAA. 2013. Commercial Arbitration Rules and Mediation Procedures (including Procedures for Large, Complex Commercial Disputes).

AAA's Code of Ethics for Arbitrators in Commercial Disputes. 2004. https://www.adr.org/aaa/ShowProperty?nodeId=/UCM/ADRSTG_003867. Accessed 25 April 2016.

About: Welcome to the Chartered Institute of Arbitrators (CIArb). http://www.ciarb.org/about/. Accessed 25 April 2016.

Application Information for Becoming an ICDR Arbitrator and Mediator. https://www.icdr.org/icdr/faces/icdrresources/icdrarbitratorsmediators?_afrLoop=316706666705919&_afrWindowMode=0&_afrWindowId=18iyqqkovq_171#%40%3F_afrWindowId%3D18iyqqkovq_171%26_afrLoop%3D316706666705919%26_afrWindowMode%3D0%26_adf.ctrl-state%3D18iyqqkovq_247 Accessed 25 April 2016.

Bond, Stephen R., Paralika Marily, and Secomb Matthew. 2010. [Exclusion of Liability] Article 34. In: Loukas A. Mistelis, ed. Concise International Arbitration. Kluwer Law International, 305–401.

CAM. Code of Ethics of Arbitrators. http://www.camera-arbitrale.it/en/Arbitration/Arbitration+Rules/Code+of+ethics.php?id=104. Accessed 25 April 2016.

CIArb: Complaints Booklet. http://www.ciarb.org/docs/default-source/default-document-library/complaints-booklet1.pdf?sfvrsn=4. Accessed 25 April 2016.

Derains, Yves, and Schwartz Eric A. 2005. A Guide to the ICC Rules of Arbitration, 2nd Edition Revised. Kluwer Law International.

Fry, Jason, Greenberg Simon, Mazza Francesca, 2012. The Secretariat's Guide to ICC Arbitration. 2012 Edition ICC Publication No. 729.

Hofbauer, Simone, Burkart Michael, Bander Lara, and Tari Mehtap. 2013. Survey On Scrutiny of Arbitral Institutions. In: Philipp Habegger, Daniel Hochstrasser, Gabrielle Nater-Bass, and Urs Weber-Stecher, eds. Arbitral Institutions Under Scrutiny. ASA Special Series 40 JurisNet, LLC, 1–35.

ICC Arbitration Rules 1998.

ICC Arbitration Rules 2012. http://www.iccwbo.org/Products-and-Services/Arbitration-and-ADR/Arbitration/ICC-Rules-of-Arbitration/. Accessed 25 April 2016.

ICC Commission on Arbitration and ADR. 2014. Effective Management of Arbitration: A Guide for In-House Counsel and Other Party Representatives. International Chamber of Commerce.

ICDR Procedures 2009.

ICDR Procedures 2014. https://www.*icdr*.org/icdr/faces/i_search/i_rule/i_rule_detail?doc=ADRSTAGE2025301&_afrLoop=318236937422936&_afrWindowMode=0&_afrWindowId=18iyqqkovq_558#%40%3F_afrWindowId%3D18iyqqkovq_558%26_afrLoop%3D318236937422936%26doc%3DADRSTAGE2025301%26_afrWindowMode%3D0%26_adf.ctrl-state%3D18iyqqkovq_618. Accessed 25 April 2016.
International Center for Dispute Resolution: ICDR Arbitrators & Mediators. https://www.icdr.org/icdr/faces/icdrresources/icdrarbitratorsmediators?_afrLoop=318198873949209&_afrWindowMode=0&_afrWindowId=18iyqqkovq_419#%40%3F_afrWindowId%3D18iyqqkovq_419%26_afrLoop%3D318198873949209%26_afrWindowMode%3D0%26_adf.ctrl-state%3D18iyqqkovq_495. Accessed 25 April 2016.
LCIA Arbitration Rules 1998. http://www.lcia.org/dispute_resolution_services/lcia_arbitration_rules.aspx. Accessed 25 April 2016.
LCIA Arbitration Rules 2014. http://www.lcia.org/Dispute_Resolution_Services/lcia-arbitration-rules-2014.aspx. Accessed 25 April 2016.
Orlandi, Chiara Giovannucci. 2012. Code of Ethics of Arbitrators. In: Ugo Draetta and Riccardo Luzzatto, eds. The Chamber of Arbitration of Milan Rules: A Commentary. Juris Net, LLC, 645–661.
Rambaud, Sandrine. 2007. French Supreme Court Strikes out Limitation of Liability Provision from an IT Contract Where the Software Publisher Has Breached a Material Obligation. Lexology Website. http://www.lexology.com/library/detail.aspx?g=64f1f21b-f865-4289-98c4-04190cb666e9. Accessed 25 April 2016.
Rogers, Catherine A. 2014. Ethics in International Arbitration. Oxford University Press.
Rutledge, Peter B. 2004. Toward a Contractual Approach to Arbitral Immunity. Georgia Law Review 39: 151–214.
Sabin, Cameron L. 2001. The Adjudicatory Boat Without a Keel: Private Arbitration and the Need for Public Oversight of Arbitrators. Iowa Law Review 87: 1337–1382.
SCC Arbitration Rules. 2010. http://sccinstitute.com/dispute-resolution/rules/. Accessed 25 April 2016.
Schöldström, Patrik. 1998. The Arbitrator's Mandate: A Comparative Study of Relationships in Commercial Arbitration under the Laws of England, Germany, Sweden and Switzerland. Elanders Gotab.
Société SNF v. International Chamber of Commerce. Cour d'appel de Paris (1. Ch.). 2009.
The Chartered Institute of Arbitrators Code of Professional and Ethical Conduct for Members. 2009. https://www.ciarb.org/docs/default-source/practice-guidelines-protocols-and-rules/code-of-professional-and-ethical-conduct-october-2009.pdf?sfvrsn=2. Accessed 25 April 2016.
The Chartered Institute of Arbitrators: Royal Charter Bye-Laws and Schedule to the Bye-Laws. 2013. http://www.ciarb.org/docs/default-source/standards-ethics-policy/9066_ciarb_bye-laws_a-pdf-jan14.pdf?sfvrsn=4. Accessed 25 April 2016.
The UK Arbitration Act 1996, Chapter 23. http://www.legislation.gov.uk/ukpga/1996/23/contents. Accessed 25 April 2016.
UNCITRAL Rules on Transparency in Treaty-Based Investor-State Arbitration. 2014. http://www.uncitral.org/uncitral/en/uncitral_texts/arbitration/2014Transparency.html. Accessed 25 April 2016.
Unfair Contract Terms Act 1977 - Chapter 50. 1977. http://www.legislation.gov.uk/ukpga/1977/50.
United Nations Convention on Transparency in Treaty-Based Investor-State Arbitration. 2014. http://www.uncitral.org/uncitral/en/uncitral_texts/arbitration/2014Transparency_Convention.html.
US National Conference of Commissioners on Uniform State Laws. 2000. Uniform Arbitration Act (Last Revisions Completed Year 2000). http://www.uniformlaws.org/shared/docs/arbitration/arbitration_final_00.pdf. Accessed 25 April 2016.
Wade, Shai, Clifford Philip , and Clanchy James. 2015. A Commentary on the LCIA Arbitration Rules 2014. London: Sweet & Maxwell.

Chapter 5
The Legal Dimension of Institutional Arbitration: On the Current National Regulations and "Visions" of Institutional Arbitral Liability

Contents

5.1 Introduction

The discussion on institutional regulations of liability in Chap. 4 demonstrated that the effectiveness and enforceability of liability clauses contained in the arbitration rules are largely dependent on the legal regulations of liability of institutional arbitration actors stemming from domestic laws. Against this background, this chapter compares the current national legal regulations of both institutional arbitration and the scope of liability of institutional arbitration actors (if any), as well as the different approaches of domestic courts to the prospective liability of arbitration

B. Warwas, *The Liability of Arbitral Institutions: Legitimacy Challenges and Functional Responses*, DOI 10.1007/978-94-6265-111-1_5

institutions (so-called "visions") as expressed in case law from jurisdictions where the leading arbitral institutions are headquartered.[1]

These issues are of particular practical importance for both arbitral institutions and the parties to institutional arbitrations. On the one hand, they provide an understanding of the interpretations of private regulations of institutional liability by domestic courts. As such, they guide the reader through the responses of domestic courts to the question of whether arbitral institutions may in fact be held liable to the parties for acts or omission in the course of arbitrations, and, if so, what categories of acts or omission can amount to institutional liability. On the other hand, the analysis of these problems serves as an explanation of the scope of protection granted to the parties under national laws in cases of misconduct in the course of the institutional arbitration proceedings.

Picture the following hypothetical situation. A party to the ICC arbitration seated in New York—being a company incorporated in the Netherlands—decides to file a liability claim against the ICC for the breach of its contractual obligations to conduct the arbitration in an expedited manner. The party claims that the series of omission on the side of the ICC counsel resulted in the delay of the arbitration proceedings that amounted to 2 years. Which laws—potentially applicable to the case in question (e.g. US law, Dutch law or French law)—would allow certain liability of the ICC if it is found in breach of its obligations resulting in an injury of the party at hand? How will the party in question decide on the court of the forum bearing in mind the broad wording of the ICC limitation of liability clause incorporated into the contract with this party? In other words, which laws applicable to the liability claim would prohibit the ICC's regulations of liability under Article 40 of the 2012 ICC Arbitration Rules?

As will be shown in this chapter, there are no straightforward answers to most questions posed above. This deepens the confusion among arbitration users as to the status and functions of arbitral institutions as interpreted by domestic courts. This, in turn, affects the forum shopping regarding the prospective liability claims, inviting the parties to seek the most favourable forum to hear their claims, often with little or no legal connection to the arbitration that gave rise to the liability claim in question.

The chapter comprises two parts. The first part of the chapter unfolds within both theoretical and practical problems related to the divergent national regulations and interpretations of both the legal nature and the scope of responsibility

[1]The analysis of the selected national provisions concerning the status and functions of institutional arbitration actors (if any), and also of the selected case law that expresses the approaches of domestic courts on the same issues does not claim to be exhaustive. Rather, it serves as guidance for the presentation of the often conflicting stances taken on the role of institutional arbitration proceedings by public authorities at national levels in the course of legal proceedings initiated against these actors by the parties.

of institutional arbitration actors. The purpose of this part is to stress the difficulty on the part of national legislators and domestic judges in determining the legal status and functions of institutional arbitration against the background of traditional contract law theories and various immunity doctrines protecting public officials under national laws. Moreover, the first part emphasizes the troubles that domestic judges have in understanding the practicalities of institutional arbitration proceedings, which indirectly affect the protection of injured parties in liability lawsuits against arbitral institutions.

The second part of the chapter concerns a more philosophical approach to the both: (1) the international dual function of institutional arbitration, and (2) the public assessment of institutional arbitral liability in view of such international institutional function. Thus, this part critically analyses the conflicting "visions" of the public courts on institutional arbitral liability (within the parameters of Gaillard's theory of representations of international arbitration).[2] In turn, this analysis serves to explain why it is necessary to harmonize these national visions of the performance of contractual obligations by arbitral institutions.

5.2 National Regulations

5.2.1 "Up in the Air": Problems with the Legal Theories of Institutional Arbitration

This part is a comparative analysis of the theoretical issues that domestic judges are faced with while dealing with institutional arbitral liability (or immunity). It is claimed that the inconsistency of the domestic judges regarding these theoretical issues mainly concerns the following: (1) the selective application of different theories of arbitration to institutional arbitration, and (2) the lack of accurate recognition of the unique, dual function of arbitral institutions, which stems from the hybridity of institutional arbitration. The discussion will thus involve questions of the legal status and functions of arbitral institutions as defined in national arbitration laws or civil codes, or as determined by judges in jurisdictions in which the law fails to regulate institutional arbitration.

[2] Sect. 3.2.2.3 of Chap. 3.

5.2.1.1 Legal Status of Arbitral Institutions: Judges or Service Providers?

None of the domestic legal regulations within the analysed jurisdictions provide for express provisions on the legal status of institutional arbitration actors, nor do they reflect on the sources of authority of institutional arbitration obligations. The analysis of the relevant case law below shows that lack of international consensus on the nature of international institutional arbitration allows incoherent domestic interpretations of the functions of arbitral institutions. French judges put more emphasis on the contractual aspect of institutional operation, while public authorities in the US and in the UK mostly recognize the jurisdictional facet of institutional activity (at least in certain stages of the arbitration proceedings). This reflects the divergent civil law and common law stances to the status and functions of the arbitration process in general. Heretofore, Swedish authorities—to the knowledge of the author—have not taken a clear stance on this matter.

5.2.1.1.1 France

French law on arbitration, recently reformed by the *Décret* no. 2011-48 of 13 January 2011,[3] neither explicitly states what the principles to be observed by arbitral institutions in the arbitration process are, nor does it reflect on the prospective legal status of such institutions. The part on domestic arbitration, which, to a certain degree, should also be applied to international arbitration, addresses the so-called "loyalty principle" only on the side of arbitrators and the parties.[4] The only references made to arbitration centres concern the provision of Article 1450 of the French Code and the general provisions of Title I that constitute certain obligations of "a person responsible for administering the arbitration" (*la personne charge d'organiser l'arbitrage*).[5] Article 1450 of the French Code states that whenever an arbitration agreement designates a legal person, such person shall have the power to only administer the arbitration.[6] The general provisions of Title I set forth limited obligations of a person responsible for administering arbitration, which usually emerges in the absence of the relevant specifications of the parties in respect of the organization of the proceedings.[7] Eventually, such obligations can

[3]"Ministry of Justice and Civil Liberties, Republic of France, Decree No. 2011-48 of 13 January 2011 Reforming the Law Governing Arbitration," translated into English by Emmanuel Gaillard, Nanou Leleu-Knobil and Daniela Pellarini of Shearman & Sterling LLP.

[4]See Article 1464 of the French Code, which states that both parties and arbitrators shall act diligently and in good faith in the conduct of the proceedings.

[5]Article 1450 of the French Code.

[6]Ibid.

[7]See the aforementioned Article 1450, Articles 1452, 1453, 1454, 1456, and 1457 of the French Code.

be borne by the "judge acting in support of arbitration" (*le juge d'appui*), that is: the President of a *Tribunal de grande instance,* in the case in which no institution was chosen to administer the proceedings.[8]

These provisions are unclear with regard to the legal nature of institutional arbitration. While some of the provisions correspond—to a certain extent—with the arguments of pure contractualists, who extoled the power of the private contract in any arbitration setting, others suggest certain prerogatives which, in the absence of an arbitral institution, can be assumed by a judge. The latter observation could suggest some jurisdictional powers of arbitral institutions, at least within the meaning of the administrative prerogatives of a judge. However, as will be shown below, the practice of the French courts suggests the opposite interpretation.

In practice, the French courts usually recognize the contractual, private nature of institutional arbitral activity. One of the first cases in which the French courts were faced with the necessity to determine the legal character of institutional relationships concerned the so-called "CEKOBANKA" case, decided in 1986, where the *Tribunal de grande instance de Paris* declared that the party to arbitration (CEKOBANKA) and the administrator of the dispute (the ICC) were contractually bound from the moment of the notification of the ICC of the request for arbitration.[9] The French Court's reasoning in CEKOBANKA was used again in the decision in *République de Guinée v. Chambre arbitrale de Paris* in which the existence of the contractual bonds between the parties and the arbitral institution was again confirmed, placing relevant contractual duties on the institutional arbitration actors.[10] Given that, it should be apparent that the French courts adopted the major assumptions of the contractual theory in defining the role of arbitral institutions in the arbitration process.

Regarding the nature of the acts of arbitral institutions (whether administrative (non-jurisdictional) or jurisdictional), the French courts issued a few relevant decisions in which they confirmed a rather uniform reasoning that the decisions rendered by the ICC in the course of ICC arbitrations should not be regarded as jurisdictional.[11] In 1986, in the case *Société Appareils Dragon*, the French *Cour de Cassation* was to decide, in the final instance, on the claim of the party to ICC arbitration to have its award set aside because of the failure of the ICC Court to dully inform the party of the reasons for its decision to extend the deadline for the issuance of the arbitral award.[12] The French *Cour de Cassation* found that the ICC Court was not in the position to give reasons for its decision on the extension of such deadline, nor to inform the parties when such a decision would be made. This judgement was

[8] Article 1459 of the French Code.

[9] *Ceskilovenska Obchodni Banka A.S. (Cekobanka) C/Chambre de Commerce Internationale.* 1986. *Rev. arb.* (1987) *Tribunal de grande instance de Paris.*

[10] *République de Guinée v. Chambre Arbitrale de Paris* 1987; Rubino-Sammartano 2001, 368.

[11] For an excellent and comprehensive discussion on the decisions of the French courts regarding the topic at hand, see Gerbay forthcoming 2016.

[12] *Société Appareils Dragon v. Empresa Central de Abastecimientas Y Vantas de Equipos, Cour de Cassation (2Ch. Civile)*, 8 June 1983; Derains and Schwartz 2005, 262.

based upon the finding that the ICC Court, unlike arbitrators, does not issue jurisdictional decisions that would require such justification.[13] Consequently, the French *Cour de Cassation* rejected the party's appeal in cassation. In a similar vein, the Paris Court of Appeal in the case *Société-Techni Import Professionel*, noticed that the ICC Court was not a jurisdictional organ and therefore there was no obligation on the side of the ICC Court to provide justification of its decisions made in the course of arbitration.[14] Here, another decision of the French courts requires particular attention, namely the judgement of the *Tribunal de grande instance de Paris* where the French court was faced with the determination of the nature of the ICC Court's decision on *prima facie* jurisdiction when deciding on the possibility of the judicial review of such decision.[15] The *Tribunal de grande instance de Paris* clearly stated there that the ICC Court was not a body issuing jurisdictional decisions that lay in the competences of arbitrators.[16] Rather, the decisions of the ICC Court should correspond with the administrative decisions that are made in the course of the proceedings to facilitate the eventual resolution of a dispute by arbitrators.[17]

The above presentation suggests that, in principle, the French courts are of the view that institutional acts should be regarded as non-jurisdictional decisions that bear resemblance to administrative acts, here made in the course of arbitration proceedings. Several questions arise as to such interpretations from the perspective of the contractual rights of the parties. How does the understanding by the French courts of institutional acts as administrative acts, translate into the parties' contractual rights to require from arbitral institutions that the contractual obligations of the latter are dully performed in the course of arbitration proceedings? Which courts, civil or administrative courts, should have jurisdiction in the parties' claims against arbitral institutions? If institutional acts could be subject to the review by administrative courts, what would be the scope of such a review in the context of institutional arbitration? Bearing in mind that the French courts confirmed the contractual nature of the relationships that emerge in institutional arbitration, how would such relationships be explained under French contract law? These questions, in the opinion of the author, have not yet been dully addressed by the French courts, specifically in the cases analysed above. This deepens the confusion among

[13]In the original language:
[…] *Et attendu que c'est par une interprétation souveraine du Règlement d'arbitrage auquel les parties étaient convenues de se soumettre que l'arrêt, abstraction faite d'un motif surabondant, énonce, hors de toute dénaturation, que la Cour d'arbitrage, qui n'avait pas elle-même la qualité d'arbitre, n'était pas tenue de motiver sa décision de prorogation qui ne présentait pas de caractère juridictionnel, et que le Règlement ne faisait pas obligation à la Cour d'arbitrage d'informer les parties de son intention de prolonger le délai ni même de les aviser de la date à laquelle la prorogation serait éventuellement décidée*. In: Gerbay, forthcoming 2016.

[14]*Société Techni-Import Professionnel v Société Electro Scientific Industries, Cour d'Appel de Paris*, 17 May 1983 with the English translation in: Gerbay, forthcoming 2016.

[15]*Société REDEC et M. Pharaon v Société Uzinexport Import et Chambre de Commerce Internationale, Tribunal de Grande Instance de Paris (Ref.)*, 13 July 1988.

[16]For the English translation in: Gerbay, forthcoming 2016.

[17]Ibid.

the institutional arbitration users regarding the role of arbitral institutions in the arbitration proceedings, at least as depicted by the French courts.

5.2.1.1.2 The US and the UK

Section 1 of the RUAA defines an "arbitration organisation" as an "association, agency, board, commission, or other entity that is neutral and initiates, sponsors, or administers arbitration proceedings or is involved in the appointment of an arbitrator".[18] In particular, the expression "sponsors" is intriguing. It could imply either the contractual support of arbitral institutions in the organization of proceedings or certain jurisdictional interference that is to ensure proper conduct in arbitration. The extension of judicial immunity to arbitration organizations by the US state and federal judges proves the recognition of jurisdictional nature of institutional arbitration in the US. Moreover, as will be analysed in detail in Sect. 5.2.1.2.2.3 below, in certain cases judicial immunity is granted to arbitration organizations *even after* acknowledgement by the courts of the contractual relationships between institutional arbitration actors.[19] This approach certainly emphasizes the jurisdictional aspect of institutional arbitration in the US.

A similar approach to arbitral institutions is found in the UK. The doctrine on judicial immunity, which—as demonstrated in the forthcoming discussion in this chapter[20]—was extended to arbitrators by the English courts, was codified in the UK Arbitration Act of 1996 also with regard to arbitral institutions while acting within the arbitrators' capacity.[21] The provisions of Section 74 of the Act are mandatory, and therefore they cannot be derogated by means of any contractual arrangements between institutional arbitration actors. This demonstrates that the English authorities share the general "common law stance" to arbitral liability. Even though the regulation of the immunity of arbitral institutions in the UK seems more moderate as compared with the US approach, it still strengthens the jurisdictional facet of arbitral institutions (at least at certain stages of the arbitration process).

5.2.1.1.3 Sweden

Swedish law does not explicitly refer to the legal nature of institutional arbitration, however two observations are relevant here. The first involves the authorization by the Swedish Arbitration Act of 1999[22] of the parties to rely on arbitral institutions

[18] The Uniform Arbitration Act (Last Revisions Completed Year 2000).

[19] *George Corey v. New York Stock Exchange* 1982.

[20] Section. 5.2.1.2.3.

[21] The UK Arbitration Act 1996, Chapter 23.

[22] The English translation of the Swedish Arbitration Act of 1999 is available on the website of the SCC Institute http://swedisharbitration.se/wp-content/uploads/2011/09/The-Swedish-Arbitration-Act.pdf. Accessed 25 April 2016.

instead of public courts in ultimate decisions concerning the removal of arbitrators.[23] The second concerns the decision in the so-called *Soyak* case, in which the Swedish Supreme Court allowed the possibility of judicial interventions in the institutional decision as to the costs of arbitration in extraordinary circumstances.[24] The first observation may imply certain jurisdictional aspects of institutional arbitration in Sweden, while the second example could, after deeper analysis, strengthen the recognition of the contractual nature—hence the commercial function—of institutional arbitration under Swedish law. These conflicting assumptions need to be analysed in order to develop a consistent interpretation of the treatment of institutional arbitration in Sweden.

Firstly, Sections 11 and 17 of the Swedish Arbitration Act allow the parties to agree on the removal of an arbitrator by an arbitral institution, even if such removal ordinarily falls within the authority of a relevant district court. The fact that the institution was granted authority to remove an arbitrator in place of a court could at first glance prove that the Swedish legislator took into account certain public functions of institutional arbitration. Although likely, it seems more convincing that such authority has been framed within the commercial function of arbitral institutions, especially given the express reference to the *agreement* between the parties by the provisions of Articles 11 and 17 of the Swedish Arbitration Act.

Secondly, it is relevant to consider what kind of approach to the functions of institutional arbitration was taken in the landmark *Soyak* decision. The Swedish Supreme Court (*Högsta domstolen*) in its decision in *Hobér, Kraus & Melis v. Soyak International Construction & Investment Inc.* of 2008 was not directly faced with a liability claim against arbitral institution but it did make a crucial determination regarding the function of institutional arbitration by deciding whether the institutional decision on the arbitrators' fees can be challenged in the courts of law.[25] In brief, the *Soyak* case arose out of the construction dispute between *Hochtief*, a German company, and *Soyak*, a Turkish company, which was arbitrated in Sweden in accordance with the Arbitration Rules of the SCC Institute. The arbitration panel rendered the arbitration award without stating the reasons therefor, which was subsequently questioned by *Soyak* before Stockholm city court. The legal action of *Soyak* concerned the prohibitive determination of the arbitrators' fees in view of the poor performance of arbitrators in the arbitration proceedings, which involved, mainly, the lack of accurate reasoning of their award. The case was finally determined by the Swedish Supreme Court that stated that, in fact, the parties were allowed to challenge the arbitrators' fees even in the situation in which such fees had been previously determined by the institution administering the proceedings and not by arbitrators themselves. Consequently, the Swedish Supreme Court provided a broad interpretation of Section 41 of the Swedish Arbitration Act of 1999.

---

[23]See Sections 11 and 17 of the Swedish Arbitration Act of 1999.

[24]The decision in *Soyak International Construction and Investment Inc. v. Hobér, Kraus and Melis*, Ö 4227-06, 3 December 2008; Baizeau 2009, 383–386.

[25]Baizeau 2009, 383–386.

The Court's interpretation was crucial to the extent that Section 41 of the Swedish Act was silent with regard to the possibility of interfering with the institutional stipulations of arbitrators' remuneration under the institutional contract.[26] In fact, by determining this case, the Court, at least indirectly, confirmed the contractual nature of the legal relationships in institutional arbitration. It was so because the issue at hand was largely rooted in the interplay between the contractual obligations of arbitral institutions to decide, in a binding manner, on the costs of arbitration (including arbitrators' fees) and the role of arbitrators in determining their own fees failing the exclusive authorization of arbitral institutions by the parties in this regard. Even if the discussion on the contractual matrix was not an essential part of the judgement, the Court was faced with the interpretation of the effects of institutional contracts binding upon arbitral institutions and the parties, on the one side, and arbitrators' contracts between the parties and arbitrators, on the other side. In this sense, we may conclude that the Court, indirectly, addressed the private regulatory powers of arbitral institutions in contract formation.[27] This happened because the Court assumed that it was the arbitral institution (the SCC) that had an ultimate authority in contractual stipulation of arbitrators' fees in the case in question and that such fees were further subject to the revision by the Court as part of the contractual arrangements between the SCC and the parties.

That being said, the proposed amendments to the Swedish Arbitration Act that are currently debated in Sweden suggest that this discussion may soon become less relevant. The recent proposals concern the exception to the rule allowing the parties to challenge the arbitrator's fees in district courts by limiting such possibility in cases in which the arbitrator's fees were determined by an arbitral institution and when such determination of the fees was not made enforceable.[28] Based on these possible amendments to the Swedish Arbitration Act, further determinations of the nature of the institutional acts remain an open issue. At the same time, it appears apparent that Swedish arbitration law has begun to recognize the private regulatory powers of arbitral institutions. This may eventually result in the inadmissibility of the parties' claims regarding institutional decisions in the Swedish courts in the future, especially when the above-mentioned amendments are adopted. By now, however, the legal nature of such decisions (whether administrative, jurisdictional, or purely contractual) has not been quite yet determined by the Swedish judges.

5.2.1.2 Lack of an Accurate Response to a Dual Function

As a natural consequence of putting different emphasis on various aspects of institutional functions by national legislators and/or courts, none of the national

---

[26]See also: Schöldström, 2008, 243–250.

[27]The Swedish Arbitration Act of 1999 Section 41.

[28]The Summary of the Parliamentary Committee's Report on the Proposed Amendments to the Swedish Arbitration Act (SOU 2015:37) http://www.sccinstitute.com/media/65386/summary-Oversyn-Av-Lagen-Om-Skiljeforfarande-English.pdf, 38. Accessed 25 April 2016.

authorities from the jurisdictions under analysis address the dual function of arbitral institutions as defined in Chap. 2. This dual function involved both the commercial and public facets of institutional activity.

5.2.1.2.1 France

The following presentation of the French understanding of the function of arbitral institutions unfolds within the confusion among French courts as to the legal character of institutional activity. The analysis of the historical French courts' decisions on the nature of institutional acts provided in Sect. 5.2.1.1.1 demonstrated that the French courts treat arbitral institutions as organizations whose acts are non-jurisdictional in nature, in most cases qualified as administrative acts. However, what was missing from these decisions concerned an exhaustive definition of institutional administrative acts together with the determination of the scope of their possible judicial and/or administrative review. At the same time, as will be presented in the analysis below, the French courts, when faced with liability claims against arbitral institutions, seem to put more emphasis on the contractual aspect of institutional obligations. Consequently, it is implied that French judges have recognized mostly the commercial function of institutional arbitration. The determination of the institutional acts as administrative, when confronted with the contractual, commercial aspects of institutional activity as upheld in the French case law presented below, reveals certain dispatch within the treatment of arbitral institutions under French law. It is striking to what extent the French courts qualify the performance of institutional obligations as contractual, whereas defining some institutional acts as administrative (as demonstrated in Sect. 5.2.1.1 above). This affects the understanding of the systemic function of institutional arbitration under French law (especially with a view to the public function of arbitral institutions defined in Sect. 2.2 of Chap. 2) and prevents the French courts from recognizing the unique nature of the arbitration service provided by arbitral institutions within their commercial function.

The following analysis will conceptualize these problems by explaining the cases on the liability of arbitral institutions that were decided in France. The three following French cases require particular attention regarding the possibility of holding arbitral institutions liable for their own conduct in the arbitration process, namely the *Cubic* case,[29] the *Cytec v. SNF* saga,[30] and the decision of 1 July 2010

[29] *Société Cubic Defense System Inc v Chambre de Commerce Internationale, (Cour d'appel de Paris (1 Ch. A)* 1998), *Rev. arb.* 1999, 103; *Société Cubic Defense System Inc v Chambre de Commerce Internationale, (Cour de Cassation (1 Ch. civile)* 2001), *Rev. arb.* 2011, 511.

[30] The *Cytec v. SNF* saga involves, inter alia, two French court decisions, namely, *Société SNF SAS v. Société Cytec Industries BV, Court d'appel de Paris, 23 March 2006, Rev. arb., 2006, 483; Cass. Civ. 1, Société SNF SAS v. Société Cytec Industries BV, 4 June 2008, no. 06-15320, Rev. arb., 2008, 346*, which resulted in filing a claim by *SNF* against the ICC Court of Arbitration; see: *Société SNF c/Chambre de Commerce Internationale, 847 Tribunal de grande instance de Paris (1 Ch.)* 2007. *Rev. arb.* 2007; *Société SNF v. International Chamber of Commerce, Cour d'appel de Paris (1. Ch.)* 2009. Moreover, the *SNF* saga involves also the decisions of Belgian courts, see, inter alia: *SNF v. Cytec, Cour d'appel de Bruxelles, 2 June 2009, RG no. 2007/AR/1742.*

of the *Tribunal de grande instance de Paris* in *Société Filature Française de Mohair c/Fédération Française des Industries Lainières et Cotonnières.*[31]

The first case relates to the plaintiff's allegation of a failure of the ICC Court to fulfil its contractual obligations owed to the plaintiff, *Cubic Defense Systems, Inc.* (*Cubic*).[32] The Paris Court of Appeal in the first instance did not, however, find the ICC in breach of its contractual duties, and, consequently, only vaguely reflected on the possible content of the ICC Court's obligations in the arbitral proceedings:

> the obligation of the ICC Court was to provide the parties with a proper structure allowing for efficient arbitration proceedings, i.e. conducted according to the expected dispatch, according to the chosen rules and which lead to the rendering of an award that is enforceable.[33]

The above decision was appealed to the French *Cour de Cassation,* which confirmed the contractual character of the relationship between the appellant and the ICC Court.[34] Moreover, the *Cour de Cassation* held that, in principle, the ICC could be held liable for the breach of its contractual obligations ordinarily aimed at ensuring the efficient and effective conduct of arbitration. However, the *Cour de Cassation* did not find such a breach on the side of the ICC Court in the case discussed here.[35]

The second case concerns the aforementioned *Cytec v. SNF* saga. The case involved two ICC awards and a fraught litigation conducted both in France and Belgium, which resulted in *SNF* suing the ICC for failure to discharge the ICC Court's obligations in the arbitration proceedings.[36] Particularly relevant for the forthcoming discussion on the problems with enforceability of the 1998 ICC exclusion of liability clause is that the Paris Court of Appeal held that such clause was unenforceable as it appeared to be invented to allow the ICC Court to avoid its essential duties assumed in the course of the arbitration proceedings.[37]

The history of the *Cytec v. SNF* saga is complex. From 1 October 1993 the Dutch company *Cytec Industries BV* (*Cytec*) and French company *SNF SAS* (*SNF*), were bound by a supply contract under which *SNF* was to purchase raw materials from *Cytec,* which, in turn, was to supply a specified amount of acrylamide monomer to *SNF.*[38] The performance of the contract was disrupted in 2000 by the parties' disagreement as to the validity of the contract under European

---

[31]*Société Filature Française de Mohair c/Fédération Française des Industries Lainières et Cotonnières, RG 07/13724, (Tribunal de grande Instance de Nanterre* 2010) .

[32]See *Société Cubic Defense System Inc v Chambre de Commerce Internationale, (Cour d'appel de Paris (1 Ch. A)* 1998), *Rev. arb.* 1999, 103; Kleiman 2009a.

[33]Translation in: Kleiman 2009a, 28.

[34]*Société Cubic Defense System Inc v Chambre de Commerce Internationale, (Cour de Cassation (1 Ch. civile)* 2001), *Rev. arb.* 2011, 511.

[35]Cf. the analysis of the decision at hand in: Rasmussen 2002, 1824.

[36]*Société SNF c/Chambre de Commerce Internationale, 847 Tribunal de grande instance de Paris (1 Ch.)* 2007. *Rev. arb.* 2007. Kleiman 2009a, 13–42; Kiffer 2009, 579–589.

[37]See also: Kleiman 2009a, 15–20.

[38]Kleiman 2009b, 15–16.

Communities (EC) competition law.[39] Consequently, the dispute was submitted to the ICC arbitral tribunal sitting in Belgium, which faced the parties' counterclaims involving: (1) the wrongful termination of the contract by *SNF* connected with the abuse of its dominant position under the former Article 81 and 82 of the EC Treaty as argued by *Cytec*; and (2) the allegation that the contract was null and void under the former Articles 81 and 82 of the EC Treaty, as raised by the *SNF*.[40] The ICC arbitral tribunal rendered two arbitral awards in this case. The first award stated that both parties contributed to the violation of EC law.[41] On these grounds, the arbitral tribunal nullified the contract inviting the parties to claim restitutions that could amount to only half of their losses, taking into account the equal contribution of *both* parties to the breach of EC law.[42] The second award, which aimed at clarifying the parties' interest rate (and the correction of an error in the first award, as claimed by *SNF*), dismissed *SNF*'s application and granted *Cytec*'s claims for damages by the ICC arbitral tribunal.[43]

Subsequently, *Cytec* obtained the enforcement of the awards before the French courts.[44] This, in turn, entailed *SNF*'s appeal in the Paris Court of Appeal based on the allegation that the recognition and enforcement of the ICC arbitral tribunal's awards were contrary to French international public policy.[45] *SNF*'s claims were dismissed by the Paris court, which was confirmed by the *Cour de Cassation* in its decision of 4 June 2008. As a result of these judgements, *SNF* initiated additional court proceedings: first, a criminal proceeding in France on the grounds that *Cytec* abused its dominant position, and second, a proceeding in Belgium which aimed at obtaining the annulment of the arbitral awards by the Court of First Instance in Brussels (thus, by the court which had territorial jurisdiction concerning the *lex loci arbitri*).[46] While the criminal action against *Cytec* was dismissed by the Paris Court of Appeal as a time-barred claim, the Brussels first instance court surprisingly agreed with *SNF* that the awards violated EU public policy, as the ICC arbitrators granted damages to one party to the contract which was performed in breach of EC competition law.[47] Consequently, the Brussels court annulled the ICC awards. *Cytec* appealed, which resulted in the abolition of the decision by the Brussels Court of Appeal, thus, also in the confirmation of the binding and final character of the ICC arbitral awards by this Court.[48]

---

[39]Kleiman 2009b,15–16; Kiffer 2009, 579–580.

[40]Kleiman 2009b, 15–16.

[41]Ibid.

[42]Ibid.

[43]Ibid.

[44]Kleiman 2009b, 15–17; Kiffer 2009, 579–581.

[45]*SNF* basically argued that a dismissal of the *SNF* claims for damages by the arbitral tribunal in the light of granting the *Cytec*'s claims was a violation of EC Competition law. Kleiman 2009b, 15.

[46]Kleiman 2009b, 15–16.

[47]Kleiman 2009b, 15–16; Kiffer 2009, 579–589.

[48]Kleiman 2009b, 16.

Accordingly, *SNF* decided to seek restitution of its rights by filing a claim against the ICC in the French court (*Tribunal de grande instance*). There, *SNF* argued that the ICC Court violated its own rules of arbitration by allowing the lengthy proceedings and prohibitive costs of arbitration, as well as by failing to act diligently while scrutinizing an arbitral award that was clearly in breach of the EC law. Thus, in this sense, it was violating EU public policy.[49] Consequently, *SNF* argued that the ICC Court should be liable for the non-performance of its essential contractual duties. Moreover, there was a misunderstanding as to the set of the ICC Arbitration Rules that should have application to the *SNF v. Cytec* arbitration proceedings.[50] This last problem, however, will be addressed in Sect. 5.2.2.1 of this chapter. What is important here is that the *SNF* claim was dismissed by the *Tribunal de grande instance de Paris*. *SNF* therefore appealed the decision.

The Paris Court of Appeal, in its judgement of 22 January 2009, stated that it was the ICC which bore the responsibility for the ICC Court's performance and proceedings, as the ICC Court was an entity of the ICC, which itself lacked the legal personality.[51] Furthermore, the Court of Appeal stated that the ICC could, in principle, be held liable for its poor performance of the institutional contract, and that the ICC exclusion of liability clause was unenforceable under French law,[52] as such a clause was invented as a means of "avoiding the responsibility for the essential institutional duties" to be carried out in the arbitration proceedings.[53] Notwithstanding the above reasoning, the Paris Court of Appeal again did not find the ICC in breach of its contractual obligations. Therefore, it did not hold the ICC liable for the misconduct for the following reasons (1) the parties themselves contributed, to a large extent, to the extension of time limits in the course of the arbitral proceedings; (2) the costs of arbitration were rightly stipulated by the ICC Court in accordance with the schedule of costs and fees in force on the date of the commencement of the arbitration proceedings; and finally (3) the ICC Court could not affect the arbitrators' decision even under the then Article 27 of the ICC Arbitration Rules and that in any event the ICC Court's scrutiny of arbitral award at stake did not violate the procedure set forth in Article 27 of the Rules.[54] While examining the prospective failure of the ICC Court to fulfil its contractual

---

[49]*Société SNF c/Chambre de Commerce Internationale, 847 Tribunal de grande instance de Paris (1 Ch.)* 2007. *Rev. arb.* 2007.

[50]Ibid.

[51]*Société SNF v. International Chamber of Commerce, Cour d'appel de Paris (1. Ch.)* 2009

[52]French law was, according to the Court, the law applicable to the institutional contract under the principles of conflict of laws. This reasoning falls within Article 4 of the Convention of 19 June 1980 on the Law Applicable to Contractual Obligations (Rome Convention) under which in the absence of choice of law by the parties the law of the country with which the contract is mostly connected should apply. French law had the closer connection with the contract at hand, as it was the law of the central administration of the ICC who acted as a party that was to effect the performance that determined the characteristics of the contract. Cf. Kleiman 2009b, 22.

[53]Kleiman 2009b, 25.

[54]Ibid.

obligations, the Paris Court of Appeal reflected on the potential scope of such obligations under the institutional arbitration contract:

> In order to require payment from the parties for the performance of its obligations, the ICC must organise and administrate arbitration proceedings and for that purpose it must provide the parties with a proper structure for efficient arbitration proceedings, conducted according to the expected dispatch, according to the chosen rules and which lead to an award that is susceptible of execution.[55]

Although the scope and content of the ICC Court's obligations assumed in the arbitration proceedings was defined rather vaguely by the Paris Court of Appeal, the Court again confirmed the contractual character of institutional operation. It also appears then that the Court emphasized the components of the commercial function of arbitral institutions in the arbitration process as defined in Sect. 2.3.1 of Chap. 2.[56]

In a nutshell, the French court established the following institutional obligations within the commercial function of arbitral institutions: (a) the "proper structure" of arbitration proceedings, which would ensure their effectiveness; (b) an expeditious character and the enforceability of the arbitration award; and (c) the proper fixing of the costs of arbitration. This suggests that the French courts consider—at least when determining the cases on liability of arbitral institutions—that the major functions of arbitral institutions should be qualified in purely contractual (commercial) terms. Albeit such reasoning is not particularly controversial with regard to institutional decisions on arbitration costs and time limits, the interpretation of the institutional rules that aim at guaranteeing the enforceability of the arbitral awards, as a purely contractual obligation of the ICC exercised solely within its commercial function, is somewhat contentious. The assurance of the enforceability of the arbitral awards, even if expressed in the arbitration rules, falls within the administrative prerogatives of arbitral institutions within the meaning of the public function of institutional arbitration as defined in Chap. 2. This means that, although the obligation of ensuring the enforceability of arbitral awards falls within the authority of institutional contracts, the content of such obligation is also determined by the specific status of arbitral institutions both within and outside the arbitration proceedings. Similar argumentation is consistent with the interpretation of some institutional decisions in the course of the proceedings that were classified as administrative by the French courts deciding on the possibility of the judicial review of institutional acts.[57] This begs the following question. How does the contractual aspect of institutional obligations correspond with the administrative nature of some acts issued by arbitral institutions in the course of the arbitration proceedings? This question appears even more relevant if one recalls the recent announcement by the ICC of its availability to communicate the reasons of the selected procedural decisions (such as, inter alia, those on the challenges to, and the replacement of, institutional arbitrators and the preliminary decisions on jurisdiction) upon the additional administrative costs to be

---

[55]Kleiman 2009a, 17.

[56]Sect. 2.3.1 of Chap. 2 and the discussion on the traditional commercial function of arbitral institutions.

[57]Sect. 5.2.1.1.1 of this chapter.

paid by the parties.[58] Would the French courts qualify such acts as a specific form of the "paid administration of justice"? Yet again, the relationship between the contractual nature of the institutional arbitration, as acknowledged by the French courts, and the administrative character of institutional acts appear as a blurred notion in the French jurisprudence.

The final relevant French case concerns the decision dated 1 July 2010 of the *Tribunal de grand instance de Nanterre* in *Société Filature Française de Mohair c/ Fédération Française des Industries Lainières et Cotonnières.*[59] This judgement will be further analysed in Sect. 7.3.5 of Chap. 7. Here it suffices to only present the French court's determination of the prospective scope of institutional liability. This decision is significant to the extent that the *Tribunal de grande instance de Nanterre* found the industrial federation that administered the arbitration between a French and a Spanish party, the *Fédération Française des Industries Lainières et Cotonnières*, liable for failure to transmit the documentary evidence to the parties, evidence which the institution itself requested to be produced.[60] The French Court found that the institution was liable to the parties for the improper performance of its own obligations and awarded monetary damages to the claimant.[61] Even though the award of damages did not correspond to the amount claimed by the claimant, as the claimant did not manage to prove the causal link between the fault of arbitral institution and the damage claimed, this judgement is particularly important as it ultimately established that an arbitral institution can in fact be held liable for the poor performance of its contractual obligations.[62]

The major controversy stemming from the preceding discussion relates to the conflict between the notions of the contractual nature of the relationship between institutional arbitration actors and the administrative nature of institutional acts presented in Sect. 5.2.1.1.1 as determined by the French courts. This controversy may imply significant confusion among the parties to the institutional arbitration proceedings. Imagine the situation in which the parties suffered injury as a result of the institutional decision either declining the jurisdiction or refusing the consolidation of the proceedings. Having in mind that the parties are bound by the contract(s) with the arbitral institution who issued the decision in question, why would they be prevented from requesting the relevant court to review such decisions based on the provisions of such contracts only upon the justification that the institutional decision in question was of administrative nature? On the one hand, it appears straightforward that the contracts between arbitral institutions and the parties incorporate the arbitration rules, which, in turn, provide rather clear-cut guidance regarding the finality of certain categories of institutional decisions. On the

[58] Sect. 2.3.1.3.5 of Chap. 2.

[59] *Société Filature Française de Mohair c/Fédération Française des Industries Lainières et Cotonnières*, RG 07/13724, (*Tribunal de Grande Instance de Nanterre* 2010).

[60] Price 2012, 187.

[61] Ibid., 188.

[62] Ibid., 193.

other hand, however, the possible interpretation of the finality of these decisions in the context of their administrative nature is no longer so clear. Moreover, the distinction between the institutional decisions that correspond to the pure facilitation of arbitration proceedings by case managers (that could be regarded as pure provision of services) and those decisions that could in fact be understood as administrative is in practice extremely muddled. The main problem underlying this discussion lies in the lack of the proper perception of all actors involved in institutional arbitration proceedings of the dual function of arbitral institutions, as presented in Chap. 2. Regrettably, these issues have not been accurately addressed in either French case law or in the existent literature.[63]

In addition, this confusion is intermittently escalated by means of other judgements of the French courts—not necessarily dealing with institutional liability—where more emphasis is in fact made on the jurisdictional aspect of institutional arbitration. This was the case with the decision of the Paris Court of Appeal in *Société Licensing Projects et autres c/société Pirelli & C. SPA et autres* (the so-called "Pirelli judgement") of 17 November 2011.[64] The case concerned the request by the party to the prior ICC arbitration proceedings, the Spanish company LP, to annul the arbitral award for the violation of access to justice. It arose out of the denial of LP's counterclaims under the then Article 30.2 in accordance with the then Article 30.4 of the 1998 ICC Arbitration Rules due to the inability of the party in question to pay the separate advance of costs to cover its further counterclaims. This was simply because this party did not have financial resources to do so as a result of being in liquidation.[65] The Paris Court of Appeal annulled the arbitral award—giving precedence to the right of the LP to access to justice—even if it meant the interference with the ICC arbitration rules in the judgement at hand. Although reversed by the French *Cour de Cassation* based on the reasoning that the French lower court should have analysed whether the counterclaims to be presented in the arbitration in question were in fact inseparable from the main claim,[66] the Pirelli case shed light on the observance of party autonomy in institutional arbitration in view of the plausible obligations falling within the administration of justice by the ICC Court and ICC arbitrators.

Therefore, it appears that the inconsistency of the French jurisprudence regarding the nature of institutional arbitral activity, especially with regard to the parties' contractual rights in the context of the principle of party autonomy, demonstrates that the French courts experience troubles when addressing the dual function of institutional arbitration. This function implies an uneasy relationship between the private regulatory powers of arbitral institutions in the course of arbitrations (that correspond to certain administrative tasks assumed by arbitral institutions) and the

[63]For a comprehensive study on these complex theoretical issues, see Gerbay, forthcoming 2016.

[64]*Société Licensing Projects et Autres C/Société Pirelli & C. SPA et autres, Cour D'appel Paris, 1e Ch., Nov. 17,* 2011, N° 09/24158.

[65]Kudrna 2013, 3.

[66]*Arrêt N° 392 Du 28 Mars* 2013 *(11-27.770)—Cour de Cassation—Première Chambre Civile—ECLI:FR:CCASS:201300392.* A summary of the judgement was also provided in: Bantekas 2015, 164.

contractual, commercial facet of institutional arbitration. However, as long as this relationship remains unaddressed, it is hard to expect that institutional arbitration will enjoy its deserved treatment, expressing its hybridity, by the French courts.

5.2.1.2.2 The US

The US courts took a different approach to the function of "organizations sponsoring arbitration" (the name that corresponds to the expression "arbitral institutions" in most jurisdictions outside of the US) by treating them as quasi-judicial bodies (quasi-judges). This resulted in granting unlimited immunity to arbitral institutions for all their acts and omission. Even though such an approach was not clearly acknowledged by statutory law, it has been expressed by US case law of precedential value.

The FAA of 1925[67] remains tacit as to the scope of responsibility of arbitration actors. However, the Uniform Arbitration Act (the UAA) promulgated in 1955, subsequently amended and renamed the RUAA in 2000 explicitly grants both arbitrators and "arbitration organizations" immunity from civil liability as well as from process.[68] Consequently, the immunity of arbitral institutions in the US

---

[67]Title 9, US Code, Section 1–14, was first enacted 12 February 1925 (43 Stat. 883), codified 30 July 1947 (61 Stat. 669), and amended 3 September 1954 (68 Stat. 1233). Chapter 2 was added 31 July 1970 (84 Stat. 692), two new Sections were passed by the Congress in October of 1988 and renumbered on 1 December 1990 (PLS 669 and 702); Chapter 3 was added on 15 August 1990 (PL 101–369); and Section 10 was amended on 15 November. See: The Federal Arbitration Act; Pub.L. 68–401, 43 Stat. 883, Enacted 12 February 1925, Codified at 9 U.S.C. § 1 et Seq.

[68]See: Section 14 of the The Uniform Arbitration Act (Last Revisions Completed Year 2000). Immunity of Arbitrators; Competency to Testify; Attorney's Fees and Costs:

(a) An arbitrator or an arbitration organization acting in that capacity is immune from civil liability to the same extent as a judge of a court of this State acting in a judicial capacity.

(b) The immunity afforded by this section supplements any immunity under other law.

(c) The failure of an arbitrator to make a disclosure required by Section 12 does not cause any loss of immunity under this section.

(d) In a judicial, administrative, or similar proceeding, an arbitrator or representative of an arbitration organization is not competent to testify, and may not be required to produce records as to any statement, conduct, decision, or ruling occurring during the arbitration proceeding, to the same extent as a judge of a court of this State acting in a judicial capacity. This subsection does not apply:

(1) to the extent necessary to determine the claim of an arbitrator, arbitration organization, or representative of the arbitration organization against a party to the arbitration proceeding; or

(2) to a hearing on a [motion] to vacate an award under Section 23(a)(1) or (2) if the [movant] establishes prima facie that a ground for vacating the award exists.

(e) If a person commences a civil action against an arbitrator, arbitration organization, or representative of an arbitration organization arising from the services of the arbitrator, organization, or representative or if a person seeks to compel an arbitrator or a representative of an arbitration organization to testify or produce records in violation of subsection (d), and the court decides that the arbitrator, arbitration organization, or representative of an arbitration organization is immune from civil liability or that the arbitrator or representative of the organization is not competent to testify, the court shall award to the arbitrator, organization, or representative reasonable attorney's fees and other reasonable expenses of litigation.

corresponds with the immunity of arbitrators, which, in turn, enjoy almost unlimited judicial immunity because of their functional comparability to the role of judges in the courts of law.

There are four important observations that relate to the legislative history of Section 14 of the RUAA. First, the regulation by the RUAA of the arbitral immunity from civil liability mimics the prior codification of the issue at stake by the State authorities of California, Florida, North Carolina, and Utah.[69] Second, the protection of arbitrators and arbitration organizations from being required to testify in court proceedings connected with arbitration (immunity from process), which was aimed at ensuring the integrity of the arbitration process, reflects the language of the California Evidence Code.[70] Third, the exception made to arbitrators and representatives of arbitration organizations, which allows them to participate in the court proceedings only in cases in which the above actors themselves filed a claim against a recalcitrant party (Section 14(d)(1) of the RUAA), distorts the balance of protection of the participants to arbitration proceedings. This rule connects with the last observation concerning the legislative history of the RUAA. Under Section 14(e) of the RUAA parties that decided to frivolously sue an arbitrator or an arbitration organization will be sanctioned to the extent that they would be required to cover the litigation costs arising from such unnecessary claim.

The revision of the UAA was directed towards the further unification of the state laws on arbitration by adopting the already existent US state's approach to the arbitration processes. It is apparent that the RUAA followed the controversial trend of state law to extensively promote arbitration by granting full protection to arbitrators and arbitration organizations, while leaving almost no possibilities for monetary claims to the parties that suffered from the possible misconduct of the arbitration actors. This approach concerns the extension of the judicial immunity on arbitrators and, subsequently, also into organizations sponsoring arbitration in the US. The following part will discuss these issues in chronological order.

5.2.1.2.2.1 Development of Judicial Immunity in the US

The legal doctrine on judicial immunity in the US originates in the English common law and was developed together with the constitution of the appellate system in the US.[71] The broad rule of the judicial immunity was confirmed in 1978 in the decision of the US Supreme Court in *Stump v. Sparkman*.[72] However, the most influential judgement regarding the issue at hand was passed by the US Supreme

[69]See accordingly: Cal. Civ. Proc. Code § 1297.119; Fla. Stat. Ann. § 44.107 (West 1995); N.C. Gen. Stat. § 7A-37.1 (1995); and Utah Code Ann. § 78-31b-4 (1994). See also: the comment to the Section 14 of the The Uniform Arbitration Act (Last Revisions Completed Year 2000).

[70]See: Cal. Evid. Code § 703.5. See also: the commentary to Section 14(d) of The Uniform Arbitration Act (Last Revisions Completed Year 2000) included in the Act.

[71]Weston 2004, 476; Feinman and Cohen 1979, 201–292.

[72]*Stump v. Sparkman* (1978) *435 U.S. 349 U.S. Supreme Court.*

Court already in 1872 in *Bradley v. Fisher*.[73] In the latter case, the Court revoked the English law's standards for judicial liability and readopted them to the US common law system.

Before analysing the decisions mentioned above, one earlier case must be considered, namely, the judgement in *Randall v. Brigham* dated 1868.[74] The decision in *Randall* is significant insofar as it addressed the basic principles underlying the doctrine on judicial immunity, extended later in *Bradley*. On the ground of the opinion delivered by Justice Feld, the US lower courts judges were granted immunity for acts provided within their jurisdiction, while the acts of supreme courts' judges were protected even if delivered in excess of jurisdiction, provided that such acts did not result from malicious conduct or corruption.[75] Such a distinction between judges from lower and supreme courts echoed the protection of English superior courts' judges granted, inter alia, in *Floyd v. Barker*, and *Yates v. Lansing*.[76] Later, in *Bradley,* Justice Feld restated the doctrine on judicial immunity by granting almost absolute protection to judges of superior courts notwithstanding the malice qualification of their acts, provided that such acts were judicial in nature[77] and were not passed without the clear absence of jurisdiction.[78]

The decision in *Bradley* is important for two reasons. First, since *Bradley*, the US courts have followed the line of reasoning related to the doctrine of almost absolute judicial immunity, which was extended to all public judges in the US including those of the lower courts. One of the most controversial decisions that was encouraged by the decision in *Bradley* concerned the ruling in *Stump v. Sparkman* in which the Indiana state judge, who had ordered a sterilization of an intellectually disabled minor, was not held liable for his act which violated the principle of due process (civil rights statute), as the judge was said to have acted

[73]*Bradley v. Fisher.* (1871) *80 U.S. 335 US Supreme Court.*

[74]*Randall v. Brigham* (1868) *74 U.S. 523 US Supreme Court.*

[75]The US Supreme Court in *Randal v. Brigham* stated that: "All judicial officers are exempt from liability in a civil action for their judicial acts done within their jurisdiction, and judges of superior or general authority are exempt from such liability even when their judicial acts are in excess of their jurisdiction, unless perhaps where the acts in excess of their jurisdiction are done maliciously or corruptly." *Randall v. Brigham* (1868) *74. U.S. 523 US Supreme Court,* page 74 US 524.

[76]See generally Feinman and Cohen 1979.

[77]The US Supreme Court in *Bradley v. Fisher* stated that: "In other words, it sets up that the order for the entry of which the suit is brought, was a judicial act, done by the defendants as the presiding justice of a court of general criminal jurisdiction. If such were the character of the act, and the jurisdiction of the court, the defendant cannot be subjected to responsibility for it in a civil action, however erroneous the act may have been, and however injurious in its consequences it may have proved to the plaintiff." *Bradley v. Fisher.* (1871) *80 U.S. 335 US Supreme Court,* page 80 US 348.

[78]Cf. the US Supreme Court in: *Bradley v. Fisher*: "[…] A distinction must be here observed between excess of jurisdiction and the clear absence of all jurisdiction over the subject matter. Where there is clearly no jurisdiction over the subject matter any authority exercised is a usurped authority, and for the exercise of such authority, when the want of jurisdiction is known to the judge, no excuse is permissible […]". *Bradley v. Fisher.* (1871) *80 U.S. 335 US Supreme Court,* page 80 US 352.

within the judicial capacity.[79] The second observation concerns the adaptation of the English regulation of judicial immunity to US law. Albeit *Bradley* was to express the exact solutions adopted by the English judiciary, some commentators claim that it, in fact, did extend the English doctrine on judicial immunity, as the English solutions provided a more moderate approach to the prospective liability of the judges.[80] This controversy will be important, in particular, in the following discussion on the standards of arbitral immunity in the UK, which will address the qualified approach to the scope of responsibility of arbitration actors under English law.

Now, the following question emerges. Is the doctrine on judicial immunity in the US in fact unlimited? It appears not. The limitations involve the following: (1) the aforementioned necessity for judges to act within their jurisdiction while delivering a decision that will be judicial in nature (*Bradley*); (2) immunity does not cover administrative or criminal acts of the judges (*Forrester v. White*[81] and *O'Shea v. Littleton,*[82] respectively); (3) there is a possibility for the action of injunctive relief against a judge who violated constitutional rights while exercising his judicial function (42 U.S. Code, § 1983[83]); and finally (4) the availability of public remedies for the judicial misconduct which can result in, inter alia, the removal of a judge from his office (e.g. the Model Code of Judicial Conduct).[84] These constraints show that the immunity granted to judges in the US is not, in fact, absolute, as it is subject to certain limitations that aim at protecting the public from judicial misconduct. Keeping in mind that there are minor limitations to the doctrine on absolute immunity of judges in the US, the fact that both arbitrators and arbitration organizations—who exercise in the arbitration processes different functions to the functions of judges—enjoy almost absolute immunity in the US seems ungrounded.

5.2.1.2.2.2 Extension of Judicial Immunity to Other Public Officials and Arbitrators

The issue of the immunity of arbitrators in the US is strongly interlinked with the extension of judicial immunity to other US public officials established in *Butz v. Economou.*[85] However, arbitrators enjoyed the broad level of public protection from any civil action long before this decision. Already in 1803, in *Shiver v. Ross* an arbitrator was released from the requirement to testify in a suit that concerned an error in the arbitral award.[86] Subsequently, in 1880 in *Jones v. Brown* an

[79] *Stump v. Sparkman* (1978) *435 U.S. 349 U.S. Supreme Court.*

[80] Block 1980, 880–881.

[81] *Forrester v. White* (1988) *484 U.S. 219 US Supreme Court.*

[82] *O'Shea v. Littleton* (1974) *414 U.S. 488 US Supreme Court.*

[83] U.S. Code, Title 42, Chapter 21, Subchapter I, § 1983—Civil action for deprivation of rights.

[84] American Bar Association, "Model Code of Judicial Conduct" 2011.

[85] *Butz v. Economou* (1978) *438 U.S. 478 US Supreme Court.*

[86] Cf.: Nolan and Abrams 1989.

arbitrator was held immune from fraud for judicial acts.[87] Furthermore, in 1884 in the decision in *Hoosac Tunnel Dock & Elevator Co. v. O'Brien*, the role of arbitrator was equalized with the function of a judge, which allowed an arbitrator to be granted immunity.[88]

Undoubtedly, the most significant judgement, which identified the functional comparability of the acts of non-judicial public officers with the acts of judges was rendered in *Butz v. Economou.*[89] In *Butz*, the US Supreme Court established a three-level test for the extension of judicial immunity to the administrative law judges of the States Department of Agriculture, which provided quasi-judicial services.[90] The so-called "*Butz* test" applied in this judgement resulted in granting immunity to the executive branch officials by the US Supreme Court providing the following justification: (1) the role of such officials was analogous to the role of judges in judicial process (functionally comparable); (2) judicial immunity was absolutely crucial for the public officials to perform their quasi-judicial function "free of harassment and intimidation"[91]; and finally (3) there was an assumption that the prospective abuse of judicial immunity was protected by other procedural safeguards in the agency of adjudication similar to the safeguards provided in judicial process. Since *Butz*, the issue of arbitral immunity was supported with even better justification, as arbitrators—similar to other non-judicial officials acting within their quasi-judicial function—were furnished with an additional safeguard which could strengthen the finality of arbitral awards and the integrity of the arbitration process.

The adoption of the *Butz* test to the work of arbitrators was controversial insomuch as it did not address the scope of procedural safeguards that secure the arbitrator's misconduct in the arbitration proceedings.[92] Taking into account the fact that the limitations regarding judicial immunity do not apply to arbitrators, as well as that the grounds for moving the arbitration award is rather narrow under the FAA, the broad extension of judicial immunity to arbitrators under the decision in *Butz* raises controversies concerning the transparency and fairness of the arbitration process in the US.[93] The issue becomes even more controversial considering the widespread adaptation of the *Butz* test to the operation of arbitration organizations in the US.

[87]*Jones v. Brown* 6 N.W. 140 (1880) with the commentary in: Weston 2004, 485. The rendering of an award by an arbitrator was analogous with a judge's decision of "reducing the opinion to writing".

[88]"[...] An arbitrator is a quasi-judicial officer (...) exercising judicial functions. There is as much reason in his case for protecting and insuring his impartiality, independence, and freedom from undue influence, as in the case of a judge or a juror [...]." *Hoosac Tunnel Dock & Elevator Co. v. O'Brien,* 137 Mass. 424, 426 (1884).

[89]*Butz v. Economou* (1978) *438 U.S. 478 US Supreme Court.*

[90]See: the commentary to the decision in Sponseller 1993, 435–440.

[91]*Butz v. Economou* (1978) *438 U.S. 478 US Supreme Court.*

[92]Sponseller 1993, 435–440.

[93]Ibid.

5.2.1.2.2.3 Extension of Arbitral Immunity to Arbitration Organizations

The first extension of the immunity doctrine to a sponsoring organization was in 1976 in *Cort v. American Arbitration Assn.*[94] The case arose out of the claim of evidence and case-handling error on the side of the arbitral institution. Following that case, the immunity of an organization sponsoring arbitration was confirmed in 1982 in *Corey v. New York Stock Exchange* where the Sixth Circuit US Court of Appeal held that the New York Stock Exchange should not be held liable for the acts committed by its own arbitrators which, in turn, enjoyed the broad immunity from suit because their function was—apparently—equivalent to the role of judges in the judicial process.[95] The justification for the arbitral immunity delivered by the Sixth Circuit Court of Appeal involved the assumption that the arbitration proceedings resemble judicial proceedings in several respects. Moreover, the Court noticed that there were a number of procedural safeguards in the arbitration process, which should provide the parties with the sufficient measures of protection.[96] What was the policy underlying the extension of arbitral immunity to the arbitration organization in *Corey*? After having confirmed the contractual character of the relationships between the institutional arbitration actors, the Sixth Circuit Court held that the plaintiff's action constituted "no more than an impermissible collateral attack on the arbitrators' award" and stated that:

> the extension of arbitral immunity to encompass boards which sponsor arbitration is natural and necessary product of the policies underlying arbitral immunity—otherwise, the immunity extended to arbitrators is illusionary. It would be of little value to the whole arbitral procedure to merely shift liability to the sponsoring organizations.[97]

It is apparent that the function of arbitration organizations, at least as established in *Corey,* was instrumental to the work of arbitrators. Moreover, the immunity of such organizations was dictated by the necessity of the protection of the institutional arbitrators, and therefore also of the integrity and finality of the whole arbitration system. Two additional cases, which also justify the extension of the arbitral immunity to the arbitral institutions, take slightly different approaches in the sense that they put more emphasis on the linkages between the arbitral immunity and the institutional arbitral acts instead of focusing mostly on the arbitrators' conduct.

The first case involves the decision in *Austerns v. The Chicago Board Options Exchange, Inc.*, in which the Second Circuit of the US Court of Appeals was faced

[94]See *Cort v. American Arbitration Assn* (1992) *795 F Supp 970 (ND CA 1992).* http://naarb.org/immunity/reference.asp#Materials. Accessed 25 April 2016.

[95]See *George Corey v. New York Stock Exchange* (1982) *691 F.2d 1205 US Court of Appeals, Sixth Circuit.*

[96]Such as the adversarial character of arbitration which allows the parties to fully present their cases, the possibility of the judicial review of both the awards and arbitrators' conduct or the very fact that arbitration is a voluntary method of dispute resolution. Cf. *George Corey v. New York Stock Exchange* (1982) *691 F.2d 1205 US Court of Appeals, Sixth Circuit.*

[97]Ibid.

with the question of whether the *contractor*, the Chicago Board Options Exchange (the CBOE), could be held immune from civil liability for *its own errors* concerning the improper notification of the arbitration hearing and the unsuitable selection of the arbitration panel.[98] It is important to stress that in the initial suit brought before the US District Court for the Sothern District of New York, Austerns argued that the CBOE acted negligently in the sense that the CBOE violated Austerns's constitutional right to procedural due process by allowing the arbitration hearing to take place even without the proper notification of the party about such a hearing.[99] The complaint was dismissed, as the lower court confirmed that the operation of arbitration organizations should be protected under the doctrine on judicial immunity.[100] Similar reasoning stood behind the decision of the Second Circuit Court of Appeals. The Second Circuit again refused to hold the CBOE liable for its own misconduct after having referred to the general policy underlying the doctrine on arbitral and judicial immunity, which aimed at protecting the whole arbitration process from "reprisals by dissatisfied litigants," as well as to the general policy of the FAA which was directed towards favouring the arbitration process.[101] Moreover, the Second Circuit stated that the acts of the CBOE "were sufficiently associated with the adjudicative phase of the arbitration to justify immunity," and that the contrary decision—allowing the liability of organizations sponsoring arbitrations—would have discouraged the CBOE's sponsorship of future arbitrations.[102] In this vein, the Second Circuit decided that the scope of institutional arbitral immunity should be defined through the function that an arbitration organization was to fulfil. Although the justification for such institutional immunity touched upon the broader context of the institutional operation, it focused solely on the economic function of arbitral institutions without referring to the legal and societal aspects of such a function. This demonstrates that the contractual obligations of arbitral institutions were not preserved (corresponding to the legal dimension of institutional arbitration as defined in this book), nor was the particular institutional commitment to the goals of the arbitration users (reflecting the societal dimension of institutional arbitration proposed in this book) addressed by the Second Circuit Court of Appeals.

The second case, which proves the absolute protection of the organizations sponsoring arbitration in the US, concerns the judgement in *Olson v. National Association of Securities Dealers.*[103] The decision in question is controversial

---

[98]See generally *Austern v. Chicago Board Options Exchange, Inc.*(1990) *898 F.2d 882 United States Court of Appeals, Second Circuit.*

[99]See generally *Austern v. Chicago Bd. Option Exchange Inc.* (1989) *716 F.Supp. 121 United States District Court, S.D. New York.*

[100]Ibid.

[101]See *Austern v. Chicago Board Options Exchange, Inc.*(1990) *898 F.2d 882 United States Court of Appeals, Second Circuit.*

[102]Ibid.

[103]See generally *Olson v. National Association of Securities Dealers.* (1996) *85 F3d 381 US Court of Appeals, Eighth Circuit.*

insofar as it provided for the unlimited immunity of the arbitration organization, the National Association of Securities Dealers (NASD), in the case arising out of the employment relationship in the securities industry, even after taking into account the organizational violation of its own rules of procedure by appointing an arbitrator without ensuring proper arbitrator disclosure.[104] The Eighth Circuit Court of Appeals granted immunity to NASD notwithstanding the prior confirmation of the institutional violation of the NASD's procedural rules. Consequently, the Eighth Circuit affirmed that arbitral immunity protects *all* acts within the scope of the arbitral process involving also the improper selection of the arbitration panel, which might constitute a violation of the institutional rules of procedure.[105]

Against this background, the discussion will now focus on the judgement in *Strategic Resources, Inc. v. BCS Life Insurance, Inc.*, which—as decided by the US Supreme Court—constituted the rule of precedential nature concerning the immunity of arbitration organizations in the US.[106] Moreover, the decision requires attention as it concerns similar controversies to those arising out of the unlimited immunity to arbitrators granted under the *Butz* test. In short, the case analysed the conduct of the AAA in the arbitration proceedings, which arose out of an unsuccessful business venture established by *Strategic Resources Inc.* (respondents) and *BCS Life Insurance Co.* (appellants).[107] Shortly after the termination of the business, the appellants, *BCS Life*, filed an action against the respondents—*Strategic Resources*—and as a result the Illinois state court compelled arbitration with regard to the parties under the arbitration agreement contained in their contract.[108]

The arbitration clause provided for an arbitration panel consisting of three arbitrators and for an appointment procedure involving the nomination of each party-appointed arbitrator by the parties' counsels, and of the presiding arbitrator by the previously chosen parties' nominees.[109] After the nominees' failure to appoint the chairman of the panel, the appellants turned to the AAA for assistance with selecting a neutral arbitrator (the chairman). They asked the AAA to prepare a list of potential candidates in accordance with the AAA's Supplementary Rules for the Resolution of Intra-Industry United States Reinsurance and Insurance Disputes (the AAA's Supplementary Rules).[110] The respondents—*Strategic Resources*—opposed

[104]Ibid.

[105]Ibid.

[106]*Strategic Resources Co. v. BCS Life Insurance Co., No. 26022, 2005 WL 1943536* (2006) with the commentary in: Eric Laufgraben, "Arbitration: South Carolina's Top Court Extends Arbitral Immunity to ADR Providers (Web)." and also Moffitt 2006.

[107]Ibid.

[108]Eric Laufgraben, "Arbitration: South Carolina's Top Court Extends Arbitral Immunity to ADR Providers (Web)".

[109]See *Strategic Resources Co. v. BCS Life Insurance Co., No. 26022, 2005 WL 1943536* (2006).

[110]Eric Laufgraben, "Arbitration: South Carolina's Top Court Extends Arbitral Immunity to ADR Providers (Web)". According to the commentator, the list of arbitrators provided pursuant to the AAA's Supplementary Rules comprised individuals with expert knowledge in the insurance industry but not necessarily in the law in more general terms.

to such request and consistently insisted on the application of the AAA's Commercial Arbitration Rules and Mediation Procedures to the arbitrator's selection process. The AAA—regardless of the respondents' preferences—decided that the parties would be provided with the list of arbitrators in accordance with the AAA's Supplementary Rules. Consequently, *Strategic Resources* filed a suit in the South Carolina state court calling for injunctive relief against the AAA's determination of the applicability of its Supplementary Rules to the selection of a neutral arbitrator. The South Carolina state court granted such a relief and ordered that the selection procedure (hence, the preparation of the list of arbitrators) shall proceed pursuant to the AAA's Commercial Rules.[111] Subsequently, *BCS Life Insurance* appealed the order of the state court to the Supreme Court of South Carolina which, in turn, reversed the decision of the lower court by finding that the AAA was protected under the doctrine of judicial immunity and, furthermore, that the injunctive relief was inappropriate, as the respondents were furnished with an adequate remedy at law which allowed them to recourse against the AAA's decision.[112]

The Supreme Court, while dealing with the arbitral immunity, referred to a number of prior decisions of lowers courts in which immunity was granted to organizations sponsoring arbitration. It restated that the doctrine of broad arbitral immunity, once extended to arbitration organizations, "insures that an arbitrator benefits from the independence necessary to protect him from bias or intimidation arising out of the exercise of judicial functions".[113] In this line, the US Supreme Court of South Carolina agreed that the extension of judicial immunity to the AAA (and to other arbitration organizations in future claims) under the *Butz* test justified the necessity for the protection of all arbitration actors while exercising their quasi-judicial functions. The US Court also noticed that the arbitral immunity was not unlimited as it covered the arbitrators' *judicial* actions that needed to be performed within the scope of arbitrators' authority.[114] The judicial character of institutional acts was therefore the ground for the prospective immunity of organizations sponsoring arbitration. In view of this, the US Supreme Court did not find the AAA to have acted in excess of its "jurisdiction" as the AAA had been authorized to assist the parties in the selection of the third arbitrator under the arbitration agreement. Furthermore, according to the Court, the organizational conduct in the arbitrator's appointment proceedings fell exactly within the organizational acts of quasi-judicial nature and therefore such acts deserved the protection under the doctrine on arbitral immunity.

The holding of the US Supreme Court of South Carolina in *Strategic Resources* is controversial for at least three reasons.[115] First, it did not provide a comprehen-

[111]Eric Laufgraben, "Arbitration: South Carolina's Top Court Extends Arbitral Immunity to ADR Providers (Web)".

[112]Ibid.

[113]See *Butz v. Economou* (1978) *438 U.S. 478 US Supreme Court.*

[114]The US Supreme Court cited the decision in *Mireles v. Waco, 502 U.S. 9, 11–12 (1991)*, which reflected on the scope of the judicial immunity.

[115]Cf. Moffitt 2006, 179–192.

sive justification for the adaptation of the *Butz* test to the operation of institutional arbitration. Given that, it is still unclear which institutional acts would ordinary fall within the quasi-judicial institutional acts and which ones would qualify as the provision of arbitration services. Notably, such a distinction simply does not matter for the US courts because all acts (or omission) of arbitral institutions appear to be covered under the doctrine on arbitral immunity. Second, the limitations to judicial immunity, as provided in the *Mireles* case,[116] on which the US Supreme Court relied in the present decision, seem to have little application to the work of arbitral institutions. The lack of proper distinction between quasi-judicial and non-judicial institutional acts implies that the institutional conduct as a whole qualifies as a particular form of the quasi-judicial performance of the institutional obligations. In this regard, the limits to the doctrine on judicial immunity become illusory with regard to the work of arbitration organizations in the US. Finally, the possibility of the parties using other procedural safeguards in the arbitration proceedings, which was stressed by the Supreme Court, appears again as a controversial issue. The FAA provides for a rather limited scope of judicial review of arbitral awards, which deals mostly with the scrutiny of the arbitrators' conduct rather than of the institutional performance in the arbitration proceedings.[117] Although this book suggests the emergence of the public function of institutional arbitration, this is not the only facet underlying institutional activity.[118] Given that, the exclusive recognition by the US courts of the judicial nature of institutional arbitration yet again seems incomplete.

All these have practical implications for the parties to arbitration proceedings. As explained in Chap. 1 with regard to the (in)famous case where the AAA, together with the individual arbitrator, were sued by the party to such proceedings for the inability to ensure the proper conduct of the arbitration underlying the lawsuit in question,[119] there has been increasing confusion as to the role of organizations sponsoring arbitration in the US. This confusion is visible both among arbitration users and local and international practitioners. The fact that the US courts do not provide a comprehensive answer to this issue under the doctrine of

---

[116]Ibid.

[117]Under the FAA the grounds for refusing the enforcement or recognition of the award are the following:

(a) In any of the following cases the United States court in and for the district wherein the award was made may make an order vacating the award upon the application of any party to the arbitration:
(1) where the award was procured by corruption, fraud, or undue means;
(2) where there was evident partiality or corruption in the arbitrators, or either of them;
(3) where the arbitrators were guilty of misconduct in refusing to postpone the hearing, upon sufficient cause shown, or in refusing to hear evidence pertinent and material to the controversy; or of any other misbehaviour by which the rights of any party have been prejudiced; or
(4) where the arbitrators exceeded their powers, or so imperfectly executed them that a mutual, final, and definite award upon the subject matter submitted was not made.

[118]Cf. Sect. 2.3 of Chap. 2 .

[119]*Malik v. Ruttenberg et al. 398 N.J. Super. 489, 495 (App. Div.* 2008).

arbitral immunity when determining liability claims only aggravates the confusion and frustration on the part of the parties to the arbitrations that enter into contractual relations with the administrators of their disputes. This frustration increases the occurrence of institutional liability claims because arbitration users keep trying to enforce their contractual rights, which stem from institutional contracts, before the US courts. The courts often appear as the *fora* of last resort to determine the breach of the contractual obligations by organizations sponsoring arbitration in the US. These determinations have been, however, continuously refused by the US courts.

5.2.1.2.3 The UK

Arbitral institutions in the UK are also treated as quasi-judges to the extent to which they act in the arbitrators' capacity. Therefore, in certain stages of institutional activity in the arbitration process, arbitral institutions enjoy qualified judicial immunity. This, in turn, stems from the immunity accorded to arbitrators under English law. In line with this, the major difficulty with the English public authorities' understanding of the function of arbitral institutions relates to the interdependency of the institutional work and the arbitrators' performance in the arbitration process.

5.2.1.2.3.1 Development of the Doctrine on Arbitral Immunity in the UK

English law has long been in favour of extending judicial immunity to arbitrators in order to protect their arbitral acts within the arbitration process (given the policy grounds).[120] However, judicial immunity in the UK was not absolute and, from the moment of the establishment of the doctrine on judicial immunity, protection was granted only to those acts that fell within the jurisdiction of a judge of a court of record.[121] Some commentators argue that the general rule established in early English common law provided for the liability of judges and not for their absolute immunity.[122]

Broad judicial immunity was acknowledged in the 17th century in two leading cases, namely, in *Floyd v. Barker*[123] and *The Case of the Marshalsea.*[124] Although Judge Coke, who delivered opinions in both decisions, stated that the protection of

---

[120]See Rasmussen 2002, 1849; Amor-Smith 1991, 6–10.

[121]Feinman and Cohen 1979, 205–206.

[122]Feinman and Cohen 1979, 203–204. The authors observe that: "English law began with a position of general judicial liability and developed only limited exceptions on the grounds that are irrelevant for the discussion of judicial liability today."

[123]*Floyd v. Barker, 77 Eng. Rep.* 1305 (Star Chamber 1607); for the comments on the case see *Rasmussen* 2002, 1851–1852; Feinman and Cohen 1979, 207–210.

[124]*The Case of the Marshalsea, 77 Eng. Rep.* 1027 *(C.P. 1610)*; for the comments on the case see Feinman and Cohen 1979, 207–214.

judges should be absolute, he pointed out two situations in which a doctrine on judicial immunity could not be applied. This involved the following situations: (1) when a judge performed his or her administrative or ministerial function, hence, he or she produced extrajudicial acts; and (2) whenever a judge exceeded his or her jurisdiction.[125] This observation is particularly important if one considers the adoption of the standards of English law on judicial immunity by the US judges in *Bradley v. Fisher*. In fact, English courts seemed to be more cautious while assessing the legal responsibility of their own public officials (as compared with their counterparts in the US) to the extent that they expressed a rather moderate approach to the scope of judicial immunity, and therefore also to the immunity of arbitrators.[126]

Once again, judicial immunity in the UK was extended to arbitrators on public policy grounds regarding the necessity of safeguarding the judicial character of the arbitrators' conduct. There are two prominent decisions in which both the judicial function of arbitrators and the extension of the judicial immunity to arbitrators were acknowledged. The first case concerns the decision in *Sutcliffe v. Thackrah*, in which Lord Reid reaffirmed the principles underlying the doctrine on arbitral immunity and stated that this doctrine should also cover the arbitrators' judicial function in the arbitration process.[127] According to Lord Reid, however, this function did not concern the investigation made by an architect while evaluating whether the work of builders had been provided with due care or in accordance with the generally established standards (which was the subject matter of the appeal analysed above).[128]

The second case relates to the judgement in *Arenson v. Casson, Beckman, Rutley & Co.* in which the House of Lords faced a claim involving the performance of accountants who were to assess the value of the shares in a private company.[129] In this regard, the issue at stake did not involve the work of arbitrators but quasi-arbitrators. The House of Lords determined that "ordinary" arbitrators should enjoy judicial immunity while exercising their judicial function. However, this was not the case in the present opinion, as the accountants whose prospective immunity was to be examined by the House of Lords assumed strictly investigative roles that did not correspond to the traditional functions of arbitrators. The ruling in *Arenson* is significant also because it raised certain doubts about the rationale behind the arbitral immunity. It inspired partially dissenting speeches delivered by Lords Kilbrandon and Fraser, in which the basis for granting immunity to arbitrators was called into question.[130] Even though the Lords ultimately agreed with the prevailing reasoning that accountants should not be granted

---

[125]Ibid.

[126]Feinman and Cohen 1979, 202–205.

[127]See *Sutcliffe v. Thackrah* [1974] 1 Lloyd's Rep. 318.

[128]Ibid.

[129]*Arenson v. Casson Beckman Rutley & Co.* [1977] *A.C. 405 et seq House of Lords.*

[130]Ibid.

immunity in the discussed case, they did so on the grounds that the judicial immunity should not be accorded to *quasi* arbitrators (neither to ordinary arbitrators), as the arbitrators' powers were derived from the parties' agreement.[131] Therefore—according to them—it would be difficult to imagine that the protection of the parties' "nominees" shall be equal to the protection of the public judges whose authority stemmed from the sovereign.[132] Although the dissenting opinion did not affect the judgement in the case at stake, it questioned the absolute protection enjoyed by arbitrators in the arbitration process in the UK. Moreover, the controversies raised in *Arenson* had an influence on the adoption of rather qualified regulation of arbitral immunity by the UK Arbitration Act of 1996, which will now be discussed.

Under Paragraph 1 of Section 29 of the Act, arbitrators were granted unlimited immunity from any civil action for anything done or omitted in the discharge or purported discharge of their functions as arbitrators unless the act or omission was shown to had been in bad faith.[133] Moreover, pursuant to paragraph 2 of the Act, arbitral immunity was also extended to arbitrators' agents or employees acting in the same capacity as arbitrators themselves.[134] Notwithstanding that, arbitral immunity has some limitations. It does not cover the unjustified resignation of arbitrators, in which case the parties are authorized to bring liability claims before the courts provided that the scope of the arbitrator's liability was previously agreed on by both the parties and the arbitrator.[135]

[131]The excerpts from the Lord's Kilbrandon opinion in: *Arenson v. Casson Beckman Rutley & Co.* 1977 (430–431) read as follows: "[...]The question which puzzled me as the argument developed was, what was the essential difference between the typical valuer (the auditor in the present case) and an arbitrator at common law or under the Arbitration Acts? It is conceded that an arbitrator is immune from suit, aside from fraud, but why? I find it impossible to put weight on such considerations as that in the case of an arbitrator (a) there is a dispute between parties, (b) he hears evidence, (c) he hears submissions from the parties, and that therefore he, unlike the valuer, is acting in a judicial capacity. As regards (a), I cannot see any judicial distinction between a dispute which has actually arisen and a situation where persons have opposed interests, if in either case an impartial person has had to be called in to make a decision which the interested parties will accept. As regards (b) and (c), these are certainly not necessary activities of an arbiter. Once the nature and the limits of the submission to him have been defined, it could well be that he would go down at his own convenience to a warehouse, inspect a sample of merchandise displayed to him by the foreman and return his opinion on its quality or value. I have come to be of the opinion that it is a necessary conclusion to be drawn from Sutcliffe v Thackrah [..] and from the instant decision that an arbitrator at common law or under the Acts is indeed a person selected by the parties for his expertise thereof and that if he is negligent in that exercise he will be liable in damages."

[132]Ibid.

[133]The UK Arbitration Act 1996, Chapter 23, Section 29.

[134]Ibid.

[135]The UK Arbitration Act 1996, Chapter 23, Section 25, in which it is stated that if the parties failed to negotiate respective provisions regarding the prospective liability of an arbitrator in the case of his resignation in the course of arbitration proceedings, an arbitrator will be capable of asking the court for granting him a relief from any liability thereby incurred by him, or for making an order within the court's discretion as to the payment or repayment of any fees and expenses which were due at the moment of the arbitrator's resignation.

The first observation which comes out of the regulation of arbitrator's immunity in the UK concerns the fact that the UK Arbitration Act of 1996 itself does not define which kind of arbitrator's acts may fall within the group of acts done in bad faith. Will such expression also involve negligent acts? Even if some commentators are negative regarding this matter,[136] the issue is still open, which, from a broader perspective, affects the accurate determination of the scope of the responsibilities of arbitrators together with their qualification under English law.

Secondly, the Act reflected on the prospective immunity of arbitral institutions in the UK. In accordance with Section 74 of the Act, an arbitral or other institution or an individual designated by the parties to act as an appointing or nominating authority should not be liable for "anything done or omitted in the discharge or purported discharge of that function unless the act or omission is shown to have been in bad faith".[137] Moreover, the aforementioned legal or natural persons shall not be liable for any acts of the arbitrators, whom such persons had appointed or nominated, neither for the acts of arbitrators' agents or employees done within the arbitral capacity.[138] The exclusion of liability in the manner defined above should also apply to an agent or employee of the institution or a person who participated in the nomination of an arbitrator or in the arbitrator's appointing procedure.[139]

The adoption of the above provisions of the Act was significant to the extent that it was the first attempt by legislative authorities in the UK to reflect on the judicial interpretations of the scope of the protection of arbitration actors as well as on the controversies associated with the function of arbitrators and the sources of arbitral power as raised in *Arenson*. Under the UK Arbitration Act of 1996, not only were arbitrators granted so-called "qualified" immunity but the doctrine on judicial immunity was also extended to arbitral institutions and their agents and employees for the acts connected with the appointment or nomination of arbitrators. Moreover, pursuant to Schedule 1 enclosed to the Act, both sections of the Act concerning the immunity of arbitrators and arbitral institutions are mandatory, therefore, the parties may not alter the scope of the arbitral immunity by way of their contractual arrangements.[140]

Here again, the institutional immunity granted by the Act, was related to the work of arbitrators in the arbitration process. This implies, *a contrario,* that arbitral institutions could be held liable for the acts or omission not directly connected with the arbitrators' conduct in the arbitration process. However, the lack of a clear definition of both the institutional involvement in the arbitration process and

[136]Cf. Rasmussen 2002, 1855.

[137]The UK Arbitration Act 1996, Chapter 23., Section 74, paragraph 1.

[138]Paragraph 2 of the Section 74 of the Act according to which: "An arbitral or other institution or person by whom an arbitrator is appointed or nominated is not liable, by reason of having appointed or nominated him, for anything done or omitted by the arbitrator (or his employees or agents) in the discharge or purported discharge of his functions as arbitrator."

[139]The UK Arbitration Act 1996, Chapter 23, Section 74, paragraph 3.

[140]Schedule 1 enclosed to the UK Arbitration Act 1996, Chapter 23.

the institutional function performed in the course of the proceedings again leaves the question of the scope of institutional responsibility unanswered. Taking into account that there is no relevant case law dealing with institutional liability in the UK, it remains unknown how the English courts would interpret the rule on institutional immunity and whether such immunity would be extended to institutional acts and omission falling beyond arbitrators' functions. The answers to these questions would be helpful for a better understanding of the stance of the English authorities on the function assumed by arbitral institutions in the arbitration process, which heretofore remains unclear. On the one hand, UK legislators seem to treat certain institutional acts as judicial acts. On the other hand, there is room for the interpretation of exclusive institutional obligations as purely contractual.

5.2.1.2.4 Sweden

The Swedish Arbitration Act of 1999 does not regulate the issue of liability of arbitrators or arbitral institutions for the acts or omission in the course of arbitration. Some commentators argue that Swedish law, in principle, recognizes the contractual nature of the relationship between the parties and arbitrators and that certain acts of the former, save those acts closely relating to the rendering of the arbitral award, could fall within the notion of contractual liability.[141] Other authors claim that the issue of civil liability of arbitrators (and of arbitral institutions) in Sweden falls within the general principles of contract law thus allowing the parties to sue an arbitrator (and possibly an arbitral institutions) if his or her negligent behaviour caused a "loss, cost or expense to one or both parties".[142] At the same time, the contractual liability of institutional arbitration actors appears to be limited to acts or omission resulting in gross negligence and wilful misconduct.[143] In addition, as Schöldström notes, if there is no express regulation of a particular issue under Swedish law of obligations, the provisions of the Contract Act and the Sale of Goods Act of 1905 could be, potentially, applied to arbitration settings by the Swedish judges facing the problem by analogy.[144] Would institutional activity fall within the scope of this Act? This assumption, again, will need to be confronted with the actual practice of the Swedish courts.

Given that, at least to the knowledge of the author, there is no case law addressing the issues at hand, the understanding by Swedish authorities (such as the legislators and courts) of the actual nature of institutional functions remains unclear. When recalling the discussion on the possibility of the parties to recourse against the decision of an arbitral institution regarding the arbitrator's fees before the relevant Swedish court as determined in the *Soyak* judgements, it could be implied

[141]Cole et al. (Annexes) 2014, 138.

[142]von Pachelbel and Oldenstam 2009, 806–807.

[143]von Pachelbel and Oldenstam 2009, 807 and Article 48 of the 2010 SCC Arbitration Rules.

[144]Schöldström 1998, 131.

that the Swedish judges place more focus on the contractual, commercial function of institutional arbitration. Thus, they provide the parties with the unrestricted right to question the performance of contractual obligations of an arbitral institution in public courts. However, as already noted in the preceding section, these issues became more complex when the proposals of the amendments to the Swedish Arbitration Act of 1999 were revealed.[145] Pursuant to the proposed changes to the Swedish Arbitration Act of 1999, the parties should be deprived of the right to apply to the relevant district court to question the decision on the arbitrator's fees if such fees had been previously determined by an arbitral institution. The last observation suggests that the Swedish legislators have begun to recognize the private regulatory powers of arbitral institutions by focusing more closely on their public function. This, together with the lack of guidance regarding the notion of gross negligence and the wilful misconduct in the context of the arbitrator's and institutional performance amounts to the conclusion that the dual function of arbitral institutions has not yet been properly acknowledged in Sweden.

5.2.1.2.5 Possible Vicarious Liability in Institutional Regulatory Arbitrations in the US?

The analysis above demonstrated that none of the public authorities from the studied jurisdictions address the dual function of institutional arbitration in a consistent manner. Some of them, including the Swedish legislators and courts, fail to address these issues entirely. While French judges emphasize the commercial facet of institutional operation, their US and UK counterparts stress the jurisdictional aspect of institutional activity, which takes different forms in the course of institutional arbitral proceedings. Moreover, in common law jurisdictions there is no separate regime of immunity for arbitrators and organizations sponsoring arbitration, which is recommendable given their distinct functions. Finally, the US approach to absolute arbitral immunity openly undermines the contractual aspect of institutional arbitration by granting legal immunity to arbitrators or institutions, regardless of the prior contractual arrangements on this matter.

All of these concerns have additional implications for the regulatory arbitration concerning disputes of a non-commercial nature. The emerging public function of institutional arbitration identified in Sect. 2.3.2 of Chap. 2 showed the increasing use of institutional arbitration in various regulatory fields. This function can be found in the case law analysed above, for example, in the *Austern* and *Olson* cases, where the arbitration proceedings arose out of the option trading partnership agreement (*Austern*) and the employment agreement providing for the NASD arbitration (*Olson*).[146] Correspondingly, the *SNF* saga proved that international

[145]Sect. 5.2.1.1.3.

[146]Sect. 5.2.1.2.2.3.

arbitrators deal with claims also falling within public regulation (i.e. the then EC competition law in the case at hand).[147] Additionally, constitutional issues emerged in the decision in *République de Guinée v. Chambre arbitrale de Paris,* in which the Paris Court of Appeal was faced with a possible violation by the arbitral tribunal and, to a certain extent, also by the arbitral institution, of the right to a fair trial under the European Convention of Human Rights.[148] Similar observations are valid in the context of the Pirelli case where the relationship between the ICC arbitration rules and the party's right to access to justice was sketched.[149] These observations imply that the protection of the statutory rights, procedural rights and possibly also constitutional rights of the parties is particularly needed in arbitration proceedings. The current national regulations of institutional liability (or immunity) do not offer satisfactory solutions to these concerns.

Two facts may allow one to think that the necessity for the protection of the weaker parties in arbitration processes has been spotted by public authorities even in countries that provide for the immunity of institutional arbitration actors. First, some decisions of the US courts have questioned the absolute extension of arbitral immunity to arbitral organizations. For example, in the decision in *Baar v. Tigerman*, the performance of arbitral institutions was explained in the context of the vicarious liability of arbitral institutions for the acts of arbitrators.[150] This implied a weakening of the doctrine of absolute arbitral immunity by assuming the need for certain liability of at least one arbitration actor—such as the organization sponsoring arbitration—for the acts performed in the course of the arbitration proceedings.

Second, regarding the exclusion of liability in consumer arbitration, the RUAA § 14(a)-(c) in California provided for the liability of "private judging companies" in consumer arbitrations "except to the extent that a private judging company's liability is predicated on a theory of vicarious liability for the acts of an arbitrator, and the arbitrator enjoys immunity from civil liability for the acts alleged".[151] This demonstrates that the provisions on liability (or immunity) of institutional arbitration actors are in fact interrelated with the scope of protection granted to the parties to arbitration proceedings under various domestic laws. The increasing acknowledgement of such relationship by the US authorities increases the likelihood of the possible room for more transparency in the institutional arbitration proceedings in the US, which is particularly required due to the democratic concerns relating to consumer and other forms of "industry-based" arbitrations in the US.

[147]Sect. 5.2.1.1.1 of this chapter.

[148]See Kleiman 2009a, 33–35.

[149]Sect. 5.2.1.1.1 of this chapter.

[150]*Baar v. Tigerman.* (1983) *140 Cal. App. 3d 979 [189 Cal. Rptr. 834] Court of Appeals of California.*

[151]Kevin G. Baker, Bill Analysis of A.B. 3030, California State Legislature, (Aug. 26, 2002), Assembly Committee on Judiciary 2011, 1.

5.2.2 *"The Jury Is Still Out!" Practical Problems with Institutional Arbitral Liability*

The divergent national treatment of the legal nature of institutional arbitration also has practical implications for the scope of the protection of the parties to the arbitration proceedings who decide to sue arbitral institutions for the breach of their contractual obligations. This connects with the theoretical issues raised in the course of the analysis of the model of contractual relationships in institutional arbitration in Chap. 3. In this vein, the following issues will be discussed now: (1) the assessment by the public courts of the moment of the emergence of institutional contracts with regard to a single party to arbitration; (2) the interplay between the legal qualification (if any) of institutional contracts under various national laws by public judges and the possible application of various doctrines of liability based on the prior legal specifications of such contracts; and finally (3) the problems with the (un)enforceability of the 1998 ICC exclusion of liability clause under French law.

5.2.2.1 Moment of the Emergence of Institutional Contracts: Does the Exclusion of Liability Apply?

The selective determination of the moment of the emergence of institutional contracts, highlighted in the following discussion, concerns, inter alia, the effects of such determinations for both the possibility of relying on the exclusion of liability clauses by the parties and the scope of the liability of arbitral institutions. These issues appear particularly significant in the context of the temporal conflict of different sets of institutional arbitration rules. These problems will be explicated with references to the judgements issued by the French courts in the CEKOBANKA case and the *Cubic v. SNF* saga.

In CEKOBANKA, the ICC Court dismissed the arbitration case at the outset because its was not *prima facie* satisfied with the existence of the arbitration agreement. That could imply the defence of the ICC Court in the subsequent court proceedings relating to this arbitration that there was no contract binding the ICC and the party in question. To the contrary, however, the Paris *Tribunal de grande instance* confirmed the contractual bonds between the claimant (CEKOBANKA) and the ICC Court:

> Considering that CEKOBANKA has notified the ICC Court of Arbitration of the request for arbitration, in accordance with the formal procedure set out in the latter's Rules and the Court of Arbitration had agreed to examine such request, contractual ties have been established including for the ICC the duty to render a decision, in accordance with its Rules (…) which have become the law between the parties, on the prima facie existence of an arbitration agreement.[152]

[152] See CEKOBANKA case with the translation in: Robine 1989, 325.

In this case, the key moment for the conclusion of the contract was said to be a notification of the ICC of the request for arbitration made by the claimant. The receipt of such request constituted the contractual bonds *only* between the claimant and the ICC Court. This determination of the Paris court should not be controversial given the analysis of the direct ties between each institutional arbitration actor under the model on contractual relations presented in Chap. 3. As will be seen from the following example, however, not all French courts follow the same logic while reflecting on the moments of the contract formation in institutional arbitration.

In the liability claim filed by *SNF* against the ICC before the *Tribunal de grande instance*, there was an issue on which set of rules (whether those of 1988 or 1998) should have application to the case at hand.[153] The Rules of 1988 were in force when the parties signed the arbitration agreement, and they did not provide for the exclusion of liability clause. To the contrary, the Rules of 1998 (which contained the exclusion of liability clause) were in effect at the moment of sending the request for arbitration to the ICC Secretariat by the claimant.

The French *Tribunal de grande instance* dismissed the *SNF*'s argument that the parties to arbitration were bound with the 1988 Rules of Arbitration, as, in the eyes of the Court, it was the date of filing of the request for arbitration which was determinative upon the commencement of the arbitral proceedings.[154] *SNF* appealed this judgement and claimed that the arbitration rules governing the relationship between the institutional arbitral actors where those of 1988, which were effective at the moment when the parties concluded their arbitration agreement (that is, in 1993). It is important to stress here that the ICC itself argued that the institutional contract was autonomous to the arbitration agreement between the parties, and therefore, the parties should be governed by the rules of arbitration that were in force when the request for arbitration reached the ICC Secretariat (the 1998 Rules).[155]

The Paris Court of Appeal followed the decision of the court of the first instance to the extent that it applied the ICC Arbitration Rules of 1998 to the contractual obligations of the disputants, even though its line of reasoning was slightly different to the argumentation that stood behind the decision of the lower court. The Paris Court of Appeal held that the parties were bound by the 1998 ICC Arbitration Rules as a result of having explicitly referred to these Rules in the ICC Terms of Reference. Without such a document, the contractual ties between

---

[153] *Société SNF c/Chambre de Commerce Internationale. Tribunal de grande instance de Paris (1 Ch.)* 2007. *Rev. arb.* 2007, 847.

[154] Ibid.

[155] Cf. Kleiman 2009b, 20–27. See also: Article 4(2) in accordance with Article 6(1) of the 1998 ICC Arbitration Rules, which states that unless the parties made an explicit reference that the Rules governing the arbitration should be the Rules in effect on the date of their arbitration agreement, the institutional relationships should be subject, by default, to the Rules in force on the date of the commencement of arbitration proceedings (hence, on the date on which the request for arbitration is received by the ICC Secretariat).

the parties and the institution presumably would have been governed by the rules which were in force at the moment of the parties' conclusion of the arbitration agreement, thus, by the ICC Arbitration Rules of 1988.

As shown in the presentation above, there is a visible disagreement among the French courts regarding the question of which document constitutes the contractual bond in institutional arbitration. The Paris *Tribunal de grande instance* in CEKOBANKA case relied on the request for arbitration while determining the emergence of the contract between the claimant and the ICC Court of Arbitration (which was, to a certain extent, confirmed by the court of the first instance in the *SNF v.* the ICC case). On the contrary, the Paris Court of Appeal in the *SNF* case referred to the Terms of Reference while considering the determinative document for the conclusion of the contract between the parties (taken collectively) and the other ICC arbitration actors because the parties to institutional contract agreed on these Rules in the Terms of Reference. If there was no such agreement, the Paris Court of Appeal would have determined the 1988 Rules as the applicable rules given the moment of the conclusion by the parties of their arbitration agreement.

Two major observations concerning the assessment by judges of the moment of the emergence of institutional contractual obligations in the arbitration processes emerge from the discussion above. The first concerns the question of which rules, and hence which provisions on liability, shall apply to the institutional arbitration contracts in situations in which the previous version of the rules was amended by the institution between the date of the arbitration agreement and the moment of the commencement of the proceedings. The fact that even the French courts seem to not have taken a consistent view in this regard implies that even a relatively straightforward provision of Article 6(1) of the 1998 ICC Arbitration Rules—stating that the parties should be deemed to have submitted their dispute *ipso facto* to the rules in effect on the date of commencement of the arbitration proceedings unless the parties have agreed to submit to the rules effective at the date of the arbitration agreement—may be interpreted in varied ways by different judges. The second point deals with the possible adoption by some judges of the triangular theory of contractual relationships when analysing the bonds coming into existence in institutional arbitration. This intensifies the confusion concerning the question of which institutional arbitration device implies the emergence of the contractual obligations of institutional arbitration actors, determining also the scope of the prospective liability of these actors. The analysis of the model of the contractual relations provided in Chap. 3 pointed out the adequacy of the theory of the individualized contractual relationships for such analyses. This could eliminate doubts regarding the emergence of contractual obligations of arbitral institutions to a *single* party to arbitration. This, in turn, could facilitate a more consistent assessment by domestic judges of the moment of the entering into the contractual obligations by institutional arbitration actors that also have an impact on their prospective liability.

5.2.2.2 Problems with the Legal Qualification of Institutional Contracts Versus Existent Doctrines on Liability

Given the specific nature of arbitration in general and of its institutional variant in particular, many practitioners and scholars have long attempted to define the institutional contractual relationships under existent theories of contract laws. French authors (i.e. Professors Robine and Fouchard) analysed the relevance of the French provisions concerning agency contracts (*contrat de mandate*) and independent contractor (*contrat d'enteprise*) to the rights and duties of the institutional arbitration actors.[156] This debate appears, however, to have mostly theoretical significance. As indicated by the French case law on institutional liability presented above, the French courts usually do not define institutional obligations in a comprehensive manner and they also fail to address the nature of institutional contracts. All these again increase the confusion about the regime of liability applicable to institutional arbitration contracts under the doctrines on liability under French law.

By way of illustration, in the decision dated 10 October 2007 in *SNF c/ Chambre de commerce internationale*, the *Tribunal de grande instance* referred to the provision of Article 1150 of the French Civil Code while analysing the prospective liability of the ICC.[157] This shows that the liability of arbitral institutions in France may, in principle, be governed by the general provisions on the liability for the non-performance of contracts under Articles 1146-1155 of the French Civil Code. In fact, the legal qualification by French judges of the institutional contracts as contracts for provision of services or agency contracts may have little significance for the determinations of the scope of institutional arbitral liability under French law. This observation is supported by other commentators who have stressed that the liability of the contractor in France should be in any case subject to the general rules of contractual liability, which largely overlap with the provisions on liability governing the contractual performance of the representative under French law[158] should the courts decide to refer to the latter provisions in the context of institutional performance. However, the fact that the qualification of institutional contracts together with the regime on liability under such contracts has not been determined in a clear manner in any jurisdiction analysed here increases the uncertainty regarding the interpretation and the enforcement of institutional liability clauses under applicable laws.

Also in the UK, the courts have not taken a position on the question of what kind of legal relationships institutional arbitrations involve. However, the debate on the nature and qualifications of the relationships between arbitrators and the parties is not uncommon in the UK. In the judgement of the UK Supreme Court in

---

[156]Robine 1989, 325–326; see also Fouchard 1987.

[157]*Société SNF c/Chambre de Commerce Internationale. Tribunal de grande instance de Paris (1 Ch.)* 2007. *Rev. arb.* 2007, 847.

[158]Kleiman 2009a, 23.

Jivraj v. Hashwani,[159] a number of different variants were discussed, including the possible employment relationship between the parties and arbitrators. Eventually, the judgement concluded that the arbitrators' contract had a very specific, *sui generis* nature that should not place such contracts next to any other types of contracts existent under English law. It is likely then that this argumentation will also be applied to institutional arbitration by the English courts.

Even though the case in question does not involve institutional arbitration, it provides sufficient guidance as to the legal character of the relationships between arbitrators and the parties to arbitration under English law. The judgement concerned the question of whether the provision of the joint venture agreement containing an arbitration clause—which required the arbitrators to be members of the Ismaili community—constituted discrimination on religious grounds under the EU Employment Equality Regulations of 2003 (the Regulations). Given the scope of this chapter, the following discussion will omit the Supreme Court's consideration of the discriminatory character of the arbitration clause, and will concentrate solely on the prospective employment relationship in arbitration.

Justice Steel, in the first instance, did not find the nature of the relationship between the parties and arbitrators able to accommodate the definition of the employment under the Regulations. Under appeal, the Court of Appeal allowed the understanding of the relationship at hand in terms of the "employment".[160] The Court of Appeal held that the appointment of arbitrators involved a contract for provision of services to be understood in a sense of a "contract personally to do any work", which corresponded to the meaning of "employment" under the Regulations.[161] Under further appeal, the Supreme Court (Lord Mance) criticized such an approach, and stated that the unique nature of the contract between arbitrator and the party did not allow for treating such contracts as contracts between an employer and an employee. Lord Mance indicated that:

> The arbitrator is in critical respects independent of the parties. His functions and duties require him to rise above the partisan interests of the parties and not to act in, or so as to further, the particular interests of either party. As the International Chamber of Commerce ("the ICC") puts it, he must determine how to resolve their competing interests. He is in no sense in a position of subordination to the parties; rather the contrary. He is in effect a "quasi-judicial adjudicator".[162]

However, Lord Mance failed to specify in an exact manner the accurate qualification of contracts arising in arbitration. The Court noted that the contract between the parties and arbitrators could be a contract for provision of personal services, yet again—in the case at hand—"they were not personal services under the direction of the parties".[163]

---

[159] See generally *Jivraj v. Hashwani* [2011] 1 WLR 1872.

[160] Ibid.

[161] Ibid.

[162] *Jivraj v. Hashwani* [2011] 1 WLR 1872,18.

[163] *Jivraj v. Hashwani* [2011] 1 WLR 1872, 20.

Lastly, while capturing the classical sense of the independent role of arbitrators, Lord Mance referred to both an early decision of the German Rechtgericht of 1904[164] and to the recent work of Gary Born on *International Commercial Arbitration*.[165] In both sources, it is understood that the contract between the parties and arbitrators is a *sui generis* contract that should be neither treated as an employment relationship nor explained in the language of any conventional contractual theories such as the theory of agency or provision of services. This approach corresponds to the preliminary proposals presented in the last part of this section for the recognition of the *sui generis* character of institutional contracts by judges in the courts of law.

The above analysis clearly does not accommodate all possible interpretations of institutional contracts or all the possible doctrines on liability that may apply to such contracts under English law. This is why, although important, the discussion on the nature of the arbitrators' contract provided in the case in question cannot serve as a comprehensive basis for the examination of all possible scenarios regarding the treatment of arbitral institutions under English law. Some commentators even call into question the existence of the contractual bonds between institutional arbitration actors by stating that qualified immunity of the LCIA (or English arbitral institutions in more general terms) under the UK Arbitration Act of 1996 corresponds with the exclusion of the third parties' liability under the Himalaya clause.[166] It also seems plausible that arbitral institutions could be qualified by the English courts as agents of the parties. This is especially so because of the fact that English law on agency does not require an agent to act in the name of or on behalf of the principal. Assuming that the parties would have different, and often conflicting, expectations regarding the ways in which their arbitration should be conducted and what the outcomes of their arbitration processes should be, the specific regime for agency contracts under English law could eliminate the possible conflict of interest of arbitral institution acting as an agent of both (or more) parties.[167]

In fact, any possible application of the provisions on general contract laws to arbitration and institutional arbitration actors bears the risk that the concept of arbitration and of the contracts coming into existence in institutional arbitration will be distorted. At the same time, however, public regulation of the obligations and standards of performance of institutional arbitration actors is required, only if to increase professional conduct in institutional arbitration.

Such regulation should, however, respect the uniqueness of both institutional nature and institutional private settings. Consider, for example, that arbitrators in the UK have been exempted from the duty to carry out their "service" with reasonable care and skill under the UK Supply and Services Act of 1982 (the UK Supply Act).[168] On first analysis, this exemption does not appear controversial

[164]Ref. No.: RGZ 59, 247, as cited to in *Jivraj v. Hashwani* [2011]1 WLR 1872.

[165]Born 2009, Vol I, pp 1607–1609, as cited in *Jivraj v. Hashwani* [2011] 1 WLR 1872.

[166]Schöldström 1998, 51.

[167]Ibid.

[168]Schöldström 1998, 48.

given the specificity of the arbitrator's mandate that largely limits the application of the provisions of general contract law to arbitration. However, what are the standards of care to be adopted in the course of arbitrations in the UK then? Imagine that such an approach is also extended to some institutional duties falling within the provisions of this Act. What would be the interpretations of the standards of duty and care of arbitral institutions by the English courts? If the application of the provisions of the UK Supply Act to institutional arbitration is also limited or somewhat excluded, and if no other legal provisions define these standards of duty and care in arbitration, would that result in judges adopting surprisingly low standards of care with regard to institutional activity and even in ultimately rejecting the liability claims against arbitral institutions?

This discussion demonstrates that any interpretations of the behaviour of institutional arbitration actors and the contracts underlying such behaviour should correspond with the unique, *sui generis* nature of arbitration. This is why none of the contract law theories presented above (agency contracts, provision of services contracts, or employment contracts) should in fact have application to institutional arbitration if they do not respect the particular aspect of institutional arbitration corresponding to its dual (commercial and public) function. The analysis below will now briefly explain why this is so.

Regarding the agency theory, three possible scenarios come to mind given the complex relationships in institutional arbitration. Namely, that: (1) the arbitral institutions will be qualified as agents of arbitrators and/or the parties; (2) the institutional arbitrators will be perceived as agents of arbitral institutions and/or the parties; and (3) that the parties will be characterized as agents of arbitral institutions and/or the arbitrators. The first scenario appears inapplicable to the proposed definition of the status and function of arbitral institutions as defined in Chap. 3. This is because arbitral institutions cannot act as agents of all parties to arbitration proceedings at the same time, given that such parties have conflicting interests in the arbitration proceedings. Even if the theory of agency could be applied to arbitral institutions in the UK (as under English law on agency the agents do not have to act in the name of or on behalf of the parties), the principle of neutrality of institutional arbitration processes (required under most institutional arbitration rules) would negate this claim. Moreover, arbitral institutions—as explained in Chap. 2—enjoy certain exclusive private regulatory powers in and outside arbitration processes that fall outside the principle of party autonomy. Additionally, arbitral institutions do not have to follow instructions from the parties at all stages of arbitration proceedings, which the agency theory implies they do under general contract laws. Finally, if it is assumed that arbitral institutions act as agents of the disputing parties and that they enter into the contracts with arbitrators within this capacity, then the contracts between arbitrators and the parties would assume a direct liability of arbitrators towards the parties. This assumption does not comply with the proposals of this book concerning the non-existence of direct contractual relationships between the parties and the institutional arbitrators after the conferment of the adjudicatory powers on arbitrators by arbitral institutions.

Regarding the second scenario—in which arbitrators are perceived as agents of arbitral institutions and/or the parties—a similar inadequacy comes to mind, especially when confronted with the adjudicatory powers that arbitrators enjoy in the arbitration processes. It is hard to imagine that the quasi-judicial functions of arbitrators could justify the agency theory with regard to arbitrators. Moreover, the parties have, in fact, no control of the work of arbitrators, and the institutional oversight of the performance of arbitrators is also limited.

The third scenario—which assumes that the parties act as agents of arbitral institution or of arbitrators while entering into institutional contracts—is also highly unlikely. Regardless of the increasing powers of arbitral institutions corresponding to their public function, one cannot ignore the fact that the authority of arbitrators and of arbitral institutions is rooted in the parties' will to submit their dispute to a particular institutional regime. This observation does not work the other way around. It is questionable that parties could be regarded as agents of other arbitration actors because the arbitration processes are initiated as a result of the parties' submission to institutional arbitration.

Furthermore, the qualification of institutional contracts as pure provision of services is also misleading. This is apparent given the discussion on the inadequacy of the mainstream definition of institutional arbitration provided in Chap. 2 as well as the preceding discussion on the lack of an accurate response by the courts of France, the US, the UK, and Sweden to the dual function assumed by arbitral institutions in and outside the arbitration proceedings. It was demonstrated that even in the context of the legal analyses of institutional settings domestic courts appear confused as to the nature of institutional activity. Some of them accord quasi-judicial immunity to arbitral institutions even after recognizing the contractual nature of institutional relationships (the US). Moreover, the French courts—although the most consistent regarding the interpretations of the legal nature of institutional contracts from all courts of the analysed jurisdictions—still experience troubles when confronted with the administrative nature of institutional acts, nota bene issued when performing contractual obligations. Moreover, these analyses of institutional contracts in the context of the legal dimension of institutional arbitration in isolation from the societal and the economic aspects of arbitral institutions are insufficient in that they are not able to grasp the unique contents of institutional obligations. Institutional arbitration is not a personal service inasmuch as it involves complex issues related to a dual, commercial and public function of institutional activity that fall within the three pillars of institutional operation. This means that the institutional obligations (and also the contracts underlying them) should be conceptualized with regard to the obligations falling within the commercial function such as speed and effectiveness of institutional arbitration proceedings. At the same time, the institutional contracts should be viewed in regards of the institutional obligations performed in the continuation of the public function. The latter observation involves the obligations falling within the institutional prerogatives in continuation of the parties' arbitration agreements and those corresponding to the private regulatory powers of arbitral institutions, often exercised contrary to the principle of party autonomy.[169] Therefore, the understanding of arbitral institutions as pure service providers distorts these comprehensive explanations of all institutional functions and the sources of their increasing powers.

In addition, the employment relationship in institutional arbitration, as analysed with regard to arbitrators in the *Jivraj v. Hashwani* judgement, should not be applied to institutional arbitration contracts. There is no subordination involved in institutional arbitration settings, and the function of arbitral institutions concerns the balancing of the competing interests of the parties. This observation excludes the possibly for arbitral institutions to be treated as an employee of any party to arbitration proceedings.

Finally, the possible interpretation of the institutional exclusion of liability clauses as "Himalaya clauses" under English law loses it rationale once confronted with the individualized theory of institutional arbitration proposed in the model on contractual relations in Chap. 3. Himalaya clauses in the context of institutional arbitration would mean the exclusion of liability of arbitral institutions (most likely the LCIA under English law) acting as third parties to the contracts between arbitrators and the parties. This assumption is inaccurate because—under the model on contractual relationships—it is unlikely that arbitral institutions will not be bound directly with the parties and institutional arbitrators, and that—instead of the arbitral institutions—the arbitrators will be directly related to the parties. This possibility was excluded under the proposed model of contractual relationships.

The discussion above demonstrated that none of the contract law theories provide exhaustive explanations of the contractual obligations of arbitral institutions. This is because at different stages of arbitration proceedings arbitral institutions perform different functions that—when separated from the institutional function taken as a whole—bear resemblance to the contractual obligations falling within different traditional contract law theories.[170] It is important, however, to stress that arbitral institutions should be analysed from a more general, systemic perspective, which allows a complete interpretation of institutional functions. This is why it is proposed here—following, to a certain extent, the *Jivraj v. Hashwani* judgement—to treat institutional arbitration contracts as *sui generis* contracts that accommodate both the provision of arbitration service (within the definition of the legal and economic dimensions of institutional activity) and some aspects of agency theories, though understood in the arbitration meaning within the societal dimension of institutional functions. This observation should also entail the unique analysis of the scope of institutional liability arising out of the *sui generis* nature of institutional arbitration contracts.

---

[169]Sects. 2.3.2.1.1 and 2.3.2.1.2 of Chap. 2.

[170]Cf. Pierre A. Karrer's observations regarding a double role of arbitral institutions that concerns administrative tasks of institutions that arbitral tribunal in *ad hoc* arbitration must perform and also the institutional assistance to the parties when institutions act as "pure mandatees" of the parties. Karrer 2008, 618–620.

5.2.2.3 Problems with the (Un)Enforceability of the 1998 ICC Exclusion of Liability Clause

Although the most recent version of the ICC Arbitration Rules makes the ICC limitation of liability clause dependent upon the applicable law to the contract between an institution and the party,[171] the previous version of the ICC Arbitration Rules did not contain such interdependency. The question therefore concerns the effectiveness of the 1998 exclusion of liability clause under applicable laws. It is sufficient to recall once again the decisions of both the Paris *Tribunal de grande instance* and the Paris Court of Appeal on the enforceability of the 1998 ICC exclusion of liability clause. The analysis of the French approach to the legal effects of such a clause aims to prove the inconsistency of the public interpretation of the legal effectiveness of this clause, which may still have significance to the pending ICC arbitrations being conducted under the 1998 version of the ICC Arbitration Rules.

While the *Tribunal de grande instance* in the *SNF v. the ICC* judgement held that the 1998 ICC exclusion of liability clause was lawful under the French law, the Paris Court of Appeal reversed this decision by stating that such a clause should be unlawful—thus—unenforceable under French law.[172] Notwithstanding such observation, the Paris Court of Appeal did not find the ICC liable for any misconduct by noticing, inter alia, that the parties contributed to the irregularities in the arbitration at hand.

Should the 1998 ICC exclusion of liability clause be enforceable or unenforceable under French law? If French law may be interpreted by French courts in an inconsistent manner, what would judges in other jurisdictions do when faced with a liability claim under the 2012 ICC limitation of liability clause? The 2012 ICC contractual immunity only aggravated the diversification of the prospective public interpretations of this "immunity" by expressly confirming the authority of the law of the judicial forum to determine the scope of liability of the ICC arbitration actors. This inconsistency has an effect on the functionality of the whole international institutional arbitration regime, and therefore calls for further reform.

5.3 Philosophical Approach to the International Institutional Function: On "Visions"

As already preliminarily demonstrated in the analysis of the domestic treatment of institutional arbitration, one question concerns if and how the domestic law regulates the activity of arbitral institutions and the other question is how domestic

[171] Sect. 3.2.1 of Chap. 3.

[172] See *Société SNF c/Chambre de Commerce Internationale. 847 Tribunal de grande instance de Paris* (1 Ch.) 2007. *Rev. arb.* 2007.

courts apply different provisions of domestic laws (whether the general principles of contract law or of the arbitration law, if at all referring to institutional liability) to institutional arbitration. The problem is that the approaches taken by domestic courts to the issues at hand will usually determine the very possibility of holding arbitral institutions liable under the laws applicable and, consequently, also the scope of institutional arbitral liability. These approaches are referred to in this section as "visions" because they correspond to the ways in which domestic courts view institutional arbitration when deciding on damages claims against arbitral institutions. Hence, those visions are more related to the understanding by domestic courts of the institutional function rather than to the literal interpretations of relevant laws in the context of institutional liability claims.

The following discussion therefore aims at pointing out the lack of the recognition by judges of the *international* function of institutional arbitration when dealing with institutional liability claims. This is done in the meaning of Gaillard's third representation of international arbitration.[173] In this sense, the following analysis also underlies the rationale of the proposals for the necessary reforms of various arbitration laws that will be presented in Chap. 7. The discussion will be organized in two parts. The first part focuses on the selective application of national *visions* (reciprocally called stances, approaches, and views) of arbitral liability to the possible liability of arbitral institutions administering *international* arbitration cases. The second part reflects on the general *visions* of national authorities to the delocalization of arbitration, which determines the national understanding of the institutional public function to be fulfilled by arbitral institutions on behalf of the *international* business community and States.

5.3.1 International Institutional Function v. the National Visions of Arbitral Liability

In order to sketch the linkages between the national stances to institutional arbitral liability and the operation of international arbitral institutions, the US District Court's decision in *Global Gold Mining LLC v Peter M. Robinson* et al. needs to be addressed.[174] The decision in *Global Gold Mining* is fundamental to the extent that it deals with the prospective application of the doctrine on arbitral immunity to an arbitral institution headquartered outside the US (in France) and regulated by French law—the ICC—together with its possible impact on the integrity of the international practice of arbitral institutions.

The judgement in the case discussed here was not a result of a direct claim of a party against the arbitral institution, as the legal action of the claimant concerned

[173]See. Sect. 3.2.2.3 of Chap.3.

[174]*Global Gold Mining, LLC v. Peter M. Robinson et al.*, No. 636 United States District Court, Southern District of New York, 6 February 2008, 07 Civ. 10492 (GEL), with a commentary in Yearbook Commercial Arbitration Vol XXXIII, 1117-1125. See Sect. 2.3.2.1.2.2.

the possibility of a review of the ICC Court's *prima facie* decision regarding the existence of the arbitration agreement with regard to a non-signatory to the ICC arbitration agreement. Nevertheless, the Southern District Court for New York made reference to the rationale of arbitral immunity in the US that can be perceived in a general context as concerning the necessary protection of international institutional arbitration actors from accidental liability claims.

Section 1 of the RUAA encourages a broad definition of "arbitration organization" under the Act. The commentary to RUAA explains that the term "arbitration organization" concerns agencies such as "the American Arbitration Association (AAA), the CPR, JAMS, the National Arbitration Forum, NASD Regulation, Inc., the American Stock Exchange, the New York Stock Exchange, and the International Chamber of Commerce".[175] On these grounds, the Southern District Court for New York in *Gold Global Mining* allowed the possibility of the extension of the doctrine on arbitral immunity in the US to include the acts performed in the course of arbitration proceedings by the ICC and by any other international arbitral institution. The Court stated that:

> In order to protect the decision-making process, courts should be wary of "claim[s] [which], regardless of [their] nominal title, effectively seek to challenge [a] decisional act" made during the arbitration process[...] That rationale extends equally to claims against arbitral administrative institutions, when they perform "functions that are integrally related to the arbitral process" [with further references]. Not does that rationale apply only to suits for damages. If administrative institutions such as the ICC or the ICC Court can be required to defend their decisions in the national courts of any country in the world, the expenses of defending such potentially far-flung suits could constrain their judgment, and increase the costs of arbitration procedures, every bit as much as potential liability for damages.[176]

This line of reasoning supports the possible extension of unlimited arbitral immunity from civil liability and of the immunity from process to foreign arbitral institutions when such institutions are being sued in the US. In other words, it demonstrates the application of the national vision (stemming from federal law) of the US judicial and legislative authorities to *international* institutional arbitration. Moreover, the justification for such an extension seems to be based on the necessity of the promotion of the finality of institutional decisions as well as on the financial concerns of both the parties (when it comes to the costs of arbitration) and the arbitral institutions (regarding prospective damages arising out of institutional liability claims).

Against this background, it seems that US judges adopt the monolocal vision—as defined by Professor Gaillard—while considering the scope of liability of international arbitral institutions. Now, what are the practical consequences of the vision of US judges for international institutional arbitration? US judges reject

[175]A comment to Section 1 of the Uniform Arbitration Act (Last Revisions Completed Year 2000).

[176]*Global Gold Mining, LLC v. Peter M. Robinson et al.*, No. 636 United States District Court, Southern District of New York, 6 February 2008, 07 Civ. 10492 (GEL) with a commentary in Yearbook Commercial Arbitration Vol XXXIII, 1117-1125, in particular 1124.

the *sui generis* nature of institutional status and international function of arbitral institutions, and they link the validity and legitimacy of international institutional arbitration with the authority of US statutory law or US case law on the functions of arbitration actors (including arbitral institutions). This means that international institutional arbitration is also treated by US judges as a national device, which diminishes the role of the collective effects of the multiple legal orders in supporting the authority of *international* institutional arbitration actors. This local (if not to say parochial) approach questions the international commitment of the US to support arbitration beyond the national ramifications for this process. This could even be understood as a violation of the values underpinning the New York Convention of 1958 by the US authorities.

5.3.2 International Institutional Function v. the National Visions of Delocalization of Arbitration

Delocalization of arbitration is largely interlinked with the autonomous theory of arbitration, as it touches upon the questions of the detachment of arbitration from: (a) the procedural rules of the place of arbitration; (b) the procedural rules of any specific national law; (c) the substantive law of the place of arbitration; and eventually from (d) the national substantive law of any specific jurisdiction.[177] More specifically, when the laws applicable to the liability of arbitral institutions are concerned, the notion of delocalization could also be found in the detachment of arbitration from any general principles of contract laws and from the provisions regulating the scope of liability (or immunity) of institutional arbitration actors. As the inadequacy of the pure autonomous theory was already addressed in Sect. 3.2.2.2 of Chap. 3, we should now examine here only the potential interplay between national visions of the delocalization of arbitration, the possible public recognition of the international function of institutional arbitration within the parameters of Gaillard's third representation, and institutional liability.

Both new domestic case law and the increasing autonomy granted to arbitration under certain domestic arbitration laws contributed to the development of scholarly literature that stresses the argument that more and more States can now be perceived as the proponents of the delocalized doctrine of international arbitration (e.g. Belgium,[178] France,[179] Switzerland[180]). This is also vaguely connected with the competition between the arbitration centres operating within

[177]The distinction follows the discussion in Janićijević 2005, 64.

[178]See Paulsson 1986.

[179]See the interplay between arbitration in France and the concept of the French *l'orde public* discussed in: von Mehren 1986.

[180]See Paulsson 1986.

these jurisdictions.[181] Under the same considerations, however, other States are regarded as opponents of the international (or transnational) nature of arbitration (e.g. the case of the UK). Even though the English approach to the transnational character of arbitration seems to evolve,[182] English judges are hesitant to recognize "the concept of arbitral procedures floating in the transnational firmament, unconnected with any municipal system of law".[183] Naturally, the main concerns about the delocalization of arbitration there are enshrined in the protection of the domestic public policy.

These observations have implications for the recognition of the international function of institutional arbitration by judges and for the determinations of the institutional arbitral liability. Although it is not proposed in this book to treat institutional arbitration as a truly delocalized instrument, it is suggested that a certain level of consistency among national judges and national legislators concerning this matter should be worked out for the two following (interrelated) reasons. First, judges should be invited to take a consistent approach to the legal nature and functions of arbitral institutions, especially with a view to the prospective liability claims against institutional arbitration actors. Second, the effectiveness of the institutional provisions on liability is dependent upon the enforcement of institutional liability clauses by domestic judges. Given the international character of the functions of arbitral institutions, the domestic visions of liability need to be harmonized in response to the calls for the integrity of international institutional arbitration. The current inconsistent domestic interpretations regarding the possibility of holding arbitral institutions liable for their breaches of institutional contracts, together with the scope of their liability, only invite the parties to forum shopping when attempting to find the forum where the liability of arbitral institutions can be upheld. In this sense, the recognition of the international function of institutional arbitration by the domestic public authorities (such as legislators and domestic courts) should also serve as an argument for those authorities to further increase the integrity of international institutional arbitration proceedings by means of the adoption of the common stance to institutional arbitral liability. Here, the notion of international public policy in the context of arbitration could be applied, in particular because the emerging public function of institutional arbitration shows the increasing administration of regulatory disputes (falling outside the traditional, commercial types of disputes) by arbitral institutions that have also begun to assume private regulatory powers in and outside the arbitration processes. This public function of arbitral institutions appears therefore to be increasingly visible at the international level due to the progressive unification of the arbitration rules of the leading arbitral institutions under analysis in this book.

---

[181]See Gharavi 2002, 137.

[182]This argument should be confronted with the statement that the UK Arbitration Act of 1996 constituted a great move forward as regards the delocalization of arbitration in England. See.: Olatawura 2003.

[183]See: *Bank Mellat v Helliniki Techniki S.A.* 1984. QB 291.

5.3.3 Divergent National Visions of Institutional Arbitral Liability and Forum Shopping

As already noted, the inconsistency within the national visions of institutional arbitration and of the prospective liability of arbitral institutions may also inform the considerations of the parties to the international institutional arbitrations regarding their selection of jurisdictions where their plausible liability claims could be determined in the most favourable manner. Although, at least to the knowledge of the author, to date there are no express provisions imposing the liability on institutional arbitration actors under any of the domestic laws, certain domestic developments presented below may serve as additional factors to be considered by the parties when deciding to sue arbitral institutions in respective jurisdictions, if not when drafting an institutional arbitration agreement. Two particular issues should be analysed in this regard. The first concerns the relationship between the institutional arbitration rules limiting liability of institutional arbitration actors and the actual sources (contractual or in tort) of such liability in the context of the domestic courts' visions of arbitration in Denmark. The second relates to the possibility of holding arbitral institutions liable for the acts of arbitrators in such jurisdictions as the Czech Republic or Spain.

Although there are no specific provisions regulating the liability of arbitral institutions (and of arbitrators) in Denmark, it is said that there is the likelihood that the liability of institutional arbitration actors may be determined by the Danish courts as tort-based (rather than contract based). Moreover, given the fact that the rules on tort in Denmark are court-driven rather than statute-based, the establishing of the sources of institutional arbitral liability will, most likely, involve the furture precedential decision of the Danish court in this regard.[184] In this context, some commentators claim that the limitation of liability clauses established by the arbitral institutions in Denmark (i.e. by the leading institution, the Danish Institute of Arbitration[185]) may, in fact, be ineffective and therefore unenforceable under Danish law.[186] This observation demonstrates that the national visions of institutional arbitration and of the liability of institutional arbitration actors may largely derogate from private regulations adopted by arbitral institutions in this regard. Although in most jurisdictions institutional arbitration has been recognized as a contractual device, it can be seen that some domestic courts may still view the acts of arbitral institutions in the context of in tort liability, even in the absence of concrete provisions of domestic laws regulating institutional arbitral liability. This conclusion may have both positive and negative consequences for the parties wishing to sue arbitral institutions in the Danish

[184] Cole et al. Annexes 2014, 28.

[185] Article 36 of the arbitration rules of the Danish Institute of Arbitration (effective as of 1 May 2013) limits the liability of all institutional arbitration actors to the extent permissible under the applicable law.

[186] Spiermann 1984, 14–15.

courts. Certainly, the parties who are able to prove before the Danish court that certain malicious acts of institutional actors contributed to their injury will likely see the court overriding the contractual provisions on limitation on liability contained in the institutional arbitration rules and the contracts emerging in institutional arbitration. This, most likely, will result in some form of liability of the institutional arbitration actors based on tort. To the contrary, hypothetically, when parties enter into contracts with arbitral institutions providing for the liability of institutional arbitration actors for specific acts or omission (for example a delay in delivering an arbitral award to the parties), it is likely that the regime for in tort liability adopted by the Danish court in the prospective liability claim will be less favourable to the parties than the contractual regime on which they had previously agreed. All these have consequences for forum shopping.

Furthermore, there are some jurisdictions in which arbitral institutions may, in principle, be held liable for some acts of institutional arbitrators. This is the case with Spain and the Czech Republic. There are different grounds, however, under which these actions are possible in these States. In Spain, the authorization to sue arbitral institutions is directly rooted in Article 21(1) of the Spanish Arbitration Act that reads as follows: "[…] In arbitration commissioned from an institution, the damaged party may file suit directly against it, irrespective of any action for indemnity lodged against the arbitrators […]".[187] This provision, although not yet interpreted by the Spanish courts in practice, clearly invites varied interpretations regarding the actual legal relationship between arbitral institutions, the parties, and arbitrators in Spain that could trigger the institutional arbitral liability. It also implies divergent interpretations of the category of arbitrator's acts for which Spanish arbitral institutions could "take responsibility" in a legal sense. At the same time, this provision serves as a guarantor for the parties that the potential misconduct in their arbitrations may in fact result in liability of certain institutional arbitration actors, be it arbitrators or arbitral institutions themselves.

A slightly different basis for institutional liability could, in principle, be relied on by the parties in the Czech Republic. Since there are no provisions on liability in the Czech Arbitration Act of 1994 (with further amendments),[188] arbitral institutions could be held liable even for the acts or omission of arbitrators simply because the Czech courts adopted the vision in which an award rendered in the course of the institutional arbitration is perceived as an award issued not in the name of arbitrators but of the arbitral institution administering the proceedings.[189] This reasoning was presented in the Resolution of the Constitutional Court of the Czech Republic of 2002 where the Court was faced with the interpretation of the nature of the arbitrator's mandate and consequently, indirectly, of the role of

[187]Spanish Act 11/2011, of 20 May, Reforming Act 60/2003, of 23 December, on Arbitration, and Regulating Institutional Arbitration within the Public Administration.

[188]Act. No 216/1994 Coll.

[189]Cole et al. 2014, 23.

arbitral institutions in arbitration proceedings.[190] The Court rejected the assumption that arbitrators could be compared to public judges, mostly because they do not render public acts since the arbitral awards deal largely with the determinations of the contractual relationships between the parties by arbitrators.[191] The Court also expressed the opinion that the arbitral awards are usually issued in the name of the administering arbitral institution and not in the name of arbitrators. The latter observation is particularly relevant for the present discussion because it shifts the responsibility for the arbitration process from arbitrators to arbitral institutions that could result in the civil liability of the Czech arbitral institutions for an unlimited category of acts done or omitted in the course of the arbitrations. Yet again, it demonstrates the significance of the national visions of institutional arbitration on the scope of liability of institutional arbitration actors, even in view of the lack of the relevant provisions in this regard contained in domestic law.

In conclusion, it can be stated that the divergent application of different visions of arbitration by domestic courts can serve as an additional consideration (on top of the understanding of the local legal framework) for the parties when deciding on the jurisdiction where the arbitral institution in question could potentially be sued. These visions involved the following: the domestic understanding of the basis of institutional liability (in tort, or contractual), the relationship between the acts of arbitrators and of arbitral institutions, and the nature of the arbitrator's mandate, as well as the role of arbitral institutions in the arbitration process. The manner in which domestic courts approach these issues may also become increasingly relevant for the parties at the pre-dispute stage, for example when deciding on a particular arbitral institution in their arbitration agreement.

5.4 Conclusion

This chapter focused on the legal consequences of the assessment of institutional arbitral liability by domestic courts. The major confusion within the national regulations of institutional arbitration (if any) and regarding their interpretations by domestic courts stems from the application of different theories of arbitration (be it contractual or jurisdictional theory) to institutional arbitration by domestic judges from the jurisdictions under analysis in this chapter. This amounts to the inaccurate determination of the dual function that arbitral institutions assume in the arbitration process. While French judges seem to regard institutions as non-judicial service providers (also recognizing the administrative nature of certain acts of arbitral institutions), UK and US legislative and judicial authorities treat arbitral institutions as judges or quasi-judges due to the judicial character of certain activities of arbitral institutions and the adjudicatory character of the work of

[190] Ref. No. IV. ÚS 174/02 of 15 July, 2002.

[191] Cole et al. 2014, 78.

arbitrators which arbitral institutions support. This resulted in the conclusion that there is no separate regime of liability (or immunity) for institutional arbitrators and arbitral institutions (at least in jurisdictions which allow the legal immunity for all arbitration actors), as the institutional operation is interconnected with the arbitrators' performance of their obligations. This not only minimises the possibility of commercial parties to institutional arbitration proceedings to sue arbitral institutions for damages in these jurisdictions but also endangers the protection of the statutory or civil rights of the parties to the so-called "regulatory" arbitration, which seems to be recently spotted even by certain authorities in the US.

The analysis of the practical problems concerning the interpretation of institutional arbitral liability proved that the judges have difficulty determining the exact moment of the emergence of institutional contracts. In turn, it showed that this confusion affects the accurate determination of the individual contractual obligations of arbitration actors towards a single party to arbitration proceedings while also preventing judges from making the proper assessment of the scope of institutional arbitral liability that could correspond to the unique, *sui generis* nature of institutional arbitration contracts. This was also shown in the analysis of the problems with the (un)enforceability of the 1998 ICC exclusion of liability clause.

Finally, the discussion on the philosophical representations of institutional arbitration and institutional arbitral liability demonstrated that most issues concerning the interpretation of the liability of international arbitral institutions arise from the application of domestic visions (also referred to as "approaches", "stances" and "views") to the responsibilities of institutional arbitration actors at the international level. This not only distorts the uniform recognition of the international function of institutional arbitration by legal, public authorities, but also jeopardizes the legality of "regulatory" arbitrations, by allowing for almost unlimited contractual immunity applicable to institutional arbitration actors participating in such arbitrations.

All these intensify the legal uncertainty stemming from the private institutional limitation of liability clauses. Just as in the previous chapter the increasing trend among arbitral institutions to limit their liability to the extent permissible under applicable law was identified, this chapter demonstrated that most "applicable laws" do not provide for clear-cut rules that would regulate this issue. In addition, there is no guidance in domestic laws as to the scope of the institutional functions, the nature of institutional acts, the types of contracts underlying the institutional activity, or the category of acts that could result in liability of arbitral institutions (including those falling within the concept of negligence, gross negligence, bad faith, wilful misconduct, etc.). It appears then that the only certain thing that judges are left with are visions of institutional arbitration that they attempt to apply to international arbitration proceedings, often without consideration of the international public policy and the effects thereon of the parochial determinations of institutional arbitral liability.

This is why the longer arbitral institutions authorize domestic laws to have the final say on their liability, the longer the legal uncertainty regarding the effectiveness and enforceability of such clauses will last. This uncertainty is detrimental to both the parties to institutional arbitration proceedings and to arbitral institutions themselves. Regarding the parties, it affects the scope of protection of their contractual rights under the limitation of liability clauses that clearly vary depending on the jurisdiction. It also deepens the confusion among the parties on the scope of institutional functions and liability because the parties that, at least accidentally, consider forum shopping when filing liability claims often make the situation worst for themselves in a longer perspective. This is so because the parties expose themselves to legal proceedings in jurisdictions whose laws and judicial system they are only vaguely familiar with, ending up with an expensive and lengthy litigation on their shoulders. Regarding the arbitral institutions, the interdependency between the private regulations of liability and the applicable laws only invites the parties to further sue arbitral institutions counting on the favourable legal window in selected jurisdictions. In fact, then, the limitation of liability clauses contained in the increasing number of private arbitration rules give arbitration users the green light to sue arbitral institutions for damages, which seems to contradict the major public rationale underlying these rules. At least certain parties seem to be accepting these invitations, which makes these arbitration users and arbitral institutions run in vicious circles on their highest turnover.

References

Act. No 216/1994 Coll.

American Bar Association. 2011. Model Code of Judicial Conduct. http://www.americanbar.org/groups/professional_responsibility/publications/model_code_of_judical_conduct.html. Accessed 25 April 2016.

Amor-Smith, John. 1991. The Immunity of Arbitrators under English and Australian Law. Australian Construction Law Newsletter 19.

Arenson v. Casson Beckman Rutley & Co. 1977. [1977] A.C. 405 et seq House of Lords.

Arrêt N° 392 Du 28 Mars 2013 (11-27.770)—Cour de Cassation—Première Chambre Civile—ECLI:FR:CCASS:201300392.

Assembly Committee on Judiciary. 2011. AB 439 Assembly Bill—Bill Analysis; Key Issue: Should California Recognize a New Affirmative Defense Against Specified Liability When a Covered Entity Has Acted Appropriately?

Austern v. Chicago Bd. Option Exchange Inc. [1989]. 716 F.Supp. 121 United States District Court, S.D. New York.

Austern v. Chicago Board Options Exchange, Inc. [1990]. 898 F.2d 882 United States Court of Appeals, Second Circuit.

Baar v. Tigerman. [1983]. 140 Cal. App. 3d 979 [189 Cal. Rptr. 834] Court of Appeals of California.

Baizeau, Domitille. 2009. Liability of Arbitral Institutions: Increased Scrutiny by the Courts of the Seat? ASA Bulletin 27, no. 2 Kluwer Law International: 383–386.

Bank Mellat v Helliniki Techniki S.A. [1984]. QB 291.

Bantekas, Ilias. 2015. An Introduction to International Arbitration. Cambridge University Press.

Block, J. Randolph. 1980. Stump v. Sparkman and the History of Judicial Immunity. Duke Law Journal 5: 879–925.

Bradley v. Fisher. [1871]. 80 U.S. 335 US Supreme Court.

Butz v. Economou. [1978]. 438 U.S. 478 US Supreme Court.

Ceskilovenska Obchodni Banka A.S. (Cekobanka) C/ Chambre de Commerce Internationale. 1986. Rev. arb. (1987) Tribunal de grande instance de Paris.

Cole, Tony, Bantekas Ilias, Feretti Federico, Riefa Christine, Warwas Barbara, Ortolani Pietro. 2014. The Legal Instruments and Practice of Arbitration in the EU, A Study for the Directorate General for Internal Policies Policy Department C: Citizens' Rights and Constitutional Affairs. http://www.europarl.europa.eu/RegData/etudes/STUD/2015/509988/IPOL_STU(2015)509988_EN.pdf. Accessed 25 April 2016.

Cole, Tony, Bantekas Ilias, Feretti Federico, Riefa Christine, Warwas Barbara, Ortolani Pietro. 2014. The Legal Instruments and Practice of Arbitration in the EU: Annexes. A Study for the Directorate General for Internal Policies Policy Department C: Citizens' Rights and Constitutional Affairs.

Cort v. American Arbitration Assn. [1992]. 795 F Supp 970 (ND CA 1992).

Derains, Yves, and Schwartz Eric A. 1998. A Guide to the New ICC Rules of Arbitration. Kluwer Law International.

Derains, Yves, and Schwartz Eric A. 2005. A Guide to the ICC Rules of Arbitration, 2nd Edition Revised. Kluwer Law International.

Feinman, Jay M., and Cohen Roy S. 1979. Suing Judges: History and Theory. South Carolina Law Review 31: 201–292.

Floyd v. Barker, 77 Eng. Rep. 1305 (Star Chamber 1607).

Forrester v. White. [1988]. 484 U.S. 219 US Supreme Court.

Fouchard, Philippe. 1987. Les Institutions Permanentes D'arbitrage Devant Le Juge étatique (A Propos D'une Jurisprudence Récente). Revue de l'Arbitrage 1987, no. 3: 225–274.

George Corey v. New York Stock Exchange. [1982]. 691 F.2d 1205 US Court of Appeals, Sixth Circuit.

Gerbay, Remy. The Functions of Arbitral Institutions: Kluwer Law International. Forthcoming 2016.

Gharavi, Hamid G. 2002. The International Effectiveness of the Annulment of an Arbitral Award. Kluwer Law International.

Global Gold Mining, LLC v. Peter M. Robinson et al., No. 636 United States District Court, Southern District of New York, 6 February 2008, 07 Civ. 10492 (GEL). Yearbook Commercial Arbitration Vol XXXIII 29: 1117–1125.

Hoosac Tunnel Dock & Elevator Co. v. O'Brien, 137 Mass. 424, 426 (1884).

ICC Arbitration Rules. 1998.

ICC Arbitration Rules. 2012. http://www.iccwbo.org/products-and-services/arbitration-and-adr/arbitration/icc-rules-of-arbitration/. Accessed 25 April 2016.

Janićijević, Dejan. 2005. Delocalization of International Commercial Arbitration. Law and Politics 3, no. 1: 63–71.

Jivraj v. Hashwani [2011] 1 WLR 1872. Trinity Term UKSC 40 Supreme Court of the United Kingdom.

Jones v. Brown 6 N.W. 140 (1880).

Karrer, Pierre A. 2008. Responsibility of Arbitrators and Arbitral Institutions. In: Lawrence W. Newman and Richard D. Hill, eds. The Leading Arbitrators' Guide to International Arbitration. Juris Publishing, 607–620.

Kiffer, Laurence. 2009. Comments on the Paris Court of Appeal Decision in SNF v. International Chamber of Commerce. Journal of International Arbitration 26, no. 4: 579–89.

Kleiman, Elie. 2009a. The SNF v. International Chamber of Commerce Case and The Obligation to Conduct Arbitration Proceedings With 'Expected Dispatch.' Stockholm International Arbitration Review no. 1, 13–42.

Kleiman, Elie. 2009b. Paris Court of Appeal Decides on Application of ICC Rules. International Law Office. http://www.internationallawoffice.com/newsletters/detail.aspx?g=b229c721-5d38-4565-9e3f-9d5f5b62c5a3#3. Accessed 25 April 2016.

Kudrna, Jaroslav. 2013. Arbitration and the Right to Access to Justice: Tips for a Successful Marriage. NYU Journal of International Law and Politics Online Forum. http://nyujilp.org/wp-content/uploads/2013/02/Jaroslav-Kudrna-Arbitration-and-Right-of-Access-to-Justice-NYU-JILP-Feb-2013.pdf. Accessed 25 April 2016.

Laufgraben, Eric. Arbitration: South Carolina's Top Court Extends Arbitral Immunity to ADR Providers (Web). International Institute for Conflict Prevention & Resolution (CPR). http://www.cpradr.org/Resources/ALLCPRArticles/tabid/265/ID/177/Arbitration-South-Carolinas-Top-Court-Extends-Arbitral-Immunity-to-ADR-Providers-Web.aspx. Accessed 25 April 2016.

Malik v. Ruttenberg et al. 398 N.J. Super. 489, 495 (App. Div. 2008).

Ministry of Justice and Civil Liberties, Republic of France, Decree No. 2011-48 of 13 January 2011 Reforming the Law Governing Arbitration.

Moffitt, W. Christian. 2006. Choice of Governing Rules of Arbitration under the Doctrine of Arbitral Immunity in Strategic Resources, Inc. v. BCS Life Insurance, Inc. The Journal of American Arbitration 5, no. 1: 179–192.

Nolan, Dennis R., and Abrams Roger I. 1989. Arbitral Immunity. Berkeley Journal of Employment and Labor Law 11, no. 2: 228–266.

Olatawura, Olakunle O. 2003. Delocalized Arbitration Under the English Arbitration Act 1996: An Evolution or a Revolution. Syracuse Journal of International Law and Commerce 30, no. 1: 49.

Olson v. National Association of Securities Dealers. [1996]. 85 F3d 381 US Court of Appeals, Eighth Circuit.

O'Shea v. Littleton. [1974]. 414 U.S. 488 US Supreme Court.

Paulsson, Jan. 1986. Arbitration Unbound in Belgium. Arbitration International 1, no. 2: 68–73.

Price, Charles. 2012. Liability of Arbitral Institutions in International Arbitration: A Comment on Société Filature Française de Mohair C/ Fédération Française Des Industries Lainières et Cotonnières. In: Patrick Wautelet, Thalia Kruger, and Govert Coppens, eds. The Practice of Arbitration: Essays in Honour of Hans van Houtte. Hart Publishing, 187–195.

Randall v. Brigham. [1868]. 74 U.S. 523 US Supreme Court.

Rasmussen, Matthew. 2002. Overextending Immunity: Arbitral Institutional Liability in the United States, England, and France. Fordham International Law Journal 26, no. 6: 1824–1875.

Ref. No. IV. US 174/02 of July 15, 2002.

République de Guinée v. Chambre Arbitrale de Paris. 1987. Tribunal de grande instance de Paris. Rev. arb., 1987 371.

Robine, Eric. 1989. The Liability of Arbitrators and Arbitral Institutions in International Arbitrations under French Law. Arbitration International 5, no. 4: 323–332.

Rubino-Sammartano, Mauro. 2001. International Arbitration Law, 1st ed. Kluwer Law International.

SCC Arbitration Rules. 2010. http://sccinstitute.com/dispute-resolution/rules/. Accessed 25 April 2016.

Schöldström, Patrik. 1998. The Arbitrator's Mandate: A Comparative Study of Relationships in Commercial Arbitration under the Laws of England, Germany, Sweden and Switzerland. Elanders Gotab.

Schöldström, Patrik. 2008. Arbitrator Fees in Institutional Arbitration Subject to Substantive Review In Court. Stockholm International Arbitration Review, 3: 243–250.

Schöldström, Patrik. 2010. Contractual Relations in Institutional Arbitration. In: Kaj Hobér, Annette Magnusson, and Marie Öhrström (eds.) Between East and West: Essays in Honour of Ulf Franke. Juris Publishing, 451–484.

Société Appareils Dragon v. Empresa Central de Abastecimientas Y Vantas de Equipos, Cour de Cassation (2Ch. Civile), 8 June 1983.

Société Cubic Defense System Inc v Chambre de Commerce Internationale. 1998. Rev. arb. 1999, 103 Cour d'appel de Paris (1Ch. A).

Société Cubic Defense System Inc v Chambre de Commerce Internationale, (Cour de Cassation (1 Ch. civile) 2001), Rev. arb. 2011, 511.

Société Filature Française de Mohair c/ Fédération Française des Industries Lainières et Cotonnières, RG 07/13724, (Tribunal de grande Instance de Nanterre 2010).

Société Licensing Projects et Autres C/ Société Pirelli & C. SPA et autres, Cour D'appel Paris, 1e Ch., Nov. 17, 2011, N° 09/24158.

Société REDEC et M. Pharaon v Société Uzinexport Import et Chambre de Commerce Internationale, Tribunal de Grande Instance de Paris (Ref.), 13 July 1988.

Société SNF c/Chambre de Commerce Internationale. Tribunal de grande instance de Paris (1 Ch.).2007. Rev. arb. 2007, 847.

Société SNF v. International Chamber of Commerce. Cour d'appel de Paris (1. Ch.). 2009.

Société Techni-Import Professionnel v Société Electro Scientific Industries, Cour d'Appel de Paris, 17 May 1983.

Soyak International Construction and Investment Inc. v. Hobér, Kraus and Melis, Ö 4227-06, 3 December 2008. Mealey's International Arbitration Report Vol. 24 No 3 March 2009 Swedish Supreme Court.

Spanish Act 11/2011, of May 20, Reforming Act 60/2003, of December 23, on Arbitration, and Regulating Institutional Arbitration within the Public Administration.

Spiermann, Ole. 1984. National Report for Denmark (2009). In: Jan Paulsson and Lise Bosman, eds. ICCA International Handbook on Commercial Arbitratio Kluwer Law International: 1–38.

Sponseller, Mark A. 1993. Redefining Arbitral Immunity: A Proposed Qualified Immunity Statue for Arbitrators. Hastings Law Journal 44: 421–447.

Strategic Resources Co. v. BCS Life Insurance Co. No. 26022, 2005 WL 1943536 (S.C. Aug. 15, 2005).

Stump v. Sparkman. [1978]. 435 U.S. 349 U.S. Supreme Court.

Sutcliffe v. Thackrah [1974] 1 Lloyd's Rep. 318.

The Case of the Marshalsea, 77 Eng. Rep. 1027 (C.P. 1610).

The Federal Arbitration Act; Pub.L. 68–401, 43 Stat. 883, Enacted February 12, 1925, Codified at 9 U.S.C. § 1 et Seq.

The Summary of the Parliamentary Committee's Report on the Proposed Amendments to the Swedish Arbitration Act (SOU 2015:37). http://www.sccinstitute.com/media/65386/summary-Oversyn-Av-Lagen-Om-Skiljeforfarande-English.pdf. Accessed 25 April 2016.

The Swedish Arbitration Act of 1999 (SFS 1999:116). http://www.sccinstitute.com/?id=23745. Accessed 25 April 2016.

The UK Arbitration Act 1996, Chapter 23. http://www.legislation.gov.uk/ukpga/1996/23/contents. Accessed 25 April 2016.

The Website of the National Academy of Arbitrators: Reference Materials. National Academy of Arbitrators. http://naarb.org/immunity/reference.asp#Materials. Accessed 25 April 2016.

US National Conference of Commissioners on Uniform State Laws. 2000. Uniform Arbitration Act (Last Revisions Completed Year 2000). http://arbitrationlaw.com/files/free_pdfs/US%20 UAA.pdf. Accessed 25 April 2016.

von Mehren, Arthur Taylor. 1986. International Commercial Arbitration: The Contribution of the French Jurisprudence. Louisiana Law Review 46, no. 5: 1046–1059.

von Pachelbel, Johann, and Oldenstam Robin. 2009. Sweden. In: Frank-Bernd Weigand, ed. Practitioner's Handbook on International Commercial Arbitration. Oxford University Press, 749–815.

Weston, Maureen. 2004. Reexamining Arbitral Immunity in an Age of Mandatory and Professional Arbitration. Minnesota Law Review 88, no. 3: 449–517.

Chapter 6
Cutting the Gordian Knot: Proposals for the Institutional Reform of Arbitral Liability

Contents

6.1 Introduction

The topic of the liability of arbitrators and, to a certain extent, of arbitral institutions, including proposals concerning the regulation of arbitral liability, has been subject to limited though stormy academic debate. Notably, most proposals were presented 10 years ago and there is clearly a gap in the most recent literature relating to the topic at hand. The lack of an accurate academic explanation of the problems stemming from institutional arbitral liability is not particularly surprising.

B. Warwas, *The Liability of Arbitral Institutions: Legitimacy Challenges and Functional Responses*, DOI 10.1007/978-94-6265-111-1_6

These problems, although invariably relevant, imply a number of controversial issues that often interfere with procedural and substantive competences of institutional arbitration actors. In this vein, the success of any proposals regarding arbitral liability is in fact contingent upon the willingness of institutional arbitration actors to open up to such proposals (in the first place) and to accept the argument that being proactive with regard to the regulations of institutional arbitral liability may, in fact, pay off long term. The current unwillingness of arbitral institutions to take up the topic is discouraging, thus affecting the decline in the number of proposals for further reforms of institutional arbitral liability.

In addition, anecdotal evidence shows that many arbitration practitioners seem to be in disagreement with academic proposals of liability or to simply ignore them, treating such proposals as a threat to their profitable legal practices. Interestingly, the issue of institutional arbitral liability often implies two types of reactions from the arbitration practitioners; the first one based on curiosity and expressing supportiveness towards the topic, and the second one, often based on prejudice and fear of the unknown, uttering hesitance towards the issue.

Notwithstanding, this chapter humbly presents a few proposals for further reform of the private regulations of liability by arbitral institutions. These proposals aim at focusing on practical issues that reflect the possible wording of the limitation of liability clauses to be taken into consideration by institutional arbitration actors. This is done with a view to both the analysis of the sources and optimal scope of institutional arbitral liability provided in Chap. 3 and the presentation of the shortcomings of the contemporary private regulations of institutional arbitral liability in Chap. 4.

The chapter is organized in two parts. The first part points out the weaknesses of the current academic proposals concerning institutional arbitral liability (Sect. 6.2). The second part focuses exclusively on the necessary amendments to institutional liability regimes and presents five different models of institutional liability that could respond to the major arguments presented in the course of this book (Sect. 6.3). It is suggested that the implementation of effective and efficient contractual liability clauses into institutional contracts is essential for the competent and professional performance of the multifaceted functions of arbitral institutions. Moreover, it is argued that due to the particular contractual regulatory powers of arbitral institutions in institutional arbitration settings, the introduction of liability clauses should be regulated "from the bottom", meaning that it should be left to the arbitral institutions. It is also claimed that arbitral institutions themselves should take a proactive approach to the reforms of institutional liability given the realistic risks related to liability suits in view of the emerging practical trends.

In this regard, the second part of the chapter (Sect. 6.3) begins by setting out the essential variables of the ideal normative model of institutional liability, and follows with five plausible liability models that could possibly accommodate these variables. All five models are based on the conclusions regarding the dual public and commercial functions to be assumed by arbitral institutions, as well as on the three pillars of institutional arbitral liability presented in this book. The second part of the chapter eventually presents the ideal, proposed model of institutional arbitration liability. Hence, this presentation concerns the most convincing accommodation by the proposed model of the dual function of institutional arbitration as well as the response of the model to the triad of institutional functions. The chapter concludes with a analysis of the risks, risk mitigation strategies, and the incentives to be taken into account by institutional arbitration actors and the parties while negotiating institutional arbitration contracts.

6.2 The Weaknesses of the Current Proposals

The major insufficiency of the existing academic proposals for the reform of arbitral liability/immunity regimes concerns the lack of accurate consideration of the prospective liability of arbitral institutions for *their own* acts or omission in general, and the necessary response to the unique functions of arbitral institutions in particular. The latter argument means that the existing proposals fail to address all possible dimensions of institutional activity, namely the legal, societal, and economic facets of institutional operation. The major shortcoming lies in the fact that most commentators focus solely on the sources and scope of the prospective liability (if any) of arbitrators (Franck, Guzman, Rudledge).[1] Meanwhile, the arbitration centres are mentioned only in the context of the arbitrators' misconduct, where it is proposed to make institutions either immune or liable as surrogates of arbitrators (Weston, Li, Rasmussen).[2]

6.2.1 Qualified Immunity, Contractual Liability and the "Surrogate Theory"

In the regime of "qualified immunity" for arbitrators defended by Professor Weston, arbitral institutions enjoy immunity in cases in which they are sued instead of arbitrators for the acts falling within the arbitrators' capacity.[3] Such an approach not only mimics the traditional common law stance to the so-called legal immunity of arbitration actors (be it as expressed in US case law or as regulated by the UK Arbitration Act of 1996),[4] but also, and more importantly, seems to disregard the very complex contractual situations coming into existence in institutional arbitration. Even though Weston allows institutional liability for, among

[1]Cf. the so-called "qualified immunity of arbitrators" as proposed by Franck 2000 with the "limited liability of arbitrators" as advocated by Guzman 1999 and finally the "contractual liability subject to waivers" as suggested by Rutledge 2004.

[2]Cf. Weston 2004; Li 1998; Rasmussen 2002.

[3]Weston 2004, 509–510.

[4]Sect. 5.2.1.2.5 of Chap. 5.

other things, a failure of the institution to fulfil its essential contractual obligations owed to the parties, her arguments justifying the legal immunity of arbitral institutions in certain circumstances seem to be insufficient.

The fact is that Weston tends to reject any responsibility of arbitral institutions for the acts of individual arbitrators. By upholding the rationale of arbitral immunity to cover arbitral institutions when it is the arbitrator's act that should be under attack, Weston detaches the individual obligations in institutional arbitration from their private, contractual context. That is to say, the solutions proposed by Weston still rely on certain public protection of arbitral institutions in the context of finality and integrity of the arbitration process. These assumptions do not correspond with the arguments of this book, especially with the analysis of the particular authority and function of arbitral institutions in contract formation, as presented in Chaps. 2 and 3, which dealt with the private regulatory powers of arbitral institutions in the contract formation.

Furthermore, Weston proposes the creation of a public body capable of overseeing arbitrators. Professor Weston fails, however, to provide a similar solution for arbitral institutions. This inconsistency undermines Weston's "surrogate theory",[5] which also disappoints due to the lack of accurate formulation of the category of acts for which institutions should be in fact granted immunity.

6.2.2 Further Surrogacy as a Doctrine of Liability?

The proposals advocated by both Rasmussen and Li could at first glance exemplify the "surrogate theory", however, and as opposed to Weston's arguments, they seem to support institutional liability rather than immunity. First, according to the line of reasoning of Rasmussen, arbitral institutions should as a general rule become liable for their failure to fulfil contractual obligations.[6] Conversely, Li argues that arbitral institutions should be held liable for the misconduct or negligence of arbitrators, which, in turn, should become mandatory "members" of arbitration centres.[7] Although some commentators put both proposed solutions on equal footing, claiming that they represent the same category of proposals in which arbitrators should enjoy broad immunity while institutions ought to be contractually liable (Rutledge), a deeper analysis suggests a different conclusion. On the one hand, the claims of Li establish a particular system of responsibility of arbitration centres that aims at protecting arbitrators that will "belong" to the relevant institutional arbitral regime. On the other hand, Rasmussen does not explicitly state that institutions should be liable for the acts of arbitrators, as he predominantly proposes to detach institutional operation from arbitrators' activity. In line with this, only Li's

[5] Weston did not use this term to define her theory. This is my own nomenclature.

[6] Rasmussen 2002, 1870–75.

[7] See generally Li 1998.

argumentation bears resemblance to the "surrogate theory", as—in addition to institutional liability for arbitrators misconduct or negligence—it allows institutions to seek redress from arbitrators. Notwithstanding this, both solutions seem somewhat incomplete.

Though insightful, Rasmussen's interpretation has some deficiencies. Rasmussen strictly claims that the institutional liability regime should not be confused with arbitrators' responsibilities or contractual obligations. Rasmussen seems unaware of the need for certain contractual liability for institutional arbitrators. By maintaining the arbitrators' absolute immunity—granted by law—Rasmussen distorts the rationale underpinning institutional contractual liability. This undermines the regulatory authority of arbitral institutions in contractual arrangements stemming from the particular status of arbitral institutions understood as the authority to re-determine the authority of institutional arbitrators.[8]

Regarding the "surrogate theory" proposed by Li, yet again the immunity of institutional arbitrators does not correspond with the particular contractual situation expressed in Chap. 3 and reiterated above. It is inaccurate to assume that arbitral institutions could be held contractually liable for *all* acts of arbitrators, involving even the preparatory stage of the pre-arbitration proceedings, at which stage institutional arbitrators do not yet assume adjudicatory functions. These functions are determined and thus confirmed by arbitral institutions at the moment when an arbitrator-to-be communicates with the arbitral institution under the aegis of which he or she is appointed. Moreover, it is unlikely that individual arbitrators become members of particular arbitral institutions. This would involve expressing conflicts of interest in cases in which international arbitrators act as private adjudicators within different institutional regimes. It is common knowledge that this happens extensively in the real world of arbitration.

6.2.3 Rutledge's Market-Based Approach to Contractual Liability

It should be stressed from the outset that the proposals for reform offered by Professor Rutledge do not explicitly refer to arbitral institutions.[9] Notwithstanding that, they seem to provide the most convincing solutions, taking into account the contractual side of arbitration.[10] Rutledge introduces a market-based approach to arbitral liability and he opts for the contractual liability of arbitrators, the scope of which (together with the necessary waivers) should be individually negotiated by the interested parties and the arbitrators themselves.[11]

[8]Sect. 3.2.1.1.2.3 of Chap. 3.

[9]Rutledge 2004, 190–197.

[10]Rutledge 2004, 156.

[11]Ibid., 190–197.

Although Rutledge tends to shift the discussion on arbitral liability from the policy-based arguments (concerning integrity and finality of arbitration awards) to market-based arguments (regarding the contractual, commercial facet of the relationships between the parties and arbitrators), yet again he does not elaborate in a comprehensive manner on the role of arbitral institutions in the formation of institutional contracts. Therefore, Professor Rutledge seems to omit the role of arbitral institutions in negotiating liability clauses. While focusing on the law and economics arguments of contractual liability (e.g. participation in the arbitration market, price distortion, disclosure of information, or market incentives), that is, on the economic dimension of liability as defined in this book, Rutledge overlooks the very authority of arbitral institutions to influence the scope of liability clauses in the context of societal, legal, and economic dimensions of institutional activity.[12] Since the model of contractual bonds in institutional arbitration is missing in Rutledge's proposal, it remains unclear how and by whom contractual liability clauses will or should be negotiated and what the implications of such negotiations will be for both the operation of institutional arbitration (supply side) and the economic incentives for arbitration users (demand side). Finally, the proposals provided by Professor Rutledge do not address the significance of the societal dimension of institutional arbitration in the context of institutional arbitral liability. This mostly concerns the failure to reflect on how the possible institutional liability clauses, especially during the negotiation stage, can increase the parties' confidence in the institutional arbitration process in the context of the early communitarian values the arbitral institutions maintained.

6.3 Institutional Liability Models: Possible Alternatives

Given the above-mentioned shortcomings of the existent proposals of institutional arbitral liability, the following discussion will focus predominantly on solutions that deal with the regulations of liability of arbitral institutions as independent arbitration actors. The references to the scope and moment of the emergence of the contractual obligations of individual arbitrators, whose breach may result in liability, will therefore be limited. They will be made solely with a view to the interconnection between the content of institutional contractual obligations and the functions of individual arbitrators within the institutional supervisory powers over arbitrators, as well as to the particular institutional authority in contract formation in institutional arbitration.

Before presenting the plausible models of standard institutional arbitral liability, it is necessary to set up a few essential variables of these models and to explain which contractual obligations of arbitral institutions fall within the commercial

[12] Rutledge 2004.

and public functions of institutional arbitration, respectively. The arguments supporting both these variables and the distinction between contractual obligations of arbitral institutions in the context of their dual function were presented in Chaps. 2 and 3.

6.3.1 Essential Variables

- Contractual institutional liability should accommodate both the traditional commercial function of arbitral institutions and the emerging public function of institutional arbitration.
- The ideal, normative contractual liability model should incorporate and respond to all three dimensions of institutional functions that involve the societal and economic objectives of institutional regimes *in addition to* a pure legal analysis of institutional contractual obligations.
- The content of substantive contractual obligations of arbitral institutions in the areas of institutional supervision over the efficient conduct in the arbitration process, complemented by the procedural authority of institutional rules in institutional contract formation, also requires certain institutional liability for the effects of negligent acts or omission of institutional arbitrators.
- Conditional on the above variable, arbitral institutions should not be liable for any acts or omission of individual arbitrators *prior* to the conferment on arbitrators of adjudicatory powers by a respective institutional organ.

6.3.2 Content of the Contractual Obligations of Arbitral Institutions

The analysis of the dual function of arbitral institutions provided in Chap. 2 distinguished between the commercial and public function of arbitral institutions. The following presentation provides examples of the contractual obligations falling within each of these functions.[13] It should be emphasized here that the rationale underlying the contractual obligations within the commercial function of arbitral institutions concern the institutional role in ensuring the effectiveness of the arbitration proceedings in terms of time and costs. In turn, the rationale underpinning the contractual obligations within the public function of arbitral institutions relate to the institutional role in securing the legality of the institutional arbitration proceedings and the enforceability of the arbitral awards issued in the course of these proceedings.

[13]The catalogue of the contractual obligations provided in this section does not claim to be exhaustive. Rather, it aims to serve as further guidance for the discussion on the possible models of limitation of institutional liability in the following sections.

Contractual obligations falling within the **commercial function** include the following:

- Institutional obligations to fix the costs of arbitration.
- Institutional obligations regarding the setting of time limits.
- Institutional obligations to enforce the arbitration rules concerning the expeditious conduct of the arbitration proceedings.
- Institutional obligations to facilitate the contractual settlement between the parties (by means of the awards by consent and mediation attempts, if the arbitration rules contain the relevant provisions on the relationship between the arbitration and mediation).

Contractual obligations falling within the **public function** include:

- Institutional obligations to ensure proper communications between and among all institutional arbitration actors (the parties, arbitrators, and the arbitral institutions themselves).
- Institutional obligations to ensure the proper composition of the arbitral tribunal (with regard to the independence, impartiality, expertise, and the availability of each individual arbitrator).
- Institutional obligations to decide on jurisdictional matters.
- Institutional obligations to decide on non-signatories, joinders, and consolidation of the proceedings.
- Institutional obligations to decide on the temporary application of the arbitration rules.
- Institutional obligations to set up the procedural framework for the issuance of the arbitral award (in particular, with regard to the arbitration rules that provide for the institutional scrutiny of arbitral awards).

6.3.3 Possible Models

There are five plausible models of institutional arbitral liability that could, on first analysis, correspond with the above essential variables underpinning the regime of contractual liability of arbitral institutions as proposed in this book.[14] Each model presented below is accompanied by a standard liability clause that could be incorporated into institutional arbitration rules, replacing the contemporary exclusion of liability or limitation of liability clauses. The examples of the clauses concerning institutional arbitral liability are based on the standard ICC limitation of liability clause.[15] The five models involve the following:

[14] The presented models are not supposed to be exhaustive. There are other possible variations of the variables set up at the outset of this part of Chap. 6. However, the presented models aim at proving in a most visible manner the interconnectedness of the major assumptions of this book, while at the same time uncovering the shortcomings of the detachment of the institutional functions from the conduct of institutional arbitrators in the area of institutional arbitral liability.

[15] As defined in Article 40 of the 2012 ICC Arbitration Rules.

(1) The model assuming: (a) no *contractual* liability of arbitral institutions for their own acts or omission in the arbitration process, (b) the contractual liability of arbitral institutions for all negligent acts or omission of institutional arbitrators *after* the conferment on arbitrators of the adjudicatory powers by an institutional organ, and (c) the blanket contractual immunity of institutional arbitrators.

Proposed Limitation of Liability Clause[16]:

> The arbitrators and the emergency arbitrator, the Court and its members, the ICC and its employees, and the ICC National Committees and Groups and their employees and representatives shall not be liable to any person for any act or omission in connection with the arbitration, *save* where the act or omission of arbitrators or the emergency arbitrator that occurred *after* the confirmation of the arbitrators by the Court or *after* the appointment of emergency arbitrator by the President of the ICC is shown by the party to be a result of negligence of arbitrators or of the emergency arbitrator, for which the party may seek redress from the ICC.
>
> In no case shall the arbitrators or the emergency arbitrator be liable to any person for any act or omission in connection with the arbitration that occurred *prior to* the confirmation of the arbitrators by the Court or *prior to* the appointment of the emergency arbitrator by the President of the ICC.

(2) The model assuming: (a) no *contractual* liability of arbitral institutions for their own acts or omission in the arbitration process, (b) the contractual liability of arbitral institutions for all negligent acts or omission of institutional arbitrators *after* the conferment on arbitrators of the adjudicatory powers by an institutional organ, and (c) the individual liability of institutional arbitrators for the acts done, or omitted, as a result of negligence or bad faith *prior to* the conferment on the individual arbitrators of the adjudicatory powers by an institutional organ.

Proposed Limitation of Liability Clause:

> The Court and its members, the ICC and its employees, and the ICC National Committees and Groups and their employees and representatives shall not be liable to any person for any act, or omission, in connection with the arbitration, *save* where the act or omission of arbitrators or the emergency arbitrator that occurred *after* the confirmation of the arbitrators by the Court or *after* the appointment of emergency arbitrator by the President of the

[16]The nomenclature used to define the proposed liability clause should not be confusing. The clause called "limitation of liability" follows the current terminology used by the ICC as well as the standard nomenclature concerning the scope of contractual liability negotiated in international commercial contracts. It should also be stressed here that the proposed limitation of liability clauses do not deal with the liability of experts, witnesses or other parties appointed by an arbitral tribunal in the course of arbitrations, which liability largely falls outside the scope of this book.

ICC is shown by the party to be a result of negligence of arbitrators or the emergency arbitrator, for which the party may seek redress from the ICC.

In no case shall the Court and its members, the ICC and its employees, and the ICC National Committees and Groups and their employees and representatives be liable to any person for any of their individual acts or omission in connection with the arbitration.

In addition, the arbitrators and the emergency arbitrator shall not be liable to any person for any act or omission in connection with the arbitration, *save* where the act or omission of arbitrators or the emergency arbitrator that occurred *prior to* the confirmation of the arbitrators by the Court or *prior to* the appointment of the emergency arbitrator by the President of the ICC is shown by the party to be a result of negligence or bad faith of arbitrators or the emergency arbitrator, in which cases the party may seek redress from an individual arbitrator or the emergency arbitrator.

(3) The model assuming: (a) the *contractual* liability of arbitral institutions for their own negligent acts or omission in the arbitration process, (b) the contractual liability of arbitral institutions for all negligent acts or omission of institutional arbitrators *after* the conferment on arbitrators of the adjudicatory powers by an institutional organ, and (c) the blanket contractual immunity of institutional arbitrators.

Proposed Limitation of Liability Clause:

The Court and its members, the ICC and its employees, and the ICC National Committees and Groups and their employees and representatives shall not be liable to any person for any act or omission in connection with the arbitration, *save* where the act or omission is shown by the party to be a result of negligence of the Court and its members, the ICC and its employees, and the ICC National Committees and Groups and their employees and representatives, in which cases the party may seek redress from the ICC.

In addition, the arbitrators and the emergency arbitrator shall not be liable to any person for any act or omission in connection with the arbitration, savewhere the act or omission of arbitrators or emergency arbitrator *after* the confirmation of the arbitrators by the Court or *after* the appointment of the emergency arbitrator by the President of the ICC is shown by the party to be a result of negligence of the arbitrators or the emergency arbitrator, in which cases the party may seek redress from the ICC.

(4) The model assuming: (a) the *contractual* liability of arbitral institutions for their own negligent acts or omission in the arbitration process, (b) the contractual liability of arbitral institutions for the effects of the acts or omission of institutional arbitrators *as a result of negligent institutional supervision of the efficient conduct in the arbitration process after* the conferment on arbitrators of the adjudicatory powers by an institutional organ, and (c) the blanket contractual immunity of institutional arbitrators.

Proposed Limitation of Liability Clause:

> The Court and its members, the ICC and its employees, and the ICC National Committees and Groups and their employees and representatives shall not be liable to any person for any act or omission in connection with the arbitration, *save* where the act or omission is shown by the party to be a result of negligence of the Court and its members, the ICC and its employees, and the ICC National Committees and Groups and their employees and representatives, in which cases the party may seek redress from the ICC.
>
> The arbitrators and the emergency arbitrator shall not be liable to any person for any act or omission in connection with the arbitration, save where the act or omission of arbitrators or emergency arbitrator *after* the confirmation of the arbitrators by the Court or *after* the appointment of the emergency arbitrator by the President of the ICC is shown by the party to be a result of negligent institutional supervision of the efficient conduct in the arbitration process, in which cases the party may seek redress from the ICC.

(5) The model assuming: (a) the *contractual* liability of arbitral institutions for their own negligent acts or omission in the arbitration process, (b) the contractual liability of arbitral institutions for the effects of the acts or omission of institutional arbitrators *as a result of negligent institutional supervision of the efficient conduct in the arbitration process after* the conferment on arbitrators of the adjudicatory powers by an institutional organ, and (c) the individual liability of institutional arbitrators for the acts or omission *prior* to the conferment on them of the adjudicatory powers by an institutional organ and a possible professional liability of arbitrators for intentional harms and wrongdoing in the arbitration processes.

Proposed Limitation of Liability Clause:

> The Court and its members, the ICC and its employees, and the ICC National Committees and Groups and their employees and representatives shall not be liable to any person for any act or omission in connection with the arbitration, *save* where the act or omission is shown by the party to be a result of negligence of the Court and its members, the ICC and its employees and the ICC National Committees and Groups and their employees and representatives, in which cases the party may seek redress from the ICC.
>
> The arbitrators and the emergency arbitrator shall not be liable to any person for any act or omission in connection with the arbitration, *save* where the act or omission of arbitrators or the emergency arbitrator *after* the confirmation of the arbitrators by the Court or *after* the appointment of the emergency arbitrator by the President of the ICC is shown by the party to be a result of negligent institutional supervision of the efficient conduct in the arbitration process, in which cases the party may seek redress from the ICC.

The above provision does not exclude the liability of individual arbitrators or the emergency arbitrator for the acts or omission *prior to* the confirmation of the arbitrators by the Court or the appointment of the emergency arbitrator by the President of the ICC, neither does it exclude professional liability of individual arbitrators and of the emergency arbitrator under the codes of conduct of the professional associations of which they are members, or under applicable law even *after* the confirmation of arbitrators by the Court or *after* the appointment of the emergency arbitrator by the President of the ICC.

It is proposed that each of these models should be also accompanied by additional mechanisms of accountability in order to respond to the societal dimension of institutional operation. Such mechanisms will be addressed in Sect. 6.4.2.1 below. Each of these models will now be analysed in order to test their compatibility with the major assumptions of this book.

6.3.4 Analysis

The first model entails that arbitral institutions—due to their emerging public function—should not be liable for any act or omission in the course of the arbitration proceedings. This excludes their liability for all contractual obligations falling within both the commercial and public function of arbitral institutions as a result of the recognition of the specific private regulatory powers of arbitral institutions, as well as the increasing role of arbitral institutions in regulatory arbitrations. The public function of arbitral institutions overrides their traditional commercial function here and to this extent the model assumes no liability of arbitral institutions whatsoever. This is because the institutional obligations corresponding to the public function are deeply rooted in the institutional obligations stemming from the commercial function of institutional arbitration (and *vice versa*). To be more specific, all contractual obligations assumed by arbitral institutions within their public function (such as those relating to the communications in the course of the arbitration, the composition of an arbitral tribunal, jurisdictional challenges, non-signatories, joinders, consolidation of arbitrations, and the decisions on the temporal application of different sets of arbitration rules) should, in principle, be performed in a timely and cost-effective manner (which rationale also underpins the contractual obligations of arbitral institutions within their commercial function).

The model assumes, however, that arbitral institutions should be liable for all negligent acts or omission of institutional arbitrators *after* the conferment of the adjudicatory powers on institutional arbitrators by relevant institutional organs due to their particular authority to re-determine the authority of institutional arbitrators.[17]

[17] Understood as the incorporation of individual obligations of arbitrators into the structures developed by arbitral institutions by means of their arbitration rules. See Sect. 3.2.1.1.2.3 of Chap. 3.

This could concern, inter alia, the institutional liability for arbitrator's error in rendering arbitral awards, for the delay in rendering arbitral awards (due to arbitrators not respecting time limits) and the failure of the arbitrator(s) to disclose conflict of interests. The institutional arbitrators, in this model, enjoy blanket contractual immunity covering all acts done or omitted in relation to arbitration, possibly including also the arbitrators' performance prior to the commencement of the proceedings. This is also plausible due to the procedural authority of institutional arbitration rules to re-determine the authority of individual arbitrators that imposes an obligation on arbitrators to comply with the institutional arbitration rules following their confirmation. Arbitrators, at the same time, still enjoy immunity protecting their adjudicatory powers that can be exercised in a manner allowing for the arbitrators' discretion.

Albeit the assumption regarding the institutional liability for certain acts or omission of arbitrators seems to stay in line with the arguments delivered in the course of the presentation of the contractual model in Chap. 3,[18] it is hard to expect arbitral institutions to take unlimited responsibility for all possible negligent acts or omission of institutional arbitrators. A liability clause that is drafted so widely seems undesirable for arbitral institutions as some of the acts or omission of arbitrators may fall outside the general supervisory authority of arbitral institutions to ensure a proper conduct in the arbitration proceedings. This could be the case in situations of legal errors of arbitrators or in cases of fraud or corruption on the side of arbitrators (which would result in criminal proceedings against arbitrators), particularly concerning, but not limited to, institutional regimes that do not provide for institutional scrutiny of the arbitral awards.[19] Moreover, the argument concerning the blanket immunity of arbitrators and the institutional liability for the acts or omission of institutional arbitrators bears the hallmarks of vicarious liability in the meaning of Li's "surrogate theory" presented in Sect. 6.2.2 above. In view of the critique of this proposal, it should be clear that this assumption does not provide for satisfactory solutions. In addition, it seems plausible that the contractual immunity of institutional arbitrators under the present model would be ineffective under some national laws applicable to liability claims, assuming that certain domestic laws provide for the liability of arbitrators for negligence. This would mean that the test of the scope of arbitral liability would be again dependent on the public determination of the private arbitration settings by domestic courts. This is one of the shortcomings of the current liability regimes that this book aims to avoid.

Furthermore, it seems counterproductive to disregard the commercial aspect of institutional activity as well as the contractual basis of such activity while

[18]Sect. 3.2.1.1.2.2 of Chap. 3.

[19]Although it seems unlikely that any institution that incorporated the mechanism of scrutiny of the arbitral awards would approve an arbitration award that contains a material error, it is advisable that, in principle, arbitral institutions should not be liable for the consequences of such an error for the parties, provided that an institution conducted the scrutiny of an arbitral award with due care, that is: that an institution exercised its supervisory powers to draw the arbitrator's attention to the fact that such material error had occurred.

determining the optimal scope of the liability of arbitral institutions. Given the professional character of institutional operation, it seems very unlikely that arbitral institutions would be allowed to totally exclude their professional responsibility for their essential contractual obligations, bearing in mind that they act as sophisticated and independent market players. In fact, all institutional obligations stem from the contract(s), even if some obligations falling within the public function stand in vast contrast to the principle of party autonomy. The assumption of this model, concerning the contractual immunity of arbitral institutions, seems to be therefore contrary to the comprehensive functional analysis of arbitral institutions. This is because it neither responds to the contractual, commercial nature of institutional activity nor does it address the problems relating to the democratic deficits of the contemporary institutional regimes. These problems constitute the major argument for the increased public control of institutional performance in the so-called regulatory arbitrations that could be exercised when domestic courts are faced with institutional liability claims. Against this background, the whole model of institutional arbitral liability discussed here seems insufficient.

In comparison with the first model, **the second model** varies in the sense that it allows liability of individual arbitrators for certain acts or omission *prior* to the conferment on them of the adjudicatory functions. Individual arbitrators are still liable for their breaches of the pre-contractual arrangements concluded beforehand with each of their nominees, at least in cases in which the composition of the arbitral tribunal involves the party-appointed arbitrators. These situations could concern the disclosure by a party's nominee of trade secrets, sensitive company information or confidential facts of a dispute, which were shared with a nominee at the stage of an informal interview. Under this model, institutional arbitrators are still immune with regard to the acts or omission that occurred after the conferment on them of the adjudicatory powers by arbitral institutions, and arbitral institutions remain immune with regard to their own acts or omission due to their public function.

This model seems to respect, to some extent, a contractual nature of the relationships between the parties and arbitrators in that it allows the parties to sue their nominees for the breach of their contractual obligations prior to the commencement of the arbitration proceedings. However, it fails to address the major variables of the ideal, normative model of arbitral liability, both from procedural and substantive grounds corresponding to the contractual nature of all institutional relationships and the content of the contractual obligations of arbitral institutions and arbitrators, accordingly. This implies the inadequacy of this model, especially in view of the concerns related to a dual function of institutional arbitration that calls for contractual institutional liability, as well as the responsibility of arbitral institutions only for specific acts and omission of individual arbitrators. The discussion related to the shortcomings of the assumptions presented in the course of the analysis of the first model remains valid in regards to the present model.

The third model differs from the first model in the area of the scope of liability of arbitral institutions for their own acts and omission. The model provides for the contractual liability of arbitral institutions for their own negligent acts and omission in the arbitration process. This stems from the contractual nature of institutional arbitration and relates to the traditional commercial function of arbitral institutions. The institutional liability for negligence also addresses the public function of institutional activity to the extent that it creates room for the increased transparency and possible oversight by public courts of the due care of arbitral institutions in the performance of their obligations. Hence, this solution accommodates the private regulatory powers exercised by arbitral institutions within the public function that generates questions of due process in all types of arbitrations and the substantive content of institutional obligations in arbitrations that involve matters of public interest (regulatory arbitrations). Irrespective of the validity of these assumptions, the model at hand still suffers from inefficiency insofar as it allows unlimited contractual liability of arbitral institutions for all acts or omission of institutional arbitrators after the conferment on arbitrators of the adjudicatory powers, as well as when it assumes the blanket contractual immunity of institutional arbitrators.

The fourth model differs from the third model to the extent that it proposes the contractual liability of arbitral institutions only for the *effects* of the acts or omission of institutional arbitrators *as a result of negligent institutional supervision of the efficient conduct in the arbitration process after* the conferment on arbitrators of the adjudicatory powers by an institutional organ. For example, arbitral institutions should be liable for the erroneous assessment of the conflict of interests following the arbitrator's disclosure in accordance with relevant institutional documents. Additionally, under this model, arbitral institutions should assume liability for delays in rendering arbitral awards as a result of the negligent extension of the time limits for arbitrators in this regard, or for procedural errors contained in the arbitral awards as a consequence of institutional negligence in providing the arbitrators with the awards' checklists, at least in institutional regimes that offer the institutional scrutiny of the arbitral awards.[20] In this view, this model respects the particular interplay between the procedural prerogatives of arbitral institutions vis-à-vis institutional arbitrators and the substantive content of institutional obligations in arbitration processes. This is so, in particular, where the institutional duties overlap with the work of arbitrators as a result of the institutional supervision of the efficient conduct in arbitration to ensure the enforceability of institutional arbitration settings.

In line with this, arbitral institutions bear contractual responsibility for the acts or omission of arbitrators that resulted in harm suffered by the injured party or parties due to negligent supervision by the arbitral institution of the conduct of arbitrators. Again, this is justified by the particular relationship between arbitral institutions and individual arbitrators already defined as institutional regulatory authority to re-determine the authority of arbitrators after the conferment on the arbitrators of adjudicatory powers. This argumentation stays in line with the major assumptions of this book reflected in the above-mentioned essential variables of the ideal institutional liability model. However, the model fails the functionality

[20]These examples are not exhaustive. They serve as the explanation of the situations in which arbitral institutions may, in fact, assume liability in the context of the work of arbitrators under the model discussed above.

test when providing for a blanket contractual immunity of institutional arbitrators, which should not be a standard for institutional arbitral liability in view of the arguments presented in the above analysis of the models one and three.

This analysis leads us to **the fifth model** of institutional arbitral liability, which this book proposes should be adopted. Under this model, arbitral institutions are—in principle—contractually liable for all *negligent* acts or omission falling within their commercial and public functions. This means that arbitral institutions are disallowed to avoid their contractual responsibility for anything done or omitted in the course of the arbitrations. This argument respects the contractual source of all obligations assumed by arbitral institutions (whether concerning the commercial or public function). It also entails an increased public accountability of institutional arbitration given the emergent external legitimacy of institutional arbitration due to their public function.[21]

Moreover, arbitral institutions are contractually liable for the *effects* of the acts or omission of institutional arbitrators *as a result of negligent institutional supervision of the efficient conduct in the arbitration process after* the conferment on arbitrators of the adjudicatory powers by an institutional organ. This assumption contributes to a better understanding of the interplay between institutional organs and bodies and individual institutional arbitrators. Arbitral institutions become liable for the effects of their own negligent supervision over the work of arbitrators due to both: the content of their substantive obligations stemming from the arbitration rules, and the peculiar procedural relationship with individual arbitrators (authority to re-determine the authority of individual arbitrator) once an arbitrator commences to rule on an arbitration case in accordance with institutional policies, rules, and soft-law codes (if any). This seems to correspond to the rationale of the contemporary arbitration rules defining the essential institutional obligations in arbitration processes, also as interpreted by the French courts in the recent decisions on potential institutional liability.[22] Finally, institutional arbitrators, under this model, enjoy only qualified contractual immunity, as the model assumes certain professional liability of arbitrators for the acts of serious professional misconduct, possibly involving intentional harms and wrongdoings in the arbitration process. In this vein, the parties could plausibly still sue individual arbitrators for their professional malpractice that could be separated from the procedural supervisory authority of arbitral institutions. Such claims would be plausible under the codes of conduct for arbitrators promulgated by national or international professional associations or institutes for arbitrators such as the National Academy of Arbitrators in the US or CIArb in the UK, or under relevant provisions of national laws (if any). In addition, institutional arbitrators are still liable for the acts that resulted in the economic or reputational losses of the party or parties that had contacted the arbitrator-to-be prior to the commencement of the arbitrations.

[21] Sect. 2.3.2 of Chap. 2.

[22] Sect. 5.2.1.2.1 of Chap. 5.

6.3.5 *Additional Assumptions of the Proposed Model*

The proposed model should be based on the following additional assumptions:

- Negotiable character of liability clauses in commercial arbitrations.
- No waivers from standard liability clauses in arbitrations of matters involving public interest (regulatory arbitrations).
- Elimination of the clauses providing for the immunity from process.
- Favourable approach to a theory of individualized relationships in institutional contracts.
- Determination of the law applicable to institutional arbitration contracts.

6.3.5.1 Negotiable Character of Liability Clauses in Commercial Arbitrations

It is advisable for arbitral institutions to resign from their policies concerning the mandatory character of institutional liability clauses, which today may result in the refusal to administer an arbitration case should the parties oppose to be bound with the standard institutional liability clause. This also means that the institutional liability clauses in the proposed model should be—in principle--negotiable, at least in traditional commercial arbitrations. The negotiations of institutional arbitral liability could take the form of possible waivers from the standard wording of the institutional liability clause concerning the scope of liability of both arbitral institutions and institutional arbitrators. Therefore, it is proposed that the standard model of institutional arbitral liability presented in this chapter be treated as a standing point for further negotiations between the parties and arbitral institutions (and also, possibly, between arbitral institutions and individual arbitrators). This means that this standard could be easily derogated by means of the private stipulations of the ideal scope of liability in the arbitration in question.

For example, arbitral institutions could bargain for a limited liability under their contract(s) with the parties that could take the form of a financial cap on the liability of arbitral institutions (i.e. reflecting the costs of institutional services). In addition, arbitral institutions could offer to the parties at the stage of negotiation that they would assume liability only for a certain category of acts or omission (i.e. negligent decisions on the extension of time limits) but not for others (i.e. the negligent decisions on jurisdiction or the replacement of arbitrators).

Arbitral institutions could even include in the liability clauses the provisions on indemnification exempting institutions from liability for certain categories of negligent acts or omission or for the negligent acts or omission of arbitrators. In return, arbitral institutions could offer to the parties respective variations of the institutional arbitration costs in accordance with the following rule: the more liability assumed by arbitral institutions agreed on during the negotiation stage, the more costly arbitration services to be offered to the parties. Conversely, if the arbitral institutions and the parties opted for the limited liability of arbitral institutions, the parties could benefit from the lower costs of the arbitration services. The costs of arbitration to be used as a bargaining argument for both the contractors (meaning the parties to the institutional arbitration contracts) would naturally reflect the difference between the administrative costs accrued in connection with the arbitration and the additional costs to be assumed by arbitral institutions due to the necessary implementation of the insurance schemes. Realistically speaking, then, the proposed model of liability would increase the costs of arbitration as compared to the current schedules of costs, with the major advantage to the parties being the possibility of reclaiming these costs in the potential liability suits against arbitral institutions.

Although negotiations of institutional liability clauses on a case-by-case basis may at first glance look unfeasible from a practical perspective, in fact such negotiations could address all three dimensions of institutional functions. That is, they could increase institutional professional responsibility under institutional arbitration contracts within the legal dimension, respond to the societal dimension by restoring the role of party autonomy in the institutional settings, and finally, support the competition between the arbitration centres within the economic dimension of institutional functions. Ideally, the invitation for the negotiations of the scope of institutional arbitral liability could be provided at the moment of sending the request for arbitration to a relevant arbitral institution (and the answer to the request in the case of a respondent), and take form of a letter from a party's counsel explaining her stance to the institutional liability issue. It also seems plausible that such negotiations could be conducted following the commencement of the arbitration proceedings, even when the potential problems concerning the conduct in the arbitration, that could imply future liability, have been identified.

However, the practical significance of this scenario for the bargaining position of the parties to arbitration in such negotiations would need to be assessed in view of the wording of the standard liability clauses subject to further negotiations. On the one hand, if the standing point for such negotiations were the standard liability clauses proposed in this book—hence, assuming the absolute liability as a general, derogative norm—it appears that the negotiations could still allow both sides at the table to achieve satisfactory solutions. On the other hand, if the liability clauses subject to negotiations resembled the existing clauses largely limiting the liability of institutional actors, the negotiations of these clauses would be detrimental to the parties. It is hard to assume that, in such cases, arbitral institutions would be eager to extend their liability following the conclusion of the institutional contracts that had already provided for almost unlimited liability of these institutions.

6.3.5.2 No Waivers from Standard Liability Clauses in Arbitrations of Matters Involving Public Interest

At the same time, it seems necessary that institutions remain reluctant to accept the waivers from standard arbitral liability in regulatory arbitrations (i.e. involving consumers, employees, or any forms of arbitrations involving States and State-like entities). This is so due to the democratically sensitive issues which such arbitration proceedings involve and/or because of the possible inequality in bargaining powers in arbitrations that result from the inclusion of the standard arbitration clauses into the contracts of adhesion used in many industry-based arbitrations. This proposal is guided by the goal to increase both transparency in arbitrations of matters involving public interest and the observance of the private rights of the weaker parties to institutional arbitration proceedings.

6.3.5.3 Elimination of the Clauses Providing for the Immunity from Process

It is also suggested that arbitral institutions, in particular the institutions who have their seats in common law jurisdictions, eliminate the provisions that prevent the parties from engaging the members of institutional organs or individual arbitrators in legal proceedings of any kind after the arbitral award has been rendered. This could, in first place, increase the transparency of institutional arbitration proceedings, and also allow the legal representatives of arbitral institutions or arbitrators to testify in liability suits, which is desirable under the proposed model. This would also permit legal counsel of institutions or individual arbitrators to effectively defend themselves in liability lawsuits, given that the burden of proof regarding negligence will be most likely bore by the injured party.

This proposal may appear controversial, as it touches upon the principle of confidentiality in arbitration. Most likely, the confidentiality problems will involve the disclosure of information produced in the arbitral proceedings, as well as further concerns related to the use of such information by judges in liability lawsuits. The judges will need to accurately assess the contractual obligations of arbitral institutions or the institutional arbitrators with a view to both the parties' rights in arbitration and the public accountability of arbitrators or institutions in more general terms. This will require a proper balance between the necessary protection of the private rights of the parties—which may not wish to have certain aspects of their arbitrations disclosed in the public forum—and the very determination of the harm or injury caused to such parties under the negligent acts of institutions or arbitrators. This assessment may be particularly difficult in regulatory arbitrations in which the private rights will have to be weighed in front of both the public interest and public policy concerns relating to the arbitration processes.[23]

[23]The problems with the disclosure in arbitration was a subject of the US Supreme Court decision in *Those Certain Underwriters at Lloyds, London v Occidental Gems, Inc.* 2007 NY Slip Op 05654 [41 AD3d 362]. There, it was stated that due to "the important public interest in protecting the rights of parties who submit to confidential arbitration, the [motion] court correctly concluded that no aspect of the Belgian arbitration, to which Occidental is not a party, may be subject to compulsory disclosure in this litigation". Even though this case involved a prospective disclosure of confidential information produced in arbitration to which the litigant was not a party, the rationale underpinning the Court's considerations should have application *a fortiori* to the prospective liability lawsuits.

It is sufficient to notice, however, that the principle of confidentiality is not absolute in arbitration, as it takes the form of the implied standard yet not the obligation unless the arbitration actors provide for the express obligation of confidentiality in their contractual settings (which is not always a common practice).[24] In view of this, it is also plausible that—once the institutional liability is introduced—the parties, institutional arbitrators, and arbitral institutions will be encouraged to deal even more expressly with the determination of the scope of confidentiality of arbitration proceedings, which may in turn increase exclusiveness of the arbitration processes within the societal dimension of institutional arbitration. This assumption, however, will only be valid under the following circumstances: the sensitive commercial information is not revealed during the liability suits, and the liability lawsuits are not open to public. Finally, it seems that once arbitral institutions resign from the absolute immunity from suit, not only can the transparency in arbitration be increased but also the detrimental consequences of institutional waivers of the right to object can be minimized.[25]

6.3.5.4 Favourable Approach to the Theory of Individualized Relationships in Institutional Contracts

It appears convincing that institutional arbitration contracts are formed under the theory of individualized relationships also proposed in the model of contractual relationships in Chap. 3. The application of this theory to institutional arbitration contracts would result in interpreting each contract between arbitral institution and each party and each individual arbitrator as a contract concluded separately. This would allow arbitral institutions to seek individual redress from an individual arbitrator in cases of possible liability of arbitral institutions for the acts of arbitrators that occurred as a result of negligent supervision of the conduct in arbitrations by the arbitral institution. Moreover, it would facilitate the accurate determinations of specific contractual obligations owed by institutions or individual arbitrators to each party to arbitration proceedings and also encourage an accurate assessment of the scope of the prospective institutional or arbitrators' liability towards a single arbitration user in liability suits. Finally, the individualized theory of contractual institutional relationships would help institutions or arbitrators claim potential contributory negligence of the party or parties to arbitration processes,

[24]For example, the ICC 2012 Rules do not provide for the implied confidentiality of the submissions. Article 22(3) authorises the ICC Arbitral Tribunal—upon a request of a party—to "make orders concerning the confidentiality of the arbitration proceedings or of any other matters in connection with the arbitration and [...] take measures for protecting trade secrets and confidential information".

[25]Sect. 4.2.3 of Chap. 4.

in particular in cases in which arbitration proceedings are obstructed by one of the parties due to, inter alia, the pending insolvency proceedings concerning such a party.

6.3.5.5 Determination of the Law Applicable to Institutional Arbitration Contracts

Finally, it is advisable for arbitral institutions to allow the parties and institutional employees to determine the law applicable to institutional arbitration contracts as a result of the negotiations of the scope and content of institutional liability clauses, or at least that the arbitration rules specify the law applicable to institutional contracts between the parties and the arbitral institutions. The latter proposal was surprisingly rejected while drafting the recent version of the ICC Arbitration Rules.[26] However, the implementation of these proposals would be sufficient, as it could diminish the uncertainty related to a prospective determination of liability by the judges in the courts of law, especially given the current inconsistency in national visions of the functions of arbitral institutions. This, in a long-term perspective, could increase the predictability of the judicial determinations of institutional liability whilst permitting the institutions to stipulate the scope of their contractual responsibility in a far-reaching manner. As a result, the negative effects of forum shopping on the side of the parties wishing to sue arbitral institutions could be minimalized.

6.4 On How the Proposed Model Responds to the Three Dimensions of Institutional Functions

This discussion deals with the implications of the proposed model of institutional arbitral liability for all three dimensions of the institutional functions presented in Chap. 2. The effects of the proposed model on the legal, societal, and economic dimensions of institutional arbitration are tested in view of the shortcomings related to the current regulations of institutional liability discussed in Chap. 4.

Hence, while considering the legal dimension, the moment of the emergence of institutional contracts under the proposed model of liability is addressed. Furthermore, while examining the response of the proposed institutional liability model to the societal dimension of institutional functions, the proposals for the incorporation by institutions of the necessary additional mechanisms of accountability within the institutional structures are set forth. Finally, the accommodation by the proposed model of the economic dimension of the institutional arbitration

[26] See generally Greenberg 2013.

deals with the analysis of the dynamics of competition within the institutional arbitration market once arbitral institutions adopt the proposed liability clauses and institutional insurance policies into their regimes.

6.4.1 The Legal Dimension

The below analysis explains the effects of the proposed model on the understanding of the moment of the emergence of the relationships between each individual institutional arbitration actor. This is done in view of the practical problems stemming from this issue, as identified in Chap. 5, that mostly concerned the implications of the determinations of the start of the contractual bonds in institutional arbitration for the possibility of holding arbitral institutions liable and determining the scope of their liability. This discussion also sets forth the framework for the proposals for the public (legal) regulations of institutional liability that will be provided in Chap. 7.

6.4.1.1 Moment of the Emergence of Institutional Contracts and the Legal Authority of Arbitral Institutions Over Institutional Arbitrators: The Role of Interviews

This section aims to prove the significance of the adoption of the theory of individualized relationships in institutional arbitration for the accurate determination of the moment of the emergence of institutional and arbitrators' obligations, the breach of which may result in their prospective liability. To this extent, the below analysis summarizes the possible moments of the emergence of institutional contracts in both the ICC regime and other institutional regimes for a better understanding of the content of contractual obligations of both arbitral institutions and individual arbitrators vis-à-vis each party to arbitration proceedings. This also serves the visualization of the legal authority of arbitral institutions over institutional arbitrators under the proposed model. This, in turn, helps assess the possible separation of the obligations owed by the institutions and individual arbitrators towards a single party to arbitration proceedings.

Under the model of contractual relationships in Chap. 3, it was proposed to distinguish between five contracts coming into existence in the ICC arbitrations after the conferment of the adjudicatory powers on institutional arbitration.[27] Let us recall these contracts: (1) the contract between the claimant (P1) and the ICC Court; (2) the contract between the respondent (P2) and the ICC Court; (3) the contract between the arbitrator (A1) and the ICC Court; (4) the contract between

[27] Sect. 3.2.1.1.2.2 of Chap. 3.

the arbitrator (A2) and the ICC Court; and finally the contract between the ICC Court and the Chairman (A3). Prior to the conferment of adjudicatory functions on arbitrators, the contracts existed also between each arbitrator-to-be (A1 and A2) and each party (P1 and P2).

Under the proposed model of liability the same number of contracts emerges, which also addresses the particular *sui generis* procedural authority of arbitral institutions to re-determine the authority of institutional arbitrators and the interplay between the content of institutional obligations to ensure efficient conduct in arbitrations and enforceability of institutional arbitration settings with the work of individual arbitrators. This implies that arbitral institutions enjoy almost absolute regulatory powers in the institutional contractual settings. This, in turn, explains the prospective institutional liability for the effects of the negligent acts or omission of arbitrators after the conferment on them of the adjudicatory powers by a relevant institutional organ insofar as they fall within the institutional obligation of professional supervision over the arbitration process.

It seems that the same number of contracts also arises in other institutional regimes. Only the moment of their emergence may be slightly different depending on the existence or non-existence of the provisions on the confirmation of arbitrators under the institutional arbitration rules. In each case, however, the decisive moment for the emergence of such obligations will involve the appointment of the chairman of an arbitral tribunal or the sole arbitrator, which determines the very emergence of the adjudicatory functions in the institutional arbitration processes. In this view—in practice—the contractual obligations both in the regimes providing for the confirmation of arbitrators and in other regimes that do not include such provisions will come into existence by means of a similar procedural action (when the adjudicatory function of the presiding member of the arbitral tribunal will be confirmed), yet only the very procedure for such confirmation will differ from one arbitral institution to another. Let us now examine this assumption in detail with regard to the ICC institutional regime (as the most representable one for the regimes providing for the confirmation of institutional arbitrators) and with regard to other institutional regimes.

For the sake of clarity, the moment of the emergence of contractual bonds in ICC arbitration (in line with the model on contractual relationships) is the following:

(1) Regarding the contracts between each party (P1 and P2) and the ICC Court it is the filing of the request of arbitration together with the non-refundable filling fee and the answer to the request to the ICC Secretariat that constitutes the contracts between the Respondent and the Claimant and the ICC Court;
(2) Concerning the contracts between the ICC Court and each arbitrator, it is the moment of the *confirmation by the Court of the Chairman* after the confirmation of each nominee and after filing by each arbitrator of the ICC's Statement of Acceptance, Availability and Independence to the ICC Court that determines the conclusion of the contracts between each ICC arbitrator and the ICC Court.

This means that, alongside the ICC Court's confirmation of the Chairman, the adjudicatory powers will be conferred on all arbitrators. This will constitute the complete contractual bonds between each party and the ICC Court, as well as between each arbitrator and the ICC Court. Additionally, after the confirmation by the ICC Court of the Chairman, certain contractual obligations of the ICC Court may overlap with the contractual obligations owed by each ICC arbitrator towards each party (see graphs).

1st Scenario: 3 Arbitrators, ICC Rules

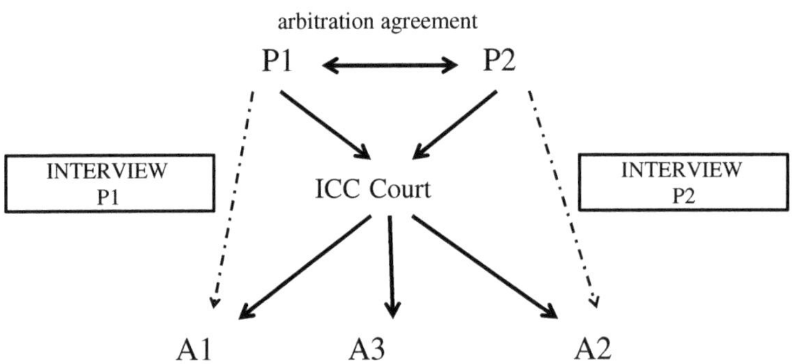

2st Scenario: Sole Arbitrator, ICC Rules

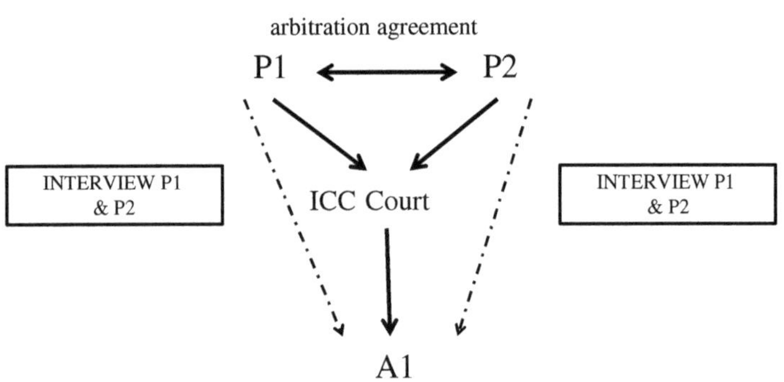

In the above graphs, it is apparent that—depending on the number of arbitrators to hear the dispute—the parties will have different influence on the choice of the members of institutional arbitral tribunals or a sole arbitrator. This is because, in cases in which the arbitral tribunal is composed of three members, each party will, most likely, focus on nominating one arbitrator. Additionally, the parties often have different views on who should be sole arbitrator and hence in practice it is difficult for the parties to reach an agreement on the nomination of a person with a background satisfying both of them. Regardless of whether the members of the arbitral tribunal or sole arbitrators are selected by arbitral institutions or the parties, it is advisable for arbitral institutions that they encourage the parties to conduct interviews with the prospective arbitrators in scenarios involving the three-member arbitration panel, and that institutions pressure the parties to agree on the name of a sole arbitrator by means of their private arrangements.[28] The latter scenario could also involve recommending to the parties to conduct an interview with the sole arbitrator-to-be.

The introduction of the interviews for arbitrators into institutional structures could have positive consequences for different institutional actors. First, from the perspective of arbitral institutions, it could diminish the prospective institutional responsibility for negligent acts or omission of institutional arbitrators by increasing the awareness of the arbitrators of the exact *expectations* of the parties already at the preliminary stages of institutional arbitrations. This would allow institutional arbitrators and also arbitral institutions to better address these expectations during the arbitration proceedings, which could have a positive impact on the "accurate" conduct of institutional arbitrators and institutions themselves in accordance with the parties' major concerns related to the ways in which their disputes should be resolved. Second, from the perspective of the parties, the interviews with prospective institutional arbitrators conducted within the institutional structures could benefit from the increased communications with the arbitrators because of the impact such dialogue could have on the performance of arbitrators. This, in turn, could increase the parties' confidence in the institutional arbitration process because the standards of the performance could be increased, and the more active involvement of arbitration users in the selection of arbitrators could restore the principle of party autonomy.

Coming back to the moment of the formation of institutional arbitration contracts, it is plausible that even in other institutional regimes which do not provide for the confirmation of arbitrators the emergence of contractual relationships between the institution and each arbitrator (or a sole arbitrator), will take place once the presiding arbitrator is chosen, and after each arbitrator accepts the arbitration rules together with the institutional policy in his or her communication with the institution. This means that once the arbitral tribunal (or an umpire) is equipped with adjudicatory powers—as a result of the institutional authority—the contractual ties will come into existence. This puts the institutions in a particular

[28]For more information and references to other sources related to the prospective interviews of arbitrators-to-be see Michael McIlwrath, 2 July 2013. "Getting to Know You." http://kluwerarbitrationblog.com/blog/2013/04/02/getting-to-know-you/. Accessed 25 April 2016.

situation in which they have the final word to approve all the relationships coming into force in institutional arbitration corresponding to the legal authority of arbitral institutions over institutional arbitrators.

Although in-depth analysis of the contractual liability of experts or other parties appointed by the arbitral tribunal does not fall within the scope of this book, it seems sufficient to refer briefly to the institutional role to shape the scope of responsibility also of these actors under the proposed model. It is advisable that arbitral institutions reconsider their authority to grant contractual immunity to all external actors to the arbitration process or that the institutions at least implement effective procedural safeguards to be invoked by the parties in cases of the misconduct of these actors. The first step could involve increased institutional control over the standards of independence and impartiality with regard to tribunal-appointed and party-appointed experts in institutional arbitration proceedings.

6.4.2 The Societal Dimension

In Sect. 3.3.1.1 of Chap. 3, the components of the early internal legitimacy of institutional arbitral regimes were defined, which concerned the following: *participation, performance,* and *moral sanctions*. As concluded in Chap. 3, the inevitable dynamics of external legitimacy (understood as the public, legal recognition of institutional arbitration) not only diminished private mechanisms of accountability of institutional arbitration actors, but also challenged the early institutional tools to oversee the *participation* and *performance* of these actors.[29] As a result, the authority of arbitral institutions was detached from the societal dimension of their activity in that arbitral institutions stopped accommodating the common values and goals of arbitration users concerning the celerity and cost-effectiveness of the arbitration proceedings and also the honourable character of early institutional arbitrations.

In view of this, it is proposed here that by looking at the contractual liability clauses—provided they are negotiable—through the lens of their societal dimension, the early dynamics of the internal institutional legitimacy might be reintroduced. It is assumed that the contractual liability as a tool of private contract law can affect the performance of institutional arbitration actors by serving as an ultimate, deterrent factor for these actors to increase the standards of their performance. This concerns the according to institutional arbitration actors the legal instrument that may increase both the *standards of performance* of such actors and their *participation* in the institutional arbitration communities, and—in the long-term perspective—also the private accountability of institutional arbitration regimes. Yet, in order for this to happen, arbitral institutions should either strengthen the existing private accountability mechanisms (understood as the means to assure internal control) or introduce additional private accountability

[29] Sect. 3.3.3 of Chap. 3.

mechanisms into their institutional arbitration regimes. This can balance the prospective legal consequences of the parties' loss or injury to be compensated in the course of prospective liability claims by allowing the parties to first refer to internal mechanisms developed by arbitral institutions. Subsequently, in cases in which the parties appear to be dissatisfied with the way in which internal institutional bodies handled their complaints or institutional procedural order, they will still have the possibility of bringing their claim before the relevant court in the form of the liability lawsuit.

It is crucial to notice here that only the accurate combination of institutional arbitral liability and the additional mechanisms of accountability are able to respond to the societal dimension of institutional operation. In other words, the understanding of contractual liability in isolation from the institutional accountability mechanisms strips the contractual liability of its societal context. Here, contractual liability remains solely a legal tool that, although responding to the legal, contractual aspect of institutional relationships does not have the ability to increase the confidence of all institutional arbitration actors in the arbitration process. In this view, the detachment of institutional accountability mechanisms from contractual liability weakens the societal relevance of such mechanisms. This is because the institutional accountability mechanisms without the possibility of holding institutions or institutional arbitrators liable for their negligence remain ordinary soft-law instruments that lack effective enforcement tools. The necessary interrelations between contractual liability and the internal accountability mechanisms were already explained in Chap. 3. It was stated that because of the increased legality of institutional arbitration that have had negative effects on the parties' confidence in arbitration, the most sufficient manner to respond to the contemporary problems (such as the legitimacy concerns on the side of traditional commercial arbitration users) requires a specific combination of the legal and societal means. Without such a combination neither of the institutional reforms (whether legal or undertaken within the societal function of institutional arbitration) will become effective. In this view, the contractual institutional liability clauses in the context of their societal dimension should also be understood as the ultimate enforcement mechanisms to ensure the effectiveness of institutional arbitration proceedings.

6.4.2.1 Additional Mechanisms of Accountability

It is advisable that the additional private mechanisms of accountability should take the following forms: (a) institutional supervision of the codes of professional conduct (or ethics) of arbitrators; (b) institutional codes of conduct for the members of institutional organs and employees; (c) separate codes of conduct for institutional arbitrators and the members of institutional organs and institutional employees in regulatory arbitrations; (d) effective statements of arbitrators' availability, independence and impartiality; (e) transparent procedures for the replacement of arbitrators on institutions' own motion; and finally, (f) institutional supervisory bodies.

These mechanisms can set up private standards for internal conduct in institutional arbitration. It appears, however, that the institutional mechanisms of accountability should be carefully balanced to respect the essential responsibilities of both arbitrators and members of institutional bodies in arbitration processes. This is necessary because the inappropriate institutional involvement in the conduct of arbitration may result in excessive litigation in situations in which the "oppressed" arbitrators (or other actors) will seek redress from institutions that interfered in the relationship between arbitrators and the parties. This was the case in one English arbitration, in which the CIArb was sued for requiring from the arbitrator, who had failed to provide sufficient reasoning of the arbitral award in question, to submit all future awards issued by this arbitrator to the CIArb for the necessary scrutiny.[30] Although in the case at hand the court found the institutional monitoring action appropriate, the prospective excess of institutional powers needs to be kept in mind, especially given that in all cases where the misperformance of institutional bodies or arbitrators comes into play the prospective contributory negligence of the party or parties to such misperformance should be taken into consideration as well.

6.4.2.1.1 Institutional Supervision of the Codes of Professional Conduct (or Ethics) of Arbitrators

As stated in Chap. 4, the current institutional arbitration regimes lack the efficient codes of conduct and ethics for arbitrators that would secure the arbitration ethos, as a societal value lying at the core of a relevant institutional system, and increase the confidence of the arbitration users in these systems. Even the AAA's Code of Ethics for Arbitrators in Commercial Disputes, discussed in Chap. 4, disappoints. This is not only because it does not appear to have any normative relevance due to a lack of enforcement means, but also because it refers solely to the arbitrators' adjudicatory authority—without the necessary focus on the contractual responsibilities of the AAA's arbitrators.[31] Against this background, it is proposed that arbitral institutions adopt their own codes of conduct and/or ethics for arbitrators, which should be of mandatory character. In principle, they should be drafted in line with the institutional arbitration rules (ideally forming the part of these rules) and with internal institutional policies. Arbitrators will then be obliged to accept the standards set forth in such codes before commencing arbitrations, preferably at the level of their appointment when disclosing their potential conflicts of interests and signing the declaration of independence, impartiality, and availability.

The distinctive character of the institutional codes of conduct/ethics, as well as the introduction of such codes to the institutional arbitration rules, will not only increase the arbitration ethos within particular institutional systems, but will also

---

[30] See Unreported English case: *Chartered Institute of Arbitrators Ex Parte Armstrong, R v. [1997] EWHC Admin 561* 1997 in Franck 2000, 55–56.

[31] Sect. 4.3.2.2 of Chap. 4.

create additional formal incentive for arbitrators to comply with the provisions of the codes under the "threat" of contractual liability. In other words, if the codes become part of formal institutional procedures, the normative authority of the codes stemming from institutional structure will secure their enforcement. This could be achieved, for example, through the provisions that (as in the case of the CAM's Code of Ethics) connect the arbitrator's performance and the compliance with the code with the removal of an arbitrator by an institution. Then, arbitral institutions could also include provisions in the codes that—in cases of an arbitrator's breach of his or her duties in the course of arbitration that result in the removal of an arbitrator—arbitral institutions should not assume liability for the negligent acts or omission of arbitrators as a result of the institutional negligent supervision of the arbitrator's conduct.

Clearly, the drafters of the codes should further specify the catalogue of acts to which the provisions of the codes would have application. It could involve both the obligations falling within the adjudicatory functions as well as the obligations corresponding to the contractual status of institutional arbitrators. The former could be exemplified by those obligations that relate to the rendering of the award by arbitrators or the obligation to ensure due process in arbitration proceedings. The latter group could involve the obligations to maintain trade secrets and confidential information about the parties and not to disclose the information acquired prior to the commencement of the arbitration proceedings. In this sense, when the codes of conduct and/or ethics also refer to contractual obligations of arbitrators in isolation from their adjudicatory function, such provisions of the codes will also serve as the provisions of the institutional arbitration contracts. This could encompass either the individual contracts between each party and each arbitrator prior to the commencement of the proceedings or the individual contracts between the arbitral institution and each party after the conferment of the adjudicatory powers on arbitrators). As such, the parties will be able to refer to the standards established by the relevant codes in their contractual arrangements, which, in turn, will link the provisions of the codes with the contractual liability clauses.

Institutional codes of conduct or ethics should also reflect on the distinctive features of institutional arbitral regimes (such as the mechanism of scrutinizing the awards in the ICC arbitration system), while not discounting the international aspect of the arbitrators' profession. This means both that the codes cannot be unnecessarily confusing and that certain uniformity is needed due to the participation of international arbitrators in various institutional arbitration systems, in which case the divergence of standards of conduct could affect the quality of the work of international arbitrators. Hence, the uniformity regarding the content of the codes should mostly concern standards for the independence and impartiality of arbitrators and the linkages between the arbitrators' ethos and the contractual aspect of the authority of institutional arbitrators. As already stated, the AAA's Code of Ethics puts emphasis solely on the adjudicatory aspect of arbitrators' performance in the view of the "public" responsibility of arbitrators for their prospective misconduct. While such an approach is certainly right, it is insufficient from the institutional, contractual perspective. Once institutions stress the importance for arbitrators to comply mainly with the provisions of the contracts with the parties, it will complement the consistent understanding by all arbitration actors of the role of institutional arbitrators in the arbitration process. Moreover, it will constitute an additional procedural safeguard for the parties to be used in cases of the arbitrators' non-compliance with their contractual duties, especially in view of the possible liability of arbitral institutions for such acts. In this sense, the codes of conduct will interact with the "threat" of contractual liability (in its societal dimension), which, in turn, will serve as an ultimate enforcement means of such codes.

6.4.2.1.2 Institutional Codes of Conduct for the Members of Institutional Organs and Institutional Employees

Furthermore, it seems crucial that arbitral institutions implement the codes of conduct or ethics for the members of institutional organs and the employees of arbitral institutions such as case managers. Today, the institutional oversight of the performance of the members of the organizational staff involves mostly the stipulation of their behaviour in institutional internal rules of procedure in view of the general obligation of confidentiality in arbitration.[32] At the same time, there are no guidelines for the members of institutional bodies nor for the case managers concerning conduct in the course of the arbitration proceedings and outside these proceedings.

The situation appears even more paradoxical when taking into account that the parties often do not know much either about who the case managers are, or about their qualifications and competences. This is not only because the case managers remain anonymous until the arbitration commences but also because most arbitral institutions do not publish any information regarding the specific qualifications of their individual employees. A similar observation is relevant with regard to the members of institutional bodies that issue decisions on a number of sensitive topics such as the challenges to arbitrators, replacement of arbitrators, and scrutiny of the awards, just to mention a few. The fact that the members of institutional bodies remain largely unknown to the public begs the question on the side of the parties of who in fact handles their arbitration case? In addition, it is not necessarily straightforward for the parties as to who may accept their complaints or requests for clarifications, and it is assumed that all discussions of this sort will need to be directed towards the counsel responsible for the management of an individual arbitration case.

It is therefore recommended that arbitral institutions devise separate codes of conduct and/or ethics for the members of institutional bodies and case managers

[32] This further concerns mostly the clarification of the competences of institutional organs vis-à-vis other institutional arbitration actors. This means that internal institutional regulations (whether in a form of institutional codes or statutes) do not expressly address the standards of behaviour of the members of institutional organs, but rather create a vague framework for the performance of the members of such organs.

in which they clarify the hierarchy in institutional decision-making and the possible consequences of the poor performance of the members of institutional bodies and case managers. For example, the codes of conduct and/or ethics of institutional bodies and employees should also include the provisions on the possible replacement of a person dealing with a case with another institutional member or employee. At the same time, arbitral institutions should consider revealing more information concerning their case managers and members of institutional bodies, possibly by posting their short bios on institutional websites containing their professional background and qualifications in the field of arbitration. In fact, the increased transparency regarding the identity of the case managers may increase the confidence of the parties in arbitration proceedings simply because the parties will feel the comfort that they can map the involvement of different actors in their case that, in turn, may allow them to be able to feel heard by a responsible professional when anything goes wrong in the course of arbitration. This can even minimize the risk of contractual liability of arbitral institutions. Such solutions will yet again build up the societal dimension of contractual liability.

6.4.2.1.3 Separate Codes of Conduct for Institutional Arbitrators and the Members of the Institutional Organs and Institutional Employees in Regulatory Arbitrations

Finally, arbitral institutions should adopt separate codes of conduct for both institutional arbitrators and the members of institutional organs that will refer separately to regulatory arbitrations. These codes could adopt more restrictive standards of performance. The performance of arbitration actors in these democratically sensitive arbitrations could also be strengthened by drafting additional due process procedures that would cover regulatory arbitration (e.g. the already existent AAA's Consumer Due Process Protocol[33]).

6.4.2.1.4 Statements of Arbitrators' Availability, Independence and Impartiality

In view of the societal dimension of contractual liability, it is also necessary that arbitral institutions adopt efficient statements of arbitrators' independence and impartiality, which will additionally expressly require the arbitrators-to-be to guarantee that they are *available* to provide the parties with a promptly rendered award. The possible improvement could encompass the obligatory disclosure by arbitrators of the number and complexity of pending arbitrations in which the arbitrators-to-be are involved at the moment of accepting the appointment. Arbitral institutions could already at this stage invite the parties to participate in

[33] The Protocol is available online on the AAA's website via: https://www.adr.org/aaa/ShowProperty?nodeId=/UCM/ADRSTAGE2009997&revision=latestreleased. Accessed 25 April 2016.

the process of the confirmation of individual arbitrators (especially in cases where arbitrators are appointed directly by arbitral institutions) by introducing the procedure of conference calls during which the parties and prospective arbitrators could conduct the conflict checks. When such conference calls are conducted in an efficient manner, there is little risk that they would unnecessarily prolong the selection process of arbitrators. This solution could, in principle, increase the parties' cooperation with an arbitral institution in the appointment of arbitrators. This is because the institution would be used as a proxy between an individual arbitrator and a single party to arbitration proceedings that could play the role of interviewee on behalf of each party with the prospective arbitrator (whether appointed by a party or directly by an arbitral institution).

Moreover, it is proposed that arbitral institutions already at this level make both the arbitrators' reimbursement and the amount of arbitrators' fees conditional on the timely and diligent conduct of arbitration. This will secure the arbitrators' fulfilment of their contractual duties (owed both towards the parties and institutions). A similar solution has been adopted by the ICC's arbitration regime, and it is encouraged that other arbitral institutions follow this pattern. It should be stressed here that transparency is particularly required in this regard. Therefore, arbitral institutions are encouraged to inform the parties to arbitration, when the institutional arbitration costs are fixed, whether the arbitrators' fees were decreased when individual arbitrators failed to diligently asses their availability that impacted the timely conduct of arbitration proceedings and/or the quality of the arbitral award. In a longer perspective, this solution could also contribute to a decline in the length of time in which institutional arbitration cases are resolved, and it could improve the quality of the institutional arbitration proceedings.

6.4.2.1.5 Transparent Procedures for Replacement of Arbitrators on Institutions' Own Motion

As concluded in Chap. 4, provisions on the replacement of arbitrators at the discretion of arbitral institutions were not adopted by all of the studied arbitral institutions. In this vein, it is proposed that all arbitral institutions introduce procedures for the replacement of arbitrators on institutions' own motion and to clarify the situations in which such provisions can actually be applied. It is advised that such procedures apply to cases in which institutional arbitrators disregard their contractual obligations by acting negligently or in bad faith in the course of the proceedings, in particularly as regards the timely and diligent rendering of awards.

Moreover, the decisions on the replacement of arbitrators on the institutions' own initiative could, plausibly, be made with the more active participation of the parties to the proceedings. This could take the form of conference calls involving both parties and their legal representatives where all necessary evidence is presented by case managers dealing with the arbitration in question and the parties are given the opportunity to comment on such evidence. Needless to say, the reasons of the decisions on the replacement of arbitrators should be communicated to the parties, ideally by reference to the codes of conduct and/or ethics for institutional arbitrators. This could not only increase the transparency of the arbitration proceedings but also provide guidance for the parties, while deciding on nominating particular arbitrators in their future arbitrations. It is also recommended that such procedures become the standard institutional service for which no additional fees apply. This solution could restore the confidence of the parties in the authority of arbitral institutions over individual arbitrators. It could also increase the feeling on the side of the parties that the arbitrations are handled in the most diligent manner possible and the parties are treated seriously by the administrators of their disputes.

With a view to the preceding discussion, arbitral institutions should also reconsider their current approaches to the effects of the replacement of individual arbitrators on an institution's own motion on the confirmation of these arbitrators in future arbitrations. The current practice does not prevent such arbitrators from serving in another arbitration proceeding administered by an institution that had previously found the arbitrator incapable to fulfil his or her duties on various grounds. As such, institutional decisions on the replacement of individual arbitrators do not, currently, constitute proper sanctions that could discourage arbitrators from similar poor performance in the future. This is simply because they do not imply any damage to the reputation of arbitrators. Here, arbitral institutions could incorporate more specific time limits for arbitrators that had been already replaced once within which these arbitrators could not be confirmed by an arbitral institution. These time limits could vary depending on the severity of the misperformance of individual arbitrators. For example, shorter time limits could apply to arbitrators who failed to assess their availability at the moment of their nomination, whereas longer time limits could concern arbitrators whose poor performance was a consequence of a number of irregularities that resulted in bad faith.

This proposal also seems practicable in view of its implications for the decrease of costs of institutional arbitration proceedings. If the experienced arbitrators who happen to contribute to a delay in the rendering of the arbitral awards are refused to participate in future arbitrations administered by a particular arbitral institution, at least for some period of time, a new pool of arbitrators can be developed. It is reasonable to assume that the fees of these new arbitrators will be comparably lower than the fees of well-established practitioners, who currently serve as repeat players. In order to refute the likely argument regarding the lesser experience of the new arbitrators that could affect the quality of arbitral awards, it appears reasonable to assume that the new arbitrators would be highly motivated to provide their service to the best of their capacity to prove their capability. In addition, these new arbitrators could have, in principle, more time to prove their qualifications in accordance with the institutional arbitration rules, because their agendas would presumably be less busy than the agendas of the well-established arbitrators. All these pertain to positive developments in institutional arbitration practices. It is therefore also recommended that the same solutions are applicable to the procedures concerning the replacement of arbitrators as a result of the challenges made by the parties.

6.4.2.1.6 Institutional Supervisory Bodies

Arbitral institutions should either develop new supervisory bodies within their institutional structures, or clarify the competences of the existent bodies to exercise thier controlling functions with a view to the proposals for internal mechanisms of control, as well as to the effects of the implementation of the contractual liability clauses to institutional contracts. While the first proposal may raise the criticism of excessive bureaucracy of institutional regimes, the second option seems convincing given the experience (be it occasional or sound) of certain institutional organs in liability lawsuits.

As far as internal control in the course of the proceedings is concerned, the controlling functions could be granted to a deputy or a lead counsel of each case management team already developed within arbitral institutions. This counsel, possibly renamed as a special counsel, would be responsible for additional screening of each arbitration case managed by his or her junior colleagues charged with a day-to-day management of the arbitration in question. Should any irregularities occur and/or should the party initiate the complaint regarding such irregularity, a special counsel would be required to liaise with his/her colleagues to decide if and how to start the enforcement procedure provided for in the rules incorporating the codes of conduct and/or ethics. This scenario would mostly involve the dissatisfaction of a party with the work of a legal counsel responsible for the arbitration in question and could take the form of a particular mediation process to be conducted by a special counsel. For example, if a legal counsel fails to communicate to the party the procedural order to extend the time limit for the rendering of the arbitral award by an arbitral tribunal, that party will have an opportunity to discuss the severity of such irregularity for the party in question with a special counsel. Depending on the outcome of such discussion, a special counsel will be able to apply relevant provisions included in the code of conduct for institutional employees and to decide how to enforce such provisions under the code. Eventually, a special counsel should be equipped with a procedural tool to even propose to the party that its case will be managed by another counsel from the relevant team. This should not affect the time of the arbitration proceedings inasmuch as the quasi mediation is conducted expeditiously and the enforcement means are implemented with immediate effect. This should also not impact the quality of the arbitration in question, provided that the new counsel cooperates with a special counsel in the conduct of the arbitration, which could correspond with the situation where a new arbitrator is called to hear the arbitration case as a result of the replacement procedure.

Regarding the effects of liability claims against arbitral institutions, it is required to specify the authority of the particular institutional organ (most likely general counsel, secretary general or the president of the arbitral institution, depending on their statutory competences) to scrutinize the arbitration that resulted in the liability claim, as well as to design a formal procedure for internal investigation. These supervisory institutional organs should enjoy the authority to enforce the relevant provisions of the proposed codes of conduct or ethics in front of both members of institutional organs and institutional arbitrators. The current internal practice of arbitral institutions may suggest that the internal investigations in the face of a filed liability suit will take place during the ordinary meetings of the institutional bodies (e.g. the weekly meetings of the ICC Court's Secretariat or monthly Court's sessions as in the case of the ICC). These investigations, if approached by relevant organs with due care and with a view to the transparency of such investigations, can additionally serve as a deterrent factor within institutional regimes to the extent that all members of the institutional organs and the employees will realize the consequences of poor performance of their counterparts in arbitrations that resulted in a liability claim (provided that such claims are filed on reasonable grounds).

The above-mentioned additional mechanisms of private accountability, complemented by contractual liability clauses, should increase the private authority of arbitral institutions over arbitrators and institutional members, which, in turn, could raise the private confidence in arbitration in the eyes of the arbitration users. The latter solution could be achieved simply because the internal controlling mechanisms would put the letter of the arbitration rules in action, which could result in the embodiment of such rules in front of the parties, who would be able to actively participate in the enforcement of arbitration rules by arbitral institutions. This is clearly not the case in contemporary institutional arbitration practice. In view of this, arbitral institutions are also encouraged to resign from the lists of institutional arbitrators, which do not have any practical value for effective conduct of arbitration processes given the lack of relevant institutional authority over the arbitrators enrolled into these lists and the unfamiliarity of the repeat and accidental arbitration users with those lists. In this vein, the lists of arbitrators remain a relict of early institutional regimes, with no relevance for the contemporary practice of institutional arbitration.

6.4.3 The Economic Dimension

This part of the chapter shows how the proposed model of contractual arbitral liability responds to the practical problems concerning the imperfect competition between arbitral institutions within the economic dimension of institutional arbitration. Given the assumption of this book that any reforms to institutional arbitral liability should be rooted in the self-regulatory practices of arbitral institutions, the following arguments will also interact with the market-based approach to contractual arbitral liability, as defined by Professor Rutledge.[34]

6.4.3.1 Waivers and the Dynamics of Competition

As already mentioned in the context of the societal dimension of institutional liability, the introduction of liability clauses into institutional contracts will bring institutional arbitration activity back to the dynamics of internal institutional

[34]Rutledge 2004, 160–165.

legitimacy because of the linkages between the proposed institutional liability clauses with the additional mechanisms of accountability. This unique combination will therefore contribute to the creation of additional moral and reputational sanctions for arbitrators and arbitral institutions to perform their duties with increased diligence and due care. In the ideal scenario, these particular reputational incentives may increase the competition within the arbitration market, as they will encourage both the arbitrators and arbitral institutions to supply the arbitration users with a higher quality of institutional arbitration services. In addition, the introduction of efficient and enforceable mechanisms of accountability (such as the replacement of arbitrators by arbitral institutions) could, presumably, contribute to the development of new arbitrators. These new players, offering the institutional arbitration users lower fees and less busy agendas (as compared to the well-established arbitrators), are likely to stimulate the competition between institutional arbitrators by encouraging arbitral institutions to open up to new actors given the continuous professionalization of international arbitration practices.

Most importantly, it is assumed here that the possible waivers of institutional arbitral liability—once negotiated within particular institutional regimes—may increase the dynamics of competition within the institutional arbitration market. As already noted in Sect. 6.3.5.1, the possibility of negotiations of institutional liability clauses with the parties implies the possible parallel reduction of the costs of institutional arbitration services once the parties agree on a broader contractual immunity with regard to arbitral institutions or institutional arbitrators. There are various possible scenarios for such negotiations. They could be conducted prior to the commencement of the arbitration proceedings (for example, before or in parallel to the moment of sending the request for arbitration and the answer to the request, accordingly) or at a later stage (i.e. at the moment of the confirmation of individual arbitrators by an arbitral institution). The latter scenario would allow institutions to assess the individual approaches to negotiations by arbitrators that, in turn, would further affect the negotiation strategies of arbitral institutions and the parties to the proceedings.

In view of the basic negotiation theories, and in particular in the context of integrative bargaining that focuses on interests instead of the positions of the negotiating parties, the negotiations of institutional arbitral liability could offer particular benefits to both the arbitral institutions and the parties. On the one hand, the arbitral institutions' interests in these types of negotiations should concern the institutional commercial goals to not have their liability regulated and/or determined purely under relevant domestic laws selectively applicable to their liability by domestic courts. This means, *a contrario*, that arbitral institutions will gain the opportunity to decide on the scope of their own liability and the possible limitations thereto. On the other hand, the parties will be able to address their commercial demands relating to the institutional arbitration (such as the length and cost-effectiveness of the proceedings), and participate in the determinations of the ideal scope of the liability of arbitral institutions and individual arbitrators depending on the significance of each of these demands in the arbitration in question. For example, when more contractual liability is decided as the outcome of the negotiations, this would correspond with the parties' choices of having their arbitration case conducted under an in-depth internal, institutional scrutiny that would affect the costs of arbitration and possibly also its length. In contrast, when the parties opt for the waiver of institutional liability, they will be able to legitimately expect their arbitration to be quicker and less expensive, yet excluding the applicability of certain internal mechanisms of institutional control to increase the performance of institutional arbitration actors. These will build up their ultimate interests during negotiations. In this vein, the negotiations between the parties and arbitral institutions, in particular under the concept of integrative bargaining, could accommodate the internal mechanisms of accountability as additional bargaining tools.

6.4.3.2 Professional Insurance and Costs of Arbitration

The introduction of institutional liability to institutional regimes will certainly need to entail professional insurance for both arbitrators and arbitral institutions. Given the main assumption of this book, concerning the self-regulatory approach to institutional arbitral liability, it is proposed that all arbitral institutions adopt insurance policies applicable to the effects of the performance of the members of institutional bodies and employees of arbitral institutions. The question emerges here: who should be responsible for the insurance schemes covering individual arbitrators, arbitral institutions, or individual arbitrators themselves?

Certain arguments falling within the present discussion were already raised in the context of the discussion on the legislative changes to the Spanish Arbitration Act of 2013. Under Article 21(1) of the Spanish Arbitration Act, both arbitrators and arbitral institutions are required to adopt insurance policies or "equivalent security for the amount established in the rules".[35] This obligation is excluded only with regard to public entities and arbitration systems incorporated under governmental structures. Moreover, under Article 21(2) arbitral institutions and arbitrators may require that the parties themselves secure the fees and expenses incurred in this regard in the form of the funds. The non-payment of the amount corresponding to these funds by the parties may even result in the termination of the arbitration proceedings. The Spanish example certainly falls within the public regulation of institutional liability, where the mandatory nature of insurance policies may involve the questions of the unnecessary interference by national legislators with the private arbitration settings.[36] Given the international character of arbitrators' activity, it therefore appears necessary that arbitrators be covered by the insurance policies of the associations of which they are members (i.e. bar associations), and that the

[35]Spanish Act 11/2011, of May 20, Reforming Act 60/2003, of December 23, on Arbitration, and Regulating Institutional Arbitration within the Public Administration with further amendments; with the translation provided by Ministerio de Justicia Secretaría General Técnica.

[36]María Pilar Perales Viscasillas, 8 January 2014. "Liability Insurance in Arbitration: The Emerging Spanish Market and the Impact of Mandatory Insurance Regimes." http://kluwerarbitrationblog.com/2014/01/08/liability-insurance-in-arbitration-the-emerging-spanish-market-and-the-impact-of-mandatory-insurance-regimes/. Accessed 25 April 2016.

institution only controls whether the arbitrator to be appointed within a particular institutional regime is covered by the necessary insurance scheme. Such solution may contribute further to the increase of competition between arbitral institutions and individual arbitrators. This is because the negotiations of the waivers of the institutional arbitral liability will need to reflect on different insurance coverage of individual arbitrators that will serve as an additional variable for the determinations of the costs of institutional arbitrations in the course of such negotiations.

Moreover, it is likely that the costs of insurance policies will interact with the possible indemnification clauses to be negotiated by the parties and arbitral institutions. Assuming the divergent insurance coverage of individual arbitrators, arbitral institutions will be equipped with further negotiation tools. By way of illustration, this could concern the exclusion of liability for certain institutional acts or the acts of the arbitrators closely related to institutional performance (such as the scrutiny of arbitral awards under the institutional arbitration rules that provide for such mechanism) when the liability insurance for individual arbitrator will not allow the institution to take the potential responsibility for arbitrator's performance. In the same vein, the financial cap on liability, the liability clauses only for certain categories of acts or omission (whether of institutions or individual arbitrators) and various indemnification clauses may serve as additional dynamics of competition between arbitral institutions (and between individual arbitrators).

In addition, bearing in mind that the liability clauses and insurance policies will influence the quality of arbitration services, institutions will likely increase the quality signalling within the institutional arbitration market. By assuming institutional liability as a standard liability clause and by incorporating additional mechanisms of accountability into institutional systems, arbitral institutions will increase the parties' awareness of the particularities of each institutional arbitration regime and their interplay with the performance of individual institutional arbitration actors. The fact that the parties may become more attentive to these particularities should also improve competition in the international arbitration market.

6.4.3.3 On Risks, Risk Mitigation Techniques, and Incentives

In view of the preceding analysis, the real risk of institutional arbitral liability necessitates a discussion of possible risk mitigation strategies adopted by arbitral institutions, as well as on the prospective incentives for arbitral institutions to assume contractual liability. The extent to which arbitral institutions undertake to rely on the proposed model of liability, or to assume liability in any other alternative manner, will depend on the development by each individual arbitral institution of a satisfactory equilibrium between the real risks associated with the liability suits and the private incentives to actually assume their own liability in the institutional arbitration contracts. Correspondingly, the arbitration users may also face certain commercial risks relating to the proposed working of the institutional liability clause. The following discussion will address both issues in turn.

6.4.3.3.1 Arbitral Institutions

The major risks related to plausible liability claims against arbitral institutions concern the increased costs to be borne by institutions due to the implementation of insurance policies and/or due to the prospective need to increase human resources and hire new staff for the sake of in-depth supervision over arbitration proceedings. Moreover, the increased costs will also most likely result from the prospective monetary damages to be paid to the party or parties if the institution is held liable for negligence. Additionally, institutions may be concerned with the intensification of the legal proceedings involving the questions of the proper conduct in arbitrations that would result in the excessive need for testimony of legal representatives of arbitral institutions in the courts of law. The second type of risk seems to be real even if institutions do not implement reforms concerning their own liability because even under contemporary limitation of liability clauses parties continue to sue arbitral institutions. To this extent, the following analysis will focus solely on the monetary risk associated with liability claims. Let us now analyse the prospective institutional strategy to make such risk less severe.

6.4.3.3.1.1 Risk Mitigation

The first step for effective risk management techniques requires the acceptance by arbitral institutions themselves of the fact that the current limitation of liability clauses does not, in fact, decrease the possibility of holding arbitral institutions liable in the courts of law. This is because of the ineffectiveness of these clauses in some jurisdictions (including, for example, France) and the lack of a uniform approach by various domestic courts to the issue in question.

The second step should entail the development by arbitral institutions of the risk mitigation units within the internal, institutional structures. These units will become responsible for the supervision of the conduct in the arbitration proceedings, disciplinary and remedial actions (provided under the codes of conduct), as well as the negotiation strategies to be applied by legal counsel charged with negotiating the liability clauses with the arbitration users (when applicable, that is, excluding the case of regulatory arbitrations). This would require additional (managerial and legal) skills from the members of risk mitigation units. As already noted, the new obligations in relation to risk mitigation could be assumed by deputy or lead legal counsel that already work within different national teams of the institutional legal staff and, as such, the excessive bureaucratization of arbitral institutions would not need to take place at all. In view of this, the administrative costs of institutional arbitrations would not increase directly because of development of risk mitigation units.

Furthermore, one of the possible ways of optimizing the liability risk should definitely involve the already-mentioned implementation of the codes of professional conduct in arbitrations, to be effective with regard to the members of institutional organs, employees, and individual institutional arbitrators. Such codes should include different disciplinary actions to be undertaken by arbitral institutions once the party contacts the institution to report the prospective misconduct or once the institution itself notices the misconduct of a member of institutional body, its employee or an institutional arbitrator. Additionally, the already-mentioned introduction into institutional arbitration rules of the mechanisms providing for the replacement of arbitrators on institution's own motion as a standard rule could also be part of the risk management with regard to the potential liability of arbitral institution as an effect of negligent supervision over the conduct of arbitrators. That is, the possibility of the replacement by an institution of an arbitrator who conducts the arbitration in an improper manner, possibly violating institutional rules, would diminish the institutional responsibility for the prospective effects of the misconduct of such an arbitrator already at an early stage of the arbitration proceedings.

Another potential risk management technique could involve the inclusion into institutional contracts of a financial cap on institutional arbitral liability, and/or the negotiation of indemnity clauses releasing arbitral institutions from responsibility for certain category of acts in return for a reduced costs of arbitration services. This solution could involve different variations given the possible indemnity for the individual institutional acts and the acts of institutional arbitrators, also in view of the divergent insurance schemes covering individual arbitrators.

Finally, in order to effectively mitigate the risk regarding institutional arbitral liability, arbitral institutions should carefully analyse the suitability of different professional liability insurance schemes based on internal institutional policies and the specificity of institutional arbitration rules. The same remains valid with regard to the assessment of the relevance of the insurance schemes of individual arbitrators prior to the confirmation of the arbitrators in the arbitration in question. Here, the risk mitigation techniques could involve the comparison of the costs of arbitration to be borne by the parties and the difference between these costs and the costs incurred by arbitral institutions as a consequence of the insurance policies.

6.4.3.3.1.2 Incentives

Now, what would be the incentives for arbitral institutions to assume liability? Coming back to the first observation on the risk management strategies, it seems convincing that once arbitral institutions accept the negative risks stemming from the ineffectiveness of the current limitation of liability clauses, the logical consequence of such assumption would involve the institutional goals to eliminate the severity of such negative effects of liability suits through the internal, institutional arrangements. This could be achieved by the already noted financial caps on institutional liability and/or indemnification clauses covering both the acts and omission of arbitral institutions and individual arbitrators. It seems unrealistic that arbitral institutions, as sophisticated market players, would continue to leave the assessment of the scope of their own liability exclusively in the hands of domestic courts, in particular in view of the possible arbitrary judgements in this regard due to differentiated domestic regulations of the issue at hand as well as divergent visions of domestic courts regarding institutional arbitral liability. This could also result in the further ineffectiveness of institutional liability clauses under certain applicable laws, which is hard to accept due to the professional nature of institutional arbitration.

The other possible incentive for arbitral institutions to regulate the scope of their own liability relates to the plausible market incentives involving the increased competition between arbitral institutions due to the negotiable character of liability clauses and the prospective divergences relating to the costs of arbitration services implied by such negotiations. Notwithstanding the progressing unification of the arbitration rules of the leading arbitral institutions, there still exist certain differences in the level of institutional supervision over the conduct in institutional arbitration among these institutions. Take, for example, the mechanism of the scrutiny of arbitral awards developed by the ICC Court that was not incorporated into the SCC or the LCIA arbitration practices. Moreover, there are certain differences in which regional arbitral institutions monitor the internal work in the course of arbitration that are not applicable to arbitration practice of the leading arbitral institutions. For example, the SCC has limited procedural competences to replace an arbitrator on its own initiative, whereas the CAM has developed its own Code of Ethics for arbitrators, whose violation by an individual arbitrator can result in the replacement of the arbitrator in question and the limitations of relying on such arbitrator in future arbitrations. These differences could be further emphasized by arbitral institutions if different institutional liability clauses are proposed to the parties and if they are combined with different internal mechanisms of accountability. Such interplay between institutional liability and internal mechanisms of accountability could be further reflected in institutional schemes of costs that would have a particular significance with regard to the self-regulatory competition between arbitral institutions within the meaning of the traditional commercial function of institutional arbitration.

Regarding the emerging public function of institutional arbitration and the increasing external legitimacy of institutional arbitration, it is also likely that the increased liability of arbitral institutions will attract the increased use of private arbitral institutions in disputes involving States or State-like entities, and in new types of regulatory arbitrations. This would be the consequence of granting arbitral institutions more competences in these kinds of arbitrations by means of legislative acts simply because arbitral institutions will be seen as more accountable actors. This will naturally increase the competition between arbitral institutions, while at the same time it will positively affect the reputational dynamics of certain institutions from the perspective of their public function (which, eventually, would also have positive effects for the parties to the regulatory institutional arbitrations).

Moreover, the possibility of redress from institutional arbitrators, at least in cases of institutional liability for negligence while supervising institutional arbitrators, should serve as additional incentive for arbitral institutions to assume their liability also for the effects of the negligent acts or omission of arbitrators as a consequence of the negligent supervision of arbitrators by arbitral institutions. Redress does not necessarily have to take a form of another liability claim in the courts of law, as arbitral institutions could possibly rely on other remedial sanctions against arbitrators, such as the reduction of the arbitrator's fees in the future arbitrations. The threat of redress may also discourage arbitrators of dubious reputation and low professional standards from acting in institutional arbitrations, which in the long-term perspective can be of benefit for the institutions for reputational reasons.

What would encourage institutional arbitrators to act in institutional arbitrations under the threat of possible institutional redress for the misconduct of an arbitrator or given the possibility of an individual liability of arbitrators for the acts of professional malpractice? It seems that some of the above-presented arguments are also valid for institutional arbitrators. The fact that contemporary institutional liability clauses exclude, to the extent possible, the liability of individual arbitrators does not mean that arbitrators are generally immune under the laws applicable to liability suits. It further implies that arbitrators should also look positively into the institutional regulations of the arbitrator's own liability in order to avoid the interference of the mandatory provisions of the applicable laws in stipulations of their professional liability. Moreover, the liability of arbitral institutions for certain acts of arbitrators should strengthen the arbitrators' comfort of unrestricted decision-making, while at the same time a risk of institutional redress should ensure that all procedural and some substantive issues in the conduct of arbitration proceedings will be observed with due care. The threat of institutional redress will be optimized when arbitrators rely on insurance schemes covering their professional conduct.

6.4.3.3.2 Arbitration Users

The following section deals with the equilibrium between the hazards of institutional arbitral liability and the potential advantages of such liability as perceived by the institutional arbitration users. The group of institutional arbitration users—referred to below—is not homogeneous, as it concerns the parties to so-called traditional commercial arbitration as well as the parties to regulatory arbitration.

6.4.3.3.2.1 Risks

Arbitration users will most likely have to bear the following risks once institutional liability has been introduced into institutional regimes: (1) the increased costs of institutional arbitration services; and (2) more lengthy arbitration proceedings due to the increased diligence in the conduct of arbitrations. Both risks might naturally result in discouraging the parties to rely on institutional arbitrations and encourage the increased use of *ad hoc* arbitrations. The below analysis of the incentives for the parties stemming from the proposed liability clauses will address these concerns.

Incentives

It seems that in the case of the incentives for arbitration users, the assessment of the balance between the risks and benefits related to the proposed reforms brings the most favourable outcomes. That being said, while considering the negative effects of the risks related to institutional liability clauses, the following incentives should be taken into account by the parties: (1) the possibility of recovering damages in liability suits; (2) the increased professional supervision in the arbitration process and the increased diligence of institutional arbitrators (potentially also increasing the efficiency of institutional arbitration proceedings); (3) the predictability of institutional arbitration processes; and finally, (4) the increased transparency of institutional arbitrations.

Naturally, some of the above incentives may not be advantageous for all institutional arbitration users. This can be the case while taking into account more transparency in institutional arbitration proceedings, which would be more desirable in regulatory arbitrations and in arbitrations involving business parties that have been recently dissatisfied with the manner in which the increasingly universalized institutional arbitration proceedings have been handled rather than in all commercial arbitrations. It seems, however, that all groups of institutional arbitration users could benefit from the increased transparency of institutional arbitration proceedings required in the context of the proposed regulations of institutional arbitral liability. The parties that have been recently criticising arbitral institutions for lack of transparency of their arbitration practices as well as the potential parties to regulatory arbitrations will be able to rely on additional, internal mechanisms of control implemented by arbitral institutions under the threat of liability. These mechanisms will certainly require arbitral institutions to adopt more transparent practices (such as the involvement of the parties themselves in the discussions leading to the decision on challenges and the replacement of arbitrators). In addition, the parties who prefer to rely on the current institutional solutions will be still left with the possibility to determine the ideal scope of institutional liability. Hence, such parties would be able to opt out from the standard liability clauses and agree on less liability for institutional arbitration actors that would presumably lead also to the opting out of the provisions on internal mechanisms of control in the course of arbitration proceedings. At the same time, this would allow these parties to rely on less costly arbitration services. At the end of the day, the parties who wish to have more transparency in their proceedings (resulting in more liability for institutional arbitration actors) will pay more arbitration costs and will, most likely, face slightly increased length of their proceedings. However, these factors will be overridden by the possibility of the parties to rely on internal control mechanisms and to eventually sue arbitral institutions in the case of their misconduct for clearly predetermined acts or omission under the institutional arbitration contracts. In turn, the parties who wish to benefit from the current status quo will be able to rely on the exclusion or limitation of liability clauses granting institutional arbitration actors contractual immunity in return for less arbitration costs (probably corresponding to the current institutional schedules of costs). All in all, the parties will have options to choose from.

6.4.4 Functions of Liability in the Proposed Model

Institutional arbitral liability in the proposed model has two main functions: the compensatory function and the preventive (deterrence) function. The compensatory function means that the parties are equipped with the possibility to be awarded damages for the poor performance of institutional arbitration actors that caused the parties' financial loss. This function has an additional dimension in the context of the regulatory arbitrations, as it increases the public accountability of institutional regimes by equipping the parties with additional procedural safeguards in the arbitration process (i.e. the internal control mechanisms in first place and the eventual court proceedings following the liability claim).

It should be emphasized here that the introduction of institutional liability clauses, in particular, when supported by the parallel implementation of the internal mechanisms of accountability aiming at increasing the scrutiny of institutional arbitrations from the bottom, will not necessarily entail the increased public interference in the conduct of arbitration proceedings or in the modes of stipulations of private arbitration settings. This is because the proposed public assessment of institutional arbitral liability will happen at the post-arbitration stage, and will aim to determine if the actual loss of the parties has been caused by the negligent acts or omission of the members of institutional organs. Similar determinations will take place internally within institutional systems prior to the liability claim, therefore minimizing the possibility of holding arbitral institutions and individual arbitrators liable in the courts of law. In this vein, institutional arbitral liability will be able to accommodate both the commercial and public functions of arbitral institutions. On the one hand, it will increase the professional responsibility of arbitral institutions under the general principles of contract law. This will serve as a response to the commercial function of arbitral institutions. On the other hand, it will increase the observance of the rule of law in regulatory arbitrations by means of both internal mechanisms of control and the eventual public oversight of the observance of the principles of procedural justice in the institutional arbitration proceedings. This will correspond to the public function of institutional arbitration.

Moreover, the proposed institutional liability should have significant preventive functions both vis-à-vis arbitral institutions themselves and individual arbitrators. The realistic threat of institutional arbitral liability would entail increased due diligence and due care on the side of arbitral institutions, while performing their functions that will also be strengthened by internal mechanisms of control within institutional regimes once equipped with effective enforcement means. At the same time, the possibility of recovery actions initiated by arbitral institutions against recalcitrant arbitrators under the grounds of possible contributory negligence of individual arbitrators while exercising their functions would require equal due care of arbitrators in the conduct of arbitration processes.

6.5 Conclusion

Against the background of the weaknesses of the contemporary academic proposals for the liability of arbitral institutions, supported by the observations on the inadequacy of the current regulations of institutional arbitral liability presented in Chap. 4, this chapter proposed a unique model of institutional arbitral liability. The proposed model involved: (a) the *contractual* liability of arbitral institutions for their own acts or omission in the arbitration process; (b) the contractual liability of arbitral institutions for the effects of the acts or omission of institutional arbitrators *as a result of negligent institutional supervision of the efficient conduct in the arbitration process after* the conferment on arbitrators of the adjudicatory powers by an institutional organ; and (c) the individual liability of institutional arbitrators for the acts or omission *prior* to the conferment on them of the adjudicatory powers by an institutional organ and a possible professional liability of arbitrators for intentional harms and wrongdoing in the arbitration process. In addition, the major assumptions of this model implied the possible waivers from liability (except from regulatory arbitrations), elimination of the clauses providing for the institutional immunity from process, a favourable approach to the theory of individualized relationships in institutional arbitration, and the possibility for the parties and institutions to negotiate the law applicable to institutional arbitration contracts. It was shown that such a model corresponds in the best manner with all three pillars of institutional arbitral liability.

Within the legal dimension, it was demonstrated that the model addresses the particular *sui generis* status and function of arbitral institutions in and outside of arbitration processes. This also explained the liability of arbitral institutions for some acts of arbitrators within the institutional obligation to provide an efficient conduct in arbitration proceedings. The analysis of the proposed model also linked the moment of the emergence of the contractual obligations of institutional arbitration actors with the confirmation or appointment of a chairman or the umpire by an arbitral institution.

The analysis of **the societal dimension** of the proposed model focused on the interplay between the proposed institutional arbitral liability and the additional private accountability mechanisms that should be implemented by institutional regimes. These proposed mechanisms concerned the following: (a) institutional supervision of the codes of professional conduct (or ethics) of arbitrators; (b) institutional codes of conduct for the members of institutional organs and employees; (c) separate codes of conduct for institutional arbitrators and the members of institutional organs and institutional employees in regulatory arbitrations; (d) effective statements of arbitrators' availability, independence, and impartiality; (e) transparent procedures for the replacement of arbitrators on institutions' own motion; and finally, (f) institutional supervisory bodies. In view of this, the contractual institutional liability was framed as a tool of private contract law to restore the informal mechanisms of compliance within institutional regimes in the sense of the early internal legitimacy of institutional regimes. Moreover, it was claimed that the introduction of internal mechanisms of accountability, once interlinked with the institutional liability clauses, could both increase the performance of institutional arbitration actors and (as a result of the former argument) increase private confidence in the institutional arbitration process on the side of traditional arbitration users. This was mostly a consequence of the increased involvement of the parties to arbitration in the internal institutional control (for example, during the procedures for challenges and replacement of individual arbitrators) that, in turn, would make the arbitration users feel like sophisticated arbitration actors who, at the end of the day, deserve to be treated seriously by arbitral institutions.

The last part focused on **the economic dimension** of the proposed model. It explained how both the professional insurance and the possible waivers of institutional liability might diminish the imperfect competition within the institutional arbitration market. Finally, the chapter presented the risks related to the adoption of the proposed model (for arbitral institutions, arbitrators, and the parties) and explained the possible strategy concerning the management of such risks to be considered by arbitral institutions. Additionally, the private incentives have been presented in order to show the possible advantages of the proposed reform for the institutional arbitration actors.

Given the fact that liability is a legal tool, the functionality of the proposed model will be dependent on the public support of the necessary reforms. In light of this, the next chapter will deal with the desirable public regulation of institutional arbitral liability.

References

AAA. 2005. AAA's Supplementary Procedures for Consumer-Related Disputes. https://www.adr.org/aaa/ShowProperty?nodeId=/UCM/ADRSTAGE2009997&revision=latestreleased. Accessed 25 April 2016.

Chartered Institute of Arbitrators Ex Parte Armstrong, R v. [1997] EWHC Admin 561.

Franck, Susan D. 2000. The Liability of International Arbitrators: A Comparative Analysis and Proposal for Qualified Immunity. New York Law School Journal of International and Comparative Law 20, no. 1: 1–60.

Greenberg, Simon. 2013. Liability of Players in Arbitration. Presented at the VIAC/ UNCITRAL/ YAAP Joint Conference, 22 March, Vienna Economic Chamber, Stubenring 8-10, 1010 Vienna.

Guzman, Andrew T. 1999. Arbitrator Liability: Reconciling Arbitration and Mandatory Rules. Duke Law Journal 49: 1279–1334.

ICC Arbitration Rules (2012). http://www.iccwbo.org/products-and-services/arbitration-and-adr/arbitration/icc-rules-of-arbitration/. Accessed 25 April 2016.

Li, Jason Yat-Sen. 1998. Arbitral Immunity: A Profession Comes of Age. Arbitration 64, no. 51: 55.

McIlwrath, Michael. 2 April 2013. Getting to Know You. http://kluwerarbitrationblog.com/blog/2013/04/02/getting-to-know-you/. Accessed 25 April 2016.

Rasmussen, Matthew. 2002. Overextending Immunity: Arbitral Institutional Liability in the United States, England, and France. Fordham International Law Journal 26, no. 6: 1824–75.

Rutledge, Peter B. 2004. Toward a Contractual Approach to Arbitral Immunity. Georgia Law Review 39: 151–214.

Spanish Act 11/2011, of May 20, Reforming Act 60/2003, of December 23, on Arbitration, and Regulating Institutional Arbitration within the Public Administration

Those Certain Underwriters at Lloyds, London v Occidental Gems, Inc. 2007 NY Slip Op 05654 [41 AD3d 362].

Viscasillas, María Pilar Perales. 8 January 2014. Liability Insurance in Arbitration: The Emerging Spanish Market and the Impact of Mandatory Insurance Regimes. Kluwer Arbitration Blog. http://kluwerarbitrationblog.com/2014/01/08/liability-insurance-in-arbitration-the-emerging-spanish-market-and-the-impact-of-mandatory-insurance-regimes/. Accessed 25 April 2016.

Weston, Maureen. 2004. Reexamining Arbitral Immunity in an Age of Mandatory and Professional Arbitration. Minnesota Law Review 88, no. 3: 449–517.

Chapter 7
The Level and Scope of the Public Regulations on Institutional Arbitral Liability: Proposals

Contents

7.1 Introduction

In Chap. 6, an ideal model of contractual institutional liability was proposed that generated the following: (a) the standard *contractual* liability of arbitral institutions for their own acts or omission in the arbitration process; (b) the standard contractual liability of arbitral institutions for the effects of the acts or omission of institutional arbitrators *as a result of negligent institutional supervision of the efficient conduct in the arbitration process* after the conferment on arbitrators of the adjudicatory powers by an institutional organ; and (c) the standard individual liability of institutional arbitrators for the acts or omission *prior* to the conferment

B. Warwas, *The Liability of Arbitral Institutions: Legitimacy Challenges and Functional Responses*, DOI 10.1007/978-94-6265-111-1_7

on them of the adjudicatory powers by an institutional organ, and a possible professional liability of arbitrators for intentional harms and wrongdoing in the arbitration process that falls beyond the institutional supervision of the conduct of arbitration. In light of all of the above, this chapter turns to normative issues related to the possible amendment to national laws concerning the operation of arbitration, as well as to the changes to the public approaches to institutional arbitration contracts and institutional liability, as determined in domestic case law.

The main assumption underlying the preceding analyses concerns the necessary support for the private regulations of institutional arbitral liability by means of legislative reforms and the harmonization of the domestic visions of institutional arbitration rather than the unnecessary interference by public authorities with the private arbitration process. This assumption stems from the approach to institutional arbitral liability taken in this book in which the current institutional regulations of liability are initiated from the bottom, that is as self-regulatory practices of arbitral institutions instead of as a result the public regulation of the issue at hand.

The major goal of this chapter, which determines also its organization, is twofold. First, this chapter aims to identify the level of the desirable public regulations that could support the proposed institutional reforms (once implemented). Second, the possible scope of such regulations is to be determined. In this vein, the chapter is organized in two main parts. The first part examines the possible level of the public reforms given the particular *sui generis* nature of private institutional arbitration settings, the incentives for legislatures and public judges to incorporate and apply the new regulations, and finally the question of why the public reforms are necessary for the better functionality of institutional arbitration. The second part focuses exclusively on the scope of national reforms in view of the suggested harmonization of national approaches to institutional arbitral liability. The discussion in this part concerns the following actions to be undertaken by the domestic legislative authorities, as well as the judges: the public regulation of arbitrability, the recognition of the particularities of institutional arbitration contracts, the implementation of domestic provisions regulating the scope of institutional and arbitrators' liability or immunity, and the accurate judicial determination of the remedies resulting from institutional liability suits that could reflect the aforementioned unique nature of institutional arbitration settings. Finally, the chapter analyses the implications of liability suits for the finality of institutional arbitration processes.

7.2 Which Level for the Public Regulation?

The institutional regulation of the contractual liability of arbitral institutions will require an adequate legal framework to accurately determine the prospective scope of institutional arbitral liability by domestic judges, while at the same time respecting the technicalities of institutional arbitration processes. The question remains whether the prospective legal reforms should be undertaken at international level or exclusively at domestic levels.

The determination of the level of the necessary legal framework is complex insofar as it involves the interplay between different bodies of law such as the general contract laws and private international laws, on the one hand, and the function of institutional arbitration exercised at the international level, on the other hand. For this reason, while searching for the appropriate level of the necessary reforms to facilitate the ideal model of contractual institutional liability proposed in this book, the accurate equilibrium between the following should be taken into account: (1) the differences between national contract laws and the doctrines on civil liability; (2) the particularity of the obligations stemming from institutional arbitration contracts that have not yet been recognized under most national contract laws; and (3) the difficulties of accurately assessing standards of care for institutional arbitration actors, given the fusion of different legal backgrounds of such actors in international arbitration proceedings, especially in view of the conflict of laws provisions to be determined by domestic courts.[1] This means that, although institutional arbitral liability would ordinarily fall within the single authority of national contract law—which would suggest the national regulations of the issue at hand—it appears that the fact that institutional liability generates the questions of procedural and substantive obligations of international arbitration actors requires the necessary harmonization to be initiated at the international level.

Against this background, and keeping in mind that any public reforms should only support prior institutional arbitration settings, it is suggested that the proposed reforms are initiated by the United Nations Commission on International Trade Law (UNCITRAL) and take the form of specific provisions incorporated in the UNCITRAL Model Law on International Commercial Arbitration of 1985 with further amendments (UNCITRAL Model Law). The amendments to the UNCITRAL Model Law should involve an express reference to the institutional and arbitrators' contracts in both institutional and *ad hoc* arbitrations, together with the necessary explanation of the essential terms of such contracts. Moreover, the above-mentioned proposals should be supported by additional changes to the UNCITRAL Arbitration Rules in the areas of institutional and arbitrators' liability. Currently, the provision of Article 16 of UNCITRAL Arbitration Rules, as revised in 2010, provides for the exclusion of liability of the arbitrators, appointing authority and any person appointed by an arbitral tribunal to the extent permissible under applicable law, save for intentional wrongdoing.[2] Such a widely drafted clause again seems insufficient given its vague character and the dependency on the effectiveness of the private regulations of liability on applicable national laws.

Considering that the UNCITRAL Model Law is directed towards States, it seems convincing that this could be a potential, yet non-binding instrument to facilitate the necessary reforms in national arbitration laws. These reforms could

[1] Cf. McIlwrath and Alvarez 2012.

[2] The United Nations Commission on International Trade, The UNCITRAL Arbitration Rules as Revised in 2010, New York 2011. The English version of the Rules is available via the UNCITRAL's website. http://www.uncitral.org/pdf/english/texts/arbitration/arb-rules-revised/arb-rules-revised-2010-e.pdf. Accessed 25 April 2016.

have effects on the more coherent treatment of liability clauses in international arbitration contracts by relevant domestic authorities. This is justifiable given the explanation of the objectives of the UNCITRAL Model Law involving the "desired harmonization and improvement of national laws" in the area of international arbitration.[3]

7.2.1 Public Incentives to Support Institutional Arbitral Liability

There are certain public incentives that domestic authorities should take into account while considering the suggested support to be granted to institutional arbitration contracts containing the reformed institutional liability clauses. In this vein, the following sections address the public incentives within the triad of the institutional arbitration functions, which is within the legal, societal, and the economic dimensions of arbitral institutions.

7.2.1.1 The *Sui Generis* Nature of Institutional Arbitration and the Legal Dimension

First, it appears recommendable for States to eliminate the current confusion as to the status, function, and scope of contractual obligations of arbitral institutions in *international* arbitration processes. This could be achieved by the recognition of the institutional arbitration contracts as *sui generis* contracts together with the specific nature of the provisions on liability contained in these contracts. The recognition of the *sui generis* character of institutional arbitration settings should accommodate dual commercial *and* public institutional functions. This could be achieved, inter alia, through the application of the contract law remedies that actually correspond to the particularity of institutional arbitration contracts, once the institution is actually held liable for negligence.[4] The discussion on the harmonization of remedies resulting from liability suits follows in Sect. 7.3.4.

States should be encouraged to implement the institutional reforms given their international obligations and commitments to recognize and foster international arbitration arising from international legal instruments such as the New York Convention. It is advisable for State authorities (i.e. legislatures or judicial authorities) to no longer adopt their local visions of arbitration to international arbitration contracts. This postulate remains valid also with regard to the discussion on

[3]See the United Nations Commission on International Trade, The UNCITRAL Model Law on International Commercial Arbitration of 1985 with Amendments as Adopted in 2006. The English version of the Model Law is available via the UNCITRAL's website. http://www.uncitral.org/pdf/english/texts/arbitration/ml-arb/07-86998_Ebook.pdf. Accessed 25 April 2016.

[4]Onyema 2010, 167.

institutional arbitral liability, especially because such liability cannot be accommodated through any current provisions of general contract laws. In addition, the new approach to the issue at hand requires emphasis to be made on the particularities of international institutional arbitration settings that the domestic laws should support, not the other way around.

Finally, it is convincing that domestic judges work out a consistent approach to institutional arbitration contracts (and liability) given the public policy concerns related to the institutional involvement in arbitrations concerning the matters of public interest (regulatory arbitrations). This could be achieved with a view to the necessary integrity of institutional arbitration (as understood from the bottom-up, internal legitimacy), yet with a view to a desirable level of accountability of institutional arbitral regimes to the public (within the parameters of the external legitimacy of arbitral institutions). These public policy concerns related to the selected institutional arbitration processes (i.e. in regulatory arbitrations) should serve as a public incentive to play a part in institutional liability claims and to further compensate the parties that suffered damage for institutional errors. These concerns involve: (1) the lack of effective procedural safeguards in institutional arbitration proceedings, and (2) the limited right to appeal that could eliminate the prospective misconduct in the management of arbitration cases in the second instance of the arbitration proceedings.

As regards the possible hesitation of domestic authorities to harmonize the laws and/or the domestic visions regarding institutional liability clauses in jurisdictions that provide for almost absolute immunity for institutional arbitration actors, such authorities should bear in mind the argument that even judicial immunity is not unlimited and there are some exceptions to such immunity.[5] Moreover, there are evident differences between the roles of arbitration actors and judges in the courts of law, which should call for different regimes of responsibility to respond to the uniqueness of the professional functions of these actors.[6]

7.2.1.2 The Private Confidence in Arbitration and the Societal Dimension

The major incentive for public authorities to support the proposed regulations on institutional liability within the societal dimension of institutional functions should be the interest of the States in fostering the functionality of arbitration. As already noted in Chap. 3, the continuous recognition of the internal legitimacy of institutional arbitration regimes by public, legal authorities is a *sine-qua-non* condition for the continuous development of arbitration. As such, both national legislators and domestic judges should further facilitate the internal developments of institutional arbitration (also concerning the proposed private reforms of institutional

[5]Cf. *Kalb v. Luce 291 N.W. 841, 234, WISC 509* where it was determined that an inferior judge may incur liability for malicious or corrupt acts.

[6]Cf. Rogers 2005, Rogers 2014.

arbitral liability). This is mostly because such support would further connect with the growth of arbitration that, in turn, has an impact on the advancement of national economies. This should also serve as an argument for the necessary public support for institutional arbitral liability, in a manner designed internally by private actors. In this vein, the reforms proposed in this book will be able to reflect on the private objectives of the arbitration users and institutional arbitration actors in the field of liability, with the support of public actors, rather than responding only to the public rationale currently standing behind the institutional arbitral liability regulations.

To illustrate the interplay between the public regulation of arbitration and the societal dimension of arbitration, let us consider the changing understanding of private arbitration settings by the US Supreme Court under the FAA. Some commentators noticed that the US Supreme Court has expressed an erred interpretation of the essential aims of the early American arbitration community, as well as of the legal framework that regulates arbitration in the US today.[7] This can be exemplified by the continuous support of the enforceability of arbitration agreements in employment and consumer arbitrations. As already explained in Chap. 2, the US Supreme Court has confirmed the arbitrability of disputes that were never of particular interest to the early arbitration society in the US. The public support of arbitration in the US has therefore progressed against the goals of early arbitration users. This excessive interpretation of early arbitration goals proves the risks of public interpretations of private arbitration values in a manner contrary to the ideas of arbitration shared by early arbitration users. This practice should no longer be repeated while enforcing provisions on liability contained in institutional arbitration contracts by diminishing the contractual rights of the parties in view of the doctrine on arbitral immunity.

7.2.1.3 Economic Efficiency and the Economic Dimension

One of the main reasons for public actors to support institutional arbitral liability relates to the economic efficiency of arbitration. This argument has dual implications. First, it concerns the mechanisms of further outsourcing new types of disputes to arbitration to underburden domestic courts, at least in the subject matters that are suited to resolution by means of institutional arbitration. Assuming the increasing external legitimacy of this form of dispute resolution as identified in Chap. 3, national legislators—encouraged by the increased accountability of institutional arbitration that the proposed institutional arbitral liability entails—may find further incentives to rely on institutional arbitration once the institutional arbitral liability is introduced. Second, with regard to the traditional, commercial function of institutional arbitration, it may be anticipated that the public support of institutional arbitral liability as implemented from the bottom, will further attract the use of institutional arbitration in jurisdictions that express an open-minded

---

[7]Szalai 2013.

and arbitration-friendly philosophy in this regard. This could simply increase the competition between States in the area of institutional arbitration by attracting new businesses, which could also be an advantage for the States for reputational reasons. The good reputation of a judicial system from a particular country stemming from the hospitable approach towards arbitration has long been an important factor considered by the parties while choosing their arbitration forum. If domestic courts in relevant States start interpreting and enforcing the liability clauses, negotiated by the parties and institutions, in line with their private, self-regulatory dynamics, the parties may increasingly become attracted to choose the laws of such liability-friendly jurisdictions as the laws governing their institutional contracts. This will also increase the selection of arbitral institutions from those jurisdictions by the parties already at the stages of drafting institutional arbitration agreements.

In fact, it is very likely that domestic authorities (such as legislators and courts) will take a favourable approach to institutional arbitral liability if we take into account that the proposed model of institutional liability prevents the parties from excluding their liability for any of their essential contractual obligations. This "public compliance" with institutional liability, in a scope agreed on or negotiated by the parties, from this perspective, could make these liability-friendly countries default places of institutional arbitrations if the parties are satisfied with the judicial support over limitation of liability clauses taken within the territory of these countries. This could have economic significance for the States, as the conduct of arbitrations within a given territory usually attracts substantive funds and contributes to the growth of the local economy.[8]

7.2.2 *Why Does Public Support Matter?*

The philosophical questions concerning the territorial jurisdiction of courts in liability claims together with the judicial determination and/or assessment of the law applicable to these claims were addressed in Chap. 5. Given that, the sections below will now turn to practicalities of the assessment of institutional arbitral liability by domestic judges that involve the following issues: (1) the significance of the choice of forum in institutional liability suits; (2) the risks related to the non-determination of the law applicable to institutional arbitration contracts by the parties to these contracts for the determination of the scope of liability by judges; and (3) the policy question of how to encourage domestic judges—while faced with liability claims—to apply a coherent approach to the role and status of arbitral institutions with the aid of national laws on arbitration.

[8]Cf. the economic impact of arbitration in the City of Toronto in Charles Rivers Advocates, "Arbitration in Toronto: An Economic Study." 2012. http://www.crai.com/sites/default/files/publications/Arbitration-in-Toronto-An-Economic-Study.pdf. Accessed 25 April 2016.

7.2.2.1 The Significance of the Choice of Forum

Institutional arbitral liability implies specific interplay between the choice of the forum, that is the choice of court to hear the institutional liability claim and the law governing the interpretation of the institutional arbitration contracts as determined (or not) by the parties to such contracts, on the one hand, and the law applicable to such contracts as determined by the court of the forum, on the other hand. All these have practical implications for the effectiveness of the proposed institutional liability clauses.

The choice of forum predetermines the outcome of the institutional liability claim, especially given the differentiated domestic regulation of institutional arbitration and divergent visions taken by domestic authorities (i.e. legislators and courts) to the issue of institutional arbitral liability. This means that—if the parties and arbitral institution did not determine the law governing the interpretations of their contracts at the drafting stage—the judge may refuse to enforce contractual terms on liability, once the mandatory provisions of the law of the forum (determined as law applicable) come into play. In addition, regardless of the fact whether the governing law is chosen by the parties or not, domestic courts may still selectively apply one of the general doctrines on liability to institutional contracts under the applicable laws due to the confusion regarding the legal nature of institutional arbitration contracts.

The interplay between the choice of forum, the law governing the interpretation of institutional arbitration contracts, and the law applicable to liability clauses is so complex because the court of the jurisdiction where an arbitral institution has its seat is not necessarily the default choice of the party aiming to sue arbitral institutions. There are other possible scenarios of choice of forum by a claimant. These concern: the court of the jurisdiction where arbitral institution performs its major functions (for example, the ICC Secretariat with its offices in New York and Hong Kong), or even the court of the jurisdiction when the actual damage had occurred in cases where some part of the arbitration proceedings is conducted elsewhere than in the seat of the arbitration in question. Take, for example, the situation where the seat of arbitration was determined as France, whereas the arbitration hearings take place in Hungary. These risks can be mitigated in the agreement between the party or parties and the arbitral institution on the law applicable to their contractual relations, or even by including the choice of law provisions related to institutional arbitration contracts in the arbitration rules.[9] Notwithstanding this, the public courts' assessments of these issues calls for further harmonization with a view to the necessary support of the prior contractual arrangements of the institutional arbitration actors.

---

[9]This is, however, not advisable, given the need for the promotion of the consensual character of institutional arbitrations.

7.2.2.2 Law Applicable, Governing Law, and the Scope of Institutional Liability

An analysis of all possible judicial interpretations of the proposed institutional liability clause under various laws applicable is a daunting task. In lieu of such a broad analysis, this section will set out two specific hypothetical scenarios for the assessment of institutional arbitral liability, as proposed in Chap. 6, by domestic judges. First, it will concern the situations in which parties to institutional arbitration contracts did not chose the law governing the interpretation of such contracts, in which cases a judge applies different doctrines of arbitral immunity or the traditional doctrines of contractual liability in institutional liability suits. Second, this section will consider the opposite scenario, where parties to institutional arbitration contracts determine the law governing the interpretation of their contracts and the judge respects the contractual provisions on liability previously agreed on by institutional arbitration actors with a view on: (1) the current provisions of the relevant applicable law, and (2) the reformed provisions of the relevant applicable law.

The first scenario is analogous to the contemporary determinations of institutional liability clauses by domestic courts. This naturally increases the negative effects of the application of the discrepancies between national laws and visions related to the judicial interpretations of the functions of *international* institutional arbitration in general, and of institutional arbitration contracts in particular. Imagine a situation where the choice of forum is generated by the seat of an arbitral institution. Here, the party to the ICC arbitration sues the ICC in France and the relevant French court, having jurisdiction in the liability claim in question, determines that French law is applicable to the case, though in the wording prior to any reforms possibly undertaken to support the institutional arbitral liability as proposed in this book. The most likely outcome of such a case would concern the French court enforcing the proposed institutional liability clause based on the approach taken heretofore by the French courts to allow the contractual liability of arbitral institutions in France. Conversely, if the proposed institutional liability clauses are decided upon by a US court or a UK court, it will likely be abolished by these courts based on the doctrine on arbitral immunity developed in the US and on the provisions of the UK Arbitration Act of 1996 providing for a qualified immunity of arbitral institutions for certain acts on behalf of arbitrators that are of mandatory character.

Moreover, if a party to arbitration administered by the DIA in Denmark files a liability claim against the DIA under the institutional arbitration contracts, it is plausible that the Danish courts will disrespect the significance of the contractual basis of institutional arbitral liability as proposed in this book to find institutions or institutional arbitrators liable (or not) in tort. All these examples within the scenario when the parties did not chose the law governing the interpretation of their institutional arbitration contracts demonstrate the necessity for the harmonization of domestic laws and visions regarding institutional arbitral liability clauses to strengthen their enforceability.

At the same time, the risks regarding the failure of the parties to determine the law governing the interpretation of their contracts, as shown above, pertain to the legal uncertainty emerging from the possible divergent outcomes of the institutional liability claims as determined by domestic courts. The latter argument should serve as an incentive for the parties to institutional arbitration contracts to choose the law governing such contracts and to draft institutional liability clauses in close connection with the relevant provisions of the governing laws. This could eliminate or at least reduce the uncertainty stemming from the application of unfavourable laws to liability disputes. This would also imply the cautious negotiation by the parties of the clauses regarding the scope of damages or indemnification clauses, and/or the accurate exclusion by the parties of some type of damages (as permissible under the governing law)[10] in institutional arbitration contracts. Additionally, it is suggested that the national laws incorporate basic provisions related to the particularity of institutional arbitration contracts to stress the *sui generis* nature of such contracts.

The second scenario has two variants. In the first variant, the parties to institutional contracts determine the law governing their interpretations; however, the law applicable to the liability claim continues to provide for the domestic protection of institutional arbitration actors. In the hypothetical scenario, the company incorporated in France, being a party to LCIA arbitration, files a liability claim against the LCIA under English law governing its contract with the LCIA. Although arbitral institutions in France are subject, in principle, to contractual liability under the proposed model, the English court determines that the mandatory provisions of English law exclude the liability of the LCIA for the negligent act in question, such as the selection of a recalcitrant arbitrator.

In the second variant of the present scenario, the English court would ideally determine that English law following its reform complies with the international understanding of the functions of arbitral institutions by respecting the prior contractual arrangements made by the party in question and the LCIA and proceed with the relevant determinations. Such an assessment, most likely, would involve the ordinary determination by the English court of the degree of institutional or arbitrator's negligence while performing institutional contracts (in the context of the concepts of wilful misconduct and gross negligence), and of the possible effects of the breach of such contracts for the remedies available to the parties that suffered damage, under the contractual terms and the provisions of the governing law chosen by the parties. It is advisable that the assessment of negligence as well as of the degree of causation accommodates the particularities of institutional arbitration contracts that should be regarded as specific *sui generis* contracts falling outside the traditional types of contracts. The English court in question should also take into account the exhaustion by the party at hand, or not, of the procedural safeguards available to such party in the course of arbitration proceedings under

[10]Some national laws will, for example, respect the indirect exclusion of consequential damages in institutional arbitration contracts once clauses on damages are drafted in line with the legal provisions regulating damages under national civil codes. This could be the case with English law, while under French law the judges would compare the contractual terms with the category of possible exclusions provided for exclusively in the French Civil Code.

the additional mechanisms of accountability developed by the LCIA before determining the type of remedies to be granted to the party. It should be evident that the second scenario providing for the carefully chosen law governing the interpretation of institutional arbitration contracts—being in line with the laws applicable to such contract—offers more certainty as to the outcome of liability lawsuits than the first scenario. Scenarios such as these should be therefore supported by the aforementioned proposed reforms to national arbitration laws and visions of institutional arbitral liability. Let us now briefly analyse the rationale standing behind the proposed reforms in this regard.

7.2.2.3 Why Public Support? The Policy Arguments

This part addresses the policy arguments concerning the reasons why public authorities should actually respect the particularities of institutional arbitration contracts and clauses on liability contained therein. In brief, the major objective to be taken into account by public actors is to actually connect the issue of institutional arbitral liability with the calls for greater public accountability of institutional arbitration, while at the same time respecting the contractual nature of institutional arbitration settings. The below discussion turns here to normative, theoretical arguments regarding the public support of the institutional liability by addressing Professor Gaillard's philosophical postulates provided within his analysis of the third representation of international arbitration.

In view of this, it is recommended that the national authorities recognize the philosophy that the legitimacy and validity, not only of arbitral awards but also of *certain facets* of the functions of institutional arbitration, derives from the international consensus of sovereign States taken collectively (the positivist model of third representation[11]). Such a transnational vision of the functions of institutional arbitration should accommodate both the emerging dual functions of arbitral institutions, as explained in Chap. 2, and the private regulatory powers of arbitral institutions to stipulate international contractual settings. Both variables pertaining to institutional functions should be understood in a more general context, namely, in a sense that they are exercised on behalf of the international arbitration community with the open support of the States that undertook certain responsibilities in the field of arbitration under the New York Convention. Once the national authorities respect this assumption, it could serve as an additional incentive for different national legal systems to enforce the contractual terms on liability even in jurisdictions that provide for contractual immunity in astounding cases involving the violation by arbitral institution of its own rules. This seems especially convincing taking into account the increasing external legitimacy of institutional arbitration and the role of this form of legitimacy on the development of new forms of (institutional) arbitration, particularly in the US.

---

[11]Gaillard 2010, 271–281. See Sect. 3.2.2.3 of Chap. 3.

The aforementioned policy arguments, however, may not be persuasive for the legislators or judges that treat the immunity doctrine as the functional argument to protect the integrity of arbitration processes. As already stated, even judicial immunity is not absolute, and, in any event, public regulations of responsibility in institutional arbitration should correspond at least to the increased prerogatives granted to institutions in the emerging forms of regulatory institutional arbitrations that necessitated certain public oversight over the performance of institutional arbitration actors. In other words, a reverse approach to the integrity of arbitration proceedings needs to be worked out by public actors. Instead of using the arbitral immunity as an argument supporting the integrity of arbitration, public actors should perceive institutional arbitral liability as the condition for securing the integrity of the arbitration. In this vein, institutional arbitral liability, together with the additional private mechanisms of accountability to be implemented by arbitral institutions with effective enforcement means, could guarantee the integrity of the arbitration processes at the international level. This would be so because the uniform public regime of institutional arbitral liability, reflecting the *sui generis* nature of institutional contracts, would decrease the legal uncertainty concerning the issues at hand that currently largely undermine the institutional activity due to the possibility of the frivolous liability claims filed by the parties against international arbitral institutions. The few American cases that at least provide for the possible vicarious liability of arbitral institutions bespeak the plausible reconsideration of the institutional functions in the arbitration processes even in the US.[12] A better explanation of institutional functions and status in the arbitration processes—even if not automatically determining the judicial understanding of the basis of institutional arbitration processes—could be contained in the increasing publications on international arbitration such as the guides for judges on the practical aspect of international arbitration processes.[13]

Additionally, regarding the commercial function of institutional arbitration, it seems necessary that the national authorities duly recognize the contractual aspect of institutional arbitration settings. This would imply the necessary reforms in the legal provisions regarding the immunity from process that protect the members of arbitral institutions and institutional arbitrators. Such reforms would necessitate changes to the legislative solutions that prevent the parties to arbitration contracts from initiating liability claims in the courts of law by imposing on them the prospective financial consequences related to "frivolous" liability claims. This is the case with the American legislation that provides for limited possibilities for the parties to exercise their procedural rights to seek redress for prospective breaches of institutional contracts or for the contractual negligence of institutional arbitration actors.[14]

[12]Sect. 5.2.1.2.5 of Chap. 5.

[13]Strong 2012.

[14]Sect. 5.2.1.2.2 of Chap. 5.

Finally, if a similar vision on institutional arbitration contracts is adopted by different national systems, the problems related to the choice of law and the choice of forum could be minimized. This could be an additional argument for different legal systems to actually protect the integrity of international institutional arbitration.

7.3 The Scope of National Reforms

As already mentioned above, institutional reforms should entail the necessary public support involving, inter alia, the harmonization of domestic laws regulating institutional arbitration, in support of the private regulations of liability. This could take the form of the following actions: (1) more accurate public regulations of arbitrability; (2) regulations of institutional arbitration contracts; (3) possible national provisions on immunity and/or liability of institutional arbitration actors; and (4) the accurate determination of remedies available to institutional arbitration actors.

7.3.1 Public Regulations of Arbitrability

Keeping in mind that arbitrability is a matter of domestic law, and given the involvement of domestic public policy in the context of arbitrability, at first glance it may not appear relevant for the analysis of institutional arbitral liability in international arbitrations. However, the interplay between domestic regulations of arbitrability and the prospective liability of arbitral institutions may also have implications for international institutional arbitration. This is because national legislators that grant exclusive prerogatives to arbitral institutions to administer certain categories of disputes involving public interest at the national level may at the same time require particular regulations of the scope of responsibility of the institutions for the performance of their functions. This, in turn, affects the domestic visions on the part of domestic courts of institutional arbitration in more general terms. In this vein, the legislative actions undertaken to outsource certain categories of disputes falling outside truly commercial matters to particular arbitral institutions or to institutional arbitration in general may also serve as a guidance for domestic judges when deciding the liability claims against all types of arbitral institutions. This argument would then be applicable regardless of whether domestic courts assess the scope of liability of the institutions involved in regulatory arbitrations in specific jurisdictions or of international arbitral institutions administering commercial arbitrations (arisen with regard to business parties or States) or the same institutions administering non-commercial disputes. In this line, the competences of arbitral institutions in all types of arbitration should be clearly defined by legislators, with a view to the specificity of the new forms of regulatory institutional arbitrations, as well as the traditional commercial function of private arbitral institutions.

In addition, once legislators extend the scope of arbitrability by allowing the resolution of new types of disputes by means of *institutional* arbitration, they should also implement regulations regarding institutional arbitral liability. Similar solutions were introduced by means of the recent amendments to the Spanish Arbitration Act, where the increased institutional competences in administering company-related disputes and the disputes within the public administration have been connected to regulations on liability to be supported with mandatory insurance schemes for arbitral institutions given the risks of institutional liability claims. Here, it should be stressed that national regulations of liability should only create a general framework for institutional liability rather than taking the form of mandatory provisions of domestic laws to allow self-regulation in the field of the institutional arbitral liability by institutional arbitration actors. These regulations—even if only concerning domestic institutional arbitration—would be able to gradually affect the judicial visions of the scope of responsibility of arbitral institutions in international proceedings, especially to the extent to which they refer to the contractual character of institutional arbitration settings. The emphasis on the contractual aspect of institutional arbitration also in regulatory arbitrations could broaden the public vision of institutional arbitral liability from the regulatory institutional arbitrations into traditional commercial institutional arbitrations in which the contractual facet should not entail major controversies.

7.3.2 Public Regulations of Institutional Contracts

Further to the discussion above, it seems convincing that national civil codes reflect on the *sui generis* nature of institutional arbitration contracts. Simply the mention and brief explanation of the essential contractual terms of institutional arbitration contracts in national civil codes could minimalize the current confusion as to the actual content of institutional contractual obligations. However, this proposal is challenging given the aforementioned fusion of different legal regimes in the area of institutional arbitral liability.

Given the territorial scope of international institutional arbitration, the standing point for the possible harmonization of different contract laws may be confusing. This confusion is even more apparent when taking into account the well-known hesitance of actors such as the EU (that could initiate relevant changes in front of EU Member States) to regulate legal instruments which arbitration generally incorporates. This natural public hesitance to interfere in arbitration settings as well as the cacophony of legal issues related to institutional arbitration are not sufficient arguments for public actors to refuse to recognize the unique *sui generis* nature of institutional contracts. This is because the recent EU regulations concerning ADR and ODR to be adopted in consumer disputes across the Union require relevant legislative responses, including in the field of institutional arbitral liability, which would certainly increase the public accountability of the recently adopted schemes for consumer arbitrations in Europe. The regulations of the *sui generis* nature of institutional contracts, as well as of the possible institutional liability could complement the EU legal framework of arbitration and ADR. Moreover, as already stated in the section above (Sect. 7.2), the policy actions in the field of institutional arbitration contracts could start with the necessary amendments to the UNCITRAL Model Law that could serve both as a guide and policy instrument in front of national legislators to better understand the practicalities of institutional arbitration contracts.

7.3.3 Public Regulations of the Scope of Institutional and Arbitrators' Liability

Furthermore, it is advisable that national laws on arbitration refer to the potential scope of the liability of arbitral institutions in addition to the liability or immunity of arbitrators. Current regulations cover mostly (if any) the scope of liability of arbitrators by leaving aside the institutional liability.[15] It is suggested that arbitral institutions be treated as independent yet equally important actors in arbitration proceedings, and that their liability is, to the extent possible, regulated in national laws. The possible policies on liability could again come from the UNCITRAL Model Law whose adoption into national laws should entail less complex issues than in the case of institutional arbitration contracts.

7.3.4 Remedies Available to Institutional Arbitration Actors

This part investigates if—in addition to monetary damages—other remedies available under general contract laws are also suitable to institutional arbitration settings. In many instances references are made to the analysis of the issue at hand provided by Emilia Onyema in her book on *International Commercial Arbitration and the Arbitrator's Contract*.[16] Onyema's proposals—related mostly to the contracts between the parties and arbitrators—are complemented by a discussion of the practicalities of the institutional arbitral liability clauses as proposed in this book. In this vein, the remedy of specific performance and the termination of the institutional contracts by domestic judges are scrutinized in the context of institutional arbitration settings. Furthermore, the necessity for an accurate understanding of the standards of diligence and due care of institutional arbitration actors is

[15]For the survey on liability of arbitrators see Ramón Mullerat "The Liability of Arbitrators: A Survey of Current Practice." Chicago: International Bar Association Commission on Arbitration, 2006.

[16]Onyema 2010.

addressed. Finally, the discussion turns to the complex issue of monetary damages as potentially awarded as a result of liability claims together with their possible consequences for the integrity and finality of institutional arbitration.

7.3.4.1 Remedy of Specific Performance

Given the exclusive nature of institutional arbitration contracts as well as the confidentiality of arbitration as such, it is assumed that the remedy of specific performance will only have limited practical relevance for institutional arbitration settings. Keeping in mind the administrative prerogatives of arbitral institutions based on institutional arbitration rules, it seems that arbitral institutions should be able to oversee the performance of both parties and institutional arbitrators out of any public interference. If this is not the case, it is still very unlikely that the parties will apply for a court's order for specific performance. Rather, they will not be interested in the further provision of the arbitration service by the institutional arbitrator or the arbitral institution, who failed to exercise their powers with due care, especially if there are monetary damages available to the parties under institutional arbitration contracts. Let us now analyse this assumption by looking at different hypothetical scenarios in which specific performance may be actually desirable by different institutional arbitration actors based on the selected national provisions on the issue at hand.[17]

The first hypothetical scenario concerns a situation in which a party or the parties to institutional arbitration seek for specific performance of the institutional arbitrator, when an arbitrator fails to comply with the contractual terms. This could involve the refusal by the arbitrator to conduct a hearing if requested by the party, a refusal to interpret the award, or even a refusal to eventually join an additional party who is not a signatory of an arbitration agreement to the arbitration proceedings. In the first two situations, parties would almost certainly rely on institutional safeguards (including the procedure on challenges to an arbitrator or the proposed removal of an arbitrator on institutions' own motion to be initiated by an institution) rather than upon the court's order. This is also because under the proposed model of institutional liability there is no direct contract between an arbitrator and a party to the proceedings. Moreover, as already noted above, the parties' major concern regarding the service of arbitrators relates to the adequate response by arbitrators to the parties' essential expectations as to the outcome of arbitration proceedings. If arbitrators do not meet such expectations, the interest of the parties to continue the arbitration with the recalcitrant arbitrators would be minimal. In the third situation, however, it is plausible that a party against whom the joinder has

[17] For a discussion on the remedy of specific performance in the context of the arbitrator's contract compare: Onyema 2010, 169.

been refused asks the court for the order to join the additional party to the arbitration proceedings. This is likely given that an arbitrator's decision regarding the joinder cannot be compelled by an arbitral institution. This was partially the case in the already analysed US judgement in *Gold Global Mining*.[18] Based on the Court's deliberation in *Gold Global Mining*, it can be surmised that a party's request for an order of specific performance will likely be rejected. As such, a party will be advised to file a motion to compel arbitration with regard to a prospective additional party rather than an action to compel arbitration *against* the arbitrator or the arbitral institution. The latter action, that could bear the resemblance of an order for specific performance, is not a common practice, even in the US.[19]

A second hypothetical scenario involves cases in which an arbitral institution seeks for specific performance by an institutional arbitrator. This action would have no grounds given the institutional rights to remove the arbitrator even on the institution's own motion—which is advisable under the proposed model of institutional arbitral liability—with a view to the institutional control over arbitrator's fees.

Finally, a third hypothetical scenario concerns a case in which a party or parties, or an institutional arbitrator, seek for specific performance of an arbitral institution whenever an institution disregards its contractual duties by contributing to the obstruction of the arbitration proceedings. Although theoretically possible, in practice it is hard to imagine arbitration actors requesting this remedy given the possibility of monetary damages under the proposed institutional liability model. This and the two other scenarios, however, should be addressed through the actual wording of the institutional liability clauses as negotiated by the parties to institutional arbitration contracts on a case-by-case basis in the future (should the proposed changes to arbitration rules be implemented).

In conclusion, the compensatory value of the remedy of specific performance in institutional arbitration seems limited due to the availability of other remedies under institutional arbitration contracts as further proposed in this chapter. This reasoning is also supported by the relevant public regulations of arbitration. For example, the UK Arbitration Act of 1996 does not seem to provide for the remedy of specific performance, although some commentators stress that such remedy is theoretically allowed.[20] The rationale behind such a provision is understandable due to the necessary limitation of any excessive public interference in the very private design of arbitration proceedings, which is one of the general principles underlying the UK Arbitration Act:

[18] *Global Gold Mining, LLC v. Peter M. Robinson et al.*, No. 636 United States District Court, Southern District of New York, 6 February 2008, 07 Civ. 10492 (GEL), with a commentary in Yearbook Commercial Arbitration Vol XXXIII, 1117–1125.

[19] Ibid.

[20] Schöldström 1998, 67.

> 1(b) the parties should be free to agree how their disputes are resolved, subject only to such safeguards as are necessary in the public interest;[21]

This also complies with the very private goals associated with the arbitration process. It is hard to imagine that the parties will voluntarily recourse to the public courts for the eventual stipulations in the arbitration proceedings that could result in an awkward type of "judicial arbitration".

7.3.4.2 Termination of Institutional Arbitration Contracts by Domestic Judges

Turning to the possible termination of the institutional arbitration contracts by domestic judges, it appears that this remedy will have equally little significance for the parties as the remedy of specific performance. Following the analysis provided for by Emilia Onyema, most institutional arbitration contracts will be terminated within institutional arbitration regimes in the following circumstances: (1) upon the full performance of institutional contracts by the contractors; (2) upon the mutual agreement between the parties to such contracts; (3) in cases of fundamental breaches of the institutional contracts; and (4) given the frustration of such contracts.[22] Let us consider each in turn.

In the first case, the contracts between each party and the arbitral institution are terminated upon the rendering of the award by institutional arbitrators, the payment by the parties of the arbitration fees to the institution, and the service of the award by an institution to the parties to arbitration. The contracts between each individual arbitrator and the arbitral institution are fully performed and then terminated once the payment by an institution of the arbitrators' fees to arbitrators is made, and once the arbitrators submit the arbitral award to the institution together with a detailed budget of the arbitrator's expenses. Onyema raises an important issue concerning the interplay between the possible correction or interpretation of the award and the exact moment of termination of arbitration contracts.[23] Onyema explains that the correction and interpretation of the award by arbitrators with the assistance of the arbitral institution may fall within the original institutional contracts, which does not necessitate entering into additional contracts by the institutional arbitration actors. That means that—under most institutional arbitration rules—the parties to arbitration proceedings are still entitled to request the correction or interpretation of arbitral awards, even if their contracts with the arbitral institution have been officially terminated upon the rendering of the award.

The second category of cases—cases terminated upon the mutual agreement between the parties to such contracts—involve the rendering of the awards by consent when the parties decide to settle a pending dispute. The settlement agreement

---

[21]The UK Arbitration Act 1996, Chapter 23.

[22]Onyema 2010, 174–179.

[23]Ibid.

underlies the award by consent. The institutional arbitration contracts in this category of cases will be terminated at the same instances as explained above.

The third category of situations—cases terminated in cases of fundamental breaches of the institutional contracts—concerns the cases of a removal of arbitrators upon the application by the party or on institution's own motion. This means that the contract between the arbitral institution and the institutional arbitrator will be terminated once the institution accepts the parties' motives related to the misconduct of an arbitrator or makes its own decision on the issue at hand.

The fourth scenario concerns the impossibility, illegality, or pointlessness of the continuation of arbitration with regard to the defaulting party.[24] For example, in the case of death or illness of arbitrators, lack of jurisdiction of an arbitral institution over the dispute, or the non-performance of institutional contracts binding the arbitral institution and the claimant, respectively.[25]

The above analysis shows that in most of these cases the institutional contracts will be terminated by means of private arrangements due to the private sources of authority in institutional arbitration settings. It is sufficient now to consider the legal provisions dealing with the possible termination of institutional arbitration contracts by domestic judges.

Certain provisions of the UK Arbitration Act of 1996 and of the French Code as amended on 13 January 2011 might—at first glance—suggest the possibility for the termination of institutional contracts by domestic judges. In accordance with Section 25 (2) and (3) of the UK Arbitration Act, if the parties did not reach an agreement with an arbitrator as to the consequences of his or her resignation, an arbitrator may apply to the court to either grant him or her relief from liability resulting from the resignation or to "make such order as it thinks fit with respect to his entitlement (if any) to fees or expenses or the repayment of any fees or expenses already paid".[26] Moreover, paragraph 1 of Section 24 of the Act states that the party may seek the removal of an arbitrator by a court in several exceptional circumstances concerning, inter alia, his or her breaches of the fundamental obligations owed towards the parties.[27] Additionally, Article 1456 of the French Code authorizes the parties that cannot agree on the removal of an arbitrator to apply to judge acting in support of arbitration if there is no person responsible for administering the arbitration.[28]

Now, will these provisions entitle a judge to terminate an arbitrator's contract in institutional arbitrations? Rather not. It seems that the above provisions will (if at all) have more implications for *ad hoc* arbitrations in which the parties have no procedural safeguards to rely on in regards to arbitrator's fees and the general

[24]Onyema 2010, 178–179.

[25]Ibid.

[26]The UK Arbitration Act 1996, Chapter 23, Section 25.

[27]The UK Arbitration Act 1996, Chapter 23, Section 24.

[28]Article 1456 of the French Code of Civil Procedure and also Section 17 of the Swedish Arbitration Act of 1999.

contractual performance of *ad hoc* arbitrators. This is confirmed in paragraph 2 of Section 24 of the same Act, which prevents the court from taking any action whenever "there is an arbitral or other institution or person vested by the parties with power to remove an arbitrator" and the recourse to the relevant authority of such actors has not been satisfied by the party or parties. Moreover, Article 1456 of the French Code expressly sets out an obligation for arbitral institution to remove, hence, terminate the contract with the institutional arbitrator. These provisions support the argument that, in institutional arbitration settings, it is the arbitral institution that has the final say on the termination of the contracts with the arbitrators. The reason for this is that parties have no direct bonds with arbitrators in the model of contractual institutional settings as also proposed in this book.

Lastly, it is necessary to analyse the prospective power of public judges to terminate the contracts in institutional regulatory arbitrations in the context of the mixed private-public authority of such institutional arbitration settings. This case is problematic as it concerns complex issues of the consent to arbitrations arising out of the mandatory pre-dispute arbitration clauses in regulatory contracts. These issues that call into question the voluntary submission of the parties to arbitrations could, on first analysis, justify the public termination of institutional contracts. It is, however, likely that even in these cases the courts in jurisdictions that generally allow the enforcement of such clauses (i.e. in the US) will be hesitant to terminate the institutional arbitration contracts. This is because there is a tendency among judges in some States (such as in the US) to uphold mandatory pre-dispute resolution clauses in regulatory arbitrations (i.e. consumer, employment, or labour arbitrations), a tendency which runs contrary to the rationale favouring the termination of the institutional arbitration contracts underlying mandatory arbitration proceedings.

The other situation worth analysing here relates to the cases in which the parties voluntarily accepted institutional arbitration clauses in regards to the disputes that involve matters of public interest and when such institutional arbitrations had been previously allowed by means of a legislative act. Here again, it seems unlikely that the very fact that the authority of arbitral institutions has been partially rooted in the public act will serve as a sufficient argument to undermine the significance of the parties' voluntary submission to institutional arbitration. This, in turn, will hardly justify the public interference in institutional arrangements in a form of public termination of institutional arbitration contracts.

7.3.4.3 Diligence and Due Care in Institutional Arbitration

The accurate understanding of the specific standards of diligence and due care in institutional arbitration will be required of judges who analyse the degree of negligence of institutional arbitration actors before awarding damages as a result of liability suits. Although such determinations will be made on a case-by-case basis, the common denominator for both institutional and arbitrator's proper performance is the professional character of institutional arbitration services, including the specific dual functions of arbitrators' mandates and institutional activity. Naturally, the performance of all institutional arbitration actors will need to be assessed based on the specificity of the arbitration rules of each arbitral institution whose actors are challenged in liability suits. The divergences of the interpretations of diligence and due care will then be dependent on the level of the involvement of institutional arbitration actors in arbitrations under the relevant rules.

In addition, in the case of arbitral institutions, standards of diligence and care will need to be assessed in relation to both the institutional supervisory powers over arbitrators and the interplay between the scope of institutional and arbitrators' duties in the course of the arbitration proceedings. The latter argument corresponds to the liability of arbitral institutions for some acts or omission of individual arbitrators as a consequence of the negligence supervision by arbitral institutions of arbitrator's performance.

Finally, it seems that some types of arbitrations (i.e. such as regulatory institutional arbitration) will involve even higher standards of care given the subject matter of the arbitrable disputes.[29] In these institutional arbitrations, the analysis of the standards of diligence and due care will therefore be required in view of the increased standards of fairness applicable to these institutional arbitration proceedings.

7.3.5 Damages Awarded as a Result of Institutional Liability Claims and Their Further Implications for the Integrity and Finality of the Institutional Arbitration Processes

The scope of damages awarded as a result of institutional liability claims will first need to be determined by the exact wording of the limitation of liability clauses as negotiated by the parties to institutional arbitration contracts under the law applicable to institutional contracts. Therefore, it is reiterated here that parties carefully consider the provisions of the appropriate governing law while drafting their limitation of liability clauses or while predetermining different types of damages (e.g. liquidated damages) in their institutional contracts.[30] Secondly, the amount of damages will be dependent on the eventual interpretation of the causal link between the damage claimed by a claimant in a liability suit and the prospective negligence of an arbitral institution. Here again, it is suggested that the judges pay due attention to the standards of due care and skill specific to institutional arbitration processes while analysing the degree of negligence of institutional arbitration

[29]Cf. the emphasis placed on the fairness in employment arbitration proceedings in: "National Academy of Arbitrators: Policy Statement on Employment Arbitration" 2009.

[30]The fact that the parties will be able to negotiate different variants of the institutional liability clauses also explains why the present discussion does not provide for an exhaustive analysis of all types of damages to be included (or not) in institutional arbitration contracts.

actors in light of the damage that occurred as a result of the poor performance of their contractual obligations.

Let us now discuss the scope of damages as determined in two separate liability cases involving an arbitral institution and an *ad hoc* arbitrator acting as defendants, respectively. This analysis will serve the forthcoming discussion on the effects of the awards of damages for the integrity and finality of institutional arbitration processes.

The first case concerns the French Court's decision in *Société Filature Française de Mohair c/Fédération Française des Industries Lainières et Cotonnières.* Since this case has been already explained in Sect. 5.2.1.2.1 of Chap. 5,[31] the following presentation will focus solely on the analysis of damages awarded as a result of this judgement. The *Tribunal de Grande Instance de Nanterre* in the case in question did not find a causal link between the damage claimed (that corresponded to the amount granted by the annulment award) and the negligence of the French industrial federation acting as a defendant given the possibility for the claimant to initiate another arbitration against the defendant to recover the amounts claimed.[32] The French Court, however, awarded to the claimant the amount of EUR 10,000 for the costs that the claimant had to bear under the annulment proceedings.[33]

The second case involves the judgement of the Finnish Supreme Court in *Roulas v Professor J Tepora* of 31 January 2005, in which damages against a presiding arbitrator (Professor Tepora) were awarded under the contract binding him towards the parties.[34] Although the case at hand concerns domestic *ad hoc* arbitration, it seems that the observations concerning the consequences of the Court's order granting excessive damages in the judgement in question will have a general applicability for the present discussion. In *Roulas v Professor J Tepora,* the key issue involved the non-disclosure by Professor Tepora that he had previously given expert opinion to the respondent company, which resulted in the nullification of the arbitral award by the Helsinki Court of Appeal.[35] Subsequently, the claimants recommenced arbitration and filed a claim against Professor Tepora in the District Court seeking damages (including for losses suffered and the interest on the claim).[36] Both the District Court and the Court of Appeal held that the Professor Tepora's non-disclosure entailed liability in tort, however, it was said that the breach at hand should be classified only as "slight negligence" and the claim was dismissed.[37] The Supreme Court expressed a different opinion, namely, that the

[31]Price 2012, 187–195.

[32]Ibid.

[33]Ibid.

[34]The case was reported by Emilia Onyema in: Onyema 2010, 170.

[35]Ibid.

[36]Ibid.

[37]Ibid.

breach was of a contractual nature and that the fault of the arbitrator contributed to the nullification of the award, for which the compensation should be awarded.[38] Eventually, Professor Tepora was ordered to pay to the claimants almost EUR 81,000 in damages.[39]

Both cases show that the exact amount of damages awarded to the claimant is conditional on many factors, including, but not limited to, the determination of the causality linking the negligence of a party in breach of its contractual obligations with the damage claimed by the claimant. The preceding discussion implies, however, the uncertainty as far as the question of to what extent the claimants in liability suits would be able to prove causality on a case-by-case basis. This is so given the above determination of the French court that made the causal relationship dependent on the possibility of the initiation of other arbitration against the opposing party in the arbitration underlying the liability claim in question. Some preliminary conclusions can be drawn in this regard. The French case, on the one hand, calls into question the willingness of public courts to interfere with the integrity of institutional arbitration settings by awarding excessive damages. On the other hand, however, it strengthens the private facet of institutional arbitration bonds within the societal dimension of institutional functions.

It is sufficient to notice that both claims analysed above were filed as a result of the nullity of the award obtained by a losing party to arbitration proceedings. This observation requires the analysis of the interaction between the annulment proceedings and the prospective liability claims against institutional arbitration actors in view of the integrity and finality of institutional arbitration processes.

It is generally said that: "in the event of a breach, in principle it is the award, and not the arbitrator that will be under attack".[40] The proposed concept of institutional arbitral liability seems to stand in opposition to this assumption. There are possible cases in which the liability claim may be filed irrespective of, or even before, the vacatur proceedings concerning the arbitral award. This involves the prospective liability claim against institutional arbitrators after the removal of an individual arbitrator by the institution, be it on its own motion or upon the mutual agreement by all the parties to arbitration proceedings. In view of this, the following discussion will concern these two scenarios: (1) the case in which the liability claim is filed as a result of the annulment proceedings, and (2) the situation in which the awards of damages are sought by the party irrespective of the post-arbitration proceedings concerning the recognition and/or enforceability of the arbitral awards.

The first example of the interplay between the nullity of arbitral awards and the awards of damages by judges as a result of liability claims is somewhat complex. This is so because the nullity of the award in the country of its origin does not necessarily mean that the same award may not be enforced in other jurisdiction where

---

[38]Ibid.

[39]Ibid.

[40]Onyema, citing *Fouchard, Gaillard and Goldman on International Commercial Arbitration* in: Onyema 2010, 168.

the enforcement is sought by the successful party in arbitration. Would it mean that each nullification of the arbitral award in the country of its origin or each refusal of the enforcement where the enforcement was sought results in the award of damages against institutional arbitration actors as a consequence of liability claims filed against these actors by the party that suffered injury? Not necessarily so. As seen from the above analysis of the French court's decision in *Société Filature Française de Mohair c/Fédération Française des Industries Lainières et Cotonnières*, in France the claimant will need to bear the burden of proof related to the relationship between the damage claimed as a result of the nullity of the arbitral award being a consequence of the negligence of the defendant in a liability suit. In turn, under English law it may be often irrelevant if the breach of the contract by a defendant in a liability suit was a result of fault (except in determinations concerning contracts for provision of service).[41] Moreover, the court of forum will likely have to assess the other possible means of redress available to the claimant in a liability suit under the institutional arbitration contracts. This claimant will have to prove the causality under the law applicable to the institutional arbitration contract that may be different from the law governing the arbitration under which the liability claim has been raised. That being said, the result of the court's determination of the degree of negligence of the defending institutional arbitration actor may differ from the outcomes of the vacatur proceedings or the enforcement proceedings. This conclusion should again prove the importance of the accurate and cautious determination of the law governing the interpretation of institutional contracts by the parties to such contracts.

Against this background, it is claimed that the awards in damages under the proposed model of liability do not necessarily have to bear detrimental effects on the integrity of the arbitration processes. It is recognized that ensuring the proper conduct of arbitration proceedings leading to the production of a legally enforceable award is the essential contractual obligation of both arbitral institutions and institutional arbitrators. However, the fact that the award will be annulled or refused enforcement does not necessarily entail the awards of damages against institutional arbitration actors corresponding to the amounts stemming from the annulled awards or by the awards that were refused enforcement. These determinations will have to be made on a case-by-case basis depending on the laws governing and the laws applicable to institutional arbitration contracts, as well as on the relevant terms of such contracts as negotiated by the parties to such contracts.

The second example tests the reverse effects of the liability claims on the finality of institutional arbitration processes (if any). This involves the impact of suing an individual arbitrator that had been previously removed on the pending arbitration proceedings related to the (in)effectiveness of an arbitration award issued in such "obstructed" arbitration proceedings. The question implies the prospective consequences of the removal of a recalcitrant arbitrator for the actual loss or injury

[41]Schöldström 1998, 48.

suffered by the parties to the proceedings (i.e. the financial loss, waste of time, necessity of repeating the arbitration proceedings in substantial part before the newly appointed arbitrator, etc.) or by the arbitral institution (i.e. financial and reputational losses). It seems that in both cases the parties to institutional arbitration contracts will need to assess the character of the breach by the removed arbitrator of his or her contractual obligations. Although the liability claims are not excluded in the above situations, it seems that in the case of the parties to arbitration, it will not be very plausible to sue the removed arbitrator under the institutional contractual settings, as there are no direct contracts between arbitrators and the parties in institutional arbitration under the proposed model. The parties could, however, bring a claim against a removed arbitrator in cases of serious malpractice of such an arbitrator under the codes of professional conduct of the arbitrators' association of which such an arbitrator is a member. Additionally, the parties would not be entitled to sue the arbitral institution either, especially when the arbitral institution complies with its own procedures related to the removal of an arbitrator understood within the meaning of the newly incorporated internal mechanism of accountability. Regarding the possible legal action against the removed arbitrator by an arbitral institution, it also does not seem very likely, given the possible alternative remedy available to arbitral institutions, namely the reduction by the institution of the fees of previously removed arbitrator in the future proceedings and/or the plausible exclusion of such an arbitrator from the pool of its arbitrators for a certain period of time as decided by an institution. Even though such claims are theoretically possible, they should not have further implications on the effectiveness of the arbitral awards, especially if the awards are in the meantime enforced in accordance with the relevant legal procedures for the recognition and enforcement in the places where such actions are sought.

A situation may arise when the losing party to arbitration proceedings decides to sue an institutional arbitrator or the arbitral institution *after* the rendering of the arbitration award, yet *prior to* the initiation of the vacatur proceedings. Once the institutional arbitration actor (acting as respondent in liability claim) is found in fault by the court, resulting in the award of damages against this actor, the party will automatically file a set-aside action against the arbitration award in the court of the origin of the award that may or may not result in the annulment of such an award. Although theoretically possible, it is again doubtful that the dissatisfied party will first seek redress against the arbitral institution or institutional arbitrator. The reason for this is that it will be extremely difficult for that party to prove the causal link between the prospective negligence of the party to institutional arbitration contract and the damage suffered if the award did not have a chance to pass the enforceability test in court of the country of the origin of the award. With this in mind, it seems that the liability claims and the awards of damages against institutional arbitration actors will not automatically negatively affect the finality of institutional arbitration processes.

7.4 Conclusion

The institutional regulations of liability as proposed in Chap. 6 require a response from the public authorities (that is from national legislators and domestic judges) to support the legal framework for private arbitration settings. This is because the effectiveness of institutional arbitration clauses depends on the accurate interpretation of such clauses by national judges that should be done in accordance with the adequate provisions of domestic laws specific to contractual arrangements in institutional arbitration.

Given the international operation of institutional arbitration, it is proposed that the necessary national reforms are initiated at international level, preferably by the authorities that recognize the unique nature of arbitration such as the UNCITRAL. This could be achieved by means of the amendments to the UNCITRAL Model Law that could provide for certain scope of liability of institutional arbitration actors or explain the specificity of institutional arbitration contracts in the explanatory note contained in the Model Law.

There seem to exist a number of prospective public incentives to implement the necessary reforms at national levels, which are able to address the triad of institutional functions presented in Chap. 3. Within the legal dimension, national legislators should encourage the *sui generis* nature of institutional arbitration contracts including the proposed liability clauses to increase the legal certainty when the scope of the liability of international institutional arbitration actors is assessed by domestic courts. Moreover, valid public policy concerns appear to support the private liability clauses insofar as the increased public accountability of institutional arbitration actors is taken into account in regulatory arbitrations, which the proposed liability clauses aim to increase. Within the societal dimension, public actors should understand the interplay between the private confidence in arbitration on the side of arbitration users and the further development of institutional arbitration. From the perspective of the economic functions of arbitral institutions, the public support for the proposed liability clauses can further increase the economic efficiency of the arbitration proceedings, which, in turn, may advance the development of the national economies in States that decide to support the private institutional contracts.

Regarding the scope of the proposed national reforms in support of the proposed model of institutional arbitral liability, public actors should put particular emphasis on the accurate determinations of the scope of arbitrability of institutional arbitration proceedings. Furthermore, national legislators and/or domestic judges should recognize the *sui generis* nature of the essential obligations of institutional arbitration actors. In addition, domestic courts should take appropriate view on the standards of diligence and due care in institutional arbitration proceedings, simply because such standards cannot be derived from any general provisions of contract laws due to the specificity of each institutional arbitration setting. Also, it appears that the monetary damages will play the major compensatory function for the parties to liability suits because of the limited practical significance of other remedies, theoretically applicable in the liability suits, such as the remedy of the specific performance and the termination of institutional contracts by domestic judges, given the exclusiveness of institutional arbitration proceedings. The type of monetary damages will need to be determined under the wordings of the respective institutional liability clauses as negotiated by the parties to institutional arbitration contracts under the governing laws.

In fact, the institutional liability suits resulting from the liability clauses under the proposed model do not necessarily have to entail negative implications for the integrity and finality of institutional arbitration. This is connected with the fact that the causal relationship between the damages claimed in liability suits and the negligent performance of the institutional arbitration actor will need to be proven by the claimant under the relevant governing law (and mandatory provisions of laws applicable) to institutional arbitration contracts on a case-by-case basis. The outcomes of such determinations will be further conditional on the stages at which the liability lawsuits are initiated in relation to the pending or already concluded institutional arbitration proceedings. This, in turn, may largely reduce the effects of liability claims on the prospective vacatur proceedings or on the enforcement proceedings that test the compliance of the arbitral awards with the procedural requirements of the place where the enforcement is sought.

References

Charles Rivers Associates. 2012. Arbitration in Toronto: An Economic Study. Toronto, Canada. http://www.crai.com/sites/default/files/publications/Arbitration-in-Toronto-An-Economic-Study.pdf. Accessed 25 April 2016.

Gaillard, Emmanuel. 2010. The Representations of International Arbitration. Journal of International Dispute Settlement 1, no. 2: 271–81.

Global Gold Mining, LLC v. Peter M. Robinson et al., No. 636 United States District Court, Southern District of New York, 6 February 2008, 07 Civ. 10492 (GEL). Yearbook Commercial Arbitration Vol XXXIII 29: 1117–25.

Kalb v. Luce 291 N.W. 841, 234, WISC 509.

McIlwrath, Michael, and Alvarez Henri. 2012. Common and Civil Law Approaches to Procedure: Party and Arbitrator Perspectives. In: Horacio A. Grigera Na6n and Paul E. Mason, eds. International Commercial Arbitration Practice: 21st Century Perspectives. LexisNexis, §§ 2.01-2.10.

Ministry of Justice and Civil Liberties, Republic of France, Decree No. 2011-48 of 13 January 2011 Reforming the Law Governing Arbitration.

Mullerat, Ram6n. 2006. The Liability of Arbitrators: A Survey of Current Practice. Chicago: International Bar Association Commission on Arbitration.

National Academy of Arbitrators: Policy Statement on Employment Arbitration. 2009. http://naarb.org/due_process.asp. Accessed 25 April 2016.

Onyema, Emilia. 2010. International Commercial Arbitration and the Arbitrator's Contract. Routledge.

Price, Charles. 2012. Liability of Arbitral Institutions in International Arbitration: A Comment on Soci6t6 Filature Française de Mohair C/ F6d6ration Française Des Industries Lainières et Cotonnières. In: Patrick Wautelet, Thalia Kruger, and Govert Coppens, eds. The Practice of Arbitration: Essays in Honour of Hans van Houtte. Hart Publishing: 187–195.

Rogers, Catherine A. 2005. The Vocation of the International Arbitrator. American University International Law Review 20, no. 5: 957–1020.
Rogers, Catherine A. 2014. Ethics in International Arbitration. Oxford University Press.
Schöldström, Patrik. 1998. The Arbitrator's Mandate: A Comparative Study of Relationships in Commercial Arbitration under the Laws of England, Germany, Sweden and Switzerland. Stockholm: Elanders Gotab.
Strong, S.I. 2012. International Commercial Arbitration: A Guide for U.S. Judges. Federal Judicial Center. http://www.fjc.gov/public/pdf.nsf/lookup/strongarbit.pdf/$file/strongarbit.pdf. Accessed 13 July 2016.
Szalai, Imre. 2013. Outsourcing Justice: The Rise of Modern Arbitration Laws in America [Kindle Edition]. Durham North Carolina: Carolina Academic Press.
The Swedish Arbitration Act of 1999 (SFS 1999:116). http://www.sccinstitute.com/?id=23745. Accessed 25 April 2016.
The UK Arbitration Act 1996, Chapter 23. http://www.legislation.gov.uk/ukpga/1996/23/contents. Accessed 25 April 2016.
United Nations Commission on International Trade. 2011. The UNCITRAL Arbitration Rules as Revised in 2010. http://www.uncitral.org/pdf/english/texts/arbitration/arb-rules-revised/arb-rules-revised-2010-e.pdf. Accessed 25 April 2016.
United Nations Commission on International Trade. 2011. The UNCITRAL Model Law on International Commercial Arbitration of 1985 with Amendments as Adopted in 2006. http://www.uncitral.org/pdf/english/texts/arbitration/ml-arb/07-86998_Ebook.pdf. Accessed 25 April 2016.

Chapter 8
Conclusion. Risk Acceptance Versus Risk Avoidance: On Why Arbitral Institutions Should Eventually Reform Their Liability

Contents

8.1 Institutional Arbitral Liability as a Recurrent Issue

The issue of institutional arbitral liability is a recurrent discussion amongst practitioners and academics. This debate usually revives when a controversial liability claim is filed against an arbitral institution in a court of law in the relevant jurisdiction. Most arbitration practitioners, including those directly involved in institutional arbitration proceedings such as members of arbitral institutions, individual arbitrators, or legal counsel, usually react with hostility towards the legal action undertaken by the party to the institutional arbitration in question. Such action is almost immediately perceived as shocking, unnecessary, and/or legally ungrounded by arbitration practitioners, even though these practitioners rarely worry themselves with the details of the case. In a sense, a liability claim being the subject of informal talks or more formal discussions is treated as an attack on the local or international arbitration community (depending upon the reputation and the level of universalization of the arbitral institution acting as respondent in the liability claim). In view of this, the party that initiates legal proceedings against an arbitral institution is almost seen as a betrayer of the arbitration values underpinning the institutional arbitration case that resulted in the liability claim.

B. Warwas, *The Liability of Arbitral Institutions: Legitimacy Challenges and Functional Responses*, DOI 10.1007/978-94-6265-111-1_8

When the emotions concerning one liability claim abate and the arbitral institution happens to be released from the threat of liability on the grounds that the institutional performance fell within the doctrine of quasi-judicial immunity, the debates among arbitration practitioners are forgotten again. Some academics still attempt to explain the plausible reasons for one party seeking damages from an arbitral institution and propose possible solutions to combat such actions in the future. Their proposals, however, remain largely unaddressed by arbitration practitioners including those involved in institutional arbitration. Consequently, academics often turn to another field of research, at least until another party to institutional arbitration proceedings risks being ostracized by asking a public judge to determine the scope of liability of an arbitral institution. The cycle then repeats itself. Scholars and academics revise their manuscripts on arbitral liability but fail to provide relevant proposals before the liability claim is decided and the interest therein seems to fade away.

The primary aim of this book was to systemize these debates on institutional arbitral liability to encourage efficient proposals on the topic. It was suggested that arbitral institutions should take a proactive approach to the contractual regulations of the scope of their own liability and, to a certain extent, to the liability of individual arbitrators that work under the aegis of those institutions on a repeat or accidental basis. There is an imperative to do so: the current trend among institutional arbitration users, as seen in the continuous institutional liability suits, is already heading towards the increased liability of arbitral institutions. The question is one of how to go about responding to that trend.

8.2 Proposals in a Nutshell

This book proposes a model of institutional arbitral liability assuming the contractual liability of arbitral institutions for their negligent acts and omission in the arbitration process in line with the limitation of liability clauses as negotiated with the parties to institutional arbitration contracts. The proposed model further suggests the liability of arbitral institutions for the effects of the acts or omission of institutional arbitrators as a result of negligent institutional supervision of the efficient conduct in the arbitration process after the conferment on arbitrators of the adjudicatory powers by arbitral institutions. Furthermore, it provides for the individual liability of institutional arbitrators for acts or omission *prior to* the conferment on them of the adjudicatory powers by an institutional organ and, possibly, the professional liability of arbitrators for intentional harms and wrongdoing in the arbitration processes.

An explanatory limitation of liability clause based on the ICC Arbitration Rules was also provided to demonstrate that the designed model could be treated as a standard for institutional arbitral liability, from which the parties to institutional arbitral contracts could derogate except in regulatory arbitrations. This clause reads as follows:

> The Court and its members, the ICC and its employees and the ICC National Committees and Groups and their employees and representatives shall not be liable to any person for any act or omission in connection with the arbitration, *save* where the act or omission is shown by the party to be a result of negligence of the Court and its members, the ICC and its employees and the ICC National Committees and Groups and their employees and representatives, in which cases the party may seek redress from the ICC.
>
> The arbitrators and the emergency arbitrator shall not be liable to any person for any act or omission in connection with the arbitration, save where the act or omission of arbitrators or the emergency arbitrator *after* the confirmation of the arbitrators by the Court or *after* the appointment of the emergency arbitrator by the President of the ICC is shown by the party to be a result of negligent institutional supervision of the efficient conduct in the arbitration process, in which cases the party may seek redress from the ICC.
>
> The above provision does not exclude the liability of individual arbitrators or the emergency arbitrator for the acts or omission *prior to* the confirmation of the arbitrators by the Court or the appointment of the emergency arbitrator by the President of the ICC, neither does it exclude professional liability of individual arbitrators and of the emergency arbitrator under the codes of conduct of the professional associations of which they are members, or under applicable law even *after* the confirmation of arbitrators by the Court or *after* the appointment of the emergency arbitrator by the President of the ICC.

The additional assumptions of the model included: (1) the aforementioned negotiable character of institutional liability clauses in commercial arbitrations; (2) no waivers from the standard liability models vis-à-vis parties to regulatory arbitrations; (3) the elimination by institutions having their seats in common law countries of the provisions on contractual immunity from process; (5) the adoption of the theory of individualized relationships in institutional contracts; and finally (6) the possibility for a determination of the law applicable to institutional contracts in the proposed model. Finally, it is recommended that arbitral institutions adopt internal control mechanisms called "additional mechanisms of private accountability". These should take the following forms: (a) institutional supervision of the codes of professional conduct (or ethics) of arbitrators; (b) institutional codes of conduct for the members of institutional organs and employees; (c) separate codes of conduct for institutional arbitrators and the members of institutional organs and institutional employees in regulatory arbitrations; (d) effective statements of arbitrators' availability, independence, and impartiality; (e) transparent procedures for the replacement of arbitrators on institutions' own motion; and finally (f) institutional supervisory bodies.

The above-mentioned additional mechanisms of private accountability, in combination with the proposed contractual institutional liability clauses, could possibly increase the performance of institutional arbitration actors in the course of arbitration proceedings. In addition, they could restore the private authority of arbitral institutions over arbitrators and institutional members, which, in turn, could raise the private confidence in arbitration in the eyes of arbitration users. It was claimed that the additional mechanisms of accountability, once equipped with transparent and effective enforcement mechanisms, could also invite the participation of arbitration users in internal controlling procedures of arbitral institutions.

8.3 Institutional Arbitral Liability and the Need for Self-Regulation

The analysis of civil, contractual liability ordinarily falls within purely legal discussions under different contract law theories. However, this book took an innovative approach to the civil liability of arbitral institutions by emphasizing the need for self-regulatory practices of arbitral institutions in the field of institutional arbitral liability. This proposal accommodated the so-called "market-based" approach to institutional arbitral liability. This implies that arbitral institutions themselves, being sophisticated players in the market for arbitration services, should reform the institutional liability clauses from the bottom (by means of their arbitration rules) in order to restore confidence in institutional arbitration in the eyes of their users.

Certainly, this is not an easy call. Any reforms relating to the proposals of this book would require taking on additional risks regarding the possible liability claims and the new institutional practices to mitigate those risks. However, as demonstrated in Chap. 6, there are a number of risk mitigation techniques available to arbitral institutions that could make the risks associated with institutional arbitral liability advantageous to arbitral institutions. This includes the negotiations of liability clauses with commercial arbitration users that could imply the agreement between arbitral institutions and these users on the financial cap on institutional liability, indemnification clauses or the narrowing down of the scope of acts for which arbitral institutions could be liable vis-à-vis these users. Moreover, arbitral institutions, by means of incorporating the additional mechanisms of accountability, inherently connected with institutional liability, could restore the confidence of the parties in institutional arbitration proceedings. This could, in fact, minimize the threat of liability claims against arbitral institutions in the courts of law. The latter observation should serve as a particular incentive for arbitral institutions to eventually reform their liability clauses. The proposed reforms could signal to their users, who increasingly complain about the lack of transparency of institutional practices, that arbitral institutions do not fear responding to this criticism. This could increase the use of institutional arbitration in the future. Arbitral institutions, given their powers and authority in and outside arbitration processes, are in an advantageous position to self-regulate their own liability. Although this call may not appear straightforward at first glance, it could certainly accommodate feasible and beneficial solutions of such sophisticated arbitration actors as arbitral institutions are today. The time has come for arbitral institutions to accept the risks regarding institutional arbitral liability instead of avoiding those risks that only diminish the position of arbitral institutions vis-à-vis other arbitration actors and public authorities.

This book further proposed that only after the reforms are initiated at the institutional level should they be subsequently supported by the relevant legal regulations. Due to the international function of most leading arbitration centres, it could be the UNCITRAL to first accommodate institutional reforms of liability to increase their functionality, as well as the effective and harmonized interpretations by legislators and judges at domestic levels. In fact, this unique combination of the self-regulation and public regulation of institutional arbitral liability[1] has the potential of increasing the status and functions of institutional arbitration settings and the usage of international institutional arbitration.

The issue of institutional arbitral liability entails a number of unregulated legal concepts and instruments including the status of institutional arbitration contracts, the content of contractual obligations emerging under such contracts, and the accountability of institutional arbitration actors. Once the discussion on these issues is triggered through the self-regulation of institutional arbitral liability, arbitral institutions would be able to further advance their position in the development of the discourse on private international law and contract law. This may increase the legitimacy of institutional arbitration whether in front of new potential arbitration users (internal legitimacy) or public authorities active in the field of arbitration (external legitimacy). On the one hand, arbitral institutions could appear as facilitators of the complex contractual relationships in institutional arbitrations vis-à-vis the parties. On the other hand, they could further influence their external legitimacy by providing guidance to the public actors on the nature of the internal, institutional arbitration settings. Until now, arbitral institutions tend to avoid the risks stemming from the lack of legal regulation of institutional arbitration that, as noted in Chap. 5, only deepens the legal uncertainty regarding the institutional liability claims. In this line, the book aimed at advancing both the private law aspect and the public law aspect of civil liability of arbitral institutions, which was required by the hybridity of institutional arbitration.

8.4 Arbitral Institutional Liability Advances the Legal, Societal, and Economic Facets of Arbitral Institutions

Although this book was devoted to the issue of institutional arbitral liability, there was a second, underlying aspect of the primary analysis. In addition to the main discussion, it concerned the debate on the status and multifaceted functions of contemporary institutional arbitration. These issues interconnect with institutional arbitral liability in that they allow one to map the sources of such liability, as well as the reasons why arbitral institutions are continuously subject to liability claims initiated by arbitration users.

In fact, arbitral institutions have become truly independent arbitration actors with enormous powers in the arbitration processes and also beyond them, in particular when policy-making in the field of arbitration is taken into account. Arbitral institutions compete for their repeat and accidental users and to this extent their major goals are to respond to the demands of the parties to arbitration. At the same time, they shape the legal framework for arbitration and have recently begun to

[1]Public regulation is meant here as the regulation outside the institutional arbitration regimes.

enter the public terrain of dispute resolution with an increased confidence. This was shown while presenting the increasing interplay between arbitral institutions and different public authorities at the international level with regard to the role of prominent arbitral institutions in shaping the legal framework for arbitration. Similar tendency to encourage new types of disputes to be outsourced to institutional arbitration by national legislators was also demonstrated at domestic levels with regard to arbitral institutions also from the countries in which arbitration is still not a preferred method of dispute resolution. The book showed the institutional arbitral power to regulate the public aspects of arbitration, including arbitrability, and which kind of tools arbitral institutions use to achieve their goals. One of the tools concerned the adaptability of the arbitration rules to arbitrations involving matters of public interest. Additionally, arbitral institutions implement various techniques to educate both junior and senior practitioners who enter or operate within international arbitration practice, in the capacity of arbitrators and legal representatives of the parties, by organizing different trainings and academic courses in cooperation with the law faculties of different universities. This proved the increasing ambitions of arbitral institutions within a globalized market of arbitration services. More importantly, it showed that arbitral institutions also deserve attention within a more advanced academic debate.

All this being said, arbitral institutions themselves fail to acknowledge some of their novel functions together with their changing position within international arbitration practice. The members of institutional organs at times mention that certain institutional tasks are at odds with the party autonomy and/or the unrestricted prerogatives of arbitrators. The guides to institutional arbitration rules, written by former institutional officials, occasionally suggest that institutional decisions should be protected through immunity because the work of case managers and institutional bodies requires so in view of the integrity of arbitration proceedings. How does this argument correspond with the actual functions of arbitral institutions? What are these functions? How should the progressive development of institutional arbitration be understood from legal, societal, and economic perspectives? Why do arbitral institutions not participate in the debates that beg the above questions?

In fact, as proposed in this book, the reforms of institutional arbitral liability could make arbitral institutions active participants in these debates. This is because the reforms of institutional arbitral liability could advance the legal, societal, and economic position of arbitral institutions in local and international arbitration communities, on the one hand, and public actors (legislators and courts), on the other hand. Arbitral institutions should accept the invitation for discussion on their own changing functions. In order to do so, they should first realize that international arbitration practice has changed drastically over the past decades, with the active involvement of arbitral institutions. The current procedural framework and mentality of institutional arbitration, rooted in the early institutional organization established at the beginning of the twentieth century, can no longer ignore these changes. New procedural responses and a new vision of institutional arbitration are required to recognize that institutional arbitration processes have developed since the foundation of the arbitral institutions and to advance these new functions of arbitral institutions. Yet again, the reforms of institutional arbitral liability could serve as the perfect opportunity to shed light on the legal, societal, and economic contexts in which contemporary arbitral institutions operate.

There are a number of **legal developments** that arbitral institutions need to embrace. Due to the progressive professionalization of both the arbitration practice and transnational business transactions, entailing the complex procedural and substantive components of institutional arbitration clauses, arbitral institutions have developed formalized arbitration rules that largely advanced the legal authority of arbitral institutions in the arbitration processes. Paradoxically, this also happened as a consequence of the fact that arbitral institutions, after their establishments, have begun to relinquish some of their early exclusive powers (e.g. nomination of arbitrators) to the parties themselves. This process required new procedural rules from contemporary arbitral institutions to be able to restore their authority in front of increasingly professionalized arbitration users. The core of the problem lies in the fact that early institutional authority was mainly based on the shared values and goals of the members of arbitration community connected with particular arbitral institutions, whereas the contemporary authority of arbitral institutions is mostly rooted in the complex, procedural matrix of arbitration rules. This suggests that the authority of contemporary arbitral institutions largely stems from the legal instruments produced in arbitration instead of the values and goals of early arbitration communities associated with a particular institution. Be that as it may, institutional arbitration entered the legal domain, which should be recognized by arbitral institutions. After such recognition, the reforms of institutional arbitral liability will appear to contemporary arbitral institutions as the only alternative to further strengthen their legal authority in front of their users. Why is this so?

It is clear that arbitral institutions work on a contractual basis. Moreover, arbitral institutions have developed *private regulatory powers* in the formation of institutional arbitration contracts. This means that arbitral institutions influence the content of contractual obligations of institutional arbitration actors (such as the parties, arbitrators, and the arbitral institutions themselves). In addition, arbitral institutions, by means of their rules, regulate the moment of the conclusion of institutional arbitration contracts, the law applicable to such contracts, and the hierarchy of legal relationships between institutional arbitration actors. In this sense, they eventually confer adjudicatory powers on institutional arbitrators, even in situations in which the parties select their nominees to act as party-nominated arbitrators. All these place arbitral institutions at the epicentre of all contractual relationships coming into existence in institutional arbitration. From the legal, contract law perspective, this makes arbitral institutions the private regulators of contract law that is generated by means of institutional arbitration. These developments, although far-reaching, have not yet been truly addressed by arbitral institutions. This is largely because arbitral institutions do not provide clarifications as to the contract law issues that arise in the course of institutional arbitration proceedings and following such proceedings, namely when the liability claims are filed against arbitral institutions in domestic courts. A number of questions have been posed in regard to these issues, including in this book. When and how are institutional contracts concluded? What are the exact obligations of arbitral institutions, arbitrators, and the parties in the course of the proceedings, and under which law should they be interpreted? Finally, what is the scope of liability of arbitral institutions and arbitrators under institutional arbitration contracts? This book provided explanatory proposals with regard to these issues. Why do arbitral institutions remain silent in this regard?

One possible answer is that the legal discussion on institutional arbitration contracts entails the debate on institutional arbitral liability. By now, it appears more sound for arbitral institutions not to open this Pandora box and to simply ignore the problem. Yet again, this practice no longer holds because the legal developments are proceeding: institutional arbitration contracts are being concluded at this moment. In this vein, arbitral institutions are invited to address the contemporary gaps relating to their private regulatory powers in institutional arbitration that result in the current situation in which private, institutional regulations of liability are dependent on the public interpretation of institutional liability, conducted by an unknown court in an unknown jurisdiction under unspecified law.

The proposed reforms of institutional arbitral liability could advance the legal position of arbitral institutions vis-à-vis the arbitration actors, while at the same time, they could strengthen the commercial aspect of institutional arbitration contracts. As noted in this book, the current institutional regulations of liability expose arbitral institutions to unknown and unquantifiable financial risks. The new regulations of liability, mostly in their negotiated terms—providing for financial caps on institutional liability, indemnification clauses, or even the categories of acts or omission for which arbitral institutions are not liable—will minimize the current risks stemming from the blanket exclusion of liability clauses. Again, the risks are already present, the question is how to go about them and minimize their far-reaching consequences. This could only be of benefit to the arbitral institutions.

The legal dimension of institutional activity was not a stand-alone pillar of institutional arbitral liability. Regardless of the fact that all institutional obligations are based on contract, an additional context for the performance of such obligations that stem from the particular status of arbitral institutions in and outside arbitration proceedings was pointed out in this book. This concerns the institutional exclusive competence in the administration of regulatory disputes *under* some national laws, but also the more systemic goals of institutional regimes vis-à-vis traditional arbitration users. Institutional arbitration has been developed as a dispute resolution mechanism outside law entailing significant **societal functions**. The latter, as presented in Chap. 3, implied the institutional role in convening the values and goals of the early traders wishing to rely on a honourable, cost-effective, fast, and procedurally flexible dispute resolution system. The professionalization of arbitration practice, however, proved not only that these early noble goals and values have diverged with time but also that arbitral institutions have failed to accommodate these values, weakening the private confidence of the arbitration users in institutional arbitration services. Arbitration communities associated with the early arbitral institutions under analysis are under the ongoing transformation from elite local societies protecting their communitarian values to less exclusive business clubs with exchangeable membership cards. Arbitral institutions, being part of these clubs, should seek novel possibilities of cooperation. The reforms of institutional arbitral liability could serve as one such possibility.

By assuming liability for negligence, arbitral institutions could reconnect their authority with the confidence in institutional arbitration processes. Moreover, the reform of institutional arbitral liability, increasing the scope of institutional liability as a standard arbitration practice, would serve as an incentive for arbitral institutions to implement additional mechanisms of accountability to increase internal performance and control in arbitration processes. The proposed mechanisms could respond to the calls for transparency of institutional practices and the parties themselves could more actively participate in those mechanisms. Arbitral institutions should be able to recognize the benefits stemming from the proposed reforms of institutional arbitral liability within the societal aspect of institutional activity. All in all, institutional arbitration was originally designed for arbitration users who need to be treated seriously by arbitral institutions to assure the continuous growth and effectiveness of this highly consensual dispute resolution system.

Finally, it appears that arbitral institutions should recognize the **economic significance** of the proposals for the reform of institutional arbitral liability. The negotiable limitation of liability clauses, together with the need for institutional insurance policies as a consequence of such clauses, has the potential to increase competition between arbitration centres. First and foremost, the different possible outcomes of the negotiations of institutional arbitral liability, in combination with the different weight put on additional mechanisms of accountability to be applied in institutional arbitrations depending on the commercial and legal preferences of the parties, will allow the parties to make rational choices about their preferred arbitral institutions. This would also affect the competition regarding the costs of institutional arbitration services. Additionally, the negotiable liability clauses could improve the quality signalling within the arbitration market (arbitral institutions, when assuming more liability, would signal to the parties the quality of their services) and therefore minimize the imperfect competition in this market.

In sum, under the proposed model, it is not only the arbitral institutions but also the parties and arbitrators that may find the new reforms advantageous. The arbitral institutions are able to negotiate and carefully determine their contractual obligations in institutional arbitration processes so as to eliminate any confusion about their role to ensure the efficient and effective arbitration (in contrast to the misleading notion of perfect arbitration). The parties gain a compensatory tool to eliminate or at least counterbalance the errors or possible unfairness of institutional arbitration settings. Individual arbitrators benefit under the proposed model to the extent that they are granted certain protection from arbitral institutions in return for the increased quality of performance in the course of arbitration processes.

The aforementioned advantages of the proposed model can restore the integrity of institutional arbitration for the parties and institutional arbitration community from the bottom, instead of relying on the integrity of arbitration system doubtfully guaranteed by the public regulations on institutional immunity (which is the case today in most common law countries). These reforms could increase the legitimacy of institutional arbitration and clarify the meaning of the efficiency of institutional arbitration regimes that will be framed by the cautiously negotiated limitation of liability clauses. Ultimately, the activity of institutional arbitration actors will not have to bring perfect and ideal outcomes to the parties (which corresponds to the contemporary expectations of the parties to institutional arbitrations), but instead will be framed by the express contractual obligations stemming from the institutional contracts. Moreover, the institutions and the parties to commercial arbitrations will have the possibility to negotiate the scope of institutional liability depending on various factors such as the institutional involvement in the conduct of arbitrations, the costs of the proceedings, and the flexibility of institutional arbitration rules vis-à-vis the parties' expectations. This means that the limitations of liability clauses providing institutional liability only to the agreed amount, the indemnification clauses, or the waivers from liability related to the conduct of institutional members or arbitrators, if allowed under the law applicable to the liability claims, could minimize the severity of institutional liability suits.

Chap. 7 demonstrated that the filing of a liability claim by an unsatisfied party does not necessarily need to amount to the automatic award of damages against arbitral institutions. There are many factors to be considered by a judge in the court of forum while determining the scope of institutional liability to be assessed under various laws applicable to the institutional contracts, which may not always result in finding institutions liable by the judges. For example, the determination of institutional fault and the causal link between the negligence of the institution and the damage suffered by the party. The effects of these assessments of institutional liability have different implications for the finality and integrity of institutional arbitration systems depending, inter alia, on the moment of the initiation of the liability suit, in relation to the stages of the arbitration proceedings. In any case, Chap. 7 showed that the possibility of ungrounded and excessive litigation against institutional arbitration actors aimed at moving the institutional arbitral awards is rather minimal under the studied scenarios. This could serve as an additional argument for institutional arbitration actors to rely on the solutions proposed in this book.

8.5 Institutional Arbitral Liability as a Response to the Dual Legitimacy Challenges

In addition to the interplay between the reforms of institutional arbitral liability and the advancement of the multifaceted functions of arbitral institutions, the reforms in question can serve as a response to the recent legitimacy pressures concerning institutional arbitration. As identified in Chap. 2, arbitral institutions have begun to assume a dual function in arbitration processes. First, arbitral institutions enjoy commercial function in the arbitration proceedings because of the traditional use of arbitration by business parties to resolve their commercial disputes. Thus, they tend to continuously respond to the commercial goals of traditional arbitration users to ensure efficiency in terms of time and costs of arbitration. Second, due to the increasing usage of arbitration by non-commercial parties (be it States, State-like entities and the so-called "regulatees" in sectorial arbitrations) to resolve their commercial or non-commercial disputes (e.g. consumer disputes, and employment, or labour disputes), arbitral institutions have started to assume a public function. Both functions entail different legitimacy pressures for arbitral institutions.

On the one hand, traditional arbitration users (meaning business parties) have recently openly criticized the institutional arbitration process as being increasingly lengthy, costly, and lacking procedural flexibility in a similar manner to court litigation. Chap. 2 concluded that although the parties to institutional arbitrations are still eager to rely on institutional regimes, whenever the outcomes of the processes turn out to be unsatisfactory to these parties, they immediately question the efficiency and effectiveness of institutional conduct. In the case of commercial arbitration users, this is because they tend to believe that sophisticated arbitral institutions are guarantors of perfect arbitrations. Moreover, the constant adaptability of the institutional rules to the demands of new institutional arbitration users (including the users involved in regulatory, more publicly oriented disputes than commercial disputes) do not serve typical commercial parties well. These parties tend to shift towards more regional arbitral institutions offering closer connections with the members of the local arbitration communities and less costly arbitration services. These can be seen as grim internal legitimacy challenges, in particular for the leading arbitral institutions, from the perspective of the traditional, commercial function of those institutions.

On the other hand, the emerging public function of institutional arbitration requires increased public accountability of arbitral institutions concerning the transparency and fairness of institutional arbitration processes. This is because the parties that indirectly consented to institutional arbitration may be unable to exercise their procedural rights due to the limited appeal mechanisms within and outside the institutional arbitration regimes. Moreover, even in institutional arbitrations concerning non-commercial parties who directly expressed their consent to be bound by an institutional arbitration clause, the requests for fairness and accountability should be addressed because of the potential criticism coming from civil society organizations or media concerned with the role of arbitral institutions in the support of the expanding business of private justice. This is in view of the complex discussion on the role of unaccountable arbitration actors in the process of the privatization of justice.[2] That is why, although traditional private, commercial arbitral institutions have not yet been directly subject of such criticism, it seems just a matter of time due to their emerging public function. New types of institutional arbitration have begun to support different private regimes (ODR, the administration of company-related disputes, or sports arbitration) and increasing

[2]Jessica Silver-Greenberg and Michael Corkery, "In Arbitration, a 'Privatization of the Justice System.'" New York Times, 1 November 2015. http://www.nytimes.com/2015/11/02/business/dealbook/in-arbitration-a-privatization-of-the-justice-system.html. Accessed 25 April 2016.

public arbitrations (e.g. the involvement of the AAA in governmental programmes or the increasing role of private arbitral institutions in investor-State arbitrations). The regulations of institutional arbitral liability by arbitral institutions should also respond to these external legitimacy challenges faced by arbitral institutions.

Institutional arbitral liability, in the scope proposed in this book, could serve as a legal tool to accommodate the dual legitimacy challenges mentioned above. Within the commercial function of institutional arbitration, entailing the internal legitimacy pressures, arbitral institutions would assume liability under the institutional contracts, just as all other sophisticated contractors assume responsibility for their essential contractual obligations. Moreover, from the perspective of the public function that implies the external legitimacy challenges, institutional arbitration actors would assume liability that could increase public oversight of the fairness and accountability of institutional processes. This could contribute to further expansion by arbitral institutions into the public terrain of dispute resolution. In this sense, institutional arbitral liability would not endanger the current institutional arbitration practice but rather facilitate its continuous development.

On the one hand, the commercial, and purely contractual function of arbitral institutions would allow for the contractual stipulations of liability. On the other hand, the public function that created more general, systemic sources of institutional arbitration rooted in the public context of institutional activity would be secured with the possibility of the public control of the conduct in institutional arbitration. Institutional arbitral liability in the proposed model thus bears mostly restorative and deterrent functions that could allow the compensation of the parties that suffered damage, and stimulate the better performance of institutional arbitration actors under the hazard of liability.

This book, in Chap. 2, recalled the early postulates of institutional regimes to create a system outside the law. The development of institutional arbitration practice shows that—regardless of the continuous accuracy of the original institutional aims—the legal, public life underlying the private context of institutional arbitration settings cannot be easily discarded. Institutional arbitral liability, as presented in this book, embodies this private–public nature of institutional arbitration.

Miles Davis once said, "if you are not making a mistake, it is a mistake".[3] It is an even bigger mistake not to minimize the consequences of making future mistakes. Arbitral institutions are powerful market players and they should realize that mistakes or errors can occur in the arbitration processes. They should assume greater responsibility for future institutional arbitration conduct. In the words of Churchill, "the price of greatness is responsibility".[4]

---

[3]An interview with Frank Barret in: Frank Barret, "What Leaders Can Learn from Jazz." Harvard Business Review IdeaCast. http://blogs.hbr.org/ideacast/2012/08/what-leaders-can-learn-from-ja.html. Accessed 25 April 2016.

[4]Winston Churchill, "The Price of Greatness" (A Speech Delivered by Winston S. Churchill While Receiving an Honorary Degree at Harvard). Finest Hour 80, Third Quarter, 1993, Speeches 1941–1945. http://www.winstonchurchill.org. Accessed 25 April 2016.

References

Barrett, Frank. 2012. What Leaders Can Learn from Jazz. Harvard Business Review IdeaCast. http://blogs.hbr.org/ideacast/2012/08/what-leaders-can-learn-from-ja.html. Accessed 25 April 2016.

Churchill, Winston. The Price of Greatness (A Speech Delivered by Winston S. Churchill While Receiving an Honorary Degree at Harvard). Finest Hour 80, Third Quarter, 1993, Speeches 1941–1945. http://www.winstonchurchill.org. Accessed 25 April 2016.

Silver-Greenberg, Jessica, and Corkery Michael. 1 November 2015. In Arbitration, a 'Privatization of the Justice System.' New York Times. http://www.nytimes.com/2015/11/02/business/dealbook/in-arbitration-a-privatization-of-the-justice-system.html. Accessed 25 April 2016.

Index

B. Warwas, *The Liability of Arbitral Institutions: Legitimacy Challenges and Functional Responses*, DOI 10.1007/978-94-6265-111-1

MIX
Papier aus verantwortungsvollen Quellen
Paper from responsible sources
FSC® C105338

If you have any concerns about our products,
you can contact us on
ProductSafety@springernature.com

In case Publisher is established outside the EU,
the EU authorized representative is:
Springer Nature Customer Service Center GmbH
Europaplatz 3, 69115 Heidelberg, Germany

Printed by Libri Plureos GmbH
in Hamburg, Germany